COCAINE ABUSE

BEHAVIOR, PHARMACOLOGY, AND CLINICAL APPLICATIONS

COCAINE

ABUSE

BEHAVIOR, PHARMACOLOGY,

AND CLINICAL

APPLICATIONS

STEPHEN T. HIGGINS

Departments of Psychiatry and Psychology
University of Vermont
Burlington, Vermont

JONATHAN L. KATZ

Department of Pharmacology and
Experimental Therapeutics
University of Maryland School of Medicine
Baltimore, Maryland

ACADEMIC PRESS
San Diego   London   Boston   New York   Sydney   Tokyo   Toronto

Academic Press
a division of Harcourt Brace & Company
525 B Street, Suite 1900, San Diego, California 92101-4495, USA
http://www.apnet.com

Academic Press Limited
24-28 Oval Road, London NW1 7DX, UK
http://www.hbuk.co.uk/ap/
Library of Congress Catalog Card Number: 98-84982

International Standard Book Number: 0-12-347360-8

PRINTED IN THE UNITED STATES OF AMERICA
98 99 00 01 02 03 BB 9 8 7 6 5 4 3 2 1

To Tamra, Tara, and Lucy Higgins for their loving support, understanding, and companionship.
—S. T. H.

To my Carol, Brian, and Matthew, who lovingly keep things in perspective; and to the memory of Roger T. Kelleher, who was an outstanding scientist, editor, and teacher, and remains a continuing source of inspiration.
—J. L. K.

CONTENTS

CONTRIBUTORS   xv
FOREWORD   xix
PREFACE   xxiii

1

BASIC PHARMACOLOGICAL MECHANISMS OF COCAINE

SARI IZENWASSER

Introduction   1
Regulation of Transporter Function   2
Neurochemical Effects of Cocaine Measured in Vivo   5
Acute and Chronic Effects of Cocaine on Receptors   8
Molecular Mechanisms of Cocaine Effects   11
Summary   13
References   13

2

NEUROANATOMICAL BASES OF THE REINFORCING STIMULUS EFFECTS OF COCAINE

S. BARAK CAINE

Introduction   21
The Mesoaccumbens Ascending Dopaminergic Pathway   22

The Medial Prefrontal Cortex   31
The Amygdala's Role in Behavioral Effects of Self-Administered
    Cocaine   35
Newly Charted Territories: Subiculum, Basal Nucleus,
    and Pedunculopontine   39
Summary and Implications for Cortico-Striato-Pallido-Thalamic
    Circuitry   41
References   44

3

BEHAVIORAL PHARMACOLOGY
OF COCAINE AND THE DETERMINANTS
OF ABUSE LIABILITY

JACK BERGMAN AND JONATHAN L. KATZ

Introduction   51
Psychomotor-Stimulant Effects of Cocaine   52
Interoceptive Effects of Cocaine   56
Contextual Determinants of the Reinforcing Effects of Cocaine   62
Alternatives to Cocaine Self-Administration   67
Suppression of Cocaine-Maintained Responding   70
Summary   74
References   74

4

BEHAVIORAL-ENVIRONMENTAL DETERMINANTS
OF THE REINFORCING FUNCTIONS
OF COCAINE

MARILYN E. CARROLL AND WARREN K. BICKEL

Introduction   81
Evaluation of Cocaine Reinforcement   82
Experimental Events Modulating Cocaine Reinforcement   87
Environmental Context   90
Processes Modulating Reinforcement   96
Summary   100
References   100

5

TOLERANCE AND SENSITIZATION TO COCAINE: AN INTEGRATED VIEW

WILLIAM L. WOOLVERTON AND SUSAN R. B. WEISS

Introduction   107
Tolerance   109
Sensitization   114
Tolerance and Sensitization in Cocaine Abuse   122
References   127

6

PRECLINICAL EVALUATION OF PHARMACOTHERAPIES FOR COCAINE ABUSE

GAIL WINGER

Introduction   135
Drug Discrimination   137
Intravenous Drug Self-Administration   141
Antibodies to Cocaine   150
Conclusions   152
References   153

7

PRENATAL EXPOSURE TO COCAINE

KEVIN F. SCHAMA, LEONARD L. HOWELL, AND LARRY D. BYRD

Introduction   159
Case Studies   160
Epidemiological Studies   162
Nonhuman Experimental Studies   166
Conclusions   171
References   172

8

COCAINE SELF-ADMINISTRATION RESEARCH: IMPLICATIONS FOR RATIONAL PHARMACOTHERAPY

MARIAN W. FISCHMAN AND RICHARD W. FOLTIN

Introduction   181
Ethical and Safety Issues Involved in Administering Cocaine to Humans   182
Assessing Cocaine Self-Administration in Human Research Participants   187
The Use of Cocaine Self-Administration Procedures to Inform Cocaine
      Pharmacotherapy   194
Conclusion   202
References   203

9

EVALUATION OF POTENTIAL PHARMACOTHERAPIES: RESPONSE TO COCAINE CHALLENGE IN THE HUMAN LABORATORY

GEORGE E. BIGELOW AND SHARON L. WALSH

Introduction   209
Mechanisms of Pharmacotherapy   210
Approaches to Pharmacotherapy Development   211
Studies of Potential Pharmacotherapies Using the Laboratory
      Challenge Method   212
Conclusions   233
References   235

10

CONTROLLED LABORATORY STUDIES ON THE EFFECTS OF COCAINE IN COMBINATION WITH OTHER COMMONLY ABUSED DRUGS IN HUMANS

CRAIG R. RUSH, JOHN M. ROLL, AND STEPHEN T. HIGGINS

Introduction   239
Patterns of Multiple Drug Abuse among Cocaine Abusers   240
Cocaine–Alcohol Combinations   241
Cocaine–Opioid Combinations   249
Cocaine–Marijuana Combinations   252

Cocaine–Nicotine Combinations   255
Summary and Directions of Future Research   257
References   258

11

COCAINE EFFECTS ON BRAIN FUNCTION

SCOTT E. LUKAS AND PERRY F. RENSHAW

Introduction   265
Effects of Cocaine on Brain Electrical Activity   266
Cocaine-Induced Euphoria—Correlates with Brain Function   269
Magnetic Resonance Imaging and Magnetic Resonance Spectroscopy   274
Coregistration of Imaging Technologies   281
Summary and Conclusions   281
References   282

12

THE CONTRIBUTION OF GENETIC FACTORS IN COCAINE AND OTHER DRUG ABUSE

GREGORY I. ELMER, LUCINDA L. MINER, AND ROY W. PICKENS

Introduction   289
Genetic Influence in Vulnerability to Drug Abuse   290
Environmental Influence in Vulnerability to Drug Abuse   300
How Do Genes and the Environment Interact?   303
References   306

13

VULNERABILITY TO COCAINE ABUSE

HOWARD D. CHILCOAT AND CHRIS-ELLYN JOHANSON

Introduction   313
Epidemiologic Studies   315
Conceptual Framework   321
Reinforcement Processes   326
Environmental Risk Factors for Cocaine Use   330

Conclusion   337
References   338

14

TREATING COCAINE ABUSE: WHAT DOES RESEARCH TELL US?

STEPHEN T. HIGGINS AND CONRAD J. WONG

Introduction   343
Treating Cocaine Abuse   344
Summary   356
References   357

15

TREATMENT OF COCAINE ABUSE IN METHADONE MAINTENANCE PATIENTS

KENNETH SILVERMAN, GEORGE E. BIGELOW, AND MAXINE L. STITZER

Introduction   363
Methadone   364
Pharmacological Treatments   368
Psychosocial and Behavioral Treatments   372
Other Treatments   380
Summary and Conclusions   380
References   389

16

RELAPSE TO COCAINE USE

SHARON M. HALL, DAVID A. WASSERMAN, BARBARA E. HAVASSY, AND PEG MAUDE-GRIFFIN

Definitions   389
Theoretical Models of Relapse   390
Prediction of Relapse to Cocaine   392
Treatments to Prevent Cocaine Relapse   400
Summary   402
References   402

17

COCAINE LEGALIZATION: DESIGNING THE EXPERIMENTS

THOMAS J. CROWLEY AND J. T. BREWSTER

Introduction   409
Brief History of Controls on Cocaine Availability   410
Cocaine Legalization: Hypotheses versus Value Statements   410
Factors Influencing Prevalence of Use   411
Cocaine Toxicity   414
What to Study: Models of Legalization   416
Research Needs   422
Conclusions   426
References   427

INDEX   431

CONTRIBUTORS

Numbers in parentheses indicate the pages on which the authors' contributions begin.

Jack Bergman (51), Harvard Medical School, McLean Hospital, Belmont, Massachusetts 02178

Warren K. Bickel (81), Human Behavioral Pharmacology Laboratory, University of Vermont, Burlington, Vermont 05401

George E. Bigelow (209, 363), Behavioral Pharmacology Research Unit, Department of Psychiatry and Behavioral Sciences, Johns Hopkins University School of Medicine, Baltimore, Maryland 21224

J. T. Brewster (409), Addiction Research and Treatment Services, Department of Psychiatry, University of Colorado School of Medicine, Denver, Colorado 80262

Larry D. Byrd (159), Yerkes Regional Primate Research Center, Emory University, Atlanta, Georgia 30322

S. Barak Caine (21), McLean Hospital, Harvard Medical School, Belmont, Massachusetts 02178

Marilyn E. Carroll (81), Department of Psychiatry, University of Minnesota, Minneapolis, Minnesota 55455

Howard D. Chilcoat (313), Departments of Psychiatry and Biostatistics, Henry Ford Health Sciences Center, Detroit, Michigan 48202

Thomas J. Crowley (409), Addiction Research and Treatment Services, Department of Psychiatry, University of Colorado School of Medicine, Denver, Colorado 80262

Gregory Elmer (289), Maryland Psychiatric Research Center, University of Maryland School of Medicine, Baltimore, Maryland 21228

Marian W. Fischman (181), Department of Psychiatry, College of Physicians and Surgeons of Columbia University, and New York State Psychiatric Institute, New York, New York 10032

Richard W. Foltin (181), Department of Psychiatry, College of Physicians and Surgeons of Columbia University, and New York State Psychiatric Institute, New York, New York 10032

Sharon M. Hall (389), Department of Psychiatry, University of California, San Francisco, San Francisco, California 94121

Barbara E. Havassy (389), Department of Psychiatry, University of California, San Francisco, San Francisco, California 94121

Stephen Higgins (239, 343), Departments of Psychiatry and Psychology, University of Vermont, Burlington, Vermont 05401

Leonard L. Howell (159), Yerkes Regional Primate Research Center, Emory University, Atlanta, Georgia 30322

Sari Izenwasser[1] (1), Psychobiology Section, National Institute on Drug Abuse, Division of Intramural Research, Baltimore, Maryland 21224

Chris-Ellyn Johanson (313), Departments of Psychiatry and Behavioral Neurosciences, Wayne State University, Detroit, Michigan 48207

Jonathan L. Katz (51), Department of Pharmacology and Experimental Therapeutics, University of Maryland School of Medicine, Baltimore, Maryland 21201

Scott E. Lukas (265), McLean Hospital, Harvard Medical School, Belmont, Massachusetts 02178

Peg Maude-Griffin (389), Department of Psychiatry, University of California, San Francisco, San Francisco, California 94121

Lucinda L. Miner (289), Office of Science Policy and Communications, National Institute of Drug Abuse, Rockville, Maryland 20857

Roy W. Pickens (289), Clinical Neurogenetics Section, Intramural Research Program, National Institute of Drug Abuse, Baltimore, Maryland 21224

Perry F. Renshaw (265), McLean Hospital, Harvard Medical School, Belmont, Massachusetts 02178

John M. Roll (239), Department of Psychiatry, University of Vermont, Burlington, Vermont 05401

Craig R. Rush (239), Departments of Psychiatry and Human Behavior and Phar-

[1] Current address: Department of Neurology, University of Miami School of Medicine, Miami, Florida 33136

macology and Toxicology, University of Mississippi Medical Center, Jackson, Mississippi 39216

Kevin F. Schama (159), Yerkes Regional Primate Research Center, Emory University, Atlanta, Georgia 30322

Kenneth Silverman (363), Department of Psychiatry and Behavioral Sciences, Johns Hopkins University School of Medicine, Baltimore, Maryland 21224

Maxine L. Stitzer (363), Department of Psychiatry and Behavioral Sciences, Johns Hopkins University School of Medicine, Baltimore, Maryland 21224

Sharon L. Walsh (209), Behavioral Pharmacology Research Unit, Department of Psychiatry and Behavioral Sciences, Johns Hopkins University School of Medicine, Baltimore, Maryland 21224

David A. Wasserman (389), Department of Psychiatry, University of California, San Francisco, San Francisco, California 94121

Susan R. B. Weiss (107), Biological Psychiatry Branch, National Institutes of Mental Health, Bethesda, Maryland 20892

Gail Winger (135), Department of Pharmacology, University of Michigan Medical Center, Ann Arbor, Michigan 48109

Conrad Wong (343), Department of Psychology, University of Vermont, Burlington, Vermont 05401

William L. Woolverton (107), Department of Psychiatry and Human Behavior, University of Mississippi Medical Center, Jackson, Mississippi 39216

FOREWORD

Scientific information on drug abuse has increased enormously during the last generation. Within living memory, drug abuse—*addiction* as it was called—was considered a relatively simple problem to understand, though hard to abate. A certain few drugs caused "euphoria" (a neologism not included in my *Oxford English Dictionary*), an ecstasy that, once experienced, forced the subject to repeat the behavior. Over days and weeks tolerance developed, and if a dose was not forthcoming at the right time, withdrawal symptoms started that forced the subject to go to any lengths to obtain a new supply. As the forces were irresistible for the subject, the only means of control was incarceration or interdiction of supply. Given these premises, the control efforts of the time were not illogical. The drug of historical concern was heroin, and the characteristics of heroin were supposed to define drugs of addiction. In particular, cocaine was not considered a drug of addiction because there was no clearly defined withdrawal syndrome. For reasons not obvious, alcohol was also not a drug of addiction; the prohibition amendment of 1919 came from concern about drunkenness, not addiction.

The pharmacology of morphine, heroin, and cocaine was studied, but until the 1950s there was almost no research on addiction except for that at the United States Public Health Service Hospital at Lexington, where some convicted addicts were studied scientifically. The research that was conducted was primarily on morphine and heroin addiction. Even though Andean Indians have chewed coca leaves since pre-Columbian times, such indulgence was regarded as a relatively harmless aid to a hard life in a harsh environment. Adventurous people such as the Conquistadors must have tried coca, but it does not seem to have become a serious abuse problem. (We use the term *drug abuse* as defined by the World Health Organization and the *Diagnostic and Statistical Manual of Mental Disorders,* 4th ed.; an agent is abused when it impairs the ability of an individual to function in society and, usually, harms the individual abuser.) Freud experimented with cocaine, as did Conan Doyle (presumably, otherwise how would Sherlock Holmes have gotten involved?), but their use was regarded as quaint and naughty, not as a dangerous, potential defiler of youth.

Such attitudes persisted until after World War II, when drug abuse was recognized as a serious problem, and opioids and even marijuana were demonized. The age-old custom of opium smoking had given way in the West to a more pernicious form of drug taking. (Opium smoking, I suppose, must be considered abuse, because sleepy men in an opium den contribute little to society, though they do not do much harm either. If they saved their opium experience until they had finished their day's work, the impact on society would be minimal. One might conjecture that there would have been no Opium Wars if importation of opium had seriously impaired the capacity of Chinese to work effectively for imperial powers.) About the time of the Civil War, the isolation of morphine, the wide availability of laudanum, the invention of the syringe for parenteral injection, and later the introduction of the much faster acting heroin were the mileposts on the road from relatively benign opium smoking to the intravenous heroin epidemic of the post World War II years. The basic pharmacological effects of morphine in opium, morphine hydrochloride, and heroin are similar: only the routes of administration and pharmacokinetics differ and lead to heroin being so harmful. In the 1940s and 1950s, a withdrawal syndrome was regarded as a necessary feature of an agent that could lead to addictive consumption. Even when the cocaine epidemic was well underway, many insisted that cocaine was not an agent of addiction, because clear-cut withdrawal symptoms on discontinuance were not reliably observed. When it became unmistakably clear that cocaine abuse was every bit as harmful as heroin abuse and even more dangerous, the term *drug addiction* lost its special meaning. Withdrawal on cessation became recognized as commonplace for agents taken regularly as are, for example, many therapeutic agents. The term *addiction* reverted to its original meaning of excessive, regular, devoted pursuit of an activity, be it work, play, watching television, gambling, or sex. All these activities, and many more, can have consequences that reinforce the behavior until it comes to dominate the lifestyle of the victim.

What does all this have to do with the present volume? In approaching a disease or a condition, one must first consider simple causes, for example, that an infectious disease is caused by a single species of organism. Drug abuse was first attributed to the "euphoric" effects of the agents. Euphoria was the hypothetical intervening construct that made people indulge in self-destructive behavior. But people (and laboratory animals) will indulge in self-destructive behavior "just" because they are subject to a schedule. People eat themselves into infirmity and early death because they are on a schedule of regular eating that leads to excessive intake of calories and no corresponding schedule of expenditure of energy. Monkeys will self-inflict noxious stimuli because such stimuli have been appropriately scheduled, not because they produce euphoria.

So attributing the mechanism of drug abuse to euphoria has failed and offers no help for coping with the problem. On the other hand, environmental influences on drug-taking behavior, such as the schedule to which the addicts are subject, have proved amenable to experimental analysis and, most importantly, have given researchers reason to hope that there will be help in coping with the problems of drug addiction.

This volume presents the state of current knowledge of cocaine abuse: from the basic pharmacology to the clinical pharmacology of vulnerability, treatment, and relapse, with a focus on behavioral analysis. Where appropriate, the chapters are multidisciplinary and include lines of research that will broaden our understanding and knowledge and lay a foundation for a rational and effective program to reduce, attenuate, and even eliminate the curse of drug abuse. Some people worry about limitations on integration across fields—chemical, anatomical, electrophysiological, behavioral, and so on. I think the worry is largely misplaced, provided no opportunities for cross-fertilization of fields are missed. We may be too ambitious in our hopes for integration. It is not the way of nature to show extensive isomorphism between structure and chemistry and structure and function across broad areas.

We have far to go along the lines we are pursuing. This volume is a start in providing a thorough understanding of how far we have come along many of these lines and where we need to go.

Peter B. Dews

PREFACE

Cocaine abuse remains a major public health problem that contributes to many of society's most disturbing social problems, including infectious disease, crime, violence, and neonatal drug exposure. Cocaine abuse results from a complex interplay of behavioral, pharmacological, and neurobiological determinants. Although a complete understanding of cocaine abuse is currently beyond us, significant progress has been made in preclinical research toward identifying fundamental determinants of this disorder. Those advances are critically reviewed in chapters 1–6 of this volume. Important advances also have been made in characterizing the clinical pharmacology of cocaine abuse, and those advances are critically reviewed in chapters 7–12. Last, and perhaps most important, those basic scientific advances have been extended to understanding individual vulnerability to cocaine abuse, to developing effective treatments for the disorder, and to forming public policy. Chapters 13–17 critically review those applications.

Contributors to this volume were selected because of their status as internationally recognized leaders in their respective areas of scientific expertise. Moreover, each is a proponent of the importance of a rigorous, interdisciplinary scientific approach to addressing the problem of cocaine abuse effectively. As such, we believe this volume offers a coherent, empirically based conceptual framework for addressing cocaine abuse that has continuity from the basic research laboratory through the clinical and policy arenas. Each chapter was prepared with the goal of being sufficiently detailed, in-depth, and current to be valuable to informed readers with specific interests while also offering a comprehensive overview for those who might be less informed or have broader interests in cocaine abuse. We hope this blend of critical review with explicit conceptual continuity that spans all of the chapters will make this volume a unique contribution to cocaine abuse in particular and substance abuse in general.

Stephen T. Higgins
Jonathan L. Katz

1

BASIC PHARMACOLOGICAL
MECHANISMS OF COCAINE

SARI IZENWASSER

Psychobiology Section
National Institute of Drug Abuse
Division of Intramural Research
Baltimore, Maryland

INTRODUCTION

Because of the widespread abuse of cocaine, there has been a considerable amount of research on its pharmacological actions, its behavioral effects, and the adaptations that occur in response to its chronic usage. Cocaine is a psychomotor stimulant that produces its major pharmacological effects by inhibiting the reuptake of the monoamines dopamine, norepinephrine, and serotonin into presynaptic terminals. Reuptake is the main mechanism by which these neurotransmitters are removed from the extracellular space, where they bind to and activate receptors (Wieczorek & Kruk, 1994). As a consequence of these actions, cocaine potentiates neurotransmission of all three monoamines (Hadfield, Mott, & Ismay, 1980; Heikkila, Orlansky, & Cohen, 1975; Ross & Renyi, 1969). In addition to these effects, cocaine acts as a local anesthetic. The major behavioral effect of cocaine is that of a psychomotor stimulant; thus it increases locomotor activity when administered to animals (for review see Johanson & Fischman, 1989). This behavior is believed to be produced primarily by its inhibition of dopamine uptake, and the effects of the drug on this system have been studied to a greater extent than have its noradrenergic or serotonergic effects. Because of this strong relationship between actions at the dopamine transporter and the behavioral effects of cocaine, the dopamine transporter has on occasion been referred to as the cocaine binding site.

This chapter will focus on the neurochemical effects of acute and chronic cocaine as measured in vitro and in vivo. The relationship between these effects and behavior will not be addressed here to a great extent but can be found in later chapters (see chapters 2, 3, and 6). For purposes of clarity, the terms *caudate putamen*

Cocaine Abuse: Behavior, Pharmacology,
and Clinical Applications

1

and *nucleus accumbens* have been used consistently in place of other terms such as *striatum* or *ventral striatum,* respectively. Only in cases where it was unclear to which regions these names referred were the original names as used in the published papers reported here.

REGULATION OF TRANSPORTER FUNCTION

DOPAMINE TRANSPORTER

Acute Effects of Cocaine

Cocaine increases dopaminergic activity by binding to the dopamine transporter and inhibiting dopamine uptake, the primary method by which dopamine is deactivated after its release into the synapse. It is thought to bind to a site on the dopamine transporter that is distinct from the substrate binding site to which dopamine binds in order to be transported (Johnson, Bergmann, & Kozikowski, 1992; McElvain & Schenk, 1992). In this manner, it blocks the uptake of dopamine via a noncompetitive mechanism and is not itself transported into the cell. The binding of uptake inhibitors to the dopamine transporter has been shown to be Na^+-dependent in the caudate putamen, nucleus accumbens, and olfactory tubercle (Izenwasser, Werling, & Cox, 1990; Kennedy & Hanbauer, 1983; Reith, Meisler, Sershen, & Lajtha, 1986), but not Cl^- dependent (Reith & Coffey, 1993; Wall, Innis, & Rudnick, 1992). This is in contrast to the ionic requirements for the actual transport of substrate, which is both Na^+- and Cl^--dependent. Transport requires the binding of two Na^+ ions and one Cl^- ion, which are cotransported with dopamine (Krueger, 1990). Using a rotating disk electroanalytical technique that can measure uptake in real time, it has been shown that cocaine binds competitively against Na^+, suggesting that it is binding to a Na^+ binding site, but noncompetitively against dopamine (McElvain & Schenk, 1992). In addition, either dopamine or Na^+ binds first, followed by Cl^-. The binding of Na^+ promotes an increased affinity for the binding of dopamine and thus promotes inward transport of the transmitter.

Autoradiographic studies using cocaine or an analog of cocaine have shown that there are high densities of dopamine transporter labeling in dopaminergic terminal regions such as the caudate putamen and nucleus accumbens of rat (Wilson et al., 1994), and the caudate, putamen, and nucleus accumbens of monkey (Canfield, Spealman, Kaufman, & Madras, 1990; Kaufman, Spealman, & Madras, 1991) and human (Biegon et al., 1992; Staley, Basile, Flynn, & Mash, 1994) brains. Because of this, many of the neurochemical studies with cocaine have been done using these brain regions. It has been suggested that dopamine uptake in the nucleus accumbens is differentially regulated by cocaine compared to the caudate putamen (Missale et al., 1985); however, the majority of the evidence suggests that the effects of cocaine in both regions are similar (Boja & Kuhar, 1989; Izenwasser et al., 1990; Wheeler, Edwards, & Ondo, 1993). These studies have shown that although there is less dopamine uptake in the nucleus accumbens (expressed as a smaller V_{max}), it is Na^+-dependent, and the IC_{50} values for cocaine to inhibit uptake are comparable in both brain regions.

The number of binding sites on the dopamine transporter for cocaine and its analogs has been the focus of much study and some controversy, with some studies reporting two binding sites and others showing evidence of only a single site. The initial studies of cocaine binding using [^{3}H]cocaine as the ligand showed that there is saturable, Na^+-dependent cocaine binding in the mouse brain (Reith 1980, 1981). In caudate putamen, a region composed predominantly of dopamine terminals, only a single binding site was apparent (Reith & Selmeci, 1992). In contrast, in monkey brain, the binding of both [^{3}H]cocaine and the more potent cocaine analog [^{3}H]WIN 35,428 is best fit by two-site binding models (Madras, Fahey, et al., 1989; Madras, Spealman, et al., 1989). Similarly, two binding sites in rat caudate putamen (Izenwasser, Rosenberger, & Cox, 1993; Schoemaker et al., 1985), human putamen (Schoemaker et al., 1985; Staley et al., 1994), and caudate (Little, Kirkman, Carroll, Breese, & Duncan, 1993) have also been reported. Recent studies have suggested that the methods used for the binding assays play an important role in the determination of one or two binding sites and that this might account for the apparent discrepancies between studies (Izenwasser et al., 1993; Kirifides, Harvey, & Aloyo, 1992; Rothman et al., 1993). It is not known whether these two binding sites represent two distinct binding sites or two conformations of a single site. What is known is that both components exist on the dopamine transporter because [^{3}H]WIN 35,428 binds to two sites on the cloned rat brain dopamine transporter expressed in COS cells (Boja, Markham, Patel, Uhl, & Kuhar, 1992).

Why is it important that cocaine might bind to two sites on the dopamine transporter? One question that has often been asked about cocaine is why it is abused so extensively, whereas other dopamine uptake inhibitors that appear to have the same functional properties (i.e., inhibition of dopamine uptake) are not. One possible explanation is that more than one binding site exists on the dopamine transporter through which uptake can be regulated, but that only one site (where cocaine binds) regulates the behavioral effects—hence the abuse potential of cocaine. Although other compounds compete against cocaine binding, they may be binding differently from cocaine and possibly only overlapping at a subset of its binding domains (for a more complete discussion see Katz, Newman, & Izenwasser, 1996).

There have been several studies suggesting that cocaine may in fact be binding to the transporter in a manner different from that of other uptake inhibitors. For example, it has been shown that cocaine and mazindol may bind to different sites on the dopamine transporter (Berger, Elsworth, Reith, Tanen, & Roth, 1990). Additionally, there is evidence that cocaine, BTCP, and GBR 12935 (two selective dopamine uptake inhibitors) may bind to mutually exclusive sites on the dopamine transporter (Reith, de Costa, Rice, & Jacobson, 1992). Similar findings of different binding domains have been reported for cocaine and GBR 12783, an analog of

GBR 12935 (Saadouni, Refahi-Lyamani, Costentin, & Bonnet, 1994). In contrast, when inward transport of dopamine is mathematically modeled from studies using rotating disk electrode voltammetry to measure dopamine levels, cocaine and GBR 12909 (another analog of GBR 12935) appear to interact in a competitive manner, whereas mazindol and nomifensine seem to bind to separate sites (Meiergerd & Schenk, 1994). Some of the best evidence that the domain to which cocaine binds is important comes from an examination of the behavioral effects of different dopamine uptake inhibitors. Functionally, there is a good correlation for cocaine and its analogs between affinities for binding to the dopamine transporter in vivo (Cline et al., 1992) or in vitro (Izenwasser, Terry, Heller, Witkin, & Katz, 1994) and ED_{50} values for producing locomotor activity. However, this correlation does not exist for compounds that are structurally dissimilar to cocaine, suggesting that the manner in which cocaine binds to the dopamine transporter might be important for the production of this behavioral effect (Izenwasser et al., 1994; Rothman et al., 1992; Vaugeois, Bonnet, Duterte-Boucher, & Costentin, 1993).

Chronic Effects of Cocaine

Chronic cocaine treatments do not appear to have neurotoxic effects like those produced by amphetamine on dopamine and serotonin neurons (for review see Seiden & Ricaurte, 1987). In fact, most studies have shown little change in transporter binding following chronic treatment of rats with cocaine, suggesting that dopamine terminals remain intact. Daily administration of cocaine for 10 days has no effect on binding to dopamine (Kula & Baldessarini, 1991), norepinephrine, or serotonin (Benmansour, Tejani-Butt, Hauptmann, & Brunswick, 1992) uptake sites. Continuous infusion of cocaine for 7 days also has no effect on dopamine transporter binding (Izenwasser & Cox, 1992). However, withdrawal from repeated administration of cocaine produces an increase in transporter binding in the rat nucleus accumbens (Sharpe, Pilotte, Mitchell, & De Souza, 1991). Because this increase only occurs after withdrawal from the drug, it is likely to be a compensatory mechanism related to some other, earlier drug effect. In contrast to these findings, an increase in the number of dopamine transporter binding sites in human striatum from cocaine-exposed subjects is seen as compared to that from normal controls (Little, Kirkman, Carroll, Clark, & Duncan, 1993). Increases are also observed in human caudate, putamen, and nucleus accumbens following fatal cocaine overdoses (Staley, Hearn, Ruttenber, Wetli, & Mash, 1994).

There are alterations in dopamine transporter function even though there are no significant alterations in ligand binding. The inhibition of dopamine uptake by cocaine changes in both the nucleus accumbens and the caudate putamen following 7 days of chronic continuous cocaine administration (Izenwasser & Cox, 1992). Daily cocaine injections (15 mg/kg/day $\times$ 3 days) have been reported to lead to a decrease in total dopamine uptake in the nucleus accumbens, with no change in the caudate putamen (Izenwasser & Cox, 1990). In contrast, a regimen of escalating doses over a 10-day period produces a transitory increase in dopamine uptake in the nucleus accumbens (Ng, Hubert, & Justice, 1991).

SEROTONIN AND NOREPINEPHRINE TRANSPORTERS

Cocaine also inhibits the reuptake of norepinephrine and serotonin into presynaptic terminals. There has been less focus on these two systems because evidence suggests that the behavioral effects of cocaine are mediated predominantly by its inhibition of dopamine uptake.

Acute administration of cocaine produces increased tissue levels of serotonin in the medial prefrontal cortex and the hypothalamus, with no changes in the nucleus accumbens, caudate putamen, hippocampus, or brain stem (Yang, Gorman, Dunn, & Goeders, 1992). With in vivo microdialysis techniques, however, it has been shown that extracellular serotonin levels are increased in some of these brain regions (see section III—Neurochemical Effects of Cocaine Measured in Vivo).

Acutely, cocaine suppresses the spontaneous activity of serotonin neurons in the dorsal raphe (Cunningham & Lakoski, 1988; Pitts & Marwah, 1987). It also decreases synthesis of serotonin in the striatum, nucleus accumbens, and medial prefrontal cortex (Galloway, 1990). Chronic cocaine administration leads to increases in the number of serotonin uptake sites in the prefrontal cortex and the dorsal raphe and in the ability of cocaine to inhibit the activity of serotonin dorsal raphe neurons (Cunningham, Paris, & Goeders, 1992). Cocaine may also have some delayed actions on serotonergic function. Following 3 months of withdrawal from seven daily injections of cocaine, there was a decrease in the amount of serotonin in the frontal cortex, which was not evident for at least 6 weeks after the treatment ended (Egan, Wing, Li, Kirch, & Wyatt, 1994). This same treatment had no effect on serotonin levels in the prefrontal cortex, nucleus accumbens, striatum, hippocampus, or hypothalamus. Similarly, twice-daily injections of cocaine for 8 days had no effect on norepinephrine, dopamine, or serotonin levels in any brain region for up to 48 days of withdrawal (Yeh & DeSouza, 1991).

STRUCTURE–ACTIVITY RELATIONSHIPS

There have been several series of compounds synthesized to bind preferentially to the dopamine transporter, and as such there is much known about the structure–activity relationships (SAR) for these binding sites. For a complete review of the SAR for binding of a large series of tropanes, including cocaine, benztropine, and WIN 35,065-2 analogs, as well as 1,4-dialkylpiperazine (GBR series), mazindol, phencyclidine, and methylphenidate analogs, see Carroll, Lewin, and Kuhar (1996).

NEUROCHEMICAL EFFECTS OF COCAINE
MEASURED IN VIVO

All dopamine uptake inhibitors appear to fully inhibit dopamine uptake in vitro. However, not all compounds have the same magnitude of effects when administered to an animal. For example, although most dopamine uptake inhibitors produce an increase in locomotor activity, they do so with different maximal efficacies (Izenwasser et al., 1994). The use of in vivo methods such as microdialysis and voltammetry to measure neurochemical responses to drugs has provided a significant amount of information on how these drugs are acting in the living animal. These methods have provided information on the time course, concentration, and neurochemical effects of a drug after administration into the animal. They have also provided some insight into how different uptake inhibitors affect dopamine uptake in vivo.

In addition to measuring dopamine levels, microdialysis has been used to measure the amount of cocaine in a brain region following either a local or systemic injection of cocaine. It has been shown that the maximal concentration of cocaine in the caudate putamen occurs within 30 min of a single intraperitoneal injection of cocaine (30 mg/kg), followed by a rapid decline in the local cocaine concentration (Nicolaysen, Pan, & Justice, 1988). In addition, extracellular levels of dopamine and cocaine were highly correlated over time.

A local infusion of cocaine produces a significant increase in dopamine, norepinephrine, and serotonin in the ventral tegmental area (VTA) in a concentration-dependent manner (Chen & Reith, 1994). At low doses of cocaine, the magnitude of the effect on all three monoamines is similar, whereas at higher doses, there is a preferential effect on dopamine. The selective dopamine uptake inhibitor GBR 12935 also produces marked increases in dopamine levels when infused locally, with a less pronounced effect on norepinephrine and serotonin observed (Chen & Reith, 1994). In contrast, 25 mg/kg of GBR 12909 (an analog of GBR 12935) has been shown to have little effect on dopamine overflow following intraperitoneal injection, an effect that might be related to its diffusional properties, since GBR 12935 is lipophilic and thus quite slow to enter the brain (Rothman et al., 1989).

An intravenous injection of cocaine produces extracellular dopamine levels approximately 400% of baseline in the nucleus accumbens and an extracellular serotonin level about 200% of basal, as measured by in vivo microdialysis (Bradberry et al., 1993). In freely moving rats, a systemic injection of cocaine (1 mg/kg sc) produces increases in extracellular dopamine in the nucleus accumbens, but not the dorsal caudate putamen. Only at a higher dose (5 mg/kg sc) is an effect seen in the caudate; however, the magnitude of the effect is not as great as that observed in the nucleus accumbens (Carboni, Imperato, Perezzani, & Chiara, 1989). These findings suggest that the nucleus accumbens may be more greatly affected by the presence of cocaine. In both brain regions, dopamine levels peak at approximately 40 min and return to normal by about 3.5 h post injection. Nomifensine, another dopamine uptake inhibitor, also produces an increase in dopamine levels in both brain regions to a magnitude similar to that of cocaine, but it is somewhat shorter acting in the caudate putamen than in the nucleus accumbens (Carboni et al., 1989).

In anesthetized rats, intravenous cocaine injections produce dose-dependent increases in extracellular dopamine levels in the caudate putamen of rats. The peak effect is observed after 10 min, and levels are back to control values by 30 min post injection (Hurd & Ungerstedt, 1989). When a second injection of cocaine is administered 90 min after the first injection, the time course of the response is similar, although somewhat diminished in magnitude. In contrast, when cocaine is administered directly into the caudate putamen and continuously infused, a diminished effect of cocaine is observed (Hurd & Ungerstedt, 1989). Nomifensine and LU 19-005, two other dopamine uptake inhibitors, produce increases in extracellular dopamine that are similar to those produced by cocaine, whereas LU 17-133 and GBR 12783 take longer to increase dopamine levels, even when perfused directly into the caudate putamen. Thus it may not be merely the distribution of these drugs into the brain that accounts for their different behavioral effects, but may have to do with the manner in which these compounds interact with the dopamine transporter.

Cocaine (15–20 mg/kg ip) produces increases in extracellular dopamine of approximately 200% in both the nucleus accumbens and the medial prefrontal cortex (Horger, Valadez, Wellman, & Schenk, 1994; Kalivas & Duffy, 1990; Parsons & Justice, 1993). In animals pretreated for 9 days with injections of amphetamine, this effect is even greater (about 450% in ventral striatum and 258% in medial prefrontal cortex). Thus, amphetamine produces cross-sensitization to cocaine (Horger et al., 1994). Pretreatment with nicotine had no effect.

Rats injected twice daily with 10 mg/kg cocaine have increased basal dopamine levels in the nucleus accumbens for the first 3 days, followed by a sharp decrease below control levels for the continuation of the treatment period (5 days) (Imperato, Mele, Scrocco, & Puglisi-Allegra, 1992). In addition, this decrease in basal levels is still present for up to 7 days of withdrawal from the cocaine injections. Basal dopamine levels are also decreased in the area of the nucleus accumbens and the striatum 1 day after 13 days of a repeated injection paradigm in which animals received three doses of cocaine daily (Maisonneuve, Keller, & Glick, 1990) and in the nucleus accumbens during withdrawal from cocaine self-administration (Weiss, Markou, Lorang, & Koob, 1992). These findings are in contrast to those of Parsons, Smith, and Justice (1991), who reported that neither basal extracellular dopamine nor serotonin levels in the nucleus accumbens or VTA are altered compared to those of control animals 1 day after the last of 10 daily cocaine injections (20 mg/kg ip), but that basal dopamine levels are significantly decreased following 10 days of withdrawal (Parsons & Justice, 1993; Parsons et al., 1991). Thus, most studies show decreases in basal dopamine levels at some time point after termination of cocaine administration. These decreases are likely to be a compensatory response to the high levels of extracellular dopamine that are produced during cocaine administration. As with many effects of cocaine, the time course for this effect to occur may depend on the cocaine administration paradigm or time course.

In response to a challenge dose of cocaine, increases in extracellular dopamine and serotonin levels are greater in both the nucleus accumbens and the VTA 1 day after either 10 days (Parsons & Justice, 1993) or 4 days (Kalivas & Duffy, 1990) of cocaine injections than after acute cocaine administration, suggesting that sensitization to the effects of cocaine occurs. The time course for the peak dopamine levels correlates temporally with the observed maximal increases in locomotor activity in response to a cocaine injection, which also appears to be sensitized (Kalivas & Duffy, 1990). In contrast, 1 week after a single injection of cocaine, a challenge dose of cocaine produces no difference in the elevation of dopamine compared to the first injection (Keller, Maisonneuve, Carlson, & Glick, 1992). These findings suggest that repeated injections, not merely withdrawal from the drug, are necessary for sensitization to occur.

The mechanism by which this sensitization to cocaine occurs is not completely understood; however, it has been shown that a challenge dose of cocaine leads to a significantly greater amount of dialysate cocaine in the nucleus accumbens following a 10-day injection regimen than it does in control animals (Pettit, Pan, Parsons, & Justice, 1990). This is only true, however, when the challenge injection of cocaine is administered intraperitoneally, as opposed to intraventricularly (Pettit & Pettit, 1994). After an intraperitoneal injection of cocaine, the amount of cocaine in both the blood and the brain is increased in cocaine-pretreated animals compared to drug-naive controls. Thus the increase appears to be in the distribution from the site of injection as opposed to a greater entry into the brain. This suggests that there is not a true sensitization of transporter function, but that more cocaine is getting into the brains of animals treated with intermittent injections of cocaine, thus producing a larger effect on dopamine overflow than in control animals. In contrast, animals receiving a continuous infusion of cocaine exhibit tolerance to the locomotor-activating effects of the drug, with no change in brain levels of cocaine either during the treatment period (Kunko, French, & Izenwasser, 1998) or following a challenge injection 1 week after the treatment period (Reith, Benuck, & Lajtha, 1987). Thus, the tolerance observed both to the continuous infusion itself and to a challenge injection after this pretreatment is not due to differences in the amount of cocaine in the brains of these animals. This suggests that it might be important for there to be drug-free periods, as are experienced during the intermittent injections, in order for this increased pharmacokinetic profile to occur.

In addition to its pronounced effects on dopamine, cocaine inhibits the reuptake of norepinephrine and serotonin. However, an intraperitoneal injection of cocaine into an anesthetized rat had no effect on norepinephrine overflow in either the frontal cortex or hippocampus, but it did produce an increase in the locus coeruleus (Thomas, Post, & Pert, 1994).

ACUTE AND CHRONIC EFFECTS OF COCAINE ON RECEPTORS

DOPAMINE RECEPTORS

The primary effect of cocaine is to inhibit dopamine uptake, thereby increasing extracellular dopamine, which remains available to act on pre- and postsynaptic dopamine receptors. Thus it is logical to assume that any long-term changes in the behavioral effects of cocaine might be due to changes in dopamine receptor number and function. There have been a number of studies looking at the effects of cocaine on dopamine D_1 and D_2 types of receptors.

There are conflicting reports of changes in dopamine D_1 receptors, with increases in receptor number observed immediately after 15 days of treatment, followed by decreases 14 days later (Kleven, Perry, Woolverton, & Seiden, 1990); and no changes seen 7 days after a 6-day treatment period (Mayfield, Larson, & Zahniser, 1992) or 1 day after either 8 days of cocaine injections (Peris et al., 1990), or 7 days of continuous infusion (Kunko, Ladenheim, Cadet, Carroll, & Izenwasser, 1997). Functional studies also produced variable results, with no change in dopamine D_1 receptor regulation of adenylyl cyclase activity reported in caudate putamen of nucleus accumbens after withdrawal from 6 days of treatment (Mayfield et al., 1992). There was, however, an increased inhibition of cell firing by D_1 agonists after 2 weeks of cocaine treatment, a sensitization that persisted for at least 1 month after cessation of treatment (Henry & White, 1991). Cocaine produces a decrease in the basal firing rate of dopamine neurons, preferentially in mesolimbic as opposed to mesocortical brain regions (White, 1990).

There were no significant changes in dopamine D_2 receptor number or mRNA level in the caudate putamen after withdrawal for 7 days from 14 days of either intermittent or continuous infusion of 40 mg/kg cocaine (King et al., 1994). In contrast, it has also been reported that intermittent daily injections of a lower dose of cocaine (10 mg/kg) for 15 days produced a decrease in dopamine D_2 receptors in the caudate putamen and an increase in the nucleus accumbens (Goeders & Kuhar, 1987). Despite the apparent lack of significant change in receptor binding, dopamine D_2 autoreceptor function appears to be increased following continuous but not intermittent cocaine administration (Chen & Reith, 1993; Gifford & Johnson, 1992; King et al., 1994).

It is important to note that these studies have differed from one another in the length of treatment, doses of cocaine administered, and time since the last drug administration when the neurochemical assays have been done. Thus it is possible that these factors might play an important role in determining what the behavioral and neurochemical consequences of chronic cocaine administration will be.

OPIOID RECEPTORS

Although much evidence suggests that dopamine is the primary system responsible for the effects of cocaine, chronic studies have implicated that cocaine has profound effects on other systems as well. Chronic treatment with cocaine has pronounced effects on opioid peptide levels. Chronic cocaine administration leads to increases in circulating β-endorphin levels (Forman & Estilow, 1988; Moldow & Fischman, 1987), striatal prodynorphin mRNA levels (Daunais, Roberts, & McGinty, 1993; Spangler, Unterwald, & Kreek, 1993), and striatonigral dynorphin content (Sivam, 1989; Smiley, Johnson, Bush, Gibb, & Hanson, 1990).

Repeated administration of cocaine can also regulate the expression of opioid receptors in discrete brain regions of rats. Two weeks of either continuous administration of cocaine via subcutaneously implanted osmotic minipumps (Hammer, 1989; Izenwasser, 1994) or repeated daily injections (Unterwald, Horne-King, & Kreek, 1992) lead to increased μ-opioid receptor and κ-opioid receptor (Unter-

wald, Rubenfeld, & Kreek, 1994) density in the nucleus accumbens, a mesolimbic terminal region that has been shown to be associated with cocaine-induced reinforcement. In contrast, continuous administration of cocaine produces no change
in opioid receptor density in the caudate putamen (Hammer, 1989; Izenwasser,
1994), whereas repeated cocaine injections increase μ-opioid receptors only in the
rostral part of the caudate putamen (Unterwald et al., 1992). One of the differences
between the nucleus accumbens and the caudate putamen is that the nucleus accumbens is a more heterogeneous region than the caudate putamen, which is almost entirely composed of dopamine terminals. Thus a possible explanation for
these findings is that it is not the dopaminergic effects of cocaine that are producing increases in opioid receptors but rather the inhibition of the other monoamines.
This hypothesis is supported by the finding that the receptor increases observed after continuous infusion of cocaine are not seen following treatment for one week
with either a selective dopamine uptake inhibitor, RTI-117, or selective inhibitors
of norepinephrine or serotonin uptake (Kunko & Izenwasser, 1996). Thus it seems
that the μ-opioid receptor upregulation following cocaine might be produced by a
combination of actions on two or possibly all three of these systems.

It is interesting to note that no changes are seen in μ-opioid receptor mRNA
levels in any brain region following the same repeated injection paradigm that produces increases in receptor number (McGinty, Kelley, Unterwald, & Konradi,
1996). Thus these increases are likely due to either posttranslational modifications
in the opioid receptors or to changes in receptor turnover or compartmentalization
(for further discussion see Unterwald et al., 1995).

The functional consequences (neurochemical and behavioral) of these changes
in opioid peptides and opioid receptor density are not well understood. Following
repeated cocaine treatment, there was no change in the inhibition of adenylyl cyclase activity (a measure of receptor-mediated effector function) by DAMGO, a
selective μ-opioid agonist, in either caudate putamen or nucleus accumbens, even
though receptor numbers were increased (Unterwald, Cox, Kreek, Cote, & Izenwasser, 1993). In contrast, in animals treated with continuous cocaine infusions
for 7 days, the increase in opioid receptor number in the nucleus accumbens was
accompanied by a significant increase in DAMGO-inhibited adenylyl cyclase activity (Izenwasser, 1994; Izenwasser, Heller, & Cox, 1996). Thus, the route or pattern of cocaine administration may influence the differences seen in receptor-mediated effector function. The latter finding with continuous cocaine administration
was similar to those obtained following chronic naltrexone treatment, where there
was an increase in μ-opioid receptor number and a concomitant increase in the inhibition of adenylyl cyclase activity by DAMGO in both whole brain (Cote, Izenwasser, & Weems, 1993) and in nucleus accumbens and caudate putamen (Izenwasser, 1994).

The role of opioid receptors in the production of cocaine's effects is not well
understood. A number of studies have shown that opioid antagonists will block the
reinforcing effects of cocaine (e.g., Bain & Kornetsky, 1987; Corrigall & Coen,
1991; Mello, Mendelson, Bree, & Lukas, 1990), although an earlier study suggested that there was no effect (Goldberg, Woods, & Schuster, 1971). Few studies

have looked at opioid effects on cocaine pharmacology. Naloxone (an opioid antagonist) has been reported to have no effect on cocaine toxicity, even though morphine will potentiate the number of seizures produced by cocaine (Derlet, Tseng, Tharratt, & Albertson, 1992). Likewise, pretreatment with naloxone has no effect on the ability of acute cocaine to stimulate either dopamine overflow or locomotor activity (Schad, Justice, & Holtzman, 1995). However, in animals treated with continuous infusions of both cocaine and naltrexone, naltrexone did partially antagonize the upregulation of μ-opioid receptors by cocaine (Izenwasser, 1994). Acutely, pretreatment with the κ-opioid agonist U50,488 attenuates cocaine-induced increases in extracellular dopamine (Maisonneuve, Archer, & Glick, 1994). When the κ-agonist is given chronically with cocaine, however, it does not diminish the sensitized effect of cocaine on dopamine overflow, yet it does block the behavioral sensitization that occurs following repeated cocaine administration (Heidbreder, Babovic-Vuksanovic, Shoaib, & Shippenberg, 1995). These apparently contradicting effects may be explained by a decrease in dopamine D_2 receptors following the κ-agonist treatment (Izenwasser, Acri, Kunko, & Shippenberg, in press). These findings together suggest that an opioid antagonist can block the indirect effects of cocaine on opioid receptors and that a κ-agonist has effects on dopamine receptors, but that neither of these drugs directly blocks the effects of cocaine on dopamine uptake and hence overflow.

OTHER RECEPTOR TYPES

Cocaine appears to interact with a number of other systems as well. Pretreatment with a protein kinase C inhibitor injected into the VTA inhibited both the ability of cocaine to stimulate locomotor activity and the cocaine-induced increase in extracellular dopamine in the nucleus accumbens, suggesting that protein kinases may be important in cocaine's effects (Steketee, 1993). Not yet known, however, is the manner in which cocaine interacts with these kinases.

Neurotensin binding is significantly decreased in the VTA both immediately following and after 10 days of withdrawal from intermittent iv cocaine administration (Pilotte, Mitchell, Sharpe, De Souza, & Dax, 1991). Significantly higher levels of binding were observed in the prefrontal cortex and substantia nigra only after withdrawal from the cocaine treatment, and no changes were seen at either time point in the nucleus accumbens. Because neurotensin and dopamine coexist in many brain regions, it may be that neurotensin plays a role in the production of cocaine's effects.

MOLECULAR MECHANISMS
OF COCAINE EFFECTS

Cloning of rat (Kilty, Lorang, & Amara, 1991; Shimada et al., 1991), bovine (Usdin, Mezey, Chen, Brownstein, & Hoffman, 1991), and human (Giros et al., 1992) dopamine transporter cDNAs has shown that the dopamine transporter is a member of the Na^+/Cl^--dependent transporter family that includes the mono-amine plasma membrane transporters for norepinephrine and serotonin, as well as carriers for a number of amino acids including γ-aminobutyric acid (GABA), glycine, betaine, and others (for review see Amara, 1995). The sequences for the dopamine transporter are highly conserved across these species. The dopamine transporter appears to have 12 transmembrane spanning domains, a large extracellular loop, and intracellular carboxy- and amino-termini, all characteristics of this family of proteins. The exact structure is still unknown, but molecular modeling studies using energy-minimizing structures show that the 12 helices may not be vertically aligned in the membrane and may actually overlap one another (Edvardsen & Dahl, 1994). In situ hybridization studies show that dopamine transporter mRNA levels are seen almost entirely in the cell body regions of dopamine neurons, such as substantia nigra and ventral tegmental area (Augood, Westmore, McKenna, & Emson, 1993; Shimada, Kitayama, Walther, & Uhl, 1992; Usdin et al., 1991).

Site-directed mutations of the cloned dopamine transporter have shown that it is possible to selectively affect dopamine uptake without altering the binding of a cocaine analog (Kitayama et al., 1992; Kitayama, Wang, & Uhl, 1993). For example, replacement by alanine or glycine of the serine residues at positions 356 and 359 of the seventh hydrophobic region leads to a selective decrease in the active transport of dopamine and MPP^+, yet it has no effect on $[^3H]WIN$ 35,428 binding (Kitayama et al., 1992). This provides further evidence that the substrate binding site is separate from the region where uptake inhibitors such as cocaine bind.

When the rat dopamine transporter cDNA is transfected into COS cells, binding consistent with the native dopamine transporter is seen. The cocaine analog $[^3H]WIN$ 35,428 identifies two binding sites on the transporter protein expressed from this cDNA, with affinities similar to those reported for binding to brain (Boja et al., 1992). These findings show that the two binding sites for cocaine and its analogs reside on the dopamine transporter protein itself. This still does not answer the question, however, of whether these two binding affinities represent binding to different locations on the dopamine transporter or to two different conformations of the same binding site. IC_{50} values for inhibition of dopamine uptake into cells containing expressed human dopamine transporters by a series of dopamine uptake inhibitors are highly correlated with uptake into cells transfected with the rat dopamine transporter cDNA (Giros et al., 1992). For the most part, there is also a good correlation between inhibition of uptake through the cloned human dopamine transporter and that in rat brain synaptosomes. It is interesting to note, however, that cocaine appears to be approximately four to five times more potent at inhibiting dopamine uptake through the cloned human transporter than it is either at the cloned rat transporter or in synaptosomes of rat caudate putamen (Giros et al., 1992).

Although only a single dopamine transporter has been cloned in rat brain, there have been suggestions of regional differences in dopamine transporters. Transporter proteins in the nucleus accumbens appear to have a higher molecular weight than those in the caudate putamen (Lew, Vaughn, Simantov, Wilson, & Kuhar, 1991). When transporters from these two brain regions are deglycosylated, the molecular weights appear to be equal, suggesting that the difference might be related to the number of glycosylation sites on each transporter (Lew et al., 1991).

The importance of the dopamine transporter in producing the effects of cocaine has been corroborated by the lack of behavioral effects following a cocaine injection in mice lacking the dopamine transporter (Giros, Jaber, Jones, Wightman, & Caron, 1996). These studies in the transporter knockout mice have clearly confirmed that the dopamine transporter is an essential component for the production of cocaine's effects.

SUMMARY

The studies have shown considerable evidence that the dopamine transporter and the inhibition of dopamine uptake by cocaine play a major role in the production of cocaine's effects. Furthermore, repeated cocaine administration can lead to many neuroadaptations in the dopaminergic system (i.e., changes to the transporter and to dopamine cell firing and receptor function), as well as to serotonergic and opioidergic function. It may be important to take into account the changes in these other systems when trying to understand what chronic cocaine treatment has done both neurochemically and behaviorally.

ACKNOWLEDGMENTS

Thanks to Dr. Amy Hauck Newman for her comments on a previous version of this chapter and to Dr. Rik Kline for his helpful discussions on molecular modeling.

REFERENCES

Amara, S. G. (1995). Monoamine transporters: Basic biology with clinical implications. *The Neuroscientist, 1,* 259–267.

Augood, S. J., Westmore, K., McKenna, P. J., & Emson, P. C. (1993). Co-expression of dopamine transporter mRNA and tyrosine hydroxylase mRNA in ventral mesencephalic neurones. *Molecular Brain Research, 20,* 328–334.

Bain, G. T., & Kornetsky, C. (1987). Naloxone attenuation of the effect of cocaine on rewarding brain stimulation. *Life Sciences, 40,* 1119–1125.

Benmansour, S., Tejani-Butt, S. M., Hauptmann, M., & Brunswick, D. J. (1992). Lack of effect of high dose cocaine on monoamine uptake sites in rat brain measured by quantitative autoradiography. *Psychopharmacology, 106,* 459–462.

Berger, P., Elsworth, J. D., Reith, M. E. A., Tanen, D., & Roth, R. H. (1990). Complex interaction of cocaine with the dopamine uptake carrier. *European Journal of Pharmacology, 176,* 251–252.

Biegon, A., Dillon, K., Volkow, N. A., Hitzemann, R. J., Fowler, J. S., & Wolf, A. P. (1992). Quantitative autoradiography of cocaine binding sites in human brain postmortem. *Synapse, 10,* 126–130.

Boja, J. W., & Kuhar, M. J. (1989). [³H]Cocaine binding and inhibition of [³H]dopamine uptake is similar in both the rat striatum and nucleus accumbens. *European Journal of Pharmacology, 173,* 215–217.

Boja, J. W., Markham, L., Patel, A., Uhl, G., & Kuhar, M. J. (1992). Expression of a single dopamine transporter cDNA can confer two cocaine binding sites. *Molecular Neuroscience, 3,* 247–248.

Bradberry, C. W., Nobiletti, J. B., Elsworth, J. D., Murphy, B., Jatlow, P., & Roth, R. H. (1993). Cocaine and cocaethylene: Microdialysis comparison of brain drug levels and effects on dopamine and serotonin. *Journal of Neurochemistry, 60,* 1429–1435.

Canfield, D. R., Spealman, R. D., Kaufman, M. J., & Madras, B. K. (1990). Autoradiographic localization of cocaine binding sites by [³H]CFT ([³H]WIN 35,428) in the monkey brain. *Synapse, 6,* 189–195.

Carboni, E., Imperato, A., Perezzani, L., & Chiara, G. D. (1989). Amphetamine, cocaine, phencyclidine and nomifensine increase extracellular dopamine concentrations preferentially in the nucleus accumbens of freely moving rats. *Neuroscience, 28,* 653–661.

Carroll, F. I., Lewin, A. H., & Kuhar, M. J. (1996). Dopamine transporter uptake blockers: Structure activity relationships. In M. E. A. Reith (Ed.), *Neurotransmitter transporters: Structure and function.* Totowa, NJ: Humana Press Publishers.

Chen, N.-H., & Reith, M. E. A. (1993). Dopamine and serotonin release-regulating autoreceptor sensitivity in A9/A10 cell body and terminal areas after withdrawal of rats from continuous infusion of cocaine. *Journal of Pharmacology and Experimental Therapeutics, 267,* 1445–1453.

Chen, N.-H., & Reith, M. E. A. (1994). Effects of locally applied cocaine, lidocane, and various uptake blockers on monoamine transmission in the ventral tegmental area of freely moving rats: A microdialysis study on monoamine interrelationships. *Journal of Neurochemistry, 63,* 1701–1713.

Cline, E. J., Scheffel, U., Boja, J. W., Carroll, F. I., Katz, J. L., & Kuhar, M. J. (1992). Behavioral effects of novel cocaine analogs: a comparison with *in vivo* receptor binding potency. *Journal of Pharmacology and Experimental Therapeutics, 260,* 1174–1179.

Corrigall, W. A., & Coen, K. M. (1991). Opiate antagonists reduce cocaine but not nicotine self-administration. *Psychopharmacology, 104,* 167–170.

Cote, T. E., Izenwasser, S., & Weems, H. B. (1993). Naltrexone-induced upregulation of mu opioid receptors on 7315c cell and brain membranes: Enhancement of opioid efficacy in inhibiting adenylyl cyclase. *Journal of Pharmacology and Experimental Therapeutics, 267,* 238–244.

Cunningham, K. A., & Lakoski, J. M. (1988). Electrophysiological effects of cocaine and procaine on dorsal raphe serotonin neurons. *European Journal of Pharmacology, 148,* 457–462.

Cunningham, K. A., Paris, J. M., & Goeders, N. E. (1992). Chronic cocaine enhances serotonin autoregulation and serotonin uptake binding. *Synapse, 11,* 112–123.

Daunais, J. B., Roberts, D. C. S., & McGinty, J. F. (1993). Cocaine self-administration increases preprodynorphin, but not c-fos, mRNA in rat striatum. *Neuroreport, 4,* 543–546.

Derlet, R. W., Tseng, C.-C., Tharratt, R. S., & Albertson, T. E. (1992). The effect of morphine and naloxone on cocaine toxicity. *American Journal of Medical Sciences, 303,* 165–169.

Edvardsen, O., & Dahl, S. G. (1994). A putative model of the dopamine transporter. *Molecular Brain Research, 27,* 265–274.

Egan, M. F., Wing, L., Li, R., Kirch, D. G., & Wyatt, R. J. (1994). Effects of chronic cocaine treatment on rat brain: Long-term reduction in frontal cortical serotonin. *Biological Psychiatry, 36,* 637–640.

Forman, L. J., & Estilow, S. (1988). Cocaine influences beta-endorphin levels and release. *Life Sciences, 43,* 309–315.

Galloway, M. P. (1990). Regulation of dopamine and serotonin synthesis by acute administration of cocaine. *Synapse, 6,* 63–72.

Gifford, A. N., & Johnson, K. M. (1992). Effect of chronic cocaine treatment on D_2 receptors regulating the release of dopamine and acetylcholine in the nucleus accumbens and striatum. *Pharmacology Biochemistry and Behavior, 41,* 841–846.

Giros, B., Jaber, M., Jones, S. R., Wightman, R. M., & Caron, M. G. (1996). Hyperlocomotion and indifference to cocaine and amphetamine in mice lacking the dopamine transporter. *Nature, 379,* 606–612.

Giros, B., Mestikawy, S. E., Godinot, N., Zheng, K., Han, H., Yang-Feng, T., & Caron, M. G. (1992). Cloning, pharmacological characterization, and chromosome assignment of the human dopamine transporter. *Molecular Pharmacology, 42,* 383–390.

Goeders, N. E., & Kuhar, M. J. (1987). Chronic cocaine administration induces opposite changes in dopamine receptors in the striatum and nucleus accumbens. *Alcohol and drug research, 7,* 207–216.

Goldberg, S. R., Woods, J. H., & Schuster, C. R. (1971). Nalorphine-induced changes in morphine self-administration in rhesus monkeys. *Journal of Pharmacology and Experimental Therapeutics, 176,* 464–471.

Hadfield, M. G., Mott, D. E. W., & Ismay, J. A. (1980). Cocaine: Effect of in vivo administration on synaptosomal uptake of norepinephrine. *Biochemical Pharmacology, 29,* 1861–1863.

Hammer, R. P., Jr. (1989). Cocaine alters opiate receptor binding in critical brain reward regions. *Synapse, 3,* 55–60.

Heidbreder, C. A., Babovic-Vuksanovic, D., Shoaib, M., & Shippenberg, T. S. (1995). Development of behavioral sensitization to cocaine: Influence of kappa opioid receptor agonists. *Journal of Pharmacology and Experimental Therapeutics, 275,* 150–163.

Heikkila, R. E., Orlansky, H., & Cohen, G. (1975). Studies on the distinction between uptake inhibition and release of [^{3}H]dopamine in rat brain tissue slices. *Biochemical Pharmacology, 24,* 847–852.

Henry, D. J., & White, F. J. (1991). Repeated cocaine administration causes persistent enhancement of D_1 dopamine receptor sensitivity within the rat nucleus accumbens. *Journal of Pharmacology and Experimental Therapeutics, 258*(1), 882–890.

Horger, B. A., Valadez, A., Wellman, P. J., & Schenk, S. (1994). Augmentation of the neurochemical effects of cocaine in the ventral striatum and medial prefrontal cortex following preexposure to amphetamine, but not nicotine: An in vivo microdialysis study. *Life Sciences, 55,* 1245–1251.

Hurd, Y., & Ungerstedt, U. (1989). Cocaine: An in vivo microdialysis evaluation of its acute action on dopamine transmission in rat striatum. *Synapse, 3,* 48–54.

Imperato, A., Mele, A., Scrocco, M. G., & Puglisi-Allegra, S. (1992). Chronic cocaine alters limbic extracellular dopamine: Neurochemical basis for addicition. *European Journal of Pharmacology, 212,* 299–300.

Izenwasser, S. (1994). Increased mu-opioid efficacy for inhibition of adenylyl cyclase induced by chronic treatment with naltrexone or cocaine. *Regulatory Peptides, 54.*

Izenwasser, S., Acri, J. B., Kunko, P. M., & Shippenberg, T. (in press). Repeated treatment with the selective kappa opioid agonist U-69593 produces a marked depletion of dopamine D_2 receptors. *Synapse.*

Izenwasser, S., & Cox, B. M. (1990). Daily cocaine treatment produces a persistent reduction of [^{3}H]dopamine uptake in vitro in rat nucleus accumbens but not in striatum. *Brain Research, 531,* 338–341.

IIzenwasser, S., & Cox, B. M. (1992). Inhibition of dopamine uptake by cocaine and nicotine: Tolerance to chronic treatments. *Brain Research, 573,* 119–125.

Izenwasser, S., Heller, B., & Cox, B. M. (1996). Continuous cocaine administration enhances μ- but not δ-opioid receptor-mediated inhibition of adenylyl cyclase activity in nucleus accumbens. *European Journal of Pharmacology, 297,* 187–191.

Izenwasser, S., Rosenberger, J. G., & Cox, B. M. (1993). The cocaine analog WIN 35,428 binds to two sites in fresh rat caudate-putamen: Significance of assay procedures. *Life Sciences/Pharmacology Letters, 52,* PL 141–145.

Izenwasser, S., Terry, P., Heller, B., Witkin, J. M., & Katz, J. L. (1994). Differential relationships among dopamine transporter affinities and stimulant potencies of various uptake inhibitors. *European Journal of Pharmacology, 263,* 277–283.

Izenwasser, S., Werling, L. L., & Cox, B. M. (1990). Comparison of the effects of cocaine and other inhibitors of dopamine uptake in rat striatum, nucleus accumbens, olfactory tubercle, and medial prefrontal cortex. *Brain Research, 520,* 303–309.

Johanson, C.-E., & Fischman, M. W. (1989). The pharmacology of cocaine related to its abuse. *Pharmacological Reviews, 41*(1), 3–52.

Johnson, K. M., Bergmann, J. S., & Kozikowski, A. P. (1992). Cocaine and dopamine differentially protect [^{3}H]mazindol binding sites from alkylation by N-ethylmaleimide. *European Journal of Pharmacology—Molecular Pharmacology Section, 227,* 411–415.

Kalivas, P. W., & Duffy, P. (1990). Effect of acute and daily cocaine treatment on extracellular dopamine in the nucleus accumbens. *Synapse, 5,* 48–58.

Katz, J. L., Newman, A. H., & Izenwasser, S. (1997). Relations between heterogeneity of dopamine transporter binding and function and the behavioral pharmacology of cocaine. *Pharmacology Biochemistry and Behavior, 57,* 505–512.

Kaufman, M. J., Spealman, R. D., & Madras, B. K. (1991). Distribution of cocaine recognition sites in monkey brain: I. In vitro autoradiography with [^{3}H]CFT. *Synapse, 9,* 177–187.

Keller, R. W., Jr., Maisonneuve, I. M., Carlson, J. N., & Glick, S. D. (1992). Within-subject sensitization of striatal dopamine release after a single injection of cocaine: An in vivo microdialysis study. *Synapse, 11,* 28–34.

Kennedy, L. T., & Hanbauer, I. (1983). Sodium-sensitive cocaine binding to rat striatal membrane: Possible relationship to dopamine uptake sites. *Journal of Neurochemistry, 41,* 172–178.

Kilty, J. E., Lorang, D., & Amara, S. G. (1991). Cloning and expression of a cocaine-sensitive rat dopamine transporter. *Science, 254,* 578–579.

King, G. R., Ellinwood, E. H., Jr., Silva, C., Joyner, C. M., Xue, Z., Caron, M. G., & Lee, T. H. (1994). Withdrawal from continuous or intermittent cocaine administration: Changes in D2 receptor function. *Journal of Pharmacology and Experimental Therapeutics, 269,* 743–749.

Kirifides, A. L., Harvey, J. A., & Aloyo, V. J. (1992). The low affinity binding site for the cocaine analog, WIN 35,428 is an artifact of freezing caudate tissue. *Life Sciences, 50,* PL-139–PL-142.

Kitayama, S., Shimada, S., Xu, H., Markham, L., Donovan, D. M., & Uhl, G. R. (1992). Dopamine transporter site-directed mutations differentially alter substrate transport and cocaine binding. *Proceedings of the National Academy of Sciences, 89,* 7782–7785.

Kitayama, S., Wang, J.-B., & Uhl, G. R. (1993). Dopamine transporter mutants selectively enhance MPP+ transport. *Synapse, 15,* 58–62.

Kleven, M. S., Perry, B. D., Woolverton, W. L., & Seiden, L. S. (1990). Effects of repeated injections of cocaine on D_1 and D_2 dopamine receptors. *Brain Research, 532,* 265–270.

Krueger, B. K. (1990). Kinetics and block of dopamine uptake in synaptosomes from rat caudate nucleus. *Journal of Neurochemistry, 55,* 260–267.

Kula, N. S., & Baldessarini, R. J. (1991). Lack of increase in dopamine transporter binding or function in rat brain tissue after treatment with blockers of neuronal uptake of dopamine. *Neuropharmacology, 30*(1), 89–92.

Kunko, P., & Izenwasser, S. (1996). Investigation of cocaine-induced changes in opioid receptors using selective monoamine uptake inhibitors. *The FASEB Journal, 10*(3), A448.

Kunko, P. M., Carroll, F. I., & Izenwasser, S. (1996). Chronic continuous administration of monoamine uptake inhibitors produces behavioral tolerance but not a cocaine-like activity pattern. *Neuroscience Abstracts, 22,* 920.

Kunko, P. M., Ladenheim, B., Cadet, J. L., Carroll, F. I., & Izenwasser, S. (1997). Reductions in dopamine transporter and D_1 receptor binding after chronic GBR 12909. *NIDA Research Monograph, Problems of Drug Dependence, 178,* 272.

Lew, R., Grigoriadis, D., Wilson, A., Boja, J. W., Simantov, R., & Kuhar, M. J. (1991). Dopamine transporter: Deglycosylation with exo- and endoglycosidases. *Brain Research, 539,* 239–246.

Lew, R., Vaughn, R., Simantov, R., Wilson, A., & Kuhar, M. J. (1991). Dopamine transporters in the nucleus accumbens and the striatum have different apparent molecular weights. *Synapse, 8,* 152–153.

Little, K. Y., Kirkman, J. A., Carroll, F. I., Breese, G. R., & Duncan, G. E. (1993). [^{125}I]RTI-55 Binding to cocaine-sensitive dopaminergic and serotonergic uptake sites in the human brain. *Journal of Neurochemistry, 61,* 1996–2006.

Little, K. Y., Kirkman, J. A., Carroll, F. I., Clark, T. B., & Duncan, G. E. (1993). Cocaine use increases [^{3}H]WIN 35428 binding sites in human striatum. *Brain Research, 628,* 17–25.

Madras, B. K., Fahey, M. A., Bergman, J., Canfield, D. R., & Spealman, R. D. (1989). Effects of cocaine and related drugs in nonhuman primates. I. [³H]Cocaine binding sites in caudate-putamen. *Journal of Pharmacology and Experimental Therapeutics, 251*(1), 131–141.

Madras, B. K., Spealman, R. D., Fahey, M. A., Neumeyer, J. L., Saha, J. K., & Milius, R. A. (1989). Cocaine receptors labeled by [³H]2β-carbomethoxy-3β-(4-fluorophenyl)tropane. *Molecular Pharmacology, 36,* 518–524.

Maisonneuve, I. M., Archer, S., & Glick, S. D. (1994). U50,488, a κ opioid receptor agonist, attentuates cocaine-induced increases in extracellular dopamine in the nucleus accumbens of rats. *Neuroscience Letters, 181,* 57–60.

Maisonneuve, I. M., Keller, R. W., & Glick, S. D. (1990). Similar effects of D-amphetamine and cocaine on extracellular dopamine levels in medial prefrontal cortex of rats. *Brain Research, 535,* 221–226.

Mayfield, R. D., Larson, G., & Zahniser, N. R. (1992). Cocaine-induced behavioral sensitization and D₁ dopamine receptor function in rat nucleus accumbens and striatum. *Brain Research, 573,* 331–335.

McElvain, J. S., & Schenk, J. O. (1992). A multisubstrate mechanism of striatal dopamine uptake and its inhibition by cocaine. *Biochemical Pharmacology, 43,* 2189–2199.

McGinty, J. F., Kelley, A. E., Unterwald, E. M., & Konradi, C. L. (1996). Symposium: Opioid-dopamine interactions. *INRC Proceedings, 49.*

Meiergerd, S. M., & Schenk, J. O. (1994). Kinetic evaluation of the commonality between the site(s) of action of cocaine and some other structurally similar and dissimilar inhibitors of the striatal transporter for dopamine. *Journal of Neurochemistry, 63,* 1683–1692.

Mello, N. K., Mendelson, J. H., Bree, M. P., & Lukas, S. E. (1990). Buprenorphine and naltrexone effects on cocaine self-administration by rhesus monkeys. *Journal of Pharmacology and Experimental Therapeutics, 254,* 926–939.

Missale, C., Castelleti, L., Govoni, S., Spano, P. F., Trabucchi, M., & Hanbauer, I. (1985). Dopamine uptake is differentially regulated in rat striatum and nucleus accumbens. *Journal of Neurochemistry, 45,* 51–56.

Moldow, R. L., & Fischman, A. J. (1987). Cocaine induced secretion of ACTH, beta-endorphin, and corticosterone. *Peptides, 8,* 819–822.

Ng, J. P., Hubert, G. W., & Justice, J. B., Jr. (1991). Increased stimulated release and uptake of dopamine in nucleus accumbens after repeated cocaine administration as measured by in vivo voltammetry. *Journal of Neurochemistry, 56,* 1485–1492.

Nicolaysen, L. C., Pan, H.-T., & Justice, J. B., Jr. (1988). Extracellular cocaine and dopamine concentrations are linearly related in rat striatum. *Brain Research, 456,* 317–323.

Parsons, L. H., & Justice, J. B., Jr. (1993). Serotonin and dopamine sensitization in the nucleus accumbens, ventral tegmental area, and dorsal raphe nucleus following repeated cocaine administration. *Journal of Neurochemistry, 61,* 1611–1619.

Parsons, L. H., Smith, A. D., & Justice, J. B., Jr. (1991). Basal extracellular dopamine is decreased in the rat nucleus accumbens during abstinence from chronic cocaine. *Synapse, 9,* 60–65.

Peris, J., Boyson, S. J., Cass, W. A., Curella, P., Dwoskin, L. P., Larson, G., Lin, L.-H., Yasuda, R. P., & Zahniser, N. R. (1990). Persistence of neurochemical changes in dopamine systems after repeated cocaine administration. *Journal of Pharmacology and Experimental Therapeutics, 253*(1), 38–44.

Pettit, H. O., & Pettit, A. J. (1994). Disposition of cocaine in blood and brain after a single pretreatment. *Brain Research, 651,* 261–268.

Pettit, H. O., Pan, H.-T., Parsons, L. H., & Justice, J. B., Jr. (1990). Extracellular concentrations of cocaine and dopamine are enhanced during chronic cocaine administration. *Journal of Neurochemistry, 55,* 798–804.

Pilotte, N. S., Mitchell, W. M., Sharpe, L. G., De Souza, E. B., & Dax, E. M. (1991). Chronic cocaine administration and withdrawal of cocaine modify neurotensin binding in rat brain. *Synapse, 9,* 111–120.

Pitts, D. K., & Marwah, J. (1987). Cocaine modulation of central monoaminergic neurotransmission. *Pharmacology Biochemistry and Behavior, 26,* 453–461.

Reith, M. E. A., & Coffey, L. L. (1993). Cationic and anionic requirements for the binding of 2beta-carbomethoxy-3beta-(4-fluorophenyl)[^{3}H]tropane to the dopamine uptake carrier. *Journal of Neurochemistry, 61,* 167–177.

Reith, M. E. A., & Selmeci, G. (1992). Radiolabeling of dopamine uptake sites in mouse striatum: Comparison of binding sites for cocaine, maxindol, and GBR 12935. *Naunyn-Schmiedeberg's Archives of Pharmacology, 345,* 309–318.

Reith, M. E. A., Benuck, M., & Lajtha, A. (1987). Cocaine disposition in the brain after continuous or intermittent treatment and locomotor stimulation in mice. *Journal of Pharmacology and Experimental Therapeutics, 243*(1), 281–287.

Reith, M. E. A., de Costa, B., Rice, K. C., & Jacobson, A. E. (1992). Evidence for mutually exclusive binding of cocaine, BTCP, GBR 12935, and dopamine to the dopamine transporter. *European Journal of Pharmacology–Molecular Pharmacology Section, 227,* 417–425.

Reith, M. E. A., Meisler, B. E., Sershen, H., & Lajtha, A. (1986). Structural requirements for cocaine congeners to interact with dopamine and serotonin uptake sites in mouse brain and to induce stereotyped behavior. *Biochemical Pharmacology, 35,* 1123–1129.

Reith, M. E., Sershen, H., & Lajtha, A. (1981). Binding of [^{3}H] cocaine in mouse brain: kinetics and saturability. *Journal of Receptor Research, 2,* 233–243.

Reith, M. E. A., Sershen, H., & Lajtha, A. (1990). Saturable [^{3}H] cocaine binding in central nervous system of mouse. *Life Science, 27,* 1055–1062.

Ross, S. B., & Renyi, A. L. (1969). Inhibition of the uptake of tritiated 5-hydroxytryptamine in brain tissue. *European Journal of Pharmacology, 7,* 270–277.

Rothman, R. B., Becketts, K. M., Radesca, L. R., de Costa, B. R., Rice, K. C., Carroll, F. I., & Dersch, C. M. (1993). Studies of the biogenic amine transporters. II. A brief study on the use of [^{3}H]DA-uptake-inhibition to transporter-binding-inhibition ratios for the in vitro evaluation of putative cocaine antagonists. *Life Sciences, 53,* 267–272.

Rothman, R. B., Greig, N., Kim, A., Costa, B. R. D., Rice, K. C., Carroll, F. I., & Pert, A. (1992). Cocaine and GBR 12909 produce equivalent motoric responses at different occupancy of the dopamine transporter. *Pharmacology Biochemistry and Behavior, 43,* 1135–1142.

Rothman, R. B., Mele, A., Reid, A. A., Akunne, H., Greig, N., Thurkauf, A., Rice, K. C., & Pert, A. (1989). Tight binding dopamine reuptake inhibitors as cocaine antagonists. *FEBS, 257,* 341–344.

Saadouni, S., Refahi-Lyamani, F., Costentin, J., & Bonnet, J.-J. (1994). Cocaine and GBR 12783 recognize nonidentical, overlapping binding domains on the dopamine neuronal carrier. *European Journal of Pharmacology, 268,* 187–197.

Schad, C. A., Justice, J. B., Jr., & Holtzman, S. G. (1995). Naloxone reduces the neurochemical and behavioral effects of amphetamine but not those of cocaine. *European Journal of Pharmacology, 275,* 9–16.

Schoemaker, H., Pimoule, C., Arbilla, S., Scatton, B., Javoy-Agid, F., & Langer, S. Z. (1985). Sodium dependent [^{3}H]cocaine binding associated with dopamine uptake sites in the rat striatum and human putamen decrease after dopaminergic denervation and in Parkinson's disease. *Archives in Pharmacology, 329,* 227–235.

Seiden, L. S., & Ricaurte, G. A. (1987). Neurotoxicity of methamphetamine and related drugs. In H. Y. Meltzer (Ed.), *Psychopharmacology: The third generation of progress* (pp. 359–366). New York: Raven Press.

Sharpe, L. G., Pilotte, N. S., Mitchell, W. M., & De Souza, E. B. (1991). Withdrawal of repeated cocaine decreases autoradiographic [^{3}H]mazindol-labelling of dopamine transporter in rat nucleus accumbens. *European Journal of Pharmacology, 203,* 141–144.

Shimada, S., Kitayama, S., Lin, C.-L., Patel, A., Nanthakumar, E., Gregor, P., Kuhar, M., & Uhl, G. (1991). Cloning and expression of a cocaine-sensitive dopamine transporter complementary DNA. *Science, 254,* 576–580.

Shimada, S., Kitayama, S., Walther, D., & Uhl, G. (1992). Dopamine transporter mRNA: Dense expression in ventral midbrain. *Molecular Brain Research, 13,* 359–362.

Sivam, S. P. (1989). Cocaine selectively increases striatonigral dynorphin levels by a dopaminergic mechanism. *Journal of Pharmacology and Experimental Therapeutics, 250,* 818–824.

Smiley, P. L., Johnson, M., Bush, L., Gibb, J. W., & Hanson, G. R. (1990). Effects of cocaine on extrapyramidal and limbic dynorphin systems. *Journal of Pharmacology and Experimental Therapeutics, 253,* 938–943.

Spangler, R., Unterwald, E. M., & Kreek, M. J. (1993). 'Binge' cocaine administration induces a sustained increase of prodynorphin mRNA in rat caudate-putamen. *Molecular Brain Research, 19,* 323–327.

Staley, J. K., Basile, M., Flynn, D. D., & Mash, D. C. (1994). Visualizing dopamine and serotonin transporters in the human brain with the potent cocaine analogue [^{125}I]RTI-55: In vitro binding and autoradiographic characterization. *Journal of Neurochemistry, 62,* 549–556.

Staley, J. K., Hearn, W. L., Ruttenber, A. J., Wetli, C. V., & Mash, D. C. (1994). High affinity cocaine recognition sites on the dopamine transporter are elevated in fatal cocaine overdose victims. *Journal of Pharmacology and Experimental Therapeutics, 271,* 1678–1685.

Steketee, J. D. (1993). Injection of the protein kinase inhibitor H7 into the A10 dopamine region blocks the acute responses to cocaine: Behavioral and in vivo microdialysis studies. *Neuropharmacology, 32,* 1289–1297.

Thomas, D. N., Post, R. M., & Pert, A. (1994). Focal and systemic cocaine differentially affect extracellular norepinephrine in the locus coeruleus, frontal cortex and hippocampus of the anaesthetized rat. *Brain Research, 645,* 135–142.

Unterwald, E. M., Cox, B. M., Kreek, M. J., Cote, T. E., & Izenwasser, S. (1993). Chronic repeated cocaine administration alters basal and opioid-regulated adenylyl cyclase activity. *Synapse, 15,* 33–38.

Unterwald, E. M., Horne-King, J., & Kreek, M. J. (1992). Chronic cocaine alters brain mu opioid receptors. *Brain Research, 584,* 314–318.

Unterwald, E. M., Rubenfeld, J. M., Imai, Y., Wang, J.-B., Uhl, G. R., & Kreek, M. J. (1995). Chronic opioid antagonist administration upregulates mu opioid receptor binding without altering mu opioid receptor mRNA levels. *Molecular Brain Research, 33,* 351–355.

Unterwald, E. M., Rubenfeld, J. M., & Kreek, M. J. (1994). Repeated cocaine administration upregulates κ and μ, but not δ, opioid receptors. *Neuroreport, 5,* 1613–1616.

Usdin, T. B., Mezey, E., Chen, C., Brownstein, M. J., & Hoffman, B. J. (1991). Cloning of the cocaine-sensitive bovine dopamine transporter. *Proceedings of the National Academy of Sciences, 88,* 11168–11171.

Vaugeois, J.-M., Bonnet, J.-J., Duterte-Boucher, D., & Costentin, J. (1993). In vivo occupancy of the striatal dopamine uptake complex by various inhibitors does not predict their effects on locomotion. *European Journal of Pharmacology, 230,* 195–201.

Wall, S. C., Innis, R. B., & Rudnick, G. (1992). Binding of the cocaine analog 2β-carbomethoxy-3β-(4-[^{125}I]iodophenyl)tropane to serotonin and dopamine transporters: Different ionic requirements for substrate and 2β-carbomethoxy-3β-(4-[^{125}I]iodophenyl)tropane binding. *Molecular Pharmacology, 43,* 264–270.

Weiss, F., Markou, A., Lorang, M. T., & Koob, G. F. (1992). Basal extracellular dopamine levels in the nucleus accumbens are decreased during cocaine withdrawal after unlimited-access self-administration. *Brain Research, 593,* 314–318.

Wheeler, D. D., Edwards, A. M., & Ondo, J. G. (1993). Dopamine uptake in five structures of the brain: Comparison of rate, sodium dependence and sensitivity to cocaine. *Neuropharmacology, 32,* 501–508.

White, F. J. (1990). Electrophysiological basis of the reinforcing effects of cocaine. *Behavioural Pharmacology, 1,* 303–315.

Wieczorek, W. J., & Kruk, Z. L. (1994). A quantitative comparison on the effects of benztropine, cocaine and nomifensine on electrically evoked dopamine overflow and rate of re-uptake in the caudate putamen and nucleus accumbens in the rat brain slice. *Brain Research, 657,* 42–50.

Wilson, J. M., Nobrega, J. N., Carroll, M. E., Niznik, H. B., Shannak, K., Lac, S. T., Pristupa, Z. B., Dixon, L. M., & Kish, S. J. (1994). Heterogeneous subregional binding patterns of ^{3}H-WIN 35,428 and ³H-GBR 12,935 are differentially regulated by chronic cocaine self-administration. *Journal of Neuroscience, 14,* 2966–2979.

Yang, X.-M., Gorman, A. L., Dunn, A. J., & Goeders, N. E. (1992). Anxiogenic effects of acute and chronic cocaine administration: Neurochemical and behavioral studies. *Pharmacology Biochemistry and Behavior, 41,* 643–650.

Yeh, S. Y., & DeSouza, E. B. (1991). Lack of neurochemical evidence for neurotoxic effects of repeated cocaine administration in rats on brain monoamine neurons. *Drug and Alcohol Dependence, 27,* 51–61.

2

NEUROANATOMICAL BASES OF THE REINFORCING STIMULUS EFFECTS OF COCAINE

S. BARAK CAINE

McLean Hospital
Harvard Medical School
Belmont, Massachusetts

INTRODUCTION

In response to the query, "What brain structure mediates the reinforcing effects of cocaine?" most behavioral pharmacologists and neuroscientists will respond, "nucleus accumbens," "ventral striatum," or "mesolimbic dopamine system." However, depending on the scientist's area of expertise, they may find it more difficult to provide the following details: What specific experiments provided the evidence to support this postulate, and against what historical context did such a discovery emerge? What are the reasonable limits of justified conclusions from those experiments? And what new concepts have emerged from recent work that extend those findings to include other brain areas, and indeed neural circuitries, that may participate in the behavioral effects of cocaine related to its abuse? The purpose of this chapter is to provide, in a concise and simple manner, some answers to these questions. This chapter will focus on neuroanatomical manipulations that alter the behavioral effects of self-administered cocaine in rats; correlative data regarding neural consequences and adaptations to cocaine administration or self-administration will not be addressed here, nor will pharmacology or behavioral pharmacology (see other chapters in this volume). Finally, this chapter is not intended to provide an exhaustive literature review, but rather to describe important discoveries and current hypotheses regarding neural substrates of the reinforcing effects of self-administered cocaine in laboratory animals.

THE MESOACCUMBENS ASCENDING
DOPAMINERGIC PATHWAY

This pathway is critical for the reinforcing effects of cocaine in rats.

BRAIN DOPAMINERGIC DEPLETIONS: MOTOR
AND CONSUMMATORY BEHAVIORS AND BEHAVIORAL
EFFECTS OF PSYCHOSTIMULANT DRUGS

At the beginning of the 1970s Breese and Traylor (1970, 1971) described a method for selectively depleting brain catecholamines (dopamine and norepinephrine) using the neurotoxin 6-hydroxydopamine (6-OHDA), and Ungerstedt (1971) reported profound adipsia and aphagia resulting from 6-OHDA lesions of the nigrostriatal pathway in rats. Fibiger, Zis, and McGee (1973) likened the behavioral effects of 6-OHDA lesions to those of the classical "lateral hypothalamic syndrome," and demonstrated that these lesions attenuated the anorectic effects of amphetamine in rats. This latter finding provided substantive evidence for the theory that the behavioral effects of psychostimulant drugs are mediated by ascending catecholaminergic pathways, and provided impetus for studies to investigate distinct roles for the nigrostriatal and mesolimbic dopamine pathways in the behavioral effects of psychostimulant drugs. Aphagia and adipsia of the lateral hypothalamic syndrome were attributed to sensorimotor deficits arising from interruption of ascending nigrostriatal dopaminergic pathways (Marshall, Richardson, & Teitelbaum, 1974; Stricker & Zigmond, 1974), whereas the mesolimbic dopamine system was hypothesized to play a role in various behavioral disorders, including those induced by psychostimulant drug administration (Anden & Stock, 1973; Horn, Cuello, & Miller, 1974; Snyder, 1973; Stevens, 1973).

Evidence for distinct behavioral functions of the nigrostriatal and mesolimbic dopaminergic pathways followed, as investigators targeted terminal regions of these pathways and isolated a role for dopamine rather than noradrenaline in behavioral effects of psychostimulants. Elegant studies demonstrated that destruction of catecholaminergic nerve terminals in the nucleus accumbens and corpus striatum attenuated amphetamine-induced hyperactivity and stereotypy, respectively (Asher & Aghajanian, 1974; Costall & Naylor, 1974; Creese & Iverson, 1974; Kelly, Seviour, & Iverson, 1975). In addition, accumbens 6-OHDA lesions actually produced some effects opposite to those of nigrostriatal lesions, inducing hyperphagia rather than aphagia; moreover, anorectic effects of amphetamine remained intact in accumbens-lesioned rats despite an attenuation of the locomotor stimulant effects of amphetamine (Koob, Riley, Smith, & Robbins, 1978). Other evidence suggested that the mechanism of the effects of 6-OHDA lesions to attenuate these psychostimulant-induced behaviors was dopaminergic rather than noradrenergic (Heffner, Zigmond, & Stricker, 1977). Thus, in less than a decade, a substantial literature provided evidence that the nigrostriatal dopaminergic pathway was critical for mediating the anorectic and stereotypic motor effects of amphetamine, whereas the mesoaccumbens dopaminergic pathway was critical for the locomotor hyperactivity produced by systemic amphetamine administration.

THE NATURE OF ALTERATIONS IN COCAINE
SELF-ADMINISTRATION PRODUCED
BY MESOACCUMBENS DOPAMINE DEPLETION IN RATS

Concurrent with the neuranatomical studies described above, results from behavioral pharmacological studies suggested that cocaine self-administration was dependent upon catecholaminergic transmission. Systemic drug treatments that depleted catecholamines, or that blocked catecholaminergic or dopaminergic receptors selectively, altered cocaine or amphetamine self-administraiton in laboratory animals (Davis & Smith, 1973, 1975; Pickens, Meisch, & Dougherty, 1968; Wilson & Schuster, 1972, 1973; Yokel & Wise, 1975, 1976). Conversely, intravenous injections of the direct dopamine agonist apomorphine maintained responding in laboratory animals (Baxter, Gluckman, Stein, & Scerni, 1974). In order to clarify the relative roles of noradrenaline and dopamine in cocaine self-administration behavior, and to localize the terminal projections involved, Roberts, Corcoran, and Fibiger (1977) evaluated the effects of 6-OHDA lesions of the dorsal or ventral noradrenergic bundles, or of the nucleus accumbens, on cocaine and apomorphine self-administration in rats.

In that study (Roberts et al., 1977), five rats that had acquired stable cocaine self-administration behavior under a fixed ratio (FR) 1 schedule subsequently received 6-OHDA infusions that depleted accumbens dopamine by an average of 90% relative to control animals. These accumbens-lesioned rats, but not rats with noradrenergic bundle lesions, exhibited significantly decreased cocaine self-administration relative to their prelesion cocaine intake. Importantly, subsequent studies indicated that dopaminergic depletions of the caudate nucleus failed to alter cocaine-maintained responding (Koob, Vaccarino, Amalric, & Bloom, 1987). Event records indicated that in at least some of the accumbens-lesioned animals, responding occurred at a slower rate and was not maintained by cocaine injections throughout the 4-h sessions. It was argued that decreased cocaine self-administration was not the result of motoric deficits, because in another group of animals similar accumbens lesions decreased responding maintained by food presentation for only a few days, whereas the decreases in responding maintained by cocaine injections lasted for 10–15 days postlesion. Moreover, the five rats exhibiting decreased cocaine self-administration exhibited comparable levels of apomorphine self-administration to that of their prelesion values. In a subsequent study, a more persuasive demonstration of decreased cocaine self-administration after accumbens 6-OHDA infusions was reported, as 4 of 11 6-OHDA-treated animals exhibited an "extinction-like" pattern of responding postlesion (Roberts, Koob, Klonoff, & Fibiger, 1980). Moreover, in some animals self-administration behavior was reinstated by apomorphine substitution for cocaine, and subsequent substitution of cocaine for apomorphine produced a pattern of responding similar to that produced

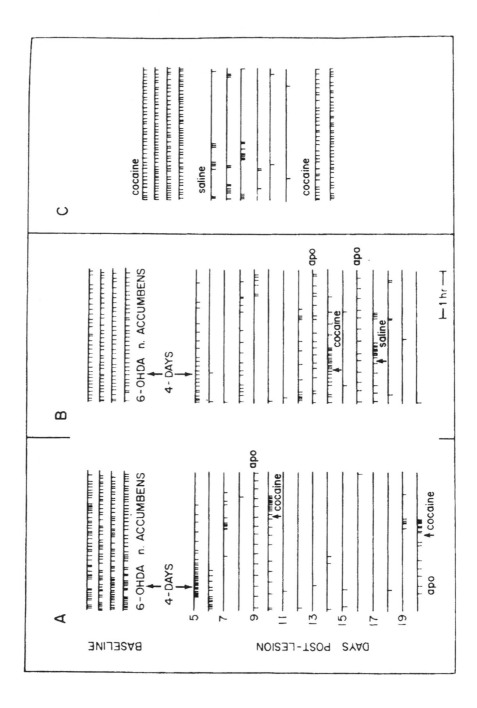

by substitution of saline for apomorphine (Figure 1). Taken together these findings are consistent with the hypothesis that nucleus accumbens dopaminergic nerve terminals are critical for the behavioral effects of self-administered cocaine.

Two alternative hypotheses to explain these results are that accumbens dopamine depletions altered cocaine self-administration by a process that is independent of changes in the behavioral effects of cocaine, or that these lesions altered general reinforcement processes that are not specific to cocaine. Although intravenous apomorphine injections maintained responding in rats with disrupted cocaine self-administration behavior (Roberts et al., 1977, 1980), administration of the direct dopamine agonist apomorphine may have restored, in part, motor or other performance deficits produced by the dopamine depletions. However, other drug reinforcers also maintained responding in animals with accumbens dopamine depletions, including intravenous heroin (Pettit et al., 1984) and oral ethanol (Rassnick, Stinus, & Koob, 1993). Furthermore, in animals trained to respond for food and cocaine reinforcers under identical schedule conditions and within the same test sessions using a multiple schedule, accumbens 6-OHDA lesions selectively decreased cocaine-maintained responding, whereas food-maintained responding remained intact (Figure 2). Taken together, the evidence suggests that accumbens dopamine depletion decreased cocaine self-administration by altering the reinforcing effects of cocaine, and that this behavioral effect of the lesion was somewhat selective for cocaine injections as the reinforcing event that maintained responding.

An unresolved issue remains regarding the nature of changes in the reinforcing effects of cocaine produced by partial versus full depletions of mesolimbic dopamine. As noted previously, only a few animals with severe ($>80\%$) accumbens dopamine depletion exhibited "extinction-like" behavior (i.e., patterns of responding resembling those observed when saline was substituted for cocaine). Moreover, Roberts and Koob (1982) reported that in animals with 6-OHDA lesions of the ventral tegmental area (VTA; the region of somatic origin of the ascending dopaminergic fibers terminating in the accumbens), *11 of 14 animals continued to self-administer cocaine at a reduced rate.* Similarly, in half of the accumbens 6-OHDA-lesioned animals shown in Figure 2, cocaine continued to maintain responding, albeit at approximately half the rate of prelesion values (Caine & Koob, 1994). The most parsimonious explanation of these data is that in some animals

---

FIGURE 2.1   Event records illustrating responding maintained by cocaine (0.75 mg/kg), apomorphine (0.06 mg/kg), or saline injections in rats before and after 6-OHDA lesions of the nucleus accumbens (A and B) or in unoperated rats (C). Each line represents one daily 3-h test session. Downward deflections indicate delivery of a single reinforcer after a single lever press. Note the "extinction-like" patterns of responding in rats self-administering saline, and similar patterns of responding in rats with 6-OHDA lesions of the accumbens self-administering cocaine, despite the reliable responding maintained by apomorphine injections. Reprinted with permission from *Pharmacology, Biochemistry and Behavior, 12,* Roberts et al. Extinction and recovery of cocaine self-administration following 6-hydroxydopamine lesions of the nucleus accumbens, p. 784, 1980. Elsevier Science Inc.

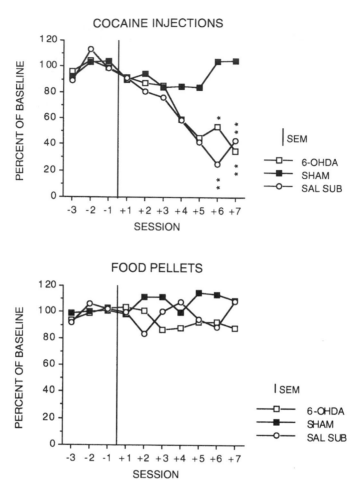

FIGURE 2.2 Effects of 6-OHDA or vehicle infusion into the nucleus accumbens and olfactory tubercle, or substitution of saline for cocaine, on the number of cocaine (top panel) or food (bottom panel) reinforcers earned in daily multiple schedule test sessions. Inset shows the average standard error of the group means (6-OHDA and sham, $n = 6$; saline substitution, $n = 4$). (Reproduced with permission from Caine & Koob, 1994a.)

with lesions of the mesolimbic dopamine pathway, cocaine continues to function as a reinforcer, but that the shape or position of the cocaine self-administration dose–effect function is altered.

Koob et al. (1987) have reported decreased rates of responding maintained by three different doses of cocaine in accumbens 6-OHDA-lesioned animals, but all three doses tested were on the descending limb of the cocaine dose–effect function, making clear interpretation of the results problematic. Contrary to the reported decrease in cocaine self-administration produced by 6-OHDA lesions of the mesolimbic pathway, LeMoal and colleagues reported accelerated acquisition of amphetamine self-administration and a *hypersensitivity* to the behavioral effects of amphetamine in rats with radiofrequency or 6-OHDA lesions of the VTA (LeMoal, Stinson, & Simon, 1979; Deminiere, Simon, Herman, & LeMoal, 1984). This apparently contradictory finding cannot be attributed to differences between the psychostimulant drugs because, similar to results from cocaine self-administration studies, severe accumbens 6-OHDA depletions (95%) impaired acquisition of amphetamine self-administration and decreased response rates in rats previously trained to self-administer amphetamine (Lyness, Friedle, & Moore, 1979). Rather, it appears that there are two variables in these different lesion studies that critically influence the resulting alterations in psychostimulant self-administration behavior: the unit dose of the drug reinforcer and the severity of the mesolimbic dopaminergic depletion. In an attempt to reconcile the apparently discrepant findings, it has been suggested that partial destruction of the mesolimbic pathway produces a hypersensitivity to stimulant drugs resulting from overactivity of the remaining neurons, whereas near complete destruction of the mesoaccumbens neurons attenuates the behavioral effects of self-administered cocaine (Koob, Stinus, & LeMoal, 1981; Roberts & Koob, 1982).

In summary, the exceptional "extinction-like" patterns of cocaine self-administration reported from a few severely accumbens dopamine-depleted animals (see Figure 1), together with the sustained responding maintained by reinforcers other than cocaine in accumbens-lesioned animals (see Figure 2), support the hypothesis that removal of the mesolimbic dopaminergic pathway, at least in some cases, *attenuates* the reinforcing effects of cocaine. However, sustained self-administration at reduced rates was observed in many mesoaccumbens-lesioned animals, and may be due in some cases to a *leftward* shift in the cocaine self-administration dose–effect function, a hypothesis that has yet to be adequately tested.

INTRA-ACCUMBENS INFUSIONS OF DOPAMINERGIC AGONISTS REPRODUCE THE STIMULUS EFFECTS OF COCAINE

Early studies by Pinjenburg et al. (1973, 1975) suggested that infusions of dopamine directly into the nucleus accumbens produced psychomotor stimulant effects, and that the locomotor stimulant effects of systemically administered amphetamine were attenuated by intra-accumbens infusions of the dopamine receptor blocker haloperidol. Nearly a decade later, Hoebel et al. (1983) demonstrated that intra-accumbens amphetamine infusions reliably maintained responding in rats. In that elegant study, several experiments provided compelling evidence for reinforcing stimulus effects of intra-accumbens amphetamine infusions. First, all nine operant-naive rats selectively acquired a response paired with intra-accumbens amphetamine infusions, but not vehicle infusions. Second, a reversal of lever responding occurred when amphetamine infusions were made contingent upon responses on the previously inactive lever. Third, responding was extinguished when infusions were directed into the ventricle, and moreover, responding was subse-

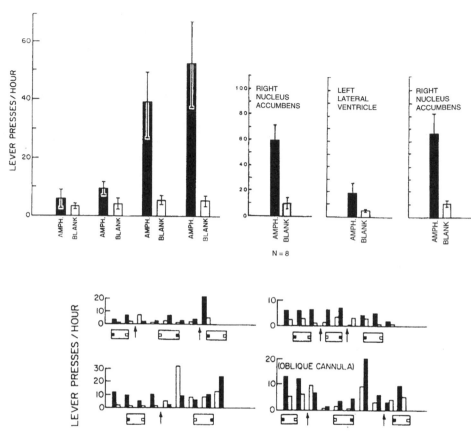

FIGURE 2.3   *Top left:* Acquisition of responding maintained by intra-accumbens amphetamine (AMPH) infusions (65 nl of 10 μg/μl) in naive rats placed in test cages with an active lever and an inactive lever (BLANK) for four consecutive sessions (*n* = 9). *Top right:* Responding maintained by amphetamine infusions into the accumbens or lateral ventricle in dual cannulated rats (*n* = 8). Each value is the group mean from three 4 hr sessions. *Bottom:* Response rates for four rats that exhibited reversal learning when the inactive lever and the lever contingent upon intra-accumbens amphetamine infusions were reversed. Each rectangle is a top view of the cage showing the position of the lever press contingent upon amphetamine infusions (solid). Arrows show reversal of contingency prior to next consecutive session. (Reprinted with permission from *Psychopharmacology, 81,* Hoebel et al., Self-injection of amphetamine directly into the brain, pp. 159–161, 1983. Copyright © 1983 by Springer-Verlag.)

quently reinstated when infusions were again made intra-accumbens (Figure 3). Despite an isolated report that intra-accumbens amphetamine infusions failed to maintain responding in rhesus monkeys (Phillips, Mora, & Rolls, 1981), the data from Hoebel's study in rats were persuasive, and have been confirmed by studies documenting intra-accumbens amphetamine or nomifensine (also an indirect dopamine agonist) self-administration in rats (Phillips, Robbins, & Everitt, 1994; Carlezon, Devine, & Wise, 1995).

The demonstration that intra-accumbens infusions of amphetamine or nomifensine maintained operant responding in rats, taken together with the observation that accumbens dopamine depletion decreased responding maintained by intravenous cocaine injections (see previous section), suggested that the stimulus effects of cocaine related to its self-administration may be mediated within the nucleus accumbens. Consistent with this hypothesis, a few studies reported that intra-accumbens infusions of cocaine reproduced the discriminative stimulus effects of systemically administered cocaine in rats, whereas infusions into other regions such as prefrontal cortex, central amygdala, caudate putamen, or lateral ventricle engendered lesser cocaine-appropriate responding (Wood & Emmett-Oglesby, 1989; Callahan, Bryan, & Cunningham, 1994, 1995). Nevertheless, there remains a paucity of compelling evidence for robust reinforcing stimulus effects of intra-accumbens cocaine. Early studies (Goeders & Smith, 1983) suggested that intracerebral cocaine infusions maintained responding when directed to the prefrontal cortex (see later section) but *not* the accumbens. In contrast, a more recent study suggested that intra-accumbens cocaine infusions maintained responding in rats, though this effect may not have been as robust as that produced by intra-accumbens nomifensine infusions (Carlezon et al., 1995). Thus, although intra-accumbens infusions of amphetamine or nomifensine clearly maintain responding in rodents, and some stimulus effects of systemic cocaine are reproduced by intra-accumbens cocaine infusions, further studies are needed to determine the range of conditions under which intra-accumbens cocaine infusions maintain responding in animals.

INTRA-ACCUMBENS INFUSIONS OF DOPAMINERGIC ANTAGONISTS ATTENUATE THE STIMULUS EFFECTS OF INTRAVENOUS COCAINE

Complementary to studies employing intra-accumbens psychostimulant administration are studies examining the behavior-modifying effects of intra-accumbens dopaminergic antagonists on responding maintained by intravenous cocaine injections. Intra-accumbens infusions of either D_{1-like} or D_{2-like} receptor antagonists dose dependently increased responding maintained by unit doses of intravenous cocaine on the descending limb of the cocaine dose–effect function, suggesting an attenuation of the behavioral effects of self-administered cocaine (Phillips, Broekkamp, & Fibiger, 1983; Robledo et al., 1992; Maldonado et al., 1993; McGregor and Roberts, 1993; Caine et al., 1995). These findings are consistent with results obtained from studies of the discriminative stimulus effects of cocaine, where intra-accumbens infusions of a D_{1-like} antagonist blocked the cocaine stimulus (Callahan et al., 1994). In some studies under certain conditions, altered rates of cocaine self-administration were observed when dopaminergic antagonists were infused into the accumbens but not into the corpus striatum (Phillips et al., 1983; Maldonado, Robledo, Chover, Caine, & Koob, 1993; Caine, Heinrichs, Coffin, & Koob, 1995); however, in other studies appropriate neuroanatomical controls were not performed.

The importance of adequate neuroanatomical control studies is evident for several reasons. First, most of the dopaminergic antagonists employed in intracerebral studies are highly lipophyllic, and may therefore spread rapidly throughout the neuraxis following local "microinjections." Second, the effective doses of the antagonists administered intra-accumbens were not markedly different from those administered subcutaneously. For example, most studies reported significant effects of 2.0 μg (1.0 μg per hemisphere, bilaterally) of the D_{1-like} antagonist SCH 23390 administered intra-accumbens, yet this dose (approximately 6.0 μg/kg) increased cocaine-maintained responding after subcutaneous administration (Caine & Koob, 1994b). Comparison of the relative potencies of SCH 23390 by different routes of administration indicated only a twofold greater potency when administered intra-accumbens rather than subcutaneously (Table 1). Third, behavioral as well as autoradiographic evidence suggested that the "local" effects of intracerebrally administered dopaminergic antagonists were time-dependent as a result of diffusion to other sites (Caine et al., 1995). Although intra-accumbens SCH 23390 altered cocaine self-administration rates in the first 20 min after infusions into the accumbens but not dorsal striatum, infusions into both sites produced similar effects over 3 h (see Figure 5). This is very important, as dopaminergic antagonists have been reported to modify the behavioral effects of cocaine after infusions into a host of different brain structures including accumbens, amygdala, bed nucleus, caudate, and neocortex (Caine et al., 1995; Callahan et al., 1995; Callahan, De La Garza, & Cunningham, 1994; Epping-Jordan, Markou, & Koob, 1998; Hurd, Mc-Gregor, & Ponten, 1997; McGregor & Roberts, 1993, 1995). In some studies qualitative or quantitive differences between the effects of infusions into different brain

TABLE 2.1   Regional Potency of Intracerebral SCH 23390 Relative to Subcutaneous Administration[a]

Region	Potency ratio	Significance
Accumbens shell	0.45	$p < 0.05$
Central amygdala	0.69	$p < 0.05$
Caudate putamen	0.96	$p > 0.1$

[a]Relative potency refers to the ratio of the amount of a drug necessary to produce an equivalent effect to some standard assigned a value of unity (Tallarida & Murray, 1987). Thus 0.45 μg in the accumbens shell or 0.69 μg in the central amygdala produced an effect equivalent to that produced by 1.0 μg administered subcutaneously. The unit dose of cocaine was 0.75 mg/kg, measured in 6 rats per group. (Reprinted with permission from *Brain Research, 692,* Caine et al., Effects of the dopamine D-1 antagonist SCH 23390 microinjected into the accumbens, amygdala or striatum on cocaine self-administration in the rat, p. 50, 1995, with kind permission of Elsevier Science-NL, Sara Burgerharstraat 25, 1055 KV Amsterdam, The Netherlands.)

regions were emphasized, for example, different effects on responding maintained under FR versus progressive ratio schedules. However, since response contingencies and cocaine intake are differently regulated under those two schedules over time, and the regional selectivity of intracerebral infusions is also time-dependent, the interaction of these factors may have contributed to the putative differential effects of SCH 23390 infusions into different brain sites on cocaine-maintained behavior.

The lack of concrete evidence for sufficient neuroanatomical resolution of intracerebral infusions of dopaminergic antagonists is a serious confound that demands caution in the interpretation of results from many studies (see also the third and fourth sections). A greater consideration of the interaction between time-dependent and putative region-dependent effects of these manipulations is strongly advised. The implementation of more sophisticated neuroanatomical control experiments, and the development of dopaminergic antagonists with lesser lipophyllicity, such as has been achieved with quaternary derivatives of opioid antagonists (Koob, Pettit, Ettenberg, & Bloom, 1984; Vaccarino, Bloom, & Koob, 1985), may improve the reliability of this technique for evaluating neuroanatomical substrates of the behavioral effects of systemically administered cocaine.

THE MEDIAL PREFRONTAL CORTEX

The medial prefrontal cortex has a modulatory role in some behavioral effects of self-administered cocaine through an interaction with the mesoaccumbens dopaminergic pathway.

MEDIAL PREFRONTAL CORTICAL DESTRUCTION

Medial prefrontal cortical destruction or dopaminergic depletion enhances acquisition and maintenance of responding maintained by low doses of intravenous cocaine. Early studies suggested that frontal cortical damage increased the sensitivity of rats and mice to the behavioral effects of amphetamine (Glick, 1972, 1973; Iverson, Wilkinson, & Simpson, 1971). For example, in experiments where responding was maintained by amphetamine injections or water presentation, large aspiration lesions of frontal cortex produced an apparent leftward shift in the dose–effect function of intravenously administered amphetamine in rats (Glick & Marsanico, 1975). More recent studies using axon-sparing excitotoxic lesions of medial prefrontal cortex generally confirm those findings (e.g., Jaskiw et al., 1990), and sophisticated studies by Weissenborn, Robbins, and Everitt (1997) demonstrated accelerated acquisition of responding maintained by intravenous cocaine injections. In that latter study, however, the authors emphasized the following important observations regarding the behavioral effects of the lesion and the modulation of the behavioral effects of cocaine. First, apart from differences in acquisition, responding maintained by cocaine injections was enhanced in medial prefrontal-lesioned rats only for a few doses of self-administered cocaine. Second, rats trained to self-administer cocaine *prior* to medial prefrontal lesions did not exhibit altered cocaine self-administration postlesion, nor did their postlesion cocaine dose–effect functions differ from those of sham-operated control animals. Third, rats with medial prefrontal lesions exhibited hyperactivity in photocell cages, as well as heightened locomotor activity after cocaine injections. Finally, in comparison to sham-opoerated controls, responding maintained by cocaine injections under a second-order schedule was heightened in medial prefrontal-lesioned rats, with patterns of responding that were unchanged by omission of the conditioned stimulus. Taken together the authors suggested that facilitated acquisition of cocaine self-administration, as well as altered response patterns under second-order schedules, resulted from deficits in behavioral inhibition induced by medial prefrontal cortical lesions, an hypothesis supported by results from other studies of prefrontal cortical function (see Robbins et al., 1994).

Studies of 6-OHDA lesions aimed at determining the role of the mesocortical dopaminergic projection in the behavioral effects of cocaine have produced results similar to those described above involving aspiration or excitotoxic lesions of medial prefrontal cortex. Thus initial studies demonstrated that in rats trained *prior* to 6-OHDA lesions of medial prefrontal cortex, postlesion rates and patterns of responding maintained by cocaine injections appeared normal (Martin-Iverson, Szostak, & Fibiger, 1986). Similarly Leccese and Lyness (1987) found no effect of prefrontal dopaminergic depletions on responding maintained by intravenous amphetamine injections. However, in subsequent studies examining a broader dose range of self-administered cocaine, accelerated acquisition of responding under a continuous reinforcement schedule (Schenk, Horger, Peltier, & Shelton, 1991) and increased responding under a progressive ratio schedule (McGregor, Baker, & Roberts, 1996) was observed in rats with medial prefrontal dopamine depletions. Importantly, however, in both of those studies, differences in the behavior of lesioned animals compared with sham-operated control animals were restricted to differences in responding maintained by low doses, but not high doses, of cocaine. The mechanism of such effects may be attributed, in part, to the increased turnover of dopamine in the nucleus accumbens following medial prefrontal excitotoxic or 6-OHDA lesions (Deutsch, Clark & Roth, 1990; Jaskiw et al., 1990; Leccese & Lyness, 1987; Martin-Iverson et al., 1986; Pycock, Carter & Kerwin 1980; Rosin, Clark, Goldstein, Roth, & Deutsch, 1992), and likely involves the cell bodies of origin (i.e., VTA) of the mesoaccumbens dopaminergic pathway (Karreman & Moghaddam, 1996).

INTRAPREFRONTAL COCAINE INFUSIONS: SELF-ADMINISTRATION AND ACCUMBENS DOPAMINERGIC TRANSMISSION

More persuasive evidence of a role for medial prefrontal cortex in the behavioral effects of self-administered cocaine comes from studies of intracranial drug self-administration. In an extraordinary study in rhesus monkeys, Phillips, Mora, and Rolls (1981) targeted sites in orbital cortex that had been used for responding maintained by intracranial self-stimulation (ICSS). They showed that in these monkeys responding was also maintained by intracortical amphetamine infusions. In two monkeys the touch response previously resulting in ICSS was first extinguished, and subsequently intracortical amphetamine infusions engendered responding on a different panel manipulandum. In one animal responding was maintained under a FR 10 (but not FR 20) schedule. Goeders and Smith (1983) subsequently demonstrated robust responding maintained by intraprefrontal cortical infusions of cocaine in rats, and in a series of elegant experiments (1986, 1993) these investigators characterized neural and pharmacological mechanisms underlying this behavioral effect of cocaine.

Responding maintained by intraprefrontal cocaine infusions in rats exhibited orderly cocaine dose–effect functions (Figure 4), and depletion of dopaminergic nerve terminals resulting from 6-OHDA lesions at the site of intracranial infusions flattened the cocaine dose–effect function (Goeders & Smith, 1986). In addition, in these 6-OHDA-lesioned animals, intraprefrontal *dopamine* infusions maintained significantly higher responding than did intraprefrontal cocaine or vehicle infusions. Moreover, the D_{2-like} dopaminergic antagonist sulpiride attenuated responding maintained by cocaine or by dopamine when coinfused into the prefrontal cortex during self-administration. Finally, dopamine turnover was significantly increased in the ipsilateral nucleus accumbens of rats that had self-administered cocaine into the medial prefrontal cortex (Goeders & Smith, 1993). Taken together the results suggest that the medial prefrontal cortex may be an important neural substrate for the reinforcing effects of cocaine, and that the mechanisms involved include presynaptic dopaminergic nerve terminals and postsynaptic D_{2-like} dopamine receptors in the medial prefrontal cortex, resulting in stimulation of the mesoaccumbens dopaminergic pathway.

INTRAPREFRONTAL INFUSIONS
OF DOPAMINERGIC ANTAGONISTS

A further bit of evidence that implicated the medial prefrontal cortex in the behavioral effects of self-administered cocaine was the observation that intraprefrontal infusions of the D_{1-like} receptor antagonist SCH 23390 increased responding maintained by intravenous cocaine injections under an FR schedule (McGregor & Roberts, 1995). However, in that study, intrastriatal infusions of SCH 23390 similarly increased cocaine-maintained responding under the same conditions, despite evidence that striatal dopamine is not critical for the behavioral effects of self-administered cocaine (Koob et al., 1987). In contrast, intraprefrontal infusions of SCH 23390, but not intrastriatal infusions, decreased cocaine-maintained responding under a progressive ratio schedule, suggesting attenuation of the behavioral effects of self-administered cocaine. Nevertheless, as discussed above, caution is advised regarding interpretation of the effects of intracerebral infusions of SCH 23390 due to the absence of compelling evidence for neuroanatomical selectivity of the infusions, the similar effective dose range of intracerebral versus

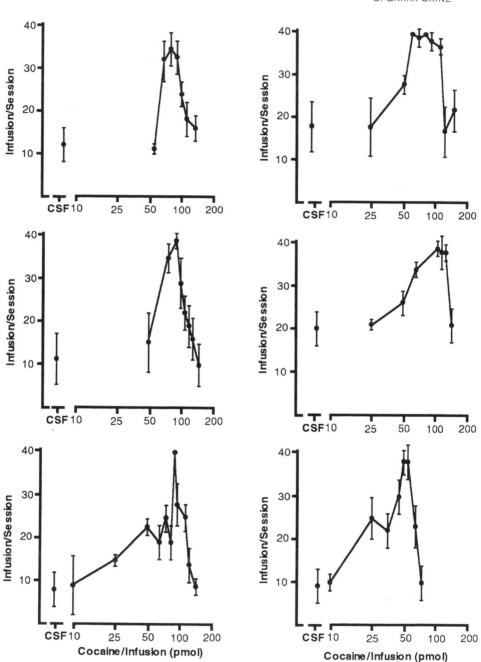

FIGURE 2.4   Cocaine dose effect functions for responding maintained by infusions of cocaine (100 nl) into the medial prefrontal cortex in six individual rats. Values are means and standard errors from an average of 62 sessions. (Reprinted with permission from *Pharmacology, Biochemistry and Behavior, 24,* Goeders et al. Neurophamacological assessment of cocaine self-administration into the medial prefrontal cortex, p. 1432, 1986. Elsevier Science Inc.)

systemic administration of SCH 23390 (see Table 1), and the complications of comparing time-dependent regional effects across conditions that differ as a function of time (e.g., FR schedules versus progressive ratio schedules).

THE AMYGDALA'S ROLE IN BEHAVIORAL EFFECTS OF SELF-ADMINISTERED COCAINE

EXCITOTOXIC LESIONS OF THE BASOLATERAL AMYGDALA UNDER A SECOND-ORDER AND AN FR 1 SCHEDULE

Amphetamine-induced increases in accumbens dopaminergic transmission enhance responding maintained by conditioned reinforcers (e.g., previously neutral stimuli that acquire motivational effects through their association with primary reinforcers), and studies have established an important role for the basolateral amygdala in conditioned reinforcement (Robbins, Cador, Taylor, & Everitt, 1989). Consistent with those findings, another study demonstrated that rats with excitotoxic lesions of the basolateral amygdala exhibited reduced performance compared with sham-operated control rats when trained to respond under a second-order schedule of cocaine-maintained behavior (Whitelaw, Markou, Robbins, & Everitt, 1996). Importantly, in that study lesions of the basolateral amygdala did not impair responding maintained by cocaine under a FR 1 schedule, but rather lesioned rats exhibited increased responding during acquisition tests and across a range of cocaine doses in subsequent tests. Thus the authors suggested that the basolateral amygdala mediates associations between previously neutral stimuli and primary reinforcers including water, sucrose, sexual interaction, and cocaine (Burns, Robbins, & Everitt, 1994; Cador, Robbins, & Everitt, 1989; Everitt, Cador, & Robbins, 1989; Whitelaw et al., 1996), but that the basolateral amygdala is not necessary for the primary reinforcing effects of cocaine. These conclusions are consistent with other results from preliminary studies that excitotoxic lesions of the basolateral amygdala attenuated responding elicited by cues paired with cocaine (Meil & See, 1995), but failed to alter cocaine-maintained responding in rats that were trained prior to the lesion (Meil & See, 1995; Caine & Koob, unpublished observations; Whitelaw & Everitt, unpublished observations).

COCAINE-MAINTAINED RESPONDING AFTER 6-OHDA LESIONS OF THE AMYGDALA

Consistent with the findings described above that excitotoxic lesions of the amygdala had little effect on cocaine-maintained responding in rats trained prior to the lesion under an FR schedule, a similar study using a progressive ratio schedule led McGregor, Baker, and Roberts (1994) to conclude that "no specific effect on cocaine reinforcement was produced by 6-OHDA lesions of the amygdala" (p. 273). In that study 6-OHDA lesions of the amygdala failed to alter responding maintained by two of three cocaine doses tested, and responding maintained by the highest cocaine dose was increased in lesioned rats compared with sham-operated rats. The latter result may be consistent with other evidence of enhanced behavioral effects of psychostimulant drugs as a result of amygdala dopaminergic depletions. Simon et al. (1988) reported enhanced locomotor responses to d-amphetamine in rats with 6-OHDA lesions of amygdala, as well as enhanced acquisition of responding maintained by a low dose of intravenous amphetamine (Deminiere, Taghzouti, Tassin, Le Moal, & Simon, 1988), effects that they attributed to increased mesoaccumbens dopaminergic transmission resulting from the amygdala lesions.

EXCITOTOXIC LESIONS OF STRUCTURES RECEIVING ACCUMBENS EFFERENTS: THE VENTRAL PALLIDUM AND "EXTENDED AMYGDALA"

Investigations into the functional output of the nucleus accumbens established the ventral pallidal region as a critical mediator of the behavioral effects of psychomotor stimulants as well as opioids (Mogenson & Nielson, 1983a,b; Swerdlow & Koob, 1985; Swerdlow, Swanson, & Koob, 1984a,b). Based on those findings and others (Zito, Vickers, & Roberts, 1985), Hubner and Koob (1990) hypothesized that the convergence of accumbens outflow through the ventral pallidum may be critical for the behavioral effects of self-administered cocaine as well as heroin. Consistent with their hypothesis, excitotoxic lesions of the ventral pallidum attenuated responding maintained by either cocaine or heroin. However, although response rates maintained by cocaine or heroin were reduced as a result of the lesion, the patterns of responding were not suggestive of "extinction" (see the second section for discussion). Nevertheless, decreased responding under the progressive ratio schedule was suggested as evidence for attenuation of the behavioral effects of self-administered cocaine and heroin.

In a subsequent study, Robledo and Koob (1993) targeted different compartments of accumbens output using excitotoxic lesions of either subcommissural ventral pallidum or sublenticular "extended amygdala." Those authors hypothesized, based upon neuroanatomical studies (Alheid & Heimer, 1988; Heimer, Zahm, Churchill, Kalivas, & Wohltmann, 1991), that different effects of the two lesions on cocaine-maintained behavior would reflect different roles of accumbens core or shell, respectively, in the behavioral effects of self-administered cocaine. Although either lesion reduced response rates maintained by cocaine under an FR schedule, only the "extended amygdala" lesion attenuated responding under a progressive ratio schedule. Thus the authors suggested that the "the sublenticular extended amygdala, which receives projections from the shell of the nucleus accumbens may be important in processing the reinforcing actions of cocaine" (p. 159). However, the authors also acknowledged that performance deficits may have contributed to the behavioral effects of the lesions in that study.

INFUSIONS OF DOPAMINERGIC ANTAGONISTS
INTO THE ACCUMBENS SHELL, CENTRAL NUCLEUS OF
AMYGDALA, OR BED NUCLEUS OF STRIA TERMINALIS

In order to further pursue the hypothesis that the "extended amygdala" functions as a neural substrate for behavioral effects of self-administered cocaine, Koob and colleagues have used intracerebral "microinjections" to chart neuroanatomical territories sensitive to the rate-increasing effects of the dopamine receptor antagonist SCH 23390 on cocaine-maintained responding (Caine et al., 1995; Epping-Jordan et al., 1998). The "extended amygdala" is proposed to comprise a forebrain continuum bordered by the central nucleus of the amygdala and the shell of the accumbens (both of which receive a dense dopaminergic innervation) and includes portions of the substantia innominata and bed nucleus of stria terminalis (Alheid and Heimer, 1988). Consistent with a role for the extended amygdala forebrain system in the behavioral effects of cocaine, local infusions of SCH 23390 into the accumbens shell, central amygdala, or bed nucleus increased rates of responding maintained by cocaine (Figure 5), an effect consistent with a rightward shift in the cocaine dose–effect function under those conditions (Caine & Koob, 1994b). Although assumptions regarding the neuroanatomical resolution of intracerebral infusions of SCH 23390 warrant scrutiny (see previous sections), several experiments aimed at addressing this important issue suggested that the increased rates of cocaine-maintained responding in those studies were attributable to actions of SCH 23390 proximal to the sites of infusions. Thus, infusions of SCH 23390 into the accumbens shell, central nucleus, or bed nucleus significantly increased response rates in the first 20 min of the session, whereas infusions into the lateral ventricle, dorsolateral caudate, or the lateral septum/medial caudate (just 1.5 mm dorsal to the bed nucleus) failed to produce such rapid effects on cocaine-maintained behavior (see Figure 5). Moreover, autoradiographic studies confirmed that the diffusion of SCH 23390 away from the site of infusion was time-dependent, providing a rationale for the comparison of rapid versus slower time course effects of intracerebral infusions of SCH 23390 (Caine et al., 1995). Nevertheless, some data suggest that caution is still warranted regarding the neuroanatomical resolution of intracerebral infusions of SCH 23390. As discussed previously, the potency of SCH 23390 infused intracerebrally is not substantially different from its potency when administered subcutaneously (Table 1). Moreover, the concentration of [3H]-SCH 23390 at the site of intracerebral infusion declined twofold in 10 min and fourfold in 20 min (Caine et al., 1995), despite a time course of effects of 90 min to 2 h, suggesting that the drug rapidly diffuses from the site of infusion.

Other investigators have also reported attenuation of the behavioral effects of cocaine after intra-amygdala infusions of SCH 23390, though the infusions were apparently aimed at the basolateral nucleus (Hurd et al., 1997; McGregor & Roberts, 1993). The central and basolateral nuclei are in close proximity to each

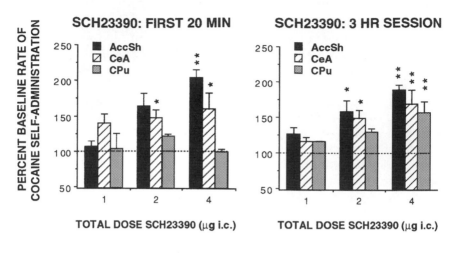

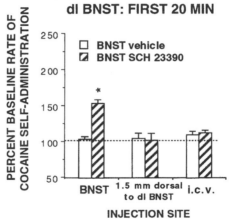

FIGURE 2.5   Effects of SCH 23390 maleate (top panels) or SCH 23390 HCl (bottom panel) microinjected into the accumbens shell (AccSh), central nucleus of the amygdala (CeA), caudate putamen (CPu), dorsolateral bed nucleus of the stria terminalis (dl BNST), 1.5 mm dorsal to the dl BNST, or into the lateral ventricle on responding maintained by intravenous cocaine (unit dose 0.75 mg/kg). Top left panel shows values from the first 20 min of the three hour sessions, and right panel shows values from the entire three hour sessions ($n = 5$–7/group). (*Top panels*—Reprinted with permission from *Brain Research, 692,* Caine et al., Effects of the dopamine D-1 antagonist SCH 23390 microinjected into the accumbens, amygdala or striatum on cocaine self-administration in the rat, p. 50, 1995, with kind permission of Elsevier Science-NL, Sara Burgerharstraat 25, 1055 KV Amsterdam, The Netherlands. *Bottom panel*—Reprinted with permission from *Brain Research,* 784, Epping-Jordan et al., The dopamine D-1 receptor antagonist SCH 23390 injected into the dorsolateral bed nucleus of the stria terminalis decreased cocaine reinforcement in the rat, p. 111, 1998, with kind permission of Elsevier Science-NL, Sara Burgerharstraat 25, 1055 KV Amsterdam, The Netherlands.

other, yet important differences exist in their neuroanatomical properties. The basolateral amygdala provides the major output pathway from the amygdala complex to the mesoaccumbens dopaminergic pathway, including a direct projection to the accumbens itself (Kelley, Domesick, & Nauta, 1982; Wright, Beijer, & Groenewegen, 1996). The central nucleus, on the other hand, receives the densest dopaminergic innervation arising from the ventral tegmental area to the amygdaloid complex (Fallon & Ciofi, 1992). Clearly, intra-amygdala infusions of SCH 23390 do not have sufficient anatomical resolution to discriminate the relative involvement of these two nuclei in the behavioral effects of cocaine. However, a recent study of excitotoxic lesions of the central nucleus provided evidence for a dissociation of functional effects of these two nuclei in the behavioral effects of intra-accumbens amphetamine. Whereas excitotoxic lesions of the basolateral nucleus attenuated responding maintained by a conditioned reinforcer but did not impair the amplification of this responding by intra-accumbens amphetamine (Robbins et al., 1989), lesions of the central nucleus produced an opposite pattern of effects such that responding maintained by the conditioned reinforcer was unaffected, yet the amplification of this responding by intra-accumbens amphetamine was attenuated (Robledo, Page, Weissenborn, Robbins, & Everitt, 1996). This latter evidence suggests a role for the central nucleus in the behavioral effects of intra-accumbens amphetamine, and though speculative, may be taken to provide some converging evidence that dopaminergic transmission in the central nucleus of the amygdala, and possibly throughout the "extended amygdala," has an important role in the behavioral effects of psychostimulants related to their reinforcing effects.

NEWLY CHARTED TERRITORIES: SUBICULUM, BASAL NUCLEUS, AND PEDUNCULOPONTINE

Hippocampal lesions have been reported to enhance the behavioral effects of amphetamine (Devenport, Devenport, & Holloway, 1981; Isaacson, 1984), and to enhance amphetamine-stimulated accumbens dopaminergic transmission (Wilkinson et al., 1993). The major projection from the hippocampal formation to the accumbens is via the subiculum (Groenewegen et al., 1987; Kelley & Domesick, 1982); however, in contrast to hippocampal lesions, excitotoxic lesions of the ventral subiculum (that spared the hippocampus proper) *attenuated* behavioral effects of intra-accumbens amphetamine (Burns et al., 1993). Consistent with this latter result, another study confirmed that lesions of the ventral subiculum attenuated the locomotor stimulant effects of i.p. amphetamine, producing a rightward shift in the amphetamine dose–effect function (Caine et al., 1996). In contrast, lesions of the dorsal subiculum produced hyperactivity and a leftward shift in the amphetamine dose–effect function. Moreover, in preliminary studies, ventral subiculum-lesioned animals exhibited heightened rates of cocaine self-administration, and conversely dorsal subiculum-lesioned rats exhibited lower rates of drug intake relative to sham-operated controls. Though preliminary, these results suggest that the hippocampal formation exerts a modulatory influence upon the behavioral effects of psychostimulants including cocaine, and that the ventral and dorsal regions of subiculum exert opposite modulatory effects.

Another recently explored neuroanatomical site of potential interest is the cholinergic nucleus basalis magnocellularis (NBM), a structure that receives projections from the nucleus accumbens, and itself projects to prefrontal cortex and basolateral amygdala. Preliminary results indicated that excitotoxic lesions of the NBM did not alter acquisition of responding maintained by intravenous cocaine injections; however, a leftward shift in the cocaine dose-effect function was observed in lesioned rats relative to sham-operated control rats (Robledo et al., 1996). Interestingly, the authors of that study suggested that the apparent increased sensitivity to low doses of cocaine may have resulted, at least in part, from a resistance to extinction of responding in the absence of cocaine reinforcers. This interpretation may be compatible with suggestions that the NBM is important for behavioral functions involving attention and discrimination (Dunnett, Everitt, & Robbins, 1991).

One further neuroanatomical site worthy of mention, despite a paucity of data related to its involvement in the behavioral effects of cocaine, is the pedunculopontine tegmental nucleus. Similar to the ventral pallidum, the pedunculopontine nucleus is hypothesized to play a role in accumbens output (see next section); moreover, the pedunculopontine nucleus may directly modulate the activity of midbrain dopamine neurons. Despite a report that excitotoxic lesions of the pedunculopontine nucleus enhanced responding maintained by intravenous amphetamine under a variety of conditions (Keating et al., 1997), caution is advised regarding interpretation of those data. First, although excitotoxic lesions of the pedunculopontine nucleus altered the amplification of responding for a conditioned reinforcer produced by intra-accumbens amphetamine, the most parsimonious explanation of those data was that the lesioned rats exhibited deficits in the discrimination between levers, or in "response selection" (Inglis, Dunbar, & Winn, 1994). Other data showed that pedunculopontine lesions produced disinhibition and perseveration of unconditioned oral motor behaviors produced by intrastriatal amphetamine (Allen & Winn, 1995). Moreover, although pedunculopontine lesions affected cholinergic stimulation of dopamine efflux in the nigrostriatal pathway, mesoaccumbens dopaminergic transmission was unaffected (Blaha et al., 1996). Finally, pedunculopontine lesions did not block cocaine-conditioned place preferences in rats (Parker & van der Kooy, 1995). Taken together, these results suggest that pedunculopontine lesions may produce behavioral abnormalities in rats, but a clear role for this brain structure in the behavioral effects of cocaine related to its abuse remains to be demonstrated.

SUMMARY AND IMPLICATIONS FOR CORTICO-STRIATO-PALLIDO-THALAMIC CIRCUITRY

Mogenson, Jones, and Yim (1980) emphasized anatomical, physiological, and behavioral results, suggesting that the nucleus accumbens might act as a functional interface between the limbic system (e.g., Maclean, 1952) and voluntary motor system (e.g., Henneman, 1974) and thus play a key role in the central nervous system processes by which actions are directed toward goals. Mogenson emphasized the accumbens as the recipient of input particularly from allocortical regions such as amygdala and hippcampal formation. Anatomical studies confirmed major sources of accumbens afferents from basolateral nucleus and subiculum, as well as prelimbic (ventromedial prefrontal) cortex (Groenewegen et al., 1991). Mogenson's own experiments demonstrated the functional role particularly of accumbens output through ventral pallidum (Mogenson & Nielson, 1984), as well as the "mesencephalic locomotor region," which includes the pedunculopontine tegmental nucleus (Swanson, Mogenson, Simerly, & Wu, 1987). Swerdlow and Koob (1987a,b) demonstrated the importance of this circuitry in mediating the locomotor stimulant effects of psychostimulant drugs, and subsequently a theme of drug self-administration studies in animals has emerged to explore the relative roles of components within this circuitry in the behavioral effects of cocaine-related to its abuse.

It is two decades since the first demonstration that nucleus accumbens dopaminergic depletion decreased cocaine self-administration, and 10 years since a neural circuitry underlying locomotor stimulant effects of psychostimulant drugs was elucidated. Now a clear role for the mesoaccumbens dopaminergic pathway in the behavioral effects of self-administered cocaine, and a modulatory role for many structures projecting to the accumbens or receiving accumbens afferents, have been demonstrated (see Figure 6). Near complete destruction of accumbens dopaminergic nerve terminals eliminated the reinforcing effects of cocaine in some rats, and damage to the mesoaccumbens dopaminergic pathway reliably altered cocaine self-administration, although some of those results were consistent with enhancement of the behavioral effects of self-administered cocaine or amphetamine. In addition, converging evidence suggested that intra-accumbens infusions of amphetamine, nomifensine, and even cocaine maintained responding in rats.

Other neuroanatomical structures may contribute to the behavioral effects of self-administered cocaine through their direct modulation of the mesoaccumbens pathway. For example, studies demonstrating robust self-administration of cocaine into the prefrontal cortex also demonstrated increased turnover of dopamine in the accumbens of these rats. Further studies may determine whether 6-OHDA lesions of the *mesoaccumbens* pathway eliminate responding maintained by intraprefrontal cocaine infusions, just as those lesions eliminate responding maintained by intravenous cocaine injections. In contrast, lesion studies suggested that destruc-

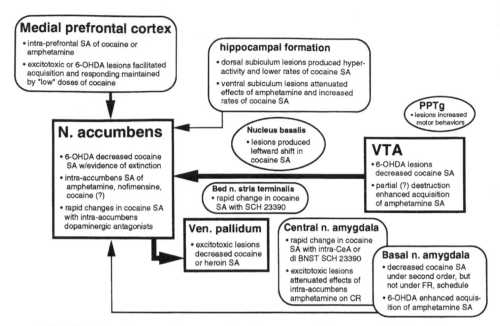

FIGURE 2.6   Diagrammatic representation of neuroanatomical structures investigated for their involvement in mediating the behavioral effects of cocaine or amphetamine related to their abuse. Abbreviations: CR, responding maintained by a conditioned reinforcer; n., nucleus; Ven., ventral; SA, self-administration; ?, controversial findings or unsubstantiated hypothesis.

tion of medial prefrontal cortex, or depletion of prefrontal dopaminergic terminals, enhanced some behavioral effects of intravenously self-administered cocaine. However, close examination of the data suggests that the effects of prefrontal lesions were critically dependent upon the dose of cocaine, and that those effects may be consistent with general decrements in behavioral inhibition.

Similarly lesions of basolateral amygdala altered cocaine-maintained responding only under certain conditions. Thus the basolateral amygdala was implicated in the process by which stimuli acquire motivational effects by virtue of their association with self-administered cocaine, just as the basolateral amygdala has been implicated in stimulus associations with other reinforcers including water, sucrose, or sexual interaction. Nevertheless, basolateral amygdala lesions did not alter cocaine-maintained responding under low FR schedules in animals that had been trained prior to the lesion. Moreover, although accelerated acquisition and amplified responding maintained by cocaine was observed in amygdala-lesioned rats, responding when saline was substituted for cocaine also appeared elevated in those animals relative to sham-operated control rats.

In other studies local intracerebral administration of dopaminergic antagonists also implicated the amygdala, and particularly the central nucleus of the amygdala and "extended amygdala," in the behavioral effects of self-administered cocaine. Nevertheless, despite attempts to validate the regional specificity of that methodology, caution is advised regarding results from those studies, because effects on cocaine self-administration have been observed after infusions of dopaminergic antagonists into a host of different brain structures, and several observations suggested rapid spread from the site of intracerebral infusion to other sites in the neuraxis.

Preliminary results also suggested that accumbens afferents originating in the subiculum of the hippocampal formation modulate the behavioral effects of amphetamine or self-administered cocaine. Importantly, different subregions of subiculum may have opposing roles in this regard, as dorsal lesions enhanced and ventral lesions attenuated the locomotor stimulant effects of amphetamine. As with other lesions, the effects of subiculum lesions on responding maintained by cocaine must be considered in the context of other behavioral effects of the lesions. Thus dorsal subiculum lesions produced hyperactivity, and ventral subiculum lesions produced gross deficits in senscrimotor gating as measured with prepulse inhibition of the startle response.

Likewise, lesions of output structures of the basal ganglia, including ventral pallidum and pedunculopontine nucleus, produced alterations in responding maintained by cocaine or amphetamine; however, some of these behavioral effects likely occurred independent of changes in the reinforcing effects of cocaine or amphetamine.

A cryptic summary of results from neuroanatomical studies of the reinforcing effects of cocaine might be that "all roads lead either to or from the mesoaccumbens dopaminergic pathway." Importantly, lesion studies suggested that activity within the mesoaccumbens pathway may be particularly critical for behavior maintained by cocaine, in comparison to behavior maintained by other drug or nondrug reinforcers. Moreover, lesion studies of anatomical structures that influence the mesoaccumbens pathway, or that participate in accumbens outflow, determined that the contribution of these different neural structures may not be restricted to modulation of the behavioral effects of cocaine, but rather may influence cocaine-maintained behavior as a result of more general behavioral abnormalities. Further studies that focus on the nature of behavioral changes resulting from manipulations of the mesoaccumbens pathway, as well as the precise modulatory roles of accumbens afferent sources and efferent targets in the behavioral effects of self-administered cocaine, should lead to a better understanding of the neuroanatomical bases underlying the behavioral effects of cocaine-related to its abuse.

ACKNOWLEDGMENT

This work was supported in part by the National Institute on Drug Abuse (T32-DA07252).

REFERENCES

Alheid, G. F., & Heimer, L. (1988). New perspectives in basal forebrain organization of special rele-
    vance for neuropsychiatric disorders: The striatopallidal, amygdaloid, and corticopetal components
    of the substantia innominata. *Neuroscience, 27,* 1–39.
Allen, L. F., & Winn, P. (1995). Excitotoxic lesions of the pedunculopontine tegmental nucleus disin-
    hibit orofacial behaviors stimulated by microinjections of d-amphetamine into rat ventrolateral cau-
    date putamen. *Experimental Brian Research, 104,* 262–274.
Anden, N. E., & Stock, G. (1973). Effect of clozapine on the turnover of dopamine in the corpus stria-
    tum and limbic system. *Journal of Pharmacy and Pharmacology, 25,* 346–348.
Asher, I. M., & Aghajanian, G. K. (1974). 6-hydroxydopamine lesions of olfactory tubercles and cau-
    date nuclei: Effect on amphetamine-induced stereotyped behaviour. *Brain Research, 82,* 1–12.
Baxter, B. L., Gluckman, M. I., Stein, L., & Scerni, R. A. (1974). Self-injection of apomorphine in the
    rat: Positive reinforcement by a dopamine receptor stimulant. *Pharmacology, Biochemistry and Be-
    havior, 2,* 387–391.
Blaha, C. D., Allen, L. F., Das, S., Inglis, W. L., Latimer, M. P., Vincent, S. R., & Winn, P. (1996). Mod-
    ulation of dopamine efflux in the nucleus accumbens after cholinergic stimulation of the ventral
    tegmental area in intact, pedunculopontine tegmental nucleus lesioned, and laterodorsal tegmental
    nucleus lesioned rats. *Journal of Neuroscience, 16,* 714–722.
Breese, G. R., & Traylor, T. D. (1970). Effect of 6-hydroxydopamine on brain norepinephrine and
    dopamine: Evidence for selective degeneration of brain catecholamine neurones. *Journal of Phar-
    macology and Experimental Therapeutics, 174,* 413–420.
Breese, G. R., & Traylor, T. D. (1971). Depletion of brain noradrenaline and dopamine by 6-hydroxy-
    dopamine. *British Journal of Pharmacology, 42,* 88–89.
Burns, L. H., Robbins, T. W., & Everitt, B. J. (1993). Differential effects of excitotoxic lesions of the
    basolateral amygdala, ventral subiculum and medial prefrontal cortex on responding with condi-
    tioned reinforcement and locomotor activity potentiated by intra-accumbens infusions of D-am-
    phetamine. *Behavioural Brain Research, 55,* 167–183.
Cador, M., Robbins, T. W., & Everitt, B. J. (1989). Involvement of the amygdala in stimulus-reward
    associations: Interaction with the ventral striatum. *Neuroscience, 30,* 77–86.
Caine, S. B., Heinrichs, S. C., Coffin, V. L., & Koob, G. F. (1995). Effects of the dopamine D-1 an-
    tagonist SCH 23390 microinjected into the accumbens, amygdala or striatum on cocaine self-ad-
    ministration in the rat. *Brain Research, 692,* 47–56.
Caine, S. B., & Koob, G. F. (1994a). Effects of mesolimbic dopamine depletion on responding main-
    tained by cocaine and food. *Journal of the Experimental Analysis of Behavior, 61,* 213–221.
Caine, S. B., & Koob, G. F. (1994b). Effects of D-1 and D-2 antagonists on cocaine self-administra-
    tion under different schedules of reinforcement in the rat. *Journal of Pharmacology and Experi-
    mental Therapeutics, 270,* 209–218.
Caine, S. B., Whitelaw, R. B., Robbins, T. W., & Everitt, B. J. (1996). Dissociable effects of dorsal vs.
    ventral subiculum lesions in animal models relevant to drug abuse and schizophrenia. *Society for
    Neuroscience Abstracts, 22,* 705.
Callahan, P. M., Bryan, S. K., & Cunningham, K. A. (1995). Discriminative stimulus effects of cocaine:
    Antagonism by dopamine D1 receptor blockade in the amygdala. *Pharmacology Biochemistry and
    Behavior, 51,* 759–766.
Callahan, P. M., De La Garza II, R., & Cunningham, K. A. (1994). Discriminative stimulus properties
    of cocaine: Modulation by dopamine D1 receptors in nucleus accumbens. *Psychopharmacology,
    115,* 110–114.
Carlezon, W. A. Jr., Devine, D. P., & Wise, R. A. (1995). Habit-forming actions of nomifensine in nu-
    cleus accumbens. *Psychopharmacology, 122,* 194–197.
Costall, B., & Naylor, R. J. (1974). Extrapyramidal and mesolimbic involvement and the stereotypic
    activity of D- and L-amphetamine. *European Journal of Pharmacology, 25,* 121–129.

Creese, I., & Iverson, S. D. (1974). The role of forebrain dopamine systems in amphetamine induced stereotyped behaviour in the rats. *Psychopharmacologia, 39*, 345–357.

Davis, W. M., & Smith, S. G. (1973). Blocking effect of alphamethyltyrosine on amphetamine based reinforcement. *Journal of Pharmacy and Pharmacology, 25*, 174–177.

Davis, W. M., & Smith, S. G. (1975). Effect of haloperidol on (+)-amphetamine self-administration. *Journal of Pharmacy and Pharmacology, 27*, 540–542.

Deminiere, J. M., Simon, H., Herman, J. P., & Le Moal, M. (1984). 6-hydroxydopamine lesions of the dopamine mesocorticolimbic cell bodies increases (+)-amphetamine self-administration. *Psychopharmacology, 83*, 281–284.

Deminiere, J. M., Taghzouti, K., Tassin, J.-P., Le Moal, M., & Simon, H. (1988). Increased sensitivity to amphetamine and facilitation of amphetamine self-administration after 6-hydroxydopamine lesions of the amygdala. *Psychopharmacology, 94*, 232–236.

Deutsch, A. Y., Clark, W. A., & Roth, R. H. (1990). Prefrontal cortical dopamine depletion enhances the responsiveness of mesolimbic neurons to stress. *Brain Research, 521*, 311–315.

Devenport, L. D., Devenport, J. A., & Holloway, F. A. (1981). Reward-induced stereotypy: Modulation by the hippocampus. *Science, 212*, 1289–1290.

Dunnett, S. B., Everitt, B. J., & Robbins, T. W. (1991). The basal forebrain-cortical cholinergic system: Interpreting the functional consequences of excitotoxic lesions. *Trends in the Neurosciences, 14*, 494–501.

Epping-Jordan, M. P., Markou, A., & Koob, G. F. (1998). The dopamine D-1 receptor antagonist SCH 23390 injected into the dorsolateral bed nucleus of the stria terminalis decreased cocaine reinforcement in the rat. *Brain Research, 784*, 105–115.

Everitt, B. J., Cador, M., & Robbins, T. W. (1989). Interactions between the amygdala and ventral striatum in stimulus-reward associations: Studies using a second-order schedule of sexual reinforcement. *Neuroscience, 30*, 63–75.

Fallon, J. H., & Ciofi, P. (1992). Distribution of monoamines within the amygdala. In J. P. Aggleton (Ed.), *The amygdala: Neurobiological aspects of emotion, memory, and mental dysfunction* (pp. 97–114). New York: Wiley-Liss.

Fibiger, H. C., Zis, A. P., & McGeer, E. G. (1973). Feeding and drinking deficits after 6-hydroxydopamine administration in the rat: Similarities to the lateral hypothalamic syndrome. *Brain Research, 55*, 135–148.

Glick, S. D. (1972). Changes in amphetamine sensitivity following frontal cortical damgage in rats and mice. *European Journal of Pharmacology, 20*, 351–356.

Glick, S. D. (1973). Impaired tolerance to the effects of oral amphetamine intake in rats with frontal cortex ablations. *Psychopharmacologia, 28*, 363–371.

Glick, S. D., & Marsanico, R. G. (1975). Time-dependent changes in amphetamine self-administration following frontal cortex ablations in rats. *Journal of Comparative Physiology and Psychiatry, 88*, 355–359.

Goeders, N. E., Dworkin, S. I., & Smith, J. E. (1986). Neuropharmacological assessment of cocaine self-administration into the medial prefrontal cortex. *Pharmacology, Biochemistry and Behavior, 24*, 1429–1440.

Goeders, N. E., & Smith, J. E. (1983). Cortical dopaminergic involvement in cocaine reinforcement. *Science, 221*, 773–775.

Goeders, N. E., & Smith, J. E. (1986). Reinforcing properties of cocaine in the medial prefrontal cortex: primary action on presynaptic dopaminergic terminals. *Pharmacology, Biochemistry and Behavior, 25*, 191–199.

Goeders, N. E., & Smith, J. E. (1993). Intracranial cocaine self-administration into the medial prefrontal cortex increases dopamine turnover in the nucleus accumbens. *Journal of Pharmacology and Experimental Therapeutics, 265*, 592–600.

Goenewegen, H. J., Berendse, H. W., Meredith, G. E., Haber, S. N., Voorn, P., Wolters, J. G., & Lohman, A. H. M. (1991). Functional anatomy of the ventral, limbic system innervated striatum. In P. Willner & J. Scheel-Kruger (Eds.), *The mesolimbic dopamine system: From motivation to action* (pp. 19–60). Chichester: Wiley.

Groenewegen, H. J., Vermeulen-Van der Zee, E., Te Kortschot, A., & Witter, M. P. (1987). Organization of the projections from the subiculum to the ventral striatum in the rat. A study using anterograde transport of PHA-L. *Neuroscience, 23,* 103–120.

Heffner, T. G., Zigmond, M. J., & Stricker, E. M. (1977). Effects of dopaminergic agonists and antagonists on feeding in intact and 6-hydroxydopamine treated rats. *Journal of Pharmacology and Experimental Therapeutics, 201,* 386–399.

Heimer, L., Zahm, D. S., Churchill, L., Kalivas, P. W., & Wohltmann, C. (1991). Specificity in the projection patterns of accumbal core and shell in the rat. *Neuroscience, 41,* 89–125.

Henneman, E. (1974). Organization of the motor system—a preview. In B. Mountcastle (Ed.), *Medical physiology, V* (pp. 603–607). St. Louis: Mosby.

Hoebel, B. G., Monaco, A. P., Hernandez, L., Aulisi, E. F., Stanley, B. G., & Lenard, L. (1983). Self-injection of amphetamine directly into the brain. *Psychopharmacology, 81,* 158–163.

Horn, A. S., Cuello, A. C., & Miller, R. J. (1974). Dopamine in the mesolimbic system of the rat brain: Endogenous levels and the effects of drugs on the uptake mechanism and stimulation of adenylate cyclase activity. *Journal of Neurochemistry, 22,* 265–270.

Hubner, C. B., & Koob, G. F. (1990). The ventral pallidum plays a role in mediating cocaine and heroin self-administration in the rat. *Brain Research, 508,* 20–29.

Hurd, Y. L., McGregor, A., & Ponten, M. (1998). In vivo amygdala dopamine levels modulate cocaine self-administration behavior: Dopamine D1 receptor involvement. *European Journal of Neuroscience, 9,* 2541–2548.

Inglis, W. L., Dunbar, J. S., & Winn, P. (1994). Outflow from the nucleus accumbens to the pedunculopontine tegmental nucleus: A dissociation between locomotor activity and the acquisition of responding for conditioned reinforcement stimulated by d-amphetamine. *Neuroscience, 62,* 51–64.

Isaacson, R. L. (1984). Hippocampal damage: Effects on dopaminergic systems of the basal ganglia. *International Review of Neurobiology, 25,* 339–359.

Iverson, S. D., Wilkinson, S., & Simpson, B. (1971). Enhanced amphetamine responses after frontal cortex lesions in the rat. *European Journal of Pharmacology, 13,* 387–390.

Jaskiw, G. E., Karoum, F., Freed, W. J., Phillips, I., Kleinman, J. E., & Weinberger, D. R. (1990). Effect of ibotenic acid lesions of the medial prefrontal cortex on amphetamine-induced locomotion and regional brain catecholamine concentrations in the rat. *Brain Research, 534,* 263–272.

Karreman, M., & Moghaddam, B. (1996). The prefrontal cortex regulates the basal release of dopamine in the limbic striatum: An effect mediated by ventral tegmental area. *Journal of Neurochemistry, 66,* 589–598.

Keating, G., Blaha, C., Winn, P., DiCiano, P., Latimer, M., & Phillips, A. (1997). Amphetamine self-administration is enhanced by excitotoxic lesions of the pedunculopontine tegmental nucleus in rats. *Society for Neuroscience Abstracts, 23,* 2145.

Kelley, A. E., & Domesick, V. B. (1982). The distribution of the projection from the hippocampal formation to the nucleus accumbens in the rat: An anterograde- and retrograde-horseradish peroxidase study. *Neuroscience, 7,* 2321–2335.

Kelley, A. E., Domesick, V. B., & Nauta, W. J. H. (1982). The amygdalostriatal projection in the rat—an anatomical study by anterograde and retrograde tracing methods. *Neuroscience, 7,* 615–639.

Kelly, P. H., Seviour, P. M., & Iverson, S. D. (1975). Amphetamine and apomorphine responses in the rat following 6-OHDA lesions of the nucleus accumbens septi and corpus striatum. *Brain Research, 94,* 507–522.

Koob, G. F., Pettit, H. O., Ettenberg, A., & Bloom, F. E. (1984). Effects of opiate antagonists and their quaternary derivatives on heroin self-administration in the rat. *Journal of Pharmacology and Experimental Therapeutics, 229,* 481–486.

Koob, G. F., Riley, S. J., Smith, S. C., & Robbins, T. W. (1978). Effects of 6-hydroxydopamine lesions of the nucleus accumbens septi and olfactory tubercle on feeding, locomotor activity and amphetamine anorexia in the rat. *Journal of Comparative and Physiological Psychology, 92,* 917–927.

Koob, G. F., Stinus, L., & Le Moal, M. (1981). Hyperactivity and hypoactivity produced by lesions to the mesolimbic dopaminergic system. *Behavioral Brain Research, 3,* 341–359.

Koob, G. F., Vaccarino, F. J., Amalric, M., & Bloom, F. E. (1987). Positive reinforcement properties of drugs: Search for neural substrates. In J. Engel & L. Oreland (Eds.), *Brain reward systems and abuse* (pp. 35–50). New York: Raven Press.

Lecesse, A. P., & Lyness, W. H. (1987). Lesions of dopamine neurons in the medial prefrontal cortex: Effects on self-administration of amphetamine and dopamine synthesis in the brain of the rat. *Neuropharmacology, 26,* 1295–1302.

Le Moal, M., Stinus, L., & Simon, H. (1979). Increased sensitivity to (+)-amphetamine self-administered by rats following meso-cortico-limbic dopamine neurone destruction. *Nature, 280,* 156–158.

Lyness, W. H., Friedle, N. M., & Moore, K. E. (1979). Destruction of dopaminergic nerve terminals in nucleus accumbens: Effect on d-amphetamine self-administration. *Pharmacology, Biochemistry and Behavior, 11,* 553–556.

Maldonado, R., Robledo, P., Chover, A. J., Caine, S. B., & Koob, G. F. (1993). D1 dopamine receptors in the nucleus accumbens modulate cocaine self-administration in the rat. *Pharmacology, Biochemistry and Behavior, 45,* 239–242.

Marshall, J. F., Richardson, J. S., & Teitelbaum, P. (1974). Nigrostriatal bundle damage and the lateral hypothalamic syndrome. *Journal of Comparative and Physiological Psychology, 87,* 808–830.

Martin-Iverson, M. T., Szostak, C., & Fibiger, H. C. (1986). 6-hydroxydopamine lesions of the medial prefrontal cortex fail to influence intravenous cocaine self-administration. *Psychopharmacology, 88,* 310–314.

Maclean, P. D. (1952). Some psychiatric implications of physiological studies of frontotemporal portions of limbic system (visceral brain). *Electroencephalography and Clinical Neurophysiology, 4,* 407–418.

McGregor, A., Baker, G., & Roberts, D. C. S. (1994). Effect of 6-hydroxydopamine lesions of the amygdala on intravenous cocaine self-administration under a progressive ratio schedule of reinforcement. *Brain Research, 646,* 273–278.

McGregor, A., Baker, G., & Roberts, D. C. S. (1996). Effect of 6-hydroxydopamine lesions of the medial prefrontal cortex on intravenous cocaine self-administration under a progressive ratio schedule of reinforcement. *Pharmacology, Biochemistry and Behavior, 53,* 5–9.

McGregor, A., & Roberts, D. C. S. (1993). Dopaminergic antagonism within the nucleus accumbens or the amygdala produces differential effects on intravenous cocaine self-administration under fixed and progressive ratio schedules of reinforcement. *Brain Research, 624,* 245–252.

McGregor, A., & Roberts, D. C. S. (1995). Effects of medial prefrontal cortex injections of SCH 23390 on intravenous cocaine self-administration under both a fixed and progressive ratio schedule of reinforcement. *Behavioral Brain Research, 67,* 75–80.

Meil, W. M., & See, R. F. (1995). Excitotoxic lesions of the basolateral amygdala attenuate the ability of drug associated cues to reinstate responding during the withdrawal from self-administration. *Society for Neuroscience Abstracts, 21,* 1958.

Mogenson, G. J., Jones, D. L., & Yim, C. Y. (1980). From motivation to action: Functional interface between the limbic system and the motor system. *Progress in Neurobiology, 14,* 69–97.

Mogenson, G. J., & Nielson, M. A. (1983). Evidence that an accumbens to subpallidal GABA-ergic projection contributes to locomotor activity. *Brain Research Bulletin, 11,* 309–314.

Mogenson, G. J., & Nielson, M. A. (1984). Neuropharmacological evidence to suggest that the nucleus accumbens and subpallidal region contribute to exploratory locomotion. *Behavioural and Neural Biology, 42,* 52–60.

Parker, J. L., & van der Kooy, D. (1995). Tegmental pedunculopontine nucleus lesions do not block cocaine reward. *Pharmacology, Biochemistry and Behavior, 52,* 77–83.

Pettit, H. O., Ettenberg, A., Bloom, F. E., & Koob, G. F. (1984). Destruction of dopamine in the nucleus accumbens selectively attentuates cocaine but not heroin self-administration in rats. *Psychopharmacology, 84,* 167–173.

Phillips, A. G., Broekkamp, C. L., & Fibiger, H. C. (1983). Strategies for studying the neurochemical substrates of drug reinforcement in rodents. *Progress in Neuropsychopharmacology and Biological Psychiatry, 7*, 585–590.

Phillips, A. G., Mora, F., & Rolls, E. G. (1981). Intracerebral self-administration of amphetamine by rhesus monkeys. *Neuroscience Letters, 24*, 81–86.

Phillips, G. D., Robbins, T. W., & Everitt, B. J. (1994). Bilateral intra-accumbens self-administration of d-amphetamine: Antagonism with intra-accumbens SCH 23390 and sulpiride. *Psychopharmacology, 114*, 47–485.

Pickens, R., Meisch, R. A., & Dougherty, J. A. (1968). Chemical interactions in methamphetamine reinforcement. *Psychological Report, 23*, 1267–1270.

Pinjenburg, A. J. J., Honig, W. M. M., & Van Rossum, J. M. (1975). Inhibition of d-amphetamine induced locomotor activity by injection of haloperidol into the nucleus accumbens of the rat. *Psychopharmacologia, 41*, 87–95.

Pinjenburg, A. J. J., & Van Rossum, J. M. (1973). Stimulation of locomotor activity following injection of dopamine into the nucleus accumbens. *Journal of Pharmacy and Pharmacology, 25*, 1003–1004.

Pycock, C. J., Carter, C. J., & Kerwin, R. W. (1980). Effect of 6-hydroxydopamine lesions of the medial prefrontal cortex on neurotransmitter systems in subcortical sites. *Journal of Neurochemistry, 34*, 91–99.

Rassnick, S., Stinus, L., & Koob, G. F. (1993). The effects of 6-hydroxydopamine lesions of the nucleus accumbens and the mesolimbic dopamine system on oral self-administration of ethanol in the rat. *Brain Research, 623*, 16–24.

Robbins, T. W., Cador, M., Taylor, J. R., & Everitt, B. J. (1989). Limbic-striatal interactions in reward-related processes. *Neuroscience and Biobehavioral Reviews, 13*, 155–162.

Robbins, T. W., Roberts, A. C., Owen, A. M., Sahakian, B. J., Everitt, B. J., Wilkinson, L., Muir, J., De Salvia, M., & Tovee, M. (1994). Monoaminergic-dependent cognitive functions of the prefrontal cortex in monkey and man. In A. M. Thierry, J. Glowinski, P. S. Goldman-Rakic, Y. Christen (Eds.), *Motor and cognitive functions of the prefrontal cortex* (pp. 83–111). Berlin: Springer-Verlag.

Roberts, D. C. S., Corcoran, M. E., & Fibiger, H. C. (1977). On the role of ascending catecholaminergic systems in intravenous self-administration of cocaine. *Pharmacology, Biochemistry and Behavior, 6*, 615–620.

Roberts, D. C. S., Koob, G. F., Klonoff, P., & Fibiger, H. C. (1980). Extinction and recovery of cocaine self-administration following 6-hydroxydopamine lesions of the nucleus accumbens. *Pharmacology, Biochemistry and Behavior, 12*, 781–787.

Roberts, D. C. S., & Koob, G. F. (1982). Disruption of cocaine self-administration following 6-hydroxydopamine lesions of the ventral tegmental area in rats. *Pharmacology, Biochemistry and Behavior, 17*, 901–904.

Robledo, P., & Koob, G. F. (1993). Two discrete nucleus accumbens projection areas differentially mediate cocaine self-administration in the rat. *Behavioural Brain Research, 55*, 159–166.

Robledo, P., Maldonado-Lopez, R., & Koob, G. F. (1992). Role of dopamine receptors in the nucleus accumbens in the rewarding properties of cocaine. *Annals of the New York Academy of Sciences, 654*, 509–512.

Robledo, P., Page, K., Weissenborn, R., Robbins, T. W., & Everitt, B. J. (1996). Effects of excitotoxic lesions of the nucleus basalis magnocellularis on the acquisition of cocaine self-administration in the rat. *Behavioral Pharmacology, 7* (suppl. 1), 95.

Robledo, P., Robbins, T. W., & Everitt, B. J. (1996). Effects of excitotoxic lesions of central amygdaloid nucleus on the potentiation of reward-related stimuli by intra-accumbens amphetamine. *Behavioral Neuroscience, 110*, 981–990.

Rosin, D. L., Clark, W. A., Goldstein, M., Roth, R. H., & Deutsch, A. Y. (1992). Effects of 6-hydroxydopamine lesions of the prefrontal cortex on tyrosine hydroxylase activity in mesolimbic and nigrostriatal dopamine systems. *Neuroscience, 48*, 831–839.

Schenk, S., Horger, B. A., Peltier, R., & Shelton, K. (1991). Supersensitivity to the reinforcing effects of cocaine following 6-hydroxydopamine lesions to the medial prefrontal cortex in rats. *Brain Research, 543,* 227–235.

Simon, H., Taghzouti, K., Gozlan, H., Studler, J. M., Louilot, A., Herve, D., Glowinski, J., Tassin, J.-P., & Le Moal, M. (1988). Lesion of dopaminergic terminals in the amygdala produces enhanced locomotor response to d-amphetamine and opposite changes in dopaminergic activity in prefrontal cortex and nucleus accumbens. *Brain Research, 447,* 335–340.

Snyder, S. H. (1973). Amphetamine psychosis: A 'model' schizophrenia mediated by catecholamines. *American Journal of Psychiatry, 130,* 61–67.

Stevens, J. R. (1973). An anatomy of schizophrenia. *Archives of General Psychiatry, 29,* 117–189.

Stricker, E. M., & Zigmond, M. J. (1974). Effects of homeostasis of intraventricular injections of 6-hydroxydopamine in rats. *Journal of Comparative and Physiological Psychology, 86,* 973–994.

Swanson, L. W., Mogenson, G. J., Simerly, R. B., & Wu, M. (1987). Anatomical and electrophysiological evidence for a projection from the medial preoptic area to the mesencephalic and subthalamic locomotor regions in the rat. *Brain Research, 405,* 108–122.

Swerdlow, N. R., & Koob, G. F. (1985). Separate neural substrates of the locomotor-activity properties of amphetamine, heroin, caffeine, and corticotropin releasing factor (CRF) in the rat. *Pharmacology, Biochemistry and Behavior, 23,* 303–307.

Swerdlow, N. R., & Koob, G. F. (1987). Dopamine, schizophrenia, mania, and depression: toward a unified hypothesis of cortico-striato-pallido-thalamic function. *Behavioral and Brain Sciences, 10,* 197–245.

Swerdlow, N. R., Swanson, L. W., & Koob, G. F. (1984a). Electrolytic lesions of the substantia innominata and lateral preoptic area attenuate the 'supersensitive' locomotor response to apomorphine resulting from denervation of the nucleus accumbens. *Brain Research, 306,* 141–148.

Swerdlow, N. R., Swanson, L. W., & Koob, G. F. (1984b). Substantia innominata: critical link in the behavioral expression of mesolimbic dopamine stimulation in the rat. *Neuroscience Letters, 50,* 19–24.

Tallarida, R. J., & Murray, R. B. (1987). *Manual of Pharmacologic Calculations with Computer Programs.* New York: Springer Verlag.

Ungerstedt, U. (1971). Adipsia and aphagia after 6-hydroxydopamine induced degeneration of the nigrostriatal dopamine system. *Acta Physiologica Scandinavia, 82* (suppl. 367), 95–122.

Vaccarino, F. J., Bloom, F. E., & Koob, G. F. (1985). Blockade of nucleus accumbens opiate receptors attenuates intravenous heroin reward in the rat. *Psychopharmacology, 85,* 37–42.

Weissenborn, R., Robbins, T. W., & Everitt, B. J. (1997). Effects of medial prefrontal or anterior cingulate cortex lesions on responding for cocaine under fixed-ratio and second-order schedules of reinforcement in rats. *Psychopharmacology, 134,* 242–257.

Whitelaw, R. B., Markou, A., Robbins, T. W., & Everitt, B. J. (1996). Excitotoxic lesions of the basolateral amygdala impair the acquisition of cocaine-seeking behaviour under a second-order schedule of reinforcement. *Psychopharmacology, 127,* 213–224.

Wilkinson, L. S., Mittleman, G., Torres, E., Humby, T., Hall, F. S., & Robbins, T. W. (1993). Enhancement of amphetamine-induced locomotor activity and dopamine release in nucleus accumbens following excitotoxic lesion of the hippocampus. *Behavioural Brain Research, 55,* 143–150.

Wilson, M. C., & Schuster, C. R. (1972). The effects of chlorpromazine on psychomotor stimulant self-administration in the rhesus monkey. *Psychopharmaocolgia, 26,* 115–126.

Wilson, M. C., & Schuster, C. R. (1973). The effects of stimulants and depressants on cocaine self-administraiton behavior in the rhesus monkey. *Psychopharmacologia, 31,* 291–304.

Wood, D. M., & Emmett-Oglesby, M. W. (1989). Mediation in the nucleus accumbens of the discriminative stimulus produced by cocaine. *Pharmacology, Biochemistry and Behavior, 33,* 453–457.

Wright, C. I., Beijer, A. V. J., & Groenewegen, H. J. (1996). Basal amygdaloid complex afferents to the rat nucleus accumbens are compartmentally organized. *Journal of Neuroscience, 16,* 1877–1893.

Yokel, R. A., & Wise, R. A. (1975). Increased lever pressing for amphetamine after pimozide in rats: Implications for a dopamine theory of reward. *Science, 187,* 547–549.

Yokel, R. A., & Wise, R. A. (1976). Attenuation of intravenous amphetamine reinforcement by central dopamine blockade in rats. *Psychopharmacology, 48,* 311–318.

Zito, K. A., Vickers, G., & Roberts, D. C. S. (1985). Disruption of cocaine and heroin self-administration following kainic acid lesions of the nucleus accumbens. *Pharmacology, Biochemistry and Behavior, 23,* 1029–1036.

3

BEHAVIORAL PHARMACOLOGY OF COCAINE AND THE DETERMINANTS OF ABUSE LIABILITY

JACK BERGMAN

Harvard Medical School
McLean Hospital
Belmont, Massachusetts

JONATHAN L. KATZ

Department of Pharmacology and
Experimental Therapeutics
University of Maryland School of Medicine
Baltimore, Maryland

INTRODUCTION

Over the two decades that comprise the most recent epidemic of cocaine use in our society, there has been an intensive effort to establish and analyze the behavioral effects of cocaine that may be related to its abuse. This effort has been at least partly based on the premise that treatment and prevention of cocaine abuse and dependence can be aided by understanding the behavioral pharmacology of cocaine. A wealth of findings has repeatedly confirmed and extended early descriptions of the stimulant effects of cocaine on unlearned and learned behavior (e.g., Barrett, 1976; Scheel-Kruger, 1972), and of its stimulus properties, including both its reinforcing and discriminative-stimulus effects (e.g., Balster & Schuster, 1973; Deneau, Yanagita, & Seevers, 1969; Ho & McKenna, 1978; Silverman & Ho, 1976). There have been excellent reviews of the behavioral effects of cocaine and other psychomotor-stimulant drugs throughout this period, and the reader is referred to those papers for a thorough account of the behavioral pharmacology of cocaine (e.g., Fischman & Johanson, 1996; Johanson & Fischman, 1989; Johanson & Schuster, 1995; Kelleher, 1977; van Rossum, 1970).

The present chapter is not an attempt to extent or update previous comprehensive reviews. Rather, we highlight the role of selected behavioral effects of cocaine and of contextual factors in experimental procedures to evaluate its abuse liability. Cocaine is a psychomotor stimulant, and a defining characteristic of this class of drugs is stimulation of either learned behavior or unlearned locomotor activity at doses below those producing convulsions (Kelleher, 1977; van Rossum, 1970). Accordingly, in the first section, we will examine the contribution of cocaine's behavioral effects in the assessment of its abuse liability. Cocaine also can be used to condition behavior. In studies involving schedule-controlled behavior, for example, cocaine is often used to establish discriminative-stimulus effects (i.e., cocaine serves as an antecedent stimulus that controls learned behavior following a history of differential reinforcement in its presence; Skinner, 1938). In studies involving classical conditioning, repeated pairings with cocaine injection have been shown to confer conditioned-stimulus effects on previously neutral stimuli. Such interoceptive effects have been linked to the reinforcing effects of cocaine and, from a clinical perspective, to relapse to drug abuse. The recognition of this linkage has encouraged considerable speculation, even theorizing, regarding the relationship between cocaine's effects and motivational or other internal states. For example, the discriminative-stimulus effects of cocaine and generalization to cocaine-associated stimuli, which may indeed play an important role in cocaine abuse and relapse, have been linked to the hypothetical construct, craving (Gawin & Kleber, 1986; Jaffe et al., 1989; Pickens & Johanson, 1992; Tiffany et al., 1993). In the second section of this chapter, we shall briefly consider the contemporary focus on such motivational constructs as explanatory principles in understanding the abuse of cocaine and other drugs. Additionally, the contribution of such constructs to the assessment of abuse liability will be briefly considered. Finally, cocaine's effectiveness in self-administration procedures have contributed to the perception that its abuse potential is unrivaled. In the final sections, we shall examine this notion by discussing how the effects of cocaine in self-administration procedures are modified by contextual factors, including the schedule of self-administration, availability of other reinforcing stimuli, and superimposition of schedules of punishment.

PSYCHOMOTOR–STIMULANT EFFECTS
OF COCAINE

Much of the behavioral pharmacology of cocaine and other psychomotor stimulant drugs has been elucidated from studies of the effects of drugs on learned behavior controlled by schedules of reinforcement (see above-mentioned reviews). Whereas the central nervous system (CNS) stimulant effects of cocaine have been long known, the first scientific studies of behavioral stimulant effects were published in the 1950s and 1960s (e.g., Dews, 1958). One of the earliest studies of the effects of cocaine on learned behavior examined alterations in performances of pigeons trained to respond under a 5-min fixed-interval schedule of food presentation (Smith, 1964). Under this schedule, all responses during the 5-min period are counted, and food is produced by the first response after the lapse of the interval. One advantage of this type of schedule is that response rates in different segments of the interval (i.e., local response rates) may differ in a predictable manner; typically, response rates are greater in the latter segments of the interval than in the earlier segments. Smith found that cocaine, like other stimulants (Dews, 1958), increased the average rates of responding throughout the 5-min fixed interval. In addition, he found that the increases in rates of responding were greatest in the early part of the fixed interval when, in the absence of drug treatment, local response rates were relatively low. In the latter part of the intervals when, in the absence of drug treatment, local response rates were relatively higher, cocaine either did not change or only decreased response rates. The effects of cocaine also were examined under a fixed-ratio schedule of reinforcement. Under this schedule, delivery of the reinforcer occurs upon completion of a fixed number of responses. Typically, fixed-ratio performance is characterized by a pause in responding followed by persistent high rates until the fixed-ratio requirement is met. Overall rates of responding tend to be greater than those obtained under the fixed-interval schedule. Smith (1964) showed that the high response rates maintained under a fixed-ratio schedule were decreased by doses of cocaine that increased rates of responding under the fixed-interval schedule.

These qualitative differences in the response to cocaine in different segments of the fixed interval or under different schedules suggested that the stimulant effects of cocaine on learned operant behavior could depend critically on control rate of responding in the absence of drug. A similar "rate dependency" had been previously proposed to characterize the effects of methamphetamine (Dews, 1958), and this type of analysis remains a major contribution of behavioral pharmacology to the understanding of the effects of drugs on behavior.

An appreciation of the rate-dependent effects of cocaine may be helpful in evaluating cocaine's reinforcing effects. In most studies of cocaine self-administration, for example, there are multiple opportunities for drug injections throughout the experimental session. As a result, behavior that is emitted as the session progresses is both maintained by the reinforcing effects of cocaine and under the influence of effects of cocaine delivered in previous injections. These latter effects are often referred to as "direct" effects, a term that is only meant to distinguish them from reinforcing or other stimulus effects of the drug in behavioral procedures. Whereas the reinforcing effects of cocaine are intimately related to the nature of the contingency between the response and the injection (see chapter 4, by Carroll & Bickel, this volume; also Katz, 1989), the direct effects may be presumed to occur independently of whether cocaine is self-administered and, as well, to influence subsequent behavior whether maintained by cocaine or another reinforcer. Thus, analysis of the reinforcing actions of cocaine in self-administration studies is hampered by the confounding influence of its effects on response rates. Moreover, these direct effects are dose related and can be changing over the course of the experimental session.

A number of investigations have examined the role of the direct effects of self-administered cocaine in cocaine-maintained behavior. In early studies, for example, Pickens and Thompson (1968) showed that cocaine self-administration under fixed-ratio schedules was characterized by relatively constant interinjection times. Each response-produced injection was followed by a pause of a duration that was directly related to the dose of the drug. The regularity of the interinjection interval in cocaine self-administration studies continues to be of interest, as it has been offered as evidence that subjects actively titrate the concentration of cocaine at relevant CNS sites to maintain a constant level of effect (e.g., Petit & Justice, 1989). However, this explanation, though seemingly plausible, may not offer the most parsimonious accounting of the observed phenomenon. Pickens and Thompson (1968) also studied the effects of response-independent iv cocaine on food-reinforced behavior. They found that the delivery of cocaine produced a pause in food-maintained responding that was directly related to cocaine dose. Further, the dose-related pause in food-maintained responding was equivalent to that which followed self-administration of the same unit doses of cocaine. As the pause following cocaine injection occurred whether food or cocaine served as the reinforcer, it appears that the pause in fixed-ratio responding in self-administraiton experiments is more parsimoniously interpreted as disruption in responding produced by the dose-related (and reinforcer-independent) direct effects of cocaine than as subject-initiated titration of cocaine's reinforcing effects (Pickens & Thompson 1968).

Spealman and Kelleher (1979) also studied the direct effects of self-administered cocaine on behavior. In their experiments, the delivery of cocaine injections or electric shock was used to maintain responding by monkeys under a multiple schedule. In the presence of one visual stimulus (cocaine component), cocaine injections could be self-administered under a 5-min fixed-interval schedule. In the presence of a second visual stimulus (shock component), responding was maintained by electric shock under a comparable fixed-interval schedule. Figure 1 shows effects of cocaine dose per injection on rates of responding maintained by electric shock (left panels) or cocaine injection (right panels). As in other studies, cocaine-maintained response rates were dose-dependent and generally described an inverted-U-shaped function of dose per injection (right panels). Rates of responding maintained by electric shock also were related to the self-administered dose of cocaine in the alternate component of the schedule and described an inverted U-shaped function of cocaine dose per injection (left panels). That is, over a low-to-intermediate range of self-administered doses, rates of responding maintained by cocaine or by electric shock were directly related to cocaine dose and comprised the ascending portion of the functions. At the higher unit doses of cocaine, rates of both cocaine- and shock-maintained responding were below the maximal rates obtained and comprised the descending limbs of the functions.

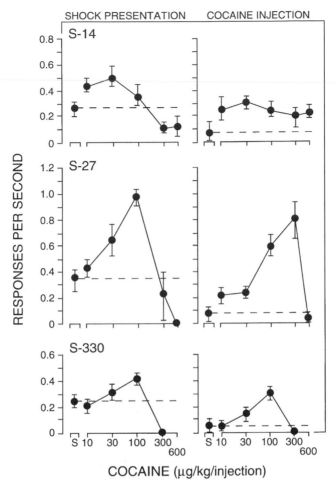

FIGURE 3.1   Effects of dose of cocaine per injection on average rates of responding maintained alternately by electric shock presentation and intravenous cocaine injection. Left panels: responding in the F1 300-sec component of electric shock presentation; right panels: responding in the F1 300-sec component of cocaine injection. Abscissae: dose, log scale; ordinates: rate of responding. Points are averages based on the last three sessions of each condition; brackets show ranges except where contained within the points. Points at S and dashed horizontal lines show responding when saline was substituted for cocaine. Squares show responding during preliminary training. (Adapted from Spealman & Kelleher, 1979.)

Spealman and Kelleher (1979) further studied the effects of response-independent (noncontingent) cocaine injections on responding in both the cocaine and shock components of the multiple schedule. They found that the effects of cocaine on responding in the shock component were similar when the drug was self-administered or delivered noncontingently. These findings indicate that changes in rates of responding in the shock component (rate increases and decreases on the ascending and descending portions, respectively, of the dose–effect function) could be ascribed to direct effects of cocaine. It seems reasonable that the direct effects of cocaine comparably influenced responding in both cocaine and shock components of the multiple schedule and, therefore, that both increases and decreases in response rates of cocaine self-administration behavior could be ascribed to the direct rate-altering effects of the accumulated self-administered dosages of cocaine. The results of these experiments provide strong evidence that responding maintained by cocaine can be influenced both by reinforcing and direct (either rate-increasing or, at higher doses, rate-decreasing) effects of self-administered cocaine.

When response rate is the measure used to evaluate the reinforcing effectiveness of cocaine, especially in comparison to different drugs that may not have comparable stimulant actions, the influence of the direct effects of cocaine needs to be considered to avoid an inaccurate analysis of self-administration data. Even when response rate is not used as a dependent measure, the contribution of direct effects of cocaine to the assessment of its reinforcing effects should be recognized. For example, many studies have employed progressive-ratio schedules as a "rate-independent" measure of the effectiveness of a reinforcer. Though the "break point" (the ratio value at which the subject stops responding within a series of systematically increasing ratio values to which the subject can be exposed) is not a response rate, it is derived from frequency of response and, thus, can be influenced by direct effects of the self-administered drug (see Katz, 1990, for discussion). Especially when such apparently "safe" rate-independent measures are used, the possibility that direct effects of cocaine spuriously contribute to observations that support claims of cocaine's superior reinforcing efficacy must be carefully evaluated.

INTEROCEPTIVE EFFECTS OF COCAINE

The pharmacological mechanisms that underlie the discriminative-stimulus effects of cocaine are reviewed elsewhere in this volume (see chapter 7 by Winger). Drug discrimination procedures have become a mainstay in behavioral pharmacology and considerable effort has been expended to study the discriminative-stimulus effects of cocaine in relation to its abuse potential. There appears to be general agreement that discriminative and other interoceptive effects of cocaine likely play important roles in its reinforcing and other behavioral effects. For example, interoceptive effects of cocaine have been proposed to mediate "priming" phenomena observed in laboratory self-administration studies. In such experiments, behavior that was previously maintained by cocaine and extinguished by substitution of saline is shown to be "reinstated" by an injection of cocaine or by the presentation of cocaine-associated stimuli at the start of the session. These findings have received substantial attention as a model of relapse to drug use as well as a model of drug craving (see Altman et al., 1996). The relationship of this phenomenon to relapse appears to reside exclusively in its face validity (i.e., as homology or formal similarity to the clinical situation in which a drug-free individual may revert to drug-taking behavior after exposure to stimuli previously associated with drug or, alternatively, after an injection of the drug itself).

The suggestion of a relationship between stimuli previously associated with a self-administered drug and relapse to self-administration behavior is not novel and was first forwarded to explain aspects of the abuse of drugs other than cocaine. For example, Wikler and others showed that previously neutral environmental stimuli could be classically conditioned to the withdrawal syndrome associated with opioids, and to its relief by opioid administration (Wikler, 1980, chapter 7). The effects of such conditioning appears to be remarkably persistent. In rats, for example, "relapse" could be triggered by stimuli associated with opioid availability for as long as 1 year after conditioning (Wikler & Pescor, 1970). In human subjects, signs of classically conditioned responses also endure despite long intervening drug-free periods (see, for example, O'Brien, 1976). Importantly, drug dependence and associated withdrawal are not necessary factors in such conditioning processes. For example, Davis and Smith (1974, 1976) found that pairings with relatively low doses of self-administered morphine conditioned subjects to the sound of a buzzer: after such pairings, responding was maintained by the sound alone, consistent with its having gained secondary reinforcing effects. These effects persisted unless they were explicitly extinguished. Moreover, following extinction, the conditioned reinforcing effects of the buzzer sound could be readily reestablished by injections of either morphine or d-amphetamine. Such findings illustrated the importance of conditioning processes in the development of opioid-maintained behavior and relapse, and encouraged the recommendation by Wikler and others that treatment of opioid drug dependence should include extinction of the relationship between drug effects and environmental stimuli to which they have become conditioned (Wikler, 1980; see also Goldstein, 1976).

More recently, O'Brien and others have extended theories and observations regarding the role of conditioning processes in the management of opioid dependence to the treatment of cocaine abuse (O'Brien et al., 1992). The idea that environmental stimuli that have been paired with cocaine play an important role in relapse to cocaine abuse has become popular and closely intertwined with speculation regarding the role of the less-easily defined internal state that may underlie self-reports of craving. For example, Ehrman et al. (1992) have shown that stimuli associated with cocaine can produce reliable decreases in skin temperature and skin resistance, reliable increases in heart rate, self-reported cocaine craving, and self-reported cocaine withdrawal in subjects with a history of free-basing and smoking cocaine. Furthermore, control subjects without the history of cocaine use did not show these responses, suggesting that the stimuli elicited these responses due to the history of cocaine abuse. The authors suggest that these results indicate that classically conditioned responses to stimuli associated with drug use play a significant role in the relapse to drug use.

Most studies of reinstatement of cocaine self-administration behavior have used drug injection as the stimulus to induce the phenomenon. For example, de

Wit and Stewart (1981) trained rats in experimental sessions that were composed of two periods: during the first period, iv injections of (1.0 mg/kg) cocaine were available for self-administration and, during the second period, saline was substituted for cocaine. Stable performance was characterized by reliable self-administration, followed by low levels of extinguished behavior. When performances were stable, subjects were tested with response-independent injections of cocaine (0.5–2.0 mg/kg) during the second period. Although only iv saline was available as a consequence of responding, rates of behavior were increased substantially by the response-independent cocaine injections. Similar results have been obtained repeatedly in a number of laboratories, and in monkeys as well as rats (e.g., Stretch & Gerber, 1973; Gerber & Stretch, 1975).

The consistency of the above findings, and the power of the conditioning processes they reveal, have encouraged the idea that reinstated self-administration behavior might serve as an experimental model for clinical relapse. However, some caution should be taken to distinguish the conditioning processes in these experiments from those that led to earlier theories and, as well, from those that may be most applicable in the clinical situation. That is, reinstatement by an unconditioned reinforcing stimulus such as a drug injection is a fundamentally distinct process from reinstatement by previously neutral stimuli that have acquired secondary reinforcing effects through pairing with drug injections. Moreover, the sequence of events in reinstatement studies differs substantially from those that occur in the clinical experience. In the latter case, relapse is rarely, if ever, preceded by the elimination of drug-seeking behavior by the type of controlled extinction process that occurs in the laboratory. Thus, the results of reinstatement studies presently provide only tangential support for theories of relapse based on classical conditioning processes, with uncertain relevance to clinical relapse phenomena. Notwithstanding these caveats, however, the reinstatement phenomenon is a reproducible one and interesting for what it may yet reveal regarding underlying behavioral processes in the reinforcing effects of drugs.

The reinstatement of self-administration behavior by a priming injection bears resemblance to the results of studies of the discriminative effects of a reinforcing stimulus. For example, Reid (1957) showed that the response-independent presentation of food following the extinction of a food-reinforced response resulted in a resumption of responding in pigeons and rats. Earlier, Bullock and Smith (1953) had shown that repeated episodes of conditioning and extinction led to increasingly rapid and relatively strong control of lever pressing by rats. That is, the consequences of responding (food reinforcement) or, alternatively, the absence of those consequences become discriminative stimuli for subsequent responding (conditioning) or no responding (extinction), respectively. These two studies clearly have implications for the studies of reinstated drug-seeking behavior, with the biggest difference being that the reinforcers in studies of reinstatement of drug seeking are drugs rather than food. It is currently unknown whether such reinstatement is reinforcer-specific (i.e., in subjects that have been trained to respond both for food presentation or drug self-administration, can the response-independent presentation of food reinstate responding under conditions associated with drug self-administration?).

In addition to interoceptive or discriminative-stimulus effects that may provoke reinstatement of behavior, the priming injection also may have direct effects on response rates. As with reinforcer specificity, the role of such direct effects probably is most easily assessed using extinguished behavior previously maintained by a nondrug reinforcer (e.g., food presentation). Indeed, Skinner and Heron (1937) showed that several stimulant drugs could increase rates of responding during extinction. More recently, investigators have attempted to control for such "nonspecific" stimulation of behavior by measuring rates of responding on a second response manipulandum on which responding never had programmed consequences. For example, Worley et al. (1994) reported that cocaine injection prior to sessions increased rates of responding to a much greater extent on one of two response keys: namely, the one on which responses previously produced cocaine injections. The authors concluded that reinstatement was a highly specific phenomenon that did not reflect the general rate-increasing effects of the priming injection. However, the effects of cocaine on responding on an alternate key not associated with consequences may not be compelling evidence for the specificity of reinstatement. For example, Verhave (1958) found that doses of methamphetamine that might be expected to increase schedule-controlled responding did not substantially increase low rates of responding that had never been reinforced. In this regard, the lack of stimulation of responding on the alternate manipulandum in the study by Worley et al. (1994) is reminiscent of the findings by Verhave. Perhaps a more salient approach than measuring responding on an alternate manipulandum might be to compare the reinstatement of cocaine-reinforced responding with the drug-induced increase in extinguished responding previously maintained by another, preferably nondrug, reinforcer. That approach would suggest that the studies by Skinner and Heron (1937) be repeated in a manner that is as closely analogous as possible to reinstatement studies with cocaine self-administration. Results under that procedure could then be compared to those obtained in the cocaine-reinstatement procedure. Differences that depend on whether behavior previously was maintained by cocaine injection or food presentation might be indicative of the role of direct effects of cocaine in the reinstatement phenomenon.

In addition to reinstatement of self-administration behavior by cocaine, some studies have established reinstatement with priming injections of other drugs. For example, de Wit and Stewart (1981) additionally reported that behavior previously maintained by cocaine was reinstated robustly by injections of the psychomotor stimulant amphetamine and only marginally by the opioid morphine or the directly acting dopamine agonist apomorphine. Reinstatement was not produced by all drugs: heroin, methohexital, and alcohol, even at doses that maintained self-administration behavior in other experiments, were not effective in reinstating responding previously maintained by cocaine. These findings have generally borne out in subsequent research and, in general, the most effective agents in these types of studies are drugs with pharmacological properties in common with cocaine, such as psychomotor stimulants (Comer et al., 1993; Slikker, Brocco, & Killam, 1984; Worley et al., 1994; but see Wise, Murray, & Bogarth, 1990 and Self et al., 1996). The weakness of reinstatement with other drugs that can maintain self-administration supports the view offered by de Wit and Stewart (1981) that reinstatement across drugs is not mediated simply by a common reinforcing effect. de Wit and Stewart (1981) also entertained the possibility that common effects of cocaine, amphetamine, and to a much lesser extent, apomorphine and morphine could be attributed to some commonality in their discriminative-stimulus effects. Thus, amphetamine and apomorphine have been shown to substitute for cocaine in drug discrimination studies (e.g., Silverman & Ho, 1976). However, there is less evidence for overlap in the discriminative-stimulus effects of cocaine and morphine in rats or monkeys (e.g., Ando & Yanagita, 1978; Colpaert et al., 1979; Negus, Gatch, & Mello, 1998; Spealman & Bergman, 1992, 1994).

De Wit and Stewart (1981) suggested that the different contingency relationships between responding and cocaine in the self-administration and extinction components of the session did not come to control behavior, as might be expected if the priming injections of cocaine were established as discriminative stimuli. In their view, the persistence of nonreinforced responding after priming injections provided evidence against the discriminative control of behavior and for a motivational interpretation of reinstatement (i.e., priming elicits craving that leads to reinstatement). Although the role of discriminative control by the priming injection in reinstatement studies probably cannot be evaluated independently of other factors, reinstatement procedures do involve differential responding in the presence and absence of stimuli associated with different reinforcement contingencies. These differential contingencies are inherent in the training procedure, with cocaine reinforcement occurring most often in the presence of the cocaine stimulus (due to previous response-produced injections) followed by extinction in its absence. These contingencies plainly engender differential responding that is appropriate to the experimental condition. When subjects are tested for reinstatement, discriminative control produced by drug injections is obscured because responding is *both* maintained by the drug during self-administration and engendered by the drug during the extinction component. Though superficially there appears to be neither differential responding nor distinctive stimulus conditions, the nondifferential performances obtained in these tests are precisely what would be expected were cocaine serving as a discriminative stimulus in a manner analogous to that described by Reid (1957) and Bullock and Smith (1953). As with the above-discussed issues of reinforcer-specificity and the contribution of direct effects of cocaine to reinstatement, the role of discriminative-stimulus effects in the reinstatement of cocaine self-administration procedures could be addressed by basic studies of the determinants of reinstated behavior. Such studies clearly would enrich a scientific understanding of this phenomenon.

In a recent application of reinstatement procedures, Self et al. (1996) showed that both D_1- and D_2-like agonists stimulated locomotor activity, whereas only D_2, and not D_1 dopamine agonists could reinstate behavior previously maintained by cocaine. Thus, reinstatement by D_2 agonists was not simply a result of psychomotor stimulant effects. On this basis, the authors suggested that D_2 agonists might be poor treatments for cocaine abuse, whereas D_1 agonists might be more promising candidate medications. More recent observations with dopamine agonists in reinstatement experiments in squirrel monkeys (Barrett-Larimore & Spealman, 1997) are consistent with the findings of Self et al. (1996). However, the relevance of this type of effect to the development of medications for cocaine dependence remains questionable. First, as described above, the relationship between experimental reinstatement and clinical relapse is ambiguous. Second, though both D_1 and D_2 agonists are reported to increase locomotor activity in rats, the effects of D1 agonists are comparatively modest (Waddington et al., 1986). Moreover, behavioral studies in monkeys indicate that only D_2, and not D_1, agonists increase schedule-controlled response rates (Bergman, Rosenzweig-Lipson, & Spealman, 1995; Katz et al., 1995). Thus, it must be considered that locomotor activity and operant behavior—as in reinstatement procedures—are not similarly affected by D_1 agonists. The argument for selectivity of reinstatement by D_2 agonists might have been better addressed by comparing the effects of priming injections of D_1 and D_2 agonists on responding previously maintained by cocaine to their effects when responding was previously maintained by another reinforcer (see above discussion).

One aspect of the findings by Self et al. (1996) is of particular interest to the analysis of reinstatement phenomena. Both D_1 and D_2 agonists have been reported to produce cocaine-appropriate responding in drug discrimination experiments (e.g., Witkin et al., 1991), though neither completely substitutes for cocaine. If reinstatement of cocaine self-administration behavior is exclusively a result of cocaine-like discriminative-stimulus effects of the priming drugs, both D_1 and D_2 agonists might have been expected to engender the reinstatement phenomenon. One possibility is that these different types of agonists mimic different aspects of the cocaine discriminative stimulus, with only those effects common to D_2 agonists and cocaine being relevant to reinstatement. Alternatively, some similarity in discriminative effects coupled with rate-increasing effects on operant behavior may be necessary conditions for reinstatement. Nevertheless, there is presently not a satisfactory explanation for the reported differences between the effects of D_1 and D_2 agonists in studies of reinstatement phenomena.

Can the reinstatement phenomenon serve as a model of relapse? Treatment of cocaine abuse can be divided into phases including detoxification followed by prevention of relapse (Mendelson & Mello, 1996). Relapse can be considered to be a Pavlovian elicitation by drug-associated stimuli of a constellation of conditioned responses (including reports of craving) that may engender renewed drug use. From a practical viewpoint, therefore, there is a need for procedures with which to better study the determinants of relapse and methods for its prevention. The face validity of reinstatement models of relapse depends on the observation that the probability with which previously reinforced behavior will occur during extinction increases upon presentation of a particular stimulus. When that stimulus is one that has been previously associated with cocaine injection, the analogy to the chain of events that may take place in actual relapse is close, though functional identity has not been established. There have been noticeably few studies of reinstatement of actual drug-seeking behavior by conditioned stimuli. When the reinstating stimulus is the injection of cocaine itself, the analogy to clinical relapse becomes less compelling. First, the salient feature of actual relapse is the transition from the drug-free to the drugged state . . . not what happens following a renewed exposure to the drug. Second, as discussed above, the phenomenon of reinstatement by injection of drug has not been satisfactorily analyzed. Despite the assertion of a role for motivational factors in renewed cocaine self-administration behavior during reinstatement, it is not firmly established that this phenomenon represents anything other than the direct effect of cocaine on operant behavior occurring at a relatively low rate due to extinction, the discriminative effect of cocaine, or a combination of the two effects.

CONTEXTUAL DETERMINANTS OF THE REINFORCING EFFECTS OF COCAINE

The discussion in the previous two sections of this essay has centered on how the measurement of cocaine's reinforcing effects in laboratory self-administration procedures may be influenced by its other behavioral effects. The emphasis in the remaining sections will be on contextual factors that may influence evaluation of the reinforcing effects of cocaine. In particular, the role of schedule conditions under which cocaine self-administration is maintained, the influence of availability of alternatives to drug-maintained responding on cocaine self-administration, and how cocaine self-administration can be modified by noxious stimuli (punishment) will be discussed.

SCHEDULES OF COCAINE
SELF-ADMINISTRATION

The role of schedules of reinforcement in the control of behavior in and out of the laboratory was first described by Skinner and his associates (Ferster & Skinner, 1957; Morse, 1966; Morse & Kelleher, 1970; Skinner, 1953), and it is clear that the schedule of reinforcement plays a prominent role in the expression of the reinforcing effects of cocaine (see Johanson & Fischman, 1989; Kelleher, 1976). In the human population, the self-administration of cocaine and other drugs occurs under a wide range of schedule conditions that likely exert powerful control over behavior. As illustrated below, the mix of schedule conditions used in the laboratory can produce varied types of performances that can provide important information regarding the controlling influences of different types of schedule conditions that may pertain to human drug self-administration. Yet, this remains a bare-ly explored area of research, and self-administration studies generally employ rel-atively simple schedules of reinforcement. It is instructive to consider the types of schedules under which cocaine self-administration is most often studied and how they may constrain the assessment of abuse liability.

For reasons of convenience and limitations on iv catheter life that may preclude more lengthy training, cocaine self-administration studies most often employ fixed-ratio schedules of reinforcement. Most often, drug delivery is arranged to occur by the iv route, although inhalation, intramuscular, and intranasal cocaine self-administraiton also have been studied (e.g., Comer, Hunt, & Carroll, 1994; Foltin & Fischman, 1991; Goldberg, Morse, & Goldberg, 1976; Grubman & Woods, 1981; Katz, 1979; Wood, Grubman, & Weiss, 1977). Fixed-ratio perfor-mance is relatively uncomplicated, and, as has been demonstrated repeatedly, ef-fective doses of cocaine maintain regular patterns of responding under such con-ditions: each completion of the fixed-ratio unit generally is characterized by sustained high rates of responding and, after drug delivery, often is followed by a period of no responding, during which the direct effects of the drug may dissipate (e.g., Dworkin & Pitts, 1994; Goldberg, 1973). Under conditions of limited daily access, such patterns of stable, spaced cocaine self-administration behavior can be maintained indefinitely. This type of performance lends itself toward an eval-uation of the relationship between response output and the dose of cocaine avail-able for self-administration which, as illustrated by behavioral economic analy-sis, can be both informative and complicated (see Carroll & Bickel, chapter 4, this volume).

As discussed earlier, the direct effects of cocaine serve to limit its intake under most conditions of drug availability. Under conditions of unlimited access (i.e., 24 h per day of cocaine availability), an interesting phenomenon may begin to occur (i.e., dysregulated cocaine intake) (Paulus & Geyer, 1991). This phenomenon has been documented most clearly in monkey self-administration studies and is char-acterized by periods of high intake with irregular interinjection intervals that al-ternate with periods of very low intake during which the subject may be exhaust-ed (Deneau et al., 1969; Johanson, Balster, & Bonese, 1976). This pattern of intake is directly a product of fixed-ratio schedule conditions that do not formally limit dosage over time. Importantly, cocaine self-administration may come to predom-inate the subject's behavioral repertoire to the exclusion of other activities, in-cluding food intake. Eventually, periods of cocaine intake may become so exces-sive that convulsions and death ensue (Deneau et al., 1969). This phasic pattern of cocaine intake also is recognized in cocaine use by humans, and has become la-beled as the "binge-and-crash" phenomenon (e.g., Gawin, 1989; Gawin & Kleber, 1986; Resnick & Schuyten-Resnick, 1976; Trinkoff, Ritter, & Anthony, 1990). Un-doubtedly, the reputation of cocaine's remarkable powers as a reinforcer can be traced, in part, to the attention that this behavioral phenomenon has received. Yet, there have been relatively few parametric self-administration studies employing fixed-ratio schedules and differing access conditions to evaluate variables that may be involved in its development. In one recent study in rats, dysregulation, as indicated by erratic patterns of fixed-ratio self-administration behavior and severe weight loss, was shown to emerge between 16 to 48 hours of continuous access to a relatively high unit dose (0.25 mg/kg) of cocaine (Mutschler & Miczek, 1997; see also Markou & Koob, 1991). Continued systematic studies of this type could contribute greatly to our understanding of cocaine-engendered behavioral dysregulation and, in turn, the binge-and-crash phenomenon among human drug users.

It is important to emphasize that the behavioral dysregulation that occurs with unlimited access under fixed-ratio schedules of iv self-administration in the laboratory or in bingeing episodes among humans is not restricted to cocaine, but may occur with amphetamines and other psychomotor stimulant drugs (Deneau et al., 1969; Johanson et al., 1976). Furthermore, the mechanism(s) underlying such dysregulation are not understood. They may involve changes in mechanisms that control satiety (see Carroll & Bickel, chapter 4, this volume), disturbances in stimulus control by contextual or physiological factors, or a more global and reinforcer-independent disruption of behavior.

Recreational cocaine use occurs under conditions other than in bingeing episodes. Analogously, the reinforcing and other behavioral effects of cocaine can be studied in the laboratory under conditions involving other than continuous availability under simple fixed-ratio schedules. One approach in such studies is to incorporate the fixed-ratio schedule of self-administration into multiple schedule conditions under which each delivery of cocaine is followed by a time-out period during which cocaine cannot be self-administered (Morse, 1976; Woods et al., 1987). The inclusion of time-out periods can limit the accumulation of cocaine yet permit high self-administration doses to be studied. Under these types of schedules, the length of the time-out period plays an obvious role in the rate of cocaine accumulation and, consequently, may determine the positon and peak of the dose–response function for cocaine self-administration (Winger, 1993a,b). For example, optimum doses of cocaine for iv self-administration may range from 0.01–0.1 mg/kg per injection in monkeys responding under fixed-ratio schedules without associated time-out components. The incorporation of a 3-h time-out period following each completion of the fixed-ratio schedule results in a rightward shift in the dose–effect function, with an at least three-fold increase in optimum doses (Griffiths, Brady, & Snell, 1978). This relationship between schedule parameters and the position of the dose–effect function is a powerful reminder that the reinforcing effects of cocaine are not a simple function of unit dose, and that direct effects of cocaine on behavior may limit its self-administration and evaluation of its reinforcing effectiveness.

Cocaine self-administration also has been studied under fixed-interval schedules of reinforcement. Unlike fixed-ratio patterning, fixed-interval performance often is characterized by an acceleration in behavior over the course of the interval, resulting in low to intermediate overall rates of responding compared to response rates under fixed-ratio schedules (Balster & Schuster, 1973; Kelleher, 1976; Nader & Bowen, 1995; Nader & Reboussin, 1994; Spealman & Kelleher, 1979). The fixed-interval schedule may present certain advantages for self-administration research. For example, one goal in the development of pharmacotherapeutics has been the identification of medications that may selectively decrease cocaine self-administration without disrupting performances maintained by nondrug reinforcers (see Balster et al., 1992; Glowa, 1996; Weissenborn et al., 1995; Winger, chapter 6, this volume). Preclinical assessment of anticocaine medications in rats and monkeys primarily utilize fixed-ratio schedules to evaluate how treatments may modify cocaine self-administration and, for comparison, food-maintained behavior. However, the use of fixed-ratio schedules, which generate high response rates and generally permit the observation only of decreases in response rates by the potential treatment agent, may provide incomplete information. For example, studies in rhesus monkeys have shown that psychomotor stimulant drugs such as GBR 12909 may decrease cocaine self-administration at doses that do not affect food-maintained performance, suggestive of a cocaine-selective effect (Glowa et al., 1995a,b). Yet, GBR 12909 is known to *increase* response rates under fixed-interval schedules (Rosenzweig-Lipson et al., 1992; Spealman, Madras, & Bergman, 1989), consistent with psychomotor stimulant actions. In the absence of a comparison of the effects of GBR 12909 on cocaine- and food-maintained performances under schedule conditions permitting increases in response rate, the suggestion that it has selective effects on cocaine self-administration and, consequently, a favorable therapeutic profile may be premature. In view of the potential for toxic consequences of pharmacological interactions between treatment drugs and cocaine, a closer analysis of the apparent selectivity of treatment effects on cocaine self-administration seems warranted.

Second-order schedules are among the more interesting schedules of reinforcement that have been used to study cocaine self-administration (Goldberg, Kelleher, & Morse, 1975; Spealman & Goldberg, 1978). Under one type of second-order schedule, the completion of each fixed-ratio unit produces a brief nondrug stimulus (e.g., light flash), and the completion of the first fixed-ratio unit after the lapse of a fixed interval produces the brief stimulus accompanied by an injection of cocaine. One advantage of this schedule is that high rates of self-administration behavior can be maintained by injections of cocaine that are spaced to limit their disruptive effects on performance. Figure 2, for example, shows performances of an individual monkey that initially responded under a 10-min fixed-interval schedule of cocaine self-administration (top panel). As can be seen, responding was maintained at relatively low rates under the fixed-interval schedule, giving little indication of cocaine's reinforcing effects. However, altering the schedule conditions so that every third and then tenth response produced a flash of light, and after the passage of the 10-min fixed-interval, the same 30 μg/kg cocaine injection resulted in a dramatic increase in response rates. Systematic studies of this type of second-order schedule have shown that similarly high rates of

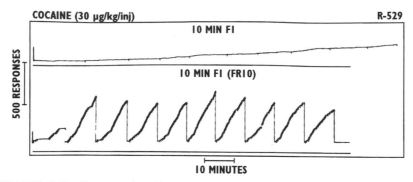

FIGURE 3.2 Representative self-administration performances in monkey R-529 maintained by cocaine under a 10-min fixed-interval schedule (top panel) and a 10-min fixed-interval second-order schedule with 10-response fixed-ratio units (bottom panel). Abscissae: time; ordinates: cumulative responses. Under the second-order schedule, the response pen resets with the completion of each 10-min fixed-interval. Diagonal marks indicate the delivery of cocaine (top panel) or the brief flash of light serving as a conditioned stimulus (bottom panel). (Adapted from Kelleher, 1976.)

responding also can be sustained for a much longer fixed-interval (e.g. 60 min) in daily sessions involving only one presentation of the fixed-interval and, consequently, only a single self-administration of cocaine (e.g., Bergman & Spealman, 1986; Goldberg et al., 1976; Katz, 1979). These types of second-order schedule performances illustrate that cocaine can maintain persistent high rates of behavior over extended periods of time. Moreover, under these conditions the effects of various drug pretreatments on the behavior maintained by cocaine can be studied without the involvement of other pharmacological interactions between cocaine and the pretreatment compound (e.g., Katz, 1980). From a behavioral—and clinically relevant—perspective, second-order schedule performances also illustrate the importance of conditioned stimuli in maintaining drug-seeking behavior and offer an experimental means for studying these relationships in an objective and quantitative manner. Such studies employing second-order conditions and other more complex types of schedules permit laboratory research conditions to more closely approximate the rich variety of schedule conditions under which the illicit use of drugs occurs. Moreover, studies of behavior under such schedules may enhance our understanding of the role of environmental stimuli in the resumption of drug-seeking behavior and self-administration (see above discussion of relapse).

In summary, the schedule of availability is an important determinant of the quantitative and qualitative effects of cocaine (and other drugs) in self-administration studies. No one set of schedule conditions is best suited for studying cocaine self-administration. Rather, each type of schedule offers distinct advantages that can be exploited to address different questions regarding the reinforcing and other behavioral effects of self-administered cocaine.

ALTERNATIVES TO COCAINE
SELF-ADMINISTRATION

Laboratory studies have contributed to the idea that cocaine is a uniquely powerful reinforcer (for discussion, see Johanson and Fischman, 1989) and, by extension, that the treatment of cocaine abuse and dependence may pose singular problems. As described above, cocaine and other stimulants, unlike abused drugs from other classes, will maintain persistent self-administration behavior under conditions of unlimited access despite life-threatening consequences of unabated intake. In combination, such lines of evidence and the perceived epidemic abuse of cocaine have fostered the view that cocaine is a uniquely powerful reinforcer. However, cocaine self-administration generally is studied under conditions that should restrict conclusions regarding its reinforcing strength and, perhaps, temper this view. Most notably, in the majority of self-administration experiments, cocaine injection is the only explicitly scheduled consequence (but see Johanson & Aigner, 1981; Johanson & Schuster, 1975, 1977). When the only option for exercising an instrumentally learned response is drug-maintained responding, the rapid onset of cocaine's effects, its relatively short duration of action, and its pronounced psychomotor stimulant actions combine with its reinforcing effects to engender high levels of self-administration behavior which, in turn, are invoked as evidence of reinforcing strength. However, the reinforcing and other behavioral effects of drug injections are subject to historical and environmental determinants (see Johanson & Fischman, 1989; Johanson & Schuster, 1981). There is no *a priori* reason to discount the influence of such determinants in the degree to which cocaine, like other drug or nondrug stimuli, may maintain behavior.

One way of evaluating reinforcing strength is in terms of choice among concurrently available consequences, and it is reasonable to ask whether the notion that cocaine possesses unusual reinforcing strength is borne out in studies in which cocaine self-administration is not the only available consequence. Direct comparisons of the reinforcing effects of cocaine and other drugs have been made using discrete-trial choice procedures in monkeys trained to self-administer cocaine. Although the time-consuming nature of such studies has restricted their widespread use, systematic comparisons have been made between cocaine and other psychomotor stimulants including methylphenidate, diethylpropion, cathinone, and procaine (Johanson & Aigner, 1981; Johanson & Schuster, 1975, 1977; Woolverton & Johanson, 1984). It is important to note that the procedures and temporal parameters in these studies were carefully chosen to minimize the influence of response bias and drug influences other than reinforcing effects of self-administered drugs. Results of studies with the above drugs indicate that higher doses of cocaine were reliably preferred to lower doses of cocaine and to low and high doses of diethylpropion. On the other hand, high doses of cocaine were not preferred over suitably high doses of methylphenidate, cathinone, or procaine. These findings are important because they indicate that the reinforcing strength of cocaine is closely related to dose and can be paralleled by the reinforcing strength of other self-administered drugs with psychomotor stimulant effects.

Studies to evaluate choice between drug and nondrug reinforcers provide another perspective from which to consider the reinforcing strength of cocaine. For example, findings of an early study using choice procedures in rhesus monkeys showed that subjects preferred cocaine over food, to the point that the experiment was stopped to avert starvation (Aigner & Balster, 1978). These findings contributed greatly to the notion that cocaine possesses extraordinary reinforcing strength. Less publicized, however, were subsequent studies in which reinforcer magnitude (dose of cocaine and number of food pellets) and response requirement (fixed-ratio value) were systematically varied (Nader & Woolverton, 1991). The results of these studies bear close attention. As shown in Figure 3, the choice of cocaine or food delivery was highly dependent on the dose of cocaine, the amount of food per delivery, and the response requirements for both cocaine and food delivery. Thus, when each trial consisted of a choice between the delivery of one food biscuit or 0.3 mg/kg cocaine, the drug injection was chosen nearly exclusively until response requirements were markedly imbalanced (FR 480 for cocaine and FR 30 for food delivery). At these last fixed-ratio values, monkeys selected food delivery over cocaine approximately 65–70% of the time. A change in preference away from cocaine injection also became apparent when either the magnitude of the food reinforcement increased to four pellets per delivery or the dosage of cocaine was decreased to 0.1 mg/kg per injection. With an increase in the magnitude of food reinforcement, the function relating choice of cocaine over food delivery to FR value shifted leftward: cocaine and food delivery were equally chosen at the response requirement of FR 120 and food delivery was selected 90% of the time when the response requirement for cocaine was increased to FR 480 (left panel). A decrease in the dosage of cocaine available each trial to 0.1 mg/kg also led to a preference for the delivery of four food biscuits over cocaine. Indicative of the dynamic relationship between the magnitude of the different reinforcers and response requirements, however, this now occurred even when response requirements were the same for cocaine and food delivery (FR 30; right panel).

Taken together, these results further support the view that assessments of the reinforcing strength of cocaine, and that of other self-administered drugs, are relativistic measures that depend on both reinforcing effects and the conditions under which the drug and other reinforcers have been, and are, currently available. From this perspective, a distinction can be made between a drug's ability to maintain self-administration and its reinforcing strength. Self-administration studies in which there is a choice between drug and a nondrug reinforcer may allow the nondrug alternative to function as a standard for subsequent comparisons of several drugs. This, in turn, may be interpreted as a reflection of reinforcing strength. However, as Morse and Kelleher noted some 20 years ago, "Comparing the levels of behavior maintained by different drugs provides information of limited generality—as, for example, in comparing the amounts eaten of oatmeal and Cream of Wheat. Under some conditions neither would be taken, and a starving person switched their preference and selected the higher unit dose of cocaine, even though responding produced electric shocks that had previously suppressed responding. These findings illustrated the dynamic nature of the relationship between the suppressant effects of noxious stimuli and the reinforcing effects of cocaine.

In both the studies described above, the suppressing stimuli were presented during single test sessions, and it was unclear whether the observed suppression of cocaine self-administration was a transient or enduring phenomenon. This issue was addressed in subsequent studies (Bergman & Johanson, 1981). In these studies cocaine self-administration under a fixed-ratio schedule was initially suppressed to approximately 50% by electric shock that accompanied the infusion of cocaine. However, the suppressant effects of the electric shock waned over repeated exposures, and within six experimental sessions cocaine-maintained responding had recovered to values obtained in the absence of punishment. Subsequent experiments showed that adaptation to the suppressant effects of electric shock occurred reliably under these conditions, except when the stimulus intensity was sufficient to fully suppress cocaine-maintained responding. These findings of adaptation to the suppression of cocaine self-administration behavior by noxious stimuli except when behavior was completely eliminated are comparable to those previously reported for the suppression of fixed-ratio responding maintained by food presentation (Azrin, 1959; for general discussion, see Azrin & Holz, 1966).

An important aspect of the studies outlined above is that both the reinforcing (cocaine) and punishing (shock) events were presented under a fixed-ratio schedule, and it was unclear whether the dominating effects of cocaine (or, perhaps, the transient punishing effects of electric shock) would be similarly evident under other conditions. Recent experiments were conducted to study the suppression of cocaine-maintained behavior more fully (Bergman & Morse, unpublished data). In these studies, schedule-controlled performances maintained by food- or iv drug injections (0.1 mg/kg cocaine or, for comparison, 3.0 mg/kg methohexital) were established in different groups of monkeys under a 10-min fixed-interval second-order schedule with fixed-ratio 30 units. When response rates were stable from day to day, dose–effect functions were determined for drug self-administration and, subsequently, response-contingent electric shock was introduced for all subjects. The introduction of electric shock resulted in an intensity-dependent suppression of responding, and, importantly, no adaptation to the rate-suppressing effects of electric shock was observed over the course of the experiments. Dose–effect functions were redetermined for cocaine and methohexital, and as shown in Figure 4, an intermediate level (approximately 40–60%) of response suppression was evident over a range of self-administered doses. The absence of adaptation to the suppressant effects of electric shock on cocaine-maintained performance under the second-order schedule indicates that the characteristics of the suppression of cocaine-maintained behavior by noxious stimuli depend fundamentally on the schedule conditions under which self-administration behavior is maintained. Moreover, the similarity in response suppression observed with pharmacologically dissimilar drugs (cocaine and methohexital) and with food illustrate that noxious stimuli

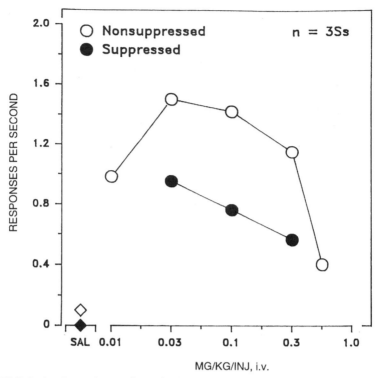

FIGURE 3.4   Rates of responding maintained by iv cocaine under a 10-min fixed-interval second-order schedule with 30-response fixed ratio units. Open symbols show response rates in a group
of three monkeys when responding to only occasional iv cocaine injections. Filled symbols show response rates maintained by cocaine in the same group of monkeys when mild electric shock stimuli
(1–3 mÅ) also were delivered upon the first response in each tenth fixed-ratio of the 10-min fixed-
interval. Symbols above SAL represent the averaged effects under both conditions when saline was
substituted for cocaine.

may modify cocaine-maintained behavior in much the same way as behavior maintained by other reinforcing events.

   Subsequently, studies were conducted to compare modification of the suppression of drug- or food-maintained responding by the antisuppressant drug chlordiazepoxide. Consistent with previously reported effects on food-maintained
responding, chlordiazepoxide attenuated the suppression of food-maintained behavior and restored rates of responding to those observed prior to the introduction
of response-suppressing electric shock. Chlordiazepoxide also attenuated the suppression of cocaine self-administration, as evident in a dose-related increase in
rates of suppressed responding (Figure 5). In contrast, however, chlordiazepoxide
did not increase suppressed rates of methohexital-maintained behavior. Rather,
pretreatment with the benzodiazepine only decreased responding and, after treat-

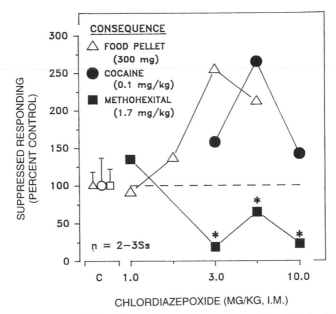

FIGURE 3.5   Effects of chlordiazepoxide on suppressed responding maintained by iv cocaine (circles), iv methohexital (squares), or food (triangles) under a second-order schedule (see Figure 3.4 for schedule details). Abscissae: pretreatment dose of chlordiazepoxide, mg/kg; ordinate: effect as percentage of suppressed control rates of responding. Symbols above C show control response rate (100% + one standard deviation) for the group of three monkeys. * indicates subjects were asleep for prolonged periods during the experimental session.

ment with doses of 3.0–10.0 mg/kg, subjects were observed to be asleep for prolonged periods (Figure 3.5). These findings indicate that, as with food-maintained responding, antisuppressant drugs like chlordiazepoxide can block or reverse the suppressant effects of noxious stimuli on cocaine-maintained behavior. However, the findings with methohexital self-administration illustrate that, under some conditions, the actions of self-administered drugs interact profoundly with pharmacological treatments. As described previously, such interactions may limit the utility of therapeutics in modifying drug self-administration.

In summary, the studies described in this section support the tenet that the suppression of behavior, like reinforcement, is a dynamic process that depends upon the magnitude and scheduling of both the punishing and reinforcing events (Morse & Kelleher, 1977). From a behavioral viewpoint, cocaine-maintained responding does not differ qualitatively in this regard from behavior maintained by other consequences, such as food delivery. Like food-maintained responding, cocaine-maintained behavior can be reliably suppressed using conventional laboratory procedures. Like other drugs, however, cocaine has pharmacological actions that can be expected to influence the effects of punishing stimuli and, as well, to alter the behavioral effects of other compounds on suppressed responding. An appreciation of these actions is as fundamental to understanding the conditions under which cocaine self-administration can be reliably suppressed as it is to understanding those under which it is reliably maintained.

SUMMARY

Throughout this chapter we have focused on aspects of the behavioral pharmacology of cocaine that have bearing on the assessment of its reinforcing effects and abuse liability. It is commonly accepted that cocaine is a uniquely powerful reinforcer and that this unique power contributes to its widespread abuse. We have attempted to explore the basis for this viewpoint in an analytic manner. Thus, we have examined how the direct effects of cocaine on operant behavior may influence results in studies of cocaine self-administration, and how the schedule of reinforcement may serve to influence performances maintained by cocaine. We have further discussed how the interoceptive effects of cocaine may contribute to laboratory assessments of relapse. In this regard, we have examined aspects of models of relapse that deserve close scrutiny. From a scientific viewpoint, an unambiguous description of the behavioral processes involved in such models of relapse are essential if they are to be credible and useful. Finally, we have examined the relatively few studies that have investigated punishment of cocaine-maintained behavior. The behaviorally dynamic effects of punishment on cocaine-maintained behavior—as on food-maintained behavior—contribute to the view that cocaine, like other reinforcing stimuli, is not invariant in its reinforcing capacity. The abuse of cocaine continues to be an important biomedical problem in contemporary society. Solutions to this problem surely will be based on analytically sound understanding of the behavioral pharmacology of cocaine.

ACKNOWLEDGMENTS

The research described and the preparation of this chapter was supported by United States Public Health Service Grants MH 07658, DA 03774, and DA 10566. The authors are indebted to Professor W. H. Morse for years of teaching, guidance, and continuous inspiration.

REFERENCES

Aigner, T. G., & Balster, R. I. (1978). Choice behavior in rhesus monkeys: cocaine versus food. *Science, 201*(4355), 534–535.
Altman, J., Everitt, B. J., Glautier, S., Markou, A., Nutt, D., Oretti, R., Phillips, G. D., & Robbins,

T. W. (1996). The biological, social and clinical bases of drug addiction: Commentary and debate. *Psychopharmacology, 125*(4), 285–345.

Ando, K., & Yanagita, T., (1978). The discriminative stimulus properties of intravenously administered cocaine in rhesus monkeys. In F. C. Colpaert, & J. A. Rosencrans (Eds.), *Stimulus properties of drugs: Ten years of progress* (pp. 125–136). Amsterdam: Elsevier.

Azrin, N. H. (1959). Punishment and recovery during fixed-ratio performance. *Journal of Experimental Analysis of Behavior, 2,* 301–305.

Azrin, N. H., & Holz, W. C. (1966). Punishment. In W. K. Honig (Ed.), *Operant behavior: Areas of research and application* (pp. 380–447). New York: Appleton-Century-Crofts.

Balster, R. L., Mansbach, R. S., Gold, L. & Harris, L. S. (1992). Preclinical methods for the development of pharmacotherapies for cocaine abuse. *NIDA Research Monograph, 119,* 160–164.

Balster, R. L., & Schuster, C. (1973). Fixed interval schedules of cocaine reinforcement: Effect of dose and infusion duration. *Journal of Experimental Analysis of Behavior, 20,* 119–129.

Barrett, J. E. (1976). Effects of alcohol, chlordiazepoxide, cocaine and pentobarbital on responding maintained under fixed-interval schedules of food or shock presentation. *Journal of Pharmacology and Experimental Therapeutics, 196,* 605–615.

Barrett-Larimore, R. L., & Spealman, R. D. (1997). Reinstatement of cocaine-seeking behavior in a nonhuman primate model of relapse: effects of preferential DA D_1 and D_3 agonists. *NIDA Research Monographs, 178,* 283.

Bergman, J., & Johanson, C. E. (1981). The effects of electric shock on responding maintained by cocaine in rhesus monkeys. *Pharmacology, Biochemistry & Behavior, 14,* 423–426.

Bergman, J., Rosenzweig-Lipson, S., & Spealman, R. D. (1995). Differential effects of dopamine D_1 and D_2 receptor agonists on schedule-controlled behavior of squirrel monkeys. *Journal of Pharmacology and Experimental Therapeutics, 273*(1), 40–48.

Bergman, J., & Spealman, R. D. (1986). Some behavioral effects of histamine H_1 antagonists in squirrel monkeys. *Journal of Pharmacology, and Experimental Therapeutics, 239,* 104–110.

Bullock, D. H., & Smith, W. C. (1953). An effect of repeated conditioning-extinction upon operant strength. *Journal of Experimental Psychology, 46,* 349–352.

Colpaert, F. C., Niemegeers, C. J. E., & Janssen, P. A. T. (1979). Discriminative stimulus properties of cocaine: Neuropharmacological characteristics as derived from stimulus generalization experiments. *Pharmacology Biochemistry & Behavior, 10*(4), 535–546.

Comer, S. D., Hunt, V. R., & Carroll, M. E. (1994). Effects of concurrent saccharin availability and buprenorphine pretreatment on demand for smoked cocaine base in rhesus monkeys. *Psychopharmacology, 115*(1–2), 15–23.

Comer, S. D., Lac, S. T., Curtis, L. K., & Carroll, M. E. (1993). Effects of buprenoprhine and naltrexone on reinstatement of cocaine-reinforced responding in rats. *Journal of Pharmacology and Experimental Therapeutics, 267*(3), 1470–1477.

Davis, W. M., & Smith, S. G. (1974). Naloxone use to eliminate opiate-seeking behavior: Need for extinction of drug-seeking behavior. *Biological Psychiatry, 4,* 181–189.

Davis, W. M., & Smith, S. G. (1976). Role of conditioned reinforcers in the initiation and extinction of drug-seeking behavior. *Pavlovian Journal of Biological Science, 11,* 222–236.

Deneau, G. A., Yanagita, T., & Seevers, M. H. (1969). Self-administration of psychoactive substances by the monkey: A measure of psychological dependence. *Psychopharmacologia, 16,* 30–48.

de Wit, H., & Stewart, J. (1981). Reinstatement of cocaine-reinforced responding in the rat. *Psychopharmacology, 75*(2), 134–143.

Dews, P. B. (1958). Studies on behavior. IV. Stimulant actions of methamphetamine. *Journal of Pharmacology and Experimental Therapeutics, 122,* 137–147.

Dworkin, S. I., & Pitts, R. C. (1994). Use of rodent self-administration models to develop pharmacotherapies for cocaine abuse. *NIDA Research Monographs, 145,* 88–112.

Ehrman, R. N., Robbins, S. J., Childress, A. R., & O'Brien, C. P. (1992). Conditioned responses to cocaine-related stimuli in cocaine abuse patients. *Psychopharmacology, 107*(4), 523–529.

Ferster, C. B., & Skinner, B. F. (1957). *Schedules of reinforcement.* New York: Appleton-Century-Crofts.

Fischman, M. W., & Johanson, C.-E. (1996). Cocaine. In C. R. Schuster & M. J. Kuhar (Eds.), *Pharmacological aspects of drug dependence: Towards an integrated neurobehavioral approach. Handbook of experimental pharmacology* (vol. 118, pp. 159–195). Berlin: Springer-Verlag.

Foltin, R. W., & Fischman, M. W. (1991). Smoked and intravenous cocaine in humans: acute tolerance, cardiovascular and subjective effects. *Journal of Pharmacology and Experimental Therapeutics, 257*(1), 247–261.

Gawin, F. H. (1989). Cocaine abuse and addiction. *Journal of Family Practice, 29,* 193–197.

Gawin, F. H., & Kleber, H. D. (1986). Abstinence symptomatology and psychiatric diagnosis in cocaine abusers. *Archives of General Psychiatry, 43*(2), 107–113.

Gerber, G. J., & Stretch, R. (1975). Drug-induced reinstatement of extinguished self-administration behavior in monkeys. *Pharmacology, Biochemistry & Behavior, 3*(6), 1055–1061.

Glowa, J. R., Wojnicki, F. H. E., Matecka, D., Bacher, J. D., Mansbach, R. S., Balster, R. L., & Rice, K. C. (1995). Effects of dopamine reuptake inhibitors on food and cocaine maintained responding. I: Dependence on unit dose of cocaine. *Experimental Clinical Psychopharmacology, 3,* 219–231.

Glowa, R. L.,Wojnicki, F. H. E., Matecka, D., Rice, K. C., & Rothman, R. B. (1996a). Effects of dopamine reuptake inhibitors on food and cocaine maintained responding. II: Comparisons with other drugs and repeated administrations. *Experimental Clinical Psychopharmacology, 3,* 232–239.

Glowa, J. R. (1996b). Dose-response analysis in risk assessment: evaluation of behavioral specificity. *Environmental Health Perspectives, 104* (suppl. 2), 391–396.

Goldberg, S. R. (1973). Comparable behavior maintained under fixed-ratio and second-order schedules of food presentation, cocaine injection, or d-amphetamine injection in the squirrel monkey. *Journal of Pharmacology and Experimental Therapeutics, 186,* 18–30.

Goldberg, S. R., Kelleher, R. T., & Morse, W. H. (1975). Second-order schedules of drug injection. *Federation Proceedings, 34*(9), 1771–1776.

Goldberg, S. R., Morse, W. H., & Goldberg, D. M. (1976). Behavior maintained under a second-order schedule by intramuscular injection of morphine or cocaine in rhesus monkeys. *Journal of Pharmacology and Experimental Therapeutics, 199,* 278–286.

Goldstein, A. (1976). Heroin addiction. Sequential treatment employing pharmacologic supports. *Archives of General Psychiatry, 33*(3), 353–358.

Griffiths, R. R., Brady, J. V., & Snell, J. D. (1978). Progressive-ratio performance maintained by drug infusions: comparison of cocaine, diethylpropion, chlorphentermine, and fenfluramine. *Psychopharmacology, 56,* 5–13.

Grove, R. N., & Schuster, C. R. (1974). Suppression of cocaine self-administration by extinction and punishment. *Pharmacology, Biochemistry & Behavior, 2,* 199–208.

Grubman, J., & Woods, J. H. (1981). Schedule-controlled behavior maintained by nitrous oxide delivery in the rhesus monkey. In S. Saito & T. Yanagita (Eds.), *Proceedings of a symposium on drugs as reinforcers.* Exerpta Medica International, Congress Series 620, Tokyo, pp. 259–274.

Ho, B. T., & McKenna, M. (1978). Discriminative stimulus properties of central stimulants. In B. T. Ho, D. W. Richards, & D. L. Chute (Eds.), *Drug discrimination and state dependent learning* (pp. 57–77). New York: Academic Press.

Jaffe, J. H., Cascella, N. G., Kumor, K. M., & Sherer, M. A. (1989). Cocaine-induced cocaine craving. *Psychopharmacology, 97*(1), 59–64.

Johanson, C. E. (1977). The effects of electric shock on responding maintained by cocaine injections in a choice procedure in the rhesus monkey. *Psychopharmacology, 53,* 277–282.

Johanson, C. E., & Aigner, T. (1981). Comparison of the reinforcing properties of cocaine and procaine in rhesus monkeys. *Pharmacology, Biochemistry & Behavior, 15,* 49–53.

Johanson, C. E., Balster, R. L., & Bonese, K. (1976). Self-administration of psychomotor stimulant drugs: The effects of unlimited access. *Pharmacology, Biochemistry & Behavior, 4*(1), 45–51.

Johanson, C. E., & Fischman, M. W. (1989). The pharmacology of cocaine related to its abuse. *Pharmacological Reviews, 41*(1), 3–40.

Johanson, C. E., & Schuster, C. R. (1975). A choice procedure for drug reinforcers: Cocaine and methylphenidate in the rhesus monkey. *Journal of Pharmacology and Experimental Therapeutics, 193,* 676–688.

Johanson, C. E., & Schuster, C. R. (1977). A comparison of cocaine and diethylpropion under two different schedules of drug presentation. In E. H. Ellinwood, Jr., & M. M. Kilbey (Eds.), *Cocaine and other stimulants* (pp. 545–570). New York: Plenum Press.

Johanson, C. E., & Schuster, C. R. (1981). Animal models of drug self-administration. In N. K. Mello (Ed.), *Advances in substance abuse: Behavioral and biological research, Vol. II.* Greenwich, CT: JAI Press.

Johanson, C.-E., & Schuster, C. R. (1995). Cocaine. In F. E. Bloom and D. J. Kupfer (Eds.), *Psychopharmacology: A generation of progress* (pp. 1685–1697). New York: Raven Press, Ltd.

Katz, J. L. (1979). A comparison of responding maintained under second-order schedules of intramuscular cocaine injection or food presentation in squirrel monkeys. *Journal of Experimental Analysis of Behavior, 32,* 419–431.

Katz, J. L. (1980). Second-order schedules of intramuscular cocaine injection in the squirrel monkey: Comparisons with food presentation and effects of d-amphetamine and promazine. *Journal of Pharmacology and Experimental Therapeutics, 212,* 405–411.

Katz, J. L. (1989). Drugs as reinforcers: Pharmacological and behavioral factors. In J. M. Liebman & S. J. Cooper (Eds.), *The neuropharmacological basis of reward* (pp. 164–213). Oxford, UK: Oxford University Press.

Katz, J. L. (1990). Models of relative reinforcing efficacy of drugs and their predictive utility. *Behavioural Pharmacology, 1,* 283–301.

Katz, J. L., Alling, K., Shores, E., & Witkin, J. M. (1995). Effects of D_1 dopamine agonists on schedule-controlled behavior in the squirrel monkey. *Behavioral Pharmacology, 6*(2), 143–148.

Kelleher, R. T. (1976). Characteristics of behavior controlled by scheduled injections of drugs. *Pharmacology Reviews, 27*(3), 307–323.

Kelleher, R. T. (1977). Psychomotor stimulants: The clinical and basic aspects. In S. N. Pradhan & S. N. Dutta (Eds.), *Drug abuse* (pp. 116–147). St. Louis, MO: C. V. Mosby Company.

Markou, A., & Koob, G. F. (1991). Postcocaine Anhedonia—An animal model of cocaine withdrawal. *Neuropsychopharmacology, 4,* 17–26.

Mendelson, J. H., & Mello, N. K. (1996). Management of cocaine abuse and dependence. *New England Journal of Medicine, 334*(15), 965–972.

Morse, W. H. (1966). Intermittent reinforcement. In W. K. Honig (Ed.), *Operant behavior: Areas of research and application* (pp. 52–108). New York: Appleton-Century-Crofts.

Morse, W. H. (1976). Introduction: The control of behavior by consequent drug injections. *Pharmacological Reviews, 27*(3), 301–306.

Morse, W. H., & Kelleher, R. T. (1970). Schedules as fundamental determinants of behavior. In W. N. Schoenfeld (Ed.), *The theory of reinforcement schedules* (pp. 139–185). Appleton-Century-Crofts.

Morse, W. H., & Kelleher, R. T. (1977). Determinants of reinforcement and punishment. In W. K. Honig & J. E. R. Staddon (Eds.), *Handbook of operant behavior* (pp. 174–200). Englewood Cliffs, NJ: Prentice Hall.

Mutschler, N. H., & Miczek, K. A. (1998). Withdrawal from iv cocaine binges in rats: Ultrasonic distress calls and startle. *Psychopharmacology, 135*(2), 161–168.

Nader, M. A., & Bowen, C. A. (1995). Effects of different food-reinforcement histories on cocaine self-administration by rhesus monkeys. *Psychopharmacology, 118*(3), 287–294.

Nader, M. A., & Reboussin, D. M. (1994). The effects of behavioral history on cocaine self-administration by rhesus monkeys. *Psychopharmacology, 115*(1–2), 53–58.

Nader, M. A., & Woolverton, W. L. (1991). Effects of increasing the magnitude of an alternative reinforcer on drug choice in a discrete-trials choice procedure. *Psychopharmacology, 105,* 169–174.

Negus, S. S., Gatch, M., & Mello, N. K. (1998). *Neuropsychopharmacology, 325–338.*

O'Brien, C. P. (1976). Experimental analysis of conditioning factors in human narcotic addiction. *Pharmacological Reviews, 27,* 533–543.

O'Brien, C. P., Childress, A. R., McLellan, A. T., & Ehrman, R. (1992). A learning model of addiction. In C. P. O'Brien & J. Jaffe (Eds.), *Advances in understanding the addictive states* (pp. 157–177). New York: Raven Press.

Paulus, M. P., & Geyer, M. A. (1991). A temporal and spatial scaling hypothesis for the behavioral effects of psychostimulants. *Psychopharmacology* (Berlin) *104,* 6–16.

Pettit, H. O., & Justice, J. B. Jr. (1989). Dopamine in the nucleus accumbens during cocaine self-administration as studied by in vivo microdialysis. *Pharmacology Biochemistry & Behavior, 34*(4), 899–904.

Pickens, R., & Thompson, T. (1968). Cocaine-reinforced behavior in rats: Effects of reinforcement magnitude and fixed-ratio size. *Journal of Pharmacology and Experimental Therapeutics, 161,* 122–129.

Pickens, R. W., & Johanson, C. E. (1992). Craving: Consensus of status and agenda for future research. *Drug & Alcohol Dependence, 30*(2), 127–131.

Reid, R. L. (1957). The role of the reinforcer as a stimulus. *British Journal of Psychology, 49,* 192–209.

Resnick, R. B., & Schuyten-Resnick, E. (1976). Clinical aspects of cocaine: Assessment of cocaine abuse behavior in man. Cleveland, OH: CRC Press.

Rosenzweig-Lipson, S., Bergman, J., Spealman, R. D., & Madras, B. K. (1992). Stereoselective behavior effects of Lu 19-005 in monkeys: Relation to binding at cocaine recognition sites. *Psychopharmacology, 107,* 186–194.

Scheel-Kruger, J. (1972). Behavioural and biochemical comparison of amphetamine derivatives, cocaine, benztropine and tricyclic anti-depressant drugs. *Europe Journal Pharmacology, 18*(1), 63–73.

Self, D. W., Barnhart, W. J., Lehman, D. A., & Nestler, E. J. (1996). Opposite modulation of cocaine-seeking behavior by D_1- and D_2-like dopamine receptor agonists. *Science, 271*(5255), 1586–1589.

Silverman, P. B., & Ho, B. T. (1976). Discriminative response control by psychomotor stimulants. *Psychopharmacology Communications, 2*(4), 331–337.

Skinner, B. F. (1938). *The behavior of organisms.* New York: Appleton-Century-Crofts.

Skinner, B. F. (1953). *Science and human behavior.* New York: Macmillan.

Skinner, B. F., & Heron, W. T. (1937). Effects of caffeine and benzedrine upon conditioning and extinction. *Psychological Records, 1,* 340–346.

Slikker, W., Jr., Brocco, M. J., & Killam, K. E., Jr. (1984). Reinstatement of responding maintained by cocaine or thiamylal. *Journal of Pharmacology and Experimental Therapeutics, 228*(1), 43–52.

Smith, C. B. (1964). Effects of d-amphetamine upon operant behavior in pigeons: Enhancement by reserpine. *Journal of Pharmacology and Experimental Therapeutics, 146,* 167–174.

Spealman, R. D. (1979). Behavior maintained by termination of a schedule of self-administered cocaine. *Science, 204,* 1231–1233.

Spealman, R. D. (1981). Environmental factors determining the control of behavior by drugs. In R. L. Balster & L. S. Seiden (Eds.), *Behavioral pharmacology: The current status* (pp. 23–38). New York: AR Liss, Inc.

Spealman, R. D., & Goldberg, S. R. (1978). Drug self-administration by laboratory animals: Control by schedules of reinforcement. *Annual Review of Pharmacology and Toxicology, 18,* 313–339.

Spealman, R. D., & Bergman, J. (1992). Modulation of the discriminative stimulus effects of cocaine by mu and kappa opioids. *Journal of Pharmacology and Experimental Therapeutics, 261*(2), 607–615.

Spealman, R. D., & Bergman, J. (1994). Opioid modulation of the discriminative stimulus effects of cocaine: comparison of mu, kappa and delta agonists in squirrel monkeys discriminating low doses of cocaine. *Behavioral Pharmacology, 5,* 21–31.

Spealman, R. D., & Kelleher, R. T. (1979). Behavioral effects of self-administered cocaine: Responding maintained alternately by cocaine and electric shock in squirrel monkeys. *Journal of Pharmacology and Experimental Therapeutics, 210*(2), 206–214.

Spealman, R. D., Madras, B. K., & Bergman, J. (1989). Effects of cocaine and related drugs in nonhuman primates. II Stimulant effects on schedule-controlled behavior. *Journal of Pharmacology and Experimental Therapeutics, 251*(1), 142–149.

Stretch, R., & Gerber, G. J. (1973). Drug-induced reinstatement of amphetamine self-administration behaviour in monkeys. *Canadian Journal of Psychology, 27*(2), 168–177.

Tiffany, S. T., Singleton, E., Haertzen, C. A., & Henningfield, J. E. (1993). The development of a cocaine craving questionnaire. *Drug & Alcohol Dependence, 34*(1), 19–28.

Trinkoff, A. M., Ritter, C., & Anthony, J. C. (1990). The prevalence and self-reported consequences of cocaine abuse: An exploratory and descriptive analysis. *Drug Alcohol Dependency, 26,* 217–225.

Van Rossum, J. M. (1970). Mode of action of psychomotor stimulant drugs. *International Review of Neurobiology, 12,* 307–383.

Verhave, T. (1958). The effect of methamphetamine on operant level and avoidance behavior. *Journal of Experimental Analysis of Behavior, 1,* 207–220.

Waddington, J. L., Molloy, A. G., O'Boyle, K. M., & Mashurano, M. (1986). Motor consequences of D-1 dopamine receptor stimulation and blockade. *Clinical Neuropharmacology, 9* (suppl. 4), 20–22.

Weissenborn, R., Yackey, M., Koob, G. F., & Weiss, F. (1995). Measures of cocaine-seeking behavior using a multiple schedule of food and drug self-administration in rats. *Drug Alcohol Dependent, 38*(3), 237–246.

Wikler, A. (1980). *Opioid dependence: Mechanisms and treatment.* New York: Plenum Press.

Wikler, A., & Pescor, F. T. (1970). Persistence of "relapse-tendencies" of rats previously made physically dependent on morphine. *Psychopharmacologia, 16*(5), 375–384.

Winger, G. (1993a). Fixed-ratio and time-out changes on behavior maintained by cocaine or methohexital in rhesus monkeys. 1. Comparison of reinforcing strength. *Experimental Clinical Psychopharmacology, 1,* 142–153.

Winger, G. (1993b). Fixed-ratio and time-out changes on behavior maintained by cocaine or methohexital in rhesus monkeys. 2. Behavioral economic analysis. *Experimental Clinical Psychopharmacology, 1,* 154–161.

Wise, R. A., Murray, A., & Bozarth, M. A. (1990). Bromocriptine self-administration and bromocriptine-reinstatement of cocaine-trained and heroin-trained lever pressing in rats. *Psychopharmacology, 100*(3), 355–360.

Witkin, J. M., Nichols, D. E., Terry, P., & Katz, J. L. (1991). Behavioral effects of selective dopaminergic compounds in rats discriminating cocaine injections. *Journal of Pharmacology and Experimental Therapeutics, 257*(2), 706–713.

Wood, R. W., Grubman, J., & Weiss, B. (1977). Nitrous oxide self-administration by the squirrel monkey. *Journal of Pharmacology and Experimental Therapeutics, 202,* 491–499.

Worley, C. M., Valadez, A., & Schenk, S. (1994). Reinstatement of extinguished cocaine-taking behavior by cocaine and caffeine. *Pharmacology Biochemistry Behavior, 48*(1), 217–221

4

BEHAVIORAL–
ENVIRONMENTAL
DETERMINANTS
OF THE REINFORCING
FUNCTIONS OF COCAINE

MARILYN E. CARROLL

Department of Psychiatry
University of Minnesota
Minneapolis, Minnesota

WARREN K. BICKEL

Human Behavioral Pharmacology Laboratory
University of Vermont
Burlington, Vermont

INTRODUCTION

It is well accepted that cocaine functions as a reinforcer in operant behavioral terminology; that is, cocaine injections or inhalations are consequences that increase the probability of behavior that produces them. Cocaine-reinforced behavior has been of great scientific and public interest for decades because of its strength, perseverance, and ability to damage productive lives. Laboratory studies in animals and humans have clearly shown how cocaine controls behavior and the importance of environmental conditions for cocaine reinforcement to occur. Thus, cocaine does not necessarily possess reinforcing properties that are guaranteed to result in drug-seeking behavior. Cocaine's behavioral effects interact with a host of experimental conditions and environmental contexts; some enhance vulnerability to cocaine use, and others offer protection from the reinforcing effects. A classic example of differential effects is a study by Spealman (1979) in which monkeys worked on a lever to self-administer cocaine, while at the same time they worked on a second lever to terminate the cocaine self-administration contingency. Cocaine's inherent physical affects are currently being revealed through neuro-chemistry and molecular biology. These advances are exceedingly important for medication development to treat cocaine abuse and for our basic understanding of how this drug effects the brain. However, an understanding of the complex inter-action between cocaine and environmental factors is also essential for the devel-opment of successful approaches for prevention and treatment of cocaine abuse.

There are many excellent reviews on the behavioral–environmental determi-nants of cocaine reinforcement (e.g., Fischman, 1988; Johanson & Fischman, 1989; Winger, Hoffman, & Woods, 1992). Therefore, this chapter is limited to is-sues regarding cocaine reinforcement that either are new developments or have re-ceived limited attention previously. First, the influence of reinforcement schedules and schedules currently used for evaluating cocaine's reinforcing effectiveness will be evaluated. Next, specific experimental conditions affecting cocaine rein-forcement will be presented, with special attention to dose and access conditions. We will then consider environmental contexts, such as drug history, alternative re-inforcing events, and stress. Finally, regulatory processes that may affect the eval-uation of cocaine reinforcement, such as direct stimulant or depressant effects ver-sus satiation, will be considered.

EVALUATION OF COCAINE REINFORCEMENT

Cocaine reinforcement occurs in a variety of species, with several routes of ad-ministration, under a range of access contingencies (reinforcement schedules) and in many environmental settings. Cocaine appears to act as an unusually efficacious reinforcer (Johanson & Fischman, 1989). Reinforcement occurs in almost 100% of animals exposed to the drug, and acquisition of cocaine self-administration is rapid. Also, as in humans, animals substitute cocaine-reinforced behavior for healthy behaviors (e.g., feeding, grooming, social), which leads to a decline in overall well-being. Thus, methods to accurately and reliably measure cocaine re-inforcement are important, so that intervention attempts can be properly evaluat-ed. The schedule of cocaine delivery, or reinforcement schedule, is an important factor in considering how to evaluate cocaine reinforcement. One concern is whether the schedule used in the laboratory is representative of the contingencies involved with drug-seeking behavior in the natural environment. Another major concern is whether the schedule used to measure cocaine reinforcement allows the nonspecific or direct effects (e.g., stimulation, stereotypy) of the drug to bias the assessment of reinforcing efficacy. The term *reinforcing efficacy* indicates that a drug has greater potential for maintaining behavior than another drug or dose across a range of different experimental conditions (Griffiths, Bradford, & Brady, 1979b).

SCHEDULES OF REINFORCEMENT

Cocaine reinforcement has been tested under most of the basic response-based [fixed-ratio (FR), variable-ratio] and time-based [fixed-interval, variable-interval, differential reinforcement of low rates (DRL)] schedules and many combinations thereof (e.g., Johanson & Fischman, 1989). The general outcome is that cocaine reinforcement occurs under all of the schedules used to study behavior maintained by food and other nondrug reinforcers. The patterns of behavior are characteristic of those generated by food (e.g., Goldberg & Kelleher, 1977); however, use of the traditional rate of responding to measure cocaine reinforcement is not satisfactory. Because cocaine has the ability to disrupt ongoing behavior, it also disrupts behavior that is reinforced by cocaine. Therefore, using simple ratio or interval schedules to compare cocaine's reinforcing effects to food or other drugs may be an underestimate. The direct effects and their distinction from drug satiation will be discussed in the final section.

In an attempt to avoid confounding measures of reinforcing efficacy by cocaine's direct, disruptive effects, three methods of arranging schedule contingencies to measure the reinforcing effects of drugs have become commonly accepted. The first method uses simple reinforcement schedules, such as a FR that arranges delivery of a specific dose of a drug after completion of a fixed number of responses. When long time-outs occur after each drug delivery, the FR schedule helps to reduce the influence of direct effects. Response rate (responses/unit time) is the measure typically employed with this method (Katz, 1989). A disadvantage of this type of analysis is that there is usually a limit to the number of cocaine deliveries earned per session, thus producing a ceiling effect and limiting the ability to measure behavioral increases.

The second method, progressive ratio (PR) schedules, divides the response requirement into orderly increments after a specified number of reinforcement deliveries (Catania, 1968). Break point—the point at which responding ceases—is the typical measure of PR schedules. A consistent finding with PR schedules using food (Hodos, 1961) or drugs (Griffiths, Brady, & Bradford, 1979a) is that an increasing magnitude of the reinforcer or drug dose increases break points. When cocaine has been compared to other drugs using PR schedules, it yields the highest break points (Griffiths, Brady, & Snell, 1978), agreeing with observational and clinical data regarding the relative reinforcing efficacy of different drugs.

The third method, concurrent schedules of reinforcement, arranges two or more independent and simultaneous schedules (Catania, 1968). Preference is the measure typically used, defined as the probability of one of two responses derived from the relative frequency of the responses (Catania, 1968). When two doses of intravenously delivered cocaine were available under concurrent fixed-interval (Johanson & Schuster, 1975) or variable-interval (Iglauer, Llewellen, & Woods, 1976) schedules, preference was usually shown for the higher dose.

Direct comparisons of drug-reinforced behavior under all three methods have not been conducted. However, three general findings have been observed with these procedures. First, response rates initially increase and later decrease as a function of drug dose under FR schedules. Second, PR schedules typically produce higher break points with larger doses, although an inverted U-shaped function can be obtained if there are shorter time-outs after each drug delivery (Griffiths et al., 1978). Third, under concurrent FR schedules of reinforcement, higher doses are generally preferred even if that dose is on the descending limb of the inverted U-shaped dose–effect function (Johanson, 1975). For a drug or dose of drug to be considered more reinforcing than some other drug or dose, it should produce a greater peak response rate, produce a larger break point, and be preferred.

BEHAVIORAL ECONOMICS

Another method used to evaluate the reinforcing efficacy of cocaine and other drugs is behavioral economics (Bickel & DeGrandpre, 1996; Bickel, DeGrandpre, Higgins, & Hughes, 1990; Bickel, DeGrandpre, & Higgins, 1993; DeGrandpre & Bickel, 1996). This is the application of economic principles (consumer demand theory) to the study of behavior, and it provides several objective, quantitative indices of reinforcing efficacy. Central to this form of behavioral economics are three primary concepts: demand, elasticity, and unit price (Bickel et al., 1990).

First, *demand* is the quantity of a good or reinforcer that an individual will purchase or consume at the prevailing price (Pearce, 1986; Samuelson & Nordhaus, 1985). When a variety of prices are assessed, demand can be displayed graphically as a *demand curve,* where the amount of goods consumed is plotted as a function of price range (Pearce, 1986). Such a curve usually demonstrates the *law of demand,* where consumption decreases as price increases (Samuelson & Nordhaus, 1985). For example, as more behavior, more money, or both are required for a fixed delivery of cocaine, consumption would decrease in a positively decelerating fashion.

The demand curve can be characterized by the intensity and elasticity of demand. *Intensity* of demand is represented by a parallel shift of the demand curve up or down. *Elasticity* is the responsiveness of the quantity of a commodity demanded to an increase in price (Pearce, 1986). According to this definition, price can refer either to the commodity's own price (*own-price elasticity*) or to the price of other available commodities (*cross-price elasticity*) (Pearce, 1986). With regard to own-price elasticity, if consumption of a reinforcer decreases to a large extent as price increases, then demand for that reinforcer is considered *elastic;* however, if consumption decreases to a limited extent as price increases, then demand for

FIGURE 4.1   Consumption of a self-administered drug is plotted as a function of unit price in each of the 10 panels. Data are placed in a log–log scale. Data were reanalyzed from DeNoble et al. (1982), Goldberg et al. (1971), Meisch et al. (1981), Goldberg (1973), Pickens et al. (1968), Lemaire et al. (1985), Marquis et al. (1989), Moreton et al. (1977), and Pickens et al. (1981). (Reprinted from Bickel et al., 1990, with permission from Elsevier Science.)

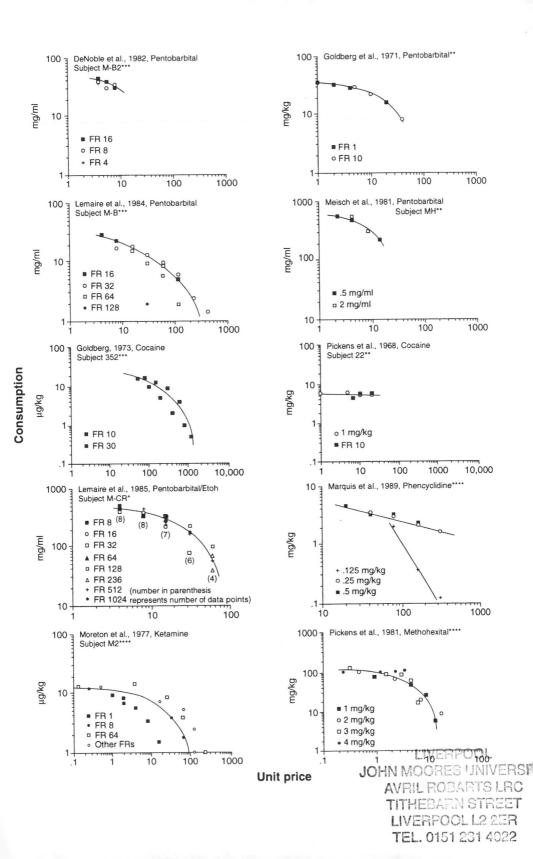

Consumption

Unit price

DeNoble et al., 1982, Pentobarbital
Subject M-B2***
■ FR 16
○ FR 8
+ FR 4

Goldberg et al., 1971, Pentobarbital**
■ FR 1
○ FR 10

Lemaire et al., 1984, Pentobarbital
Subject M-B***
■ FR 16
○ FR 32
□ FR 64
● FR 128

Meisch et al., 1981, Pentobarbital
Subject MH**
■ .5 mg/ml
□ 2 mg/ml

Goldberg, 1973, Cocaine
Subject 352***
○ FR 10
■ FR 30

Pickens et al., 1968, Cocaine
Subject 22**
○ 1 mg/kg
■ FR 10

Lemaire et al., 1985, Pentobarbital/Etoh
Subject M-CR*
■ FR 8 (8)
○ FR 16 (8)
□ FR 32 (7)
▲ FR 64
□ FR 128
△ FR 236 (6)
+ FR 512   (number in parenthesis
● FR 1024 represents number of data points) (4)

Marquis et al., 1989, Phencyclidine****
+ .125 mg/kg
○ .25 mg/kg
■ .5 mg/kg

Moreton et al., 1977, Ketamine
Subject M2****
■ FR 1
● FR 8
□ FR 64
○ Other FRs

Pickens et al., 1981, Methohexital****
■ 1 mg/kg
○ 2 mg/kg
□ 3 mg/kg
● 4 mg/kg

that reinforcer is considered *inelastic* (Hursh & Bauman, 1987). A commodity with inelastic demand at the lower range of prices and elastic demand at higher prices is considered to have *mixed elasticity* (Bickel et al., 1990; DeGrandpre & Bickel, 1996; DeGrandpre et al., 1995; Hursh & Bauman, 1987). Cocaine and other self-administered drugs (see Figure 1) demonstrate mixed elasticity of demand. In terms of analyzing drug abuse with behavioral economic measures, a treatment goal would be to increase the elasticity of demand and/or reduce the intensity of demand.

Another metric that can be used to characterize changes in a demand function is referred to as P_{max}, that is, the price associated with the maximal responding. P_{max} measures the point at which the demand function moves from being inelastic to elastic. P_{max} has been demonstrated to quantify shifts in the demand curve for cocaine and other drugs after treatment interventions such as providing alternative reinforcers or providing experimental pharmacotherapies (Bickel, DeGrandpre, Higgins, Hughes, & Badger, 1995; Rawleigh, Rodefer, Hansen, & Carroll, 1996). P_{max} can be used as an estimate of the reinforcing efficacy of a drug. Changes in P_{max} can occur following a change in the intensity of demand, a change in elasticity of demand, or changes in both intensity and elasticity (Bickel et al., 1995).

Cross-price elasticity refers to a continuum of interaction between different reinforcers or commodities. When reinforcers are *substitutes,* as the price of one reinforcer increases (and consumption declines, e.g., price of movie tickets), consumption of a fixed-price second reinforcer (i.e., the substitute) increases (e.g., video rentals). In contrast, reinforcers can be *complements.* As the cost of one reinforcer increases (e.g., soup), the consumption of a second reinforcer (i.e., the complement) decreases (e.g., soup crackers). There are also *independent* reinforcers. As the cost of one reinforcer increases, consumption of the second reinforcer is unchanged (Hursh & Bauman, 1987). A goal in the treatment of cocaine abuse would be to demonstrate that nondrug reinforcers can serve as economic substitutes for cocaine; for example, in monkeys smoking cocaine base (crack), a preferred dietary substance substituted for cocaine (Comer, Hunt, & Carroll, 1994). As the price of cocaine increased and corresponding cocaine smoking decreased, intake of a fixed-price sweetened liquid increased.

Another concept in behavioral economies is *unit price* (UP) (Bickel et al., 1990, 1991; DeGrandpre et al., 1993; Hursh, Raslear, Shurtleff, Bauman, & Simmons, 1988), which integrates cost and benefit factors that affect demand into a single term. First, unit price (responses/mg) suggests that the same consumption should occur at the same price regardless of change in the constituents of which it is composed (responses or mg). For example, if 10 mg/kg of cocaine were administered for every 100 responses, or 30 mg of cocaine were administered for every 300 responses, consequences should be the same because the unit price is the same (10 responses/mg). Second, consumption when plotted as a function of unit price should conform to a single demand curve. These assumptions about unit price have been demonstrated with a variety of drug reinforcers as well as with food. That cocaine intake is similar at the same unit prices (made of different response requirements and drug doses) suggests that satiation or some form of regulation is playing a role in drug taking. Cocaine satiation will be discussed later in this chapter.

EXPERIMENTAL EVENTS MODULATING COCAINE REINFORCEMENT

Aspects of the experimental setting used to study drug abuse can have a profound effect on the extent to which cocaine functions as a reinforcer. This section will briefly review variables that are typically controlled in the animal and human experimental setting, such as dose, route of administration, duration of access, and stimulus conditions.

COCAINE DOSE AND REGULATION OF DRUG INTAKE

Generally, the reinforcing effects of cocaine and other drugs are considered to increase when the magnitude of the reinforcing stimulus or dose increases (Katz, 1989). Dose size is typically predetermined by the experimenter and held constant during experimental sessions. However, there are a few examples in which the animal regulates its own dose. One case would be in a concurrent choice and discrete-trial choice design where two doses are concurrently or sequentially available, respectively (e.g., Iglauer et al., 1976; Johanson & Schuster, 1975). In these studies larger doses were preferred to smaller doses. In a recent study rats could increase their cocaine dose up to 2.5 mg/kg by pressing one lever and decrease their dose to 0 mg/kg by pressing the other lever (Lynch, La Bounty, & Carroll, 1997). Both levers initially produced a 1.25 mg/kg dose. Although there was no clear preference for the larger doses, as there was in the discrete-trial choice studies, the rats precisely regulated their interdose interval during the 5-h session so that the postinjection interval was highly correlated with the previous dose size. Others have reported similar regulation when doses were randomly presented by the experimenter, and infusions were predicted by a fall in dopamine levels in the nucleus accumbens (Wise et al., 1995).

ROUTE OF ADMINISTRATION

The intravenous route has been most commonly used in animals and humans to study cocaine-reinforced behavior (e.g., Johanson & Schuster, 1975). Cocaine self-administration in animals has also been established as a reinforcer via the intragastric (Altshuler, Weaver, & Phillips, 1975), intramuscular (Goldberg, Morse, & Goldberg, 1976), oral (Meisch, Kliner, & Henningfield, 1981) and smoking (Carroll, Krattiger, Gieske, & Sadoff, 1990) routes. Rats self-administer cocaine via intracerebral cannulae directly into the medial prefrontal cortex (Goeders & Smith, 1983). The intravenous, intranasal, and smoking routes of self-administration have been used in the human laboratory (Foltin & Fischman, 1992), and the behavioral and pharmacokinetic effects are similar for smoking and intravenous (iv) self-administration. Pharmacokinetic data also indicate that cocaine base smoking in rhesus monkeys is similar to that obtained in the human laboratory (Carroll et al., 1990).

DURATION OF ACCESS

Session Length

When intravenously delivered cocaine is limited to sessions consisting of a few hours per day, there is a consistent rate of evenly spaced responding and little variability in total infusions per day (Fischman, 1988). A steady circadian pattern of cocaine self-administration is also observed when access throughout a 24-h period is limited by discrete trials and time-out periods that limit infusions to no more than 2 per hour (Fitch & Roberts, 1993). However, when monkeys were allowed unlimited access to iv cocaine self-administration, a cyclic pattern developed whereby periods of high and low intake alternated (Deneau, Yanagita, & Seevers, 1969), and the circadian rhythm was disturbed (Fitch & Roberts, 1993). Negus and co-workers (1995) found diurnal variation in cocaine self-administration in monkeys. Cocaine self-administration during the evening and morning sessions was more sensitive to a decrease in reinforcer magnitude than during afternoon sessions. Factors that can reduce the high level of cocaine intake under long-term access conditions in rats and monkeys, respectively, are more palatable food (Carroll, Lac, & Nygaard, 1989) increased amounts of food in a choice situation (Nader & Woolverton, 1991), or both.

Period of Access

In rats, long-term iv cocaine produced periods of excessive self-administration alternating with periods of abstinence, whereas heroin resulted in a stable pattern of self-administration that gradually increased over the first 2 weeks of testing, suggesting tolerance development (Bozarth & Wise, 1985). The rats self-administering cocaine also showed a much higher mortality rate (90%) during 30 days of continuous testing than the rats that self-administered heroin (36%). Cocaine self-administration is particularly sensitive to the duration of access and potentially to the time of day compared with other drugs of abuse. With greater duration of access there is more potential for toxic consequences.

STIMULUS CONDITIONS

The environmental stimulus conditions present during cocaine reinforcement (discriminative stimuli) gain considerable control over drug-maintained behavior. There are several reviews describing this effect with cocaine, other drugs, and food reinforcement (e.g., Bickel & Kelly, 1988; Branch, 1991). There have been powerful demonstrations showing that drug-paired stimuli maintained long sequences (several hours) of high rates of behavior leading to a cocaine-injection reinforcement (e.g., Goldberg, Spealman, & Kelleher, 1979). Stimulus control also plays an important role in human drug abuse (Bickel & Kelly, 1988) producing conditioned tolerance to opiates (Siegel, 1989) and self-reported cocaine and opiate craving (Childress, McLellan, Ehrman, & O'Brien, 1987). Most studies have focused on exteroceptive cues such as lights, sounds, and odors; however, interoceptive cues such as saline infusions (Schuster & Brady, 1964) or feeding conditions (Carroll, 1985b) can also serve as conditioned stimuli.

One area that has received recent attention is the role of stimuli in the study of reinstatement of extinguished cocaine-reinforced behavior (relapse). External and internal stimuli both elicit reinstatement of responding during an extinction period, although the focus recently has been on the role of internal stimuli such as a single cocaine injection (for a review see Carroll & Comer, 1996). This paradigm is comparable to the first drink in an abstinent alcoholic (e.g., Ludwig & Wikler, 1974) or a puff on a cigarette for an ex-smoker (Chornock, Stitzer, Gross, & Leischow, 1992). The typical animal model used to simulate relapse provides 2-h daily access to iv cocaine self-administration followed by about 5 h of extinction (saline substitution) (e.g., Wise, Murray, & Bozarth, 1990). After responding has extinguished during hour 3, an experimenter-administered priming injection of cocaine is given at the beginning of hour 4. Responding on a lever that previously resulted in a drug infusion serves as a measure of reinstatement of drug-seeking behavior or relapse, and responding in the hour after the priming injection is often as high as during the previous self-administration period.

A number of variables alter reinstatement of extinguished cocaine responding, such as dose, temporal aspects, and crossover effects with other drugs. Cocaine-priming doses ranging from 0.32 to 3.2 mg/kg result in dose-dependent increases in extinction responding. De Wit and Stewart (1981) reported reinstatement of responding when the priming injection was given at intervals of 10, 30, 60, 120, and 180 min after cocaine responding extinguished, but the magnitude of the effect decreased with interval length. Others have shown reinstatement of responding in cocaine-trained animals after a long period (43 days) of time (e.g., Meil & See, 1996).

When cocaine was used as the self-administered drug, reinstatement of responding was generated by priming injections of several other drugs, including morphine (de Wit & Stewart, 1981). However, rats trained to self-administer heroin (de Wit & Stewart, 1983) did not show reinstatement of responding after a cocaine-priming injection. Thus, an asymmetrical crossover exists between the opioid and psychomotor drug classes on this measure. Reinstatement is most likely to occur with priming drugs from the same pharmacological class as the self-administered drug. In general, all of the drugs that reinstate extinguished responding independently function as reinforcers (Carroll, 1996a) (see Table 1).

Attempts to block reinstatement responding in cocaine-trained animals have also been studied as a model for treating relapse. Treatment drugs have also been given as priming injections in cocaine-trained animals to determine whether they promote relapse. Some drugs that could be used therapeutically, such as

TABLE 4.1   Priming Drugs That Have Been Tested in the Reinstatement Model

Drugs that produced a priming effect *and* function as reinforcers	Drugs that produced *no* priming effect *and* function as reinforcers	Drugs that produced *no* priming effect *and do not* function as reinforcers
Amphetamine[a,b]	Buprenorphine[c]	Chlorpromazine[d]
Apomorphine[a,b]	Diazepam[d]	Clonidine[b]
Bromocriptine[e]	Ethanol[a,e]	Desipramine[f]
Caffeine[g]	Etonitazene[c]	Desmethyltryptamine[d]
Cocaine[a–d]	Heroin[a,b]	Nalorphine[h]
Codeine[d]	Methylamphetamine[d]	Naloxone[d]
Morphine[a,b,d,g]	Secobarbital[d]	Naltrexone[c,g]

[a]deWit and Stewart, 1981.
[b]deWit and Stewart, 1983.
[c]Comer et al., 1993.
[d]Slikker et al., 1983.
[e]Wise et al., 1990.
[f]Comer et al. (unpublished data).
[g]Worley et al. 1994.
[h]Stewart and Wise, 1992.

bromocriptine, a dopamine D_2 receptor agonist (Wise et al., 1990), and desipramine, an antidepressant (Weiss, 1988), reinstate behavior when used as priming agents, whereas others, such as buprenorphine (Comer et al., 1993), naltrexone, and nalorphine (Stewart & Wise, 1992), do not reinstate responding. Buprenorphine did, however, dose dependently block the cocaine priming effect (Comer et al., 1993).

ENVIRONMENTAL CONTEXT

Human cocaine abuse occurs in a much richer environmental context than the sterile atmosphere of animal and human laboratory self-administration experiments. Although considerable generality exists across laboratory and naturalistic behaviors, environmental variables add another dimension to our understanding of cocaine reinforcement. Factors such as previous and current exposure to other drugs, feeding status, access to alternative nondrug reinforcers, and stress are environmental conditions that significantly affect cocaine reinforcement.

DRUG HISTORY

Drug history affects the rate of acquisition of cocaine-reinforced behavior. Drug exposure may occur prenatally, perinatally, or immediately before a specific drug exposure in adult rats. Ramsey (1991) showed that prenatal exposure to morphine enhanced the rate of cocaine- and heroin-reinforced behavior in rats. Keller et al. (1996) exposed rats to cocaine and tested the offspring as adults for acquisition of iv cocaine self-administration. The prenatally cocaine-exposed group showed more rapid acquisition and a greater number of cocaine infusions than a control group prenatally exposed to saline.

Several studies demonstrate that pretreatment (e.g., 10 days) with a drug such as cocaine (Horger, Shelton, & Schenk, 1990), amphetamine (Piazza, Demeniere, LeMoal, & Simon, 1989), or methamphetamine (Woolverton, Cervo, & Johanson, 1984) produced sensitization and more rapid acquisition of self-administration of that same drug. Preexposure effects have also been reported under conditions in which the pretreatment drug and the self-administration drug were different. For example, rats pretreated with amphetamine (Horger, Giles, & Schenk, 1992), caffeine (Horger, Wellman, Morien, Davies, & Schenk, 1991), cocaine (Horger et al., 1990), naltrexone (Ramsey & van Ree, 1990), and nicotine (Horger et al., 1992) that ended before the test for cocaine acquisition acquired cocaine-reinforced responding more rapidly than saline-treated controls. These results suggest that a brief pretreatment period may have a long-lasting effect on the vulnerability to acquisition of drug reinforcement.

CONCURRENT EXPOSURE TO OTHER DRUGS

Cocaine-reinforced responding was also enhanced when animals were exposed to another drug while their behavior was maintained by cocaine. For example, when monkeys trained to smoke cocaine base had caffeine (200 mg) added to their daily diet, they showed a significant increase in smoke deliveries when the response cost for cocaine was high (FRs 1024, 2048) (Comer, Lac, Wyvell, & Carroll, 1996). When monkeys smoked a combination of cocaine and heroin (speedball), the number of smoke deliveries also increased at higher response requirements (FRs 512, 1024) (Mattox, Thompson, & Carroll, 1997). In the human laboratory Higgins and co-workers (1996) tested concurrently available cocaine and alcohol in humans and found that alcohol increased the preference for cocaine over an alternative monetary reinforcer. Cocaine also increases the rate of cigarette smoking (Higgins et al., 1994; Roll, Higgins, & Tidey, 1997).

FEEDING CONDITIONS

Food restriction increases rates of cocaine and other drug self-administration in rats, monkeys, and human subjects (e.g., Carroll, 1996b). This finding has been widely generalized across all of the drug classes abused by humans, different routes of self-administration (oral, iv, and smoking), and many different experimental protocols and behavioral schedules. The effects of feeding conditions on cocaine reinforcement have also been studied in other phases of the addiction process, such as the acquisition phase (Carroll & Lac, 1993), withdrawal (Carroll

& Carmona, 1991), and with an animal model of relapse (Comer et al., 1994). In the acquisition study (Carroll & Lac, 1993) groups of rats were exposed to iv cocaine self-administration using an autoshaping procedure (Brown & Jenkins, 1968). One group had unlimited access to food, a second group was limited to 20 g of food per day, and a third group had 8–12 g of food per day. The mean number of days to meet the acquisition criterion were 16.1, 9.5, and 6, respectively. In another study female rats had their food restricted on three brief occasions during their development and later were allowed to feed freely for several months. Compared to a control group that was not food restricted, they showed an accelerated rate of acquisition of cocaine-reinforced behavior (Specker, Lac, & Carroll, 1994). Thus, current feeding conditions as well as feeding history play a role in the rate of acquisition of cocaine reinforcement.

Feeding conditions are also an important determinant of reinstatement of extinguished cocaine-reinforced responding (Comer et al., 1994). Three groups of rats were fed 8–12 g, 20 g, or unlimited amounts (24.5 g mean intake) of food after their daily 7-h relapse session. Figure 2 shows that although the different feeding conditions had no effect on the number of cocaine infusions during hours 1 and

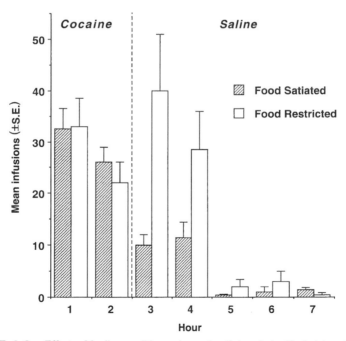

FIGURE 4.2   Effects of feeding condition on iv cocaine (0.4 mg/kg) self-administration (hours 1 and 2), saline substitution and extinction (hour 3), and reinstatement of responding (hour 4) after a cocaine (3.2 mg/kg) priming infusion (arrow) in rats under conditions of food restriction (open bars) and food satiation (filled bars). Each point represents a mean (±SE) of five rats. (Redrawn from Comer et al., 1995.)

2, there was a marked increase in saline infusions (reinstatement behavior) in the group fed 8–12 g during hour 3, the first hour of saline substitution (extinction), and hour 4 after the cocaine priming (0.32) injection (reinstatement).

ACCESS TO ALTERNATIVE NONDRUG REINFORCERS

Restricting food access can be viewed as an example of a more general case of limiting alternative nondrug reinforcers. In a study of the acquisition and maintenance of cocaine reinforcement, Carroll et al. (1989) exposed a group of rats to an alternative nondrug reinforcer, a drinking solution of glucose and saccharin (G + S) (in addition to water), and another group only to water. The G + S-exposed group had more difficulty acquiring cocaine self-administration and maintained self-administration with fewer daily infusions than the water-only group. When water was substituted for G + S, cocaine infusions nearly doubled. Previous work with cocaine (Nader & Woolverton, 1991) and PCP (Carroll, 1985a) in monkeys and cocaine (Higgins, Roll, & Blekel, 1996) and alcohol (Zacny, Divane, & de Wit, 1992) in humans suggests that alternative nondrug reinforcers become more effective at suppressing drug intake as their magnitude increases.

Studies in rats suggest that the most viable approach to treating cocaine abuse with alternative nondrug reinforcers would be in the acquisition phase. In a systematic study of acquisition of iv cocaine reinforcement, four groups of 12 rats each were exposed to an automated autoshaping protocol until acquisition criteria were met or until 30 days elapsed (Carroll & Lac, 1993). In a 2×2 factorial design, two groups were exposed to either G + S or water for 2 weeks before the acquisition procedure began, and two groups had concurrent access to G + S or water during the entire acquisition period. Figure 3 shows that the group that acquired cocaine self-administration most rapidly had no G + S exposure, the group that had the longest G + S exposure (before and during autoshaping) was the slowest to acquire, and only 50% of the animals met the acquisition criterion in 30 days. The group with G + S available during autoshaping showed a 75% rate of acquisition. The group that had G + S history but only water during autoshaping acquired at a rate of 100%. Thus, current access but not a history of exposure to a palatable dietary substance reduced the rate of acquisition.

EFFECTS OF COMBINING PHARMACOLOGICAL TREATMENT AND ALTERNATIVE NONDRUG REINFORCERS ON COCAINE REINFORCEMENT

Recent approaches to treating drug abuse have focused on pharmacological as well as behavioral approaches, such as offering competing nondrug alternative rewards contingent upon cocaine abstinence (Higgins et al., 1996). A recent series of animal studies combined pharmacological and behavioral interventions and compared the result to the effect of each treatment alone. Buprenorphine was used as the treatment drug, as it reduces cocaine use in humans and animals (Carroll,

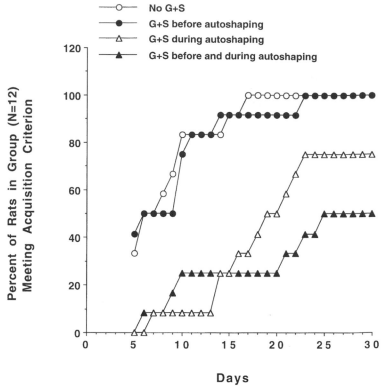

FIGURE 4.3 Percentage of rats meeting the acquisition criterion of a mean of 100 cocaine (0.2 mg/kg) infusions per day for 5 days over the 30-day acquisition period as a function of whether an alternative nondrug reinforcer, glucose and saccharin (G + S), was available before and/or during the acquisition (autoshaping) training. Each point represents a mean of 12 rats. (Redrawn from Carroll & Lac, 1993.)

Carmona, May, Buzalski, & Larson, 1992; Kosten, Rosen, Schottenfeld, & Ziedonis, 1992; Mello, Mendelson, Bree, & Lukas, 1990). In these experiments injections were given 30 min prior to drug self-administration sessions for 3–5 days. Rats or monkeys always had access to water, but at some times there was also access to a sweetened solution of saccharin or G + S. The demand for the drug was also evaluated by an increasing FR schedule.

In the first experiment, groups of five rats self-administered iv cocaine during daily 12-h sessions (Comer et al., 1996). One group had a G + S solution continuously available, and the other group had only water. Either 2, 8, or 32 responses were required per injection. Figure 4 shows that the buprenorphine or the alternative reinforcer (G + S) reduced cocaine infusions by 37 or 21%, respectively, at the lowest FR, but the combined treatments reduced cocaine responding by 70%. This experiment was replicated in five monkeys trained to smoke crack during daily 3-h sessions under FRs ranging from 64 to 1024 (Rodefer et al., 1997). Figure

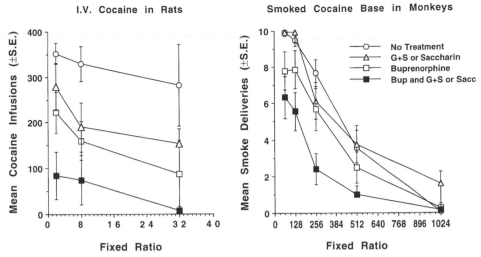

FIGURE 4.4   Mean (±SE) cocaine (0.2 mg/kg) infusions (left) and cocaine base (1 mg/kg) smoke deliveries (right) are presented for rats and monkeys, respectively, as a function of the fixed ratio requirement for drug delivery and whether buprenorphine pretreatment was given and/or an alternative nondrug reinforcer (G + S for rats, saccharin for monkeys) was concurrently available with drug access. Each point represents a mean of five rats (left) or five monkeys (right). [Redrawn from Comer et al., 1996 (left), and Rodefer et al., 1997 (right).]

4 shows that at FR 64 buprenorphine and saccharin alone resulted in a 3 and 21% reduction in smokes taken, respectively, but the combination reduced crack smoking by 36%. At the higher FRs the maximum reduction was 41%.

STRESS

Accumulating evidence suggests that stress may be an important environmental factor in the initiation, maintenance, and reinstatement of cocaine reinforcement. Vulnerability to acquire cocaine- or amphetamine-reinforced behavior is enhanced by physical stress, such as footshock (Goeders & Guerin, 1994) and repeated tail pinch (Piazza, Deminiere, LeMoal, & Simon, 1990), and social stress, such as isolation (Schenk et al., 1987), unstable housing conditions (Maccari et al., 1991), exposure to other rats placed on a hot plate (Ramsey & van Ree, 1993), social defeat (Tidey & Miczek, 1997), and exposure to an aggressive male or lactating female (Haney, Maccari, LeMoal, Simon, & Piazza, 1995).

A recent series of studies indicates that there is a relationship between stress, dopamine, and drug reinforcement. For example, levels of the stress hormone corticosterone are elevated during cocaine reinforcement (Goeders & Guerin, 1996), and increased levels of corticosterone potentiate the reinforcing and motor-activating effects of psychomotor stimulants (Piazza et al., 1991). Also, subjects that are more vulnerable to acquisition of amphetamine self-administration show a longer stress-induced corticosterone secretion (Piazza et al., 1991). Finally, corticosterone increases the release of dopamine, which is thought to be critical for cocaine reinforcement (Rouge-Pont et al., 1993). Depletion of corticosterone by bilateral adrenalectomy in rats resulted in a blockade of enhanced motor activity produced by amphetamine (Deroche, Piazza, Casolini, LeMoal, & Simon, 1993), and it abolished the acquisition of cocaine-reinforced behavior over a wide range of doses (Goeders & Guerin, 1996). Administration of corticosterone partially reversed the effects. In other studies corticosterone synthesis was blocked by pretreatment with metyrapone, and this resulted in dose-related decreases in ongoing cocaine self-administration (Goeders & Guerin, 1996) as well as in decreases in reinstatement of extinguished cocaine responding after a priming injection of cocaine (Piazza et al., 1994). Stress (e.g., corticosterone) has been suggested as the factor mediating the effects of food restriction on the psychomotor and reinforcing effects of psychomotor stimulants (Deroche et al., 1993). Food restriction increased corticosterone levels 3–5 times those of normally fed rats (Broocks, Liu, & Pirks, 1990), and adrenalectomy blocked the food-restriction-induced amplification of the psychomotor response to amphetamine (Deroche et al., 1993).

PROCESSES MODULATING REINFORCEMENT

As discussed earlier, the processes involved in cocaine reinforcement include reinforcing effects and direct effects, such as the stimulant or depressant effects that may nonspecifically alter behavior. In contrast, the processes invoked with traditional reinforcers, such as food and water, include reinforcement and a modulating process referred to as satiation or regulation. Satiation is rarely considered relevant to drug-reinforced behavior. Determining whether cocaine reinforcement is modulated by satiation and/or direct effects has important consequences for evaluating cocaine-reinforced behavior as a model of drug dependence. If satiation is operating, then the processes of drug reinforcement are similar to those involved with more conventional reinforcers, such as food and water. However, if the direct effects of drugs are the predominant modulating factor, then drugs may be a special case of reinforcement that departs from more traditional reinforcers.

Satiation refers to the reduction in a reinforcer's effectiveness that follows from the continued presentation of the reinforcer (Catania, 1968). Satiation is most likely a continuous process, coextensive with reinforcement, and more likely to be observed as the number of obtained reinforcers increases. The direct effects of drugs refer to the unconditioned or "intoxicating" effects. Direct effects are most likely a continuous process, coextensive with drug dose, and may also be observed more frequently with higher doses, a greater number of reinforcement deliveries, or both. The phenomenon of direct effects is supported by two observations: (a) numerous experimental studies demonstrate that drugs modify the ongoing rates of responding under schedules of food presentation; and (b) an inverted U-Shaped function is observed under FR schedules of drug delivery. This latter observation is inconsistent with the expectation that increases in dose lead to increases in reinforcing efficacy unless the descending limb of the dose–response function is interpreted as direct effects masking the reinforcing effects of drugs (Skjoldager, Winger, & Woods, 1991). Because many of the same conditions can be explained by either drug satiation or direct effects, what will distinguish these processes and permit a determination of their contribution to cocaine-reinforced behavior?

DISTINGUISHING BETWEEN SATIATION AND DIRECT EFFECTS

The first question to ask is whether these generalities are accurate. Studies examining conventional reinforcers typically reported increases in response rate with increases in reinforcer magnitude instead of inverted U-shaped magnitude (dose) response curves. However, just as many early studies of drug self-administration reported only the descending limb because large doses were used (Katz, 1989). The relationship between response rate and reinforcer magnitude with conventional reinforcers such as food may result from using small magnitudes that may have only captured the ascending limb.

Goldberg (1973) compared behavior maintained by cocaine and food across a broad range of reinforcement magnitudes under FR 10 and 30 schedules of reinforcement. As shown in Figure 5, an inverted U-shaped function was obtained as reinforcement magnitude increased for both cocaine and food. These data first demonstrate that descending limbs can be obtained with food-maintained behavior and second pose a paradox; namely, the descending limb (rate decreases) occurs in both food- and drug-maintained responding, with the food case typically interpreted as satiation and the drug case often interpreted as direct (disruptive) effects of drugs. The following are three ways that can be used to distinguish between these two processes that decrease responding.

Within-Session Response Patterning

Direct effects are assumed to result in disruption in the local response rates on FR schedules, whereas satiation only increases postreinforcement pause (Katz, 1989). Sidman and Stebbins (1954) found satiation decreased overall response rates on FR schedules by increasing the postreinforcement pause without disruptions in the local rates of responding. In contrast, Skjoldager and colleagues (1991) found disruption in local rates of responding in the descending limb of the dose–response functions when cocaine and ketamine served as reinforcers under FR schedules. However, these differential results may be due to the limited ranges of the independent variables used in the study of conventional reinforcers. A classic study of satiation by Ferster and Skinner (1957) supports the possibility that Sidman and Stebbins used a limited range.

Drug Intake across Changes in Doses

Satiation would be supported if responding began to cease when approximately the same amount of drug was consumed. This observation would also pose some

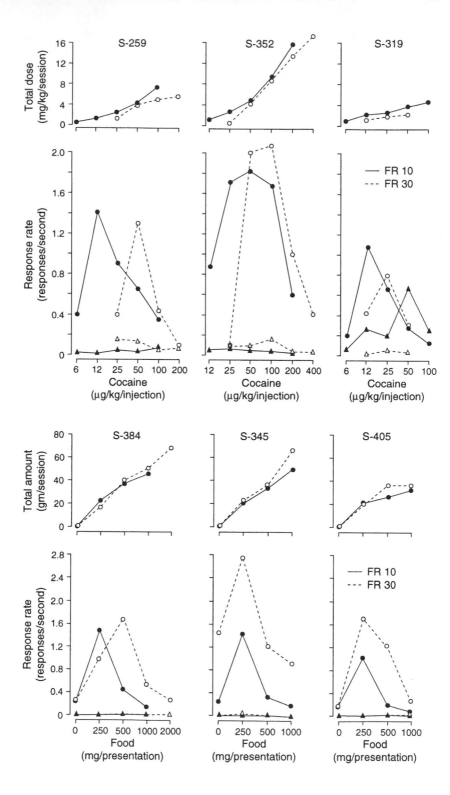

difficulty for a direct effect interpretation because it would suggest that the same total drug intake or proportionally small dose increases somehow progressively decreased responding. Several studies have addressed this issue by examining blood levels of drug. For example, Yokel and Pickens (1974) examined the body levels of amphetamine resulting from the pattern of intravenous infusion. They found that early high rates of within-session responding rapidly increased blood levels, with the remaining administrations preventing drug levels from decreasing below some value. Young and Herling (1986) noted that because higher doses elevate the blood level for a longer period of time than do lower doses, the higher doses are taken less frequently. However, similar procedures used with β-phenethylamine have not produced similar effects (Cone, Risner, & Neidert, 1978). This raises the question of whether drugs vary in the extent to which they can produce satiation.

Satiation is also a process that is responsive to cumulative administrations of unit doses of drug across a session, and this may have implications for understanding the reinforcing effects along the ascending limb of the dose–effect curve. Specifically, if cumulative drug intake is a determinant of drug reinforcement, then the number of times a drug is permitted to be self-administered must contribute to the process of drug reinforcement. Low unit doses should only maintain self-administration above control levels under circumstances where drug can accumulate and should not result in drug reinforcement if they cannot accumulate. Thus, from a satiation perspective, long duration sessions should permit lower doses to accumulate sufficiently to maintain drug-reinforced behavior above control values, whereas short sessions should lead to drug-reinforced behavior above control values for only larger doses. This suggests an inverse relationship between the drug dose that functions as a reinforcer and the session duration. The direct effect interpretation does not make specific predictions about this relationship. Such an analysis of session duration and dose of cocaine and other drugs that functioned as reinforcers was conducted in a classic chapter by Young and Herling (1986). Low doses that did not maintain self-administration under short sessions were able to maintain responding when sessions were longer. This finding suggests the relevance of satiation for cocaine self-administration.

Within-Session Changes in the Magnitude of Drug Dose

Perhaps the strongest method of differentiating between satiation and direct effects is to conduct a within-session change in the unit dose of drug. Carney, Llewellyn, and Woods (1976) employed a dose of drug (e.g., codeine or ethanol) that had been previously established to be on the descending limb and made it contingent upon completing an FR schedule. In the middle of the session a lower dose of drug was then substituted. If direct effects were operating, a decrease in unit

FIGURE 4.5   Effects of varying the amount of cocaine and food per presentation and the fixed ratio response requirement on mean rates of responding and on total amount of cocaine and food received per session. (Reprinted from Goldberg, 1973, with permission.)

dose at this point should not change response rate, and response rate should remain at the same level associated with intoxication or impairment. However, if satiation was relevant and a lower dose was substituted resulting in less intake, then response rate increases would be expected to compensate for that lower dose. An increase in response rate was precisely what was observed, supporting satiation as a relevant process. This interesting and important method can clearly differentiate the two processes; however, it will have to be replicated with cocaine and other drugs before any strong conclusion about the two processes can be drawn.

SUMMARY

Various methods of assessing reinforcing efficacy of cocaine were compared. Progressive ratio schedules and behavioral economic measures are currently used most often, and findings are concordant across these measures. Experimental conditions that are important in assessing cocaine's reinforcing effects are dose, reinforcement schedule, route of administration, duration of access, and feeding stimulus conditions. Recent studies have also shown that the environmental context in which cocaine is taken is related to its reinforcement potential. Environments that are rich with alternative nondrug reinforcers prevent or reduce cocaine-maintained behavior, whereas other variables, such as a history or current exposure to other drugs (e.g., caffeine, ethanol), restricted feeding, and stress, enhance cocaine reinforcement. This chapter emphasizes that reinforcing properties are not inherent to cocaine or other drugs, but they emerge through an interaction with the organism and its environment.

ACKNOWLEDGMENTS

Preparation of this chapter was supported by grants R01 DA02486, R37 DA03240 (MEC) and R01 DA06526 (WKB) from the National Institute on Drug Abuse.

REFERENCES

Altshuler, H., Weaver, S., & Phillips, P. (1975). Intragastric self-administration of psychoactive drugs by the rhesus monkey. *Life Science, 17,* 883–890.

Bickel, W. K., & DeGrandpre, R. J. (1996). Modeling drug abuse policy in the behavioral economics laboratory. In L. Green & J. Kagel (Eds.), *Advances in behavioral economics* (Vol. 3, pp. 69–95). New York: Ablex.

Bickel, W. K., DeGrandpre, R. J., & Higgins, S. T. (1993). Behavioral economics: A novel experimental approach to the study of drug dependence. *Drug and Alcohol Dependence, 33,* 173–192.

Bickel, W. K., DeGrandpre, R. J., & Higgins, S. T. (1995). The behavioral economics of concurrent drug reinforcers: A review and reanalysis of drug self-administration research. *Psychopharmacology, 118,* 250–259.

Bickel, W. K., DeGrandpre, R. J., Higgins, S. T., & Hughes, J. R. (1990). Behavioral economics of drug self-administration. I. Functional equivalence of response requirement and drug dose. *Life Sciences, 47,* 1501–1510.

Bickel, W. K., DeGrandpre, R. J., Higgins, S. T., Hughes, J. R., & Badger, G. J. (1995). Effects of simulated employment and recreation on drug taking: A behavioral economic analysis. *Experimental and Clinical Psychopharmacology, 3,* 467–476.

Bickel, W. K., DeGrandpre, R. J., Hughes, J. R., & Higgins, S. T. (1991). Behavioral economics of drug self-administration. II. A unit-price analysis of cigarette smoking. *Journal of the Experimental Analysis of Behavior, 55,* 145–154.

Bickel, W. K., & Kelly, T. H. (1988). The relationship of stimulus control to the treatment of substance abuse. In B. A. Ray (Ed.), *Learning factors in substance abuse* (pp. 122–140). (NIDA Research Monograph 84, DHHS). Washington, DC: U.S. Government Printing Office.

Bozarth, M. A., & Wise, R. A. (1985). Toxicity associated with long-term intravenous heroin and cocaine self-administration in the rat. *Journal of the American Medical Association, 254,* 81–83.

Branch, M. N. (1991). Behavioral pharmacology. In I. H. Iversen & K. A. Lattal (Eds.), *Experimental analysis of behavior, Part 2* (pp. 21–77). Amsterdam: Elsevier Science Publishers.

Broocks, A., Liu, J., & Pirke, K. M. (1990). Semistarvation-induced hyperactivity compensates for decreased norepinephrine and dopamine turnover in the mediobasal hypothalamus of the rat. *Journal of Neural Transmission—General Section, 79,* 113–124.

Brown, P. L., & Jenkins, H. M. (1968). Auto-shaping of the pigeon's key-peck. *Journal of the Experimental Analysis of Behavior, 11,* 1–8.

Carney, J. M., Llewellyn, M. E., & Woods, J. H. (1976). Variable interval responding maintained by intravenous codeine and ethanol injections in the rhesus monkey. *Pharmacology, Biochemistry and Behavior, 5,* 577–582.

Carroll, M. E. (1996a). Acquisition and reacquisition (relapse) of drug abuse: Modulation by alternative reinforcers. In C. L. Wetherington & J. L. Falk (Eds.), *Laboratory and behavioral studies of vulnerability to drug abuse* (NIDA Research Monograph). Washington, DC: U.S. Government Printing Office.

Carroll, M. E. (1996b). Reducing drug abuse by enriching the environment with alternative nonddrug reinforcers. In L. Green & J. Kagel (Eds.), *Advances in behavioral economics* (Vol. 3, pp. 37–68). Norwood, NJ: Ablex Publishing Co.

Carroll, M. E. (1985a). Concurrent phencyclidine and saccharin access: Presentation of an alternative reinforcer reduces drug intake. *Journal of Experimental Analysis of Behavior, 43,* 131–144.

Carroll, M. E. (1985b). The role of food deprivation in the maintenance and reinstatement of cocaine-seeking behavior in rats. *Drug and Alcohol Dependence, 16,* 95–109.

Carroll, M. E., & Carmona, G. N. (1991). Effects of food FR and food deprivation on disruption in food-maintained performance of monkeys during phencyclidine withdrawal. *Psychopharmacology, 104,* 143–149.

Carroll, M. E., Carmona, G. N., May, S. A., Buzalski, S., & Larson, C. (1992). Buprenorphine's effects on self-administration of smoked cocaine-base and orally-delivered phencyclidine, ethanol and saccharin in rhesus monkeys. *Journal of Pharmacology and Experimental Therapeutics, 261,* 26–37.

Carroll, M. E., & Comer, S. D. (1996). Animal models of relapse. *Experimental and Clinical Psychopharmacology, 4,* 61–67.

Carroll, M. E., Krattiger, K. L., Gieske, D., & Sadoff, D. A. (1990). Cocaine-base smoking in rhesus monkeys: Reinforcing and physiological effects. *Psychopharmacology, 102,* 443–450.

Carroll, M. E., & Lac, S. T. (1993). Autoshaping i.v. cocaine self-administration in rats: Effects of nondrug alternative reinforcers on acquisition. *Psychopharmacology, 110,* 5–12.

Carroll, M. E., Lac, S. T., & Nygaard, S. L. (1989). A concurrently available nondrug reinforcer prevents the acquisition or decreases the maintenance of cocaine-reinforced behavior. *Psychopharmacology, 97,* 23–29.

Catania, A. C. (1968). Glossary. In A. C. Catania (Ed.), *Contemporary research in operant behavior* (pp. 327–349). Glenview, IL: Scott Foreman.

Childress, A. R., McLellan, A. T., Ehrman, R. N., & O'Brien, C. P. (1987). Extinction of conditioned responses in abstinent cocaine or opioid users. *NIDA Research Monographs, 76,* 189–195.

Chornock, W. M., Stitzer, M. L., Gross, J., & Leischow, S. (1992). Experimental model of smoking re-exposure: Effects on relapse. *Psychopharmacology, 108,* 495–500.

Comer, S. D., Hunt, V. R., & Carroll, M. E. (1994). Effects of concurrent saccharin availability and buprenorphine pretreatment on demand for smoked cocaine base in rhesus monkeys. *Psychopharmacology, 115,* 15–23.

Comer, S. D., Lac, S. T., Curtis, L. D., & Carroll, M. E. (1993). Effects of buprenorphine and naltrexone in a model of cocaine relapse in rats. *Journal of Pharmacology and Experimental Therapeutics, 267,* 1470–1477.

Comer, S. D., Lac, S. T., Curtis, L. D, & Carroll, M. E. (1995). Food deprivation affects extinction and reinstatement of responding in rats. *Psychopharmacology, 121,* 150–151.

Comer, S. D., Lac, S. T., Wyvell, C. L., & Carroll, M. E. (1996). Combined effects of buprenorphine and a nondrug alternative reinforcer on i.v. cocaine self-administration in rats maintained under FR schedules. *Psychopharmacology, 125,* 355–360.

Cone, E. J., Risner, M. E., & Neidert, G. L. (1978). Concentrations of phenethylamine in dog following single doses and during intravenous self-administration. *Research Communications in Chemical Pathology and Pharmacology, 22,* 211–232.

DeGrandpre, R. J., & Bickel, W. K. (1996). Drug dependence as consumer demand. In L. Green & J. Kagel (Eds.), *Advances in behavioral economics* (Vol. 3, pp. 1–36). New York: Ablex.

DeGrandpre, R. J., Bickel, W. K., Hughes, J. R., Layng, M., & Badger, G. (1993). Unit price as a useful metric in analyzing effects of reinforcer magnitude. *Journal of Experimental Analysis of Behavior, 60,* 641–666.

Deneau, G. W., Yanagita, T., & Seevers, M. H. (1969). Self-administration of psychoactive substances by the monkey: A measure of psychological dependence. *Psychopharmacology, 16,* 30–48.

Deroche, V., Piazza, P. V., Casolini, P., LeMoal, M., & Simon, H. (1993). Sensitization to the psychomotor effects of amphetamine and morphine induced by food restriction depends on corticosterone secretion. *Brain Research, 611,* 352–356.

de Wit, H., & Stewart, J. (1981). Reinstatement of cocaine-reinforced responding in the rat. *Psychopharmacology, 75,* 134–143.

de Wit, H., & Stewart, J. (1983). Reinstatement of heroin-reinforced responding in the rat. *Psychopharmacology, 79,* 29–31.

Ferster, C. B., & Skinner, B. F. (1957). *Schedules of reinforcement.* Englewood Cliffs, NJ: Prentice-Hall, Inc.

Fischman, M. W. (1987). Cocaine and the amphetamines. In H. Y. Meltzer (Ed.), *Psychopharmacology: The third generation of progress* (pp. 1543–1553). New York: Raven Press.

Fischman, M. W. (1988). Behavioral pharmacology of cocaine. *Journal of Clinical Psychiatry, 49* (suppl.), 7–10.

Fischman, M. W., Schuster, C. R., & Hatano, Y. (1983). A comparison of the subjective and cardiovascular effects of cocaine and lidocaine in humans. *Pharmacology, Biochemistry and Behavior, 18,* 123–127.

Fitch, T. E., & Roberts, D. C. S. (1993). The effects of dose and access restrictions on the periodicity of cocaine self-administration in the rat. *Drug and Alcohol Dependence, 33,* 119–128.

Foltin, R. W., & Fischman, M. W. (1992). The cardiovascular and subjective effects of intravenous cocaine and morphine combinations in humans. *Journal of Pharmacology and Experimental Therapeutics, 261,* 623–632.

Goeders, N. E., & Guerin, G. F. (1994). Non-contingent electrical footshock facilitates the acquisition of intravenous cocaine self-administration in rats. *Psychopharmacology, 114,* 63–70.

Goeders, N. E., & Guerin, G. F. (1996). Effects of surgical and pharmacological adrenalectomy on the initiation and maintenance of intravenous cocaine self-administration in rats. *Brain Research, 722,* 145–152.

Goeders, N. E., & Smith, J. E. (1983). Cortical dopaminergic involvement in cocaine reinforcement. *Science, 221,* 773–775.

Goldberg, S. R. (1973). Comparable behavior maintained under fixed-ratio and second-order schedules of food presentation, cocaine injection or *d*-amphetamine injection in the squirrel monkey. *The Journal of Pharmacology and Experimental Therapeutics, 186,* 18–30.

Goldberg, S. R., Hoffmeister, F., Schlichting, U. U., & Wuttke, W. (1971). A comparison of pentobarbital and cocaine self-administration in rhesus monkeys: effects of dose and fixed-ratio parameters. *Journal of Pharmacology and Experimental Therapeutics, 179,* 277–283.

Goldberg, S. R., Morse, W. H., & Goldberg, D. M. (1976). Behavior maintained under a second-order schedule by intramuscular injection of morphine or cocaine in rhesus monkeys. *Journal of Pharmacology and Experimental Therapeutics, 199,* 278–286.

Goldberg, S. R., Spealman, R. D., & Kelleher, R. T. (1979). Enhancement of drug-seeking behavior by environmental stimuli associated with cocaine or morphine injections. *Neuropharmacology, 18,* 1015–1017.

Goldberg, S. R., & Kelleher, R. T. (1977). Reinforcement of behavior by cocaine injections. In E. H. Ellinwood, Jr. & M. M. Kilbey (Eds.), *Cocaine and other stimulants* (pp. 523–544). New York: Plenum Press.

Griffiths, R. R., Bradford, L. D., & Brady, J. V. (1979a). Progressive ratio and fixed ratio schedules of cocaine-maintained responding in baboons. *Psychopharmacology, 65,* 25–136.

Griffiths, R. R., Brady, J. V., & Bradford, L. D. (1979b). Predicting the abuse liability of drugs and animal drug self-administration procedures: Psychomotor stimulants and hallucinogens. In T. Thompson & P. B. Dews (Eds.), *Advances in behavioral pharmacology* (pp. 163–208). New York: Academic Press, Inc.

Griffiths, R. R., Brady, J. V., & Snell, J. D. (1978). Progressive-ratio performance maintained by drug infusions: Comparison of cocaine, diethylpropioin, chlorphentermine, and fenfluramine. *Psychopharmacology, 56,* 5–13.

Haney, M., Maccari, S., LeMoal, M., Simon, H., & Piazza, P. V. (1995). Social stress increases the acquisition of cocaine self-administration in male and female rats. *Brain Research, 698,* 46–52.

Higgins, S. T., Budney, A. J., Hughes, J. R., Bickel, W. K., Lynn, M., & Mortenson, A. (1994). Influence of cocaine use on cigarette smoking. *Journal of the American Medical Association, 272,* 1724.

Higgins, S. T., Roll, J. M., & Bickel, W. K. (1996). Alcohol pretreatment increases preference for cocaine over monetary reinforcement. *Psychopharmacology, 123,* 1–8.

Hodos, W. (1961). Progressive ratio as a measure of reward strength. *Science, 134,* 943–944.

Horger, B. A., Giles, M., & Schenk, S. (1992). Preexposure to amphetamine and nicotine predisposes rats to self-administer a low dose of cocaine. *Psychopharmacology* (Berlin), *107,* 271–276.

Horger, B. A., Shelton, K., & Schenk, S. (1990). Preexposure sensitizes rats to the rewarding effect of cocaine. *Pharmacology, Biochemistry and Behavior, 37,* 707–711.

Horger, B. A., Wellman, P. J., Morien, A., Davies, B. T., & Schenk, S. (1991). Caffeine exposure sensitizes rats to the reinforcing effects of cocaine. *Neuro Report, 2,* 53–56.

Hursh, S. R., & Bauman, R. A. (1987). The behavior analysis of demand. In L. Green & J. H. Kagel (Eds.), *Advances in behavioral economics* (Vol. 1, pp. 117–165). Norwood, NJ: Ablex.

Hursh, S. R., Raslear, T. G., Shurtleff, D., Bauman, R., & Simmons, L. (1988). A cost-benefit analysis of demand for food. *Journal of Experimental Analysis of Behavior, 50,* 419–440.

Iglauer, C., Llewellyn, M. E., & Woods, J. H. (1976). Concurrent schedules of cocaine injection in rhesus monkeys: Dose variations under independent and non-independent variable-interval procedures. *Pharmacological Reviews, 27,* 367–383.

Johanson, C. E. (1975). Pharmacological and environmental variables affecting drug preference in rhesus monkeys. *Pharmacological Reviews, 27,* 343–355.

Johanson, C. E., & Fischman, M. W. (1989). The pharmacology of cocaine related to its abuse. *Pharmacological Reviews, 41,* 3–52.

Johanson, C. E., & Schuster, C. R. (1975). A choice procedure for drug reinforcers: Cocaine and methylphenidate in the rhesus monkey. *Journal of Pharmacology and Experimental Therapeutics, 193,* 676–688.

Katz, J. L. (1989). Drugs as reinforcers: pharmacological and behavioural factors. In J. M. Liebman &

S. J. Cooper (Eds.), *The neuropharmacological basis of reward* (pp. 164–213). New York: Oxford University Press.

Keller, R. W., LeFevre, R., Raucci, J., Carlson, J. N., & Glick, S. D. (1996). Enhanced cocaine self-administration in adult rats prenatally exposed to cocaine. *Neuroscience Letters, 205,* 153–156.

Kosten, T. R., Rosen, M. I., Schottenfeld, R., & Ziedonis, D. (1992). Buprenorphine for cocaine and opiate dependence. *Psychopharmacology Bulletin, 28,* 15–19.

Ludwig, A. M., & Wikler, A. (1974). "Craving" and relapse to drink. *Quarterly Journal of Studies on Alcohol, 35,* 45–53.

Lynch, W. J., LaBounty, L. P., & Carroll, M. E. (1997). A novel paradigm to investigate regulation of drug intake in rats self-administering i.v. cocaine or heroin. *Experimental and Clinical Psychopharmacology, 6,* 22–31.

Maccari, S., Piazza, P. V., Deminiere, J. M., Lemaire, V., Mormede, P., Simon, H., Angelucci, L., & LeMoal, M. (1991). Life events-induced decrease of corticosteroid type I receptors is associated with reduced corticosterone feedback and enhanced vulnerability to amphetamine self-administration. *Brain Research, 547,* 7–12.

Mattox, A. J., Thompson, S. T., & Carroll, M. E. (1997). Smoked heroin and cocaine base combinations (speedball) in rhesus monkeys. *Experimental and Clinical Psychopharmacology, 5,* 113–118.

Meil, W. M., & See, R. E. (1996). Conditioned cue recovery of responding following prolonged withdrawal from self-administered cocaine in rats: An animal model of relapse. *Behavioral Pharmacology, 7,* 754–763.

Meisch, R. A., Kliner, D. J., & Henningfield, J. E. (1981). Pentobarbital drinking by rhesus monkeys: Establishment and maintenance of pentobarbital-reinforced behavior. *Journal of Pharmacology and Experimental Therapeutics, 217,* 114–119.

Mello, N. K., Mendelson, J. H., Bree, M. P., & Lukas, S. E. (1990). Buprenorphine and naltrexone effects on cocaine self-administration by rhesus monkeys. *Journal of Pharmacology and Experimental Therapeutics, 254,* 926–939.

Nader, M. A., & Woolverton, W. L. (1991). Effects of increasing the magnitude of an alternative reinforcer on drug choice in a discrete-trials choice procedure. *Psychopharmacology, 105,* 69–174.

Negus, S. S., Mello, N. K., Lukas, S. E., & Mendelson, J. H. (1995). Diurnal patterns of cocaine and heroin self-administration in rhesus monkeys responding under a schedule of multiple daily sessions. *Behavioural Pharmacology, 6,* 763–775.

Pearce, D. W. (1986). *The MIT dictionary of modern economics.* Cambridge, MA: The MIT Press.

Piazza, P. V., Deminière, J-M., LeMoal, M., & Simon, H. (1989). Factors that predict individual vulnerability to amphetamine self-administration. *Science, 245,* 1511–1513.

Piazza, P. V., Deminière, J-M., LeMoal, M., & Simon, H. (1990). Stress- and pharmacologically-induced behavioral sensitization increases vulnerability to acquisition of amphetamine self-administration. *Brain Research, 514,* 22–26.

Piazza, P. V., Maccari, S., Deminière, J-M., LeMoal, M., Mormede, P., & Simon, H. (1991). Corticosterone levels determine vulnerability to amphetamine self-administration. *National Academy of Science, 88,* 2088–2092.

Piazza, P. V., Marinelli, M., Jodogne, C., Deroche, V., Rouge-Pont, F., Maccari, S., Le Moal, M., & Simon, H. (1994). Inhibition of corticosterone synthesis by Metyrapone decreases cocaine-induced locomotion and relapse of cocaine self-administration. *Brain Research, 658,* 259–264.

Ramsey, N. F. (1991). *Cocaine dependence: Factors in the initiation of self-administration in rats* (pp. 125–136). Rudolf Magnus Institute, University of Utrecht, Utrecht, The Netherlands.

Ramsey, N. F., & van Ree, M. (1990). Chronic pretreatment with naltrexone facilitates acquisition of intravenous cocaine self-administration in rats. *European Journal of Neuropharmacology, 1,* 55–61.

Ramsey, N. F., & van Ree, M. (1993). Emotional but not physical stress enhances intravenous cocaine self-administration in drug naive rats. *Brain Research, 608,* 216–222.

Rawleigh, J. M., Rodefer, J. S., Hansen, J. J., & Carroll, M. E. (1996). Combined effects of buprenorphine and an alternative nondrug reinforcer on phencyclidine self-administration in rhesus monkeys. *Experimental and Clinical Psychopharmacology, 4,* 68–76.

Rodefer, J. S., Mattox, A. J., Thompson, S. S., & Carroll, M. E. (1997). Effects of buprenorphine and an alternative nondrug reinforcer, alone and in combination, on smoked cocaine self-adminstration in monkeys. *Drug and Alcohol Dependence, 45,* 27–29.

Roll, J. M., Higgins, S. T., & Tidey, J. (1997). Cocaine use can increase cigarette smoking: Evidence from laboratory and naturalistic settings. *Experimental and Clinical Psychopharmacology, 5,* 263–268.

Rougè-Pont, F., Piazza, P. V., Kharouby, M., Le Moal, M., & Simon, H. (1993). Higher and longer stress-induced increase in dopamine concentrations in the nucleus accumbens of animals predisposed to amphetamine self-administration: A microdialysis study. *Brain Research, 602,* 169–174.

Samuelson, P. A., & Nordhaus, W. D. (1985). *Economics.* New York: McGraw-Hill.

Schenk, S., Lacell, G., Gorman, K., & Amit, Z. (1987). Cocaine self-administration in rats influenced by environmental conditions: Implications for the etiology of drug abuse. *Neuroscience Letters, 81,* 227–231.

Schuster, C. R., & Brady, J. V. (1964). The discriminative control of a food-reinforced operant. *Pavlov Journal of Higher Nervous Activity, 14,* 448–458.

Sidman, M., & Stebbins, W. C. (1954). Satiation effects under fixed-ratio schedules of reinforcement. *Journal of Comparative and Physiological Psychology, 47,* 114–116.

Siegel, S. (1989). Pharmacological conditioning and drug effects. In A. J. Goudie and M. W. Emmet-Oglesby (Eds.), *Psychoactive drugs: Tolerance and sensitization* (pp. 115–180). Clifton, NJ: Humana.

Skjoldager, P., Winger, G., & Woods, J. H. (1991). Analysis of fixed-ratio behavior maintained by drug reinforcers. *Journal of Experimental Analysis of Behavior, 56,* 331–343.

Slikker, W., Brocco, M. J., & Killam, K. F. (1983). Reinstatement of responding maintained by cocaine or thiamylal. *Journal of Pharmacology and Experimental Therapeutics, 228,* 43–52.

Spealman, R. D. (1979). Behavior maintained by termination of a schedule of self-administered cocaine. *Science, 204,* 1231–1233.

Specker, S. M., Lac, S. T., & Carroll, M. E. (1994). Food deprivation history and cocaine self-administration: An animal mode of binge eating. *Pharmacology, Biochemistry and Behavior, 48,* 1025–1029.

Stewart, J., & Wise, R. A. (1992). Reinstatement of heroin self-administration habits: Morphine prompts and naltrexone discourages renewed responding after extinction. *Psychopharmacology, 108,* 79–84.

Tidey, J. W., & Miczek, K. A. (1997). Acquisition of cocaine self-administration after social stress: Rle of accumbens dopamine. *Pschopharmacology, 130,* 203–212.

Weiss, R. D. (1988). Relapse to cocaine abuse after initiating desipramine treatment. *Journal of the American Medical Association, 260,* 2545–2546.

Winger, G., Hoffman, F. G., & Woods, J. H. (1992). Central nervous system stimulants: Cocaine, In *A Handbook on drug and alcohol abuse: The biological aspects* (3rd ed.) (pp. 150–163). Cambridge, UK: Oxford University Press.

Wise, R. A., Murray, A., & Bozarth, M. A. (1990). Bromocriptine self-administration and bromocriptine reinstatement of cocaine-trained and heroin-trained lever pressing rats. *Psychopharmacology, 100,* 355–360.

Wise, R. A., Newton, P., Leeg, K., Burnette, B., Pocock, D., & Justice, J. B., Jr. (1995). Fluctuations in nucleus accumbens dopamine concentration during intravenous cocaine self-administration in rats. *Psychopharmacology, 120,* 10–20.

Woolverton, W. L., Cervo, L., & Johanson, C. E. (1984). Effects of repeated methamphetamine administration on amphetamine self-administration. *Pharmacology, Biochemistry and Behavior, 21,* 737–741.

Worley, C. M., Valadez, A., & Schenk, S. (1994). Reinstatement of extinguished cocaine-taking behavior by cocaine and caffeine. *Pharmacology, Biochemistry and Behavior, 48,* 217–221.

Yokel, R. A., & Pickens, R. (1974). Drug level of *d*- and *l*-amphetamine during intravenous self-administration. *Psychopharmacologia, 34,* 255–264.

Young, A. M., & Herling, S. (1986). Drugs as reinforcers: Studies in laboratory animals. In S. R. Goldberg & I. P. Stolerman (Eds.), *Behavioral analysis of drug dependence* (pp. 9–67). Orlando, FL: Academic Press.

Zacny, J. P., Divane, W. T., & de Wit, H. (1992). Assessment of magnitude and availability of a nondrug reinforcer on preference for a drug reinforcer. *Human Psychopharmacology, 7,* 281–286.

5

TOLERANCE AND SENSITIZATION TO COCAINE: AN INTEGRATED VIEW

WILLIAM L. WOOLVERTON

Department of Psychiatry and Human Behavior
University of Mississippi Medical Center
Jackson, Mississippi

SUSAN R. B. WEISS

Biological Psychiatry Branch
National Institutes of Mental Health
Bethesda, Maryland

INTRODUCTION

Tolerance refers to diminished sensitivity to the effects of a drug upon repeated exposure (see Kalant, LeBlanc, & Gibbins, 1971; O'Brien, 1996). Conversely, sensitization refers to enhanced sensitivity to a drug upon repeated exposure. Tolerance is demonstrated by a decrease in the effect of a drug dose or, preferably, by a shift to the right in a dose–response function with repeated administration; sensitization is demonstrated by an increase in the effect of a drug dose or shift to the left in a dose–response function. Either change in drug sensitivity may be due to changes in pharmacokinetics (i.e., drug absorption, metabolism, or excretion) or pharmacodynamics (i.e., changes in the effector system's response to the drug). Additionally, behavioral mechanisms can play a crucial role in determining changes in sensitivity to drugs. Although pharmacokinetic changes may play a role in the effects of chronic cocaine abuse (Pan & Menacherry, 1991), because of space limitations we will consider only pharmacodynamic and behavioral mechanisms.

Cocaine Abuse: Behavior, Pharmacology,
and Clinical Applications

Tolerance has long been felt to play a major role in drug abuse. It is widely held that drug abusers seek and consume ever larger amounts of drugs to compensate for diminished euphorigenic effects, and that the increasing preoccupation with drugs results from ever-increasing demands for higher doses to achieve the desired effect (Koob & Bloom, 1988; Wikler, 1973). Interestingly, however, it was long thought that tolerance did not develop to cocaine. In 1924, Lewin stated that "as opposed to morphia, animals cannot become accustomed to cocaine; they even exhibit an increasing sensibility to the drug" (Byck, 1974, p. 245). Tatum and Seevers (1929) reported increased sensitivity to the central stimulant effects of cocaine in dogs and monkeys. It has been stated that sensitization is a consistent finding in animal studies of cocaine (O'Brien, 1996). Obviously, the simultaneous belief that tolerance plays a central role in drug abuse but that sensitization develops to the effects of cocaine, a drug that is extensively abused in ever-increasing amounts, requires some thought. It has recently been hypothesized that sensitization may be the primary change contributing to increased drug seeking and drug taking seen with cocaine and other stimulants (Robinson & Berridge, 1993). The Incentive-Sensitization Theory of addiction posits that repeated drug use sensitizes the mesolimbic dopamine (DA) system to drugs and drug-associated stimuli in a way that changes ordinary "wanting" of drugs into excessive craving, which drives excessive drug-seeking and drug-taking behavior. In fact, both tolerance and sensitization have been reported to develop upon repeated administration of cocaine to animals. A comprehensive view of the determinants of cocaine abuse should incorporate both findings.

The purpose of the present chapter is to review basic research on the phenomena and mechanisms of changes in sensitivity to cocaine. It is not our intention to review the extensive literature on cocaine tolerance and sensitization. This has been done previously (Hammer, Egilmez, & Emmett-Oglesby, 1997; Kalivas & Stewart, 1991; Robinson & Berridge, 1993), and the interested reader is referred to one of these excellent reviews. Rather, our primary goal is to begin to assmilate into a comprehensive view the empirical phenomena of tolerance and sensitization to cocaine with changes in sensitivity that occur with repeated cocaine use, and discuss how these phenomena may interact in the evolution of cocaine abuse. In our view, in the development of tolerance and sensitization to cocaine, behavioral and neurobiological mechanisms interact in a way that includes not only neuronal systems directly affected by cocaine, which mediate many of its behavioral effects, but also neuronal systems involved in learning and memory. Although much of this formulation is speculative, the evolving data suggest that systems affected both directly and indirectly by cocaine may play a crucial role in the overall contribution of tolerance and sensitization to cocaine abuse.

Although it may be obvious that behavioral and neurobiological mechanisms interact in the development of tolerance and sensitization to cocaine, the specifics of this interaction are largely unknown. Furthermore, the major focus of tolerance studies has been behavioral mechanisms, whereas, for sensitization, the focus has been neurobiological substrates. In this way, these two areas have proceeded fairly independently. The present chapter reflects this difference in emphasis. However, in our opinion, future studies should attempt to correct this imbalance and begin to integrate behavioral and neurobiological mechanisms of both tolerance and sensitization into a more comprehensive understanding of how changes in sensitivity to cocaine occur, how or whether they may be modulated, and their role in cocaine abuse.

TOLERANCE

Tolerance to cocaine was initially reported in animal studies conducted in the 1970s. Thompson (1977) reported that tolerance developed to the effects of cocaine on complex schedule-controlled behavior. Woolverton, Kandel, and Schuster (1978a,b) reported tolerance to the effects of cocaine on food consumption and schedule-controlled behavior, and cross-tolerance to *d*-amphetamine. Perhaps the most comprehensive analysis of tolerance to cocaine has been undertaken by Branch and his colleagues investigating cocaine's effects on schedule-controlled behavior (Stafford & Branch, 1996). Recent research has also established that tolerance develops to effects of cocaine that play a central role in its abuse, both subjective and reinforcing effects. This tolerance has been reported both in humans studied in a laboratory setting and in animal subjects.

SUBJECTIVE AND DISCRIMINATIVE STIMULUS EFFECTS

Subjective effects are those effects that humans report feeling after taking a drug. Positive subjective effects are presumed to be critical to the maintenance of drug taking. Tolerance to the subjective effects of a drug would logically seem a significant determinant of the escalation in dose that occurs in drug abusers. Ethical considerations limit laboratory investigation of long-term exposure to high doses of cocaine in humans. Therefore, information concerning changes in sensitivity to cocaine in humans with chronic administration is largely anecdotal. The textbook view has varied. Jaffe (1970) stated, accurately, that "there is some question whether tolerance develops to cocaine" (p. 295). Indeed, Jaffe (1985) maintained that there is increased sensitivity to many of the effects of cocaine when it is administered repeatedly. Jaffe (1990) reported that there is tolerance to some of the effects of cocaine, based largely on the fact that cocaine abusers report that they require more cocaine to produce the same pleasurable effects that were achieved with initial cocaine use. O'Brien (1996) states that sensitization to the euphoric effect of cocaine is "not typically seen."

Acute tolerance to the subjective effects of cocaine has been reported in human subjects in the laboratory. Acute tolerance is defined as a decrease in the effects of a drug across a single session of drug administration. Fischman, Schuster, Javaid, Hatano, and Davis (1985) studied the effects of pre-exposure to cocaine on the subjective effects of intravenous (i.v.) cocaine. Subjects were prepared with i.v. lines and, after a 30-min baseline period, were allowed to intranasally inhale 100 mg of cocaine (96 mg cocaine + 4 mg lactose) or placebo (4 mg cocaine + 96 mg lactose). One hour later, saline or cocaine (0, 16, 32, or 48 mg) was injected i.v. Subjective effects were measured using the Profile of Mood States (POMS) and Addiction Research Center Inventory (ARCI). Cocaine induced the expected subjective effects. However, the subjective effects were decreased or eliminated relative to placebo in subjects who received cocaine pretreatment (i.e., acute tolerance occurred to its subjective effects). These differences could not be accounted for by differences in plasma levels of cocaine, suggesting pharmacodynamic rather than pharmacokinetic mechanisms. Acute tolerance was reversed within 24 h, as evidenced by the fact that subjects did not need a larger dose of cocaine to achieve the same initial effect the day after a cocaine session. Surprisingly, people continued to self-administer cocaine at the same rate even as the subjective effects of the injection waned. Acute tolerance has been reported repeatedly (Ambre et al., 1988; Foltin & Fischman, 1991) and may play a role in cocaine binging (but see Kumor et al., 1988, 1989).

A discriminative stimulus (DS) is one that sets the occasion for a particular behavior to be reinforced. The stimulus may be exteroceptive (e.g., a light) or interoceptive (e.g., a drug). Animals can be trained to a high level of accuracy to emit one behavior after receiving a drug and another behavior after receiving another drug or saline. An animal trained in this way makes the drug-appropriate response when given adequate doses; the drug itself is functioning as a DS. DS effects in animals are used to model the subjective effects in humans (Holtzman, 1990). That is, drugs that have similar DS effects in animals also have similar subjective effects. Therefore, studies investigating tolerance to the DS effect of cocaine in animals are particularly relevant to the question of whether tolerance develops to its subjective effects. In addition, since DS effects can be studied in animals, parameters of the exposure regimen that may affect changes in sensitivity can be readily investigated.

Tolerance to the DS effect of cocaine was first reported by McKenna and Ho (1977). Rats were trained to discriminate cocaine from saline. When 20 mg/kg cocaine was administered every 8 h for 7 days, the dose–response function for cocaine shifted to the right, indicative of tolerance. This phenomenon has been replicated and studied in detail by Emmett-Oglesby and his colleagues. Wood, Lal, and Emmett-Oglesby (1984) found that tolerance was maximal after 6 days of repeated injections and was reversed with a similar time course. In a second experiment (Wood & Emmett-Oglesby, 1986), administration of 10 mg/kg of cocaine every 8 h for 7 days produced a twofold shift to the right in the cocaine dose–response function. This magnitude of shift appeared to be maximal since the same shift was observed when 20 mg/kg was given every 8 h for either 7 or 14 days. A dose of 5.0 mg/kg every 8 h did not change the cocaine dose–response function, even when given for 14 days. Cocaine tolerance was reversed gradually over 18 days (Wood & Emmett-Oglesby, 1986). Cross-tolerance between cocaine and other psychomotor stimulants has been found for DS effects. Repeated administration of cocaine induced tolerance to the effects of methamphetamine, phenmetrazine, methylphenidate, and phentermine, and repeated exposure to *d*-amphetamine induced tolerance to cocaine (Wood et al., 1984; Wood & Emmett-Oglesby, 1988). In contrast, repeated administration of morphine did not induce tolerance to cocaine (Wood & Emmett-Oglesby, 1986).

Thus, laboratory data from both humans and nonhumans as well as anecdotal reports suggest that tolerance develops to the subjective effects of cocaine upon repeated administration. It is important to note differences between the tolerance that, to this point at least, has been described in humans and that found in animals. The studies of Fischman and colleagues involved acute tolerance that developed within a single session of cocaine availability and apparently required the presence of cocaine in the body to be expressed. Acute tolerance was reversed within 24 h. It seems likely that this sort of tolerance plays a role in cocaine self-administration during a binge. In contrast, in the studies of Emmett-Oglesby and colleagues, tolerance took several days to develop, at least a comparable amount of time to be reversed, and was observed after cocaine had been cleared from the body. It seems likely that this sort of tolerance is involved in long-term escalation in dose. This type of tolerance has not been reported in human subjects except anecdotally.

REINFORCING EFFECTS

Reinforcing effects of drugs are those effects that increase the probability of repeated drug self-administration. Therefore, reinforcing effects are essential to the repeated drug administration that is necessary for tolerance to develop. Early observations concerning tolerance to the reinforcing effect of cocaine were based on results of experiments not specifically designed to assess tolerance. Balster and Schuster (1973a) observed that rate of self-administration of a baseline dose of cocaine under a simple fixed-ratio (FR 10) schedule usually decreased over repeated periods of self-administration. Since rate of self-administration under these conditions is higher when lower doses are available, this result was noted by the authors not to be consistent with tolerance development. Indeed, the animals may have been sensitized to cocaine. On the other hand, Yanagita (1973) used a progressive-ratio (PR) schedule to evaluate the reinforcing efficacy of cocaine in "cocaine-dependent" monkeys. A PR schedule begins with a low response requirement that increases for subsequent injections until the subject stops taking injections. This is called the breaking point or breakpoint (BP). PR schedules are believed to measure the magnitude or intensity of the reinforcing effect (Hodos, 1961), a measure that for drugs has been called reinforcing efficacy (see Woolverton & Nader, 1990). Yanagita (1973) reported a decrease in the BP maintained by cocaine in cocaine-exposed monkeys, suggesting tolerance to the reinforcing effect.

Several more recent experiments were designed to more specifically address the development of tolerance to the reinforcing effect of cocaine. Emmett-Oglesby and Lane (1992) allowed rats to self-inject cocaine i.v. under a schedule that required two lever presses per injection and had a 30-s time-out after each injection (FR2 TO 30). Daily sessions lasted until 15 injections of 0.25 mg cocaine were taken or until 6 hours had elapsed. Cocaine dose–response functions were determined. Next, behavioral sessions were stopped, and for 7 days rats received 20 noncontingent infusions (one/minute) of 0.25 mg cocaine or saline (control) every 8 hours, a regimen similar to that used in the drug discrimination experiments. Eight hours after the last injection of cocaine, experimental sessions resumed and dose–response functions for cocaine were redetermined over 4 days. Rats self-administered cocaine at a higher rate. Since a decrease in the unit dose of cocaine results in an increased rate of self-injection, this finding suggests that the chronic regimen had functionally decreased the unit dose of cocaine. This could be because tolerance developed to the reinforcing effect of cocaine or because tolerance developed to other effects of cocaine that influence rate (e.g., satiation, motor effects). These latter effects have been referred to as "nonspecific effects." To address this second possibility, the investigators determined the lowest dose of cocaine that would maintain maximal responding after the chronic regimen of cocaine exposure. Logically, the lowest dose that maintains maximal behavior should be a dose where responding is least determined by nonspecific effects. When the dose–response function was determined after repeated cocaine exposure, the lowest dose of cocaine that maintained behavior was twofold higher in cocaine-treated rats relative to control rats given saline under the same injection regimen, consistent with tolerance to the reinforcing effect. Tolerance was reversed over 6 days.

Emmett-Oglesby and colleagues followed up this initial experiment with several experiments designed to further examine the development of tolerance to the reinforcing effect of cocaine. In one (Emmett-Oglesby et al., 1993), they evaluated the onset and duration of tolerance to cocaine in a self-administration paradigm. Regardless of whether cocaine was given noncontingently or self-administered during chronic exposure, tolerance was maximal after 4 consecutive days of cocaine exposure and was lost by 6 days after termination of exposure. Because of ambiguity as to whether reinforcing effects or nonspecific effects of cocaine were changed by the chronic regimen, these investigators also assessed the development of tolerance to cocaine under a PR paradigm (Li, Depoortere, & Emmett-Oglesby, 1994). When the cocaine dose–response function was initially determined, there was a dose-related increase in responding, presumably reflecting a dose-related increase in reinforcing efficacy (i.e., tolerance to the reinforcing effect). The asymptote of the dose–response function was shifted downward (i.e., BP was decreased in the PR test after repeated cocaine exposure), suggesting diminished reinforcing efficacy of cocaine. It is important to note that in this study three of the seven rats showed no tolerance (i.e., a statistically significant effect was due to changes in four of seven rats). In another study, Peltier, Li, Lytle, Taylor, & Emmett-Oglesby (1996), using both an FR and a PR schedule, reported similar shifts in the cocaine dose–response function when *d*-amphetamine or methamphetamine were administered repeatedly, suggesting cross-tolerance among stimulants in this measure.

Laboratory data from nonhumans, then, suggest that tolerance develops to the reinforcing effect of cocaine and that cross-tolerance develops to other stimulants. The development of tolerance to the reinforcing effect of cocaine might be expected to contribute to escalating cocaine intake, consistent with the findings in animals in studies using simple FR schedules. On the other hand, reinforcing effects are, by definition, those effects that increase the probability of repeating a response. In this context, an increase in self-administration might reflect an increased sensitivity to the reinforcing effect. In any case, several points need to be considered in evaluating these findings. It is well known that rate of responding under simple FR schedules is not a reliable measure of intensity of reinforcing effects (see Young & Herling, 1986, for discussion). As noted, rate of responding under these conditions is determined by a combination of reinforcing effects and nonspecific effects. Therefore, changes in FR rate of self-administration cannot alone be relied upon to provide a measure of changes in sensitivity to the reinforcing effect. If rate increases with chronic administration, it may be because tolerance developed to the reinforcing effect. However, it is also possible that tolerance developed to the nonspecific drug effects that decrease the rate of responding. This is an especially vague possibility, because we lack a good idea of what these latter effects might be. Although a decrease in rate of self-administration occurs at high unit doses and is typically thought of as reflecting disruption of motor performance, it may also reflect factors such as drug satiation (Carney, Llewellyn, & Woods, 1976) or some unspecified sensory disruption. Moreover, drugs may differ in the mechanism by which they decrease responding (Young & Herling, 1986). Combinations of changes in sensitivity are also a possibility. Given the complexity of this issue, it is difficult or impossible to interpret changes in rate of responding under a simple FR schedule. As noted by Emmett-Oglesby and colleagues, the least ambiguous finding is that rats given chronic cocaine failed to self-administer a low dose that maintained responding in rats given chronic saline. The basis for the argument that tolerance develops to the reinforcing effect of cocaine, then, is strongest at a single dose.

It should be emphasized that the ambiguity in these studies is not a flaw in design or execution, nor is it exclusive to the study of cocaine. It is inherent to a methodological approach that relies on absolute rate of self-administration as a measure of reinforcing effects. There are several approaches to decreasing the ambiguity in these data. Emmett-Oglesby and colleagues used a combination of methodological approaches, both FR and PR schedules and Occam's razor. As discussed, results with the FR schedule may reflect tolerance to reinforcing effects, tolerance to the nonspecific effects, or a combination. In the PR experiment reported by Li et al. (1994), it could be that animals were tolerant to the reinforcing effect of cocaine or that the chronic regimen sensitized them to nonspecific effects of cocaine, causing BP to decrease. That is to say, the single overlapping account of the results using these two types of schedules is tolerance to the reinforcing effect. A second approach is to maintain cocaine self-administration under conditions that eliminate, or at least minimize, the influence of nonspecific effects as a determinant of self-administration. Conditions can be arranged that isolate the reinforcing effect as the determinant of behavior (e.g., by programming a drug-free period—time-out—between injections). We have used this approach to examine the dose–response function of the reinforcing effect of cocaine and to compare cocaine to other drugs (Rowlett, Massey, Kleven, & Woolverton, 1996; Woolverton, 1995). Although this approach has not yet been used to study tolerance, it might be useful in clarifying some of the ambiguities that have been described.

SENSITIZATION

Sensitization to cocaine's effects has been reported in a number of species, including mice (Reith, 1986; Shuster, Yu, & Bates, 1977), rats (Downs & Eddy, 1932; Post, 1980), dogs (Tatum & Seevers, 1929), and monkeys (Post, Kopanda, & Black, 1976). It occurs in a variety of behaviors, including locomotion, convulsions, aggression, and various stereotypies (for reviews, see Kalivas & Stewart, 1991; Post, Weiss, & Pert, 1988; Robinson & Berridge, 1993; Stewart & Badiani, 1993). It has been suggested that people who abuse cocaine become sensitized to its anxiogenic, psychotomimetic, and convulsant effects (Gay, Inaba, Sheppard, & Neumeyer, 1975; Pose et al., 1988; Segal & Schukit, 1983; Washton & Gold, 1984). However, sensitization has not been reported in laboratory studies of cocaine in humans. Regardless, sensitization's robustness, persistence (greater than 1 year in some rodent models; Robinson & Becker, 1986), and ubiquity across species and behaviors, obligate us to consider its role in relation to any circumstance in which repeated drug administration occurs.

A number of variables have been shown to be important determinants of sensitization. These include gender (Post, 1983), dose (Shuster et al., 1977), method and schedule of drug administration (King, Joyner, Lee, Kuhn, & Ellinwood, 1992; Post, 1980), behavioral and pharmacological history (Kalivas & Duffy, 1989), and conditioning factors (Falk & Feingold, 1987; Stewart, de Wit, & Eikelboom, 1984; Weiss, Post, Pert, Woodward, & Murman, 1989). Conditioning factors will be our focus because they may provide a link between sensitization and cocaine abuse (Childress, McLellan, Ehrman, & O'Brien, 1987; Ehrmen et al., 1992; Stewart et al., 1984).

NEUROBIOLOGY OF REPEATED COCAINE
ADMINISTRATION AND SENSITIZATION

The underlying neurobiology of sensitization involves changes in function in the mesocorticolimbic DA system, initially involving the midbrain cell body region (ventral tegmental area—VTA; Kalivas & Stewart, 1991) and subsequently the terminal areas, particularly the nucleus accumbens (NAC; Henry & White, 1995; Kalivas & Stewart, 1991). Increases in extracellular DA have been reported in the NAC of sensitized animals (Kalivas & Duffy, 1993; Petit, Pan, Parsons,

& Justice, 1990; Weiss, Paulus, Lorang, & Koob, 1992), as have increases in D1 receptor function (Henry & White, 1995). The roles of other neurotransmitter and peptide systems have also generated interest (e.g., Heidbreder, Babovic-Vuksanovic, Shoaib, & Shippenberg, 1995; White, Hu, Zhang, & Wolf, 1995; Wolf & Jeziorski, 1993), with particular emphasis on the contribution of glutamate, as it has already been linked to other forms of neural plasticity (e.g., Malenka & Nicole, 1993; Morris, 1989).

The prefrontal cortex, probably through glutamatergic input to the VTA (or NAC), has been implicated in both the development and expression of sensitization (Wolf, Dahlin, Hu, & Xue, 1995). Pierce, Bell, Duffy, and Kalivas (1996) observed that the alterations in glutamate function that indicate its involvement in sensitization (i.e., a sustained, increased release of glutamate in the core region of the NAC following cocaine, and the ability of the AMPA antagonist CNQX to block the expression of cocaine sensitization) were only observed in animals that were sensitized. Likewise, behavioral cross-sensitization to AMPA microinjected into the NAC occurred only in animals that were sensitized. The distinction between development and expression seems to have functional significance in terms of pharmacological responsivity and neuroanatomical substrates of sensitization (Cador, Bijou, & Stinus, 1995). Blockade of N-methyl-D-aspartate (NMDA) glutamate receptors inhibits the development of cocaine sensitization but does not block its expression (Karler, Calder, Chaudhry, & Turkanis, 1997; Wolf & Jeziorski, 1993). Similarly, DA antagonists can block the development of conditioned sensitization to cocaine but not its expression (Beninger & Herz, 1986; Mattingly, Rowlett, Ellison, & Rase, 1997; Weiss et al., 1989). AMPA/kainate receptors, on the other hand, may be important to the expression of cocaine sensitization (Bell & Kalivas, 1996; Pierce et al., 1996). Researchers interested in the treatment of drug abuse have largely shifted their focus to the mechanisms underlying the expression of sensitization, which are more likely to be relevant to the situation encountered in chronic drug abusers, who have already been extensively exposed to cocaine.

Alterations in intracellular processes have also been reported following repeated administration of cocaine. These include changes in gene and protein expression (Graybiel, Moratella, & Robertson, 1990; Hyman, 1996; Moratella, Elbol, Vallejo, & Graybiel, 1996), second messenger systems, and G proteins (Self & Nestler, 1995; Terwilliger, Beitner-Johnson, Sevarino, Crain, & Nestler, 1991). Many of these effects differ for repeated versus acute drug administration (e.g., Hope et al., 1994; Moratella et al., 1996; Nye, Hope, Iadorola, & Nestler, 1995). In some cases, a different pattern of expression of immediate early genes (e.g., *c-fos, jun B,* zif268) has been observed following chronic treatment (Moratella et al., 1996). In other cases, induction of novel genes (e.g., chronic *fos*-related antigens) has been reported (Hope et al., 1994; Nye et al., 1995). It is notable that for many of these effects, especially on immediate early genes, the dorsal rather than ventral striatum appears to be more sensitive (e.g., Graybiel et al., 1990; Moratella et al., 1996; Steiner & Gerfen, 1996). For the most part, these changes have not yet been specifically linked to behavior, sensitization, or tolerance. Nevertheless, because changes in gene expression can lead to long-lasting alterations in function, it would seem an important avenue to pursue.

THE IMPORTANCE OF CONDITIONING
TO SENSITIZATION

The differential effects found when cocaine is administered in a specific and unique environment versus in the home cage make clear the importance of conditioning in cocaine-induced sensitization. If procedural and pharmacological factors are identical (species, age, drug, dose, experimental history, injection regimen), and the only difference between groups is the novelty of the environment in which drug is given, then any behavioral differences are likely attributable to associative learning (Weiss et al., 1989; Stetwart et al., 1984; Pert, Post, & Weiss, 1990; Post et al., 1988). Sensitization that occurs more readily in an environment with which drug has been differentially associated is referred to as context-dependent sensitization. These effects are in addition to whatever nonassociative changes in responsivity might result simply from repeated exposure to a particular environment or drug.

An interesting demonstration of the power of associative factors in the establishment of sensitization to drugs has been reported by Badiani, Browman, and Robinson (1995). They studied sensitization to the rotational effects of cocaine in novel and home environments in rats with unilateral 6-hydroxydopamine (6-OHDA) lesions of the substantia nigra. When direct DA agonists (e.g., apomorphine) are given to rats with these lesions, rotational behavior contralateral to the side of the lesion is observed, whereas indirect DA agonists (e.g., cocaine) produce ipsilateral rotation (Ungerstedt, 1971a,b). Badiani et al. (1995) found that animals injected with cocaine in a novel environment developed a greater degree of sensitization than those injected in their home cage. In addition, animals administered drug in the home cage exhibited a significant negative correlation between their rotational response to the first drug dose and their degree of subsequent sensitization, whereas animals receiving cocaine in the novel environment showed no such relationship. Lack of certain control groups did not permit this experiment to conclusively demonstrate that differences between the novel- and home-cage-injected animals were due solely to conditioning. However, an extensive literature as well as later work from the same laboratory with additional controls (Anagnostaras & Robinson, 1996) leave little doubt that conditioning not only enhanced the degree of sensitization in the novel-cage injected animals, but may even have overridden whatever genetic or other factors contributed to the home-cage group's inverse relationship between initial drug response and ultimate level of sensitization. To the extent that these findings are pertinent to humans, they imply that although differing genetic vulnerabilities to drug abuse likely exist, these may be overridden by environmental circumstances that favor conditioning, thus extending the susceptibility to drug abuse to a more diverse population than might otherwise be the case.

The duration and scope of this sort of conditioning is further illustrated in work from Silverman's laboratory (Silverman & Ho, 1981; Silverman & Bonate, 1997). Using the same unilateral lesion model, Silverman et al. (1977) observed conditioned rotation up to a year after only a single pairing of previously neutral stimuli with a low dose of the direct DA agonist apomorphine. Further, Silverman (1990) demonstrated that through conditioning, cocaine could come to elicit a response opposite to its unconditioned pharmacological effect. In this experiment, when cocaine and apomorphine were given together to lesioned rats, apomorphine-like contralateral rotation resulted. After several more cocaine-apomorphine pairings, cocaine alone came to elicit apomorphine-like contralateral rotation, an effect that lasted for 2 weeks. Thus, cocaine's direct pharmacological action of eliciting ipsilateral rotation was overridden simply by a history of pairing cocaine with a drug with different unconditioned properties.

In our studies of cocaine sensitization, we have observed a continuum for the induction of sensitization in relation to conditioning (Post et al., 1988). In a single-injection sensitization paradigm, cocaine sensitization was completely dependent upon conditioning factors (i.e., totally context-dependent). In procedures using higher and/or repeated doses, sensitization occurred irrespective of where the animals were treated. Even so, the persistence of sensitization was generally enhanced in context-treated animals. In a single-injection paradigm, the resulting sensitization lasted less than a week; in a 3-day injection paradigm, sensitization persisted at least 2 weeks. Parallel to these findings were our observations that lesions of the amygdala blocked cocaine sensitization in a single injection but not a 3-day injection paradigm (Post, Weiss, & Smith, 1995; Post et al., 1988). These findings imply that distinct or additional mechanisms come into play in the single-versus repeated-injection regimens.

In considering the role of conditioning, it should be emphasized that simply administering drug in the familiar surroundings of the home cage does not rule out the possible occurrence of conditioning, just as the pairing of drug with a novel environment doesn't insure that conditioning will take place. The injection itself, the weighing of the animals, their handling by the experimenter—any or all of these may come to influence behavior through association with drug administration irrespective of the specific location in which the drug is administered. In fact, it may well be that the lack of more extensive knowledge of or control over the variables relevant to conditioning contributes to the variability often observed in sensitization experiments.

The rather frequent finding of individual variability, in which some proportion of subjects does not show sensitization, proved to be a significant factor in recent studies of Kalivas and associates (Bell & Kalivas, 1996; Pierce et al., 1996). Initially, Pierce et al. (1996) observed that after repeated exposure to cocaine, enhanced glutamate function in the nucleus accumbens occurred only in rats that had become behaviorally sensitized to the drug. This was about two-thirds of their subjects when sensitization was defined as an increase in locomotor activity of greater than 20% over the baseline response to cocaine. In their experimental procedure, cocaine was administered initially in a novel test chamber (for recording of loco-motor activity), and then for the next 5 days in the home cage. The animals were then evaluated for sensitization with a cocaine challenge in the same test chamber used on the first day of the experiment. These authors speculated that the animals that sensitized may have been those that were most readily conditioned.

Bell and Kalivas (1996) examined this possibility by administering cocaine each day to one group of subjects in the test chamber and to another group in the home cage. Surprisingly, despite their substantially greater exposure to drug-spe-cific cues, the test-chamber group failed to show a higher rate of sensitization than did the animals in the Pierce et al. (1996) study. In addition, Bell and Kalivas (1996) found cross-sensitization to intra-NAC AMPA only in animals treated with cocaine in the test cage and of these again only in those showing sensitization to cocaine. In animals comparably exposed to cocaine but without the opportunity for conditioning to the test environment, the response to intra-accumbens AMPA was not enhanced. In fact, the AMPA response of home-cage injected animals was identical to that of saline-pretreated controls. This degree of selectivity is in no-table contrast to previous microdialysis studies reporting changes in DA function 2–3 weeks after cocaine irrespective of the occurrence of sensitization (Kalivas & Duffy, 1993). Based on these findings, Kalivas and associates suggested that glu-tamate is likely involved in the learned component of sensitization, whereas DA probably is involved in a less specific manner that is principally attributable to the pharmacology of cocaine.

Dovetailing with these observations, Schwarzschild, Cole, and Hyman (1997) reported that striatal changes in cell phenotype that occur after chronic stimulant administration are dependent on glutamate receptor activation. Whereas DA pro-duced changes in several immediate early genes (*c-fos, jun-b, zif*-268), activa-tion of AP1 proteins in the medium spiny neurons of the striatum depended upon the immediate early gene *c-jun,* which was expressed following exposure to glu-tamate but not DA. Together with the findings from numerous other studies in-dicating that glutamate is important for learning (e.g., Malenka & Nicoll, 1993; Morris, 1989), these data suggest that glutamate may also be critical to some long-term changes in the striatum associated with chronic cocaine, supporting the no-tion that learning or conditioning may be important for some of cocaine's effects after repeated use.

CONDITIONED STIMULI ELICIT EFFECTS SIMILAR
TO THOSE PRODUCED BY THE DRUG

In light of such strong conditioning effects, it should come as no surprise that previously neutral stimuli associated with cocaine can come to elicit some of the neurochemical, physiological, and behavioral effects of the drug. For the most part, neurochemical studies have focused on measures of DA function. Fontana and Post (1993), using a single-injection sensitization paradigm and *in vivo* mi-crodialysis, observed a cocaine-related increase in DA in NAC that was greater in conditioned animals than in unconditioned or saline-treated animals tested on the following day. That this difference was not simply due to the corresponding enhanced locomotor activity of the conditioned animals was suggested by their observation that MK-801, a noncompetitive NMDA glutamate receptor antagonist, caused locomotor activation but did not increase NAC DA levels. However, conditioned increases in extracellular DA are not universally reported in sensitization studies. Brown and Fibiger (1992) reported enhanced locomotor activity, but no differential increase in DA levels in conditioned animals compared to those that received cocaine in an environment different than the one in which the DA was measured. Among the differences between these two studies was that Brown and Fibiger (1992) did not administer cocaine (or saline) to the animals before the microdialysis samples were collected. Conditioned subjects were simply placed in the environment previously paired with cocaine. It may be that the conditioned stimulus (i.e., the injection ritual) must be present for conditioning-related enhancement of extracellular DA to occur. Pert, Post, and Weiss (1990) have discussed this issue in relation to the importance of the interoceptive stimuli produced by the drug, particularly in situations where the conditioning effects may not be robust.

Conditioned increases in DA function have also been reported in self-administration studies. Maldonado-Irizarry et al. (1996) trained rats to self-administer cocaine and paired a specific stimulus with the availability of drug; a different stimulus indicated the availability of saline. Following a period of unreinforced responding, they reexposed these "abstinent" animals to the cocaine-related stimulus and observed both a reinstatement of extinguished lever pressing and an increase in DA in the NAC and central amygdala. This was not observed with the stimulus paired with saline. Furthermore Gratton and Wise (1994), using *in vivo* voltammetry, found a changing pattern of DA responsiveness that evolved within and across self-administration sessions. On the first day of the experiment, a neutral stimulus had no effect, but there was a large and sustained decrease in DA after cocaine injection. From the second day, DA increased in the presence of the previously neutral stimulus before cocaine was delivered. Following cocaine, DA decreased below then quickly returned to baseline levels. The decrease in DA in the presence of cocaine is surprising, given that dialysis studies usually show an increase. However, dialysis studies also typically involve longer time frames of analysis than voltammetry, presumably reflecting a more integrated response. In any case, this study indicates that the NAC DA response was modulated by stimuli paired with the drug, by the acquisition of the cocaine self-administration behavior, and by the occasional administration of a priming dose at the initiation of a session.

Also noteworthy is the investigation of Bowman, Aigner, and Richmond (1995) of electrophysiological responses of neurons in the ventral striatum of monkeys working to obtain cocaine or juice. Monkeys were trained to release a lever on a variable-ratio schedule. A distinctive visual stimulus indicated whether juice or cocaine would be delivered on each trial. In addition, the stimulus brightened during the trial as responding progressed toward the reinforcer delivery. Whereas the conditioned stimuli for each reinforcer elicited increased responses of neurons in the ventral striatum, all stimuli paired with cocaine were effective over a greater proportion of the trial, even during the earliest component. The stimulus associated with juice tended to alter firing immediately preceding reinforcement. Thus, there may have been a greater generalization of the conditioned neuronal responses to cocaine than to juice in animals, showing comparable behavior in relation to the two reinforcers. These data demonstrate that cocaine can facilitate conditioned physiological changes in brain.

In light of the recent data implicating glutamate in sensitization, it will be interesting to learn whether, in addition to these DA effects, conditioned psychomotor stimulant effects will be linked to glutamate systems. It may be that the conditioned effects observed so far either are secondary to changes in glutamate systems, reflect a critical role of DA in the conditioned effects of cocaine, or, as is most likely, occur in both neurotransmitter systems (and others as well).

NEUROANATOMY OF CONDITIONING AND CONDITIONED DRUG EFFECTS

Since conditioning and sensitization can be very persistent, it might be useful to explore the substrates of other well-investigated forms of long-term neuroplasticity. A great deal of research has been done to establish the mechanisms of memory in humans and nonhuman primates. The recognition that multiple forms of memory exist initially arose from observations of amnestic patients with damage to the medial temporal lobes following surgery for temporal lobe epilepsy (Scoville & Milner, 1957; Zola-Morgan & Squire, 1993). Research with these individuals led to the notion that there are at least two forms of memory: representational and habit memory. Representational memory is conscious, forms quickly, and dissipates with time (Squire, Knowlton, & Musen, 1993; Zola-Morgan & Squire, 1993). Habit memory is nonconscious, develops gradually, and is related to "the changed probability that a specific stimulus or specific environment will evoke a specific response, purely as a result of the reinforcement contingencies operating in the situation" (Mishkin & Petrie, 1984, p. 288). Habit memory requires repeated exposures to stimulus–response–reinforcement contingencies and does not appear to degrade with time. The neuroanatomical substrates of these types of memory also differ. Habit memory is thought to involve cortical-striatal interactions (Mishkin & Appenzeller, 1987; Wang, Aigner, & Mishkin, 1990) as well as the cerebellum (Thompson, 1986). Representational memory utilizes cortical input to the perirhinal, parahippocampal, and hippocampal cortices (Mishkin & Appenzeller, 1987; Squire & Zola-Morgan, 1991).

It was initially thought that the amygdala played a role in representational memory (Mishkin & Appenzeller, 1987) and cross-modal learning (Murray & Mishkin, 1985). However, many effects reported in early studies are now attributed to damage to the cortex surrounding the amygdala (Squire & Zola-Morgan, 1991; Zola-

Morgan, Squire, Clower, & Rempel, 1993). The amygdala's role in appetitive and aversive conditioning has also been studied for many years (e.g., Cador, Robbins, & Everitt, 1989; Davis, 1992; LeDoux, 1992). After initial observations that amygdala-lesioned monkeys did not exhibit species-typical responses to environmental stimuli (Weiskrantz, 1956), it was postulated that they would also have an impaired capacity to modify their behavior based on changing behavioral contingencies. The amygdala has been shown to be critically involved in the development of conditioned fear responses in a manner independent of the stimulus modality used for conditioning. The lateral nucleus of the amygdala receives convergent sensory information from all modalities from thalamic and cortical afferent inputs (LeDoux, 1992). The central nucleus provides the output of the system with efferent projections to hypothalamus, brain stem, and spinal cord that modulate autonomic and behavioral responses (Davis, 1992; Davis, Hitchcock, & Rosen, 1987; LeDoux, 1992). Whereas the amygdala is necessary for the acquisition of fear conditioning, the cortex appears to play a role in its extinction, providing behavioral flexibility (LeDoux, 1992; LeDoux, Romanski, & Xagoraris, 1989). Thus, following lesions of the visual cortex, fear conditioning to a visual cue could not be extinguished following 1 month of unreinforced exposure to the conditioning stimulus. Along with a variety of other data, these findings have been interpreted to indicate a role for the amygdala in fear conditioning, presumably through its "emotional valencing" of stimuli. Once established, amygdala responses persist and cortical influences are required to modify subsequent behavior (LeDoux, 1992; Rolls, 1992). With regard to appetitive conditioning, Everitt et al. (1992) showed that lesions of the basolateral amygdala impaired responding maintained by a conditioned reinforcer and abolished conditioned place preference (CPP). Under a variety of conditions, amygdala lesions disrupted appetitive conditioning. The amygdala may serve as a link between reinforcement-related stimuli and motor output (Everitt & Robbins, 1992; Robbins, Cador, Taylor, & Everitt, 1989). Moreover, direct connections of the amygdala with the ventral striatum, VTA, thalamus, cortex, and brain stem nuclei offer avenues of potential influence over many behavioral responses.

There is accumulating evidence for the involvement of limbic cortical structures and the amygdala in conditioned responses to cocaine. Brown and Fibiger (1992) found increases in *c-fos* expression in the cingulate cortex, claustrum, septum, paraventricular nucleus of the thalamus, and amygdala when rats were exposed to an environment previously paired with cocaine. Recently, Grant et al. (1996) found that glucose metabolism selectively increased in several cortical areas, in the cerebellum, and in certain medial temporal regions, including the amygdala in cocaine abusers exposed to conditioned stimuli associated with cocaine that elicited reports of "craving." This occurred even though the unconditioned stimulus (cocaine) produces a decrease in glucose metabolism of cocaine users. Thus, the conditioned stimuli may be activating circuits distinct from those specifically related to the drug's pharmacological effects. If, in fact, the amygdala is involved in development of drug-related conditioned responses, and if its responses remain intact even under changing environmental consequences and contingencies (LeDoux, 1992; LeDoux et al., 1989; Rolls, 1992), then it may play a role in the persistence of conditioning and, in turn, the high susceptibility to relapse that characterizes drug abusers. In addition, other limbic circuits that relate to memory functions may also be important for triggering of drug craving and/or relapse.

This, of course, is not the entire story. Our data (Post & Weiss, 1988) and those of Brown and Fibiger (1993) Indicate that even in the absence of the amygdala, cocaine-conditioned responses can emerge. In our study, amygdala lesions failed to block conditioned sensitization produced by 3 days of cocaine treatment. Brown and Fibiger (1993) found that amygdala lesions did not inhibit conditioned loco-motion to saline but did interfere with CPP. Other structures (e.g., the striatum) may be able to compensate for the amygdala or may be involved in parallel with conditioning related to cocaine, or perhaps both. This reiterates the notion that con-ditioned (and unconditioned) drug effects are likely to involve multiple and chang-ing neuronal pathways. Additionally, as indicated above, many changes in gene and protein expression are found within the dorsal striatum following chronic stim-ulant administration (Graybiel et al., 1990; Hyman, 1996; Moratella et al., 1996). Therefore, this structure may be involved in long-term neural adaptations to drugs of abuse. Since the striatum is thought to be the seat of habit memory and less sus-ceptible to forgetting and may play a role in compulsive behaviors (Rosenberg, Dick, O'Hearne, & Sweeney, 1997), it may be that some of the long-term behav-ioral consequences of cocaine abuse relate to this system.

In summary, sensitization to a subject of cocaine's behavioral effects is widely reported across species and paradigms. Although not all sensitization depends upon conditioning, it can be a major factor. Stimuli paired with cocaine can pro-duce behavioral and physiological responses similar to the drug and enhance the drug's effects. Investigation of the circuitry underlying sensitization has focused on the mesolimbic DA (and glutamate) systems, but other regions have been im-plicated in drug-associated conditioning as well. Some of these areas have been linked to different forms of neural plasticity, including learning and memory. The data suggest that with repeated drug use, changes in the brain become more wide-spread, so that areas not affected at all on initial administration may be recruited.

TOLERANCE AND SENSITIZATION
IN COCAINE ABUSE

Thus, there is convincing evidence for both tolerance and sensitization to the behavioral effects of cocaine. Taken at face value, these data present different views of the changes that can occur with cocaine abuse. We suggest that, rather than being mutually exclusive, tolerance and sensitization can develop simultane-ously or sequentially, or perhaps both, and may develop differentially to different behavioral effects. Without question, a complete understanding of the sequelae of cocaine abuse should incorporate both phenomena. Our conceptualization of the roles of tolerance and sensitization in cocaine abuse relies, in addition to neurobiology, on basic principles of operant and respondent conditioning. Operant conditioning refers to the modulation and control of what is usually referred to as voluntary behavior by its consequences. Drugs can control voluntary behavior through operant conditioning. Respondent or classical conditioning refers to a change in the likelihood that a response, voluntary or involuntary, will be elicited by an originally neutral stimulus as a consequence of repeated pairing with an unconditioned stimulus. For drugs, both "drug-like" or "drug-opposite" conditioned responses can develop (see Eikelboom & Stewart, 1982).

We propose that initiation of drug use is under operant control of the consequences arranged by factors such as peer pressure or medical circumstance in a situation in which drug is available. Subsequent drug use comes under operant control of the drug itself, which serves as a reinforcer to maintain and strengthen drug seeking and drug taking. As drug use continues, tolerance may develop to the reinforcing and positive subjective effects, thus necessitating higher doses and/or increasing frequency of drug use to achieve and maintain the effect. Concurrently, through respondent conditioning, both interoceptive and exteroceptive stimuli associated with drug administration come to elicit a variety of neurochemical and behavioral responses. Some of these may be "drug-opposite" and contribute to tolerance development. Others are "drug-like" and appear to have the dual effect of activating the nervous system and sensitizing the organism to certain drug effects. As drug use continues, more and more stimuli are paired with the drug and come to elicit the sensitized response. By this mechanism cocaine abuse may be facilitated, even with reinforcing and positive subjective effects diminished or absent (see Mello, 1977). It follows then, that by the time treatment is invoked, extinction of responses to all possible cocaine-associated cues is exceedingly difficult if not impossible. Moreover, even if all conditioned responses could be abolished through extinction, Pavlov (1960/1927) observed that, once established, conditioned reflexes will sooner or later reemerge at their original strength (spontaneous recovery). In addition, with brief periods of abstinence, tolerance to cocaine is lost and a more powerful drug effect can again be achieved, providing an additional mechanism by which cocaine abuse is perpetuated. The long-term nature of learning, and its role in sensitization, accounts for the persistence of phenomena such as craving and relapse.

This view of the sequelae of cocaine abuse has the virtue of incorporating tolerance and sensitization into the larger context of learning theory. In this way, it may have generality beyond cocaine abuse. Cocaine is not unique in the findings of both tolerance and sensitization and the important role of environmental conditions in both. Similar effects have been known for many years for morphine (Siegel, 1977). A process, such as conditioning, that is operative across drugs of abuse would help account for the generality of sensitization across drugs. Importantly, cross-sensitization has been reported between stimulants and opiates (Kalivas, 1985; Vezina & Stewart, 1990), implying common mechanisms. The VTA has been established as a common substrate for the sensitizing effects of opiates and stimulants, albeit through different neurochemical mediators (e.g., Kalivas, 1985; Kalivas, Duffy, Abhold, & Dilts, 1988; Vezina & Stewart, 1990). Nevertheless, cross-sensitization may also reflect a common learning mechanism that could be important in polydrug abuse. Interestingly, cross-tolerance, usually suggestive of a common pharmacological mechanism, has been reported not to develop between cocaine and morphine (Wood & Emmett-Oglesby, 1986).

Of course, much of this scenario is speculative. One of the limitations that has not been adequately addressed empirically is the demonstration of both tolerance and sensitization in the same organism. A study by Gui-Hua and Woolverton (unpublished) provides data on this issue. Two groups of rats ($N = 9$/group) were trained in a food-reinforced drug discrimination paradigm to discriminate cocaine (8.0 mg/kg, i.p.) from saline. After the initial cumulative dose–response function for cocaine was determined, one group was given cocaine under the same regimen used by Wood and Emmett-Oglesby (1986: 20 mg/kg, every 8 h, i.p.) for 7 days. The other group was given saline (1 ml/kg, every 8 h, i.p.) under identical conditions. The cocaine dose–response function was redetermined at various points after the cocaine regimen. In addition, locomotor behavior (rearing, sniffing, gnawing, licking, grooming, and ambulation) was observed after saline or 8.0 mg/kg cocaine three times: before discrimination training, before, and after the chronic regimen. As had been reported, the cocaine regimen significantly shifted the dose–response function for DS effects to the right (Figure 1, upper panel; $p < .05$), whereas saline treatment did not (data not shown). That is, tolerance developed to the DS effects of cocaine and had begun to dissipate after 2 weeks without cocaine. Additionally, both groups of rats were more sensitive to cocaine-induced ambulation (Figure 1; lower panel; $p < .05$) and rearing ($p < .05$, data not shown) after cocaine discrimination training. Sensitivity was not further changed by the chronic regimen. Thus, discrimination training (8.0 mg/kg cocaine every other day) sensitized rats to the motor effects of cocaine, whereas the chronic regimen made them tolerant to the DS effects. That is, it appears that both tolerance and sensitization can develop to different effects of cocaine within the same animal. It may be that some behaviors and/or neural systems are more likely to develop tolerance and others sensitization. A similar conclusion was reached by French and Izenwasser (1996). Obviously, additional data need to be collected on this point.

A complete understanding of these disparate changes in sensitivity to cocaine requires other issues to be resolved. It is important to consider that the conditions of drug exposure under which tolerance or sensitization have been studied are quite different. Sensitization has been found to develop with intermittent injections, whereas tolerance has been reported with more frequent or even continuous exposure to cocaine. Indeed, it may be that somewhere along the transition from intermittent to continuous cocaine, the effect of chronic administration changes from sensitization to tolerance (Reith, Benuck, & Lajtha, 1987). Additionally, most regimens that have been used do not reflect the progression to cocaine abuse in humans (i.e., a more intermittent early pattern toward more continuous use, still separated by periods of drug abstinence). Parametric investigation of the effect of

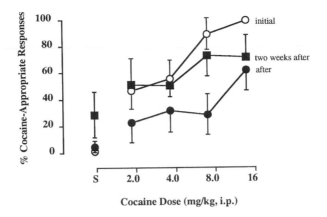

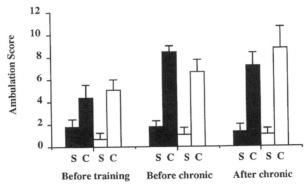

FIGURE 5.1   Changes in sensitivity to the effects of cocaine in rats. Top panel: Tolerance to the discriminative stimulus effects of cocaine. Dose–response functions were determined after training rats to discriminate 8.0 mg/kg cocaine (initial), after a chronic regimen of cocaine injection (8.0 mg/kg, i.p., 3 times/day for 1 week), and 2 weeks after repeated cocaine injections had stopped. Bottom panel: Locomotor effects of saline (S) and 8.0 mg/kg cocaine (C) in the same rats before training the cocaine discrimination, before the chronic regimen, and after the chronic regimen. Solid bars represent data from rats that received the chronic regimen of cocaine; open bars are from rats that received injections of saline under the same regimen (see text). In both panels, vertical lines represent the SEMs.

exposure conditions on changes in sensitivity to the effects of cocaine is needed. It may be, for example, that sensitization can develop to the reinforcing effect of cocaine, but we haven't yet established the conditions. Indeed, it has been reported that preexposure to cocaine under conditions that sensitize rats to its motor effects can enhance acquisition of cocaine self-administration, arguably because the animals were sensitized to the reinforcing effect of cocaine (Horger, Shelton, & Schenck, 1990). It has also been reported that rats can be sensitized to the effects of cocaine in a CPP paradigm (Shippenberg & Heidbreder, 1995). It may also be significant that both tolerance and sensitization have been studied, almost entirely, using noncontingent drug exposure (i.e., cocaine administered by the experimenter). The contingency relationship has been reported to be important in sensitivity to the lethal effects of cocaine (Dworkin, Volkmer, & Dworkin, 1988) and may be a determinant of changes in sensitivity. Since cocaine administration is almost always contingent on behavior in humans, the development of sensitization needs to be examined when cocaine is self-administered by the subject (see Hooks, Duffy, Striplin, & Kalivas, 1994).

Similar concerns can be raised with regard to central nervous system (CNS) mechanisms. In contrast to the extensive literature assessing the neurobiology of sensitization to cocaine, there has been little effort to examine the CNS mechanisms of tolerance (see, e.g., Wood & Emmett-Oglesby, 1987; Katz, Griffiths, Sharpe, De Souza, & Witkin, 1993). This needs to be remedied. In addition, mechanisms that mediate tolerance need to be distinguished from those that mediate sensitization and from epiphenomena. For example, Terwilleger et al. (1991) reported similar changes in G-proteins and cAMP in the brains of animals given continuous morphine and those given intermittent cocaine. Those two regimens have been reported in other studies to produce tolerance and sensitization, respectively, suggesting that the reported CNS changes are not specifically related to either tolerance or sensitization but may represent changes induced by any form of chronic drug exposure. It is extremely important to design studies that directly relate any CNS changes to tolerance and/or sensitization. One approach would be to use conditioning paradigms as discussed earlier. A CNS change that occurs in sensitized animals but not in nonsensitized animals following the same cocaine exposure seems more likely to be a mechanism of sensitization. Similarly, Woolverton et al. (1978a) found that tolerance developed to the effects of cocaine in animals given drug before, but not after, a behavioral session. This sort of paradigm might prove useful for isolating mechanisms related to tolerance.

It is also crucial to determine whether the changes in sensitivity to cocaine that have been described in animals occur in humans. There are a variety of reasons why it is difficult to demonstrate tolerance or sensitization in humans, among them ethical concerns that arise with laboratory studies of chronic cocaine in humans, unreliable data obtained from self-reports of users, and the confound of polydrug abuse. With regard to tolerance, although acute tolerance to the effects of cocaine has been reported, it remains an open question whether more long-lasting tolerance of the type described in rats in the studies of Emmett-Oglesby and colleagues develops in humans. Sensitization in humans has not been unequivocally demonstrated, although it has been demonstrated in other primates. One of the strongest arguments that has been made is that stimulant-induced psychosis, once established, can be retriggered by a low dose of drug long after last drug use (Sato, Chen, Yakiyama, & Otsuki, 1983). With regard to CNS changes, Volkow et al. (1996) used positron emission tomography (PET) to visualize the brains of human cocaine users compared to drug-naive subjects. The binding of raclopride, a competitive D_2 receptor antagonist, was decreased following administration of methylphenidate, a DA-potentiating drug. In cocaine users, the efficacy of methylphenidate in displacing raclopride was reduced as compared to cocaine-naive subjects. Furthermore, there were regional differences as a function of drug history, the most prominent being a decrease in raclopride binding in the thalamus of cocaine abusers relative to controls. These data support not only the notion that some systems may become tolerant to the drug's effects (indicated by a decreased efficacy of methylphenidate to displace raclopride), while others may be sensitized, but also that additional and changing neuronal substrates may be part of the process of cocaine abuse.

A substantial percentage of the population is exposed to drugs, but only a small portion become drug abusers. If, in fact, tolerance and sensitization play a major role in drug abuse, individual differences in the development of tolerance and sensitization should be linked to individual differences in susceptibility to drug abuse. There has been a growing interest in investigation of those factors that affect differences in individual responsivity to drugs, including tolerance and sensitization. Some of this research was alluded to earlier (e.g., Pierce et al., 1996). Other work is seeking to uncover the experiential (Nader & Reboussin, 1994), molecular (Perisco, Bird, Gabbay, & Uhl, 1996), and neuroendocrine (Goeders & Guerin, 1994, 1996; Piazza et al., 1993) bases of individual differences in drug intake. Investigation of the determinants of behavioral responsivity, and how their interplay affects abuse susceptibility, seems a promising direction for future research. At the very least, studies of tolerance and sensitization can inform us about the nature and mechanisms of behavioral and neural plasticity. Ultimately, this may be of use in designing treatment strategies for drug abuse, and, more globally, in providing a greater understanding of the brain's ability to adapt to and modulate responses to a changing set of environmental contingencies.

REFERENCES

Ambre, J. J., Belknap, S. M., Nelson, J., Ruo, T. I., Shin, S. G., & Atkinson, A. J. (1988). Acute tolerance to cocaine in humans. *Clinical Pharmacology and Therapeutics, 44,* 1–8.

Anagnostaras, S., & Robinson, T. (1996). Sensitization to the psychomotor stimulant effects of amphetamine: Modulation by associative learning. *Behavioral Neuroscience, 110,* 1397–1414.

Badiani, A., Browman, K., & Robinson, T. (1995). Influence of novel versus home environments on sensitization to the psychomotor stimulant effects of cocaine and amphetamine. *Brain Research, 674,* 291–298.

Balster, R. L., & Schuster, C. R. (1973a). A comparison of *d*-amphetamine, *l*-amphetamine and methamphetamine self-administration in rhesus monkeys. *Pharmacology, Biochemistry and Behavior, 1,* 67–71.

Bell, K., & Kalivas, P. (1996). Context-specific cross sensitization between systemic cocaine and intra-accumbens AMPA infusion in rats. *Psychopharmacology, 127,* 377–383.

Beninger, R. J., & Herz, R. S. (1986). Pimozide blocks establishment but not expression of cocaine-produced environment-specific conditioning. *Life Sciences, 38,* 1425.

Bowman, E., Aigner, T., & Richmond, B. (1995). Neural signals in the monkey ventral striatum related to motivation for juice and cocaine rewards. *Journal of Neurophysiology, 75,* 1061–1073.

Brown, E., & Fibiger, H. (1993). Differential effects of excitotoxic lesions of the amygdala on cocaine-induced conditioned locomotion and conditioned place preference. *Psychopharmacology, 113,* 123–130.

Brown, E. E., & Fibiger, H. C. (1992). Cocaine-induced conditioned locomotion: Absence of associated increases in dopamine release. *Neuroscience, 48,* 621–629.

Byck, R. (1974). *The cocaine papers, (by Sigmund Freud).* New York: Stonehill Publishing Co.

Cador, M., Bijou, Y., & Stinus, L. (1995). Evidence of a complete independence of the neurobiological substrates for the induction and expression of behavioral sensitization to amphetamine. *Neuroscience, 65,* 385–395.

Cador, M., Robbins, T., & Everitt, B. (1989). Involvement of the amygdala in stimulus-reward associations: Interaction with the ventral striatum. *Neuroscience, 30,* 77–86.

Carney, J. M., Llewellyn, M. E., & Woods, J. H. (1976). Variable interval responding maintained by intravenous cocaine and ethanol injections in the rhesus monkey. *Pharmacology, Biochemistry and Behavior, 5,* 577–582.

Childress, A. R., McLellan, A. T., Ehrman, R. N., & O'Brien, C. P. (1987). *Extinction of conditioned responses in abstinent cocaine or opioid users* (pp. 189–195). Washington, DC: U.S. Government Printing Office.

Davis, M. (1992). The role of the amygdala in conditioned fear. In J. Aggleton (Ed.), *The amygdala: Neurobiological aspects of emotion, memory, and mental dysfunction* (pp. 255–306). New York: Wiley-Liss.

Davis, M., Hitchcock, J., & Rosen, J. (1987). Anxiety and the amygdala: Pharmacological and anatomical analysis of the fear-potentiated startle paradigm. In G. Bower (Ed.), *The psychology of learning and motivation* (pp. 263–305). San Diego: Academic Press.

Downs, A. W., & Eddy, N. B. (1932). The effect of repeated doses of cocaine on the rat. *Journal of Pharmacology and Experimental Therapeutics, 46,* 199.

Dworkin, S. M., Volkmer, C., & Dworkin, S. I. (1988). Toxic consequences of cocaine are augmented by noncontingent drug administration. *Society for Neuroscience Abstracts, 14,* 961.

Ehrman, R. N., Robbins, S. J., Childress, A. R., & O'Brien, C. P. (1992). Conditioned responses to cocaine-related stimuli in cocaine abuse patients. *Psychopharmacology, 107,* 523–529.

Eikelboom, R., & Stewart, J. (1982). Conditioning of drug-induced physiological responses. *Psychological Review, 89,* 507–528.

Emmett-Oglesby, M. W., & Lane, J. D. (1992). Tolerance to the reinforcing effects of cocaine. *Behavioural Pharmacology, 3,* 193–200.

Emmett-Oglesby, M. W., Peltier, R. L., Depoortere, R. Y., Pickering, C. L., Hooper, M. L., Gong, Y. H., & Lane, J. D. (1993). Tolerance to self-administration of cocaine in rats: Time course and dose–response determination using a multi-dose method. *Drug and Alcohol Dependence, 32,* 247–256.

Everitt, B., & Robbins, T. (1992). Amygdala-ventral striatal interactions and reward-related processes. In J. Aggleton (Ed.), *The amygdala: Neurobiological aspects of emotion, memory, and mental dysfunction* (pp. 401–429). New York: Wiley-Liss, Inc.

Falk, J., & Feingold, D. (1987). Environmental and cultural factors in the behavioral action of drugs. In H. Meltzer (Ed.), *Psychopharmacology: The third generation of progress* (pp. 1503–1510). New York: Raven Press.

Fischman, M. W., Schuster, C. R., Javaid, J., Hatano, Y., & Davis, J. (1985). Acute tolerance development to the cardiovascular and subjective effects of cocaine. *Journal of Pharmacology and Experimental Therapeutics, 235,* 667–682.

Foltin, R. W., & Fischman, M. W. (1991). Smoked and intravenous cocaine in humans: Acute tolerance, cardiovascular and subjective effects. *Journal of Pharmacology and Experimental Therapeutics, 257,* 247–261.

Fontana, D., & Post, R. A. P. (1993). Conditioned increases in mesolimbic dopamine overflow by stimuli associated with cocaine. *Brain Research, 629,* 31–39.

French, D., & Izenwasser, S. (1996). Tolerance and sensitization to cocaine are mediated via independent mechanisms. *Society for Neuroscience Abstracts, 22,* 921.

Gay, G. R., Inaba, D. S., Sheppard, C. W., & Neumeyer, J. A. (1975). Cocaine: History, epidemiology, human pharmacology and treatment: A perspective on a new debut for an old girl. *Clinical Toxicology, 8,* 149–178.

Goeders, N. E., & Guerin, G. F. (1994). Non-contingent electric footshock facilitates acquisition of intravenous cocaine self-administration in rats. *Psychopharmacology, 114,* 63–70.

Goeders, N. E., & Guerin, G. F. (1996). Role of corticosterone in intravenous cocaine self-administration in rats. *Neuroendocrinology, 64,* 337–348.

Grant, S., London, E., Newlin, D., Villemagne, V., Liu, X., Contoreggi, C., Phillips, R., Kimes, A., & Margolin, M. (1996). Activation of memory circuits during cue-elicited craving. *Proceedings of the National Academy of Sciences, 93,* 12040–12045.

Gratton, A., & Wise, R. (1994). Drug- and behavior-associated changes in dopamine-related electrochemical signals during intravenous cocaine self-administration in rats. *Journal of Neuroscience, 14,* 4130–4146.

Graybiel, A., Moratella, R., & Robertson, H. (1990). Amphetamine and cocaine induce drug-specific activation of the c-fos gene in striosome-matrix and limbic subdivisions of the striatum. *Proceedings of the National Academy of Sciences, 87,* 6912–6916.

Hammer, R. P., Egilmez, Y., & Emmett-Oglesby, M. W. (1997). Neural mechanisms of tolerance to the effects of cocaine. *Behavioural Brain Research, 84,* 225–239.

Heidbreder, C., Babovic-Vuksanovic, D., Shoaib, M., & Shippenberg, T. (1995). Development of behavioral sensitization to cocaine: Influence of kappa opioid receptor agonists. *Journal of Pharmacology and Experimental Therapeutics, 275,* 150–163.

Henry, D., & White, F. (1995). The persistence of behavioral sensitization parallels enhanced inhibition of nucleus accumbens neurons. *Journal of Neuroscience, 15,* 6287–6299.

Hodos, W. (1961). Progressive-ratio as a measure of reward strength. *Science, 134,* 943–944.

Holtzman, S. G. (1990). Discriminative stimulus effects of drugs: Relationship to potential for abuse. In M. W. Adler & A. Cowan (Eds.), *Testing and evaluation of drugs of abuse: Modern Methods in Pharmacology,* (Vol. 6, pp. 193–210). New York: Wiley-Liss.

Hooks, M. S., Duffy, P., Striplin, C., & Kalivas, P. W. (1994). Behavioral and neurochemical sensitization following cocaine self-administration. *Psychopharmacology, 115,* 265–272.

Hope, B., Nye, H., Kelz, M., Self, D., Iadarola, M., Nakabeppu, Y., Duman, R., & Nestler, E. (1994). Induction of long-lasting AP-1 complex composed of altered Fos-like proteins in brain by chronic cocaine and other chronic treatments. *Neuron, 13,* 1235–1244.

Horger, B. A., Shelton, K., & Schenck, S. (1990). Preexposure sensitizes rats to the rewarding effects of cocaine. *Pharmacology, Biochemistry and Behavior, 37,* 707–711.

Hyman, S. (1996). Addiction to cocaine and amphetamine. *Neuron, 16,* 901–904.

Jaffe, J. H. (1970). Drug addiction and drug abuse. In L. S. Goodman & A. Gilman (Eds.), *The pharmacological basis of therapeutics* (pp. 276–313). New York: The Macmillan Co.

Jaffe, J. H. (1985). Drug addiction and drug abuse. In A. G. Gilman, L. S. Goodman, T. W. Rall, & F. Murad (Eds.), *The pharmacological basis of therapeutics* (pp. 532–581). New York: Macmillan.

Jaffe, J. H. (1990). Drug addiction and drug abuse. In A. G. Gilman, T. W. Rall, A. S. Nies, & P. Taylor (Eds.), *The pharmacological basis of therapeutics* (pp. 522–573). New York: Pergamon Press.

Kalant, H., LeBlanc, A. E., & Gibbins, B. J. (1971). Tolerance to, and dependence on, some non-opiate psychotropic drugs. *Pharmacological Reviews, 23,* 135–191.

Kalivas, P. W. (1985). Sensitization to repeated enkephalin administration into the ventral tegmental area of the rat. II. Involvement of the mesolimbic dopamine system. *Journal of Pharmacology and Experimental Therapeutics, 235,* 544–550.

Kalivas, P. (1993). Neurotransmitter regulation of dopamine neurons in the ventral tegmental area. *Brain Research Reviews, 18,* 75–113.

Kalivas, P., Duffy, P., Abhold, R., & Dilts, R. (1988). Sensitization of mesolimbic dopamine neurons by neuropeptides and stress. In P. Kalivas & C. Barnes (Eds.), *Sensitization in the nervous system* (pp. 119–143). Caldwell, NJ: Telford.

Kalivas, P., & Duffy, P. (1993). Time course of extracellular dopamine and behavioral sensitization to cocaine. I. Dopamine axon terminals. *Journal of Neuroscience, 13,* 266–275.

Kalivas, P., & Stewart, J. (1991). Dopamine transmission in the initiation and expression of drug- and stress-induced sensitization. *Brain Research Reviews, 16,* 223–244.

Kalivas, P. W., & Duffy, P. (1989). Similar effects of daily cocaine and stress on mesocorticolimbic dopamine neurotransmission in the rat. *Biological Psychiatry, 25,* 913–928.

Karler, R., Calder, L., Chaudhry, I., & Turkanis, S. (1989). Blockade of "reverse tolerance" to cocaine and amphetamine by MK-801. *Life Sciences, 45,* 599–606.

Katz, J. L., Griffiths, J. W., Sharpe, L. G., De Souza, E. B., & Witkin, J. M. (1993). Cocaine tolerance and cross-tolerance. *Journal of Pharmacology and Experimental Therapeutics, 264,* 183–192.

King, G., Joyner, C., Lee, T., Kuhn, C., & Ellinwood, E. Jr. (1992). Intermittent and continuous cocaine administration: Residual behavioral states during withdrawal. *Pharmacology, Biochemistry and Behavior, 43,* 243–248.

Koob, G. F., & Bloom, F. E. (1988). Cellular and molecular mechanisms of drug dependence. *Science, 242,* 715–723.

Kumor, K. M., Sherer, M., Thompson, L., Cone, E., Mahaffey, J., & Jaffe, J. H. (1988). Lack of cardiovascular tolerance during intravenous cocaine infusions in humans volunteers. *Life Science, 42,* 2063–2071.

Kumor, K. M., Sherer, M., Gomez, J., Cone, E., & Jaffe, J. H. (1989). Subjective response during continuous infusion of cocaine. *Pharmacology, Biochemistry and Behavior, 33,* 443–452.

LeDoux, J. (1992). Brain mechanisms of emotion and emotional learning. *Current Opinions in Neurobiology, 2,* 191–198.

LeDoux, J. (1992). Emotion and the amygdala. In J. Aggleton (Ed.), *The amygdala: Neurobiological aspects of emotion, memory and mental dysfunction* (pp. 339–351). New York: Wiley-Liss, Inc.

LeDoux, J., Romanski, L., & Xagoraris, A. (1989). Indelibility of subcortical emotional memories. *Journal of Cognitive Neuroscience, 1,* 238–243.

Li, D. H., Depoortere, R. Y., & Emmett-Oglesby, M. W. (1994). Tolerance to the reinforcing effects of cocaine in a progressive ratio paradigm. *Psychopharmacology, 116,* 326–332.

Maldonado-Irizarry, C., Parsons, L., Markou, A., Smith, D., Koob, G., & Weiss, F. (1996). Involvement of mesolimbic dopamine transmission in cocaine-seeking behavior elicited by drug-related environmental cues in rats. *ACNP Abstracts,* 226.

Malenka, R. C., & Nicoll, R. A. (1993). NMDA-receptor-dependent synaptic plasticity: Multiple forms and mechanisms. *Trends in Neuroscience, 16,* 521–527.

Mattingly, M. A., Rowlett, J. K., Ellison, T., & Rase, T. (1996). Cocaine-induced behavioral sensitization: Effects of haloperidol and SCH 23390 treatments. *Pharmacology, Biochemistry and Behavior, 53*(3), 481–486.

McKenna, M., & Ho, B. T. (1977). Induced tolerance to the discriminative stimulus effects of cocaine. *Pharmacology, Biochemistry and Behavior, 7,* 273–276.

Mello, N. K. (1977). Stimulus self-administration: Some implications for prediction of drug abuse liability. In T. Thompson & K. R. Unna (Eds.), *Predicting dependence liability of stimulant and depressant drugs.* Baltimore: University Park Press.

Mishkin, M., & Appenzeller, T. (1987). The anatomy of memory. *Science, 256,* 80.

Mishkin, M., & Petri, H. (1984). Memories and habits: Some implications for the analysis of learning and retention. In L. Squire & N. Butters (Eds.), *Neuropsychology of memory* (pp. 287–296). New York: Guilford Press.

Moratella, R., Ellbol, B., Vallejo, M., & Graybiel, A. (1996). Network-level changes in expression of inducible fos-jun proteins in the striatum during chronic cocaine treatment and withdrawal. *Neuron, 17,* 147–156.

Morris, R. G. M. (1989). Synaptic plasticity and learning: Selective impairment of learning in rats and blockade of long-term potentiation in vivo by the *N*-methyl-D-aspartate receptor antagonist AP5. *Journal of Neuroscience, 9,* 3040–3057.

Murray, E. A., & Mishkin, M. (1985). Amygdalectomy impairs crossmodal association in monkeys. *Science, 228,* 604.

Nader, M. A., & Reboussin, D. M. (1994). The effects of behavioral history on cocaine self-administration by rhesus monkeys. *Psychopharmacology, 115,* 53–58.

Nye, H., Hope, B., Kelz, M. B., Iadorola, M., & Nestler, E. (1995). Pharmacological studies of the regulation of chronic FOS-related antigen induction by cocaine in the striatum and nucleus accumbens. *Journal of Pharmacology and Experimental Therapeutics, 275,* 1671–1680.

O'Brien, C. P. (1996). Drug addiction and drug abuse. In J. G. Hardman, L. Limbird, P. B. Molinoff, R. W. Ruddon, & A. G. Gilman (Eds.), *The pharmacological basis of therapeutics* (pp. 557–577). New York: McGraw-Hill.

Pan, H. T., & Menacherry, S., Jr. (1991). Differences in the pharmacokinetics of cocaine in naive and cocaine-experienced rats. *Journal of Neurochemistry, 56,* 1299–1306.

Pavlov, I. P. (1960). *Physiological reflexes* (G. V. Anrep, Trans.). New York: Dover. (Original work published 1927)

Perisco, A. M., Bird, G., Gabbay, F. H., & Uhl, G. (1996). D2 dopamine receptor gene Taq1 A1 and B1 restriction fragment length polymorphisms: Enhanced frequencies in psychostimulant-preferring polysubstance abusers. *Biological Psychiatry, 40,* 776–784.

Piazza, P. V., Deroche, V., Demeuniere, J. M., Maccari, S., Lemoal, M., & Simon, H. (1993). Corticosterone in the range of stress-induced levels possesses reinforcing properties—implications for sensation-seeking behaviors. *Proceedings of the National Academy of Sciences* (USA), *90,* 11738–11742.

Peltier, R. L., Li, D. H., Lytle, D., Taylor, C. M., & Emmett-Oglesby, M. W. (1996). Chronic d-amphetamine or methamphetamine produces cross-tolerance to the discriminative and reinforcing stimulus effects of cocaine. *Journal of Pharmacology and Experimental Therapeutics, 277,* 212–218.

Pert, A., Post, R., & Weiss, S. (1990). Conditioning as a critical determinant of sensitization induced by psychomotor stimulants. In L. Erinoff (Ed.), *NIDA Research Monograph* (pp. 208–241), Washington, DC: Government Printing Office.

Petit, H., Pan, H-T., Parsons, L., & Justice Jr. J. (1990). Extracellular concentrations of cocaine and dopamine are enhanced during chronic cocaine administration. *Journal of Neurochemistry, 55,* 798–804.

Piazza, R., Deminiere, J., Le Moal, M., & Simon, H. (1989). Factors that predict individual vulnerability to amphetamine self-administration. *Science, 245,* 1511–1513.

Pierce, R., Bell, K., Duffy, P., & Kalivas, P. (1996). Repeated cocaine augments excitatory amino acid transmission in the nucleus accumbens only in rats having developed behavioral sensitization. *Journal of Neuroscience, 16,* 1550–1560.

Post, R., Weiss, S., & Smith, M. (1995). Sensitization and kindling: Implications for the evolving neural substrates of PTSD. In M. Friedman, D. Charney, & A. Deutch (Eds.), *Neurobiology and clinical consequences of stress from normal adaptation to PTSD* (pp. 203–224). New York: Raven Press.

Post, R. M. (1980). Intermittent versus continuous stimulation: Effect of time interval on the development of sensitization or tolerance. *Life Sciences, 26,* 1275–1282.

Post, R. M. (1981). Central stimulants: Clinical and experimental evidence on tolerance and sensitization. In Y. Israel, F. Glaser, H. Kalant, R. E. Popham, W. Schmidt, & R. Smart (Eds.), *Research advances on alcohol and drug problems* (pp. 1–65). New York: Plenum Press.

Post, R. M. (1983). Contel NR. Human and animal studies of cocaine: Implications for development of behavioral pathology. In I. Creese (Ed.), *Stimulants: Neurochemical, behavioral, and clinical perspective* (pp. 169–203). New York: Raven Press.

Post, R. M., Kopanda, R. T., & Black, K. E. (1976). Progressive effects of cocaine on behavior and central amine metabolism in rhesus monkeys: Relationship to kindling and psychosis. *Biological Psychiatry, 11,* 403–419.

Post, R. M., & Weiss, S. R. B. (1988). Sensitization and kindling: Implications for the evolution of psychiatric symptomatology. In P. W. Kalivas & C. D. Barnes (Eds.), *Sensitization of the nervous system* (pp. 257–291). Caldwell, NJ: Telford Press.

Post, R. M., Weiss, S. R. B., & Pert, A. (1988). Cocaine-induced behavioral sensitization and kindling: Implications for the emergence of psychopathology and seizures. In P. W. Kalivas & C. B. Nemeroff (Eds.), *The mesocorticolimbic dopamine system* (pp. 292–308). New York: New York Academy of Science.

Reith, M. (1986). Effect of repeated administration of various doses of cocaine and WIN35,065-2 on locomotor behavior in mice. *European Journal of Pharmacology, 130,* 65–72.

Reith, M. E., Benuck, M., & Lajtha, A. (1987). Cocaine disposition in the brain after continuous or intermittent treatment and locomotor stimulation in mice. *Journal of Pharmacology and Experimental Therapeutics, 243,* 281–287.

Robbins, T., Cador, M., Taylor, J., & Everitt, B. (1989). Limbic-striatal interactions in reward-related processes. *Neuroscience Biobehavioral Reviews, 13,* 155–162.

Robinson, T. E., & Berridge, K. C. (1993). The neural basis of drug craving: An incentive-sensitization theory of addiction. *Brain Research Reviews, 18,* 247–291.

Robinson, T. E., & Becker, J. B. (1986). Enduring changes in brain behavior produced by chronic amphetamine administration: A review and evaluation of animal models of amphetamine psychosis. *Brain Research Reviews, 11,* 157–198.

Rolls, E. (1992). Neurophysiology and functions of the primate amygdala. In J. Aggleton (Ed.), *The amygdala: Neurobiological aspects of emotion, memory, and mental dysfunction* (pp. 143–166). New York: Wiley-Liss Inc.

Rosenberg, D. R., Dick, E. L., O'Hearn, K. M., & Sweeney, J. A. (1997). Response-inhibition deficits in obsessive compulsive disorder: an indicator of dysfunction in frontostriatal circuits. *Journal of Psychiatry and Neuroscience, 22,* 29–38.

Rowlett, J. K., Massey, B. W., Kleven, M. S., & Woolverton, W. L. (1996). Parametric analysis of cocaine self-administration under a progressive-ratio schedule in rhesus monkeys. *Psychopharmacology, 125,* 361–370.

Sato, M., Chen, C. C., Akiyama, K., & Otsuki, S. (1983). Acute exacerbation of paranoid psychotic state after long-term abstinence in patients with previous methamphetamine psychosis. *Biological Psychiatry, 18,* 429–440.

Schwarzschild, M. A., Cole, R. I., & Hyman, S. E. (1997). Glutamate, but not dopamine, stimulates stress-activated protein kinase and AP-1-mediated-transcription in striatal neurons. *Journal of Neuroscience, 17,* 3455–3466.

Scoville, W., & Milner, B. (1957). Loss of recent memory after bilateral hippocampal lesions. *Journal of Neurology, Neurosurgery and Psychiatry, 20,* 11–21.

Segal, D., & Schukit, M. (1983). Animal models of stimulant-induced psychosis. In I. C (Ed.), *Stimulants: Neurochemical behavioral and clinical aspects* (pp. 131–167). New York: Raven Press.

Self, D., & Nestler, E. (1995). Molecular mechanisms of drug reinforcement and addiction. *Annual Review of Neuroscience, 18,* 483–496.

Shippenberg, T. S., & Heidbreder, Ch. (1995). Sensitization to the conditioned rewarding effects of cocaine: Pharmacological and temporal characteristics. *Journal of Pharmacology and Experimental Therapeutics, 273,* 808–815.

Shuster, L., Yu, G., & Bates, A. (1977). Sensitization to cocaine stimulation in mice. *Psychopharmacology, 52,* 185–190.

Siegel, S. (1977). Morphine tolerance acquisition as an associative process. *Journal of Experimental Psychology, 3,* 1–13.

Silverman, P. (1990). Direct dopamine agonist-like activity conditioned to cocaine. *Pharmacology, Biochemistry and Behavior, 37,* 231–234.

Silverman, P., & Bonate, P. (1997). Role of conditioned stimuli in addiction. In B. Johnson & J. Roache (Ed.), *Drug addiction and its treatment: Nexus of neuroscience.* Philadelphia: Lippincott-Raven.

Silverman, P., & Ho, B. (1981). Persistent behavioral effect of apomorphine in 6-hydroxydopamine-lesioned rats. *Nature, 294,* 475–477.

Squire, L., Knowlton, B., & Musen, G. (1993). The structure and organization of memory. *Annual Review of Psychology, 44,* 453–495.

Squire, L., & Zola-Morgan, S. (1991). The medial temporal lobe memory system. *Science, 253,* 1380–1386.

Stafford, D., & Branch, M. N. (1996). Relations between dose magnitude, subject sensitivity, and the development of tolerance to cocaine-induced behavioral disruptions in pigeons. *Behavioural Pharmacology, 7*, 324–333.

Steiner, H., & Gerfen, C. (1996). Dynorphin opioid inhibition of cocaine-induced D1 dopamine receptor-mediated immediate-early gene expression in the striatum. *Journal of Comparative Neurology, 353*, 200–212.

Stewart, J., & Badiani, A. (1993). Tolerance and sensitization to the behavioral effects of drugs. *Behavioural Pharmacology, 4*, 289–312.

Stewart, J., de Wit, H., & Eikelboom, R. (1984). Role of unconditioned and conditioned drug effects in the self-administration of opiates and stimulants. *Psychological Review, 91*, 251–268.

Tatum, A. L., & Seevers, M. H. (1929). Experimental cocaine addiction. *Journal of Pharmacology and Experimental Therapeutics, 36*, 401.

Terwilliger, R., Beitner-Johnson, D., Sevarino, K., Crain, S., & Nestler, E. (1991). A general role for adaptations in G-proteins and cyclic AMP system in mediating the chronic actions of morphine and cocaine on neuronal function. *Brain Research, 548*, 100–110.

Thompson, D. M. (1977). Development of tolerance to the disruptive effects of cocaine on repeated acquisition and performance of response sequences. *Journal of Pharmacology and Experimental Therapeutics, 203*, 294–302.

Thompson, R. (1986). The neurobiology of learning and memory. *Science, 233*, 941–947.

Ungerstedt, U. (1971a). Postsynaptic supersensitivity after 6-hydroxydopamine induced degeneration of the nigro-striatal dopamine system. *Acta Physiologica Scandinavia, Supplementum, 367*, 69–93.

Ungerstedt, U. (1971b). Striatal dopamine release after amphetamine or nerve damage revealed by rotational behavior. *Acta Physiologica Scandinavia, Supplementum, 367*, 49–68.

Vezina, P., & Stewart, J. (1990). Amphetamine administered into the ventral tegmental area but not to the nucleus accumbens sensitizes rats to systemic morphine. *Brain Research, 516*, 99–106.

Volkow, N. D., Wang, G. J., Fowler, J. S., Logan, J., Gatley, S. J., Hitzeman, R., Chen, A. D., & Pappas, N. (1996). Decreased striatal dopaminergic responsivity in detoxified cocaine abusers. *Nature*.

Wang, J., Aigner, T., & Mishkin, M. (1990). Effects of neostriatal lesions on visual habit formation in rhesus monkeys. *Society for Neuroscience Abstracts, 16*, 617.

Washton, A. M., & Gold, M. S. (1984). Chronic cocaine abuse: Evidence for adverse effects on health and functioning. *Psychiatry Annals, 14*, 733.

Washton, A. M., & Gold, M. S. (1986). Recent trends in cocaine abuse: A review from the National Hotline, "800-COCAINE". *Advances in Alcohol and Substance Abuse, 6*, 31–47.

Weiskrantz, L. (1956). Behavioral changes associated with ablation of the amygdaloid complex in monkeys. *Journal of Comparative and Physiological Psychology, 49*, 381–391.

Weiss, F., Paulus, M., Lorang, M., & Koob, G. (1992). Increases in extracellular dopamine in the nucleus accumbens by cocaine are inversely related to basal levels: Effects of acute and repeated administration. *The Journal of Neuroscience, 12*, 4372–4380.

Weiss, S. R. B., Post, R. M., Pert, A., Woodward, R., & Murman, D. (1989). Context-dependent cocaine sensitization: Differential effect of haloperidol on development versus expression. *Pharmacology, Biochemistry and Behavior, 34*, 655–661.

White, F., Hu, X-T, Zhang, X-F., & Wolf, M. (1995). Repeated administration of cocaine or amphetamine alters neuronal responses to glutamate in the mesoaccumbens dopamine system. *Journal of Pharmacology and Experimental Therapeutics, 273*, 445–454.

Wikler, A. (1973). Dynamics of drug dependence: Implications of a conditioning theory for research and treatment. In S. Fisher & A. M. Freedman (Eds.), *Opiate addiction: Origins and treatment* (pp. 7–21). Washington, DC: VH Winston.

Wolf, M., Dahlin, S., Hu, X-T., & Xue, C-J. (1995). Effects of lesions of prefrontal cortex, amygdala, or fornix on behavioral sensitization to amphetamine: Comparison with *N*-methyl-D-aspartate antagonists. *Neuroscience, 69*, 417–439.

Wolf, M., & Jeziorski, M. (1993). Coadministration of MK-801 with amphetamine, cocaine or morphine prevents rather than transiently masks the development of behavioral sensitization. *Brain Research, 613*, 291–294.

Wood, D. M., & Emmett-Oglesby, M. W. (1986). Characteristics of tolerance, recovery from tolerance and cross-tolerance for cocaine used as a discriminative stimulus. *Journal of Pharmacology and Experimental Therapeutics, 237,* 120–125.

Wood, D. M., & Emmett-Oglesby, M. W. (1987). Evidence for dopaminergic involvement in tolerance to the discriminative stimulus properties of cocaine. *European Journal of Pharmacology, 138,* 155–157.

Wood, D. M., & Emmett-Oglesby, M. W. (1988). Substitution and cross-tolerance profiles of anorectic drugs in rats trained to discriminate the discriminative stimulus properties of cocaine. *Psychopharmacology, 95,* 364–368.

Wood, D. M., Lal, H., & Emmett-Oglesby, M. W. (1984). Acquisition and recovery of tolerance to the discriminative stimulus properties of cocaine. *Neuropharmacology, 23,* 1419–1423.

Woolverton, W. L. (1995). Comparison of the reinforcing efficacy of cocaine and procaine in rhesus monkeys responding under a progressive-ratio schedule. *Psychopharmacology, 120,* 296–302.

Woolverton, W. L., Kandel, D. A., & Schuster, C. R. (1978a). Tolerance and cross-tolerance to cocaine and *d*-amphetamine. *Journal of Pharmacology and Experimental Therapeutics, 205,* 525–536.

Woolverton, W. L., Kandel, D. A., & Schuster, C. R. (1978b). Effects of repeated administration of cocaine on schedule-controlled behavior in rats. *Pharmacology, Biochemistry and Behavior, 9,* 327–337.

Woolverton, W. L., & Nader, M. A. (1990). Experimental evaluation of the reinforcing effects of drugs. In M. W. Adler & A. Cowan (Eds.), *Testing and evaluation of drugs of abuse* (pp. 165–192). New York: Wiley-Liss, Inc.

Yanagita, T. (1973). An experimental framework for evaluation of dependence liability of various types of drug in monkeys. *Proceedings of the 5th International Congress on Pharmacology, 1,* 7–17.

Young, A. M., & Herling, S. (1986). Drugs as reinforcers: Studies in laboratory animals. In S. R. Goldberg & I. P. Stolerman (Eds.), *Behavioral analysis of drug dependence* (pp. 9–67). Orlando, FL: Academic Press.

Zola-Morgan, S., & Squire, L. (1993). Neuroanatomy of memory. *Annual Review of Neuroscience, 16,* 547–563.

Zola-Morgan, S., Squire, L., Clower, R., & Rempel, N. (1993). Damage to the perirhinal cortex but not the amygdala exacerbates memory impairment following lesions to the hippocampal formation. *The Journal of Neuroscience, 13,* 251–265.

6

PRECLINICAL EVALUATION
OF PHARMACOTHERAPIES
FOR COCAINE ABUSE

GAIL WINGER

Department of Pharmacology
University of Michigan Medical Center
Ann Arbor, Michigan

INTRODUCTION

The weight of preclinical evaluation of pharmacotherapies for cocaine abuse falls most heavily on two procedures: that measuring the ability of potential therapeutic drugs to modify the discriminative stimulus effects of drugs of abuse, and that measuring a similar ability to modify the reinforcing stimulus effects of drugs of abuse. The discriminative stimulus effects of drugs is thought to be relevant to the subjective effect of the drug in clinical situations (Bigelow & Preston, 1989; Holtzman, 1990; Spealman, 1992), whereas measures of the reinforcing effect of drugs of abuse may indicate more directly the behavioral or pharmacological basis of drug taking by humans. The evidence for this comes from data that demonstrate that most drugs that are abused by humans serve as reinforcing stimuli in animals (Griffiths, Bigelow, & Henningfield, 1980).

Although these procedures have been used extensively to test the ability of potential therapeutic compounds to modify relevant properties of cocaine, evaluation of the validity of the procedures is limited by the fact that no effective therapy for cocaine abuse currently exists. There are, however, medications that are effective in the treatment of opioid abuse. It is possible, therefore, to evaluate the preclinical tests using opioid drugs and effective medications, and to compare these data with those obtained in studies of cocaine.

Two approaches that have been successful in reducing illicit opioid use by humans are (a) to administer a drug that can substitute for the abused opioid (i.e., an opioid agonist), and (b) to administer a drug that is a selective antagonist of the abused opioid (i.e., an opioid antagonist). Methadone is the prototypic opioid agonist treatment drug and is the option most used today for the treatment of opioid abuse. Its mechanism of therapeutic action is probably to provide a sustained opioid agonist effect that reduces the likelihood that an opioid abuser will continue to seek and take illicit opioid drugs. Methadone has several pharmacological properties that appear critical to its effectiveness as a treatment drug. One is that it is bioavailable following oral administration. Because its onset of action is gradual with this route, it is less subject to the patterns of compulsive abuse than is intravenously delivered heroin. Methadone also has a long duration of agonist action; discontinuation of methadone in dependent individuals results in more prolonged but less intense withdrawal signs. Furthermore, methadone can be given once daily and have maintained effectiveness in reducing heroin abuse. The relatively long duration of action also means that the receptor occupation by methadone is maintained for a considerable period of time, during which the person is neither "high," as he or she would be immediately following iv heroin administration, nor "sick," which he or she would be several hours following iv heroin administration, but is more likely to remain in a stable state that is more conducive to productive function in the community (Dole, Nyswander, & Kreek, 1991).

The opioid buprenorphine is also being evaluated as a treatment for opioid abuse, and it has been studied more extensively than methadone in animal models. Buprenorphine is a low efficacy μ-agonist and, as such, it may not be able to provide a full opioid response. Although this means that buprenorphine acts as an antagonist of opioids that are full agonists in a particular response system, the data in humans in which buprenorphine has been compared with methadone indicate that these two drugs are reducing opioid abuse in these people by similar mechanisms (e.g., Bickel & Amass, 1995).

The prototypic opioid antagonist that is used in the treatment of heroin abuse is naltrexone. Naltrexone is a competitive antagonist of μ-opioids such as heroin and methadone, and as such it produces a surmountable blockade of the effects of heroin. Its effects can be overcome by administration of larger doses of heroin, as has been demonstrated experimentally, but this requires additional resources on the part of the addict and is rarely a problem in the population that uses naltrexone therapeutically. In situations where naltrexone administration can be enforced, it is effective and its effectiveness has encouraged the search for a similar antagonist of the reinforcing effects of cocaine.

As documented in other chapters of this book, cocaine's effects are thought to be primarily through blocking reuptake of dopamine into synaptic terminals, and the resultant increase in dopamine levels in critical areas of the brain is thought to be responsible for the reinforcing effects of the drug. Cocaine has several other effects, including a local anesthetic action and blockade of both serotonin and norepinephrine reuptake. Although there are data that indicate an involvement of serotonin and noradrenergic systems in the discriminative effects of cocaine (e.g., Callahan & Cunningham, 1995; Spealman, 1993, 1995a), most available information suggests that the actions on dopamine are by far the most important with respect to the abuse liability of this stimulant. Thus, the search for drugs that might be useful in treating cocaine abuse, using the models described for treatment of opioid abuse, has focused, to a large extent, on dopamine agonists and dopamine antagonists.

When investigators began studying the effects of dopamine agonists and antagonists on cocaine actions, only two types of dopamine receptors had been described, namely D_1 and D_2. Their characteristics were differentiated primarily on the basis of opposite effects on second messenger systems and on the relative affinity of various drugs for the two types. Since these early efforts, additional dopamine receptors have been identified using cloning methods, and there are currently five acknowledged dopamine receptor types. Two of these, the D_1 and the D_5 receptors, have apparently similar structures and effects on second messenger systems and are usually classified as D_1-like. Also, there are apparently few D_5 receptors in the brain, making them less relevant for the current discussion. The D_2, D_3, and D_4 receptor types have similar molecular biological properties and the classification of D_2-like is generally useful for these three types. The finer distinctions will become much more useful as pharmacological agents are developed that differentiate among these receptor types and help uncover their individual functions. This is beginning to occur with the D_2 and the D_3 types, but the selectivities of the currently available ligands are not very good. It is rare to find differences of more than two orders of magnitude between relative binding affinities at D_2 versus D_3 receptors with any of the compounds that are available at the present time.

Although the development of drugs that are more selective for dopamine receptor types will certainly move us a long way toward understanding whether the stimulus effects of cocaine are mediated selectively through action at one of the several dopamine receptor types, it should be noted that even drugs that differentiate well between the classical D_1 and D_2 types are not very different in their effects on cocaine's behavioral actions. The reasons for this may include poor pharmacological tools, inappropriate behavioral measures, or a true lack of a differential effect. It is unfortunate that research on the use of dopamine antagonists to reduce cocaine abuse tends to focus on splitting receptor type hairs than in attempting to understand the extant data and making certain that the models, tools, and hypotheses that are being used are, in fact, appropriate.

A great deal of information on the effects of opioid drugs, antidepressant drugs, and anticonvulsant drugs on cocaine use and abuse will go largely unreviewed in this chapter, despite the fact that some of these drugs have had some success in both preclinical and clinical studies. The early excitement surrounding their potential usefulness has been tempered considerably by the more negative results in carefully controlled clinical trials. A brief review of the exciting new information on the ability of antibodies to modify the effects of drugs is included at the end of this review.

DRUG DISCRIMINATION

Drug discrimination procedures involve training animals in an appetitively or aversively controlled operant procedure to use the interoceptive effect of an injected drug as a stimulus to control distribution of responding on two manipulanda. Following administration of an active dose of the training drug, responses on one of these manipulanda result in reinforcement. If a saline injection or no injection is given, responses on the other manipulandum result in reinforcement. Once established, this discrimination behavior has characteristics that make it useful for evaluating potential therapeutic drugs. Dose–effect curves (distribution of responses on the "drug-associated" lever as a function of drug dose) are easily generated. Drugs that antagonize the effects of the training drug typically produce a decrease in the potency of the training drug, shifting the dose–effect curve in a parallel fashion to the right. Agents that produce sustained agonist effects should have discriminative stimulus effects in common with the drug of abuse, with a slow onset and long duration of action. Ideally, they are also effective by the oral route of administration.

OPIOID DRUGS AND INTERACTIONS WITH POTENTIAL TREATMENT MEDICATIONS

Methadone and buprenorphine had discriminative stimulus effects in common with other μ-opioid agonists in both nonhuman primates and in rodents (e.g., Hoffmeister, 1988; Holtzman, 1979; Miksic, Sherman, & Lal, 1978; Schaefer & Holtzman, 1977; Shannon, Cone, & Gorodetzky, 1986; Young et al., 1984). Largely lacking are studies that demonstrate the aspects of the discriminative stimulus effects of methadone and buprenorphine that seem to make them effective treatment agents (i.e., a slow onset of opioid discriminative stimulus effects following oral administration, and a long duration of action). Very long duration of agonist effects of buprenorphine was reported in pigeons (France, Jacobson, & Woods, 1984), but in other species, the agonist effects appeared to be replaced rapidly by opioid antagonist effects (e.g., Winger & Woods, 1996).

Buprenorphine has been evaluated as a discriminative stimulus in humans and when the procedures were similar to those used in animals, it usually had stimulus properties in common with the μ-agonist hydromorphone (Preston et al., 1992). In humans trained to discriminate among three stimulus states—saline, hydromorphone, and pentazocine—buprenorphine produced nearly equal choice of the hydromorphone and pentazocine options (Preston & Bigelow, 1994; Preston et al., 1989).

Naltrexone served as a competitive antagonist of the discriminative stimulus effects of μ-agonists including morphine, buprenorphine, and fentanyl (e.g., Walker et al., 1994). An example of the interaction between naltrexone and opioid agonists is shown in Figure 1. This figure demonstrates that naltrexone's antagonism of the discriminative stimulus effects of opioid agonists could be overcome by increasing the dose of the agonists, and a series of rightward shifts in the agonist dose–response curves could be drawn as the dose of naltrexone was increased.

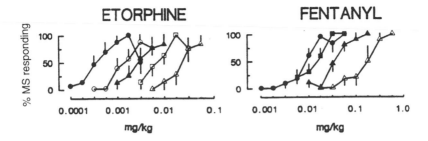

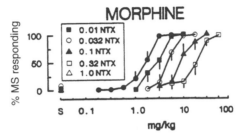

FIGURE 6.1   The effects of several doses of naltrexone (NTX) on the discriminative stimulus effects of the opioid agonists etorphine, fentanyl, and morphine in rats trained to discriminate 3.2 mg/kg morphine from saline. Ordinates: the percent of the total responses made on the morphine-appropriate lever. Abscissae: cumulative dose of each agonist in mg/kg. The closed circles represent the potency of the agonists when they were given alone. (Reprinted with permission from the *Journal of Pharmacology and Experimental Therapeutics, 271,* Walker, E. G., Makhay, M. M., House, J. D., and Young, A. M. In vivo apparent pA2 analysis for naltrexone antagonism of discriminative stimulus and analgesic effects of opiate agonists in rats, pp. 959–998, 1994.)

COCAINE AND INTERACTIONS WITH POTENTIAL TREATMENT MEDICATIONS

Dopamine Agonists

Drugs that block reuptake of dopamine (e.g., GBR-12909, mazindol, d-amphetamine, bupropion, and several cocaine analogs), produced cocaine-like discriminative stimulus effects in nonhuman primates (Balster et al., 1991; Kleven, Anthony, & Woolverton, 1990a; Mansbach & Balster, 1993; Spealman et al., 1991). However, drugs that act directly on dopamine receptors or drugs that act selectively and with high efficacy on the D_1-like (e.g., SKF 81297) or the D_2-like site (e.g., quinpirole or bromocriptine), either alone or together, did not produce a full cocaine-like stimulus in monkeys (Katz & Witkin, 1992a; Kleven et al., 1990a; Spealman, 1996; Spealman et al., 1991). Agonists with greater selectivity for the D_3 site, including 7-OH-DPAT, and PD 128907 also produced substantial but less than complete generalization to cocaine in squirrel monkeys at doses that suppressed responding to a considerable extent (Lamas et al., 1996; Spealman, 1996). However, the dopamine autoreceptor agonist PD 128483 produced a full cocaine-like discriminative stimulus in three of four rhesus monkeys (Vanover & Woolverton, 1994).

Rats that have been trained to discriminate cocaine tend to be more variable than monkeys in their responses to various dopamine agonists and antagonists. They generalized to dopamine reuptake inhibitors such as GBR 12909, nomifensine, and bupropion, but not to directly or indirectly acting dopamine receptor agonists such as bromocriptine and amantadine (Broadbent et al., 1991; Witkin et al., 1991). Witkin et al. (1991), however, found complete generalization between cocaine and the general dopamine agonist apomorphine. In rats, a partial D_1-like receptor agonist SKF 77434 resulted in cocaine-appropriate responding (Kantak, Edwards, & Spealman, 1995). The D_2-like agonist quinpirole also occasioned cocaine-approrpiate responding (Barrett & Appel, 1989; Callahan et al., 1991) and the partial D_1-like agonist SKF-38393 produced considerable but not complete cocaine-appropriate responding in some studies (Callahan et al., 1991; Witkin et al., 1991), but very little cocaine-appropriate responding in others (Barrett & Appel, 1989). Recent studies indicated that several novel dopamine agonists with selective effects on the D_3 receptor (PD 128907 and 7-OH-DPAT) had cocaine-like discriminative stimulus effects in rats at doses that suppressed rates of responding (Acri et al., 1995).

Dopamine Antagonists

Compounds that are selective antagonists at the D_1-like receptor, the D_2-like receptor, or both of these receptors all produce surmountable antagonism of the discriminative stimulus effects of cocaine. The D_1-like antagonists, SCH 23390, SCH 39166, and A-66359 each produced a 4- to 16-fold decrease in the potency of cocaine as a discriminative stimulus in rhesus monkeys (Kleven et al., 1988, 1990a; Vanover, Kleven, & Woolverton, 1991). There seemed to be a mutual antagonism between cocaine and the D_1-like antagonists in that, whereas cocaine reversed the rate-decreasing effect of the antagonists, the antagonists also reversed the discriminative stimulus effects of cocaine. Kleven et al. (1990a) also found a twofold surmountable antagonism of cocaine's discriminative stimulus effect following administration of the D_2-like antagonist haloperidol. In squirrel monkeys, Spealman et al. (1991) found that SCH 39166 as well as the D_2-like antagonist YM 09151-2 and the D_1-like/D_2-like antagonist *cis* flupenthixol produced a rightward, surmountable shift in the discriminative stimulus effects of cocaine. The partial D_2-like agonists terguride, SDZ 208-911, and SDZ 208-912, however, did not produce a marked antagonism of cocaine's discriminative stimulus effects in squirrel monkeys (Spealman, 1995b). The dopamine autoreceptor antagonist $(+)$ AJ 76, which has slight preferential affinity for the D_3 over the D_2 receptor site, attenuated the discriminative stimulus effects of cocaine across a narrow dose range in two of four monkeys. In the remaining monkeys, the rate-suppressing effects appeared to interfere with the evaluation, although cocaine was able to reverse some of these effects (Vanover, Piercey, & Woolverton, 1993).

Similar studies have been published using rats as subjects, although in these studies, cocaine dose–response curves have not been obtained in the presence of dopamine antagonists, so the nature of the interaction between cocaine and these drugs is less clear. SCH 23390 produced a substantial (50–70%) attenuation of the cocaine cue in rats (Barrett & Appel, 1989; Callahan et al., 1991; Witkin et al., 1991). Callahan et al. (1991) found that haloperidol also attenuated the discriminative stimulus effects of cocaine, although Barrett and Appel (1989) and Witkin et al. (1991) were among those who did not find haloperidol able to modify cocaine's discriminative effect. Other D_2-like antagonists such as spiperone produced only partial blockade of cocaine's cue in rats (Barrett & Appel, 1989; Callahan et al., 1991). A recent study investigated the effects of a dopamine autoreceptor antagonist on cocaine's discriminative stimulus effects in rats (Clark et al., 1995). This drug (DS121) did not produce a cocaine-like effect, and it did not antagonize the effects of cocaine.

SUMMARY

In preclinical studies, dopamine reuptake blockers mimic the discriminative stimulus effects of cocaine, but directly acting dopamine agonists tend to produce incomplete generalization, or variable results. It is not yet clear whether these agonists are of insufficient efficacy, or whether the cocaine cue involves more than stimulation of these receptors. There is consistent evidence that antagonists at both the D_1-like and the D_2-like dopamine receptor sites are effective in decreasing the potency of cocaine as a discriminative stimulus. However, the interaction between the dopamine antagonists and cocaine is quite unlike the interaction between opioid antagonists and opioids in this system. In the former instance, the dopamine antagonists have direct, rate-decreasing effects themselves that preclude their administration in increasingly large doses. Thus, they can produce only small (2- to 14-fold) decreases in the potency of cocaine as a discriminative stimulus. These effects of the dopamine antagonists can be reversed to some extent by cocaine, indicating a mutual antagonism between cocaine and dopamine antagonists. In the opioid system, the antagonists have little behavioral effect of their own at doses that modify a wide range of doses of the agonist drugs. Opioid antagonists can produce decreases of 100-fold or more in the potency of opioids as discriminative stimuli.

INTRAVENOUS DRUG SELF-ADMINISTRATION

Measuring rates of responding or number of injections taken by rodents or nonhuman primates under conditions in which iv drug administration is contingent on responses made by the animal is one of several methods for estimating the abuse liability of drugs. Others, including conditioned place preference and drug-induced decreases in threshold levels of electrical brain stimulation, have also been used extensively in preclinical evaluation of potential therapeutic agents. Results from these latter studies are frequently at variance with results from direct measures of reinforcing effects, a situation that raises some interesting questions. Space limitations, however, preclude consideration of any but the iv model of the reinforcing effects of drugs.

We are extremely fortunate to have a recent and thorough review by Mello and Negus (1996) of the effects of various pharmacotherapeutics on behavior maintained by cocaine and by opioids. That review includes an excellent discussion of the dose–effect curves generated by drugs that serve as reinforcers, and how these curves can be modified by presession administration of potential treatment agents. Suffice it to say here that low doses of reinforcing drugs produce little behavioral output. As the dose is increased, behavior increases as well, probably due to a dose-related increase in the reinforcing effects of the drug, until a maximum is reached. With further increases in dose, behavior decreases, due to negative feedback of administered drug on the behavior required to produce administration. Ideally, the effect of a potential therapeutic medication is evaluated on a range of doses of the stimulant or opioid, so that the nature of the dose–response curve change can be evaluated. Practically, however, this can be difficult, especially in rats where the ascending limb of the dose–response curve seems particularly difficult to define.

It is important to know whether the medication being evaluated is having specific effects on drug-maintained responding or is having more general effects on behavior. An ideal treatment compound is one that decreases only drug-taking behavior, allowing more productive behaviors to increase. In many studies of the effects of medications on drug self-administration, this evaluation is made by determining the effect of the medication on behavior maintained by a reinforcer in addition to the drug of interest. The other reinforcer is usually food, which, in some of the more interesting studies, is available to the same experimental animal in the same paradigm in which drug is available. The aim is to identify a medication that reduces drug self-administration while leaving food-maintained responding intact. Although using food as a control may not answer all the questions raised about the specificity of the treatment medication, having a control of this type provides much needed information about the direct effect of the medication on behavior in general.

OPIOIDS

Opioid Agonists

Methadone, unfortunately, has been used infrequently as a pretreatment in studies of opioid self-administration. One of the best studies was published by Griffiths, Wurster, and Brady (1976). These investigators allowed baboons to make a mutually exclusive choice between an injection of heroin or delivery of food every 3 h throughout the day. When the animals were selecting each reinforcer equally frequently, an infusion of 8.3 mg/kg/24 h of methadone was initiated for as long as 14 days. This treatment had the effect of reducing the choice of heroin and increasing the choice of food, and this differential was maintained throughout the period of methadone administration. In other studies of the effects of methadone on opioid self-administration there is less evidence of a selective suppression. Harrigan and Downs (1981) and Mello, Bree, and Mendelson (1983) were both unable to produce suppression of heroin self-administration in rhesus monkeys by chronic administration of methadone without also producing behavioral toxicity, which included decreased food intake, psychomotor and respiratory depression, and death. Jones and Prada (1975) reported that methadone initially suppressed morphine self-administration in dogs, but the behavior gradually returned over a 2-week period of methadone infusion.

Two of the studies described above that evaluated the effects of methadone on this behavior also studied the effects of chronic infusions of buprenorphine. Both Mello et al. (1983) and Harrigan and Downs (1981) reported that buprenorphine reduced self-administration of μ-opioids. Mello et al. (1983) found that, in contrast to methadone, buprenorphine spared food-reinforced behavior. Harrigan and Downs (1982) did not indicate the specific nature of buprenorphine's effects, but apparently did not observe the toxicity with this drug that they found with methadone. Winger, Skjoldager, and Woods (1992) found that with acute administration, buprenorphine was more potent in reducing alfentanil-maintained responding than in suppressing cocaine-maintained responding. In more recent work (Winger & Woods, 1996), a clear rightward shift in alfentanil and heroin dose–response curves was observed, suggesting that, under conditions of acute administration, buprenorphine suppresses the reinforcing effects of opioids through an opioid antagonist effect. As noted above, this is not the mechanism that appears to be relevant to the pharmacotherapeutic action of buprenorphine in humans. Whether the difference is due to acute versus chronic administration conditions, route of administration, species, or test condition is unfortunately unclear.

Opioid Antagonists

The effect of an antagonist on behavior maintained by an opioid depends on the dose of the opioid being used to maintain behavior. When large doses are used, the effect of an antagonist is to increase the amount of behavioral output; with doses of agonist at or below those that maintain peak responding, the effect of an antagonist is to decrease behavior. The ability of opioid antagonists such as naltrexone or quadazocine, an antagonist with a similar spectrum of action as naltrexone but with a different chemical structure, to block the reinforcing effects of opioids has been shown in a number of situations. Bertalmio and Woods (1989) and Winger et al. (1992) have shown the clearest examples of a competitive interaction between opioid agonists and antagonists in a self-administration paradigm, as shown in the bottom of Figure 2. Here, the ascending limb of the agonist dose–response curve

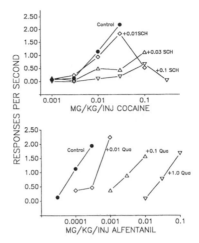

FIGURE 6.2   Top: the effects of several doses of the D_1-like antagonist SCH-39166 (SCH) on rates of responding maintained by intravenous cocaine in rhesus monkeys. Bottom: the effects of several doses of the opioid antagonist quadazocine (Qua) on rates of responding maintained by intravenous alfentanil using a similar paradigm in rhesus monkeys. Ordinates: rates of lever-press responding. Abscissae: doses in mg/kg/injection of cocaine (top) or alfentanil (bottom). (The alfentanil data are reprinted with permission from the *Journal of Pharmacology and Experimental Therapeutics, 261*, Winger, G. D., Skjoldager, P. and Woods, J. H. Effects of buprenorphine and other opioid agonists and antagonists on alfentanil- and cocaine-reinforced responding in rhesus monkeys. pp. 311–317, 1992.)

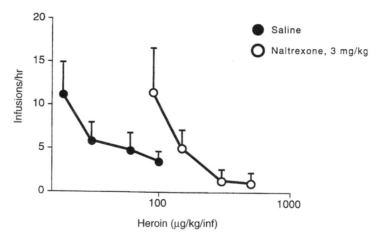

FIGURE 6.3   The effects of 3 mg/kg naltrexone on rates of heroin infusion in rats trained to self-administer a range of doses of heroin. (Reprinted from *Drug and Alcohol Dependence, 41*, Martin, T. J., Walker, L. E., Sizemore, G. M., Smith, J. E. and Dworkin, S. I. Within-session determination of dose-response curves for heroin self-administration in rats: Comparison with between-session determination and effects of naltrexone. pp. 93–100, 1996, with kind permission from Elsevier Science Ireland Ltd., Bay 15K, Shannon Industrial Estate, Co. Clare. Ireland.)

is shifted in a classically competitive manner to the right by presession administration of quadazocine. These data demonstrate that the reinforcing effects of alfentanil and presumably other μ-opioid agonists can be surmountably blocked by an opioid antagonist. In a procedure similar to that used by Winger et al. (1992), Martin et al. (1996) studied the effect of naltrexone on behavior maintained by heroin in rats. A decrease in the potency of heroin was shown (Figure 3) by a rightward shift in heroin's dose–response curve in the presence of naltrexone. In this case, the heroin doses were on the descending limb of the dose–response curve. Taken together, these studies indicate that both limbs of opioid dose–effect curves can be shifted to the right by opioid antagonists in rats and monkeys.

COCAINE

Dopamine Agonists

The ability of several dopamine agonists with various mechanisms of action to modify iv self-administration of cocaine have been evaluated. Cocaine itself has been evaluated in several studies. Skjoldager, Winger, and Woods (1993), Herling, Downs, and Woods (1979) and Mansbach and Balster (1993) each reported that cocaine decreased self-administration of cocaine in rhesus monkeys. Skjoldager et al. (1993) reported a very short duration of cocaine-induced suppression of cocaine self-administration. Mansbach and Balster found that cocaine decreased food-maintained responding at the same doses that decreased cocaine-maintained responding, and Herling et al. (1979) found similarly, that cocaine's effects on behavior, whether it was maintained by cocaine or by food, depended more on the rate of responding than on the event maintaining responding.

Acute doses of mazindol and d-amphetamine decreased rates of cocaine self-administration in rhesus monkeys at doses that also decreased similar rates of food-maintained responding (Mansbach & Balster, 1993). In several studies, the dopamine agonist was given continuously to the experimental animal by an iv drip. In each of these cases, when the infused dose was high, agonists produced psychomotor stimulation, reduction in food intake, and other signs of stimulant overdose. Interestingly, however, under these conditions, the agonists either did not affect cocaine self-administration (amantadine in baboons, Sannerud & Griffiths, 1988) or, in most animals, produced decreased food intake at the same doses that decreased cocaine self-administration (bromocriptine in rhesus monkeys, Kleven & Woolverton, 1990; mazindol in rhesus monkeys, Kleven & Woolverton, 1993). Bromocriptine was tested in acute doses in rats in an iv self-administration paradigm and found to produce dose-related, selective decreases in cocaine self-administration (Hubner & Koob, 1990). Despite the provocative results in rats that were at variance with data obtained in monkeys with bromocriptine, there have been no published attempts to resolve these differences, which may have involved obvious procedural differences.

The autoreceptor agonist, PD 128483 suppressed cocaine self-administration in rhesus monkeys in a manner that suggested it was enhancing the effect of cocaine

(Vanover & Woolverton, 1994). It was not itself self-administered, but it did have discriminative stimulus effects in common with cocaine in three of four monkeys, as mentioned above. Since a true autoreceptor agonist would act through presynaptic reduction of dopamine release and would not be expected to have any cocaine-like effects, the authors concluded that the profile of action of PD 128483 was more like that of a dopamine receptor partial agonist than of a dopamine autoreceptor agonist in their evaluation in the monkey.

One of the most interesting compounds to be evaluated as a substitution compound in the treatment of cocaine abuse is GBR 12909. As described above, GBR 12909 has stimulus properties in common with dopamine. Its mechanism of action is that of a dopamine reuptake blocker that may act in a competitive manner at the transporter site (Meiergerd & Schenk, 1994). It appears to bind tightly to the reuptake site and prevents binding of other dopamine reuptake inhibitors (Rothman et al., 1989). It has reinforcing effects in monkeys; it maintained rates that were somewhat below those that are maintained by cocaine in rhesus monkeys (Skjoldager et al., 1993) and were equal to those maintained by cocaine in squirrel monkeys (Bergman et al., 1989). It was found to initiate responding if relatively large doses were used, and to maintain responding at smaller doses in monkeys with a history of cocaine self-administration (Wojnicki & Glowa, 1996).

GBR 12909 was found to produce short-lived effects, similar to those of cocaine on cocaine self-administration by Skjoldager et al. (1993). Other investigators, however, have found that it had selective effects on cocaine self-administration that were not mimicked by other dopamine agonists, such as GBR 12935, WIN 35,428, or d-amphetamine (Glowa et al., 1995b). Under conditions in which monkeys could respond and receive iv cocaine under one stimulus condition, and respond and receive food under another stimulus condition, intermediate doses of GBR 12909 produced a decrease in behavior maintained by cocaine with little effect on behavior maintained by food (Glowa et al., 1995a). Large doses or injections of cocaine were more resistant to the suppressing effects of GBR 12909 than were smaller doses, suggesting that the larger injection doses of cocaine may have been able to override the substitution effect of GBR 12909. In subsequent research, Glowa et al. (1995b) found that chronic administration (12 days) of GBR 12909 did not lead to an attenuation of the ability of this drug to produce a selective decrease in cocaine-maintained responding. Administration of a single dose of a long-acting decanoate derivative of GBR 12909 suppressed cocaine-maintained responding selectively over food for 26 days (Glowa et al., 1996).

The partial D_2-like agonist terguride was found to produce a rightward shift in the cocaine reinforcement function in rats. Terguride did not, however, maintain self-administration behavior in rats (Pulvirenti et al., 1996).

In an extensive evaluation of interactions between 7-OH-DPAT and cocaine, Caine and Koob (1995) reported that the D_3 agonist increased the potency of cocaine as a reinforcer in rats. This was similar to the effect observed with the D_2-like agonist bromocriptine reported by Hubner and Koob (1990). The increased potency of cocaine was noted on both the ascending and descending limb of cocaine's dose–effect curve under several different experimental conditions. 7-OH-DPAT itself served as a reinforcer, although it appeared to be less efficacious than cocaine in progressive ratio tests, and it decreased food-reinforced responding at doses that enhanced the effects of cocaine.

Some of the dopamine agonists that have been evaluated in experimental models have also been tested for their ability to reduce cocaine use in human abusers. This research has been reviewed by Mendelson and Mello (1996) and by Wallace and Kosten (1996) and these reviews are summarized here. Double-blind studies of bromocriptine administration to human cocaine abusers indicated that bromocriptine reduced craving more than did placebo during cocaine withdrawal (Giannini, Baumgartel, & DiMarzio, 1987). Bromocriptine appeared to antagonize some cardiovascular effects of cocaine and to enhance others (Kumor, Sherer, & Jaffe, 1989). Despite the fact that bromocriptine produced less subjective effect than cocaine, it did not block cocaine's subjective effects, suggesting it might be of little benefit in the treatment of cocaine abuse (Preston et al., 1992). Similarly, mazindol did not attenuate cocaine's subjective effects or reduce reports of craving for cocaine (Preston et al., 1993). Amantadine did not reduce cocaine craving when studied in an appropriately controlled manner (Gawin et al., 1989). The antidepressant dopamine agonist bupropion did not reduce cocaine use by clients in a methadone-maintenance program (Margolin et al., 1995).

Dopamine Antagonists

Several dopamine antagonists (e.g., chlorpromazine, flupenthixol, pimozide, haloperidol, thioridazine, metoclopramide, and sulpiride) produced an increase in high-dose cocaine self-administration in rats and monkeys (see review by Mello & Negus, 1996, and introduction in Koob, Lee, & Creese, 1987). Some of these drugs (i.e., metoclopramide, sulpiride, pimozide, haloperidol) have more D_2-like than D_1-like antagonist effects. Others are relatively nonselective, acting at both receptor subtypes. This ability to increase cocaine self-administration when the dose of cocaine is on the descending limb of the dose–response curve has been taken as an indication of antagonism of cocaine's reinforcing effects. However, when the interaction between a range of doses/injection of cocaine has been used in the absence and presence of several doses of dopamine antagonists, it is clear that, rather than a simple blockade by the antagonist of cocaine's effects, there is mutual antagonism of these compounds for each other (Glowa & Wojnicki, 1996; Herling & Woods, 1980). Dopamine antagonists have marked, nonselective, rate-suppressing effects that can be partially reversed by cocaine, whereas cocaine's rate-suppressing effect can be partially reversed by dopamine antagonists. This rather complicated interaction makes interpretation of dose–response curves difficult and also makes it difficult to predict what effect these agents might have on illicit cocaine use in humans.

The relatively lower doses of cocaine that make up the ascending limb of the dose–response curve of self-administered drug might be more amenable to interactions with dopamine antagonists. In addition, the discovery of agents that act more selectively on either D_1-like or D_2-like dopamine receptors has greatly increased our ability to interpret interaction studies. The first tested D_1-like antagonist SCH 23390 produced only decreases in cocaine self-administration in rhesus monkeys (Woolverton, 1986). Woolverton and Virus (1989) compared the effects of SCH 23390 on behavior maintained by food with behavior maintained by the dose of cocaine that maintained peak levels of responding. The D_1-like antagonist produced decreases in both behaviors. Only occasionally was a selective effect of SCH 23390 observed on cocaine-maintained responding. Because cocaine doses were selected that maintained peak rates of responding, SCH 23390-induced decreases in cocaine-maintained responding could reflect a decrease in cocaine's reinforcing effects. The nonselective nature of the interaction indicated that this effect was unlikely to be limited to cocaine-maintained responding. When SCH 23390 was delivered by a continuous iv infusion, it produced a selective decrease in cocaine-maintained as compared with food-maintained responding in two of four rhesus monkeys (Kleven & Woolverton, 1990).

Glowa and Wojnicki (1996) evaluated SCH 23390 in a multiple schedule paradigm in which food availability and cocaine availability alternated. The effect of the D_1-like antagonist depended on the dose of cocaine that was used to maintain responding, but both food- and cocaine-maintained responding were altered in the same fashion by SCH 23390.

Bergman, Kamien, and Spealman (1990) established the reinforcing effects of several doses of cocaine in squirrel monkeys responding under a second-order schedule. Chronic administration of the D_1-like receptor antagonist SCH 39166 typically produced a rightward and, with larger doses, a downward shift in cocaine's effectiveness as a reinforcer. The maximum shift in cocaine's effects was sixfold, indicating a fairly narrow dose range across which SCH 39166's effects could be surmounted by increasing doses of cocaine. A similar evaluation was done by Winger (1994) with rhesus monkeys as subjects under a simple fixed ratio schedule of cocaine delivery. In this study, the primary effect of acute administration of SCH 39166 was to decrease the maximum rates of cocaine-maintained responding, and there was little evidence of the ability of cocaine to surmount the effects of D_1-like antagonism. This interaction is shown at the top of Figure 2. Similar behavior maintained by alfentanil was affected in a like manner by SCH 39166, although smaller doses were often necessary to suppress alfentanil-maintained as compared with cocaine-maintained responding.

In rats self-administering large doses of cocaine, D_1-like antagonists produced an increased number of cocaine injections (Caine & Koob, 1994; Hubner & Moreton, 1991; Koob et al., 1987). When the dose of injected cocaine produced maximum rates of responding under the schedule conditions employed, these same drugs (SCH 23390 and SCH 39166) only decreased cocaine-maintained responding. At a single, small dose of each antagonist, a 30–40% decrease in number of cocaine rewards was observed with no effect on the number of food rewards obtained (Caine & Koob, 1994). Larger doses decreased both behaviors. SCH 23390 produced dose-related decreases in breakpoints engendered by cocaine under a progressive ratio schedule (Depoortere et al., 1993; Hubner & Moreton, 1991). This indicated that some aspect of cocaine's effects was being antagonized by this D_1-like antagonist.

By virtue of having low efficacy at the D_1 site, SKF 38393—although frequently referred to as an agonist—has the capability of blocking the effects of agonists with greater efficacy at the D_1 receptor. Katz and Witkin (1992b) reported that SKF 38393 produced a decrease in the potency of cocaine as a reinforcer in squirrel monkeys. The ascending limb of the cocaine dose–response curve was shifted to the right approximately threefold in what appeared to be a surmountable fashion.

In most of the above studies, a D_2-like antagonist was compared to the D_1-like antagonist employed, and the effect was usually nearly the same although occasionally across a narrower dose range. Woolverton (1986) observed a very similar pattern of effect of the D_2-like antagonist primozide on cocaine self-administration as he found with SCH 23390, principally a decrease in responding. Pimozide decreased behavior maintained by both food and by the peak rate-maintaining dose of cocaine in rhesus monkeys (Woolverton & Virus, 1989). Glowa and Wojnicki (1996) found in their multiple schedule of either food- or cocaine-maintained responding that pimozide and chlorpromazine had effects similar to and as nonselective as those of SCH 23390. Eticlopride produced rightward and downward shifts in cocaine dose–response curves that were similar to those produced by D_1-like antagonists during chronic administration to squirrel monkeys (Bergman et al., 1990) and with acute administration to rhesus monkeys (Winger, 1994). Koob et al. (1987) found that spiperone also increased the number of cocaine injections taken by rats, but this effect occurred at only one dose of spiperone and appeared less robust than the effects of SCH 23390. Hubner and Moreton (1991) noted that spiperone increased the number of cocaine injections and decreased the breakpoint in the progressive ratio schedule in much the same way as SCH 23390. Caine and Koob (1994) observed that both eticlopride and spiperone increased the number of cocaine injections taken when a relatively "rich" schedule of cocaine administration was used, and decreased the number of injections taken when a "leaner" schedule was used. Both of these results paralleled findings with D_1-like antagonists, but the D_2-like antagonists more consistently suppressed food-maintained responding at doses that also suppressed cocaine-maintained responding.

The dopamine autoreceptor antagonist (+)-AJ 76 enhanced the behavioral effects of small doses of cocaine, but antagonized the effects of larger doses of cocaine in the rat (Piercey et al., 1992). Vanover et al. (1993) reported that (+)-AJ 76 produced a dose-related increase in number of cocaine injections taken by each of four monkeys. It did not alter the regular pattern of cocaine self-administration behavior, so the effect did not appear to be like that of extinction as much as like decreasing the reinforcing dose of cocaine. In rats, (+)-AJ 76 did not maintain iv self-administration behavior. It reduced the break point maintained by cocaine, similar to dopamine antagonists, but increased the time before animals obtained their first injection of cocaine, an effect like that produced by dopamine agonists

(Richardson et al., 1993). (+) AJ 76 thus appeared to reduce the effect of cocaine as a reinforcer in both rats and monkeys.

SUMMARY

Preclinical studies of the effects of opioid agonists on opioid-reinforced responding have not provided good models of how agonist therapy should modify cocaine-reinforced responding. The ideal result, one of a selective suppression of heroin's reinforcing effects by methadone, was revealed in only one study; the toxic effects of methadone appeared to predominate in the other studies. Buprenorphine was effective and selective against opioid-reinforced behavior in at least two studies, but the selectivity was due to an antagonist effect in at least one of the studies.

Despite the absence of a validated model, a great many studies of dopamine agonists on cocaine-maintained behavior have been published. The majority of dopamine agonists that have been evaluated in preclinical tests have been shown to be ineffective, and these data are nicely paralleled in negative clinical studies. GBR 12909 is unusual in that it has been shown in monkeys consistently to modify cocaine-maintained behavior while sparing similar food-maintained behavior that is occurring at similar rates and patterns. GBR 12909 has not been evaluated in human cocaine abusers.

Opioid antagonists are clearly effective in reducing the reinforcing effects of opioid agonists in self-administration paradigms, suggesting the validity of this model for demonstrating antagonist effects. Using this model, little preclinical evidence has been generated to indicate that dopamine antagonists, whether general or receptor selective, can produce an effect on cocaine-maintained responding in the absence of effects on behavior maintained by other reinforcers. Furthermore, the effect of these antagonists seems to be surprisingly similar no matter if they are selective at the D_1-like site, the D_2-like site, or act nonselectively. As was indicated in studies of the effects of these drugs on the discriminative stimulus effects of cocaine, some studies showed a rightward shift in cocaine's potency as a reinforcer following administration of dopamine antagonists. The shift was relatively small, compared to that shown by opioid antagonists on opioid-maintained responding. Large doses of the antagonists produced general decreases in behavior that could be reversed to a considerable extent if sufficient doses of cocaine were administered. Studies of the effects of D_3 antagonists have not progressed sufficiently to allow conclusions to be drawn, but there is some hope that actions at this site, or more selective actions at one of the other dopamine receptors will yield more promising results.

ANTIBODIES TO COCAINE

A totally new approach to the treatment of cocaine abuse may be required, one with better selectivity and fewer side effects than modification of the dopamine system. Antibodies that are directed specifically to cocaine are currently the best hope for this type of selectivity. The notion that it might be possible to generate an antigen–antibody reaction to drugs of abuse, and thereby produce a vaccine against specific drugs, was put forward by Bonese et al. (1974) many years ago. These investigators administered morphine-6-hemisuccinyl-bovine serum albumin (M-6 HS-BSA) conjugate to a rhesus monkey every 2 weeks for 20 weeks. The morphine-binding capacity of the animal in the IgG fraction of the serum increased during the period of immunization. Although the monkey's cocaine self-administration behavior continued unabated following this 20-week immunization period, its heroin-maintained behavior decreased to saline levels. It was necessary to increase the dose of heroin approximately 16-fold in order to recover opioid self-administration. The reduced sensitivity to heroin decreased rather rapidly following discontinuation of the M-6 HS-BSA administration.

More recently, Carrera et al. (1995) synthesized a hapten (GNC) based on cocaine and coupled to keyhole limpet hemocyanin (KLH). The aim was to produce an antibody–antigen reaction with cocaine that would result in a complex that would be unable to enter the central nervous system. Immunization with this compound in rats was accomplished on days 1, 21, and 35. The locomotor stimulant effects of cocaine were evaluated on days 3, 7, and 10 following the final administration of GNC-KLH. Animals who were actively immunized against cocaine showed a decreased locomotor stimulant response to 15 mg/kg cocaine that was significantly different from that shown by animals receiving KLH alone on days 3 and 7. Immunized animals also showed no sensitization to cocaine, as was demonstrated to some extent in the control animals receiving cocaine under this regimen. A lower concentration of cocaine in the brain was found in the immunized animals.

Fox and colleagues (1996) synthesized a cocaine antigen by conjugating the cocaine derivative, norcocaine, to bovine serum albumin. This conjugate was given to BALB/c mice, who responded with high serum titers of anticocaine antibodies. These antibodies bound to cocaine in the blood of the mice and caused the cocaine to be retained in the blood rather than entering the central nervous system (CNS). The inhibition of cocaine entry into the brain 30 sec after administration was dependent on the amount of cocaine administered, indicating that the antibody was saturable. The percent inhibition ranged from approximately 65% at a small dose of 0.018 mg/kg cocaine to approximately 30% at a dose of about 1.8 mg/kg cocaine. Despite the apparently small inhibitory effect of the antibody, iv administration of 4 mg produced a decrease in cocaine self-administration over a 5-day period in rats receiving 1 mg/kg/injection cocaine during daily sessions. The decline in behavior closely approximated that observed when saline was substituted for cocaine in these rats. As the antibody was cleared from the system, cocaine-maintained responding returned to control levels. This occurred over an 8- to 20-day period. Although the results of this study indicated that the antibody eliminated the reinforcing effects of 1 mg/kg/injected cocaine, reducing the dose of cocaine to 0.3 mg/kg/injection had a similar effect in the particularly lean schedule of cocaine delivery used. It's somewhat difficult to evaluate the full effectiveness of the antibody because a half-log unit dose reduction in cocaine was equivalent to full antagonism of cocaine's effect, but the results appeared promising.

The antibody studies described above make use of the fact that when cocaine is tied to an antibody, it is too large to enter the CNS and therefore cannot produce its reinforcing effects. A different approach to immunization against cocaine was taken by Landry et al. (1993). In this effort, a catalytic monoclonal antibody was synthesized that greatly increased the breakdown of cocaine in the blood, thereby reducing the amount of cocaine that entered the CNS. In addition, the catalytic nature of the antibody meant that once it had done its job of breaking down cocaine, it was freed to attack other cocaine molecules. The advantage of this system is that the antibody would not be depleted by repeated administration of cocaine. This antibody markedly increased the amount of cocaine required to produce seizure-induced death, although there was a similar amount of cocaine in the serum of rats at death whether or not they received the antibody (Mets et al., 1997). Rats with a history of cocaine and saline self-administration demonstrated a saline-like pattern of responding when they had been given the antibody and permitted to self-administer cocaine; the antibody did not alter rates or patterns of responding maintained by milk or the dopamine reuptake blocking buproprion (Mets et al., submitted).

CONCLUSIONS

Measures of the discriminative and reinforcing stimulus effects of cocaine have been used extensively to evaluate a number of potentially useful pharmacotherapies. It is difficult to validate these procedures because there are no pharmacotherapies currently available for cocaine abuse in humans, and therefore no way to compare effective therapies in preclinical and clinical studies. When direct comparisons can be made using the few dopamine agonists or uptake blockers that have been evaluated in both types of studies, preclinical information parallels the clinical data. These studies are generally negative in that none of the drugs that have been tested produce consistent decreases in cocaine use in humans, and they are generally unable to modify cocaine effects in animals without also modifying behavior maintained by other reinforcers. (GBR 12909, a dopamine uptake blocker, may be an exception to this latter rule, but it has not been evaluated in human drug abusers.) There is, therefore, no reason yet to doubt the validity of these models of preclinical pharmacotherapies with respect to dopamine agonists. It is difficult to be as positive about the models when noting their validity as indicators of preclinical effectiveness of opioid agonists against heroin abuse. Methadone, the most popular agonist treatment of heroin abuse, does not produce decreases in opioid effects in most of the preclinical models of opioid abuse, a fact that has been neither explained nor examined. Buprenorphine, another effective opioid agonist treatment, does have selective effects on opioid self-administratin in some preclinical studies, but these seem to be due to its antagonist, rather than its agonist effects. Thus, with respect to opioid agonist treatment, the preclinical models in current use appear to be flawed.

When examining antagonist treatment of cocaine and heroin abuse, the picture with respect to preclinical evaluation is quite different. Opioid antagonist therapy, which is effective in humans if compliance is ensured, is also effective and specific with respect to opioid agonist effects in preclinical measures of both discriminative and reinforcing stimulus effects. If these measures are, therefore, valid with respect to evaluation of antagonist therapy, then it appears as though dopamine antagonists are unlikely to be able to produce appropriate decreases in cocaine abuse in humans; they are unable to produce the large decreases in the potency of cocaine that are seen with opioid agonists in the presence of opioid antagonists. This is demonstrated clearly in Figure 2, where the effects of the D_1-like antagonist SCH 39166 on the reinforcing effects of cocaine are compared with the effects of the opioid antagonist quadazocine on the reinforcing effects of alfentanil. The inability of dopamine antagonists to decrease the potency of cocaine is correlated with the direct effects of the dopamine antagonists themselves. This may reflect the importance of dopamine in ongoing, normal behavior and suggests that it will be very difficult to produce selective disruption of cocaine's stimulus effects by antagonism of dopamine.

A novel approach to cocaine pharmacotherapy seems warranted, and the development of very selective antibodies, particularly catalytic antibodies, against cocaine may represent a superior approach. The interaction of these antibodies with cocaine should be very much like the interaction between opioid antagonists and heroin. The antibody should have little behavioral effect on its own, but should selectively decrease the potency of cocaine as a stimulus. Further development of these approaches is eagerly awaited, not only because they may represent an effective treatment mechanism, but also because they may allow us to validate some of the preclinical models that are designed to identify therapeutic drugs.

REFERENCES

Acri, J. B., Carter, S. R., Alling, K., Geter-Douglass, B., Dijkstra, D., Wikstrom, H., Katz, J. L., & Witkin, J. M. (1995). Assessment of cocaine-like discriminative stimulus effects of dopamine D3 receptor ligands. *European Journal of Pharmacology, 281,* R7–9.

Balster, R. L., Carroll, F. I., Graham, J. H., Mansbach, R. S., Rahman, M. A., Philip, A., Lewin, A. H., & Showalter, V. M. (1991). Potent substituted-3 beta-phenyltropane analogs of cocaine have cocaine-like discriminative stimulus effects. *Drug and Alcohol Dependence, 29,* 145–151.

Barrett, R. L., & Appel, J. B. (1989). Effects of stimulation and blockade of dopamine receptor subtypes on the discriminative stimulus properties of cocaine. *Psychopharmacology, 99,* 13–16.

Bergman, J., Madras, B. K., Johnson, S. E., & Spealman, R. D. (1989). Effects of cocaine and related drugs in nonhuman primates, III. Self-administration by selective dopamine D_1 and D_2 antagonists. *Journal of Pharmacology and Experimental Therapeutics, 251,* 150–155.

Bergman, J., Kamien, J. B., & Spealman, R. D. (1990). Antagonism of cocaine self-administration by selective dopamine D_1 and D_2 antagonists. *Behavioural Pharmacology, 1,* 355–363.

Bertalmio, A. J., & Woods, J. H. (1989). Reinforcing effect of alfentanil is mediated by mu opioid receptors: Apparent pA_2 analysis. *Journal of Pharmacology and Experimental Therapeutics, 251,* 455–460.

Bickel, W. K., & Amass, L. (1995). Buprenorphine treatment of opioid dependence: a review. *Experimental and Clinical Psychopharmacology, 3,* 477–489.

Bigelow, G. E., & Preston, K. L. (1989). Drug discrimination: Methods for drug characterization and classification. *NIDA Research Monograph, 92,* 101–122.

Bonese, K. F., Wainer, B. H., Fitch, F. W., Rothberg, R. M., & Schuster, C. R. (1974). Changes in heroin self-administration by a rhesus monkey after morphine immunisation. *Nature, 252,* 708–710.

Broadbent, J., Michael, E. K., Riddle, E. E., & Appel, J. B. (1991). Involvement of dopamine uptake in the discriminative stimulus effects of cocaine. *Behavioural Pharmacology, 2,* 187–197.

Caine, S. B., & Koob, G. F. (1995). Pretreatment with the dopamine agonist 7-OH-DPAT shifts the cocaine self-administration dose-effect function to the left under different schedules in the rat. *Behavioural Pharmacology, 6,* 333–347.

Caine, S. B., & Koob, G. F. (1994). Effects of D_1 and D_2 antagonists on cocaine self-administration under different schedules of reinforcement in the rat. *Journal of Pharmacology and Experimental Therapeutics, 270,* 209–218.

Callahan, P. M., Appel, J. B., & Cunningham, K. A. (1991). Dopamine D_1 and D_2 mediation of the discriminative stimulus properties of d-amphetamine and cocaine. *Psychopharmacology, 103,* 50–55.

Callahan, P. M., & Cunningham, K. A. (1995). Modulation of the discriminative stimulus properties of cocaine by 5-HT1B and 5-HT2C receptors. *Journal of Pharmacology and Experimental Therapeutics, 274,* 1414–1424.

Carrera, M. R. A., Ashley, J. A., Parsons, L. H., Wirsching, P., Koob, G. F., & Janda, K. D. (1995). Suppression of psychoactive effects of cocaine by active immunization. *Nature, 378,* 727–730.

Clark, D., Exner, M., Furmidge, L. J., Svensson, K., & Sonesson, C. (1995). Effects of the dopamine autoreceptor antagonist ($-$)-DS121 on the discriminative stimulus properties of d-amphetamine and cocaine. *European Journal of Pharmacology, 275,* 67–74.

Depoortere, R. Y., Li, D. H., Lane, J. D., & Emmett-Oglesby, M. W. (1993). Parameters of self-administration of cocaine under a progressive ratio schedule. *Pharmacology, Biochemistry and Behavior, 45,* 539–548.

Dole, V. P., Nyswander, M. E., & Kreek, M. J. (1966). Narcotic blockade. *Journal of Psychoactive Drugs, 23,* 232–.

Fox, B. S., Kantak, K. M., Edwards, M. A., Black, K. M., Bollinger, B. K., Botka, A. J., French, T. L., Thompson, T. L., Schad, V. C., Greenstein, J. L., Gefter, M. L., Exley, M. A., Swain, P. A., & Briner, T. J. (1996). Efficacy of a therapeutic cocaine vaccine in rodent models. *Nature Medicine, 2,* 1129–1132.

France, C. P., Jacobson, A. E., & Woods, J. H. (1984). Discriminative stimulus effects of reversible and irreversible opiate agonists: morphine, oxymorphazone and buprenorphine. *Journal of Pharmacology and Experimental Therapeutics, 230,* 652–657.

Gawin, F. H., Riordan, C., & Kleber, H. D. (1985). Methylphenidate treatment of cocaine abusers without attention deficit disorder: a negative report. *American Journal of Drug Alcohol Abuse, 11,* 193–197.

Gawin, F. H., Morgan, C., Kosten, T. R., & Kleber, H. D. (1989). Double-blind evaluation of the effect of acute amantadine on cocaine craving. *Psychopharmacology, 97,* 402–403.

Giannini, A. J., Baumgartel, P., & DiMarzio, L. R. (1987). Bromocriptine therapy in cocaine withdrawal. *Journal of Clinical Pharmacology, 27,* 267–270.

Glowa, J. R., Fantegrossi, W. E., Lewis, D. B., Matechka, D., Rice, K. C., & Rothman, R. B. (1996). Sustained decrease in cocaine-maintained responding in rhesus monkeys with 1-[2-[Bis(4-fluorophenyl)methyoxy]ethyl]-4-(3-hydroxy-3-phenylpropyl)piperazinyl decanoate, a long-acting ester derivative of GBR 12909. *Journal of Medical Chemistry, 39,* 4689–4691.

Glowa, J. R., & Wojnicki, F. H. E. (1996). Effects of drugs on food- and cocaine-maintained responding. III: Dopaminergic antagonists. *Psychopharmacology, 128,* 351–358.

Glowa, J. R., Wojnicki, F. H. E., Matecka, D., Bacher, J. D., Mansback, R. S., Balster, R. L., & Rice, K. (1995a). Effects of dopamine reuptake inhibitors on food-and cocaine-maintained responding: I. dependence on unit dose of cocaine. *Experimental Clinical Psychopharmacology, 3,* 219–231.

Glowa, J. R., Wojnicki, F. H. E., Matecka, D., Rice, K., & Rothman, R. B. (1995b). Effects of dopamine reuptake inhibitors on food- and cocaine-maintained responding: II Comparisons with other drugs and repeated administrations. *Experimental Clinical Psychopharmacology, 3,* 232–239.

Griffiths, R. R., Wurster, R. M., & Brady, J. V. (1976). Discrete-trial choice procedure: Effects of naloxone and metadone on choice between food and heroin. *Pharmacology Review, 27,* 357–365.

Griffiths, R. R., Bigelow, G., & Henningfield, J. (1980). Similarities in animal and human drug taking behavior. In N. K. Mello (Ed.), *Advances in substance abuse, behavioral and biological research* (pp. 1–90). Grenwich, CT: JAI Press.

Harrigan, S. E., & Downs, D. A. (1981). Pharmacological evaluation of narcotic antagonist delivery systems in rhesus monkeys. In R. E. Willette, & G. Barnett (Eds.), *Narcotic antagonists: Naltrexone pharmacochemistry and sustained-release preparations* (pp. 77–92). *NIDA Research Monograph 28.* Washington, DC: U.S. Government Printing Office.

Herling, S., Downs, D. A., & Woods, J. H. (1979). Cocaine, d-amphetamine, and pentobarbital effects on responding maintained by food or cocaine in rhesus monkeys. *Psychopharmacology, 64,* 261–269.

Herling, S., & Woods, J. H. (1980). Chlorpromazine effects on cocaine-reinforced responding in rhesus monkeys: Reciprocal modification of rate-altering effects of the drugs. *Journal of Pharmacology and Experimental Therapeutics, 214,* 354–361.

Hoffmeister, F. (1988). A comparison of the stimulus effects of codeine in rhesus monkeys under the contingencies of a two lever discrimination task and a cross self-administration paradigm: tests of generalization to pentazocine, buprenorphine, tilidine, and different doses of codeine. *Psychopharmacology, 94,* 315–320.

Holtzman, S. G. (1990). Discriminative stimulus effects of drug: relationship to potential for abuse. In *Modern methods in pharmacology, testing and evaluation of drugs of abuse* (Vol. 6, pp. 193–210). New York: Wiley-Liss.

Holtzman, S. G. (1979). Discriminative stimulus properties of levo-alpha-acetylmethadol and its metabolites. *Pharmacology, Biochemistry and Behavior, 10,* 565–568.

Hubner, C. B., & Koob, G. F. (1990). Bromocriptine produces decreases in cocaine self-administration in the rat. *Neuropsychopharmacology, 3,* 101–108.

Hubner, C. B., & Moreton, J. E. (1991). Effects of selective D_1 and D_2 dopamine antagonists on cocaine self-administration in the rat. *Psychopharmacology, 105,* 151–156.

Jones, B. E., & Prada, J. A. (1975). Drug-seeking behavior during methadone maintenance. *Psychopharmacologia, 41,* 7–10.

Kantak, K. M., Edwards, M. A., & Spealman, R. D. (1995). Effects of N-methyl-D-aspartate antagonists in rats discriminating different doses of cocaine: Comparison with direct and indirect dopamine agonists. *Journal of Pharmacology and Experimental Therapeutics, 274,* 657–665.

Katz, J. L., & Witkin, J. M. (1992a). Effects of quinpirole and SKF 38393 alone and in combination in squirrel monkeys trained to discriminate cocaine. *Psychopharmacology, 107,* 217–220.

Katz, J. L., & Witkin, J. M. (1992b). Selective effects of the D_1 dopamine receptor agonist, SKF 38393, on behavior maintained by cocaine injection in squirrel monkeys. *Psychopharmacology, 109,* 241–244.

Kleven, M. S., Anthony, E. W., Goldberg, L. I., & Woolverton, W. L. (1988). Blockade of the discriminative stimulus effects of cocaine in rhesus monkeys with the D_1 dopamine antagonist SCH 23390. *Psychopharmacology, 95,* 427–428.

Kleven, M. S., Anthony, E. W., & Woolverton, W. L. (1990). Pharmacological characterization of the discriminative stimulus effects of cocaine in rhesus monkeys. *Journal of Pharmacology and Experimental Therapeutics, 254,* 312.

Kleven, M. S., & Woolverton, W. L. (1990). Effects of bromocriptine and desipramine on behavior maintained by cocaine or food presentation in rhesus monkeys. *Psychopharmacology, 101,* 208–213.

Kleven, M. S., & Woolverton, W. L. (1993). Effects on three monoamine uptake inhibitors on behavior maintained by cocaine or food presentation in rhesus monkeys. *Drug and Alcohol Dependence, 31,* 149–158.

Koob, G. F., Le, H. T., & Creese, I. (1987). The D_1 dopamine receptor antagonist SCH 23390 increases cocaine self-administration in the rat. *Neuroscience Letters, 79,* 315–320.

Kumor, K., Sherer, M., & Jaffe, J. (1989). Effects of bromocriptine pretreatment on subjective and physiological responses to i.v. cocaine. *Pharmacology Biochemistry and Behavior, 33,* 829–837.

Lamas, X., Negus, S. S., Nader, M. A., & Mello, N. K. (1996). Effects of the putative O_3 receptor agonist 7-OH-DPAT in rhesus monkeys trained to discriminate cocaine from saline. *Psychopharmacology, 4,* 306–314.

Landry, D. W., Zhao, K., Yang, G X.-Q., Glickman, M., & Georgiadis, T. M. (1993). Antibody-catalyzed degredation of cocaine. *Science, 259,* 1899–1901.

Mansbach, R. S., & Balster, R. L. (1993). Effects of mazindol on behavior maintained or occasioned by cocaine. *Drug and Alcohol Dependence, 31,* 183–191.

Margolin, A., Kosten, T. R., Avants, S. K., Wilkins, J., Ling, W., Beckson, M., Arndt, I. O., Cornish, J., Ascher, J. A., Li, S-H., & Bridge, P. (1995). A multicenter trial of bupropion for cocaine dependence in methadone-maintained patients. *Drug and Alcohol Dependence, 40,* 125–131.

Martin, T. J., Walker, L. E., Sizemore, G. M., Smith, J. E., & Dworkin, S. I. (1996). Within-session determination of dose-response curves for heroin self-administration in rats: Comparison with between-session determination and effects of naltrexone. *Drug and Alcohol Dependence, 41,* 93–100.

Meiergerd, S. M., & Schenk, J. O. (1994). Kinetic evaluation of the commonality between the site(s) of action of cocaine and some other structurally similar and dissimilar inhibitors of the striatal transporter for dopamine. *Journal of Neurochemistry, 63,* 1683–1692.

Mello, N. K., Bree, M. P., & Mendelson, J. H. (1983). Comparison of buprenorphine and methadone effects on opiate self-administration in primates. *Journal of Pharmacology and Experimental Therapeutics, 225,* 378–386.

Mello, N. K., & Negus, S. S. (1996). Preclinical evaluation of pharmacotherpies for treatment of cocaine and opioid abuse using drug self-administration procedures. *Neuropsychopharmacology, 14,* 375–424.

Mendelson, J. H., & Mello, N. K. (1996). Management of cocaine abuse and dependence. *New England Journal of Medicine, 334,* 965–972.

Mets, B., Winger, G., Cabrera, C., Seo, S., Jamdar, S., Yang, G., Zhao, K., Briscoe, R. J., Woods, J. H., & Landry, O. W. *A catalytic antibody against cocaine prevents cocaine's reinforcing and toxic effects in rats.* Unpublished manuscript.

Miksic, S., Shearman, G., & Lal, H. (1978). Generalization with some narcotic and nonnarcotic drugs in rats trained for morphine-saline discrimination. *Psychopharmacology, 60,* 103–104.

Piercey, M. F., Lum, J. T., Hoffmann, W. E., Carlsson, A., Ljung, E., & Svensson, K. (1992). Antagonism of cocaine's pharmacological effects by the stimulant dopamine antagonists (+)-AJ76 and (+)-UH232. *Brain Research, 588,* 217–222.

Preston, K. L., & Bigelow, G. E. (1994). Drug discrimination assessment of agonist-antagonist opioids in humans: a three-choice saline-hydromorphone-butorphanol procedure. *Journal of Pharmacology and Experimental Therapeutics, 271,* 48–60.

Preston, K. L., Sullivan, J. T., Berger, P. C., & Bigelow, G. E. (1993). Effects of cocaine alone and in combination with mazindol in human cocaine abusers. *Journal of Pharmacology and Experimental Therapeutics, 267,* 296–307.

Preston, K. L., Sullivan, J. T., Strain, E. C., & Bigelow, G. E. (1992). Effects of cocaine alone and in combination with bromocriptine in human cocaine abusers. *Journal of Pharmacology and Experimental Therapeutics, 262,* 279–291.

Preston, K. L., Bigelow, G. E., Bickel, W. K., & Liebson, I. A. (1989). Drug discrimination in human post-addicts: Agonist–antagonist opioids. *Journal of Pharmacology and Experimentsl Therapeutics, 250,* 184–196.

Pulvirenti, L., Balducci, Piercy, M., & Koob, G. F. (1996). The effects of the dopamine partial agonist terguride on cocaine self-administration. *Society for Neuroscience Abstracts, 22,* 704.

Richardson, N. R., Piercey, M. F., Svensson, K., Collins, R. J., Myers, J. E., & Roberts, D. C. (1993). Antagonism of cocaine self-administration by the preferential dopamine autoreceptor antagonist, (+)-AJ 76. *Brain Research, 619,* 15–21.

Rothman, R. B., Mele, A., Reid, A. A., Akunne, H., Greig, N., Thurkauf, A., Rice, K. C., & Pert, A. (1989). Tight binding dopamine reuptake inhibitors as cocaine antagonists. *Federal Europe Biochemistry Society Letters, 57,* 341–344.

Sannerud, C. A., & Griffiths, R. R. (1988). Amantadine: evaluation of reinforcing properties and effect on cocaine self-injection in baboons. *Drug and Alcohol Dependence, 21,* 195–202.

Schaefer, G. J., & Holtzman, S. G. (1977). Discriminative effects of morphine in squirrel monkeys. *Journal of Pharmacology and Experimental Therapeutics, 201,* 67–75.

Shannon, H. E., Cone, E. J., & Gorodetzky, C. W. (1986). Morphine-like discriminative stimulus effects of buprenorphine and dimethoxybuprenorphine in rats: quantitative antagonism by naloxone. *Journal of Pharmacology and Experimental Therapeutics, 229,* 768–774.

Skjoldager, P., Winger, G., & Woods, J. H. (1993). Effects of GBR 12909 and cocaine on cocaine-maintained behavior in rhesus monkeys. *Drug and Alcohol Dependence, 33,* 31–39.

Spealman, R. D. (1992). Use of cocaine-discrimination techniques for preclinical evaluation of candidate therapeutics for cocaine dependence. *NIDA Research Monograph, 119,* 175–179.

Spealman, R. D. (1993). Modification of the behavioral effects of cocaine by selective serotonin and dopamine uptake inhibitors in squirrel monkeys. *Psychopharmacology, 112,* 93–99.

Spealman, R. D. (1995a). Noradrenergic involvment in the discriminative stimulus effects of cocaine in squirrel monkeys. *Journal of Pharmacology and Experimental Therapeutics, 275,* 53–62.

Spealman, R. D. (1995b). Discriminative stimulus effects of cocaine in squirrel monkeys: lack of antagonism by the dopamine D_2 partial agonists terguride, SDZ 208-911, and SDZ 208-912. *Pharmacology, Biochemistry, and Behavior, 51,* 661–665.

Spealman, R. D. (1996). Dopamine D_3 receptor agonists partially reproduce the discriminative stimulus effects of cocaine in squirrel monkeys. *Journal of Pharmacology and Experimental Therapeutics, 278,* 1128–1137.

Spealman, R. D., Bergman, J., Madras, B. K., & Melia, K. F. (1991). Discriminative stimulus effect of cocaine in squirrel monkeys. *Journal of Pharmacology and Experimental Therapeutics, 258,* 945–953.

Vanover, K. E., Kleven, M. S., & Woolverton, W. L. (1991). Blockade of the discriminative stimulus effects of cocaine in rhesus monkeys with the D_1 dopamine antagonists SCH-39166 and A-66359. *Behavioural Pharmacology, 2,* 151–159.

Vanover, K. E., Piercey, M. F., & Woolverton, W. L. (1993). Evaluation of the reinforcing and discriminative stimulus effects of cocaine in combination with (+) AJ76 or clozapine. *Journal of Pharmacology and Experimental Therapeutics, 266,* 780–789.

Vanover, K. E., & Wooverton, W. L. (1994). Behavioral effects of the dopamine autoreceptor agonist PD 128483 alone and in combination with cocaine. *Journal of Pharmacology and Experimental Therapeutics, 270,* 1049–1056.

Walker, E. A., Makhay, M. M., House, J. D., & Young, A. M. (1994). In vivo apparent pA2 analysis for naltrexone antagonism of discriminative stimulus and analgesic effects of opiate agonists in rats. *Journal of Pharmacology and Experimental Therapeutics, 271,* 959–968.

Wallace, E. A., & Kosten, T. R. (1996). Pharmacotherapies for cocaine dependence. In C. R. Schuster & M. J. Kuhar (Eds.), *Pharmacological aspects of drug dependence, handbook of experimental pharmacology* (Vol. 118, pp. 627–644). Berlin: Springer.

Winger, G. (1994). Dopamine antagonist effects on behavior maintained by cocaine and alfentanil in rhesus monkeys. *Behavioural Pharmacology, 5,* 141–152.

Winger, G. D., Skjoldager, P., & Woods, J. H. (1992). Effects of buprenorphine and other opioid agonists and antagonists on alfentanil- and cocaine-reinforced responding in rhesus monkeys. *Journal of Pharmacology and Experimental Therapeutics, 261,* 311–317.

Winger, G., & Woods, J. H. (1996). Effects of buprenorphine on behavior maintained by heroin and alfentanil in rhesus monkeys. *Behavioural Pharmacology, 7,* 155–159.

Witkin, J. M., Nichols, D. E., Terry, P., & Katz, J. L. (1991). Behavioral effects of selective dopaminergic compounds in rats discriminating cocaine injections. *Journal of Pharmacology, 257,* 706–713.

Wojnicki, F. H., & Glowa, J. R. (1996). Effects of drug history on the acquisition of responding maintained by GBR 12909 in rhesus monkeys. *Psychopharmacology, 123,* 34–41.

Woolverton, W. L. (1986). Effects of a D_1 and a D_2 dopamine antagonist on the self-administration of cocaine and piribedil by rhesus monkeys. *Pharmacology, Biochemistry and Behavior, 24,* 531–535.

Woolverton, W. L., & Virus, R. M. (1989). The effects of a D_1 and a D_2 dopamine antagonist on behavior maintained by cocaine or food. *Pharmacology, Biochemistry and Behavior, 32,* 691–697.

Young, A. M., Stephens, K. R., Hein, D. W., & Woods, J. H. (1984). Reinforcing and discriminative stimulus properties of mixed agonist-antagonist opioids. *Journal of Pharmacology and Experimental Therapeutics, 229,* 118–126.

7

PRENATAL EXPOSURE
TO COCAINE

KEVIN F. SCHAMA, LEONARD L. HOWELL,
AND LARRY D. BYRD

Yerkes Regional Primate Research Center
Emory University
Atlanta, Georgia

INTRODUCTION

Cocaine has been the focus of considerable scientific attention in recent years due, in part, to its increased use in North America. In the United States, it is estimated that more than 30 million people have tried cocaine, and up to 8 million use it regularly (Abelson & Miller, 1985). Of these users, a considerable number are pregnant women. In many urban areas in North America, reported or detected cocaine use in pregnant women typically ranges from 10–18% (Forman et al., 1994; Frank et al., 1988; McCalla et al., 1991; Streissguth et al., 1991). In suburban and rural areas, however, the rate can be considerably lower (Forman et al., 1994; Sloan, Gay, Snyder, & Boles, 1992; Weeman, Zanetos, & DeVoe, 1995). Cocaine has been associated with a number of complications during pregnancy, and may produce an estimated $500 million in additional medical costs due to more intensive care and longer hospital stays required by cocaine-exposed neonates (Phibbs, Bateman, & Miller, 1991). It is therefore important to determine what effects, if any, cocaine may have on mothers and their children.

The amount of exposure that a fetus may receive when the mother uses cocaine is critical in assessing whether there may be significant risks. Cocaine readily transferred across the human placenta (Krishna, Levitz, & Dancis, 1993; Schenker et al., 1993), and was not significantly metabolized during the transfer (Schenker et al., 1993). During in vitro analysis, cocaine has been detected on the fetal side of the placenta 10–15 min after perfusion started, suggesting rapid transfer (Malek, Ivy, Blann, & Mattison, 1995). Cocaine and benzoylecognine, a potentially neurotoxic cocaine metabolite (Konkol, Murphy, Ferriero, Dempey, & Olsen, 1994), have been detected in human fetal brain, scalp, liver, kidney, heart, blood, and hair,

Cocaine Abuse: Behavior, Pharmacology, and Clinical Applications

suggesting fairly widespread distribution (Klein, Greenwald, Becker, & Koren, 1992), although benzoylecognine does not cross the placental barrier as readily as cocaine (Simone, Derewlany, Oskamp, Knie, & Koren, 1994). In rhesus monkeys the amount of fetal cocaine exposure was about a third of maternal exposure (Binienda, Bailey, Duhart, Slikker, & Paule, 1993). Similarly, in rats, fetal brain and plasma levels were 2–3 times less than maternal levels (Spear, Frambes, & Kirstein, 1989), indicating significant cocaine exposure in the fetus. It is clear that there is a potential for significant fetal exposure due to cocaine use by the mother.

During the past decade there has been a considerable amount of research on the consequences of cocaine use during pregnancy for the mother and child. This chapter will review that research, and attempt to draw conclusions where possible and highlight areas in need of further study. However, it is difficult to understand fully the biological and psychological consequences of cocaine use during pregnancy without first understanding the social contexts of cocaine use. There are a number of social and lifestyle factors that are associated with cocaine use by pregnant women. Women in North America who report or test positive for cocaine use during pregnancy were less likely to have adequate, if any, professional prenatal care (McCalla et al., 1991, 1992; Vaughn et al., 1993), were less likely to maintain adequate nutrition (Frank et al., 1988; Knight et al., 1994), were more likely to use other drugs such as opiates, nicotine, alcohol, and marijuana (Frank et al., 1988; McCalla et al., 1992; Vaughn et al., 1993), were lower on socioeconomic scales (Graham & Koren, 1991), were more likely to be infected with sexually transmitted diseases (Amaro, Zuckerman, & Cabral, 1989; Frank et al., 1988), and were more likely to have a history of elective abortions (Amaro et al., 1989; Graham & Koren, 1991). In addition, mothers who abuse cocaine were more likely to report incidents of violence or stressful life events during pregnancy (Amaro et al., 1989), were less likely to be married (Frank et al., 1988; Graham & Koren, 1991), were younger (Graham & Koren, 1991), less educated (Streissguth et al., 1991), and had more children previously (McCalla et al., 1991).

Many of the lifestyle and socioeconomic factors that are correlated with cocaine use may produce gestational effects on their own, or interact with cocaine's effects on gestation (Coles & Platzman, 1993). Accordingly, many studies of prenatal cocaine exposure in humans have attempted to ascertain the role of cocaine independent of many of these correlated factors, either by carefully selecting matched control groups, or by performing post hoc statistical analyses. The sheer number of possible confounds, however, makes this very difficult. The human literature presented in this chapter should therefore be evaluated within the socioeconomic and cultural contexts in which cocaine use takes place.

CASE STUDIES

Case study reports often present the first indication of a problem in need of attention from the medical sciences. In case studies, researchers usually report one or more incidents in which a particular set of medical circumstances are identified and possibly treated. Often, detailed information is presented that is lacking in many epidemiological studies that compare groups of subjects. Much of the early indication that cocaine may be the cause of difficulties during pregnancy and in newborns has come from case studies.

A brief review of the case study literature presents a host of problems that have been associated with cocaine use during pregnancy. In particular, cocaine exposure has been associated with cardiovascular problems in neonates, including myocardial calcification (Yap, Diana, Herson, Chameides, & Rowe, 1994), acute infarction of a cerebral artery and episodes of apnea and cyanosis (Chasnoff, Bussey, Savich, & Stack, 1986), hypertension (Horn, 1992), and ventricular tachycardia (Geggel, McInerny, & Estes, 1989). Decreased amounts of amniotic fluid, premature rupture of membranes, and umbilical cord anomalies were observed using ultrasonography during the 24th week of gestation (Martinez et al., 1994). Cocaine use has also been associated with limb malformation (Hannig & Phillips, 1991), including missing digits (Sheinbaum & Badell, 1992), and two cases of limb–body wall complex, a syndrome in which body-wall disruption and limb abnormalities are present (Viscarello, Ferguson, Nores, & Hobbins, 1992). Good, Ferriero, Golabi, and Kobori (1992) studied 13 infants exposed to cocaine prenatally and found optic nerve abnormalities, delayed visual maturation, and prolonged eyelid edema.

Prenatal cocaine exposure also has been implicated in case studies of brain anatomy and function. An autopsy of four cocaine-exposed fetuses showed that three had hemorrhages involving the germinal matrix (Kapur, 1991). In another study, 16 neonates prenatally exposed to cocaine showed postdelivery tremulousness, irritability, and increased startle responses (Kramer, Locke, Ogunyemi, & Nelson, 1990). Eight of these infants continued to have seizures 1 month postdelivery. In an ultrasound study of the behavioral state organization of 20 fetuses with mothers who used cocaine during pregnancy, 13 produced abnormal scores, and 16 produced abnormal scores at birth (Hume, O'Donnell, Stanger, Killam, & Gingras, 1989).

There are a few case studies, however, which did not report significant anomalies on a number of measures (Gilbert, Lafferty, Benirschke, & Resnick, 1990; Horn, 1992; Link, Weese-Mayer, & Byrd, 1991). For instance, one study used magnetic resonance imaging (MRI) to examine the brains of 0.6–12-month-old infants whose mothers used cocaine, but not marijuana, phencyclidine, alcohol, narcotics, or amphetamine (Link et al., 1991). There was normal brain and brainstem anatomy, and myelination was found to be consistent with age-matched norms.

Overall, the case study literature implicates a host of problems associated with the use of cocaine during pregnancy. These problems are often observed and presented in a detailed and careful fashion, with suggestions about detection and treatment. However, the case-study approach has a number of shortcomings. Small samples, a lack of matched control subjects for comparison, and the absence of "blind" observers make it difficult to attribute abnormalities to the effects of prenatal cocaine exposure, per se, or to ascertain the overall extent of complications presented by prenatal cocaine exposure.

EPIDEMIOLOGICAL STUDIES

A considerable number of epidemiological studies have been conducted that attempt to ascertain more directly the role of cocaine exposure during pregnancy. Epidemiological studies typically employ larger numbers of subjects, and feature a control group for direct comparison. Factors correlated with cocaine use during pregnancy are frequently taken into account through selection of control subjects that are matched along particular parameters, or through post hoc statistical analyses. Although the particular parameters selected often vary from study to study, socioeconomic status (SES), age, race, and polydrug use are employed frequently. The use of "blind" observers who are not aware of the particular prenatal exposure condition can also vary from study to study, as well as the definition of "cocaine exposure." For example, inclusion in a cocaine exposure group can be based on the mother's verbal reports, detection of cocaine in the mother at any time during pregnancy, detection of cocaine in the mother at birth, and detection of cocaine in the neonate. Often, some combination of criteria are established. Even though there is considerable variation in study design, there are some useful conclusions that can be drawn from the epidemiological literature.

GESTATION AND DELIVERY

Cocaine use during pregnancy has been associated with a number of complications during gestation. Bingol, Fuchs, Diaz, Stone, and Gromisch (1987) found that women using cocaine were more likely to experience still births, but not spontaneous abortions, than drug-free mothers who were matched for SES, cigarette smoking, and ethnicity. In another study, which controlled for SES, age, and number of pregnancies, cocaine was associated with increases in the frequency of spontaneous abortion (Chasnoff, Burns, Schnoll, & Burns, 1985). In a meta-analysis of 45 studies, few effects of prenatal cocaine exposure were revealed, although cocaine exposure was associated with increased *in utero* death (Lutiger, Graham, Einarson, & Koren, 1991). However, another study of interactions between drug use, including cocaine, and prenatal care during gestation, found that the association between fetal death and drug use was minimal when subjects received at least five prenatal care visits (Broekhuizen, Utrie, & Van Mullem, 1992). The pattern of cocaine abuse by pregnant women may also affect gestation. Erratic, but frequent, cocaine binging was more associated with increases in acute problems, including still births, in comparison to daily or cyclic binging patterns (Burkett, Yasin, Palow, LaVoie, & Martinez, 1994).

Cocaine also has been associated with decreases in gestation length. In a study which controlled for the mother's age, parity (number of pregnancies), SES, tobacco use, and medical complications, mothers who used cocaine during pregnancy produced children whose average gestational age was about 15 days less than drug-free mothers (MacGregor et al., 1987). A number of other studies, which controlled for various factors, have repeated these general findings (Bateman, Hansen, & Heagarty, 1993; Cohen, Green, & Crombleholme, 1991; Little, Snell, Klein, & Gilstrap, 1989; Neerhof, MacGregor, Retzky, & Sullivan, 1989). Chasnoff, Lewis, Griffin, and Willey (1989) reported shortened gestational lengths in mothers who used cocaine throughout pregnancy, while use during the first trimester did not affect gestation lengths. In addition, a statistical analysis of eleven independent variables identified cocaine use near delivery as a principle factor in prematurity (Kliegman, Madura, Kiwi, Eisenberg, & Yamashita, 1994). Providing further evidence that cocaine use later in pregnancy may be related to preterm labor, in two groups of fetuses that were exposed to cocaine during gestation, the group that tested positive for cocaine at birth had a greater incidence of preterm labor (Mastrogiannis, Decavalas, Verna, & Tejani, 1990). Consistent with findings relating to fetal death, prenatal care was associated with reductions in the effects of prenatal cocaine exposure on gestation length in one study (MacGregor, Keith, Bachicha, & Chasnoff, 1989). Not all studies have identified a role for cocaine in gestation length, however. In a more recent study of 7,470 women, 2.3% of whom used cocaine during pregnancy, no association was found between cocaine use and preterm delivery, although many of the users in this study claimed to have used cocaine infrequently (Shiono et al., 1995). In a related study of cocaine's effects on the duration of labor, cocaine initially was associated with shorter labor, but when type of delivery, parity, birthweight, and prenatal care were controlled, there were no differences due to cocaine use (Wehbeh, Matthews, McCalla, Feldman, & Minkoff, 1995).

Abruptio placentae (premature detachment of the placenta) and premature rupture of membranes also have been associated with cocaine use in some, but not all, studies. In a study that used control subjects matched for age, race, and parity, mothers exposed to cocaine alone, determined by two urine screens, had an increased incidence of abruptio placentae (Cohen et al., 1991). Other studies have repeated this finding (Dusick et al., 1993; Miller, Boudreaux, & Regan, 1995; Neerhof et al., 1989; Shiono, 1995). However, there are a number of studies that did not find a significant effect of cocaine use on abruptio placentae or premature rupture of membranes (Chouteau, Namerow, & Leppert, 1988; Gillogley, Evans, Hansen, Samuels, & Batra, 1990; Mayes, Bornstein, Chawarska, & Granger, 1993). Consistent with findings about gestation length, mothers of neonates that were exposed to cocaine during gestation and tested positive at birth were at higher risk for abruptio placentae than mothers of neonates who were exposed to cocaine but did not test positive (Mastrogiannis et al., 1990).

EFFECTS ON THE NEONATE

Neonates exposed to cocaine prenatally have been considered at risk for a number of problems, including retarded physical measurements, neuropsychological abnormalities, withdrawal symptoms, genitourinary tract malformations, cardiorespiratory anomalies, optical irregularities, and increased incidence of sudden infant death syndrome (SIDS). Of these potential difficulties, physical measurements have been studied frequently, and many studies have found that prenatal cocaine exposure is associated with abnormal physical measurements at birth (MacGregor et al., 1987; Chasnoff et al., 1989; Cherukuri, Minkoff, Feldman, Parekh, & Glass, 1988; Cohen et al., 1991; Coles, Platzman, Smith, James, & Falek, 1992; Gillogley et al., 1990; Hadeed & Siegel, 1989; Mayes, Granger, Frank, Schottenfeld, & Bornstein, 1993; Neerhof et al., 1989). For instance, in a relatively early study, birthweight was lower, and body length and head circumference were smaller in a group of neonates exposed to cocaine, as opposed to control subjects matched for estimated gestation length (Bingol et al., 1987). Bateman et al. (1993) controlled for the mother's prenatal care, race, tobacco, alcohol, marijuana, and phencyclidine use, and the infant's sex and estimated gestation length, and also found that prenatal cocaine exposure was related to decreased physical measurements at birth. In addition, the concentration of the cocaine metabolite, benzoylecognine, in neonate meconium was associated with smaller physical measurements (Mirochnik, Frank, Cabral, Turner, & Zuckerman, 1995), suggesting a dose–response relationship between cocaine exposure and decreased physical measurements at birth.

However, not all studies have found a strong association between cocaine use and neonatal physical measurements (Chasnoff et al., 1985; Richardson & Day, 1991; Shiono et al., 1995). When SES, race, age, polydrug use, and marital status were controlled, there was no significant relationship between cocaine exposure and physical measurements at birth (Richardson & Day, 1994). Other studies have shown that prenatal care can reduce or eliminate clinically significant effects of cocaine exposure on physical measurements (Broekhuizen et al., 1992; Feldman, Minkoff, McCalla, & Salwen, 1992; MacGregor et al., 1989). For instance, when prenatal care and cigarette smoking were controlled, differences in birthweight associated with cocaine exposure were eliminated (Miller et al., 1995). Additional studies indicate that early deficits in physical growth may be overcome during postnatal development. At 1.6 years of age, body weight was not related to prenatal cocaine exposure (Graham et al., 1992), and only head circumference was smaller at 3 years of age (Griffith, Azuma, & Chasnoff, 1994). In longitudinal studies, children prenatally exposed to cocaine and other drugs were significantly smaller at birth, but no different than control subjects in measurements of body weight and length at 1 year of age (Chasnoff, Griffith, Freier, & Murray, 1992; Weathers, Crane, Sauvain, & Blackhurst, 1993).

In addition to physical characteristics, prenatal exposure to cocaine may have significant effects on early neurobehavioral development (Chasnoff et al., 1989). For instance, infants prenatally exposed to cocaine exhibited poorer feeding and increased tremulousness and irritability (Neerhof et al., 1989), and decreased scores on the neonatal behavioral assessment scale (NBAS) (Chasnoff et al.,

1989). The NBAS (Brazelton, 1984) rates neonates on a number of measures of reflex development (e.g., rooting, placing), and behavioral traits (e.g., orientation, irritability). Abnormalities in NBAS scores have been reported in other studies, including decreased interactive behavior and poor organizational response (Chasnoff et al., 1985), and retarded development of orientation, motor ability, state regulation, and reflexes (Chasnoff et al., 1989). Some studies, however, have found that only habituation is impaired by prenatal cocaine exposure (Eisen et al., 1991; Mayes et al., 1993). Cocaine-exposed infants that were 3 months old had difficulty starting a habituation test procedure, and were more irritable once started, but were not different than control subjects in habituation or recovery to a novel stimulus once criterion was reached (Mayes et al., 1995). In a study of auditory brainstem responses, which did not control for gestational age, prenatal cocaine exposure was associated with prolonged interpeak and absolute latencies in neonates recently exposed to cocaine (Shih, Cone-Wesson, & Reddix, 1988). Corwin et al. (1992) found that cocaine-exposed infants exhibited fewer cry utterances, and more short cries than nonexposed subjects with similar demographic backgrounds. In addition, Mayes et al. (1995) found decreased motor, but not mental, scores in Bayley Scales of Infant Development (BSID) tests. BSID scores reflect motor, reflex, and behavioral state characteristics of neonates (Bayley, 1969).

However, not all studies have found a significant relationship between prenatal cocaine exposure and neurobehavioral development. In a study which matched age, parity, SES, alcohol use, and the presence or absence of prenatal care, only modest and infrequent neurobehavioral symptoms were attributable to cocaine exposure (Cherukuri et al., 1988). Other studies have not found cocaine-related differences in NBAS scores (Coles et al., 1992; Neuspiel, Hamel, Hochberg, Greene, & Campbell, 1991), or the BSID (Chasnoff et al., 1992). In a recent study of the neurobehavioral and physiological effects of prenatal cocaine exposure in 1- and 2-day-old neonates using gestational age- and race-matched controls, no differences were found in body tone and reflexes, anterior or middle cerebral arterial blood flow velocity, rates of sonographic abnormalities, intraventricular hemorrhage, and neonatal stroke (King et al., 1995). Consistent with findings relating to physical measurements, some neurobehavioral effects do not persist. For instance, EEG abnormalities (in comparison to normative data) present in 17 of 38 cocaine-exposed neonates were not present when these neonates were tested again at 3–12 months (Doberczak, Shanzer, Senie, & Kandall, 1988). Although hypertonia and coarse tremors were observed in cocaine-exposed infants (Chiriboga, Bateman, Brust, & Hauser, 1993), hypertonia decreased with age, and initial differences associated with cocaine exposure were almost gone by 2 years of age (Chiriboga et al., 1995). In another study, infants prenatally exposed to cocaine exhibited increased auditory-evoked brainstem transmission times compared to control subjects, but these differences disappeared by 2 months of age (Salamy, Eldredge, Anderson, & Bull, 1990). Lastly, no differences were found between cocaine-exposed and control subjects in BSID at 1.6 years of age (Graham et al., 1992).

LONG-TERM EFFECTS

The long-term effects of prenatal cocaine exposure on physical measures and simple neurobehavioral tasks have been discussed, but there are few studies of the long-term effects of prenatal cocaine exposure on more complex neurobehavioral tasks. The effects of possible confounding influences increase as a developing child is exposed to many of the disadvantages of being born to a mother who uses cocaine. The ability to isolate the effects of prenatal cocaine exposure, *per se,* is difficult, but the information is important given early predictions of the strains that "crack" babies would place on school systems and social service agencies. Some early signs of neurobehavioral abnormalities appear to be transient phenomena (Chiriboga et al., 1995; Graham et al., 1992). However, the long-term consequences of prenatal cocaine exposure on more complex behavioral performances are unclear. In a longitudinal study, 3-year-old children exposed to cocaine and other drugs had IQ scores in the normal range, with mean IQ scores about 5 points below the nonexposed group (Azuma & Chasnoff, 1993). In another study, 3-year-old children prenatally exposed to cocaine and other drugs had lower mean verbal reasoning scores (Griffith et al., 1994). These studies do not identify the effects of individual drugs, but they are consistent with modest, long-term effects of prenatal cocaine exposure. In a retrospective study, 21% of 2–4-year-old children with language delays had a history of prenatal cocaine exposure, compared to only 7% of children without language delays (Angelilli et al., 1994). In an attempt to ascertain more directly the effects of prenatal cocaine exposure in the absence of postnatal confounding influences, Nulman et al. (1994) studied adopted children, 14 months to 6.5 years old, who were cocaine-exposed during gestation. Observers were "blind" to the conditions of the study, control groups were age-matched, and the adoptive mothers were matched for IQ and SES. The groups were no different in overall IQ scores, but cocaine-exposed children exhibited lower verbal competence and expressive language. More studies need to be completed in order to delineate the ability of prenatal cocaine exposure to produce long-term behavioral deficits.

NONHUMAN EXPERIMENTAL STUDIES

Nonhuman studies have been conducted that supplement epidemiological studies in humans. Epidemiological studies have investigated a broad spectrum of effects of prenatal cocaine exposure, and these studies are often conducted in the overall social and medical contexts in which cocaine is reputed to produce harmful effects. Because the overall context is not controlled, however, it is often difficult to attribute deleterious effects to cocaine use, *per se.* Many studies have attempted to verify the causative role of cocaine independent of possible confounds by comparing cocaine-exposed groups with nonexposed control groups that are matched for certain factors that are correlated with cocaine abuse and may influence gestational development and outcome. Unfortunately, these potential confounds, along with the amount and frequency of cocaine exposure, are sometimes difficult to measure. In addition, large subject pools are often required to obtain the necessary statistical power to conduct meaningful statistical tests.

In order to address these issues, a number of nonhuman experimental studies have been conducted to investigate more directly the role of cocaine in the absence of potential confounds. By using nonhuman subjects, researchers can study the effects of prenatal cocaine exposure under conditions where the amount, frequency, and method of cocaine administration are controlled. In addition, certain potential confounds, such as polydrug use, nutritional status, and prenatal care, may be eliminated under properly arranged laboratory conditions. In a typical experiment using nonhuman subjects, one group of pregnant females is administered cocaine in a controlled fashion, while a control group receives saline in the same manner. Many studies also employ pair-fed control groups, in which the amount of food given to control mothers is yoked proportionately to the amount of food consumed by the cocaine-exposed mothers. Pair-fed control groups are designed to control for deleterious outcomes due to effects of cocaine on food consumption of the mothers, as opposed to the direct effects of cocaine on the fetus. All studies described below used pair-fed control groups, unless otherwise indicated. Another advantage of nonhuman experimental studies is that subjects can be monitored easily over a longer time span, making longitudinal studies possible without many of the often difficult interpretive problems associated with subject attrition or continued exposure to potential confounds when studying humans. In addition, fetuses can be obtained in various stages of development for more direct observation and analysis. A drawback to nonhuman studies in that interspecies generalizations should be made cautiously. For instance, many nonhuman studies employ rodents, whose gestation lengths are considerably shorter than humans, and it is not clear how this may affect outcomes of prenatal cocaine exposure. Epidemiological studies of human prenatal exposure and nonhuman experimental studies should be viewed as complementary, and each evaluated in the context of the other relative to its strengths and weaknesses.

GESTATION AND DELIVERY

In general, most studies have not found an effect of prenatal cocaine exposure on gestation and delivery in nonhuman subjects, including rats (El-Bizri, Guest, & Varma, 1991; Hutchings et al., 1989; Kunko, Moyer, & Robinson, 1993; Spear et al., 1989; Tonkiss et al., 1995) and rhesus monkeys (Morris et al., 1996a). For instance, rats exposed to cocaine (up to 60 mg/kg/day) prenatally showed no significant effect on offspring mortality (Hutchings et al., 1989). There are exceptions, however. An early study in rats, which did not use pair-fed control subjects, found that larger doses of cocaine (up to 90 mg/kg/day) produced increases in fetal death and *abruptio placentae* (Church, Dintcheff, & Gessner, 1988). Another study in rabbits found increased numbers of still births, but not spontaneous abortions

(Weese-Mayer, Klemka-Walden, Chan, & Gingras, 1991). In a study using rats, at the highest dose administered through gestation and into the postnatal period (90 mg/kg/day), rats exposed to cocaine prenatally had higher postnatal mortality (Wiggins & Ruiz, 1990). However, the authors attributed the increased mortality to the undernourishment and poor maternal care of cocaine-exposed dams (Wiggins & Ruiz, 1990).

EFFECTS ON NEONATE

Few nonhuman studies have found significant effects of prenatal cocaine exposure on neonatal physical measurements. Morris et al. (1996a) studied rhesus monkeys prenatally exposed to three daily (weekday) injections of 0.3 mg/kg, 1.0 mg/kg, or escalating doses up to 8.5 mg/kg cocaine. When compared to pair-fed control subjects, no significant differences were found in physical measurements at birth, including body weight, crown-rump length, and crown circumference (Morris et al., 1996a). In a follow-up study, cocaine-exposed offspring did not exhibit differences in postnatal growth (Morris, Gillam, Allen, & Paule, 1996b). A number of other studies have also found no effect of prenatal cocaine exposure on neonatal physical measurements in rats (El-Bizri et al., 1991; Hutchings et al., 1989; Kunko et al., 1993; Laviola, Fiore, Loggi, & Alleva, 1994; Riley & Foss, 1991a; Smith, Mattran, Kurkjian, & Kurtz, 1989; Spear et al., 1989) and rabbits (Murphy et al., 1995; Weese-Mayer et al., 1991). A study that investigated the interactions of nutritional status and cocaine on fetal development in rats found that malnutrition (low protein diet), but not cocaine exposure, decreased fetal body-weights (Tonkiss et al., 1995). However, both cocaine and malnutrition individually impaired skeletal maturation, with no additive effect. Another study found that prenatally exposed mouse fetuses were smaller than control subjects in middevelopment, but no different at full-term (Arpasi & Chakraborti, 1993). Church, Overbeck, and Andrzejczak (1990) found dose-dependent decreases in body weights and postnatal weight gain in both cocaine-exposed and pair-fed control groups of rats, indicating that body-weight differences at birth can be influenced by cocaine's effects on the dam's nutritional status. However, a more recent study found dose–dependent decreases in body weight of rat fetuses examined on gestational day 20, which suggests a more direct role for cocaine (Church, Mohrbach, & Subramanian, 1995).

In contrast to nonhuman studies investigating physical measurements, a number of studies have found significant influences of prenatal cocaine exposure on neurobehavioral assessments. In one study, prenatal cocaine exposure decreased immobility in a forced-swim test in 60-day-old rats, and prenatally exposed subjects were less sensitive to the effects of shock on behavior in an open-field test, suggesting altered response to stressors (Molina, Wagner, & Spear, 1994). In a neurobehavioral study in mice, prenatally exposed subjects did not differ from controls in a number of early postnatal tests, but post-weaning behaviors were affected (Smith et al., 1989). For instance, cocaine-exposed subjects obtained more reinforcers on a differential-reinforcement-of-low-rate schedule as the testing progressed, and prenatally exposed males exhibited decreases in spontaneous alternation in a T-maze (Smith et al., 1989). In a separate study, mice that were prenatally exposed to a relatively high dose of cocaine (50 mg/kg/day) showed accelerated development of responses to strong tactile stimulation, although there were no differences in morphine-induced increases in locomotor activity (Laviola, Fiore, Loggi, & Allevy, 1994). Prenatal cocaine exposure has also reduced sensitivity to the discriminative-stimulus effects of cocaine (Heyser, Rajachandran, Spear, & Spear, 1994), and produced deficits in learning an odor/milk association in rats (Spear et al., 1989). In addition, 3-month-old rats prenatally exposed to cocaine were more sensitive to the effects of acute cocaine administration on measures of stereotypy and locomotion (Peris, Coleman-Hardee, & Millard, 1992). In tests of open-field activity, rats exposed to cocaine were less likely to enter an open-field apparatus on postnatal day 60, and were hyperactive while in the open-field apparatus, but there were no differences in spontaneous alternation, or acquisition of a water maze task (Johns, Means, Means, & McMillen, 1992). In a study where rats were exposed to cocaine daily during most of gestation, hypoactivity was observed in offspring (Church & Overbeck, 1990a). A number of other studies have indicated differences in behaviors of rat offspring prenatally exposed to cocaine, including increased postweaning locomotor activity, rearing, and hole-poke behavior (Vorhees et al., 1995), decreased exploratory behavior (Kunko et al., 1993), retarded acquisition of a discrimination reversal (Heyser, Spear, & Spear, 1992), and an increase in fetal motor activity (Simonik, Robinson, & Smotherman, 1994).

However, not all studies have found significant behavioral effects in nonhuman subjects prenatally exposed to cocaine. In a study of rhesus monkeys, there was no effect of prenatal cocaine exposure on the early development of reflexes (Morris et al., 1996a). In a follow-up study when the subjects were 6–18 months old (Morris et al., 1996b), no differences were found between cocaine-exposed and control subjects in acquisition or terminal performance on various operant tasks designed to test learning, memory, attention, motivation, and color and position discriminations. In a series of experiments in rats (Foss & Riley, 1991a,b; Riley & Foss, 1991a,b), prenatally exposed subjects were similar to control subjects in measures of passive or active avoidance, spatial navigation, open-field activity, sensitivity of open-field activity to acute cocaine administration, acoustic startle responses, prepulse inhibition of acoustic startle responses, and habituation of startle responses. Other studies have found no effects of prenatal cocaine exposure on passive or active avoidance (Church, Holmes, Overbeck, Tilac, & Zajac, 1991) or locomotor activity (Heyser et al., 1994) in rats.

An advantage of using nonhuman subjects is that central nervous system (CNS) structure and function can be observed more directly through various invasive techniques. For instance, subjects can be sacrificed at certain levels of development, and brains can be studied directly, or substances with specific pharmacological actions can be administered and observations made. In terms of gross measurements, brain–weight was not affected by administration of cocaine during the postnatal brain growth spurt in rats (Chen, Anderson, & West, 1993). In another study, brain–weight was only slightly affected by prenatal cocaine exposure in rats, and there were no differences between exposed and control groups on postnatal day 20 (Wiggins & Ruiz, 1990). Brain stem auditory response latencies were prolonged in rats prenatally exposed to cocaine (Salamy et al., 1992), although the authors implicated maternal, fetal, and postnatal nutritional status in production of the increased latencies. In another study using rats, the highest dose of cocaine administered prenatally induced prolonged brain stem auditory evoked potentials and decreased amplitude on postnatal day 35, but no differences were found at 6–10 months (Church & Overbeck, 1990b). Sixty-day-old male rats that were prenatally exposed to cocaine exhibited decreases in brain glucose metabolism in the primary somatosensory and motor cortices, although no size differences were found in the cortical and subcortical structures (Dow-Edwards, Freed, & Fico, 1990). In addition, rats prenatally exposed to cocaine were less sensitive to the convulsant actions of bicuculline and pentylenetetrazol at 10 days postpartum, but not at 20 or 30 days postpartum (de Feo, Del Priore, & Mecarelli, 1995).

A number of studies have investigated the effects of prenatal cocaine exposure on specific neurotransmitter systems. El-Bizri et al. (1991) found no changes in dopamine (DA), epinephrine, or norepinephrine concentrations in the brains of rat fetuses or newborn pups. However, in another study using microdialysis, 10–30-day-old rat pups prenatally exposed to cocaine exhibited increased basal levels of DA, in addition to increased levels of DA in response to a tail pinch or acute cocaine administration (Keller, Maisonneuve, Nuccio, Carlson, & Glick, 1994). Stadlin, Ling Choi, and Tsang (1994) found decreases in DA-binding sites in rats prenatally exposed to cocaine at postnatal weeks 3 and 4, but values were normal by week 8. Prenatal cocaine exposure increased amphetamine-stimulated release of [^{3}H]DA from the striatum of 3-month-old female rats, but not male rats (Peris et al., 1992). In prenatally exposed rabbits, the spontaneous release of [^{3}H]DA was elevated in the frontal and cingulate cortices, but not the striatum, in 10-day-old subjects (Wang, Yeung, & Friedman, 1995). However, the differences in [^{3}H]DA release were no longer present when the rabbits were 50 or 120 days old (Wang et al., 1995). In prenatally exposed rhesus monkeys that were 60 days old, there was a similar distribution of neurons containing tyrosine hydroxylase compared to controls, but tyrosine hydroxylase mRNA content was reduced in the substantia nigra and ventral tegmental area, which the authors attributed to reduced DA synthesis (Ronnekleiv & Naylor, 1995). Studies of other neurotransmitter systems have found a presynaptic serotonin (5-HT) deficit in male rats prenatally exposed to cocaine, as well as elevated 5-HT neuroendocrine responses in males, but not females (Cabrera et al., 1993; Cabrera, Levy, Li, Van de Kar, & Battaglia, 1994; Cabrera & Van de Kar, 1995). Akbari, Kramer, Whitaker-Azmitia, Spear, & Azmitia (1992) found that rats prenatally exposed to cocaine exhibited attenuated 5-HT terminal fiber density at days 1 and 7 postdelivery, but not at 1 month.

CONCLUSIONS

SUMMARY AND SYNTHESIS OF HUMAN
AND NONHUMAN LITERATURE

Many early studies have implicated prenatal cocaine exposure in a variety of obstetric complications, including preterm delivery, fetal death, retarded physical growth and development, neurobehavioral abnormalities, learning disabilities, genitourinary malformations, and increased incidence of SIDS. However, in retrospect, early predictions and dire warnings appear to have been premature. A considerable number of studies have been conducted recently, and it appears as if deleterious effects of cocaine, per se, are in many instances not demonstrated consistently, or are mitigated by other factors such as polydrug use and prenatal care. The relationship between cocaine exposure and complications during pregnancy, such as preterm delivery, appears to be exacerbated by the use of other substances (Miller et al., 1995), most prevalent when cocaine is used late in pregnancy (Kliegman et al., 1994; Mastrogiannis et al., 1990), dependent on pattern of exposure (Burkett et al., 1994), and reduced substantially by adequate prenatal care (Feldman et al., 1992; MacGregor et al., 1989). In addition, physical abnormalities that have been detected and monitored during development generally did not persist and presented no long-term clinical difficulties (Graham et al., 1992; Weathers et al., 1993). These conclusions are supported by nonhuman experiments, which have not generally found effects of cocaine on gestation and delivery, except at very high doses (Church et al., 1988; Kunko et al., 1993; Spear et al., 1989). However, the effects of pattern of exposure should be studied further. These same conclusions can be drawn with respect to the relationship between cocaine and physical maturation.

Neurobehavioral tests with infants that were prenatally exposed to cocaine have produced mixed results. Some studies have reported abnormalities associated with prenatal cocaine exposure (Chasnoff et al., 1989; Neerhof et al., 1989), while others have not (Cherukuri et al., 1988; Coles et al., 1992). In addition, some effects that have been observed early in development do not persist in human (Chiriboga et al., 1995) and nonhuman subjects (Church & Overbeck, 1990b; Wiggins & Ruiz, 1990). Nonhuman studies have more consistently shown alterations in neurobehavioral function as a consequence of prenatal cocaine exposure (Molina et al., 1994; Spear et al., 1989). However, specific tests used in nonhuman studies often do not have corresponding tests that are used routinely with humans. Some of the tests used with nonhuman subjects should, where feasible, be repeated with human subjects, especially tests of habituation, where there is some concordance between the human (Mayes et al., 1993) and nonhuman literature (Johns et al., 1992).

Human studies of the long-term effects of prenatal cocaine exposure are difficult to conduct while taking into account potential confounds such as polydrug use and poor maturational environment, and, consequently, there are few studies of this kind. Studies that have been conducted indicate that there may be verbal deficits in prenatally exposed children (Angelilli et al., 1994; Griffith et al., 1994), although at this point much more work needs to be done in order to draw firm conclusions. Studies of the long-term behavioral effects of prenatal cocaine exposure in nonhuman subjects have been conducted mostly in rodents, and effects have been found using a number of measures (Molina et al., 1994; Heyser et al., 1994). However, one study in rhesus monkeys did not detect long-term effects of prenatal cocaine exposure on a variety of complex behavioral tasks (Morris et al., 1996b). More studies should be conducted using a variety of species in order to evaluate the species generality of findings using rodents.

GENERAL CONCLUSIONS AND FUTURE DIRECTIONS

It appears as if early indications of widespread abnormalities and profound dysfunction caused by cocaine use during pregnancy generally have not been supported by subsequent research. In many cases the abnormalities are not detected consistently across studies, are not clinically significant, are related to polydrug use, and certain risks can be reduced considerably by adequate prenatal care. There may be some substantial risks involved, however. Use of large amounts of cocaine late in pregnancy may produce difficulties with labor. A number of controlled nonhuman studies indicate abnormal neurobehavioral and neurotransmitter function as a consequence of prenatal cocaine exposure. These studies should be followed by more thorough investigations of these phenomena in other species, including humans. In addition, effects of prenatal cocaine exposure on long-term development of complex behavioral processes should be investigated more fully.

ACKNOWLEDGMENTS

The authors gratefully acknowledge the secretarial assistance of P. M. Plant. Work on this manuscript was supported, in part, by U.S. Public Health Service grants DA-06264 and RR-00165 (Division of Research Resources, National Institutes of Health).

REFERENCES

Abelson, H. I., & Miller, J. D. (1985). A decade of trends in cocaine use in the household population. In N. J. Kozel & E. H. Adams (Eds.), *Cocaine use in America: Epidemiologic and clinical perspectives* (pp. 35–49). NIDA Research Monograph Series 61. Washington, DC: U.S. Government Printing Office.

Akbari, H. M., Kramer, H. K., Whitaker-Azmitia, P. M., Spear, L. P., & Azmitia, E. C. (1992). Prenatal cocaine exposure disrupts the development of the serotonergic system. *Brain Research, 572,* 57–63.

Amaro, H., Zuckerman, B., & Cabral, H. (1989). Drug use among adolescent mothers: Profile of risk. Source. *Pediatrics, 84,* 144–151.

Angelilli, M. L., Fischer, H., Delaney-Black, V., Rubinstein, M., Ager, J. W., & Sokol, R. J. (1994). History of *in utero* cocaine exposure in language-delayed children. *Clinical Pediatrics, 33,* 514–516.

Arpasi, P., & Chakraborty, J. (1993). Effects of cocaine on fetal and postnatal development in mice. *Life Sciences, 52,* 2063–2069.

Azuma, S. D., & Chasnoff, L. J. (1993). Outcome of children prenatally exposed to cocaine and other drugs: A path analysis of three-year data. *Pediatrics, 92,* 396–402.

Bateman, D. A., Ng, S. K. C., Hansen, C. A., & Heagarty, M. C. (1993). The effects of intrauterine cocaine exposure in newborns. *American Journal of Public Health, 83,* 190–193.

Battaglia, G., Cabrera, T. M., & Van de Kar, L. D. (1995). Prenatal cocaine produces biochemical and functional changes in brain serotonin systems in rat progeny. In P. V. Thadani (Ed.), *Biological mechanisms and perinatal exposure to drugs.* NIDA Research Monograph Series 158. Rockville, MD: National Institute on Drug Abuse.

Battin, M., Albersheim, S., & Newman, D. (1995). Congenital genitourinary tract abnormalities following cocaine exposure *in utero. American Journal of Perinatology, 12,* 425–428.

Bauchner, H., Zuckerman, B., McClain, M., Frank, D., Fried, L. E., & Kayne, H. (1988). Risk of sudden infant death syndrome among infants with *in utero* exposure to cocaine. *Journal of Pediatrics, 113,* 831–834.

Bayley, N. (1969). *The Bayley Scales of Infant Development.* New York: Psychological Corp.

Bingol, N., Fuchs, M., Diaz, V., Stone, R. K., & Gromisch, D. S. (1987). Teratogenicity of cocaine in humans. *Journal of Pediatrics, 110,* 93–96.

Binienda, Z., Bailey, J. R., Durhart, H. M., Slikker, W., Jr., & Paule, M. G. (1993). Transplacental pharmacokinetics and maternal/fetal plasma concentrations of cocaine in pregnant macaques near term. *Drug Metabolism and Disposition, 21,* 364–368.

Brazelton, T. B. (1984). *Neonatal Behavioral Assessment Scale, 2nd edition: Clinic in Developmental Medicine 88.* Philadelphia: Lippincott.

Broekhuizen, F. F., Utrie, J., & Van Mullem, C. (1992). Drug use or inadequate prenatal care? Adverse pregnancy outcome in an urban setting. *American Journal of Obstetrics and Gynecology, 166,* 1747–1756.

Burkett, G., Yasin, S. Y., Palow, D., LaVoie, L., & Martinez, M. (1994). Patterns of cocaine binging: Effect on pregnancy. *American Journal of Obstetrics and Gynecology, 171,* 372–379.

Cabrera, T. M., Levy, A. D., Li, Q., Van de Kar, L. D., & Battaglia, G. (1994). Cocaine-induced deficits in ACTH and corticosterone responses in female rat progeny. *Brain Research Bulletin, 34,* 93–97.

Cabrera, T. M., Yracheta, J. M., Li, Q., Levy, A. D., Van de Kar, L. D., & Battaglia, G. (1993). Prenatal cocaine produces deficits in serotonin mediated neuroendocrine responses in adult rat progeny: Evidence for long-term functional alterations in brain serotonin pathways. *Synapse, 15,* 158–168.

Carraccio, C., Papadimitriou, J., & Feinburg, P. (1994). Subcutaneous fat necrosis of the newborn: Link to maternal use of cocaine during pregnancy. *Clinical Pediatrics, 33,* 317–318.

Chan, K., Dodd, P. A., Day, L., Kullama, L., Ervin, M. G., Padbury, J., & Ross, M. G. (1992). Fetal catecholamine, cardiovascular, and neurobehavioral responses to cocaine. *American Journal of Obstetrics and Gynecology, 167,* 1616–1623.

Chasnoff, I. J., Burns, W. J., Schnoll, S. H., & Burns, K. A. (1985). Cocaine use in pregnancy. *New England Journal of Medicine, 313,* 666–669.

Chasnoff, I. J., Bussey, M. E., Savich, R., & Stack, C. M. (1986). Perinatal cerebral infarction and maternal cocaine use. *Journal of Pediatrics, 108,* 456–459.

Chasnoff, I. J., Chism, G. M., & Kaplan, W. E. (1988). Maternal cocaine use and genitourinary tract malformations. *Teratology, 37,* 201–204.

Chasnoff, I. J., Griffith, D. R., Freier, C., & Murray, J. (1992). Cocaine/polydrug use in pregnancy: Two-year follow-up. *Pediatrics, 89,* 284–289.

Chasnoff, I. J., Lewis, D. E., Griffith, D. R., & Willey, S. (1989). Cocaine and pregnancy: Clinical and toxicological implications for the neonate. *Clinical Chemistry, 35,* 1276–1278.

Chazotte, C., Forman, L., & Gandhi, J. (1991). Heart rate patterns in fetuses exposed to cocaine. *Obstetrics and Gynecology, 78,* 323–325.

Chen, W. A., Andersen, K. H., & West, J. R. (1993). Cocaine exposure during the brain growth spurt: Studies of neonatal survival, somatic growth, and brain development. *Neurotoxicology and Teratology, 15,* 267–273.

Chen, C., Duara, S., Neto, G. S., Tan, S., Bandstra, E. S., Gerhardt, T., & Bancalari, E. (1991). Respiratory instability in neonates with *in utero* exposure to cocaine. *Journal of Pediatrics, 119,* 111–113.

Cherukuri, R., Minkoff, H., Feldman, J., Parekh, A., & Glass, L. (1988). A cohort study of alkaloidal cocaine ("crack") in pregnancy. *Obstetrics and Gynecology, 72,* 147–151.

Chiriboga, C. A., Bateman, D. A., Brust, J. C. M., & Hauser, W. A. (1993). Neurologic findings in neonates with intrauterine cocaine exposure. *Pediatric Neurology, 9,* 115–119.

Chiriboga, C. A., Vibbert, M., Malouf, R., Suarez, M. S., Abrams, E. J., Heagarty, M. C., Brust, J. C. M., & Hauser, W. A. (1995). Neurological correlates of fetal cocaine exposure: Transient hypertonia of infancy and early childhood. *Pediatrics, 96,* 1070–1077.

Chouteau, M., Namerow, P. B., & Leppert, P. (1988). The effect of cocaine abuse on birth weight and gestational age. *Obstetrics and Gynecology, 72,* 351–354.

Church, M. W., Dintcheff, B. A., & Gessner, P. K. (1988). Dose-dependent consequences of cocaine on pregnancy outcome in the Long-Evans rat. *Neurotoxicology and Teratology, 10,* 51–58.

Church, M. W., Holmes, P. A., Overbeck, G. W., Tilak, J. P., & Zajac, C. S. (1991). Interactive effects of prenatal alcohol and cocaine exposures on postnatal mortality, development and behavior in the Long-Evans rat. *Neurotoxicology and Teratology, 13,* 377–386.

Church, M. W., Morbach, C. A., & Subramanian, M. G. (1995). Comparative effects of prenatal cocaine, alcohol, and undernutrition on maternal/fetal toxicity and fetal body composition in the Sprague-Dawley rat with observations on strain-dependent differences. *Neurotoxicology and Teratology, 17,* 559–567.

Church, M. W., & Overbeck, G. W. (1990a). Prenatal cocaine exposure in the Long-Evans rat: II. Dose-dependent effects on offspring behavior. *Neurotoxicology and Teratology, 12,* 335–443.

Church, M. W., & Overbeck, G. W. (1990b). Prenatal cocaine exposure in the Long-Evans rat: III. Developmental effects on the brainstem auditory-evoked potential. *Neurotoxicology and Teratology, 12,* 345–351.

Church, M. W., Overbeck, G. W., & Andrzejczak, A. L. (1990). Prenatal cocaine exposure in the Long-Evans rat: I. Dose-dependent effects on gestation, mortality, and postnatal maturation. *Neurotoxicology and Teratology, 12,* 327–334.

Cohen, H. R., Green, J. R., & Crombleholme, W. R. (1991). Peripartum cocaine use: Estimating risk of adverse pregnancy outcome. *International Journal of Gynecology and Obstetrics, 35,* 51–54.

Coles, C. D., & Platzman, K. A. (1993). Behavioral development in children prenatally exposed to drugs and alcohol. *International Journal of the Addictions, 28,* 1393–1433.

Coles, C. D., Platzman, K. A., Smith, I., James, M. E., & Falek, A. (1992). Effects of cocaine and alcohol use in pregnancy on neonatal growth and neurobehavioral status. *Neurotoxicology and Teratology, 14,* 23–33.

Corwin, M. J., Lester, B. M., Sepkoski, C., McLaughlin, S., Kayne, H., & Golub, H. L. (1992). Effects of *in utero* cocaine exposure on newborn acoustical cry characteristics. *Pediatrics, 89,* 1199–1203.

Czyrko, C., Del Pin, C. A., O'Neill, J. A., Jr., Peckham, G. J., & Ross, A. J., 3rd. (1991). Maternal cocaine abuse and necrotizing enterocolitis: Outcome and survival. *Journal of Pediatric Surgery, 26,* 414–418 (Discussion 419–421).

de Feo, M. R., Del Priore, D., & Mecarelli, O. (1995). Prenatal cocaine: Seizure susceptibility in rat offspring. *Pharmacological Research, 31,* 137–141.

Derks, J. B., Owiny, J., Sadowsky, D., Ding, X. Y., Wentworth, R., & Nathanielsz, P. W. (1993). Effects of repeated administration of cocaine to the fetal sheep in the last days of pregnancy. *American Journal of Obstetrics and Gynecology, 168,* 719–723.

Doberczak, T. M., Shanzer, S., Senie, R., & Kandall, S. R. (1988). Neonatal neurologic and electroencephalographic effects of intrauterine cocaine exposure. *Journal of Pediatrics, 113,* 354–358.

Dow-Edwards, D. L., Freed, L. A., & Fico, T. A. (1990). Structural and functional effects of prenatal cocaine exposure in adult rat brain. *Developmental Brain Research, 57,* 263–268.

Dusick, A. M., Covert, R. F., Schreiber, M. D., Yee, G. T., Browne, S. P., Moore, C. M., & Tebbett, I. R. (1993). Risk of intracranial hemorrhage and other adverse outcomes after cocaine exposure in a cohort of 323 very low birth weight infants. *Journal of Pediatrics, 122,* 438–445.

Eisen, L. N., Field, T. M., Bandstra, E. S., Roberts, J. P., Morrow, C., Larson, S. K., & Steele, B. M. (1991). Perinatal cocaine effects on neonatal stress behavior and performance on the Brazelton Scale. *Pediatrics, 88,* 477–480.

El-Bizri, H., Guest, I., & Varma, D. (1991). Effects of cocaine on rat embryo development *in vivo* and in cultures. *Pediatric Research, 29,* 187–190.

Feldman, J. G., Minkoff, H. L., McCalle, S., & Salwen, M. (1992). A cohort study of the impact of perinatal drug use on prematurity in an inner-city population. *American Journal of Public Health, 82,* 726–728.

Fisher, J. E., Potturi, R. B., Collins, M., Resnick, E., & Zimmerman, E. F. (1994). Cocaine-induced embryonic cardiovascular disruption in mice. *Teratology, 49,* 182–191.

Forman, R., Klein, J., Barks, J., Mehta, D., Greenwald, M., Einarson, T., & Koren, G. (1994). Prevalence of fetal exposure to cocaine in Toronto, 1990–1991. *Clinical and Investigative Medicine, 17,* 206–211.

Foss, J. A., & Riley, E. P. (1991a). Failure of acute cocaine administration to differentially affect acoustic startle and activity in rats prenatally exposed to cocaine. *Neurotoxicology and Teratology, 13,* 547–551.

Foss, J. A., & Riley, E. P. (1991b). Elicitation and modification of the acoustic startle reflex in animals prenatally exposed to cocaine. *Neurotoxicology and Teratology, 13,* 541–546.

Frank, D. A., Zuckerman, B. S., Amaro, H., Aboagye, K., Bauchner, H., Cabral, H., Fried, L., Hingson, R. S. D., Kayne, H., Levenson, S. M., Parker, S., Reece, H., & Vinci, R. (1988). Cocaine use during pregnancy: Prevalence and correlates. *Pediatrics, 82,* 888–895.

Geggel, R. L., McInerny, J., & Estes, M. (1989). Transient neonatal ventricular tacychardia associated with maternal cocaine use. *American Journal of Cardiology, 63,* 383–384.

Gilbert, W. M., Lafferty, C. M., Benirschke, K., & Resnik, R. (1990). Lack of specific placental abnormality associated with cocaine use. *American Journal of Obstetrics and Gynecology, 163,* 998–999.

Gillogley, K. M., Evans, A. T., Hansen, R. L., Samuels, S. J., & Batra, K. K. (1990). The perinatal impact of cocaine, amphetamine, and opiate use detected by universal intrapartum screening. *American Journal of Obstetrics and Gynecology, 163,* 1535–1542.

Gleason, C. A., Iida, H., O'Brien, T. P., Jones, M. D., Jr., Cone, E. J., & Traystman, R. J. (1993). Fetal responses to acute maternal cocaine injection in sheep. *American Journal of Physiology, 265* (Pt. 2), H9–H14.

Good, W. V., Ferriero, D. M., Golabi, M., & Kobori, J. A. (1992). Abnormalities of the visual system in infants exposed to cocaine. *Ophthalmology, 99,* 341–346.

Graham, K., Feigenbaum, A., Pastuszak, A., Nulman, I., Weksberg, R., Einarson, T., Goldberg, S., Ashby, S., & Koren, G. (1992). Pregnancy outcome and infant development following gestational cocaine use by social cocaine users in Toronto, Canada. *Clinical and Investigative Medicine, 15,* 384–394.

Graham, K., & Koren, G. (1991). Characteristics of pregnant women exposed to cocaine in Toronto between 1985 and 1990. *Canadian Medical Association Journal, 144,* 563–568.

Greenfield, S. P., Rutigliano, E., Steinhardt, G., & Elder, J. S. (1991). Genitourinary tract malformations and maternal cocaine abuse. *Urology, 37,* 455–459.

Griffith, D. R., Azuma, S. D., & Chasnoff, I. J. (1994). Three-year outcome of children exposed prenatally to drugs. *Journal of the American Academy of Child and Adolescent Psychiatry, 33,* 20–27.

Hadeed, A. J., & Siegel, S. R. (1989). Maternal cocaine use during pregnancy: Effect on newborn infant. *Pediatrics, 84,* 205–210.

Hannig, V. L., & Phillips, J. A., 3rd. (1991). Maternal cocaine abuse and fetal anomalies: Evidence for teratogenic effects of cocaine. *Southern Medical Journal, 84,* 498–499.

Heyser, C. J., Rajachandran, L., Spear, N. E., & Spear, L. P. (1994). Responsiveness to cocaine challenge in adult rats following prenatal exposure to cocaine. *Psychopharmacology, 116,* 45–55.

Heyser, C. J., Spear, N. E., & Spear, L. P. (1992). Effects of prenatal exposure to cocaine on conditional discrimination learning in adult rats. *Behavioral Neuroscience, 106,* 837–845.

Ho, J., Afshani, E., & Stapleton, F. B. (1994). Renal vascular abnormalities associated with prenatal cocaine exposure. *Clinical Pediatrics, 33,* 155–156.

Horn, P. T. (1992). Persistent hypertension after prenatal cocaine exposure. *Journal of Pediatrics, 121,* 288–291.

Hume, R. F., Jr., O'Donnell, K. J., Stanger, C. L., Killam, A. P., & Gingras, J. L. (1989). *In utero* cocaine exposure: Observations of fetal behavioral state may predict neonatal outcome. *American Journal of Obstetrics and Gynecology, 161,* 685–690.

Hutchings, D. E., Fico, T. A., & Dow-Edwards, D. L. (1989). Prenatal cocaine: Maternal toxicity, fetal effects and locomotor activity in rat offspring. *Neurotoxicology and Teratology, 11,* 65–69.

Iriye, B. K., Bristow, R. E., Hsu, C.-D., Bruni, R., & Johnson, T. R. B. (1994). Uterine rupture associated with recent antepartum cocaine abuse. *Obstetrics and Gynecology, 83* (Suppl.), 840–841.

Johns, J. M., Means, L. W., Means, M. J., & McMillen, B. A. (1992). Prenatal exposure to cocaine. I: Effects on gestation, development, and activity in Sprague-Dawley rats. *Neurotoxicology and Teratology, 14,* 337–342.

Kain, Z. N., Chinoy, M. R., Antonio-Santiago, M. T., Marchitelli, R. N., & Scarpelli, E. M. (1991). Enhanced lung maturation in cocaine-exposed rabbit fetuses. *Pediatric Research, 29,* 534–537.

Kandall, S. R., Gaines, J., Habel, L., Davidson, G., & Jessop, D. (1993). Relationship of maternal substance abuse to subsequent sudden infant death syndrome in offspring. *Journal of Pediatrics, 123,* 120–126.

Kapur, R. P., Shaw, C. M., & Shepard, T. H. (1991). Brain hemorrhages in cocaine-exposed human fetuses. *Teratology, 44,* 11–18.

Keller, R. W., Maisonneuve, I. M., Nuccio, D. M., Carlson, J. N., & Glick, S. D. (1994). Effects of prenatal cocaine exposure on the nigrostriatal dopamine system: An *in vivo* microdialysis study in the rat. *Brain Research, 634,* 266–274.

King, T. A., Perlman, J. M., Laptook, A. R., Rollins, N., Jackson, G., & Little, B. (1995). Neurologic manifestations of *in utero* cocaine exposure in near-term and term infants. *Pediatrics, 96,* 259–264.

Klein, J., Greenwald, M., Becker, L., & Koren, G. (1992). Fetal distribution of cocaine: Case analysis. *Pediatric Pathology, 12,* 463–468.

Kliegman, R. M., Madura, D., Kiwi, R., Eisenberg, I., & Yamashita, T. (1994). Relation of maternal cocaine use to the risks of prematurity and low birth weight. *Journal of Pediatrics, 124*(Pt. 1), 751–756.

Knight, F. M., James, H., Edwards, C. H., Spurlock, B. G., Oyemade, U. J., Johnson, A. A., West, W. L., Cole, O. J., Westney, L. S., & Westney, O. E. (1994). Relationships of serum illicit drug concentrations during pregnancy to maternal nutritional status. *Journal of Nutrition, 124*(Suppl.), 973S–980S.

Konko, R. J., Murphey, L. J., Ferriero, D. M., Dempsey, D. A., & Olsen, G. D. (1994). Cocaine metabolites in the neonate: Potential for toxicity. *Journal of Child Neurology, 9,* 242–248.

Kramer, L. D., Locke, G. E., Ogunyemi, A., & Nelson, L. (1990). Neonatal cocaine-related seizures. *Journal of Child Neurology, 5,* 60–64.

Krishna, R. B., Levitz, M., & Dancis, J. (1993). Transfer of cocaine by the perfused human placenta: The effect of binding to serum proteins. *American Journal of Obstetrics and Gynecology, 169,* 1418–1423.

Kunko, P. M., Moyer, D., & Robinson, S. E. (1993). Intravenous gestational cocaine in rats: Effects on offspring development and weanling behavior. *Neurotoxicology and Teratology, 15,* 335–344.

LaViola, G., Fiore, M., Loggi, G., & Alleva, E. (1994). Prenatal cocaine potentiates the effects of morphine in adult mice. *Neuropharmacology, 33,* 825–831.

Lezcano, L., Antia, D. E., Sahdev, S., & Jhaveri, M. (1994). Crossed renal ectopia associated with maternal alkaloid cocaine abuse: A case report. *Journal of Perinatology, 14,* 230–233.

Link, E. A., Weese-Mayer, D. W., & Byrd, S. E. (1991). Magnetic resonance imaging in infants exposed to cocaine prenatally: A preliminary report. *Clinical Pediatrics, 30,* 506–508.

Lipshultz, S. E., Frassica, J. J., & Orav, E. J. (1991). Cardiovascular abnormalities in infants prenatally exposed to cocaine. *Journal of Pediatrics, 118,* 44–51.

Little, B. B., Snell, L. M., Klein, V. R., & Gilstrap, L. C., III. (1989). Cocaine abuse during pregnancy: Maternal and fetal implications. *Obstetrics and Gynecology, 73,* 157–160.

Lutiger, B., Graham, K., Einarson, T. R., & Koren, G. (1991). Relationship between gestational cocaine use and pregnancy outcome: A meta-analysis. *Teratology, 44,* 405–414.

MacGregor, S. N., Keith, L. G., Bachicha, J. A., & Chasnoff, I. J. (1989). Cocaine abuse during pregnancy: Correlation between prenatal care and perinatal outcome. *Obstetrics and Gynecology, 74,* 882–885.

MacGregor, S. N., Keith, L. G., Chasnoff, I. J., Rosner, M. A., Chisum, G. M., Shaw, P., & Minogue, J. P. (1987). Cocaine use during pregnancy: Adverse perinatal outcome. *American Journal of Obstetrics and Gynecology, 157,* 686–690.

Malek, A., Ivy, D., Blann, E., & Mattison, D. R. (1995). Impact of cocaine on human placental function using an in vitro perfusion system. *Journal of Pharmacological and Toxicological Methods, 33,* 213–219.

Martinez, J. M., Fortuny, A., Comas, C., Puerto, B., Borrell, A., Palacio, M., & Coll, O. (1994). Body stalk anomaly associated with maternal cocaine abuse. *Prenatal Diagnosis, 14,* 669–672.

Mastrogiannis, D. S., Decavalas, G. O., Verma, U., & Tejani, N. (1990). Perinatal outcome after recent cocaine usage. *Obstetrics and Gynecology, 76,* 8–11.

Mayes, L. C., Bornstein, M. H., Chawarska, K., & Granger, R. H. (1995). Information processing and developmental assessments in 3-month-old infants exposed prenatally to cocaine. *Pediatrics, 95,* 539–545.

Mayes, L. C., Granger, R. H., Frank, M. A., Schottenfeld, R., & Bornstein, M. H. (1993). Neurobehavioral profiles of neonates exposed to cocaine prenatally. *Pediatrics, 91,* 778–783.

McCalla, S., Minkoff, H. L., Feldman, J., Delke, I., Salwin, M., Valencia, G., & Glass, L. (1991). The biologic and social consequences of perinatal cocaine use in an inner-city population: Results of an anonymous cross-sectional study. *American Journal of Obstetrics and Gynecology, 164,* 625–630.

McCalla, S., Minkoff, H. L., Feldman, J., Glass, L., & Valencia, G. (1992). Predictors of cocaine use in pregnancy. *Obstetrics and Gynecology, 79,* 641–644.

Mehta, S. K., Finkelhor, R. S., Anderson, R. L., Harcar-Sevcik, R. A., Wasser, T. E., & Bahler, R. C. (1993). Transient myocardial ischemia in infants prenatally exposed to cocaine. *Journal of Pediatrics, 122,* 945–949.

Miller, J. M., Jr., Boudreaux, M. C., & Regan, F. A. (1995). A case-control study of cocaine use in pregnancy. *American Journal of Obstetrics and Gynecology, 172,* 180–185.

Mirochnick, M., Frank, D. A., Cabral, H., Turner, A., & Zuckerman, B. (1995). Relation between meconium concentration of the cocaine metabolite benzoylecognine and fetal growth. *Journal of Pediatrics, 126,* 636–638. Mishra, A., Landzberg, B. R., & Parente, J. T. (1995). Uterine rupture in association with alkaloidal ("crack") cocaine abuse. *American Journal of Obstetrics and Gynecology, 173,* 243–244.

Molina, V. A., Wagner, J. M., & Spear, L. P. (1994). The behavioral response to stress is altered in adult rats exposed prenatally to cocaine. *Physiology and Behavior, 55,* 941–945.

Morris, P., Binienda, Z., Gillam, M. P., Harkey, M. R., Zhou, C., Henderson, G. L., & Paule, M. G. (1996). The effect of chronic cocaine exposure during pregnancy on maternal and infant outcomes in the rhesus monkey. *Neurotoxicology and Teratology, 18,* 147–154.

Morris, P., Gillam, M. P., Allen, R. R., & Paule, M. G. (1996). The effects of chronic cocaine exposure during pregnancy on the acquisition of operant behaviors by rhesus monkey offspring. *Neurotoxicology and Teratology, 18,* 155–166.

Murphy, E. H., Hammer, J. G., Schumann, M. D., Groce, M. Y., Wang, X. H., Jones, L., Romano,

A. G., & Harvey, J. A. (1995). The rabbit as a model for studies of cocaine exposure *in utero. Laboratory Animal Science, 45,* 163–168.

Neerhof, M. G., MacGregor, S. N., Retzky, S. S., & Sullivan, T. P. (1989). Cocaine abuse during pregnancy: Peripartum prevalence and perinatal outcome. *American Journal of Obstetrics and Gynecology, 161,* 633–638.

Neuspiel, D. R., Hamel, S. C., Hochberg, E., Greene, J., & Campbell, D. (1991). Maternal cocaine use and infant behavior. *Neurotoxicology and Teratology, 13,* 229–233.

Nulman, I., Rovet, J., Altmann, D., Bradley, C., Einarson, T., & Koren, G. (1994). Neurodevelopment of adopted children exposed *in utero* to cocaine. *Canadian Medical Association Journal, 151,* 1591–1597.

Peris, J., Coleman-Hardee, M., & Millard, W. J. (1992). Cocaine *in utero* enhances the behavioral response to cocaine in adult rats. *Pharmacology Biochemistry and Behavior, 42,* 509–515.

Phibbs, C. S., Bateman, D. A., & Schwartz, R. M. (1991). The neonatal costs of maternal cocaine use. *JAMA, 266,* 1521–1526.

Richardson, G. A., & Day, N. L. (1991). Maternal and neonatal effects of moderate cocaine use during pregnancy. *Neurotoxicology and Teratology, 13,* 455–460.

Richardson, G. A., & Day, N. L. (1994). Detrimental effects of prenatal cocaine exposure: Illusion or reality? *Journal of the American Academy of Child and Adolescent Psychiatry, 33,* 28–34.

Riley, E. P., & Foss, J. A. (1991a). The acquisition of passive avoidance, active avoidance, and spatial navigation tasks by animals prenatally exposed to cocaine. *Neurotoxicology and Teratology, 13,* 559–564.

Riley, E. P., & Foss, J. A. (1991b). Exploratory behavior and locomotor activity: A failure to find effects in animals prenatally exposed to cocaine. *Neurotoxicology and Teratology, 13,* 553–558.

Ronnekleiv, O. K., & Naylor, B. R. (1995). Chronic cocaine exposure in the fetal rhesus monkey: Consequences for early development of dopamine neurons. *Journal of Neuroscience, 15,* 7330–7343.

Salamy, A., Dark, K., Salfi, M., Shah, S., & Peeke, H. V. (1992). Perinatal cocaine exposure and functional brainstem development in the rat. *Brain Research, 598*(1–2), 307–310.

Schenker, S., Yang, Y., Johnson, R. F., Downing, J. W., Schenken, R. S., Henderson, G. I., & King, T. S. (1993). The transfer of cocaine and its metabolites across the term human placenta. *Clinical Pharmacology and Therapeutics, 53,* 329–339.

Sehgal, S., Ewing, C., Waring, P., Findlay, R., Bean, X., & Taedsch, H. W. (1993). Morbidity of low-birthweight infants with intrauterine cocaine exposure. *Journal of the National Medical Association, 85,* 20–24.

Sheinbaum, K. A., & Badell, A. (1992). Psychiatric management of two neonates with limb deficiencies and prenatal cocaine exposure. *Archives of Physical Medicine and Rehabilitation, 73,* 385–388.

Shih, L., Cone-Wesson, B., & Reddix, B. (1988). Effects of maternal cocaine abuse on the neonatal auditory systsm. *International Journal of Pediatric Otorhinolaryngology, 15,* 245–251.

Shiono, P. H., Klebanoff, M. A., Nugent, R. P., Cotch, M. F., Wilkins, D. G., Rollins, D. E., Carey, J. C., & Behrman, R. E. (1995). The impact of cocaine and marijuana use on low birth weight and preterm birth: A multicenter study. *American Journal of Obstetrics and Gynecology, 172,* 19–27.

Simone, C., Derewlany, L. O., Oskamp, M., Knie, B., & Koren, G. (1994). Transfer of cocaine and benzoylecgonine across the perfused human placental cotyledon. *American Journal of Obstetrics and Gynecology, 170,* 1404–1410.

Simonik, D. K., Robinson, S. R., & Smotherman, W. P. (1994). Central administration of cocaine produces age-dependent effects on behavior in the fetal rat. *Behavioral Neuroscience, 108,* 1179–1187.

Sloan, L. B., Gay, J. W., Snyder, S. W., & Bales, W. R. (1992). Substance abuse during pregnancy in a rural population. *Obstetrics and Gynecology, 79,* 245–248.

Smith, R. F., Mattran, K. M., Kurkjian, M. F., & Kurtz, S. L. (1989). Alterations in offspring behavior induced by chronic prenatal cocaine dosing. *Neurotoxicology and Teratology, 15,* 35–38.

Spear, L. P., Frambes, N. A., & Kirstein, C. L. (1989). Fetal and maternal brain and plasma levels of cocaine and benzoylecgonine following chronic subcutaneous administration of cocaine during gestation in rats. *Psychopharmacology, 97,* 427–431.

Stadlin, A., Ling Choi, H., & Tsang, D. (1994). Postnatal changes in [³H]mazindol-labeled dopamine uptake sites in the rat striatum following prenatal cocaine exposure. *Brain Research, 637,* 345–348.

Streissguth, A. P., Aase, J. M., Clarren, S. K., Randels, S. P., LaDue, R. A., & Smith, D. F. (1991). Cocaine and the use of alcohol and other drugs during pregnancy. *American Journal of Obstetrics and Gynecology, 164,* 1239–1243.

Sztulman, L., Ducey, J. J., & Tancer, M. L. (1990). Intrapartum, intranasal cocaine use and acute fetal distress. A case report. *Journal of Reproductive Medicine, 35,* 917–918.

Telsey, A. M., Merrit, T. A., & Dixon, S. D. (1988). Cocaine exposure in a term neonate: Nectotizing enterocolitis as a complication. *Clinical Pediatrics, 27,* 547–50.

Tonkiss, J., Shultz, P. L., Shumsky, J. S., Blease, S. J., Kemper, T. L., & Galler, J. R. (1995). The effects of cocaine exposure prior to and during pregnancy in rats fed low or adequate protein diets. *Neurotoxicology and Teratology, 17,* 593–600.

Toubas, P. L., Sekar, K. C., Wyatt, E., Lawson, A., Duke, J. C., & Parker, M. D. (1994). Respiratory abnormalities in infants of substance-abusing mothers: Role of prematurity. *Biology of the Neonate, 66,* 247–253.

van de Bor, M., Walther, F. J., & Ebrahimi, M. (1990). Decreased cardiac output in infants of mothers who abused cocaine. *Pediatrics, 85,* 30–32.

Vaughn, A. J., Carzoli, R. P., Sanchez-Ramos, L., Murphy, S., Khan, N., & Chiu, T. (1993). Community-wide estimation of illicit drug use in delivering women: Prevalence, demographics, and associated risk factors. *Obstetrics and Gynecology, 82,* 92–96.

Viscarello, R. R., Ferguson, D. D., Nores, J., & Hobbins, J. C. (1992). Limb-body wall complex associated with cocaine abuse: Further evidence of cocaine's teratogenicity. *Obstetrics and Gynecology, 80*(Suppl.), 523–526.

Vorhees, C. V., Reed, T. M., Acuff-Smith, K. D., Schilling, M. A., Cappon, G. D., Fisher, J. E., & Pu, C. (1995). Long-term learning deficits and changes in unlearned behaviors following *in utero* exposure to multiple daily doses of cocaine during different exposure periods and maternal plasma cocaine concentrations. *Neurotoxicology and Teratology, 17,* 253–264.

Wang, H. Y., Yeung, J. M., & Friedman, E. (1995). Prenatal cocaine exposure selectively reduces mesocortical dopamine release. *Journal of Pharmacology and Experimental Therapeutics, 273,* 1211–1215.

Ward, S. L. D., Bautista, D., Chan, L., Derry, M., Lisbin, A., Durfee, M. J., Mills, K. S. C., & Keens, T. G. (1990). Sudden infant death syndrome in infants of substance-abusing mothers. *Journal of Pediatrics, 117,* 876–881.

Weathers, W. T., Crane, M. M., Sauvain, K. J., & Blackhurst, D. W. (1993). Institution cocaine use in women from a defined population: Prevalence at delivery and effects on growth in infants. *Pediatrics, 91,* 350–354.

Weeman, J. M., Zanetos, M. A., & DeVoe, S. J. (1995). Intensive surveillance for cocaine use in obstetric patients. *American Journal of Drug and Alcohol Abuse, 21,* 233–239.

Weese-Mayer, D. E., Klemka-Walden, L. M., Chan, M. K., & Gingras, J. L. (1991). Effects of prenatal cocaine exposure on perinatal morbidity and postnatal growth in the rabbit. *Developmental Pharmacology and Therapeutics, 16,* 221–30.

Wehbeh, H., Matthews, R. P., McCalla, S., Feldman, J., & Minkoff, H. L. (1995). The effect of recent cocaine use on the progress of labor. *American Journal of Obstetrics and Gynecology, 172,* 1014–1018.

Wiggins, R. C., & Ruiz, B. (1990). Development under the influence of cocaine. I. A comparison of the effects of daily cocaine treatment and resultant undernutrition on pregnancy and early growth in a large population of rats. *Metabolic Brain Disease, 5,* 85–99.

Yap, T. E., Diana, D., Herson, V., Chameides, L., & Rowe, J. C. (1994). Fetal myocardial calcification associated with maternal cocaine use. *American Journal of Perinatology, 11,* 179–83.

Zuckerman, B., Frank, D. A., Hingson, R., Hortensia, A., Levenson, S. M., Kayne, H., Parker, S., Vinci, R., Aboagye, K., Fried, L. E., Cabral, H., Timperi, R., & Bauchner, H. (1989). Effects of maternal marijuana and cocaine use on fetal growth. *New England Journal of Medicine, 320,* 762–768.

8

Cocaine Self-Administration Research: Implications for Rational Pharmacotherapy

Marian W. Fischman and Richard W. Foltin

Department of Psychiatry
College of Physicians and Surgeons of Columbia University, and
New York State Psychiatric Institute
New York, New York

INTRODUCTION

Although cocaine abuse has been a serious public health problem for well over a decade, a generally effective approach for treating it has not yet been developed. The severity, intractability, and complexity of this problem suggest that a combination of pharmacological and behavioral interventions will have to be developed to implement and maintain cocaine abstinence. Although behavioral interventions have shown some remarkable successes (see chapters 14, by Higgins & Wong, and 15, by Silverman et al., this volume), it is likely that, for many individuals, medications in combination with well-designed behavioral interventions will be necessary. Neurobiological research has provided information about the brain regions and neurotransmitter systems on which to focus and the kinds of medications that might be efficacious in treating cocaine abusers. To date, however, the results of clinical trials testing pharmacotherapies with cocaine abusers have generally been disappointing, suggesting a poor understanding of this disorder.

Cocaine abuse is a complex phenomenon, with etiology that varies across individuals, use patterns that vary by dose, route, and drug history, and effects that, although generally similar, are multiply determined. Most cocaine abusers use a number of drugs, including nicotine (in tobacco cigarettes), caffeine, alcohol, marijuana, and heroin (Foltin, Fischman, Cornell, & Butler, 1996). As has been reported for methamphetamine (Kramer, Fishman, & Littlefield, 1967), the typical cocaine user self-administers cocaine in multiple dose bouts often lasting hours or days, separated by periods when no cocaine is used (binge–crash cycles; e.g., Gawin & Kleber, 1986; Siegel, 1985), although daily cocaine use has also been described (Schnoll, Karraigan, Kitchen, Daghestani, & Hansen, 1985; Levin, Foltin, & Fischman, 1996). It is possible that pattern of use is affected by other substances being used concurrently, and cocaine abusers with current or prior opiate dependence may well be simply including cocaine in their ongoing pattern of daily drug use. It is also possible that the decreasing cost of cocaine in the 1990s, and its ready availability in smokable form, makes more likely the daily use of this drug.

Because the salient feature of cocaine abuse is multiple-dose bouts, even in those who use almost daily, research on the variables controlling cocaine abuse has the greatest likelihood of success if repeated drug use and/or its predictors are studied. Laboratory studies, using nonhuman research participants given access to multiple doses of cocaine within a test session, have developed, refined, and validated the drug self-administration paradigm to serve as a model of drug abuse by humans (see chapter 3, by Bergman & Katz, this volume). Using the drug self-administration model, it has been demonstrated that cocaine functions as a reinforcer across virtually all species tested, over a broad range of doses, and via a number of different routes of administration. Although cocaine can exert substantial control over behavior, research with nonhumans has shown that cocaine taking is malleable. Modification of cocaine self-administration has been accomplished by varying environmental, behavioral, and organismic factors (see Johanson & Fischman, 1989). The identification of factors that can modulate cocaine self-administration by humans is essential for the development of rational and effective treatment interventions for cocaine abusers. One approach to doing this is to include a measure of cocaine taking in research with humans, although other laboratory models are also being developed (e.g., Bigelow and Walsh, chapter 9, this volume).

ETHICAL AND SAFETY ISSUES INVOLVED IN ADMINISTERING COCAINE TO HUMANS

Research in which drugs such as cocaine are made available to humans requires considerable care and thoughtful design for a number of reasons. As with all research with humans, and consistent with the Nuremburg Code and the Belmont Report (National Commission for the protection of human subjects of biomedical and behavioral research, 1978; discussed by Kleber, 1989; Mendelson, 1991), the basic ethical principles guiding such research are (a) respect for persons, (b) beneficence, and (c) equity. The legal and regulatory aspects of clinical research have been well described by Levine (1986), and will not be repeated here. In addition, a number of professional organizations have published statements or are preparing guidelines that cover general ethical and safety issues related to research with human participants (e.g., College on Problems of Drug Dependence, 1995). The present discussion will focus on the considerably more narrow issue of administering cocaine to human research volunteers within a research laboratory setting. It is clear that there is a substantial need to improve our understanding and treatment of cocaine abuse, because of the enormous individual and societal costs of this problem. Research with nonhumans is extremely important, but cannot, for several reasons, provide a complete answer to the complex questions being asked. First of all, we are still learning about the generalizability of data from complex animal models, such as those modeling subtle abstinence effects (e.g., Carroll & Lac, 1987), and we need cross-species information to validate them. Second, we do not know how to model many aspects of human behavior, such as drug craving, and may be more successful working directly with humans. In addition, careful validation of the safety and efficacy of pharmacotherapies in humans before they are placed in expensive and time-consuming clinical trials is imperative to protect those who enter these trials, where monitoring cannot be as concentrated as in laboratory studies. Therefore, laboratory studies with humans are an integral part of research into the treatment and prevention of drug abuse.

RESEARCH VOLUNTEER RECRUITMENT

Since laboratory research in which cocaine is being administered has no immediate therapeutic value to the participant, the safety of these procedures and the appropriateness of the volunteers is of paramount importance. Carefully screened volunteers capable of providing informed consent should be active participants in the ongoing consent process. Investigators must take care that no real or perceived coercion exists, and that the consent process is sufficiently extensive to assure that each volunteer is fully informed. Screening of volunteers is generally accomplished through the use of medical and psychiatric evaluations prior to enrollment into research protocols. Screening should include (a) a current medical evaluation, with attention to the cardiovascular and central nervous systems, and exclusion of those individuals with abnormalities that might put them at risk when given cocaine, even though they administer cocaine to themselves regularly (b) an assessment of any preexisting medical or psychiatric conditions that might predict an adverse response to cocaine or any pharmacotherapy being tested in association with cocaine; and (c) exclusion of those with a history of adverse response to stimulant drugs.

It is generally accepted, because cocaine is such an efficacious reinforcer, that researchers should not administer cocaine to cocaine-naive volunteers, and that cocaine should be administered only in doses and routes approximating those used by the volunteer outside the laboratory, although it is clearly appropriate to use a route of administration that has less toxicity than the one currently being used (i.e., intranasal or oral cocaine could be given to those who only smoke or use cocaine intravenously). Routes and patterns of cocaine use can be validated through multiple interviews, and verification of cocaine use can be achieved through urine screens. Because research participants will have histories of similar or more intense cocaine exposure, and all cocaine administration is carried out under careful medical monitoring, the laboratory experience is not likely to place participants at any incremental risk from cocaine administration. In fact, studies include placebo administration, days when no drugs are administered, and lower doses than are generally used outside the laboratory, suggesting that cocaine exposure is likely to be lower than prior to study participation. Since so much is dependent on knowing the participants' drug use histories, careful screening prior to acceptance into a cocaine administration study is of prime importance.

An important issue, unique to drugs of abuse and certainly relevant to cocaine administration, has to do with the propensity of cocaine to serve as a stimulus for continued cocaine use. The concern here is that volunteers receiving a dose of cocaine in the laboratory might be more likely to leave the laboratory and take additional cocaine. Some studies require participants to live on a Clinical Research Center for the study duration (e.g., Fischman & Schuster, 1982; Fischman, Foltin, Pearlson & Nestadt, 1990; Foltin & Fischman, 1996), whereas other studies are conducted outpatient, with no drug administered unless presession drug screens indicate compliance with instructions to refrain from all drug use during study participation (e.g., Higgins, Bickel, & Hughes, 1994). In outpatient studies, participants generally may not leave the laboratory unless drug effects are dissipated.

In addition to the concern that cocaine administered during a study might lead to additional cocaine use when volunteers leave the laboratory that day, there is always a concern that administration of cocaine in the laboratory will impact on volunteers' cocaine use after they complete the study. Unpublished data from our laboratory suggest that nontherapeutic cocaine research had virtually no effect on subsequent cocaine use by research participants, all of whom were not seeking treatment. This is based on a comparison of data collected during prestudy interviews with data from interviews carried out 1 and 3 months after study completion. Since participants' cocaine use in studies is equal to, or less than what they report prior to the study, and since study use occurs under conditions different from those associated with cocaine use outside of the laboratory (e.g., in isolation rather than social settings), it does not seem likely that study participation will result in higher levels of use. Further, study participation is only a relatively short period in a cocaine users drug-taking history (generally less than a month's duration as compared with participant's multiple-year cocaine-use histories). It is difficult enough to change cocaine-taking behavior in a treatment setting and with cocaine abusers seeking treatment. Changing such behavior fortuitously is considerably less likely.

Although participation in cocaine self-administration research is not risk-free, care in matching participants to protocols and repeated review by local (Institutional Review Board, IRB) and Federal Agencies (Food and Drug Administration, FDA; National Institute on Drug Abuse, NIDA) ensures, insofar as possible, that safety and ethical issues are addressed. Voluntary and fully informed consent must be obtained from all participants, and procedures for obtaining that consent are reviewed by the IRB. Because all volunteers selected to participate in these studies have prior histories of cocaine use at or greater than the doses being studied, and therefore are fully aware of the effects of the drug being studied, consent is even more fully informed than in clinical trials in which investigational medications are being studied and volunteers have never experienced the effects of those medications.

The issue of whether or not to include treatment seekers in studies in which cocaine is being administered remains unresolved. The self-administration studies described in this chapter all excluded volunteers seeking treatment for their cocaine use. The rationale for this approach is that these protocols are nontherapeutic, and those seeking treatment should not continue to be exposed to cocaine, particularly under conditions in which they can self-administer it repeatedly for a number of days. There is also a concern that the message they receive from such an approach may be that their treatment seeking is being ignored and their continued cocaine use endorsed. Some investigators will include participants seeking treatment, providing the treatment at the protocol conclusion or as a requirement of protocol participation, so that participants are committing to treatment at the same time that they are committing to participation in the study. The decision about whether or not to include treatment seekers in cocaine administration studies should include an assessment of the risk–benefit ratio of administering cocaine to this population in the specific protocol in question. For example, it may be appropriate to enroll treatment seekers in studies evaluating blockade medications, particularly after preliminary data with nontreatment seekers suggested efficacy. Regardless of the decision about whether or not to include treatment seekers, the consent process should clearly indicate that the study has no therapeutic value to the individual, and that participants always have the option to request referral to treatment, an option that should be offered again at the conclusion of the study.

MEDICAL SAFETY

In addition to assuring that volunteers are appropriate for the doses and routes being studied, other medical safety issues must be addressed. There is now a body of literature available on the safety of cocaine administration as well as the precautions that should be taken (Foltin, Fischman, & Levin, 1995; Pentel, Thompson, Hatsukami, & Salerno, 1994). Cardiovascular monitoring during and immediately after cocaine administration and competent medical back-up are always necessary. Cardiovascular guidelines should be written into any cocaine administration protocol, and care should be taken that participants are free of all other drugs and medications not covered in the protocols. When studies are conducted outpatient, monitoring of urines is important in order to assure safe administration of cocaine during experimental sessions.

COMPENSATION

Research volunteers who are not receiving treatment should be adequately, but not excessively compensated for their time. Assessment of the adequacy of compensation is, to a large extent, a local issue, with payment scales related to geographical area. However, it is important to keep in mind that payment must neither be so high that it is coercive nor so low that only one segment of the socioeconomic stratum would be attracted to participate. There is always the concern that drug abusers will use any money they receive to purchase drugs, but this is no different than if a drug abuser were being hired to any other job. Some investigators have been concerned that if money is used as payment there is no way to be sure what will be purchased. One option is to limit the amount of money paid at any one time and require the research volunteer to return repeatedly for all earned money. This has several advantages. First of all, participants can be required to return in a non-intoxicated, although not necessarily drug-free state, since these are not treatment seekers. In addition, frequent follow-up can be carried out immediately after termination of a study. An alternative approach has recently become more popular: vouchers that can be exchanged for merchandise (e.g., Higgins et al., 1993) are being offered as partial payment in an effort to decrease the likelihood that payment will be used for drug purchase. This is a population, however, that has demonstrated repeatedly a skill at acquiring the necessary money to purchase the drugs they use, and study participation is only one source of acquiring money.

CONFIDENTIALITY

Because of the information being evaluated, data on illegal activities such as drug use and sale of drugs or other criminal activities will be collected during the recruiting process. It is therefore important that investigators prevent harm to their research volunteers by making every effort to keep such information confidential or, at least, to indicate to potential research participants the limits of the confidentiality that can be offered. Investigators can obtain Certificates of Confidentiality for specific protocols from the Department of Health and Human Services, which allow investigators to turn down requests or subpoenas for research information. However, there are limits to this protection (e.g., reporting participant's earnings to the IRS under some conditions), and investigators should inform themselves of these limits and carefully monitor staff and affiliated personnel to ensure that participant confidentiality is not breached (e.g., contacting participants who have not agreed to be contacted, discussing volunteers outside of the research environment). Personnel should be trained to keep all identifying information in research files and avoid having them read by those not listed on the Confidentiality Certificates. There are also state and local reporting requirements that take precedence over Confidentiality Certificates (e.g., issues related to child abuse, sexually transmitted diseases), and researchers should inform themselves about local rules and regulations.

ASSESSING COCAINE SELF-ADMINISTRATION IN HUMAN RESEARCH PARTICIPANTS

GENERAL METHODOLOGY

Access to cocaine has been studied under a number of different conditions in non-humans, all of which take advantage of the fact that cocaine is an efficacious reinforcer and can therefore be used to maintain behavior leading to its delivery. The simplest self-administration paradigm is one in which cocaine is made available contingent on a fixed number of responses or some other response "cost." Cocaine-maintained responding occurs readily under this free-access procedure, with the patterns of intake dependent on variables such as the contingencies in effect and the dose of cocaine available. For example, there is an inverse relationship between dose and rate of responding related to the interaction between cocaine's reinforcing and direct rate-suppressant effects (e.g., Herling, Downs, & Woods, 1979). The reinforcement schedule under which responding is maintained influences response rate, as has been shown with interval schedules (e.g., Balster & Schuster, 1973) and second-order schedules (e.g., Goldberg, Morse, & Goldberg, 1976). These parametric schedule manipulations using cocaine as a reinforcer have not, however, been carried out with humans, with the exception of a pilot study with two participants, using a second-order schedule of cocaine (25 mg/injection or 2.5, 7.9, and 25 mg/injection) delivery (Henningfield, Nemeth-Coslett, Katz, & Goldberg, 1987). Completion of 100 responses was followed by a visual and an auditory stimulus, and completion of the first 100 responses after 1 h had elapsed was followed by the visual and auditory stimuli plus a cocaine infusion. The session continued for three cocaine injections or $3\frac{1}{2}$ h. Response rates for both participants were high, with rate greater under cocaine than saline for only one of the two participants. Furthermore, self-reported effects were not predictive of the rate of responding for cocaine or saline. Because so little data on behavior maintained under complex schedules of reinforcement in humans are available, it is difficult to reach a firm conclusion about this paradigm, but it does suggest that a model based on response rate does not hold great promise as a viable model for evaluating drug use by humans.

An alternative procedure for studying drug abuse by humans is a choice procedure. Understanding the determinants of the reinforcing effects of drugs in an environment in which alternative reinforcers are available has great relevance for developing therapeutic interventions for cocaine abusers. A better understanding of the factors controlling the choice to use drugs should suggest approaches to modifying that choice. Laboratory research with nonhumans has delineated some of the determinants of choice both between different drugs and between drug and nondrug reinforcers. For example, the frequency of drug choice depends on dose (Johanson, 1975; Nader & Woolverton, 1991), as well as environmental factors such as the availability of a nondrug option (Carroll, Carmona, & May, 1991), simultaneous delivery of electric shock (Johanson, 1977), or an increased response requirement for drug (Nader & Woolverton, 1992).

Although data obtained using a cocaine self-administration paradigm in nonhumans have important scientific and clinical implications, understanding the level of their generalizability to humans requires research in humans. Much research studying drugs of abuse with humans has been accomplished using a single-dose, experimenter-administered drug paradigm (e.g., Jasinski, Nutt, & Griffith, 1974; Preston & Jasinski, 1991; Preston, Sullivan, Strain, & Bigelow, 1992), measuring subjective, physiological, and sometimes performance effects of the drug being tested. The assumption has been that certain measures of subjective effects (e.g., "euphoria," drug liking) predict the likelihood that a drug will function as a reinforcer (Fischman, 1989; Fischman & Foltin, 1991). Although it is certainly the case the drugs that readily serve as reinforcers in humans also have effects that lead to self-reports of "liking" or "euphoria," these self-reported effects can dissociate from drug taking under some conditions (Fischman, 1989; Fischman & Foltin, 1992). Understanding the relationship between drug taking and the behavioral context in which it occurs has the potential to provide information about modifying that behavior. The collection of subjective effects data in the self-administration paradigm can delineate the relationship between self-reported effects and drug self-administration.

ROUTES OF ADMINISTRATION

Cocaine is generally self-administered for nonmedical purposes via the intranasal, intravenous, or smoked routes of administration. Although 95% of users reported past-year cocaine use by the intranasal route in 1985 (NIDA, 1988), by 1993 the percentage reporting past-year intranasal cocaine use had decreased to 77% (SAMHSA, 1995). The percent reporting past-year intravenous use declined from 17% to 7% over that period, with only smoking cocaine maintaining popularity over this period (between 36% and 39%). Once absorbed, the pharmacokinetics of cocaine are quite similar regardless of the route administered (see Hatsukami & Fischman, 1996), and the pharmacological effects of the drug are the same regardless of the route. However, the rate of onset, intensity, and duration of cocaine's effects are route dependent. Oral ingestion, not generally used for nonmedical purposes, achieves maximal blood (and therefore brain concentration) most slowly, followed by the intranasal route (Figure 8.1). Intravenous and smoked cocaine achieve maximal concentrations most rapidly, providing maximal cocaine plasma levels within seconds of ingestion. The popularity of smoked cocaine can thus be understood because it provides a route of administration that is both socially acceptable and requires minimal paraphernalia, while still providing the possibility of a drug effect comparable in magnitude to the intravenous route. Thus, administering intranasal cocaine to an intravenous or smoked cocaine user would not be considered a risk because of the lower rate of onset of the effect and the smaller amount of route-related toxicity (e.g., HIV). Until the mid-1980s cocaine hydrochloride, which is destroyed at the temperatures required to vaporize it, was virtually the only form of illicit cocaine available. Cocaine base ("crack"), however, can be smoked at much lower temperatures, and, for the past 10–12 years, has been available for illicit purchase. Furthermore, the unit price of crack makes it popular with those who have little money to spend. Although drug prices can vary, even within a city, cocaine hydrochloride sells for approximately $25–$100/gram, whereas crack cocaine can sell for as little as $1–$5/rock, with 30–40 rocks obtained from a gram of cocaine (Hatsukami & Fischman, 1996).

Research with humans has investigated cocaine taking by the intranasal, intravenous, and smoked routes of administration. Prior to beginning studies in which multiple doses were made available for self-administration, it was necessary to conduct single-dose and experimenter-administered multiple-dose studies to assure that the schedules of administration were safe and to understand more thoroughly the consequences of repeated cocaine in the dose range being proposed (e.g., Fischman et al., 1976; Fischman, Schuster, Javaid, Hatano, & Davis, 1985; Foltin, Fischman, Pedroso, & Pearlson, 1988; Foltin, Fischman, Nestadt, Stromberger, Cornell & Pearlson, 1990; Hatsukami et al., 1994). Under such conditions, it was found that cocaine's rate of metabolism and metabolic profile remains generally the same despite route or dose. Furthermore, acute tolerance development has been documented via the intravenous (Fischman et al., 1985), intranasal (Foltin et al., 1988), and smoked routes of administration (Foltin & Fischman, 1991; chapter 5, by Woolverton & Weiss, this volume). Because cocaine is frequently taken repeatedly over days or even weeks, its chronic effects clearly impact self-administration. The chronic effects of many drugs can be substantial, in-

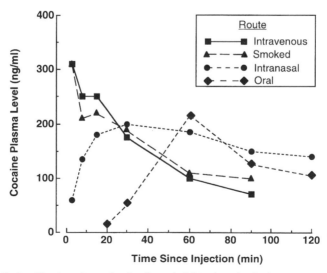

FIGURE 8.1   Cocaine plasma levels after administration via the intravenous, smoked, intranasal, and oral routes. (Figure redrawn from Fischman, M. W., Behavioral pharmacology of cocaine, *The Journal of Clinical Psychiatry,* 1988, *49,* 7–10. Copyright 1989, Physicians Postgraduate Press. Reprinted by permission.)

cluding tolerance, physical dependence, and sensitization. Tolerance and physical dependence can increase drug-seeking and drug-taking behavior, although the relationship is a complex one. However, although research on these topics has been carried out in nonhumans, most studies evaluating drug self-administration by humans do not focus on these issues (see chapter 5, by Woolverton & Weiss, this volume).

With the exception of one study described above (Henningfield et al., 1987), there has been no published research on cocaine self-administration under conditions in which single doses of cocaine are the only programmed reinforcers available. Instead, cocaine self-administration research with humans has focused on the effects of competing alternatives (e.g., a second dose of cocaine or placebo or money). These paradigms, often called "drug choice" procedures, are self-administration procedures in which cocaine taking is measured under conditions in which more than one stimulus is available for self-administration, and the options are made available in discrete trials. First used to study cocaine self-administration by rhesus monkeys (Johanson & Schuster, 1975) to eliminate the direct effects of cocaine on response rate, this paradigm has been used productively since then to study cocaine-taking behavior in several species. The terms *choice* and *self-administration* will be used interchangeably in this discussion.

CHOICE: COCAINE DOSE AND ROUTE OF ADMINISTRATION

When research participants who are not maintained on any treatment medication are given the opportunity to choose between intravenous injections of cocaine and saline or between two doses of cocaine, they reliably choose cocaine over saline and higher doses of cocaine over lower doses (Fischman & Schuster, 1982), as might be anticipated of those who choose to take cocaine repeatedly outside of the laboratory. Similarly, research participants tested on an outpatient basis and allowed to choose between intranasal cocaine and placebo choose cocaine over placebo and, when the alternative reinforcer is money, show lawful dose response functions related to the amount of money versus drug available (Higgins et al., 1994). However, when research participants who consistently chose high-dose intravenous cocaine over low doses had the low doses paired with money, they were inconsistent in shifting their choices to the low-dose plus money combinations (Foltin & Fischman, unpublished). Participants in this latter study lived on a hospital unit, with standard hospital food and recreation available, and had no way to spend money while in the hospital, which might account for the discrepancy between the Higgins et al. (1994) study and this one, although dose and route of administration also differed. When participants were given the opportunity to choose between intravenous cocaine (0, 8, 16, 32 mg/70 kg) and tokens exchangeable for commodities available on their research unit (e.g., videotaped movies, cassette tapes, snacks), their choice was dependent on both the dose of cocaine and the number of tokens available (Mayr, Foltin, & Fischman, 1998). Increasing the number of tokens/choice while keeping the dose choice constant had the effect of shifting cocaine choice to tokens, while holding the number of tokens constant and increasing the dose of intravenous cocaine had the effect of decreasing the number of tokens chosen. Similar data were reported by Hatsukami et al. (1994), who provided cocaine smokers with 10 tokens each session and allowed them to choose smoked cocaine (0.5 mg, 0.2 mg/kg, 0.4 mg/kg) at 30-min intervals up to 10 times/day, after sampling the dose available that day. Unused tokens could be exchanged for money ($2, $3, $5, or $7, depending on the test group). More cocaine was self-administered by participants in the groups in which tokens had lower monetary value as compared with the group with the highest monetary value. The data from these studies suggest that cocaine use, in this model, can be modified, providing the opportunity to study a range of manipulations that might modify cocaine self-administration (i.e., test potential treatment interventions).

The drug-choice procedure can also be used to elucidate some of the similarities and differences in cocaine taken by different routes of administration. This is particularly useful in obtaining information about smoked cocaine (i.e., "crack"), a route that has achieved substantial popularity. We have examined cocaine self-administration when participants could choose between a smoked dose or an iv dose (Foltin & Fischman, 1992). After sampling a smoked (0, 25, 50 mg) and an iv dose (0, 16, 32 mg/70 kg), participants could choose up to five doses of either of the two samples. Participants (a) reliably chose active doses of cocaine compared to placebo, (b) chose to self-administer the low-smoked cocaine dose about as often as either the low *or* high iv cocaine doses, and (c) reliably chose the high-smoked cocaine dose when compared to either active iv dose. With few exceptions, both low doses and both high doses produced similar subjective and cardiovascular effects as well as peak plasma levels after the initial dose, regardless of the route of administration. This suggests that initial effects were not predictive of subsequent choice (Figure 8.2). Cumulative doses of smoked cocaine increased scores on a number of subjective-effects measures (e.g., Visual Analog Scale [VAS] Sedated score; Lysergic Diethylamide [LSD] score of the Addiction Research Center Inventory [ARCI]; and the Confusion, and Positive Mood scores of the Profile of Mood States [POMS]) that were not similarly increased by cumulative doses of iv cocaine. These differences were predictive of smoked cocaine self-administration. After-session ratings of drug "Liking" and "Quality" differentiated smoked from iv cocaine, reflecting route choice. However, there were no significant differences between these ratings for low and high doses. The results provide information about the relationship between subjective drug effects and drug self-administration, and demonstrate the utility of a choice procedure in analyzing these relationships.

The smoked cocaine research by Fischman, Foltin, and colleagues and by Hatsukami et al. (1994) was carried out with male cocaine abusers. Although the majority of cocaine abusers are male, the National Household Survey on Drug Abuse (NIDA, 1988; Substance Abuse and Mental Health Services Administration; SAMHSA) found that approximately 32% of current cocaine users are female, and this percentage has remained constant for at least 9 years. As Dudish, Pentel, and

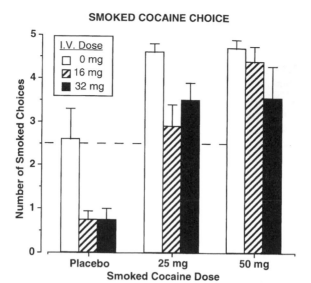

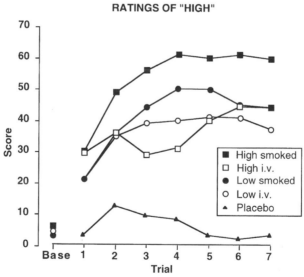

FIGURE 8.2   Relationship between initial ratings of "High" and choice to self-administer smoked or intravenous cocaine. (Figure redrawn using data from Figures 1 and 3 in Foltin, R. W., & Fischman, M. W., Self-administration of cocaine by humans: Choice between smoked and intravenous cocaine. *Journal of Pharmacology and Experimental Therapeutics*, 1992, 261, 841–849. Reprinted with permission).

Hatsukami (1996) have pointed out, it is possible that males and females may have differential responses to cocaine both because sex hormones may affect behavioral and physiological responsivity to cocaine and because cocaine may modify its own effects by altering the hormonal cycles. Dudish et al. (1996) in a paradigm similar to that used by Hatsukami et al. (1994), gave female participants the opportunity to choose to purchase smoked cocaine or $5 every 30 min, using tokens earned earlier that day. As with males, there was a dose–response relationship between cocaine administration and the dose available. Furthermore, as in other studies, acute tolerance developed to cocaine's heart-rate increasing and subjective ("High," "Stimulated") effects. The authors noted that there were fewer significant self-reported effects of cocaine by females in this study compared to an earlier one with males by Lexau, Hatsukami, Pentel, and Flygare (1995), although the studies were not designed to be compared directly.

Drug abusers who restrict their use to cocaine only are extremely rare. Polydrug use or abuse is the general rule, with alcohol, cannabis, nicotine cigarettes, and caffeinated beverages being most commonly used with cocaine (Higgins, Roll, & Bickel, 1996). In addition, many cocaine abusers combine cocaine with opiates such as heroin. Because such drug combinations are commonplace, it is important to understand the way in which they interact, and if use of one impacts the likelihood that another drug will be abused. For example, if an individual is in treatment, are there empirical reasons why use of other psychoactive substances should be proscribed? Because the drug self-administration model is believed to model drug use outside of the laboratory, it has the potential to provide useful information about the interactions of drugs of abuse. Such interactions have been studied with single doses of cocaine combined with alcohol (Foltin & Fischman, 1988; Farre et al., 1993; Higgins et al., 1992), marijuana (Foltin & Fischman, 1990), and an opiate (Foltin & Fischman 1992), but rarely in a cocaine self-administration study, although such studies have the potential to identify more accurately the behavioral and physiological consequences of polydrug use in cocaine abusers than do single-dose studies. Higgins and his colleagues (1996) demonstrated that alcohol pretreatment (0.5 and 1.0 g/kg) resulted in increased preference for intranasal cocaine (10-mg unit doses), providing a clear rationale for the generally accepted clinical approach of counseling cocaine abusers to cease alcohol use in conjunction with their attempts to maintain cocaine abstinence. (e.g., Carroll, Rounsaville, & Bryant, 1993).

The data collected with human research participants in a number of different choice paradigms, giving participants the opportunity to choose between intranasal, intravenous, or smoked cocaine and alternative reinforcers (drug or nondrug), have been remarkably consistent and impressively similar to data collected with nonhuman research subjects. Parametric manipulations have yielded systematic shifts in behavior (e.g., dose–response functions, shifts related to magnitude of alternative reinforcers, etc.). Such consistency suggests that these procedures should be useful in predicting shifts in behavior related to pharmacological and nonpharmacological treatment interventions.

THE USE OF COCAINE SELF-ADMINISTRATION PROCEDURES TO INFORM COCAINE PHARMACOTHERAPY

The general approach for testing new medications for the treatment of cocaine abuse has been to investigate a compound that has been shown promising in neuroscience research or self-administration research with nonhumans, by carrying out a few case studies or initiating an open-label trial, in which both physician and patient know the medication being tested. These trials have been impressively successful, suggesting in many cases that the medication being studied will have great promise for the treatment of cocaine abusers (e.g., Berger, Gawin, & Kosten, 1989, testing mazindol). The successful open-label trials have been followed by double-blind placebo-controlled trials, which can take 2–3 years to complete and require a patient population of several hundred cocaine abusers. To date, little success has been reported following this approach to clinical testing (e.g., Stine, Krystal, Kosten, & Charney, 1995, testing mazindol).

LABORATORY MODELS

There is no procedure currently available in which data collected in the laboratory can directly predict clinical efficacy in treating cocaine abuse. Neurobiological research has provided us with extremely useful information about the areas of the brain affected by cocaine use and the general drug class to test, but the behavior of cocaine use is multiply determined, and potential treatment medications require careful behavioral testing. Self-administration research using nonhumans has even more predictive validity, but, again, studies must be carried out in humans in order to evaluate their efficacy. Ultimately these medications must be tested in humans in order to assess their efficacy. Two general laboratory approaches for testing medications in humans have been developed. They are (a) experimenter-controlled challenge studies (described by Bigelow & Walsh, chapter 9, this volume) and (b) subject-controlled self-administration studies, described in this chapter. Because we do not have prototype-effective medications to treat cocaine abuse, it is not possible to validate these laboratory models through controlled clinical trials. Nevertheless, both laboratory models, using human research participants, appear to have some predictive validity. Despite a difference in the focus of these procedures, they share many measures and many advantages. Because multiple measures are taken under controlled conditions, fewer research participants are required. The laboratory studies include a placebo comparison, are less expensive, are relatively more rapid than controlled clinical trials, and provide information on the behavioral mechanism of action of a potential medication. We believe that the self-administration laboratory model has face validity as well, with the potential to be a useful adjunct to clinical trials research. When a clinical trial is successful, it is often difficult to say more about the medication than drug use was decreased, and further studies must be carried out to elucidate the results. The laboratory self-administration model, which measures both drug use and other drug effects can be more specific in describing this clinical outcome. Medications can modify cocaine use in a number of different ways, such as by decreasing craving, initiating abstinence, decreasing the positive effects of the drug, substituting for cocaine, or blocking cocaine's effects. Differentiation of these effects can best be effected through use of multiple laboratory measures.

COCAINE CRAVING

A challenge to laboratory research, whether the model focuses on self-administration or experimenter-administered drug, is the objective measurement of transient, often situation-specific self-reports by patients in treatment programs. One example of this is the feeling of craving, described by many patients as an irresistible motivation to continue use despite firm resolutions to remain abstinent. From the perspective of the drug abuser, craving is a major impediment to abstinence, and its presence is the major predictor of drug use. If this is the case, it could be an important measure to include in any self-administration study. Although the concept of craving may have importance from a descriptive perspective, it is an extremely difficult concept to measure in the laboratory because studies attempting to correlate reports of "wanting" or "craving" cocaine with actual use of cocaine in a laboratory setting have not been successful. Under some conditions cocaine use remained unchanged as reports of "wanting" cocaine decreased (Fischman et al., 1990); under other conditions when cocaine use decreased, "wanting" cocaine remained unchanged (Foltin & Fischman, 1994). Similar dissociations have been found with tobacco smokers (Nemeth-Coslett & Henningfield, 1986) and are supported by a report by Stephen Higgins (personal communication, 1995), suggesting that craving reports by cocaine abusers during the first week of treatment participation were only weakly predictive of treatment outcome (correlation of 0.25). In addition, changes in craving over the course of the treatment intervention were not correlated with success abstaining from cocaine use. Further, Negrete, and Emil (1992) measured cue reactivity in cocaine users entering treatment and found that level of reactivity to cocaine-related cues did not predict success in treatment. The implication from these data is that craving and the increased probability of drug self-administration may both be related to other variables (e.g., withdrawal states, drug-associated environmental cues), but that craving is not causally related to drug taking. Thus, although craving measures may be a part of the overall study design, they should not be used as surrogates for cocaine taking in predicting pharmacotherapeutic efficacy.

TESTING PHARMACOTHERAPIES

A major concern in the development of new psychotropic medications, as well as in the use of those already on the market, has been to maximize their therapeutic efficacy under conditions in which no adverse consequences result from their use in combination with the drugs that people are abusing. An added benefit of testing potential pharmacotherapies in the laboratory under conditions of repeated dose use is that the effects of the medication in combination with cocaine, approximating the doses and patterns generally used, can be assessed, and evaluation of safety with estimates of the likelihood of efficacy carried out.

Desipramine

The first medication to be tested in the cocaine choice/self-administration paradigm was the tricyclic antidepressant, desipramine, based on both positive clinical reports (Gawin & Kleber, 1986), and the hypothesis that desipramine might be effective by reversing some of the neurochemical changes produced by chronic exposure to cocaine (Fischman et al., 1990). Participants were tested with iv cocaine while inpatients, but were maintained as outpatients for 3–4 weeks on doses of desipramine, which achieved blood levels reported to be clinically effective in cocaine abusers (125 ng/ml). Maintenance on desipramine was not effective in reducing the amount of cocaine self-administered in the laboratory: participants chose to take the same amount of cocaine whether or not they were maintained on desipramine (Figure 8.3). However, desipramine maintenance did have an effect on a number of cocaine's subjective effects as well as on reports of "I Want Cocaine," used as an operational measure of craving. Some of cocaine's "positive" or stimulant-like effects (e.g., Positive Mood, Vigor and Arousal on the POMS; the Benzedrine Group Scale on the ARCI) were attenuated under desipramine maintenance, whereas other more generally negative effects (e.g., Anxiety, Anger, and Confusion on the POMS) were increased. Other self-reported effects were unchanged by desipramine maintenance although they showed cocaine dose-response sensitivity (e.g., Morphine Benzedrine Group, [MBG] scale of the ARCI and VAS ratings for "High," "Stimulated"). In addition, reports of wanting or craving cocaine were substantially reduced, similar to reports of reduced cocaine craving in the clinical literature, but this reduction in craving was not accompanied by a reduction in use. This dissociation of cocaine craving and actual cocaine taking again supports the utility of including a measure of cocaine use in the laboratory model, because the self-report data alone would have overestimated desipramine's effectiveness in treating cocaine abusers. The data suggest that desipramine by itself is not an adequate pharmacological intervention for treating cocaine abusers: cocaine remains a potent reinforcer. It may, however, sufficiently alter cocaine's profile of effects so that users participating in a behavioral treatment intervention will learn to use other reinforcers in their environment rather than continue to take cocaine. Controlled clinical trials with desipramine have generally been consistent with the laboratory data, showing both positive (Gawin et al., 1989) and negative results (O'Brien et al., 1988; Weiss, 1988). It is likely that desipramine is most effective under conditions of less severe cocaine dependence or with cocaine abusers who do not have other psychopathology. Kleber (1988) suggested that desipramine provides a treatment "window of opportunity"; these laboratory data describing desipramine's effect suggest a possible mechanism for that "window."

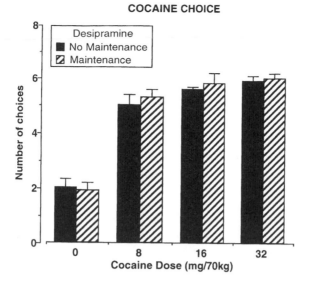

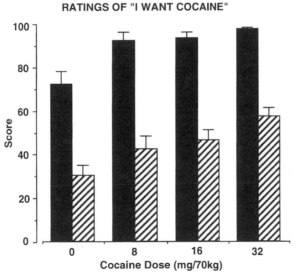

FIGURE 8.3   Effects of desipramine maintenance on choice to self-administer cocaine and ratings of cocaine craving. (Figure redrawn using data from Figures 1 and 5 in Fischman, M. W., Foltin, R. W., Pearlson, G., & Nestdat, G. Effects of desipramine maintenance on cocaine self-administration. *Journal of Pharmacology and Experimental Therapeutics,* 1990, 253, 760–770. Reprinted with permission).

Pergolide

A recent study (Haney, Foltin, & Fischman, in press) using pergolide, a potent long-lasting D_2 dopaminergic agonist, was based on the hypothesis that repeated cocaine use results in dopaminergic receptor supersensitivity and decreased release of endogenous dopamine, such that drugs that facilitate dopaminergic neurotransmission would "normalize" the dopaminergic system. The possibility of dopaminergic dysfunction has provided the basis for the development of several medications for the treatment of cocaine abuse and their evaluation in clinical trials (see Fischman & Johanson, 1995); pergolide is one of them. In addition, data from open-label trials suggested that pergolide both reduced cocaine craving and reduced cocaine use in cocaine abusers (Malcolm, Hutto, Philips, & Ballenger, 1991). In contrast, maintenance on 0.05-mg pergolide twice daily, as compared with placebo, did not result in any changes in iv cocaine-taking behavior in our laboratory, but was associated with increases in reports of cocaine craving. Interestingly, the data also suggested that cocaine self-administration differed between women and men, with women taking more cocaine while showing less responsivity to some self-reported measures (e.g., "High"). As described earlier, this reduced sensitivity in women to some of cocaine's effects has been reported by Lukas and his colleagues (Lukas, Sholar, Fortin, Wines, & Mendelson, 1995; Lukas, et al., 1996) for intranasal cocaine, and was suggested by Dudish et al. (1996) for smoked cocaine, although no direct comparisons between males and females was carried out in the latter study. Thus, despite some promising open-label trial data, this medication does not warrant further testing as a cocaine pharmacotherapy. Further, the data from Haney et al. (in press) add to a growing body of data suggesting that research on the efficacy of potential treatment medications clearly should be carried out for both men and women, since sensitivity to a range of cocaine's behavioral effects appears to be sexually dimorphic (Lukas et al., 1995; 1996; Roberts, Bennett, & Vickers, 1989).

Cis-flupenthixol

Cis-flupenthixol was also tested because of evidence that cocaine's reinforcing effects are mediated by dopamine. Gawin, Allen, and Humblestone (1989) reported successful treatment of intransigent crack smokers in the Bahamas in an open-label trial. However, in a 30–35-day laboratory study with cocaine users tested after oral placebo, 2.5 mg of 5.0 mg flupenthixol, and then repeatedly after intramuscular depot cis-flupenthixol (10 or 20 mg), there was no change in iv cocaine use (Evans, Foltin, & Fischman, 1997). Although the data collected do not support a clinical trial for flupenthixol with cocaine abusers, there is a subpopulation of cocaine abusers who might benefit from maintenance on this medication. Flupenthixol is an effective neuroleptic; in addition, it appears to reduce cocaine use in schizophrenic cocaine abusers (Frances Levin, personal communication, 1996). Thus, this medication may be the treatment of choice for this target population.

Fluoxetine

Cocaine, in addition to blocking reuptake of dopamine and norepinephrine, also blocks the reuptake of serotonin. In fact, the potency of cocaine to inhibit serotonin uptake is 2–4 times greater than for dopamine, suggesting that serotonergic regulation might be an effective target of medication development for cocaine abusers. Fluoxetine is a selective serotonin reuptake inhibitor that has been shown to reduce cocaine self-administration in nonhuman research subjects (Carroll, Lac, Ascenso, & Kragh 1990). In addition, there have been mixed reports of success with fluoxetine in open-label trials with methadone-maintained cocaine abusers. Pollack and Rosenbaum (1991) reported improvement in 63% of the participants who completed their study, and Batki, Manfredi, Jacob, and Jones (1993) reported a significant decrease in self-reported cocaine use, which was verified by weekly urinalysis in a larger group of individuals. Mayr, Fischman, and Foltin (1998), maintained research participants on 20-mg fluoxetine for at least 3 weeks prior to conducting the cocaine laboratory sessions testing that medication. Unfortunately, in comparison to placebo maintenance, neither iv cocaine use nor any of its subjective effects was modified under conditions of fluoxetine maintenance. In addition, research participants demonstrated some adverse reactions (such as substantially increased blood pressure) to cocaine in combination with fluoxetine, suggesting that fluoxetine should not be recommended as a treatment medication for cocaine abusers. Participant attrition due to an inability to tolerate fluoxetine maintenance along with their cocaine use made it impossible to test a higher dose of fluoxetine in this study. This contrasts with laboratory data from Walsh, Preston, Sullivan, Fromme, and Bigelow (1994; see chapter 9, by Bigelow & Walsh, this volume) who reported that participants briefly maintained on 40-mg fluoxetine demonstrated no adverse interaction with single doses of cocaine and, in fact, demonstrated changes in subjective response to cocaine under fluoxetine. Although recent data from controlled clinical trials suggest that fluoxetine may not be a useful adjunct for the treatment of cocaine abusers, the influence of serotonergic regulation on cocaine abuse has not yet been fully described, and the data reported by Walsh and her colleagues are an important contribution to this area.

Buprenorphine

It is well known that endogenous opioid and dopamine systems interact in the central nervous system, and it has been shown that buprenorphine, a mixed opiate agonist/antagonist specifically reduced cocaine self-administration in rhesus monkeys (Comer, Hunt, & Carroll 1994; Mello, Mendelson, Bree, & Lukas, 1989; Winger, Skjoldager, & Woods, 1992). Two cocaine self-administration studies with humans have been carried out to evaluate the interaction between buprenorphine and cocaine. The first study evaluated buprenorphine effects (2 and 4 mg sublingual) in nonopiate-dependent cocaine abusers (Foltin & Fischman, 1994). Because buprenorphine has opioid agonist properties, maintenance results in physical dependence, so participants were pretreated with buprenorphine prior to cocaine sessions only on weekdays. As anticipated, buprenorphine in combination with iv cocaine had effects similar to other opiate-cocaine combinations (i.e., "speedball"; e.g., Foltin & Fischman, 1992). There was no evidence that buprenorphine attenuated any of the "positive" subjective effects associated with cocaine use. In fact, under many of the dosing conditions, significantly greater ratings of "high" were obtained than following cocaine alone. In addition, no change in ratings of cocaine craving occurred when participants were pretreated with buprenorphine. Despite this lack of effect on cocaine craving, and the increased positive effect of cocaine in combination with buprenorphine, high-dose cocaine self-administration was decreased under both doses of buprenorphine. Figure 8.4 presents data from the 4-mg buprenorphine dose. This was the first time that a significant decrease in cocaine-taking behavior had been reported in our laboratory during testing of a potential pharmacotherapy, but was not the first time that effects on self-reports and effects on cocaine-taking dissociated, providing additional support for collecting data on both subjective and drug-taking behaviors. The pattern of results suggested that buprenorphine does not block either cocaine craving or the positive subjective effects associated with cocaine self-administration, and it does not alter ratings of cocaine dose quality. Instead, buprenorphine appears to facilitate some of the subjective effects of cocaine. Despite this facilitation and the lack of change in cocaine craving, choice to take cocaine decreased. Foltin and Fischman (1994) hypothesized that the cocaine-buprenorphine combination has the effect of making the cocaine more opiate-like. Therefore, the repeated dose pattern typical for cocaine might well have shifted to a more opiate-like pattern, in which dosing occurs with longer time intervals between doses. Regardless of the mechanism, however, buprenorphine looked promising in the self-administration protocol and the data supported testing it in a population of opiate-dependent cocaine users.

Up to 75% of methadone-maintained individuals occasionally use cocaine (Kolar, Brown, Weddington, & Ball, 1990; Condelli, Fairbank, Dennis, & Rachal, 1991; see chapter 15, by Silverman et al., in this volume). Continued cocaine use, either by iv injection or smoking, poses a significant health risk with respect to the spread of HIV, and undermines the goals of drug abuse treatment. Therefore, if buprenorphine were to be an effective treatment for cocaine abusers, the logical population to test is methadone-maintained cocaine abusers. Using a controlled double-dummy procedure in which opiate-dependent participants were blind as to which medication they were receiving, Foltin and Fischman (1996) compared the effects of maintenance on either 8-mg sublingual buprenorphine or 60-mg oral methadone on iv cocaine taking, cocaine craving, and cocaine's subjective effects. Half of the participants began the study under methadone maintenance and half began it under buprenorphine maintenance. After testing under one medication was completed, participants were crossed over to the other medication and the study repeated (Levin, Fischman, Connerney, & Foltin, 1997). Buprenorphine maintenance had a small but significant effect on choice to take cocaine, decreasing it relative to cocaine taking under methadone. The decrease was limited to the

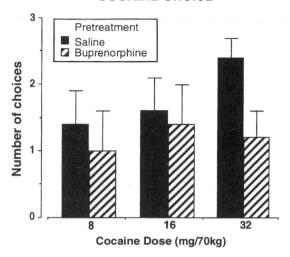

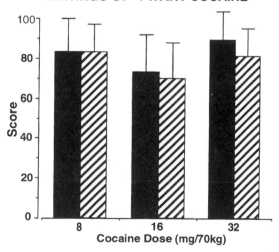

FIGURE 8.4 Effects of 4-mg sublingual buprenorphine pretreatment on choice to self-administer cocaine and ratings of cocaine craving (Figure redrawn using data from Figures 1 and 5 in Foltin, R. W., & Fischman, M. W., Effects of buprenorphine on the self-administration of cocaine by humans, *Behavioral Pharmacology,* 1994, 5, 79–89, Rapid Science Publishers Ltd. Reprinted with permission.

lower doses of cocaine tested (16, 32 mg/70 kg), with no effect on choice to self-administer 48 mg/70 kg/injection, suggesting that the effects of buprenorphine can be overcome with sufficiently large doses of cocaine. In addition, buprenorphine slightly reduced cocaine craving, although neither medication had any effect on cocaine's subjective effects. The data from controlled treatment trials with buprenorphine are still unclear in this area, with some data suggesting that buprenorphine is efficacious (e.g., Gastfriend, Mendelson, Mello, Teoh, & Reif, 1993; Schottenfield, Pakes, Ziedonis, & Kosten, 1993), but a direct comparison between these maintenance medications has demonstrated no difference in effects on cocaine use (Strain, Stitzer, Liebson, & Bigelow, 1994). There are many reasons why individuals maintained on methadone use cocaine (e.g., as one of many drugs being used, because of the opiate-cocaine combination, relieving depression, etc.) such that cocaine use in this population cannot be viewed as a unitary phenomenon. In fact, Foltin and Fischman (1996) reported that cocaine administration eliminated the differential increases in ratings of "Sedated" and "Tired" observed during methadone maintenance, suggesting one mechanism for use of cocaine in the methadone-maintained opiate abuser. The data from this study suggest that for some populations of methadone-maintained individuals, buprenorphine maintenance could be the pharmacotherapy of choice, effectively treating both heroin and cocaine abuse.

CONCLUSION

Despite the explosion in basic neurophysiological research, progress towards the development of an effective pharmacologic treatment for cocaine abuse has been slow. In contrast to opiate and alcohol abuse, where known efficacious medications have played a substantial role in treatment, therapeutic interventions for cocaine abuse have been hindered by the absence of efficacious medications. The need, however, is great and the problem compounded by the fact that there is increased concurrent use of heroin with cocaine, and many methadone clients abuse cocaine. Because much of this drug use is intravenous, the risk of toxicity is substantial, including the risk of infection to iv cocaine users and the increased risk of sexually transmitted HIV common to crack smokers. The data collected thus far using a laboratory model of cocaine abuse have shown the procedure capable of differentiating, in a relatively rapid fashion, the effects of buprenorphine, fluoxetine, cis-flupenthixol, desipramine, and pergolide on cocaine taking as well as on cocaine craving and other subjective effects, with findings that point to potential efficacy of some, but not all, of these medications under varying circumstances. Use of this model provides a prediction of medication efficacy within a shorter period of time than using more expensive and time-consuming controlled clinical trials and with far fewer participants. It also allows investigators to address safety issues in an environment where more intense participant monitoring is available. Although the laboratory model appears to be a useful one, and data from treatment studies continue to provide validation of the laboratory results, the lack of an effective cocaine pharmacotherapy makes thorough validation of this model impossible. However, the inclusion of a measure of cocaine taking in the model provides important information about the relation between maintenance on a specific medication and the likelihood that cocaine use will be modified. Clearly, we do not anticipate a 1:1 correlation between the laboratory and the clinic. However, these data can inform clinical trials, so that dosing and other clinical issues can be more intelligently addressed. An additional point that has clearly been made in these studies is that cocaine taking is extremely robust and difficult to modify. As such, behavioral interventions that can be combined with the appropriate medications must be developed in parallel to the pharmacotherapies. Utilization of multiple measures in the self-administration procedure has the potential to elucidate the focus of these parallel interventions.

ACKNOWLEDGMENTS

This manuscript was prepared with the support of research grants DA-06234, DA-03818 and DA-08105 from the National Institute on Drug Abuse of the National Institutes of Health. We appreciate the editorial assistance of Drs. Eric Collins, Sandra Comer, Margaret Haney, and Amie Ward.

REFERENCES

Balster, R. L., & Schuster, C. R. (1973). Fixed-interval schedule of cocaine reinforcement: Effect of dose and infusion duration. *Journal of the Experimental Analysis of Behavior, 20,* 119–129.

Batki, S. L., Manfredi, L., Jacob, P., & Jones, R. (1993). Fluoxetine for cocaine dependence in methadone maintenance: Quantitative plasma and urine cocaine/benzoylecognine concentrations. *Journal of Clinical Psychopharmacology, 13,* 243–250.

Berger, P., Gawin, F., & Kosten, T. R. (1989). Treatment of cocaine abuse with mazindol. *Lancet, 1,* 283.

Carroll, K. M., Rounsaville, B. J., & Bryant, K. J. (1993). Alcoholism in treatment-seeking cocaine abusers: Clinical and prognostic significance. *Journal of the Study of Alcohol, 54,* 199–208.

Carroll, M. E., & Lac, S. T. (1987). Cocaine withdrawal produces behavioral disruptions in rats. *Life Science, 40,* 2183–2190.

Carroll, M. E., Carmona, G. G. & May, S. A. (1991). Modifying drug-reinforced behavior by altering the economic conditions of the drug and a nondrug reinforcer. *Journal of the Experimental Analysis of Behavior, 56,* 361–376.

Carroll, M. E., Lac, S. T., Acensio, M., & Kragh, R. (1990). Fluoxetine reduces intravenous cocaine self-administration in rats. *Pharmacology Biochemistry and Behavior, 35,* 237–244.

College on Problems of Drug Dependence (1995). Human subject issues in drug abuse research. *Drug and Alcohol Dependence, 37,* 167–175.

Comer, S. D., Hunt, V. R., & Carroll, M. E. (1994). Effects of concurrent saccharine availability and buprenorphine pretreatment on demand for smoked cocaine base in rhesus monkeys. *Psychopharmacology, 115,* 15–23.

Condelli, W. S., Fairbank, J. A., Dennis, M. L., & Rachal, J. V. (1991). Cocaine use by clients in methadone programs: Significance, scope and behavioral interventions. *Journal of Substance Abuse Treatment, 8,* 203–212.

Dudish, S. A., Pentel, P. R., & Hatsukami, D. K. (1996). Smoked cocaine self-administration in females. *Psychopharamcology, 123,* 79–87.

Farre, M., De La Torre, R., Llorente, M., Lamas, X., Ugena, B., Segura, J., & Cami, J. (1993). Alcohol and cocaine interactions in humans. *Journal of Pharmacology and Experimental Therapeutics, 266,* 1364–1373.

Fischman, M. W. (1988). Behavioral pharmacology of cocaine. *The Journal of Clinical Psychiatry* (suppl.), 7–10.

Fischman, M. W. (1989). Relationship between self-reported drug effects and their reinforcing effects: Stimulant drugs. In M. W. Fischman & N. H. Mello (Eds.), *Testing for abuse liability of drugs in humans* (pp. 211–230). NIDA Research Monograph #92, Washington, DC: U.S. Government Printing Office.

Fischman, M. W., & Foltin, R. W. (1991). Utility of subjective-effects measurements in assessing abuse liability of drugs in humans. *British Journal of Addiction, 86,* 1563–1570.

Fischman, M. W., & Foltin, R. W. (1992). Self-administration of cocaine by humans: A laboratory perspective. In *Cocaine: scientific and social dimensions* (pp. 165–180). Ciba Foundation Symposium 166. Chichester: Wiley.

Fischman, M. W., & Johanson, C. E. (1995). Cocaine. In C. R. Schuster, S. Gust, & M. Kuhar (Eds.), *Handbook of experimental pharmacology, pharmacological aspects of drug dependence: Toward an integrated neurobehavioral approach* (pp. 159–195). Heidelberg: Springer-Verlag.

Fischman, M. W., & Schuster, C. R. (1982). Cocaine self-administration in humans. *Federation Proceedings, 41,* 241–246.

Fischman, M. W., Foltin, R. W., Pearlson, G., & Nestadt, G. (1990). Effects of desipramine maintenance on cocaine self-administration. *Journal of Pharmacology and Experimental Therapeutics, 253,* 760–770.

Fischman, M. W., Schuster, C. R., Javaid, J. I., Hatano, Y., & Davis, J. (1985). Acute tolerance development to the cardiovascular and subjective effects of cocaine. *Journal of Pharmacology and Experimental Therapeutics, 235,* 677–682.

Fischman, M. W., Schuster, C. R., Krasnegor, N. A., Shick, J. F. E., Resnekov, L., Fennell, W. & Freedman, D. X. (1976). Cardiovascular and subjective effects of intravenous cocaine in humans. *Archives of General Psychiatry, 33,* 983–989.

Foltin, R. W., & Fischman, M. W. (1988). Ethanol and cocaine interactions in humans: Cardiovascular consequences. *Pharmacology Biochemistry and Behavior, 31,* 877–883.

Foltin, R. W., & Fischman, M. W. (1990). The effects of combinations of intranasal cocaine, smoked marijuana, and task performance on heart rate and blood pressure. *Pharmacology Biochemistry and Behavior, 36,* 311–315.

Foltin, R. W., & Fischman, M. W. (1991). Smoked and intravenous cocaine in humans: Acute tolerance, cardiovascular and subjective effects. *Journal of Pharmacology and Experimental Therapeutics, 257,* 247–261.

Foltin, R. W., & Fischman, M. W. (1992). The cardiovascular and subjective effects of intravenous cocaine and morphine combinations in humans. *Journal of Pharmacology and Experimental Therapeutics, 261,* 623–632.

Foltin, R. W., & Fischman, M. W. (1994). Effects of buprenorphine on the self-administration of cocaine by humans. *Behavioral Pharmacology, 5,* 79–89.

Foltin, R. W., & Fischman, M. W. (1996). Effects of methadone or buprenorphine maintenance on intravenous cocaine self-administration by humans. *Journal of Pharmacology and Experimental Therapeutics, 278,* 1153–1164.

Foltin, R. W., Fischman, M. W., & Levin, F. L. (1995). Cardiovascular effects of cocaine in humans: Laboratory studies. *Drug and Alcohol Dependence, 37,* 193–210.

Foltin, R. W., Fischman, M. W., Cornell, E. L., & Butler, L. (1996). Characteristics of nontreatment sample of heavy cocaine users volunteering for studies involving cocaine administration in Baltimore (USA). *Addiction Research, 4,* 139–149.

Foltin, R. W., Fischman, M. W., Nestadt, G., Stomberger, H., Cornell, E. E., & Pearlson, G. D. (1990). Analysis of naturalistic methodologies for cocaine smoking by human volunteers. *Drug and Alcohol Dependence, 26,* 145–154.

Foltin, R. W., Fischman, M. W., Pedroso, J. J., & Pearlson, G. D. (1988). Repeated intranasal cocaine administration: Lack of tolerance to pressor effects. *Drug and Alcohol Dependence, 22,* 169–177.

Gastfriend, D. R., Mendelson, J. H., Mello, N. K., Teoh, S. K., & Reif, S. (1993). Buprenorphine pharmacotherapy for concurrent heroin and cocaine dependence. *American Journal of Addiction, 2,* 1–11.

Gawin, F., Allen, D., & Humblestone, B. (1989). Outpatient treatment of "crack" cocaine smoking with flupenthixol decanoate. *Archives of General Psychiatry, 46,* 322–325.

Gawin, F. H., & Kleber, H. D. (1986). Abstinence symptomatology and psychiatric diagnosis in cocaine abusers. *Archives of General Psychiatry, 43,* 107–113.

Gawin, F. H., Kleber, H. D., Byck, R., Rounsaville, B. J., Kosten, T. R., Jatlow, P. I., & Morgan, C. (1989). Desipramine facilitation of initial cocaine abstinence. *Archives of General Psychiatry, 46,* 117–121.

Goldberg, S. R., Morse, W. H., & Goldberg, D. M. (1976). Behavior maintained under a second-order schedule by intramuscular injection of morphine or cocaine in rhesus monkeys. *Journal of Pharmacology and Experimental Therapeutics, 199,* 278–286.

Haney, M., Foltin, R. W., & Fischman, M. W. (In press). Effects of pergolide on cocaine self-administration by men and women. *Psychopharmacology.*

Hatsukami, D. K., & Fischman, M. W. (1996). Crack cocaine and Cocaine hydrochloride: Are differences a myth or reality? *Journal of the American Medical Association, 276,* 1580–1588.

Hatsukami, D. K., Pentel, P. R., Glass, J., Nelson, R., Brauer, L. H., Crosby, R., & Hanson, K. (1994). Methodological issues in the administration of multiple doses of smoked cocaine-base in humans. *Pharmacology, Biochemistry and Behavior, 47,* 531–540.

Henningfield, J. E., Nemeth-Coslett, R., Katz, J., & Goldberg, S. R. (1987). Intravenous cocaine self-administration by human volunteers: Second order schedules of reinforcement. In L. S. Harris (Ed.), *Problems of drug dependence 1986* (pp. 266–273). National Institute on Drug Abuse Research Monograph #76, Washington, DC: U.S. Government Printing Office.

Herling, S., Downs, D. A., & Woods, J. H. (1979). Cocaine, d-amphetamine, and pentobarbital effects on responding maintained by food or cocaine in rhesus monkeys. *Psychopharmacology, 64,* 261–269.

Higgins, S. T., Bickel, W. K., & Hughes, J. R. (1994). Influence of an alternative reinforcer on human cocaine self-administration. *Life Sciences, 55,* 179–187.

Higgins, S. T., Budney, A. J., Bickel, W. K., Hughes, J. R., Foerg, F., & Badger, G. (1993). Achieving cocaine abstinence with a behavioral approach. *American Journal of Psychiatry, 150,* 763–769.

Higgins, S. T., Roll, J. M., & Bickel, W. K. (1996). Alcohol pretreatment increases preference for cocaine over monetary reinforcement. *Psychopharmacology, 123,* 1–8.

Higgins, S. T., Rush, C. R., Hughes, J. R., Bickel, W. K., Lynn, M., & Capeless, M. A. (1992). Effects of cocaine and alcohol, alone and in combination, on human learning and performance. *Journal of the Experimental Analysis of Behavior, 58,* 87–105.

Jasinski, D. R., Nutt, J. G., & Griffith, J. D. (1974). Effects of diethylpropion and d-amphetamine after subcutaneous and oral administration. *Clinical Pharmacology and Therapeutics, 16,* 645–652.

Johanson, C. E. (1975). Pharmacological and environmental variables affecting drug preference in rhesus monkeys. *Pharmacological Review, 27,* 343–355.

Johanson, C. E. (1977). The effects of electric shock on responding maintained by cocaine injections in a choice procedure in the rhesus monkey. *Psychopharmacology, 53,* 277–282.

Johanson, C. E., & Schuster, C. R. (1975). A choice procedure for drug reinforcers: Cocaine and methylphenidate in the rhesus monkey. *Journal of Pharmacology and Experimental Therapeutics, 193,* 676–688.

Johanson, C. E., & Fischman, M. W. (1989). The pharmacology of cocaine related to its abuse. *Pharmacological Reviews, 41,* 3–52.

Kleber, H. D. (1988). Introduction—cocaine abuse: Historical, epidemiological, and psychological perspectives. *Journal of Clinical Psychiatry, 49,* 3–6.

Kleber, H. D. (1989). Drug abuse liability testing: Human subject issues. In M. W. Fischman & N. K. Mello (Eds.), *Testing for abuse liability of drugs in human* (pp. 341–356). NIDA Research Monograph Series No. 92, Washington, DC: U.S. Government Printing Office.

Kolar, A. F., Brown, B. S., Weddington, W. W., & Ball, J. C. (1990). A treatment crisis: Cocaine use by clients in methadone maintenance programs. *Journal of Substance Abuse Treatment,* 101–107.

Kramer, J. C., Fishman, V. S., & Littlefield, D. C. (1967). Amphetamine abuse. *Journal of the American Medical Association, 201,* 89–93.

Levin, F. R., Fishman, M. W., Connerney, I., & Foltin, R. W. (in press). A protocol to switch high-dose methadone-maintained participants to buprenorphine. *American Journal of the Addictions.*

Levin, F. R., Foltin, R. W., & Fischman, M. W. (1996). Pattern of cocaine and other drug use in methadone-maintained individuals applying for research studies. *Journal of Addictive Disorders, 15,* 97–106.

Levine, R. J. (1986). *Ethics and regulation of clinical research.* Baltimore-Munich: Urban & Schwarzenberg.

Lexau, B. J., Hatsukami, D. K., Peentel, P. R., & Flygare, B. K. (1995). Self-administration of smoked cocaine. In L. S. Harris (Ed.), *Problems of drug dependence 1994* (p. 224). NIDA Research Monograph #153, Washington, DC: U.S. Government Printing Office.

Lukas, S. E., Sholar, M. B., Fortin, M., Wines, J., & Mendelson, J. H. (1995). Gender and menstrual cycle influences on cocaine's effects in human volunteers. In L. S. Harris (Ed.), *Problems of drug dependence 1994* (p. 490). NIDA Research Monograph #153, Washington, DC: U.S. Government Printing Office.

Lukas, S. E., Sholar, M., Lundahl, L. H., Lamas, X., Kouri, E., Wines, J. D., Kragie, L., & Mendelson, J. H. (1996). Sex differences in plasma cocaine levels and subjective effects after acute cocaine administration in human volunteers. *Psychopharmacology, 125,* 346–354.

Malcolm, R., Hutto, B. R., Phillips, J. D., & Ballenger, J. C. (1991). Pergolide mesylate treatment of cocaine withdrawal. *Journal of Clinical Psychiatry, 52,* 39–40.

Mayr, M. T., Foltin, R. W., & Fischman, M. W. (1998). *Cocaine choice: Effects of dose, alternative reinforcers and fluoxetine.* Unpublished manuscript.

Mello, N. K., Mendelson, J. H., Bree, M. P., & Lukas, S. E. (1989). Buprenorphine supresses cocaine self-administration by rhesus monkeys. *Science, 245,* 859–861.

Mendelson, J. H. (1991). Protection of subjects and experimental design in clinical abuse liability testing. *British Journal of Addiction, 86,* 1543–1548.

Nader, M. A., & Woolverton, W. L. (1991). Effects of increasing the magnitude of an alternative reinforcer on drug choice in a discrete-trials choice procedure. *Psychopharmacology, 105,* 169–174.

Nader, M. A., & Woolverton, W. L. (1992). Effects of increasing response requirement on choice between cocaine and food in rhesus monkeys. *Psychopharmacology, 108,* 293–300.

National Commission for the Protection of Human Subjects of Biomedical and Behavioral Research. (1978). *The Belmont Report: Ethical Principles and Guidelines for the Protection of Human Subjects of Research.* DHEW Publication No. (OS) 78–0012, Appendix I, DHEW Publication No. (OS) 78–0013, Appendix II, DHEW Publication (OS) 78–0014. Washington, DC: U.S. Government Printing Office.

National Institute on Drug Abuse. (1988). *National Household Survey on drug abuse: Main findings 1985.* U.S. Department of Health and Human Services, Washington, DC: U.S. Government Printing Office.

Negrete, J. C., & Emil, S. (1992). Cue-evoked arousal in cocaine users: A study of variance and predictive use. *Drug and Alcohol Dependence, 30,* 187–192.

Nemeth-Coslett, R., & Henningfield, H. E. (1986). Effects of nicotine chewing gum on cigarette smoking and subjective and physiologic effects. *Clinical Pharmacology and Therapeutics, 39,* 625–630.

O'Brien C. P., Childress, A. R., Arndt, I. O., McLellan, A. T., Woody, G. E., & Maany, I. (1988). Pharmacological and behavioral treatments of cocaine dependence: Controlled studies. *Journal of Clinical Psychiatry, 49,* (suppl.), 17–22.

Pentel, P. R., Thompson, T., Hatsukami, D. K., & Salerno, D. M. (1994). 12-lead and continuous ECG recordings of subjects during inpatient administration of smoked cocaine. *Drug and Alcohol Dependence, 35,* 107–116.

Pollack, M. H., & Rosenbaum, J. F. (1991). Fluoxetine treatment of cocaine abuse in heroin addicts. *Journal of Clinical Psychiatry, 52,* 31–33.

Preston, K. L., & Jasinski, D. R. (1991). Abuse liability studies of opioid agonist-antagonists in humans. *Drug and Alcohol Dependence, 28,* 49–82.

Preston, K. L., Sullivan, J. T., Strain, E. C., & Bigelow, G. E. (1992). Effects of cocaine alone and in combination with bromocriptine in human cocaine abusers. *Journal of Pharmacology and Experimental Therapeutics, 262,* 279–291.

Roberts, D. C. S., Bennett, S. A. L., & Vickers, G. J. (1989). The estrous cycle affects cocaine self-administration on a progressive ratio schedule in rats. *Psychopharmacology, 98,* 408–411.

Schnoll, S. H., Karrigan, J., Kitchen, S. B., Daghestani, A., & Hansen, T. (1985). Characteristics of cocaine abusers presenting for treatment. In N. J. Kozel & E. H. Adams (Eds.), *Cocaine use in America: Epidemiologic and clinical perspectives* (pp. 171–181). National Institute on Drug Abuse Research Monograph #61, Washington, DC: U.S. Government Printing Office.

Schottenfeld, R. S., Pakes, J., Ziedonis, D., & Kosten, T. R. (1993). Buprenorphine dose-related effects on cocaine and opioid use in cocaine-abusing opioid-dependent humans. *Biological Psychiatry, 34,* 66–74.

Siegel, R. K. (1985). New patterns of cocaine use: Changing doses and routes. In E. H. Adams and N. J. Kozel (Eds.), *Cocaine use in America: Epidemiologic and clinical perspectives* (pp. 204–220). National Institute on Drug Abuse Research Monograph #92, Washington, DC: U.S. Government Printing Office.

Stine, S. M., Krystal, J. H., Kosten, T. R., & Charney, D. S. (1995). Mazindol treatment for cocaine dependence. *Drug and Alcohol Dependence, 39,* 245–252.

Strain, E. C., Stitzer, M. L., Liebson, I. A., & Bigelow, G. E. (1994). Buprenorphine versus methadone in the treatment of opioid-dependent cocaine users. *Psychopharmacology, 116,* 401–406.

Substance Abuse and Mental Health Services Administration (1995). *National Household Survey on Drug Abuse: Main Findings 1993.* U.S. Department of Health and Human Services. Washington, DC: U.S. Government Printing Office.

Walsh, S. L., Preston, K. L., Sullivan, J. T., Fromme, R., & Bigelow, G. E. (1994). Fluoxetine alters the effects of intravenous cocaine in humans. *Journal of Clinical Psychopharmacology, 14*(6), 396–407.

Weiss, R. D. (1988). Relapse to cocaine abuse after initiating desipramine treatment. *Journal of the American Medical Association, 260,* 2545–2546.

Winger, G., Skjoldager, P., & Woods, J. H. (1992). Effects of buprenorphine and other opioid agonists and antagonists on alfentanil- and cocaine-reinforced responding in rhesus monkeys. *Journal of Pharmacology and Experimental Therapeutics, 261,* 311–317.

9

EVALUATION OF POTENTIAL PHARMACOTHERAPIES: RESPONSE TO COCAINE CHALLENGE IN THE HUMAN LABORATORY

GEORGE E. BIGELOW AND SHARON L. WALSH

Behavioral Pharmacology Research Unit
Department of Psychiatry and Behavioral Sciences
Johns Hopkins University School of Medicine
Baltimore, Maryland

INTRODUCTION

The aim of this chapter is to discuss the rationale for, the methods, and to summarize human laboratory research in which cocaine challenges have been administered to volunteers as part of an effort to identify potential pharmacotherapies for cocaine abuse. Two general approaches have been used in this field of research; both study the effects of pretreatments with potential pharmacotherapies, but one focuses upon cocaine self-administration or choice behavior as the dependent variable, whereas the other focuses on subjective and physiological response to cocaine administration as the dependent variable. In both approaches the laboratory-dependent variable is used as an index for assessing the likelihood of illicit cocaine abuse outside the laboratory under the various pharmacological pretreatment conditions studied. Chapter 8 by Fischman and Foltin (this volume) reviews studies that have focused upon cocaine self-administration as the dependent variable. The present chapter provides a comprehensive review of human laboratory medication–cocaine interaction studies published in peer-reviewed journals in which the dependent variable has been the subjects' response to the cocaine challenge. Most studies using the self-administration approach have concurrently collected data regarding response to the cocaine administration also. In those cases, this chapter is limited to discussion of the cocaine-response data. The chapter concludes by summarizing what has so far been learned regarding potential pharmacological approaches to cocaine-dependence treatment, and by discussing optimal methods for conducting medication–cocaine interaction evaluations.

MECHANISMS OF PHARMACOTHERAPY

In devising methods to search for effective pharmacotherapies for cocaine dependence, it can be instructive to consider experience with pharmacotherapies for other varieties of drug dependence. Table 9.1 summarizes various behavioral pharmacological approaches to substance abuse pharmacotherapy and lists examples of pharmacotherapies that utilize each of these approaches.

Agonist substitution approaches have been most successful overall. These pharmacotherapies provide pharmacological effects similar to those of the abused drug, but in a dosage that is safer, of slower onset, and of longer duration. Via the pharmacological mechanism of tolerance, response to the abused drug is typically attenuated. These pharmacotherapies provide both satiation and positive reinforcement and, at the same time, reduce reinforcement from illicit drug use; they are generally well accepted by patients and sustain relatively good treatment retention and medication adherence.

Pharmacotherapies such as naltrexone, which have no agonist activity in their own right but block or attenuate the pharmacological effects of the abused drug,

TABLE 9.1   Behavioral Pharmacological Mechanisms and Examples of Substance Abuse Pharmacotherapies

Substitution
- Methadone, LAAM, buprenorphine for opioid abuse
- Nicotine gum or patch for smoking cessation
- Benzodiazepines for alcohol withdrawal

Blockade or attenuation
- Naltrexone for opioid abuse
- Naltrexone for alcohol abuse

Deterrence
- Disulfiram for alcohol abuse

Palliation
- Benzodiazepines for opioid withdrawal
- Clonidine for opioid withdrawal

have limited patient acceptance and adherence. They have no reinforcing effects of their own, and their mechanism is to prevent or reduce reinforcement from illicit drug use.

Disulfiram (Antabuse®) is a pharmacotherapeutic deterrent of alcohol drinking. It has little direct psychopharmacological action of its own, but it inhibits the metabolism of ethanol at the acetaldehyde step, resulting in toxic and subjectively aversive accumulation of acetaldehyde if the patient consumes alcohol. The behavioral mechanism of its efficacy is through avoidance/escape behavior.

A final category of pharmacotherapy is that of palliation, or symptomatic relief of distress. This approach is used in withdrawal and detoxification treatment, but it is relatively infrequently considered in regard to cocaine abuse. Palliative care is intended simply to provide immediate symptomatic and humanitarian relief to the patient and is not directed at changing the complex behavior patterns related to dependence and addiction.

All four of these types of pharmacotherapy—but especially the first three—would be desirable for cocaine dependence, for which no pharmacotherapy of any type or mechanism has yet been developed and recognized as effective.

APPROACHES TO PHARMACOTHERAPY DEVELOPMENT

Perhaps in the most logical and linear of worlds, science would progress in an orderly fashion—first from mechanistic knowledge at the basic laboratory science level, then to controlled animal and human laboratory research testing the safety and generalization of relationships and procedures to whole organisms, and only then to therapeutic clinical trials in patients. But this is not the nature of scientific practice. The cocaine abuse problem is too urgent, and linear progress is too slow, so science pursues multiple strategies and methodologies simultaneously. Thus, with diverse data available from a broad array of scientific approaches, a critical issue becomes the basis for selection of medications for comprehensive evaluation in controlled clinical trials.

Controlled clinical trials are the gold standard of therapeutic effectiveness. They are the usual final common path by which potential pharmacotherapies progress from "investigational" to the status of being recognized, accepted, and officially approved for a specific therapeutic indication. However, well-designed controlled clinical trials are very costly and must compete for access to limited clinical research resources. Therefore, the method is most efficiently and productively used when it is limited to testing medications for which there is a sound scientific foundation documenting their relevant pharmacological activity. Human laboratory medication–cocaine interaction studies can be a valuable screening tool for ensuring that test medications have relevant pharmacological activity, and for guiding selection of medications for controlled clinical trial evaluation.

Human laboratory studies are significantly more sensitive than clinical trials for detecting relevant pharmacological activity. All of the substance abuse pharma-cotherapies yet developed (see Table 9.1) are more easily and sensitively detected as interacting with their target drug of abuse in the laboratory than in the clinic. In fact, with typical pharmacotherapy clinical trial procedures it is difficult to detect any efficacy of naltrexone treatment for opioid dependence (NRC Committee, 1978) or of disulfiram treatment for alcoholism (Fuller & Roth, 1979), and these medications received official approval largely on the basis of pharmacological in-teractions documented in the laboratory.

The types of pharmacological interactions that are most relevant to substance abuse pharmacotherapy are those relating to modulation of indices of abuse lia-bility. A useful conceptual framework is to view the goal of drug abuse pharma-cotherapy as being to reduce the abuse liability of the drug of abuse. An extensive and well-validated experimental literature exists concerning assessment of drug abuse liability in humans (Jasinski, 1977; Cami, Bigelow, Griffiths, & Drummond, 1991). The human laboratory medication-cocaine interaction approach builds upon this experience and methodology and assesses whether test medications al-ter the abuse liability profile of cocaine challenges.

STUDIES OF POTENTIAL PHARMACOTHERAPIES USING THE LABORATORY CHALLENGE METHOD

This section provides an overview of the pharmacodynamic effects of cocaine in humans, including measurement procedures commonly employed in the labo-ratory. Common methodological approaches used for evaluating potential cocaine pharmacotherapies in combination with cocaine are described. Human laboratory studies that have employed both acute and chronic pretreatment procedures are then reviewed. A table of results from these studies is provided as a summary.

PHARMACODYNAMIC PROFILE OF COCAINE IN HUMANS

Controlled laboratory procedures make possible the collection of continuous data on a variety of pharmacodynamic measures before and following cocaine ad-ministration. Cocaine produces a characteristic constellation of physiological and subjective effects; these are reliable, reproducible, and their magnitude is typical-ly proportional to dose. In the moderate dose range that is commonly employed in the human laboratory (i.e., 20–60 mg iv, or equivalent), cocaine produces limited observable signs of drug intoxication and, thus, observer-rated measures are not as sensitive as physiological and subject-rated indices. Careful assessment of physiological interactions between cocaine and proposed pharmacotherapeutics can provide important safety information relevant to the clinical utility of the test medication and its safety in a cocaine-abusing population. Modification of the subjective response to cocaine may reflect the ability of the test medication to increase or decrease the abuse liability of cocaine; subjective data can also reveal untoward somatic or psychoactive effects or interactions that could limit acceptability to patients.

Figure 9.1 illustrates representative data from a single physiological measure (i.e., heart rate) and a subjective index of abuse liability (i.e., liking scores). Re-

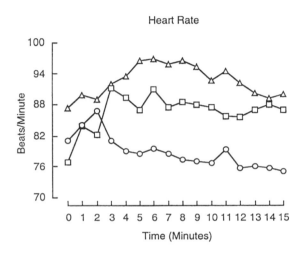

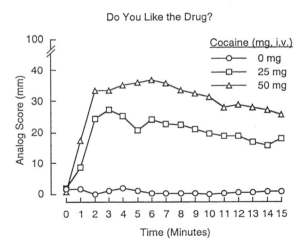

FIGURE 9.1   The mean response (*n* = 8) to single intravenous doses of 0, 25-, and 50-mg cocaine administered in ascending order 1 h apart. Infusions were delivered over 1 min. Data shown illustrate the heart rate response (top) and the subjects' ratings on a 100-mm visual analog measure that posed the question "Do you like the drug?" (bottom) for the first 15 min after infusion.

TABLE 9.2   An Overview of the Prototypic Subjective and Physiological Responses to Cocaine

Pharmacodynamic response	Direction of effect
Physiological measure	
Heart rate	↑
Diastolic blood pressure	↑
Systolic blood pressure	↑
Pupil diameter	↑
Skin temperature	↓
Subjective responses	
Global ratings of abuse liability	
Drug effect	↑
Liking	↑
High	↑
Rush	↑
Craving for cocaine	↑/—
Addiction Research Center Inventory (ARCI)	
Morphine-Benzedrine Group (MGB) Scale	↑
Lysergic Acid Diethylamide (LSD) Scale	↑
Benzedrine and Amphetamine (BG/Amph) Scales	↑
Profile of Mood Status (POMS)	
Vigor Scale	↑
Fatigue Scale	↓

sponses to cocaine are reliably dose- and time-dependent and reproducible. This type of data can be collected in drug interaction studies under a range of dosing conditions. The ability of a putative treatment agent either to reduce or enhance the peak response to cocaine, or to alter the onset or duration of cocaine effects can be measured and used to make predictions about the safety and efficacy of a particular treatment. Table 9.2 provides an overview of the prototypic pharmacodynamic responses to cocaine that are typically recorded in the laboratory.

The robust physiological responses to cocaine can be readily monitored in the laboratory; it is possible to collect most physiological data through the use of computerized and automated monitoring devices. The profile of physiological responses to cocaine includes increased heart rate, increased systolic and diastolic blood pressure, decreased skin temperature, and increased pupil diameter (mydriasis). Although cocaine produces this qualitative constellation of effects regardless of route of administration, as with most drugs, the time–action profile of cocaine's dynamic effects is dependent upon the route of administration. Routes of administration that deliver the drug more rapidly to the site of action produce a faster onset of effects. Pharmacokinetic studies have shown that the onset and peak effects of cocaine correspond closely to the plasma concentration of cocaine and parallel the expected distribution of the drug by various routes of administration (Javaid, Fischman, Schuster, Dekirmenjian, & Davis, 1978; Resnick, Kestenbaum, & Schwartz, 1977; Van Dyke, Jatlow, Ungerer, Barash, & Byck, 1978), although a more recent study reported that arterial concentrations of cocaine are better correlated with the pharmacodynamic time course of cocaine than venous concentrations (Evans, Cone, & Henningfield, 1996). Thus, the rank order for the speed of onset for cocaine effects from fastest to slowest delivery is as follows: inhalation (e.g., smoking) ≥ intravenous > intranasal > oral.

Using the rise in heart rate as an illustrative physiological response (Figure 9.1), the onset of tachycardia occurs within the first 2 min, and the peak response occurs shortly thereafter when cocaine is smoked or administered intravenously (Javaid et al., 1978; Perez-Reyes, Di Guiseppi, Ondrusek, Jeffcoat, & Cook, 1982). Due to the rapid metabolism of cocaine in plasma (Barnett, Hawks, & Resnick, 1981; Inaba, Stewart, & Kalow, 1978), the effects dissipate rather quickly and typically return to baseline within 30 min of intravenous administration. The onset of intranasal cocaine effects is slower than that of smoked or intravenous cocaine; heart rate increases within 5 min but generally does not peak until 20–30 min after administration (Javaid et al., 1978; Resnick et al., 1977; Van Dyke, Jatlow, Barash & Byck, 1980). Finally, the onset of oral cocaine effects is slowest; rises in heart rate are seen at approximately 30 min following drug administration and peak at 1–1.5 h after ingestion (Van Dyke et al., Wilkinson et al., 1980); the effects of oral cocaine are more sustained than those of intravenous or intranasal cocaine.

The subjective or mood-altering properties of cocaine are as robust as its physiological effects and can also be measured in the laboratory. Because the mood-altering properties of drugs are believed to contribute significantly to their abuse liability and reinforcing efficacy, incorporation of subjective effect measures is critical to the evaluation of a pharmacotherapy aimed at reducing the abuse liability of cocaine. The most widely used procedure for evaluating the subjective response to cocaine, as well as other drugs of abuse, is to collect self-reports using structured questionnaires (e.g., checklists, rating scales). These can be designed to provide descriptive information regarding the qualitative characteristics and magnitude of the subjective drug experience.

In most cocaine interaction studies, volunteers respond to a number of different questionnaires before and at multiple time points after drug administration in order to characterize completely the time–action curve and qualitative features of the drug experience. Various subjective instruments have been used to assess the effects of cocaine in humans and these vary widely in their content and format; they can be used to detect the euphorigenic, stimulant, and/or anxiogenic properties of cocaine as well as any relevant psychoactive or side effects of the putative pharmacotherapeutic agent. The profile of subjective responses to cocaine has been characterized following administration of oral (Oliveto, Rosen, Woods & Kosten, 1995; Van Dyke et al., 1978), intravenous (Foltin & Fischman, 1991; Javaid et al., 1978; Resnick et al., 1977), intranasal (Javaid et al., 1978; Resnick et al., 1977), and smoked cocaine (Foltin & Fischman, 1991; Hatsukami, Thompson, Pentel, Flygare, & Carroll, 1994; Perez-Reyes et al., 1982). As with the physiological responses to cocaine, subjective responses can vary in their onset and duration depending upon the route of administration, but the profile of effects is generally similar regardless of route. Thus, the onset and peak subjective responses to cocaine are correlated with the concentration of cocaine in plasma and follow a similar route-dependent time course as described above. Although cocaine administered by any route is associated with abuse liability, routes producing the most rapid delivery of cocaine to the central nervous system (i.e., intravenous and smoking) produce more pronounced subjective responses and are associated with a higher abuse liability (Hatsukami & Fischman, 1996). Even modest variations in the speed of intravenous infusion can significantly alter the magnitude of the subjective response to cocaine; two studies have reported that a faster infusion speed can enhance the subjective response to cocaine when cocaine dose is held constant but infusion speed is varied (Abreu, Walsh, Bonson, Ginn, & Bigelow, 1997; Fischman & Schuster, 1984). Thus, it is important to control the rate of cocaine delivery and to choose a route of administration that has kinetic characteristics relevant to illicit use when evaluating parameters of abuse liability in the laboratory.

Cocaine produces a profile of subjective effects that reflects both its euphorigenic and stimulant properties. Measures of euphoria elevated by cocaine administration include "high," "rush," "good effects," and "liking" for the drug. Ratings of these indices are typically dose related regardless of route of administration (e.g., Perez-Reyes et al., 1982; Resnick et al., 1977; Van Dyke et al., 1978). Responses on these measures of global drug effects tend to be very sensitive, reliable, and reproducible and have been widely used in abuse liability test procedures (Bigelow, 1991; Jasinski, Johnson, & Henningfield, 1984); however, more specific questionnaires may be required in order to distinguish cocaine from other drugs with euphorigenic properties, such as opioids (Walsh, Sullivan, Preston, Garner, & Bigelow, 1996). More qualitatively descriptive adjective rating scales are commonly employed for this purpose and can be tailored to assess specific cocaine-induced psychoactive and somatic symptoms as well as effects specific to the pharmacotherapeutic test medication. Ratings on items that are descriptive or symptomatic of psychomotor stimulation (e.g., stimulated, excited, fidgety, energetic, and nervous) are elevated by cocaine, whereas ratings on measures of sedation (e.g., fatigued or drowsy) are usually decreased by cocaine (Foltin, Fischman, Pedroso, & Pearlson, 1988; Preston, Sullivan, Strain, & Bigelow, 1992; Sherer, 1988). Cocaine also produces a number of somatic sensations that can be detected, including increased ratings of lightheadedness/dizziness, numbness or tingling sensations, dry mouth, sweating, and decreased ratings of hunger (Foltin et al., 1988; Preston et al., 1992; Resnick et al., 1977).

Another global measure of interest is the degree of craving for cocaine that a subject is experiencing. Many researchers and clinicians believe that craving, while difficult to define objectively (see Pickens & Johanson, 1992), may play an important role in continued drug use and relapse. In the laboratory, craving can be assessed using standard rating scales. Craving can be assessed during the absence of drug administration (i.e., baseline levels of cocaine craving) or, because administration of cocaine itself can enhance cocaine craving (Jaffe, Cascella, Kumor, & Sherer, 1989), it can be measured as a response to the cocaine challenge. Researchers have employed descriptors other than "craving," such as "want," "desire," or "need" for cocaine and these have been used interchangeably, with recognition that their specific connotations to cocaine abusers may differ in subtle but meaningful ways.

Another subjective instrument commonly used in cocaine studies is the Addiction Research Center Inventory (ARCI). The original form of this empirically derived structured questionnaire consisted of 550 items (Haertzen, 1974; Hill, Haertzen, Wolbach, & Miner, 1963); however, a shortened 49-item version (Martin, Sloan, Sapira, & Jasinksi, 1971) is most commonly used. This instrument consists of true/false questions that are scored into five subscales: the Morphine-Benzedrine Group (MBG; an index of euphoria); the Pentobarbital-Chlorpromazine-Alcohol Group (PCAG; an index of sedation); the Lysergic Acid Diethylamide scale (LSD; an index of somatic and dysphoric changes), and the Benzedrine Group (BG) and Amphetamine (A or AMPH) scales (empirically derived stimulant-sensitive scales). Cocaine increases ratings on the MBG-euphoria scale and on those scales empirically derived for sensitivity to psychomotor stimulants (the BG and A scales), whereas scores on the PCAG-sedation scale are decreased by cocaine. Scores on the LSD scale are increased by acute doses of cocaine; this may reflect the anxiogenic (e.g., "I feel anxious and upset") or somatic responses (e.g., "I have a weird feeling") to cocaine. Another structured questionnaire that has been widely employed is the Profile of Mood States (POMS) (McNair, Lorr, & Droppleman, 1971). This questionnaire consists of adjective items (65- or 72-item scales) that are rated from "not at all" (0) to "extremely" (4). The weighted items are grouped by factor analysis to form eight subscales including tension-anxiety, depression-dejection, anger-hostility, vigor, fatigue, confusion-bewilderment, friendliness, and elation. Cocaine typically decreases scores on the fatigue scale and increases scores on the vigor, friendliness, and elation scales. The effects of cocaine on the ARCI and POMS scales are usually dose-related regardless of route of administration (Fischman et al., 1976; Haberny et al., 1995; Kumor, Sherer, & Jaffe, 1989; Oliveto et al., 1995; Perez-Reyes et al., 1982; Preston et al., 1992; Sherer, 1988).

DESIGN CONSIDERATIONS FOR PHARMACOLOGICAL INTERACTION STUDIES

Numerous laboratory studies have been conducted with human subjects to evaluate putative pharmacotherapies for cocaine abuse. Two strategies that have been employed are to evaluate the dynamic interaction between an acute pretreatment dose of the test medication followed closely in time by administration of a cocaine challenge, or to evaluate the effects of chronic administration of the test medication alone and in combination with cocaine challenges at various time points in treatment. Although various methodologies have been used, most studies share some essential experimental features. A within-subject crossover design in which all subjects are exposed to every experimental condition is frequently used. Because of the experimental control and the inherent power of the within-subject design (i.e., decreased variability), only a small number of subject ($n = 5$–10) are typically evaluated. The interval between administration of the test medication and administration of cocaine is usually determined based on the pharmacokinetic features of the test medication, such that administration of cocaine occurs during peak plasma concentrations of the test medication. When possible, it is valuable to collect pharmacokinetic data in order to (a) measure plasma concentrations of the test medication (this is particularly relevant when chronic dosing procedures are used), and (b) evaluate whether the test medication modifies critical pharmacokinetic characteristics of cocaine, such as the rate of metabolism.

One of the most critical factors that may influence the outcome and interpretation of these studies is the range of doses that are tested for both the test medication and the cocaine challenge. Ideally, a range of doses for both drugs, including placebo controls for both drugs, should be evaluated. Such a procedure enables one to characterize the effects of the pretreatment agent alone, the effects of cocaine alone, and the effects of the two drugs in combination over a range of safely tolerated doses. Unfortunately, some studies have evaluated only a single test dose of cocaine or the test medication or both, or failed to include appropriate placebo controls; this renders the task of interpreting the clinical significance of findings very difficult and sometimes impossible (for further discussion on this topic see Mello & Negus, 1996). It is preferable to evaluate the interaction of drugs over a broad range of doses for both the pretreatment agent and the cocaine challenges whenever possible. The results of both acute and chronic medication interaction studies with cocaine are discussed below, and an overview of results is provided in Table 9.3.

STUDIES USING AN ACUTE INTERACTION DESIGN

The acute interaction procedure can be useful when little is known about the effects of a putative treatment in humans (i.e., evaluation of an investigational drug). In this case, evaluation of the acute interaction is prudent and may yield important safety data that could support subsequent testing involving chronic administration. There are some disadvantages of the acute interaction design that should also be recognized. First, an acute interaction design may not be appropriate or efficient when the medication under study has a particularly long duration of action and does not lend itself to repeated testing. Second, because most pharmacotherapies are administered chronically in treatment settings, the acute interaction design does not mimic the conditions under which the medication would likely be used clinically. Third, some medications may have a delayed onset of therapeutic action; thus a medication with clinical utility during chronic treatment may be erro-

TABLE 9.3 Compounds Tested in Combination with Cocaine in the Laboratory Setting with Human Subjects and Their Interaction, if Any, and Direction of the Interactive Effects

Test compound	Mechanism of drug action	Route of cocaine administration[a]	Subjective effects	Cardiovascular effects	Adverse effects detected	Reference
Acute interaction studies						
Bromocriptine	Dopamine D$_2$ agonist	iv	—	↓bp/↑h	Fainting/Nausea	Kumor et al., 1989; Preston et al., 1992
Mazindol	Dopamine uptake inhibitor	iv	—	↑		Preston et al., 1993
Haloperidol	Dopamine antagonist	iv	↓	↓	EPS[b]	Sherer et al., 1988
Buprenorphine	Opioid μ partial agonist	iv	↑	—		Foltin & Fischman, 1995
Naloxone	Opioid antagonist	iv	—	↓		Byck et al., 1982
Trazodone	Nontricyclic antidepressant	po	↓	↑		Rowbotham et al., 1984
Nifedipine	Ca^{++} channel blocker	iv	—	↓/—		Muntaner et al., 1991
Disulfiram	Alcohol dehydrogenase inhibitor	in	—	—	Paranoia	Hameedi et al., 1995
Tryptophan depletion	Decreased 5-HT synthesis	in	—	↑		Aronson et al., 1995
Selegiline	MAO-B inhibitor	iv	—	—		Haberny et al., 1995
Chronic interaction studies						
Desipramine	Tricyclic antidepressant	iv	↓	↑		Fischman et al., 1990; Kosten et al., 1992
Fluoxetine	5-HT uptake inhibitor	iv	↓	—		Walsh et al., 1994
Carbamazepine	Anticonvulsant	smk	—	↓		Hatsukami et al.,1991
Methadone	Opioid agonist	iv	↑	↑		Foltin et al., 1995; Preston et al., 1996
Buprenorphine	Opioid-μ partial agonist	iv, in	—/↑	—		Rosen et al., 1993; Strain et al., 1994; Teoh et al., 1994; Foltin & Fischman, 1996
Naltrexone	Opioid antagonist	iv	—	—		Kosten et al., 1992; Walsh et al., 1996

[a]iv, intravenous; po, oral; in, intranasally; smk, smoked.
[b]Extrapyramidal side effects.

neously dismissed as ineffective when evaluated with acute administrations. Finally, some medications may have therapeutic action only at doses higher than those tolerated in acute administration, but well tolerated when achieved by gradual dose escalation during chronic treatment; such medications also could be erroneously dismissed with only acute testing.

Bromocriptine

Several studies have utilized the acute interaction design to explore the potential modulation of cocaine effects by medications whose actions are mediated by central monaminergic systems, particularly the dopamine system. Two studies have evaluated the effects of bromocriptine when administered in combination with cocaine in volunteers with cocaine abuse histories. Bromocriptine possesses prominent dopamine D_2 receptor agonist properties, as well as other CNS pharmacological effect. In the first study (Kumor et al., 1989), seven volunteers were initially exposed to test doses of cocaine alone and bromocriptine alone using an ascending dose ranging procedure as a safety precaution. This phase was followed by a randomized, double-blind interaction evaluation of response to cocaine (0 & 40 mg iv) given 2 h after oral administration of bromocriptine (0 & 2.5 mg). Bromocriptine alone produced modest but significant decreases in blood pressure and pulse but did not alter cocaine-induced pressor or tachycardic effects. Moreover, bromocriptine pretreatment failed to alter significantly any of the subjective responses to cocaine that are considered relevant to its abuse liability.

A second study also evaluated the effects of cocaine alone and in combination with bromocriptine but tested both drugs over a range of dose combinations (Preston et al., 1992). This study employed a 3 x 4 within-subject design (3 doses of bromocriptine: 0, 1.2, and 2.5 mg po; 4 doses of cocaine: 0, 12.5, 25 & 50 mg iv). Following an initial dose ranging safety run-up phase, the effects of cocaine were evaluated in combination with bromocriptine in randomized order under double-blind conditions. Similar to the findings of Kumor and colleagues (1989), bromocriptine alone decreased blood pressure; however, in this study, bromocriptine also significantly reduced the pressor action of cocaine (Preston et al., 1992). Moreover, bromocriptine alone increased pulse rate and significantly potentiated the tachycardic effect of cocaine. In agreement with the earlier data, bromocriptine produced few subjective effects and failed to significantly modify the subjective response to cocaine. Moreover, administration of bromocriptine alone caused fainting in two of eight subjects. In summary, the results of these two studies suggested that acute administration of bromocriptine did not modify either the physiological or subjective effects of cocaine in a therapeutic direction, and its use was associated with undesirable side effects. Both studies are limited by having studied bromocriptine doses substantially lower than those achieved in chronic treatment clinically.

Mazindol

Mazindol, a potent dopamine reuptake inhibitor, has been evaluated in combination with cocaine using methodology similar to that described above (Preston,

Sullivan, Berger, & Bigelow, 1993). Acute doses of cocaine (0, 12.5, 25, and 50 mg iv) were administered 2 h after mazindol (0, 1, and 2 mg po) using a randomized, double-blind procedure. Unlike bromocriptine, mazindol produced stimulant-like effects when given alone; these included increased heart rate and blood pressure and increased subjective ratings of some prototypic stimulant effects (e.g., "stimulated" and "dry mouth"). However, subjective indices commonly used to assess abuse liability, such as "rush" or "liking" for the drug, were not altered by mazindol alone, which is consistent with its low incidence of abuse. While mazindol significantly potentiated the heart rate and systolic blood pressure response to cocaine, it did not modify the subjective response to cocaine in either direction. Thus, this study demonstrated that mazindol, administered under acute dosing conditions, showed no evidence of any therapeutic action against cocaine but appeared to enhance the cardiovascular risks of cocaine.

Haloperidol

Haloperidol, a dopamine receptor antagonist in clinical use as a neuroleptic, has been examined for its ability to modulate cocaine effects (Sherer, Kumor & Jaffe, 1988). In this study, all doses of cocaine and haloperidol were initially evaluated alone in a dose-rising sequence in order to assess their safety and tolerability in the study population. Subsequently, a 2 x 2 design was utilized in which the effects of cocaine (0 and 40 mg iv) were evaluated 20 min after intramuscular administration of haloperidol (0 and 8 mg) in five cocaine abusers; the four test conditions were presented in randomized order under double-blind conditions. Haloperidol attenuated the pressor response to cocaine without modifying the heart rate response; these data suggested that haloperidol would not enhance the potential cardiotoxicity of cocaine. While subjective ratings of "rush" were not differentially affected by haloperidol pretreatment, the peak ratings of "good effects" were significantly lower when cocaine was administered following haloperidol pretreatment compared to placebo pretreatment. Similar trends were seen on other indices of abuse liability (i.e., the MBG scale of the ARCI, ratings of "high"), suggesting that acute administration of haloperidol could decrease the euphorigenic effects of cocaine.

Buprenorphine

Buprenorphine is a mixed opioid agonist–antagonist that acts as a partial agonist at μ-receptor sites and as an antagonist at κ-receptor sites. Buprenorphine has been undergoing evaluation as a substitution agonist therapy for opioid dependence, and preclinical studies have suggested that it may have therapeutic action against cocaine (Mello, Mendelson, Bree, & Lukas, 1989, 1990). The interaction of single acute doses of sublingual buprenorphine (2 and 4 mg) with cocaine (0, 8, 16, and 32 mg/70 kg) was examined in sixteen subjects with histories of both opioid and cocaine abuse (Foltin & Fischman, 1995). This study did not employ a placebo control for buprenorphine, but rather included data collected from a previous study under similar conditions as a historical control for the effects of cocaine alone. Because this study also examined the interaction of buprenorphine with morphine alone and morphine–cocaine combinations, drug conditions were presented in a constrained order such that low–dose combinations preceded high-dose combinations; only the results of the cocaine challenges are described here. Sublingual buprenorphine (2 or 4 mg) administered 50 min before intravenous cocaine did not alter the cardiovascular effects of cocaine. Buprenorphine alone increased ratings on numerous subjective measures including "high," opiate symptoms, "stimulated," "sedated" as well as ratings of Positive Mood on the POMS and PCAG scores on the ARCI. Cocaine administered alone also produced some of the same subjective responses. However, in combination, buprenorphine neither potentiated nor attenuated the majority of subjective effects of cocaine with only one exception; the opiate symptoms scores were higher following the high-dose combination (i.e., 4 mg buprenorphine/32 mg cocaine) compared to the 32 mg cocaine alone condition. This study concluded that buprenorphine alone possessed significant abuse liability and did not modify the abuse liability of cocaine in a therapeutic fashion.

Naloxone

An early study, described as a brief report, examined the acute interaction between naloxone, a short-acting opioid antagonist, and cocaine in seven volunteers (Byck, Ruskis, Ungerer, & Jatlow, 1982). This study varied the pretreatment time (5, 15, or 25 min) between administration of a large dose of intravenous naloxone (20 mg) and challenge with a single dose of intranasal cocaine (2 mg/kg), but included no placebo controls. The results were described as indicating that naloxone, when administered at 15 min prior to cocaine only, potentiated the euphoric effects and enhanced the depression of "lethargy" ratings produced by cocaine; no physiological or statistical results were reported.

Trazodone

Trazodone is a nontricyclic antidepressant that inhibits serotonin reuptake and acts as an adrenergic antagonist. The interaction between trazodone (0 and 100 mg po) and oral cocaine (2 mg/kg) was evaluated in a counterbalanced design with eight cocaine-experienced subjects; no placebo for oral cocaine was included (Rowbotham, Jones, Benowitz, & Jacob, 1984). Trazodone pretreatment attenuated many cocaine-induced physiological responses, including mydriasis, pressor effects, and the decline in skin temperature. Although trazodone did not modify any of the subjective euphoric effects of cocaine, it did diminish scores on the Tension/Anxiety scale of the POMS scale after cocaine as well as somatic responses to cocaine including sweating and shakiness. Under these dose conditions, trazodone did not modify the pharmacokinetics of oral cocaine. This study was aimed at evaluating the safety of trazodone for treatment of depression in patients who were likely to use illicit cocaine and concluded that trazodone could be safely tolerated in this population and would not enhance the abuse liability of cocaine.

Nifedipine

Nifedipine is a calcium channel blocker clinically used as an antihypertensive agent and for the treatment of angina. Because calcium channel blockers can diminish some of the cardiotoxic effects of cocaine overdose, there has been some interest in their evaluation as potential pharmacotherapies for cocaine abuse. One study examined the interaction between nifedipine and cocaine with the aim of determining whether nifedipine could modulate the acute cardiovascular response to cocaine (Muntaner, Kumor, Nagoshi, & Jaffe, 1991). Initial safety evaluations with single ascending-dose administrations of cocaine alone and nifedipine alone were conducted to preclude idiosyncratic responses to the drugs when later administered in combination. Subsequently, the response to single acute intravenous cocaine challenges (0, 20, and 40 mg) were measures 20–25 min after pretreatment with nifedipine (0 and 10 mg po) in ten subjects. The order of drug condition presentation was randomized in this phase of the study. As expected, nifedipine alone decreased blood pressure but did not significantly attenuate cocaine pressor effects; nifedipine tended to decrease the heart rate response to cocaine. Nifedipine decreased subjective responses to cocaine, including global ratings of "drug effect" and "rush" and scores on the Tension and Confusion scales of the POMS; in some cases, the attenuation was more pronounced for the 40-mg cocaine challenge. Observer ratings failed to detect any significant nifedipine–cocaine interactions.

Disulfiram

One study examined the acute interaction between disulfiram and cocaine using a within-subject crossover design (Hameedi, et al., 1995). Disulfiram is approved for use in the treatment of alcoholism as described earlier. By inhibiting acetaldehyde dehydrogenase, the enzyme primarily responsible for alcohol metabolism, disulfiram causes the toxic accumulation of acetaldehyde, producing nausea and hypotension and thereby reducing alcohol use. Of the eight subjects who participated, all were cocaine abusers and seven also abused alcohol. Disulfiram (250 mg) and placebo were each administered for 2 consecutive days; the order of presentation of the treatment conditions was counterbalanced. A single administration of intranasal cocaine (2 mg/kg) was given 1 h after oral drug or placebo treatment, but no cocaine placebo control was included. Disulfiram did not modify subjective measures of cocaine-induced euphoria nor did it alter the physiological response to cocaine. Interestingly, disulfiram pretreatment significantly enhanced peak plasma concentrations of cocaine and also produced paranoid and agitated behavior in three of the eight subjects. These data do not provide evidence of any therapeutic effect of disulfiram against cocaine and suggest that disulfiram may produce undesirable and adverse psychological responses to cocaine.

Tryptophan Depletion

In order to evaluate the potential role of serotonin in mediating or modulating the effects of cocaine, a recent study employed a dietary, rather than a pharmacological, intervention to examine the effects of cocaine following modification of serotonin concentrations (Aronson et al., 1995). This study employed a noninvasive procedure in which central serotonin concentrations were experimentally manipulated by administration of a solution containing high concentrations of amino acids excluding tryptophan. The sudden increase of circulating exogenous amino acids induces protein synthesis causing consumption of the available circulating tryptophan; this procedure has been proven reliably to decrease concentrations of serotonin in the brain (Biggio, Fadda, Fanni, Tagliamonte, & Gessa, 1974). In this study, Aronson and colleagues (1995) evaluated the subjective and physiological response to a single dose of intranasal cocaine (2 mg/kg) following administration of a sham placebo drink and a tryptophan-depleting cocktail. These pretreatments were delivered in randomized order to twelve inpatient volunteers. Free plasma tryptophan was reduced by 78% following administration of the active amino acid mixture compared to the placebo treatment. Subjective ratings on the measure of "high" were significantly decreased when intranasal cocaine was administered 5 h after tryptophan depletion, although no other changes were observed on either subjective, observer-rated, or physiological responses to cocaine. These data suggested that serotonin may play a role in modulating some of the subjective responses to cocaine and that serotonergic agents may be a relevant class of drugs to target for pharmacotherapy development.

Selegiline

Selegiline, an irreversible monoamine oxidase-B (MAO-B) inhibitor, has also been evaluated in combination with cocaine (Haberny et al., 1995). This study was conducted as a preliminary safety assessment to enable the launching of a multisite clinical trial of selegiline as a relapse-prevention treatment for cocaine abuse. Because selegiline irreversibly inhibits MAO-B activity, an acute administration functions like a chronic treatment; effects of a single dose persist for up to 2 weeks or until de novo enzyme is synthesized. This study examined the interaction between selegiline (0 and 10 mg, sustained release oral formulation) and cocaine in five subjects. This study used a repeated cocaine dosing procedure in which multiple doses of intravenous cocaine (0, 20, and 40 mg, 1 h apart) were administered within a single session to generate a cocaine dose–effect curve. Cocaine produced dose-related effects on prototypic subjective and physiological measures; selegiline produced virtually no effects of its own, nor did it alter any of cocaine's effects. These data suggested that selegiline could be safely administered in the presence of cocaine without risk of adverse cardiovascular interactions.

STUDIES USING A CHRONIC INTERACTION DESIGN

Chronic interaction studies, in which the test medication is administered for a sustained period, rather than acutely, provide a more complete simulation of how medications would likely be used clinically. Chronic designs are especially important if therapeutic benefits are cumulative or of gradual onset, or if progressive tolerance and gradual dose escalation are necessary to achieve appropriate dose levels of the test medication.

Desipramine

In a study intended primarily to examine effects on cocaine self-administration, Fischman, Foltin, Nestadt, and Pearlson (1990) tested six volunteer cocaine abusers in the laboratory before and after 3–4 weeks of nonblinded maintenance on the tricyclic antidepressant desipramine. Individualized titration of desipramine doses (mean = 175 mg/day po) was successful in achieving blood levels in the target range of 80–150 ng/ml (mean achieved = 121–134 ng/ml). Cocaine was administered intravenously in doses of 0, 8, 16, and 32 mg. There were no desipramine-associated changes in cocaine self-administration, but there were changes in subjective response to cocaine administration. Desipramine was described as disrupting the profile of cocaine's subjective effects; it appeared to dampen a number of cocaine's positive effects (ratings of positive mood and vigor), and to exaggerate some of its negative effects (mood-rating indices of anxiety and confusion). There were also significant cardiovascular interactions, with peak heart rate and peak diastolic blood pressure in response to cocaine being higher during desipramine maintenance; this was interpreted as indicating a risk of adverse cardiovascular events with cocaine in combination with desipramine. In addition, desipramine maintenance was associated with a substantial reduction in baseline craving for cocaine (i.e., prior to cocaine administration) as assessed by a 100-point visual analog scale (VAS) rating of "I want cocaine"; mean ($\pm$SEM) ratings were 84 ($\pm$4) before beginning desipramine maintenance versus 32 ($\pm$5) during desipramine maintenance. Intravenous cocaine administration produced an increase in this index of cocaine craving; the magnitude of the cocaine-produced increase was similar under both desipramine and nondesipramine conditions but, perhaps because of the reduced baseline, the absolute levels of craving were significantly lower during desipramine treatment.

A second study also examined the interactions of cocaine and desipramine in the laboratory (Kosten et al., 1992). In a within-subject crossover design, five volunteer cocaine abusers were tested for their response to intravenous cocaine challenges of 0, 0.125, 0.25, and 0.50 mg/kg following 10 days or more of placebo maintenance, and again later following 10 days or more of desipramine maintenance (150 mg/day po). Cocaine doses were double-blind and in a mixed order, but the placebo–desipramine order was fixed and single-blind. Subjective ratings of "high" and "rush" in response to cocaine were not affected by desipramine treatment. However, subjective rating of desire for cocaine following the 0.5 mg/kg cocaine challenge was significantly reduced during desipramine treatment; this difference was based on an area-under-the-curve analysis, and reflects both a reduced baseline desire-for-cocaine score and a shorter duration of elevated desire in response to cocaine challenge. These effects on indices of craving are similar to those reported in the Fischman et al. (1990) study of cocaine–desipramine interactions. The cardiovascular findings of the two studies are also similar. Kosten et al. (1992)

also found desipramine to increase baseline heart rate (by a mean of about 18 bpm) and baseline blood pressure (by a mean of less than 5 mmHg), and concluded that desipramine–cocaine combinations may present increased risk of serious cardiovascular events compared to either drug alone.

Fluoxetine

Fluoxetine is a selective serotonin reuptake inhibitor that has received extensive attention as a potential treatment for cocaine abuse in both perclinical studies and in clinical trials. The possible interaction between fluoxetine and cocaine has been evaluated by Walsh, Preston, Sullivan, Fromme, and Bigelow (1994) in a 4-week residential human laboratory study of five volunteer cocaine abusers. Volunteers received oral medication capsules daily containing either placebo (weeks 1 and 4) or fluoxetine (weeks 2–3). During the active fluoxetine treatment weeks the daily fluoxetine dose progressively ascended—10, 20, 30, and 40 mg/day—with each dose given for 3–4 consecutive days. Periodic cocaine challenge sessions were superimposed upon this medication schedule. Challenge sessions were conducted twice weekly, once at each active fluoxetine dose level and twice during both the initial and the washout placebo phases. In challenge sessions, subjects received three ascending doses of cocaine (0, 20, and 40 mg iv) 1.5 h apart. Fluoxetine (40 mg) significantly decreased subjective ratings of cocaine's positive mood effects on several VAS measures. Selected results for two measures commonly used as indices of cocaine's abuse liability (subjective ratings of "any drug effect" and of "liking") are presented in Figure 9.2. As can be seen, the cocaine dose–effect curves were progressively suppressed and flattened as fluoxetine dose increased. Fluoxetine also attenuated the mydriatic effect of cocaine. The extent of attenuation of cocaine's effects was significantly correlated with blood levels of fluoxetine and its major (active) metabolite norfluoxetine. No adverse interactions between fluoxetine and cocaine were observed on cardiovascular measures. The authors conclude that fluoxetine can be safely used in the presence of cocaine use, and that its substantial attenuation of cocaine's abuse liability profile indicates that fluoxetine and other serotonergic agents should be investigated further as potential pharmacotherapies for cocaine abuse. An attractive feature of this study design is that it provides dose–effect characterizations both for cocaine and for the test medication—in this case, fluoxetine. The orderliness of the dose–effect relationships in the results contributes substantially to enhancing the persuasiveness of the results. The single-session determination of each cocaine dose–effect evaluation makes this an efficient testing procedure.

Carbamazepine

Hatsukami, Keenan, Halikas, Pentel, and Brauer (1991) used a within-subject crossover design to evaluate the effects of carbamazepine treatment on response to smoked cocaine base (40 mg). Participants were six volunteer cocaine abusers. After an initial adaptation-session exposure to the cocaine challenge, subjects par-

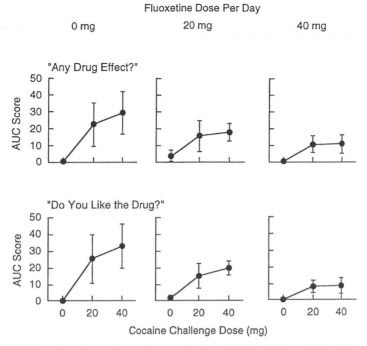

FIGURE 9.2   The effects of successive cocaine doses (0, 20, and 40 mg iv infused over 1 min) given 90 min apart are shown for the visual analog scales of "any drug effect" (upper panel) and "liking" (lower panel) at three successive fluoxetine dose levels (0, 20, and 40 mg po) during chronic treatment. Each data point represents the mean area-under-the-curve score for 5 subjects; vertical bars represent ± 1 standard error of the mean. The effects of cocaine 40 mg were significantly reduced by the 40 mg pretreatment dose of fluoxetine ($p < .05$). (Adapted from Walsh et al., 1994.)

ticipated in two experimental challenge test sessions—one after 5 days placebo treatment, and the other after 5 days carbmazepine treatment (200, 200, 400, 400, 400 mg po). The order of exposure was randomized, and procedures were double-blind. There were no significant carbamazepine effects on any subjective indices of response to cocaine, including ratings of craving for cocaine. However, there were significant cardiovascular effects of carbamazepine. Heart rate, diastolic blood pressure, and the rate-pressure product (HR x systolic BP) following cocaine were all significantly elevated by carbamazepine treatment. The authors conclude that carbamazepine may increase the risk of adverse cardiovascular events in cocaine abusers.

Methadone

Foltin, Christiansen, Levin, and Fischman (1995) examined the effects of intravenous cocaine challenges in 16 volunteer cocaine abusers who were receiving methadone-maintenance treatment. They experimentally manipulated and studied a number of variables—the cocaine challenge dose (0, 8, 16, 32, 48 mg/70kg iv); whether challenge doses were administered singly or as four consecutive identical injections at 14-min intervals; and whether challenges were administered 1 h or 22 h following the daily oral methadone dose (i.e., the times of peak and trough methadone levels). Results were also examined in relation to patients' methadone-maintenance dose (clinically determined, not experimentally assigned; range = 20–100 mg/day). There was no evidence of any attenuation of cocaine's subjective effects by methadone, but rather higher methadone doses increased some cocaine effects. Cardiovascular measures showed no evidence of any adverse cardiovascular interaction, but rather there appeared to be some protective effect of methadone (e.g., lower peak heart rate following cocaine when combined with higher methadone doses). The authors conclude that any reductions in cocaine use associated with methadone-maintenance treatment are likely the result of behavioral factors associated with methadone treatment and not due to any pharmacological attenuation of cocaine's effects.

Preston, Sullivan, Strain, and Bigelow (1996) evaluated the possible interactions of cocaine with chronic methadone maintenance by comparing responses to cocaine challenge in volunteers receiving versus not receiving concurrent methadone-maintenance treatment. Participants were 22 volunteer cocaine abusers, 11 of whom were maintained on methadone (50 mg/day po) as treatment for their opioid dependence. The other 11 volunteers had similar cocaine-use and illicit opioid-use histories, but were not opioid dependent and were not receiving methadone treatment. Each participant received acute cocaine challenges of 0, 12.5, 25, and 50 mg iv in random order under double-blind conditions in separate test sessions. In the methadone-maintenance group, cocaine challenge sessions occurred 15.5 h after the daily methadone dose. Two types of significant differences between the methadone and nonmethadone groups were found: (a) resting-level differences related to chronic methadone administration and not associated with cocaine administration (lower respiration rate, smaller pupil diameter, higher skin temperature); and (b) differences in response to cocaine administration. The cocaine-induced increases in subjective ratings of positive cocaine effects ("drug effect," "rush," "good effects," "liking"), in ratings of cocaine craving ("desire for cocaine"), and in heart rate were greater in the methadone-maintenance subjects than in the nonmethadone subjects. The authors conclude that methadone maintenance can enhance the abuse liability profile of cocaine, and that this may provide a pharmacological basis for the high rates of cocaine abuse often observed among methadone-maintenance patients. However, they note also that nonpharmacological factors associated with methadone treatment may still produce an overall decrease in cocaine abuse during methadone-maintenance treatment.

Buprenorphine

Buprenorphine is an opioid μ-receptor partial agonist that is marketed as an analgesic and under development as a treatment of opioid dependence. Rosen et al. (1993) evaluated the interaction of intranasal cocaine challenges with buprenorphine in a within-subject crossover study. The five participants were dually dependent on both opioids and cocaine. Following initial opioid detoxification they participated in two 5-day test cycles (separated by a 2-day washout) in which they received daily placebo or buprenorphine (2 mg/day, sl); the order of conditions was randomized and double-blind. On days 3 and 5 of each cycle, cocaine challenges (2 mg/kg in) were performed 2 h after the daily buprenorphine or placebo administration. Buprenorphine significantly enhanced the positive mood effects (e.g., ratings of "pleasant") and the heart rate increase produced by cocaine, and it appeared to reduce—though nonsignificantly—negative mood ratings (anxiety, anger, depression). The magnitude of buprenorphine's interaction with cocaine appeared to lessen from day 3 to day 5, suggesting the lessening was related to opioid-tolerance development to buprenorphine.

Strain, Preston, Stitzer, Liebson, and Bigelow (1994) evaluated possible buprenorphine–cocaine interactions in four volunteer abusers of both opioids and cocaine by testing their response to cocaine challenge before and after a period of buprenorphine maintenance. Volunteers were studied as outpatients. Following initial challenge with cocaine (40 mg iv), they were inducted to buprenorphine maintenance (8 mg/day, sl), and then subsequently rechallenged after an average of 43 days of daily buprenorphine treatment. There were no statistically significant buprenorphine–cocaine interactions on any subjective or physiological indices. On a number of subjective indices related to abuse liability (ratings of "liking," "good effects," and "desire for cocaine"), there were nonsignificant trends for ratings in response to cocaine to be higher during buprenorphine treatment. The authors concluded that, while there appeared to be no adverse cardiovascular interactions between buprenorphine and cocaine, neither did buprenorphine appear likely to be effective in reducing cocaine abuse.

Teoh et al. (1994) evaluated the possible interaction of buprenorphine with cocaine (and with morphine) by challenging subjects, in separate sessions, with cocaine, morphine, and placebo both before and after a period of buprenorphine maintenance. The 26 participants were treatment-seeking volunteers with concurrent dual dependence on both opioids and cocaine. The initial challenges occurred after 6 days of residential drug-free status; in a randomized, double-blind procedure participants were challenged with intravenous administration of cocaine (30 mg), morphine (10 mg), and saline. Participants were then randomized to 4 mg or 8 mg/day sublingual buprenorphine maintenance, and after 10–12 days were rechallenged. Buprenorphine produced dose-related attenuation of the subjective detection and certainty-of-detection of morphine, but had no effects on the detection of cocaine or on ratings of the intensity of cocaine effects.

A fourth study (Foltin & Fischman, 1996) has also evaluated cocaine response during buprenorphine maintenance. Participants were 12 opioid-dependent, methadone-maintained volunteers who were tested, under double-blind conditions and in randomized and counterbalanced order, both while maintained on methadone (60 mg/day po) and while maintained on buprenorphine (8 mg/day sl). Challenge sessions consisted of four consecutive identical injections of 0, 16, or 48 mg/70 kg iv cocaine at 14-min intervals. In general, the subjective effects of cocaine relevant to its abuse liability ("high," "stimulated," "good drug effect") were rated similarly under both buprenorphine maintenance and methadone maintenance. Ratings of "I want cocaine" were lower during buprenorphine treatment than during methadone treatment, but these differences were present at baseline (prior to cocaine administration); cocaine administration resulted in no evident change in these ratings under either treatment condition. During a cocaine self-administration component of the study some subjective responses to some doses of cocaine were lower during buprenorphine treatment than during methadone treatment (ratings of "friendly," "alert," "tired," "talkative," "good drug effect," and "I want cocaine"). The authors interpret the study as indicating that buprenorphine reduces cocaine craving, and cocaine self-administration varied in patterns consistent with the craving indices; see Fischman and Foltin (chapter 8, this volume) for discussion of the self-administration aspects of this study. However, it should be noted that the observed differences could reflect an enhancing effect of methadone rather than an attenuating effect of buprenorphine, and that they could reflect lack of equivalence of the single-dose levels used for comparing the two medications.

Naltrexone

Naltrexone is a long-acting opioid antagonist that is currently approved and marketed as a treatment both for opioid dependence and for alcohol dependence. Kosten et al. (1992) investigated the effect of naltrexone maintenance on response to cocaine using a method similar to their previously discussed study of cocaine–desipramine interactions. In a within-subject crossover design, five volunteer cocaine abusers were tested for their response to iv cocaine challenges of 0, 0.125, 0.25, and 0.50 mg/kg following 10 days or more of placebo maintenance, and again following 10 days or more of naltrexone maintenance (50 mg/day po). Cocaine doses were double-blind and in random order. Subjective effect results were mixed and somewhat contradictory. There was no effect of naltrexone on ratings of "high" or of the "quality" of the cocaine administered, but it did significantly decrease area-under-the-curve ratings of the dollar value of the cocaine challenges, and it decreased peak rating of unpleasant effects (this peak occurred at 90 min postinjection and was interpreted as an index of the postcocaine "crash"). The authors concluded that because naltrexone appeared to decrease both positive and negative cocaine effects the net result would likely be limited treatment effectiveness.

Possible interactions of naltrexone with cocaine have been further evaluated in a study by Walsh et al. (1996). The study design was similar to that described earlier for the Walsh et al. (1994) fluoxetine–cocaine interaction study—participants were maintained initially on placebo and then on progressively increasing daily doses of the test medication (naltrexone), and repeated single-session cocaine dose–effect challenge evaluations were superimposed on this test medication schedule. An additional refinement of the design in this study was that at each dose level of test medication there were three types of challenge sessions—cocaine alone (0, 20, 40 mg iv), hydromorphone alone (0, 1.5, 3 mg iv), and their so-called "speedball" combination (0 cocaine plus 0 hydromorphone; 20 mg cocaine plus 1.5 mg hydromorphone; 40 mg cocaine plus 3 mg hydromorphone). Participants were volunteers who abused both opioids and cocaine but who were not physically dependent. The double-blind, within-subject crossover study was conducted while participants resided for 7 weeks on a closed research unit. Oral test medication capsules were given each morning containing either placebo (weeks 1, 6, and 7) or ascending doses of naltrexone (3.125, 12.5, 50, & 200 mg/day, during weeks 2, 3, 4, and 5, respectively). In each study week there were three experimental sessions in which subjects received intravenous injections of either hydromorphone, cocaine, or their combination. Within each session the three ascending doses of challenge drug (zero, low, high) were given 1 h apart. The order of the challenge drugs was randomized across weeks. The magnitude of effects produced by the hydromorphone–cocaine combination was greater than that produced by either hydromorphone or cocaine alone. Selected interaction results are shown in Figure 9.3. Naltrexone produced dose-related blockade of the subjective and physiological effects of hydromorphone. All doses of naltrexone produced partial attenuation of the speedball effects, which appeared attributable to selective blockade of the opioid component of the combination's effects. Naltrexone had no effect on any of the physiological or subjective effects of cocaine. These data provide no evidence of a therapeutic effect of naltrexone for the treatment of cocaine abuse, but suggest that naltrexone may be partially effective in treating so-called speedball abusers who use cocaine in combination with heroin. As with the previously discussed fluoxetine–cocaine interaction study, this study design has the attractive feature of characterizing the dose–effect functions both of the challenge drug(s) and of the test medication. The present study has the added attractive feature of including three different challenge drugs and of documenting within a single study what a strong medication–drug interaction looks like (naltrexone–hydromorphone), what a modest interaction looks like (naltrexone–speedball), and what a negligible or noninteraction looks like (naltrexone–cocaine). These naltrexone–cocaine data also make an important scientific contribution by documenting the reliability and replicability of the cocaine response in the absence of any relevant pharmacological interaction. A final point worth noting about this study is that it suggests that this type of human laboratory interaction study can be very sensitive at detecting relevant pharmacological interactions; substantial attenuation of hydromorphone effects and of speedball effects is apparent at naltrexone doses of only 3 mg/day po despite the fact that the therapeutically recommended antiopioid dose is 50 mg/day.

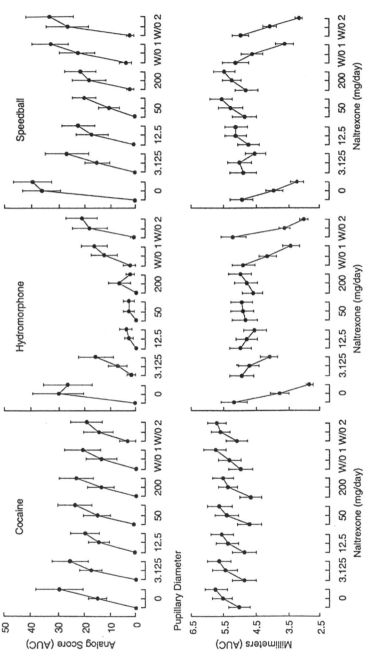

FIGURE 9.3   The effects of cocaine (left), hydromorphone (center), and the "speedball" combination of cocaine and hydromorphone (right) are shown during treatment with placebo, a range of chronic naltrexone doses, and during washout. Data are shown for a visual analog measure of "high" (upper panel) and pupil diameter (lower panel). Each set of three connected data points represents the three ascending doses for that challenge drug (0, 20, and 40 mg cocaine; 0, 1.5, and 3 mg hydromorphone; cocaine/hydromorphone combinations 0/0 mg, 20/1.5 mg, and 40/3 mg). Each data point represents the mean ($\pm$ 1 standard error of the mean) for 8 subjects. Naltrexone did not alter any of the effects of cocaine, but significantly attenuated the effects of hydromorphone ($p < .05$). The effects of the hydromorphone/cocaine combination were significantly ($p < .05$), but only partially, modified but only to the extent that the contributions of hydromorphone to the combination's effects were reduced. (Adapted from Walsh et al., 1996.)

CONCLUSIONS

No medication has yet been found with clear and recognized efficacy against cocaine abuse. In the absence of such a "known positive" case, it is difficult to evaluate with certainty the utility of any of the various research methods that have been contributing to the search for anticocaine pharmacotherapies. However, human laboratory interaction studies such as those reviewed here are known to be effective and sensitive for detecting pharmacotherapies for other varieties of substance abuse and dependence. It is likely they will be similarly effective and sensitive for detecting anticocaine pharmacotherapies. Certainly, they appear to provide an efficient procedure for identifying medications with relevant pharmacological interactions with cocaine that are suggestive of potential therapeutic utility. This human laboratory approach is likely to provide a cost-effective strategy for selecting those medications most deserving of further evaluation in outpatient clinical trials. Pharmacologically relevant interactions in the laboratory may not be sufficient for a medication to have clinical effectiveness, but they are likely necessary. The laboratory can be a sensitive tool for identifying medications with this necessary feature. Once medications are identified that have relevant pharmacological efficacy, it will be necessary to find clinical treatment contexts in which that efficacy can display itself to clinical benefit. Clinical treatment procedures may need to be adapted and changed from the traditional models in order for medications to be clinically effective. The identification of pharmacologically promising medications will renew the need for designing concurrent behavioral procedures that maximize the benefit to be derived from pharmacotherapy.

PHARMACOLOGY

The clinical pharmacology of anticocaine pharmacotherapy is in its infancy. A substantial number of different compounds and different pharmacological mechanisms have been tested in the human laboratory. Many of these evaluations have been in less-than-optimal designs. Of necessity, human testing to date has focused on a limited array of convenient and/or marketed compounds. Many more compounds and mechanisms are being developed and tested preclinically, and many of these will need to receive thorough evaluation in well-designed human laboratory studies. Well-designed human laboratory interaction studies such as those reviewed here offer the potential to screen and to triage test medications, and thereby to promote efficient allocation of research resources.

One valuable application of human laboratory testing would be to the selection of medications for evaluation in controlled clinical trials. Based upon experience with pharmacotherapies developed for other varieties of substance abuse, it seems extremely likely that any cocaine-dependence pharmacotherapy will pharmacologically interact with cocaine in some way. The research reviewed above, and summarized in Table 9.3, well documents the sensitivity of these human laboratory evaluations for detecting such interactions. The procedure is sensitive both to safety indices (e.g., cardiovascular effects) and to efficacy indices (e.g., subjective effects). For both categories of indices the procedure is sensitive bidirectionally (i.e., it can detect both increases and decreases). In addition, it is able to detect and to characterize possible unexpected adverse effects.

The human laboratory evaluations reviewed above provide some useful pharmacological guidance. These studies suggest two general differential conclusions for which there is some consistency of support. First, opioids—regardless of whether they are agonists or antagonists—appear to have little therapeutic potential in the treatment of cocaine abuse. Second, tricyclic antidepressants (desipramine) and serotonergic antidepressants (fluoxetine) seem consistently to show pharmacological interactions suggestive of therapeutic potential. These effects are often modest, but these compounds remain more consistently promising than any other pharmacological class yet studied. Clinical trial results with these compounds have been mixed (Batki, Manfredi, Jacob, & Jones, 1993; Levin & Lehman, 1991; Grabowski et al., 1995), and recent opinion has been that these medications should be dropped from further consideration (Grabowski et al., 1995; Johanson & Schuster, 1995). This could be a mistake; while it is appealing to hope for the discovery of a dramatically effective pharmacotherapy, it may be prudent to continue working also with these less-dramatic agents to develop behavioral treatment conditions under which their efficacy might be maximized.

METHODOLOGY

Medication–cocaine interaction studies will be most informative if they assess interactions under a broad range of parameters. In this regard, chronic interaction designs have several advantages over acute interaction designs. Chronic interaction studies more closely simulate how medications are used clinically. If there are changes in interaction effects over time (e.g., either slow-onset therapeutic effects or gradual tolerance development) the chronic design is more likely to detect those effects. The chronic design also makes it possible to increase the medication dose gradually and thereby to reach and to test doses that might not be feasible in acute-interaction procedures. This gradual increase in the medication dose can result in a dose–effect evaluation of the test medication that is far more informative than is testing of a single-lose level. Crossovers from chronic active treatment to chronic placebo treatment are desirable, but this can be difficult when testing medications with long half-lives. Testing of multiple dose levels of cocaine challenge is certainly desirable, and single-session cocaine dose–effect evaluations appear to be a safe and efficient way to accomplish this. Intravenous challenges provide better standardization and uniformity of biodelivery than do the intranasal or smoked routes of administration. Using ascending dose sequences for both the test medication and the cocaine challenge may be a valuable safety procedure, in that it ensures that each individual volunteer has safely tolerated lower doses before exposure to higher doses.

Overall, this general approach of examining the effects of cocaine challenges in interaction with putative therapies offers substantial promise for guiding the safe and efficient development of new treatments for cocaine abuse and dependence. The present review has focused on its application to evaluating potential pharmacological treatments. But the approach is also applicable to nonpharmacological treatments (e.g., immunologic, vaccine approaches) that seek to alter the abuse liability profile of cocaine. That the procedure simultaneously assesses safety indices and efficacy indices is an especially useful feature as research moves forward to assess previously untested interactions.

ACKNOWLEDGMENT

Preparation of this chapter was supported by U.S. Public Health Service Grants from the National Institute on Drug Abuse R01 DA-05196 (GEB & SLW), K05 DA-00050 (GEB) and R29 DA-10029 (SLW).

REFERENCES

Abreu, M. E., Walsh, S. L., Bonson, K. R., Ginn, D., & Bigelow, G. E. (1997). Effects of intravenous injection speed on responses to cocaine or hydromorphone in humans. In L. S. Harris (Ed.), *Problems of Drug Dependence 1996, Proceedings of the 58th Annual Scientific Meeting, The College on Problems of Drug Dependence, Inc* (p. 139). NIDA Research Monograph Series, *174*, (NIH Publication No. 97–4236). Rockville, MD: National Institute on Drug Abuse.

Aronson, S. C., Black, J. E., McDougle, C. J., Scanley, B. E., Jatlow, P., Kosten, T. R., Heninger G. R., & Price L. H. (1995). Serotonergic mechanisms of cocaine effects in humans. *Psychopharmacology, 119*, 179–185.

Barnett, G., Hawks, R., & Resnick, R. (1981). Cocaine pharmacokinetics in humans. *Journal of Ethnopharmacology, 3*, 353–366.

Batki, S. L., Manfredi, L. B., Jacob, P., & Jones, R. T. (1993). Fluoxetine for cocaine dependence in methadone maintenance: Quantitative plasma and urine cocaine/benzoylecgonine concentrations. *Journal of Clinical Psychopharmacology, 13*, 243–250.

Bigelow, G. E. (1991). Human drug abuse liability assessment: Opioids and analgesics. *British Journal of Addiction, 86*, 1615–1628.

Biggio, G., Fadda, D., Fanni, P., Tagliamonte, A., & Gessa, G. L. (1974). Rapid depletion of serum tryptophan, brain tryptophan, serotonin and 5-hydroindolacetic acid by a tryptophan-free diet. *Life Science, 14*, 1321–1329.

Byck, R., Ruskis, A., Ungerer, J., & Jatlow, P. (1982). Naloxone potentiates cocaine effect in man. *Psychopharmacology Bulletin, 18*, 214–215.

Cami, J., Bigelow, G. E., Griffiths, R. R., & Drummond, D. C. (Eds) (1991). Special issue: Clinical testing of drug abuse liability. *British Journal of the Addictions, 86*, No. 12.

Evans, S. M., Cone, E. J., & Henningfield, J. E. (1996). Arterial and venous cocaine plasma concentrations in humans: Relationship to route of administration, cardiovascular effects and subjective effects. *Journal of Pharmacology and Experimental Therapeutics, 279*, 1345–1356.

Fischman, M. W., Foltin, R. W., Nestadt, G., & Pearlson, G. D. (1990). Effects of desipramine maintenance on cocaine self-administration by humans. *Journal of Pharmacology and Experimental Therapeutics, 253*, 760–770.

Fischman, M. W., & Schuster, C. R. (1984). Injection duration of cocaine in humans. *Federation Proceedings, 43*, 570.

Fischman, M. W., Schuster, C. R., Resnekov, L., Schick, J. F. E., Krasnegor, N. A., Fennell, W., & Freedman, D. X. (1976). Cardiovascular and subjective effects of intravenous cocaine administration in humans. *Archives of General Psychiatry, 33,* 983–989.

Foltin, R. W., Christiansen, I., Levin, F. R., & Fischman, M. W. (1995). Effects of single and multiple intravenous cocaine injections in humans maintained on methadone. *Journal of Pharmacology and Experimental Therapeutics, 275,* 38–47.

Foltin, R. W., & Fischman, M. W. (1991). Smoked and intravenous cocaine in humans: Acute tolerance, cardiovascular and subjective effects. *Journal of Pharmacology and Experimental Therapeutics, 257,* 247–261.

Foltin, R. W., & Fischman, M. W. (1995). Interaction of buprenorphine with cocaine-morphine combinations. *Experimental and Clinical Psychopharmacology, 3,* 261–269.

Foltin, R. W., & Fischman, M. W. (1996). Effects of methadone or buprenorphine maintenance on the subjective and reinforcing effects of intravenous cocaine in humans. *Journal of Pharmacology and Experimental Therapeutics, 278,* 1153–1164.

Foltin, R. W., Fischman, M. W., Pedroso, J. J., & Pearlson, G. D. (1988). Repeated intransal cocaine administration: Lack of tolerance to pressor effects. *Drug and Alcohol Dependence, 22,* 169–177.

Fuller, R. K., & Roth, H. P. (1979). Disulfiram for the treatment of alcoholism. *Annals of Internal Medicine, 90,* 901–904.

Grabowski, J., Rhoades, H., Elk, R. Schmitz, J., David, C., Creson, D., & Kirby, K. (1995). Fluoxetine is ineffective for treatment of cocaine dependence or concurrent opiate and cocaine dependence: Two placebo-controlled, double-blind trials. *Journal of Clinical Psychopharmacology, 15,* 163–174.

Haberny, K. A., Walsh, S. L., Ginn, D. H., Wilkins, J. N., Garner, J. E., Setoda, D., & Bigelow, G. E. (1995). Absence of cocaine interactions with the MAO-B inhibitor selegiline. *Drug and Alcohol Dependence, 39,* 55–62.

Haerzten, C. A. (1974). *An overview of the Addiction Research Center Inventory (ARCI): An appendix and manual of scales.* DHEW Pub. No. 79, Department of Health Education and Welfare, Washington, DC: Government Printing Office.

Hameedi, F. A., Rosen, M. I., McCance-Katz, E. F., McMahon, T. J., Price, L. H., Jatlow, P. I., Woods, S. W., & Kosten, T. R. (1995). Behavioral, physiological and pharmacological interaction of cocaine and disulfiram in humans. *Biological Psychiatry, 37,* 560–563.

Hatsukami, D. K., & Fischman, M. W. (1996). Crack cocaine and cocaine hydrochloride: Are the differences myth or reality? *Journal of the American Medical Association, 276,* 1580–1588.

Hatsukami, D., Keenan, R., Halikas, J., Pentel, P. R., & Brauer, L. H. (1991). Effects of carbamazepine on acute responses to smoked cocaine-base in human cocaine abusers. *Psychopharmacology, 104,* 120–124.

Hatsukami, D. K., Thompson, T. N., Pentel, P. R., Flygare, B. K., & Carroll, M. E. (1994). Self-administration of smoked cocaine. *Experimental and Clinical Psychopharmacology, 2,* 115–125.

Hill, H. E., Haertzen, C. A., Wolbach, A. B., & Miner, E. J. (1963). The Addiction Research Inventory: Standardization of scales which evaluate subjective effects of morphine, amphetamine, pentobarbital, alcohol, LSD-25, pyrahexyl and chlorpromazine. *Psychopharmacologia, 4,* 167–183.

Inaba, T., Stewart, D. J., & Kalow, W. (1978). Metabolism of cocaine in man. *Clinical Pharmacology and Therapeutics, 23,* 547–552.

Jaffe, J. H., Cascella, N. G., Kumor, K. M., & Sherer, M. A. (1989). Cocaine-induced cocaine craving. *Psychopharmacology, 97,* 59–64.

Jasinski, D. R. (1977). Assessment of the abuse potential of morphine-like drugs (methods used in man). In Martin W. R. (Ed.), *Drug Addiction I* (vol. 45/1, pp. 197–258). Heidelberg: Springer-Verlag.

Jasinski, D. R., Johnson, R. E., & Henningfield, J. E. (1984). Abuse liability assessment in human subjects. *Trends in Pharmacological Sciences, 5,* 196–200.

Javaid, J. I., Fischman, M. W., Schuster, C. R., Dekirmenjian, H., & Davis, J. M. (1978). Cocaine plasma concentration: Relation to physiological and subjective effects in humans, *Science, 202,* 227.

Johanson, C-E., & Schuster, C. R. (1995). Cocaine. In F. E. Bloom & D. J. Kupfer (Eds.), *Psychopharmacology: The fourth generation of progress* (pp. 1685–1697). New York: Raven Press.

Kosten, T., Gawin, F. H., Silverman, D. G., Fleming, J., Compton, M., Jatlow, P., & Byck, R. (1992). Intravenous cocaine challenges during desipramine maintenance. *Neuropsychopharmacology, 7,* 169–176.

Kosten, T., Silverman, D. G., Fleming, J. Kosten, T. A., Gawin, F. H., Compton, M., Jatlow, P., & Byck, R. (1992). Intravenous cocaine challenges during naltrexone maintenance: A preliminary study. *Biological Psychiatry, 32,* 543–548.

Kumor, K., Sherer, M., & Jaffe, J. (1989). Effects of bromocriptine pretreatment on subjective and physiological responses to IV cocaine. *Pharmacology, Biochemistry and Behavior, 33,* 829–837.

Levin, F. R., & Lehman, A. F. (1991). Meta-analysis of desipramine as an adjunct in the treatment of cocaine addiction. *Journal of Clinical Psychopharmacology, 11,* 374–378.

Martin, W. R., Sloan, B. S., Sapira, J. D., & Jasinksi, D. R. (1971). Physiologic, subjective and behavioral effects of amphetamine, methamphetamine, ephedrine, phenmetrazine and methylphenidate in man. *Clinical Pharmacology and Therapeutics, 12,* 245–258.

McNair, D. M., Lorr, M., & Droppleman, L. F. (1971). *EDITS Manual for the Profile of Mood States.* San Diego: Educational and Industrial Testing Service.

Mello, N. K., Mendelson, J. H., Bree, M. P., & Lukas, S. E. (1989). Buprenorphine suppresses cocaine self-administration by rhesus monkeys. *Science, 245,* 859–862.

Mello, N. K., Mendelson, J. H., Bree, M. P., & Lukas, S. E. (1990). Buprenorphine and naltrexone effects on cocaine self-administration by rhesus monkeys. *Journal of Pharmacology and Experimental Therapeutics, 254,* 926–939.

Mello, N. K., & Negus, S. S. (1996). Preclinical evaluation of pharmacotherapies for treatment of cocaine and opioid abuse using drug self-administration procedures. *Neuropsychopharmacology, 14,* 375–424.

Muntaner, C., Kumor, K. M., Nagoshi, C., & Jaffe, J. H. (1991). Effects of nifedipine pretreatment on subjective and cardiovascular responses to intravenous cocaine in humans. *Psychopharmacology, 105,* 37–41.

NRC Committee on Clinical Evaluation of Narcotic Antagonists (1978). Clinical evaluation of naltrexone treatment of opiate-dependent individuals. *Archives of General Psychiatry, 35,* 335–340.

Oliveto, A., Rosen, M. I., Woods, S. W., & Kosten, T. R. (1995). Discriminative stimulus, self-reported and cardiovascular effects of orally administered cocaine in humans. *Journal of Pharmacology and Experimental Therapeutics, 272,* 231–241.

Perez-Reyes, M., Di Guiseppi, S., Ondrusek, G., Jeffcoat, A. R., & Cook, C. E. (1982). Free-base cocaine smoking. *Clinical Pharmacology and Therapeutics, 32,* 459–465.

Pickens, R. W., & Johanson, C-E. (1992). Craving: consensus of status and agenda for future research. *Drug and Alcohol Dependence, 30,* 127–131.

Preston, K. L., Sullivan, J. T., Berger, P., & Bigelow, G. E. (1993). Effects of cocaine alone and in combination with mazindol in human cocaine abusers. *Journal of Pharmacology and Experimental Therapeutics, 267,* 296–307.

Preston, K. L., Sullivan, J. T., Strain, E. C., & Bigelow, G. E. (1992). Effects of cocaine alone and in combination with bromocriptine in human cocaine abusers. *Journal of Pharmacology and Experimental Therapeutics, 262,* 279–291.

Preston, K. L., Sullivan, J. T., Strain, E. C., & Bigelow, G. E. (1996). Enhancement of cocaine's abuse liability in methadone maintenance patients. *Psychopharmacology, 123,* 15–25.

Resnick, R. B., Kestenbaum, R. S., & Schwartz, L. K. (1977). Acute systemic effects of cocaine in man: A controlled study by intranasal and intravenous routes. *Science, 195,* 696–698.

Rosen, M. I., Pearsall, H. R., McDougle, C. J., Price, L. H., Woods, S. W., & Kosten, T. R. (1993). Effects of acute buprenorphine on responses to intranasal cocaine: A pilot study. *American Journal of Drug and Alcohol Abuse, 19,* 451–464.

Rowbotham, M. C., Jones, R. T., Benowitz, N. L., & Jacob, P. (1984). Trazodone-oral cocaine interactions. *Archives of General Psychiatry, 41,* 895–899.

Sherer, M. A. (1988). Intravenous cocaine: Psychiatric effects, biological mechanisms. *Biological Psychiatry, 24,* 865–885.

Sherer, M. A., Kumor, K. M., & Jaffe, J. H. (1988). Effects of intravenous cocaine are partially attenuated by haloperidol. *Psychiatry Research, 27,* 117–125.

Strain, E. C., Preston, K. L., Stitzer, M. L., Liebson, I. A., & Bigelow, G. E. (1994). The effects of cocaine in buprenorphine-maintained outpatient volunteers. *The American Journal on Addictions, 3,* 129–143.

Teoh, S. K., Mello, N. K., Mendelson, J. H., Kuehnle, J., Gastfriend, D. R., Rhoades, E., & Sholar, W. (1994). Buprenorphine effects on morphine- and cocaine- induced subjects responses by drug-dependent men. *Journal of Clinical Psychopharmacology, 14,* 15–27.

Van Dyke, C., Jatlow, P., Ungerer, J., Barash, P. G., & Byck, R. (1978). Oral cocaine: Plasma concentrations and central effects. *Science, 200,* 211–213.

Walsh, S. L., Preston, K. L., Sullivan, J. T., Fromme, R., & Bigelow, G. E. (1994). Fluoxetine alters the effects of intravenous cocaine in humans. *Journal of Clinical Psychopharmacology, 14,* 396–407.

Walsh, S. L., Sullivan, J. T., Preston, K. L., Garner, J. E., & Bigelow, G. E. (1996). Effects of naltrexone on response to intravenous cocaine, hydromorphone, and their combination in humans. *Journal of Pharmacology and Experimental Therapeutics, 279,* 524–538.

Wilkinson, P., Van Dyke, C., Jatlow, P., Barash P., & Byck, R. (1980). Intranasal and oral cocaine kinetics. *Clinical Pharmacology and Therapeutics, 3,* 386–394.

10

CONTROLLED LABORATORY STUDIES ON THE EFFECTS OF COCAINE IN COMBINATION WITH OTHER COMMONLY ABUSED DRUGS IN HUMANS

CRAIG R. RUSH

Departments of Psychiatry and Human Behavior and Pharmacology and Toxicology
University of Mississippi Medical Center
Jackson, Mississippi

JOHN M. ROLL

Department of Psychiatry
University of Vermont
Burlington, Vermont

STEPHEN T. HIGGINS

Departments of Psychiatry and Psychology
University of Vermont
Burlington, Vermont

INTRODUCTION

Multiple drug use and abuse is well documented among drug abusers in general and cocaine abusers in particular. Multiple drug use among cocaine abusers is a significant public health concern because it is associated with increased morbidity and mortality relative to the use of cocaine alone (Drug Abuse Warning Network [DAWN], 1991, 1996). In this chapter we characterize common patterns of multiple drug abuse among cocaine abusers, and then review the extant literature on the behavioral and cardiovascular consequences associated with using cocaine in combination with alcohol, marijuana, nicotine, and opioids. We focused on these forms of other drug use because of their prevalence among cocaine abusers. This chapter focuses on studies with humans conducted under controlled laboratory conditions. Preclinical research is reviewed in other chapters in this volume. Because drug interactions are often complex, laboratory studies permit the rigorous experimental control that is essential to obtaining an accurate characterization of their effects.

PATTERNS OF MULTIPLE DRUG ABUSE AMONG COCAINE ABUSERS

The probability of having ever used cocaine increases as a function of experience with other drug use, especially illicit drugs (Kandel & Yamaguchi, 1993). In national surveys, for example, those who reported cigarette, alcohol, or marijuana use in the past month were 5, 12, and 51 times more likely, respectively, to report having used cocaine than respondents who did not report using these substances in the past month (SAMHSA, 1995).

Emergency-room admission and medical-examiner data from the DAWN illustrate the adverse and potentially life-threatening consequences of using cocaine in combination with other drugs (DAWN, 1991, 1996). In the most recent DAWN results, cocaine was mentioned in approximately 123,000 emergency-room admissions, which was the single most frequently mentioned drug (DAWN, 1996). However, approximately 70% of these mentions involved cocaine in combination with at least one other drug. Cocaine–alcohol (44%) and cocaine–opioid (15%) combinations were the first and second most commonly mentioned two-way combinations, respectively. Consistent with the emergency-room admissions data, cocaine was the single most frequently mentioned drug in drug-related deaths reported by medical examiners (DAWN, 1991). Approximately 76% of these drug-related deaths involved cocaine in combination with at least one other drug. Cocaine–alcohol (40%) and cocaine-opioid (30%) combinations were the first and third most commonly mentioned two-way combinations, respectively. Although striking, these results are conservative estimates of the extent of multiple drug use among cocaine abusers. For example, nicotine was not listed among drugs mentioned in DAWN emergency-room or medical-examiner data. As discussed below, regular cigarette smoking is quite prevalent among cocaine abusers, and cocaine–nicotine combinations have the potential to produce serious adverse effects.

Data from clinical samples also document high levels of multiple drug use and abuse among cocaine abusers (e.g., Higgins et al., 1991, Higgins, Budney, Bickel, Foerg, & Badger, 1993, 1994; Miller, Gold, & Millman, 1989; Miller, Millman, & Keskiner, 1989). Cocaine is often administered simultaneously or in close temporal proximity with alcohol, and the vast majority of cocaine users consume alcohol regularly (Higgins, Budney, Bickel, et al., 1994; Jatlow, 1993; Weiss, Mirin, & Griffin, 1988). Approximately 60% of cocaine-dependent patients meet diagnostic criteria for alcohol dependence (Carroll, Rounsaville, & Bryant, 1993; Higgins, Budney, Bickel, et al., 1994; Miller, Gold, & Millman, 1989; Miller, Millman & Keskiner, 1989; Miller, Summer, & Gold, 1993). Cocaine is also often administered simultaneously or in close temporal proximity with heroin or other opioids (i.e., "speedballing"), and like alcohol, dependence on both cocaine and opioids is common among patients in drug abuse treatment programs (Avants, Margolin, & Kosten, 1994; Condelli, Fairbank, Dennis & Rachal, 1991; Kosten, Gawin, Rounsaville, & Kleber, 1986; Strain, Stitzer, Liebson, & Bigelow, 1993). Rates of cocaine use and abuse among methadone-maintained patients, for example, are reportedly as high as 75% (Condelli et al., 1991; see Silverman et al., Chapter 15,this volume). Estimates of marijuana use among cocaine abusers range from 25–90% (Budney, Higgins, Delaney, Kent, & Bickel, 1991; Budney, Higgins, & Wong, 1996; Kreek, 1987; Miller et al., 1993; Schnoll, Daghertani, Kerrigan, Kitchen, & Hansen, 1985; Smart, Ogborne, & Newton-Taylor, 1990), while 30–50% of cocaine-dependent patients meet diagnostic criteria for cannabis dependence (Budney et al., 1991; Miller, Gold, & Belkin, 1990; Miller, Gold, & Klarh, 1990). Finally, regular cigarette smoking is significantly more prevalent in cocaine-dependent patients than in community samples (75 vs. 22%) (Budney, Higgins, Hughes, & Bickel, 1993).

As with the emergency-room admission and medical-examiner data, results from clinical samples may be conservative estimates of multiple drug use among cocaine abusers. In a comparison of treatment-seeking and community samples of cocaine abusers, for example, the treatment-seeking sample reported 35%, 54%, and 48% fewer days of alcohol, marijuana, and multiple drug abuse, respectively, during the past month than did the community sample (Carroll & Rounsaville, 1992)

Conservative or not, these epidemiological and clinical data leave little doubt about the prevalence of multiple drug use among cocaine abusers and the serious adverse effects associated with these practices. We review next published laboratory studies in humans that experimentally examined the behavioral and cardiovascular consequences associated with the use of cocaine in combination with alcohol, opioids, marijuana, and nicotine.

COCAINE–ALCOHOL COMBINATIONS

EFFECTS OF ALCOHOL ON COCAINE
SELF-ADMINISTRATION

Patients who report combined cocaine and alcohol use also report using more cocaine than those patients who use cocaine alone, which suggests that alcohol may modify the reinforcing or other behavioral effects of cocaine (Kidorf & Stitzer, 1993). We are aware of only one report that explicitly examined the effects of alcohol on cocaine self-administration under controlled laboratory conditions (Higgins, Roll, & Bickel, 1996). In the first phase of this experiment, subjects chose between cocaine (10 mg unit does of intranasal cocaine) and placebo. The majority (80%) of subjects chose cocaine over placebo, demonstrating that cocaine functioned as a reinforcer in these subjects. In the second phase of the experiment, subjects were pretreated with placebo or active doses of alcohol (0.5 or 1 g/kg) and allowed to choose between cocaine and varying amounts of money (0–$4.00). Cocaine choice decreased as the amount of money in the monetary option increased (Figure 1). However, pretreatment with the active doses of alcohol increased preference for cocaine over money. Alcohol's ability to increase cocaine preference was most discernible in the high-money condition. These results provide experimental evidence that alcohol can enhance the relative reinforcing effects of cocaine.

SUBJECT-RATED EFFECTS OF COCAINE–ALCOHOL COMBINATIONS

Cocaine and alcohol both produce interoceptive-stimulus effects (i.e., subject-rated effects) that are thought to contribute to their widespread use and abuse (e.g., Fischman, 1989; Higgins, Rush, et al., 1992, 1993, 1996; Rush, Higgins, Bickel, Wiegner, & Hughes, 1994; Rush & Griffiths, 1996). The common practice of ingesting cocaine and alcohol concurrently or in close temporal proximity suggests that the drug combination may produce subject-rated effects that are qualitatively or quantitatively different from those produced by the constituent drugs alone. Cocaine users report using cocaine and alcohol in combination because (a) alcohol enhances the cocaine high, (b) alcohol prolongs the cocaine high, and (c) alcohol at-

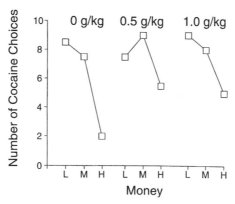

FIGURE 10.1 Number of cocaine choices during sessions that involved alcohol pretreatment are shown as a function of the three monetary conditions (L, low, M, medium, and H, high), with separate functions for each of the three alcohol conditions (0, 0.5 and 1 g/kg). x-axis: monetary condition. y-axis: number of cocaine choices. Data points show means of seven subjects. (Redrawn with permission from Higgins, Roll, & Bickel, 1996, © Springer-Verlag.)

tenuates cocaine-induced anxiety and agitation (Gorelick, 1992; Miller & Gold, 1988).

To our knowledge, there are eight published reports of studies examining the subject-rated effects of cocaine-alcohol combinations in humans under controlled laboratory conditions (Farre et al., 1993; Foltin, Fischman, Pippen, & Kelly, 1993; Higgins, Rush, et al., 1993; Higgins, et al., 1996; Mannelli, Janiri, Tempests, & Jones, 1993; McCance-Katz et al., 1993; Perez-Reyes, 1994; Perez-Reyes & Jeffcoat, 1992). Across these studies, the subject-rated effects of the cocaine–alcohol combination often differed from those of the constituent drugs alone in three important respects. First, the magnitude of the positive-mood effects (e.g., "Feeling good") was often greater following the administration of the cocaine–alcohol combination than cocaine alone (Farre et al., 1993; McCance-Katz et al., 1993; Mannelli et al., 1993; Perez-Reyes & Jeffcoat, 1992). In one study, for example, both cocaine (5 and 100 mg/70 kg) and alcohol (0 and 1 g/kg) administered alone increased ratings of "Feeling good" (Figure 2, top panel) (Farre et al., 1993). Combining cocaine and alcohol increased these ratings significantly above levels observed with either drug alone.

Second, the effects of cocaine–alcohol combinations are often of longer duration than are observed with cocaine alone. In one study, for example, subject ratings of "cocaine high" were no longer significantly different from placebo 180 min after the administration of intranasal cocaine alone (2 mg/kg) (McCance-Katz et al., 1993). However, when combined with alcohol (1 g/kg) these ratings remained significantly different from placebo for as long as 360 min after cocaine administration (Figure 2, bottom panel).

Third the magnitude of the subject-rated effects are often less following the administration of the cocaine–alcohol combination relative to alcohol alone. In one study, for example, alcohol (0., 0.5, or 1.0 g/kg) alone increased subject ratings of "Drunk" as a function of dose, whereas cocaine (4, 48, or 96 mg/70 kg) alone did not affect these ratings (Figure 3, top panel). Combining cocaine and alcohol attenuated alcohol-induced increases in subject–ratings of "Drunk." Similar effects were observed with subject ratings of "Slurred speech" and "Drowsy."

These studies document significant alterations in the profile of subject-rated effects observed with cocaine–alcohol combinations relative to those produced when the drugs are ingested alone. Whether these effects are due to pharmacokinetic or pharmacodynamic interactions is unclear. Cocaine-plasma levels were assayed in three of the experiments discussed above, and in each case cocaine-plasma levels were greater following the administration of the cocaine–alcohol combination compared to cocaine alone (Farre et al., 1993; McCance-Katz et al., 1993; Perez-Reyes & Jeffcoat, 1992). These findings are concordant with studies conducted with rodents suggesting that alcohol pretreatment increases cocaine-plasma levels above those observed with cocaine alone (Hedaya & Pan, 1996). Future studies with human cocaine abusers need to further characterize the pharmacokinetic interaction of cocaine and alcohol, and how such interactions influence the pharmacodynamic effects of the drug combination.

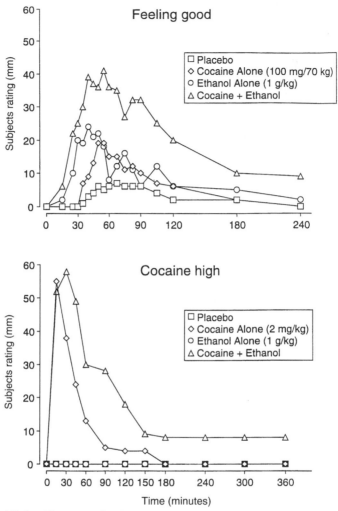

FIGURE 10.2   Time-course functions for cocaine and ethanol, alone and in combination, on subject ratings of "Feeling good" and "Cocaine high." x-axis: time after drug administration in hours; P indicates predrug. Data points in top panel show means of nine subjects, whereas data points in bottom panel show means of six subjects. (Top panel was redrawn with permission from Farre et al., 1993, copyright American Society of Pharmacology and Experimental Therapeutics; the bottom panel was redrawn with permission from McCance-Katz et al., 1993, copyright Springer-Verlag.)

PERFORMANCE EFFECTS

Acute administration of cocaine can significantly improve performance in sleep-deprived and rested subjects (Fischman & Schuster, 1980; Higgins et al., 1990, 1992, Higgins, Rush, et al., 1993; Stillman, Jones, Moore, Walker, & Welm, 1993), while alcohol generally impairs human performance (e.g., Higgins et al.,

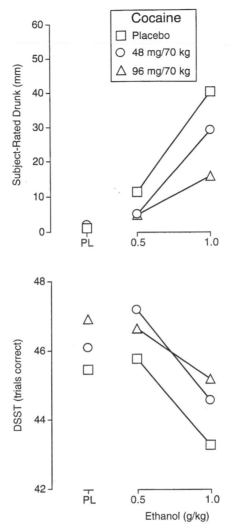

FIGURE 10.3 Dose–response functions for cocaine and ethanol, alone and in combination, on subject ratings of "Drunk" (top panel) and trials correct on the Digit-Symbol-Substitution Test (DSST) (bottom panel). Symbols above PL represent values when one of the three doses of cocaine (i.e., 4, 48, and 96 mg/70 kg) was administered alone (i.e., 4, 48, and 96 mg/70 kg) administered in combination with the two active doses of alcohol (0.5 and 1 g/kg). Data are expressed as marginal means. Data points show means of eight subjects (Both panels were redrawn with permission from Higgins, Rush et al., 1993, copyright Springer-Verlag.)

1992, Higgins, Rush, et al., 1993; Rush et al., 1994; Rush & Griffiths, 1996). To our knowledge, there are five published reports on the effects of cocaine and alcohol, alone and in combination, on human performance (Farre et al., 1993; Foltin & Fischman, 1989; Foltin et al., 1993; Higgins et al., 1992, Higggins, Rush, et al.,

1993). Cocaine administered alone enhanced or did not affect performance (Farr et al., 1993; Foltin & Fischman, 1989; Higgins et al., 1992; Higgins, Rush et al., 1993), although in one instance it impaired performance (Foltin et al., 1993). Cocaine–alcohol combinations produced less performance impairment than was observed with alcohol alone in 4 of 5 studies (Farre et al., 1993; Foltin et al., 1993; Higgins et al., 1992; Higgins, Rush, et al., 1993). In the fifth study, cocaine did not attenuate alcohol's deleterious effects to a statistically significant degree, but the graphic presentation of the results suggested a trend in that direction (Foltin & Fischman, 1989).

The study by Higgins and colleagues illustrates the performance effects of cocaine and alcohol, alone and in combination (Higgins, Rush, et al., 1993). In this study, intranasal cocaine (4, 48, and 96 mg/70 kg) administered alone improved performance on the Digit-Symbol-Substitution Test (DSST), whereas oral alcohol (0, 0.5 and 1.0 g/kg) administered alone impaired performance (Figure 3, bottom panel). Combining cocaine and alcohol significantly attenuated the disruptive effects of alcohol, and, to a lesser extent, alcohol attenuated the performance-enhancing effects of cocaine. Breath-alcohol levels were similar when alcohol was administered alone or in combination with cocaine in this study, but cocaine plasma levels were not examined. These effects were replicated in a second experiment with five volunteers that was included in the same report. The ability of cocaine and alcohol to mutually attenuate some of the behavioral effects of the drugs administered alone may explain some of the popular allure of this drug combination.

CARDIOVASCULAR EFFECTS

The cardiovascular effects of cocaine are well documented. Cocaine increases coronary vasoconstriction and myocardial oxygen demand (Boehrer, Moliterno, & Willard, 1992; Brogan, Lange, Glamann, & Hillis, 1992; Flores, Lange, Cigarroa, & Hillis, 1990; Lange, Cigarroa & Yancy, 1989), and can induce myocardial ischemia and infarction (e.g., Hadjimiltiades, Covalesky, Manno, Haas, & Mintz, 1988; Rod & Zucker, 1987; Smith et al., 1987; Zimmerman, Gustafson & Kemp 1987), ventricular arrhythmias (Banchimol, Bartall, & Dresser, 1978; Karch & Billingham, 1988; Nanji & Filipenko, 1984), pulmonary edema (Allred & Ewer, 1981; Welti & Wright, 1979), and left ventricular dysfunction (Bertolet et al., 1990; Chokshi, Moore, Pandian, & Isner, 1989). These cardiovascular effects undoubtedly play a prominent role in cocaine-related deaths, and may be enhanced by alcohol (Escobedo, Ruttenber, Agocs, Anda, & Welti, 1991; Henning et al., 1994).

Controlled laboratory studies that examined the cardiovascular effects of cocaine–alcohol combinations in humans generally support the position that the effects of the drug combination are of larger magnitude than those observed with cocaine alone (Farre et al., 1993; Foltin & Fischman, 1989; Higgins, Rush, et al., 1993; Higgins et al., 1996; Mannelli et al., 1993; McCance-Katz et al., 1993; Perez-Reyes & Jeffcoat, 1992; but see Perez-Reyes, 1994; Pirwitz et al., 1995). Across these studies, cocaine alone, and to a lesser extent alcohol alone, increased heart rate and pressure-rate product (a measure of myocardial oxygen demand) above levels observed with placebo. Combining cocaine and alcohol produced greater increases in heart rate and pressure-rate product than either drug alone (for representative data see Figure 4). The combined effects of the cocaine–alcohol combinations on blood pressure were qualitatively similar, but of smaller magnitude.

In one report, the combined cardiovascular effects of cocaine and alcohol did not differ significantly from those observed with cocaine alone (Perez-Reyes, 1994). Importantly, cocaine was administered *before* alcohol in this experiment (Perez-Reyes, 1994) and *after* alcohol in each of the other studies discussed above (Farre et al., 1993; Foltin & Fischman, 1989; Higgins, Rush, et al., 1993; Higgins et al., 1996; Mannelli et al., 1993; McCance-Katz et al., 1993; Perez-Reyes & Jeffcoat, 1992). The failure of alcohol to alter the cardiovascular effects of cocaine in this study may be due to the pharmacokinetics of cocaine–alcohol combinations differing depending on whether cocaine is administered *before* or *after* alcohol ingestion (Perez-Reyes, 1994). As was noted above, cocaine-plasma levels are generally greater with cocaine–alcohol combinations compared to cocaine alone when cocaine is administered *after* alcohol ingestion. By contrast, cocaine-plasma

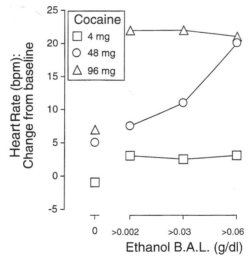

FIGURE 10.4   Dose–response functions for cocaine and ethanol, alone and in combination, on heart rate. *x*-axis: ethanol breath–alcohol level (g/dl). Symbols above zero represent values when one of the three doses of intranasal cocaine (i.e., 4, 48, and 96 mg/70 kg) was administered alone (i.e., breath–alcohol level was zero). Connected data points represent the effects of the doses of intranasal cocaine (i.e., 4, 48,and 96 mg/70 kg) administered in combination with the three breath-alcohol-level conditions (>0.002,, >0.03, and >0.06). Data are expressed change from baseline. Data points show means of nine subjects. (Redrawn from *Pharmacology, Biochemistry and Behavior, 31,* R. W. Foltin and M. W. Fischman, Ethanol and cocaine interactions in humans: Cardiovascular consequences, p. 879, Copyright c1989, with permission of Elsevier Science.)

levels were unchanged across the cocaine–alcohol and cocaine-alone conditions in this study when cocaine was administered *before* alcohol ingestion (Perez-Reyes, 1994). Future studies with humans should attempt to replicate this finding and determine if the order of drug administration is a critical determinant of the cardiotoxic effects of cocaine–alcohol combinations.

ROLE OF COCAETHYLENE IN MEDIATING THE EFFECTS

Cocaethylene, the ethyl ester of benzoylecgonine, is formed after the concurrent administration of cocaine and alcohol (Bailey, 1993; Jatlow et al., 1991; Landry, 1992; Rose, 1994). Preclinical studies suggest that the behavioral pharmacology of cocaethylene is generally similar to that of cocaine (Katz, Terry, & Witkin, 1992; Schechter, 1994), although its median half-life is significantly longer than that of cocaine, and it may be more potent in terms of lethality and other acute toxic reactions (Hearn, Rose, Wagner, Ciarleglio, & Mash, 1991; Henning & Wilson, 1996; Katz et al., 1992).

There are three reports on the role of cocaethylene in mediating the behavioral and cardiovascular effects of cocaine–alcohol combinations in humans (McCance, Price, Kosten & Jatlow, 1995; Perez-Reyes, Jeffcoat, Myers, Sihler, & Cook, 1994; Perez-Reyes, 1993). In the first study, the acute subject-rated and cardiovascular effects of intravenous cocaethylene (0.025, 0.05, 0.1, 0.15, 0.20 and 0.25 mg/kg) and cocaine (0.25 mg/kg) were compared in three volunteers (Perez-Reyes, 1993). The second study compared the acute subject-rated and cardiovascular effects of equal doses (0.25 mg/kg) of intravenously administered cocaethylene and cocaine in six volunteers (Perez-Reyes et al., 1994). The third study compared the acute subject-rated and cardiovascular effects of intranasally administered cocaethylene (0.48 and 0.95 mg/kg), cocaine (0.92 mg/kg) and placebo in eight volunteers (McCance et al., 1995).

Cocaethylene and cocaine both produced prototypical stimulant-like subject-rated drug effects (e.g., increased rating of "Cocaine high") in these studies, but the magnitude of these ratings was generally lower with cocaethylene. Similarly, the cardiac effect of cocaethylene were of comparable or smaller magnitude than those observed with cocaine (McCance et al., 1995; Perez-Reyes et al., 1993, 1994). However, in one of these studies, both the subject-rated and heart-rate effects of cocaethylene were of longer duration than those of cocaine (McCance et al., 1994). The greater duration of cocaethylene's action compared to cocaine may contribute to at least some of the increased subject-rated and cardiovascular effects of cocaine–alcohol combinations described above.

SUMMARY

At least six conclusions can be drawn concerning the behavioral and cardiovascular effects of cocaine–alcohol combinations. First, alcohol can enhance the relative reinforcing effects of cocaine under some conditions. Second, alcohol can enhance some of the subject-rated effects of cocaine, which is concordant with anecdotal reports from cocaine users. Third, cocaine attenuates some of the subject-rated effects of alcohol. Fourth, the subject-rated effects of cocaine–alcohol combinations generally are of longer duration than effects observed with cocaine alone. Fifth, combining cocaine and alcohol can attenuate some of the performance-impairing effects of alcohol. Sixth, cocaine–alcohol combinations often produce greater increases in heart rate, blood pressure, and pressure-rate product than either drug alone. Interestingly, the interactive effects of cocaine and alcohol on cardiovascular and perhaps other measures may depend on the order of drug administration.

Findings that alcohol enhances and prolongs the subject-rated effects of cocaine, and that cocaine functionally antagonizes some of the performance-impairing effects of alcohol, may explain, in part, the popularity of this drug combination. However, alcohol-induced increases in cocaine use and the greater cardiotoxicity of the cocaine–alcohol combination observed under some conditions may contribute to the prominence of this drug combination in drug-related emergency-room admissions and deaths, and underscores the potential life-threatening consequences of combined drug use.

Finally, recently published studies have begun to explore the role of cocaethylene in mediating the behavioral and cardiovascular effects of cocaine–alcohol combinations in humans. The behavioral and cardiotoxic effects of cocaethylene are generally similar to those of cocaine, but have a longer duration of action. This longer duration of cocaethylene's action may contribute to the increased toxicity of cocaine–alcohol combinations.

COCAINE–OPIOID COMBINATIONS

As was noted above, cocaine is often administered simultaneously or in close temporal proximity with opioids like heroin and morphine (i.e., speedballing) (Meandzija, O'Connor, Fitzgerald, Rounsaville, & Kosten, 1994; Nemoto, 1994; Siegal et al., 1994). Patients who report using cocaine with heroin on the same day also report using more cocaine than those who use cocaine alone, suggesting that opioids may modify the reinforcing or other behavioral effects of cocaine (Kidorf & Stitzer, 1993). Emergency-room admission data suggest that combined cocaine and opioid use increases potentially life-threatening adverse effects compared to cocaine alone (DAWN, 1996).

We review next the effects of commonly abused opioids on the self-administration, subject-rated, performance, and cardiovascular effects of cocaine. This review is limited to full agonist at the μ-opioid receptor that are commonly abused (e.g. morphine). The effects of full agonist at the μ-opioid receptor that are used therapeutically in the management of opioid abuse (e.g., methadone) as well as mixed agonist-antagonists (e.g., buprenorphine) on the behavioral effects of cocaine are reviewed in detail in other chapters in this volume (see chapter by

Bigelow & Walsh, and Fischman & Foltin, this volume). To the best of our knowledge, there are no published reports that examined the effects of other commonly abused opioids on cocaine self-administration in humans.

SUBJECT-RATED EFFECTS OF COCAINE–OPIOID COMBINATIONS

We know of two published reports characterizing the subject-rated effects of a full μ-agonist in combination with cocaine under controlled laboratory conditions in humans (Foltin & Fischman, 1992; Walsh, Sullivan, Preston, Garner, & Bigelow, 1996). In these studies, the subject-rated drug effects of the cocaine–opioid combination were greater than those observed with the constituent drugs alone, or the drug combinations produced effects that were not observed when the drugs were administered alone. For example, the study by Foltin and colleagues assessed the effects of intravenous cocaine (0, 8, 16, and 32 mg/70 kg) and morphine 0, 5, and 10 mg/70 kg), alone and in combination, in nine volunteers (Foltin & Fischman, 1992). Cocaine alone increased visual-analog ratings of "Stimulated" and Amphetamine (A) scores on the Addiction Research Center Inventory (ARCI). Morphine alone increased visual-analog ratings of "Sedated" and opiate symptoms. Both cocaine and morphine alone increased ratings of "high," "drug quality," and "drug liking" (for representative data see Figure 5, top panel). Combining cocaine and morphine produced greater effects on many of these measures, including subject ratings of "High", than the constituent drugs alone (Figure 5, top panel). These findings are consistent with reports that cocaine effects are enhanced in methadone-maintained versus nonmethadone-maintained opioid abusers (Preston, Sullivan, Strain, & Bigelow, 1996) (for more details see Bigelow & Walsh, Chapter 9, this volume).

PERFORMANCE EFFECTS

The study by Foltin and colleagues described above also assessed the performance effects of cocaine–opioid combinations (Foltin & Fischman, 1992). Intravenous cocaine (0, 8, 16, and 32 mg /70 kg) and morphine (0, 5, and 10 mg/70 kg) did not significantly affect accuracy of performance on a serial acquisition task when administered alone or in combination (Foltin et al., 1992).

CARDIOVASCULAR EFFECTS

The study by Foltin and colleagues described above also assessed the cardiovascular effects of cocaine–opioid combinations (Foltin & Fischman, 1992). Intravenous cocaine (0, 8, 16, and 32 mg/70 kg) and morphine (0, 5, and 10 mg/70 kg) administered alone increased heart rate and blood pressure as a function of dose. Combining these doses of cocaine and morphine increased heart rate and

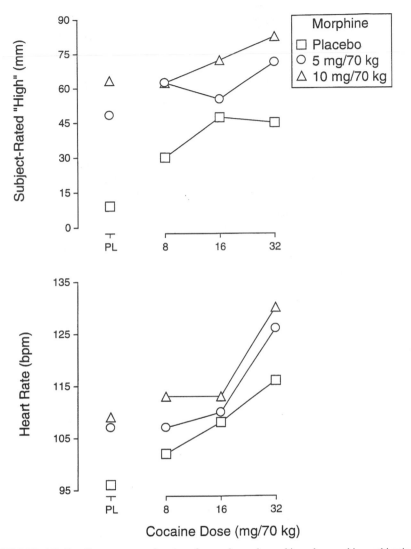

FIGURE 10.5   Dose–response functions for cocaine and morphine, alone and in combination, on heart rate. *x*-axis: cocaine dose (mg/70 kg). Symbols above PL represent values when one of the three doses of intravenous morphine (i.e., 0, 5, and 10 mg/70 kg) was administered alone (i.e., with placebo cocaine). Connected data points represent the effects of the three active doses of intravenous cocaine (i.e., 8, 16, and 32 mg/70 kg) administered in combination with the three doses of intravenous morphine (0, 5, and 10 mg/70 kg). Data are expressed as the maximal drug effect observed across the time–action function. Data points show means of nine subjects. (Both panels redrawn from Foltin & Fischman, 1992.)

diastolic blood pressure significantly above levels observed with the constituent drugs alone (for representative data see Figure 5, bottom panel). These findings are also consistent with reports that cocaine produced greater increases in heart rate and blood pressure in methadone-maintained versus nonmethadone-maintained volunteers (Preston et al., 1996). These findings suggest cocaine's cardiotoxic effects may be enhanced by opioids.

SUMMARY

Three tentative conclusions can be drawn concerning the behavioral and cardiovascular effects of cocaine–opioid combinations. First, commonly abused opioids like morphine appear to enhance some of the subject-rated effects of cocaine. Second, there is no evidence that cocaine–opioid combinations impair performance. Third, cocaine-opioid combinations may produce greater cardiovascular effects than are observed with either drug alone. These increased subject-rated effects of cocaine–opioid combinations may contribute to the prominence of this drug combination in drug-related emergency-room admissions and deaths.

COCAINE–MARIJUANA COMBINATIONS

As noted above, estimates of marijuana use among cocaine abusers range from 25–90%, and 30–50% of cocaine-dependent patients meet diagnostic criteria for cannabis dependence (Budney et al., 1991; Kreek, 1987; Miller et al., 1993; Schnoll et al., 1985; Smart et al., 1990). Perhaps because marijuana is considered to be less dangerous than alcohol or opioids, its effects in combination with cocaine have received less scientific attention. However, approximately 10% of cocaine-related emergency-room admissions involve marijuana or hashish, suggesting that combining cocaine and marijuana can sometimes produce serious adverse consequences (DAWN, 1996).

We review next the subject-rated performance, and cardiovascular effects of cocaine–marijuana combinations. We are not aware of any published reports on the effects of marijuana on cocaine self-administration in humans, nor are we aware of any published reports on the effects of cocaine on marijuana self-administration.

SUBJECT-RATED EFFECTS

We know of only two controlled, laboratory studies that examined the subject-rated effects of cocaine–marijuana combinations in humans (Foltin et al., 1993; Lukas, Sholar, Kouri, Fukuzako, & Mendelson, 1994). The first study examined the effects of intravenous cocaine (0, 16, and 32 mg) and smoked marijuana (0, 1.3, 1.84, and 2.7% Δ^9-THC), alone and in combination, in seven volunteers (Foltin et al., 1993). Both doses of cocaine alone increased visual-analog ratings of "Stimulated" and "High" and increased lysergic acid diethylamide (LSD) scores on the ARCI. Marijuana alone increased these measures as a function of THC bloodlevel. Combining cocaine and marijuana did not alter these effects. The second study examined the combined effects of intranasal cocaine (0.9 mg/kg) and smoked marijuana (0.004 [placebo], 1.24 or 2.64% Δ^9-THC) in five volunteers (Lukas et al., 1994). The dependent measure was the number of positive (i.e., "euphoric") and negative (i.e., "dysphoric") events reported, and the latency and duration of those effects following drug administration. Combining cocaine and marijuana significantly increased the duration of the positive events reported relative to cocaine alone, but did not increase the absolute number of these events. Cocaine-plasma levels were significantly greater when cocaine and marijuana were administered in combination compared to cocaine alone in this study. Thus, the increased duration of the positive subject-rated effects observed with the cocaine–marijuana combinations relative to cocaine alone may have resulted from marijuana increasing the bioavailability of cocaine.

PERFORMANCE EFFECTS

We know of only two published studies on the performance effects of cocaine–marijuana combinations (Foltin & Fischman, 1990; Foltin et al., 1993). In the first study, there were no significant effects of intranasal cocaine (4–96 mg) and smoked marijuana (0–2.9% Δ^9-THC) on a serial acquisition task, whether administered alone or in combination (Foltin & Fischman, 1990). In the second study, there was a significant interaction of intravenous cocaine (0–32 mg) and smoked marijuana (0–2.7% $\Delta/9$-THC) on a repeated acquisition task (Foltin et al., 1993). Only the high dose of cocaine (32 mg) combined with the high THC-bloodlevel condition significantly impaired performance on this task. Performance on a simple-reaction-time, choice-reaction-time, DSST, list-learning, or recognition-memory task were not significantly affected by any of the cocaine–marijuana dose combinations (Foltin et al., 1993).

CARDIOVASCULAR EFFECTS

To our knowledge, there are three published reports on the cardiovascular effects of cocaine–marijuana combinations and the results are relatively consistent (Foltin, Fischman, Pedroso, & Pearlson, 1987; Foltin & Fischman, 1990; Lukas et al., 1994). The first study assessed the effects of intravenous cocaine (0–32 mg) and smoked marijuana (0.27% Δ^9-THC) (Foltin et al., 1987); the second study assessed the effects of intranasal cocaine (4–96 mg) and smoked marijuana (0–2.9% Δ^9-THC) (Foltin & Fischman, 1990); and the third study assessed the effects of intranasal cocaine (0.9 mg/kg) and smoked marijuana (0–2.53% Δ^9-THC) (Lukas et al., 1994). Cocaine and marijuana alone increased heart rate above levels observed with placebo in each of these studies. Combining cocaine and marijuana increased heart rate above levels observed with the drug alone in each of these studies, although these differences generally did not achieve statistical significance (for representative data see Figure 6). The blood-pressure effects of the cocaine–marijuana combinations were similar to those observed with cocaine alone. Cocaine-plasma levels were significantly greater when cocaine and marijuana were administered in combination compared to cocaine alone, which may explain the greater cardiac effects observed with the drug combination relative to cocaine or marijuana alone (Lukas et al., 1994).

SUMMARY

Based on the available studies examining cocaine–marijuana combinations, three conclusions can be drawn. First, marijuana may prolong the subject-rated effects of cocaine, but it does not appear to effect the absolute magnitude of these

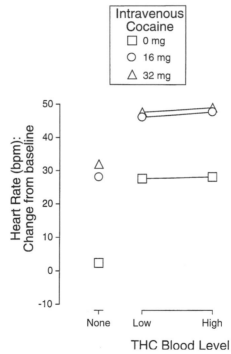

FIGURE 10.6   Dose–response functions for cocaine and marijuana, alone and in combination, on heart rate. x-axis: THC blood level. Symbols above None represent values when one of the three doses of cocaine (i.e., 0, 16, and 32 mg/70 kg) was administered alone (i.e., with placebo marijuana). Connected data points represent the effects of the three doses of cocaine (i.e., 0, 16, and 32 mg/70 kg) administered in combination with the 2 THC-blood-level conditions (i.e., Low and High). Data points in top panel show means of seven subjects. (Redrawn from Foltin et al., 1987, with permission from Elsevier Science.)

effects. Second, under some conditions and only on some tasks, cocaine–marijua-na combinations may produce significant performance impairment that is not ob-served when the drugs are administered alone. Finally, combining cocaine and marijuana produces greater increases in heart rate than either drug alone.

COCAINE–NICOTINE COMBINATIONS

As was noted above, regular cigarette smoking is more common among cocaine abusers than the general population (Budney et al., 1993). Although not listed among the drugs mentioned in DAWN emergency-room and medical-examiner data, a review of 114 case reports indicate that 83% of patients with cocaine-in-duced myocardial infarction were moderate to heavy cigarette smokers (Minor, Scott, Brown, & Winniford, 1991). Of course, that study permits no inferences about whether the liklihood of cocaine-induced myocardial infarction is greater in smokers versus nonsmokers. Few laboratory studies have characterized the be-havioral and cardiovascular effects of cocaine–nicotine combinations.

SELF-ADMINISTRATION STUDIES

We know of no published studies examining the effects of nicotine pretreatment on subsequent cocaine self-administration. To our knowledge, there are three re-ports on the effects of cocaine on cigarette smoking (i.e., nicotine self-adminis-tration) in humans. In the first study, subjects were given the opportunity to self-administer either intravenous cocaine or saline and then allowed to smoke tobacco cigarettes *ad libitum* (Nemeth-Coslett, Henningfield, Katz, & Goldberg, 1986). Subjects smoked more cigarettes following cocaine self-administration than place-bo. In the second study, four volunteers were alowed to smoke *ad libitum* for 1.75 h after having the opportunity to make ten discrete choices between intranasal co-caine and varying amounts of money (Higgins, Budney, Hughes, et al., 1994b). The number of cigarettes smoked during these 1.75-h periods increased signifi-cantly as a function of whether subjects ingested the maximum dose (100 mg), only part of the maximum dose (mean = 42.5 mg), or no cocaine during the self-administration period. In the third study, 10 volunteers were given 10 mg of co-caine or placebo (0.4-mg cocaine plus 9.6-mg lactose) every 2 min for a 20-min period so that the total dose accumulated over 20 minutes was 100-mg cocaine or placebo (i.e., 4-mg cocaine) (Roll, Higgins, & Kennedy, 1996). Following cocaine administration, subjects were allowed to smoke *ad libitum* for 3 h. Relative to placebo, cocaine significantly increased the number of cigarettes smoked, and de-creased the latency to initiate smoking and the interval between successive ciga-rettes.

These studies suggest that cocaine may increase the reinforcing effects of nico-tine, although this effect could be the result of a nonspecific increase in overall ac-tivity levels. These results are consistent with data from clinical samples. For example, cigarette-smoking cocaine abusers report using more cocaine than non-smoking abusers and report smoking cigarettes at a greater frequency when under the influence of cocaine (Roll, Higgins, & Kennedy, 1996; Roll, Higgins, Budney, Bickel, & Badger, 1996). Similarly, nicotine levels are higher in cocaine-dependent patients on days when urine toxicology screens indicate recent cocaine use than when results indicate recent cocaine abstinence (Roll, Higgins, Budney, et al., 1996). Future studies should explore possible mechanisms for this effect and determine if a reciprocal relationship exists, that is, whether cigarette smoking or other forms of nicotine use increase cocaine self-administration.

SUBJECT-RATED EFFECTS

We are aware of only one published study that examined the influence of cigarette smoking on the subject-rated effects of cocaine (Lukas, Lindahl, Sholar, & Wines, 1996). In this study, male and female cigarette smokers and nonsmokers inhaled 0.9 mg/kg cocaine or placebo. Cocaine and placebo were administered on different days under double-blind conditions, and order of drug administration was counterbalanced across subjects. Subjects reported the number of positive ("euphoric") and negative ("dysphoric") events they experienced following drug administration. Male smokers reported fewer "euphoric" events from cocaine than male nonsmokers. Female smokers, by contrast, reported more "euphoric" events from cocaine than female nonsmokers. These data suggest that cigarette smoking (i.e., nicotine self-administration) may modify the subject-rated effects of cocaine, but the direction of that effect depends on gender.

CARDIOVASCULAR EFFECTS

We are aware of only one study that experimentally examined the cardiovascular effects of cocaine–nicotine combinations in humans (Moliterno et al., 1994). Separate groups of subjects received 2 mg/kg doses of intranasal cocaine ($N = 6$), smoked one cigarette but received no cocaine ($N = 12$), or received 2 mg/kg doses of intranasal cocaine and smoked one cigarette ($N = 24$). Relative to baseline, mean pressure-rate product increased by 11% after cocaine alone, 12% after one cigarette alone, and by 45% after combining cocaine and one cigarette. These data suggest that cocaine–nicotine combinations produce supra-additive effects on cardiac output, and thereby may increase the risk of adverse cardiac effects above levels observed with either drug alone.

SUMMARY

Experimental results of cocaine–nicotine interactions in humans are sparse, but three tentative conclusions can be drawn. First, acute ingestion of cocaine increases the frequency of cigarette smoking (i.e., nicotine self-administration). Second, a history of cigarette smoking (i.e., nicotine dependence) may alter the subject-rated effects of cocaine, but the interaction of cocaine and nicotine on self-report measures is complex and possibly dependent on gender. Finally, cocaine–nicotine combinations appear to be more cardiotoxic than either drug alone. More research is clearly needed in each of these important areas.

SUMMARY AND DIRECTIONS
OF FUTURE RESEARCH

The prevalence of multiple drug abuse among cocaine abusers is striking (Miller, Gold, & Milman, 1989; Miller, Millman, & Keskinen, 1989; Grant & Harford 1990; Budney et al., 1993; Roll et al., 1996). Cocaine abusers report regularly ingesting alcohol, opioids, marijuana, and other drugs in combination with cocaine (Gorelick, 1992; Miller & Gold, 1988). Furthermore, street samples of cocaine often contain adulterants such that cocaine is ingested with other drugs unbeknownst to the user (Siegel, 1980). Experimentally characterizing the effects of drug combinations is important because their behavioral and cardiovascular effects cannot necessarily be predicted based on the effects observed when the constituent drugs are ingested alone and, more importantly, the combined effects are often more toxic than those of the constituent drugs alone. Characterizing the effects of drug combinations under controlled laboratory conditions is an important first step in understanding multiple drug use and abuse. Such studies need to test a wide range of drug doses using different behavioral and physiological measures. The precise control that laboratory settings afford is necessary for such complex dose–response analyses.

Determining the effects of other abused drugs on subsequent cocaine use is a very important area for further research. In one study, for example, alcohol increased preference for cocaine over monetary reinforcement (Higgins et al., 1996). Those results provided experimental evidence that is concordant with results from clinical studies suggesting that alcohol abuse predicts poorer treatment outcome in cocaine abusers (Carroll, Ziedonis, et al., 1993; Higgins, Budney, Bickel, Hughes, & Foerg, 1993). Future laboratory studies that examine the influence of other abused drugs on cocaine self-administration, as well as the influence of cocaine use on the self-administration of those drugs, would provide sorely needed information.

Subject-rated drug-effect questionnaires have been used extensively to characterize the interoceptive-stimulus effects of cocaine in combination with other abused drugs. Alcohol and opioids have been shown to enhance or prolong the subject-rated effects of cocaine. Marijuana, by contrast, may prolong the effects of cocaine by increasing its bioavailability, but does not appear to increase their absolute magnitude. We know of no published studies on the direct effects of nicotine on the subject-rated effects of cocaine. A history of nicotine dependence may modify the subject-rated effects of cocaine, but this interaction is complex and appears to depend on gender. Future studies on the interoceptive-stimulus effects of cocaine in combination with other drugs would benefit from efforts to standardize the subject-rated items and methods used. Standardized procedures would greatly facilitate comparisons across studies. Employing procedures other than self-reports to characterize the interoceptive effects of drug combinations would also be useful. The drug-discrimination paradigm, for example, may be particularly well suited for this purpose as subjects are carefully trained to detect the presence or absence of a particular drug (e.g., cocaine) before initiating testing with other doses, drugs, or drug combinations (Oliveto, Rosen, Woods, & Kosten, 1995). Although subject-rated and discriminative-stimulus effects of drugs generally covary (Preston & Bigelow, 1991; Schuster & Johanson, 1988; Schuster, Fischman, & Johanson, 1981; Woolverton & Schuster, 1983), use of the more rigorous drug-discrimination procedures may provide a better characterization of the interoceptive-stimulus effects of cocaine in combination with other drugs. For example, recent evidence suggests that human drug-discrimination procedures may be more sensitive than the traditional subject-rated drug-effect questionnaires (Perkins, DiMarco, Grobe, Scierko, & Stiller, 1994; Rush, Critchfield, Troisi, & Griffiths, 1995).

Finally, more research is needed to characterize better the cardiovascular effects of cocaine in combination with other abused drugs. Combining cocaine with alcohol, opioids, marijuana, and nicotine generally produces greater cardiotoxicity than is observed with the constituent drugs alone. Interestingly, the greater cardiotoxicity observed with cocaine–alcohol combinations appears to depend on the order in which the constituent drugs are administered (Perez-Reyes & Jeffcoat, 1992; Perez, 1994). Whether similar order-dependent effects would be observed with other commonly abused drugs in combination with cocaine is unknown but should be examined. Order of drug administration is just one variable that may influence the cardiovascular effects of cocaine in combination with other drugs. The influence of other variables (e.g., acute vs. chronic administration, route of cocaine administration) also await systematic investigation. Such studies are essential to achieving a comprehensive understanding of the cardiovascular and other risks associated with multiple drug abuse among cocaine abusers.

ACKNOWLEDGMENTS

Preparation of this manuscript was supported, in part, by the National Institute on Drug Abuse Grant DA 10325 (CRR), 5T32 DA 07267 (JMR), DA 08076 (STH), and GCRC Grant RR-109. The authors are grateful to Catherine A. Hayes for her expert technical assistance in redrawing the figures.

REFERENCES

Allred, R. J., & Ewer, S. (1981). Fatal pulmonary edema following intravenous free-base cocaine use. *Annals of Emergency Medicine, 10,* 441–442.
Avants, S. K., Margolin, A., & Kosten, T. R. (1994). Cocaine abuse in methadone maintenance programs: Integrating pharmacotherapy with psychosocial interventions. *Journal of Psychoactive Drugs, 26,* 137–146.
Bailey, D. N. (1993). Serial plasma concentrations of cocaethylene, cocaine, and ethanol in trauma victims. *Journal of Analytical Toxicology, 17,* 79–83.

Banchimol, A., Bartall, H., & Dresser, K. B. (1978). Accelerated ventricular rhythm and cocaine abuse. *Annals of Internal Medicine, 88,* 419–420.

Bertolet, B. D., Freund, G., Martin, C. A., Perchalski, D. L., Williams, C. M., & Pepine, C. J. (1990). Unrecognized left ventricular dysfunction in an apparently healthy cocaine abuse population. *Clinical Cardiology, 13,* 323–328.

Boehrer, J. D., Moliterno, D. J., & Willard, J. E. (1992). Hemodynamic effects of intranasal cocaine in humans. *Journal of the American College of Cardiology, 20,* 90–93.

Brogan, W. C. I., Lange, R. A., Glamann, D. B., & Hillis, L. D. (1992). Recurrent coronary vasoconstriction caused by intranasal cocaine: Possible role for metabolites. *Annals of Internal Medicine, 116,* 556–561.

Budney, A. J., Higgins, S. T., Delaney, D. D., Kent, L., & Bickel, W. K. (1991). Contingent reinforcement of abstinence with individuals abusing cocaine and marijuana. *Journal of Applied Behavior Analysis, 24,* 657–665.

Budney, A. J., Higgins, S. T., Hughes, J. R., & Bickel, W. K. (1993). Nicotine and caffeine use in cocaine-dependent individuals. *Journal of Substance Abuse, 5,* 117–130.

Budney, A. J., Higgins, S. T., & Wong, C. J. (1996). Marijuana use and treatment outcome in cocaine-dependent patients. *Journal of Experimental and Clinical Psychopharmacology, 4,* 396–403.

Carroll, K. M., & Rounsaville, B. J. (1992). Contrast of treatment seeking and untreated cocaine abusers. *Archives of General Psychiatry, 49,* 464–471.

Carroll, K. M., Rounsaville, B. J., & Bryant, K. J. (1993a). Alcoholism in treatment-seeking cocaine abusers: Clinical and prognostic significance. *Journal of Studies on Alcohol, 54,* 199–208.

Carroll, K. J., Ziedonis, D., O'Maley, S., McCance-Katz, E., Gordon, L., & Rounsaville, B. (1993b). Pharmacologic interventions for alcohol- and cocaine-abusing individuals. *American Journal of Addictions, 2,* 77–79.

Chokshi, S. K., Moore, R., Pandian, N. G., & Isner, J. M. (1989). Reversible cardiomyopathy associated with cocaine intoxication. *Annals of Internal Medicine, 11,* 1039–1040.

Condelli, W. S., Fairbank, J. A., Dennis, M. L., & Rachal, J. V. (1991). Cocaine use by clients in methadone programs: Significance, scope, and behavioral interventions. *Journal of Substance Abuse Treatment, 8,* 203–212.

DAWN (1996). *Annual Emergency Room Data, 1993: Data from the Drug Abuse Warning Network,* Public Health Service: Substance Abuse and Mental Health Services Administration, U.S. Department of Health and Human Services. CHHS Publication No. (ADM) 92-1955, Rockville, MD.

DAWN (1991). *Annual Medical Examiner Data 1990: Data from the Drug Abuse Warning Network,* Rockville, Maryland: National Institute on Drug Abuse. Public Health Service: Alcohol, Drug Abuse, and Mental Health Administration. U.S. Department of Health and Human Services. CHHS Publication No. (ADM) 91-1840. Washington, DC: U.S. Government Printing Office.

Escobedo, L. G., Ruttenber, A. J., Agocs, M. M., Anda, R. F., & Welti C.V. (1991). Emerging patterns of cocaine use and the epidemic of cocaine overdose deaths in Dade County, Florida. *Archives of Pathology and Laboratory Medicine, 115,* 900–905.

Farre, M., De La Torre, R., Llorente, M., Lamas, X., Ugena, B., Seguar, J., & Cami, J (1993). Alcohol and cocaine interactions in humans. *Journal of Pharmacology and Experimental Therapeutics, 266,* 1364–1373.

Fischman, M. W. (1989).*Relationship between self-reported drug effects and their reinforcing effects: Studies with stimulant drugs* (Vol. (ADM) 89-1613). Rockvill: National Institute on Drug Abuse. Public Health Service: Alcohol, Drug Abuse, and Mental Health Administration. U.S. DHHS (ADM) 89-1613. Washington, DC: U.S. Government Printing Office.

Fischman, M. W., & Schuster, C. R. (1980). Cocaine effects in sleep-deprived humans. *Psychopharmacology, 72,* 1–8.

Flores, E. D., Lange, R. A., Cigarroa, R. G., & Hillis, L. D. (1990). Effect of cocaine on coronary artery dimensions in atherosclerotic coronary artery disease: Enhanced vasoconstriction at sites of significant stenoses. *Journal of the American College of Cardiology, 16,* 74–79.

Foltin, R. W., & Fischman, M. W. (1992). The cardiovascular and subjective effects of cocaine and morphine combinations in humans. *Journal of Pharmacology and Experimental Therapeutics, 261,* 623–632.

Foltin, R. W., & Fischman, M. W. (1990). The effects of combinations of intranasal cocaine, smoked marijuana, and task performance on heart rate and blood pressure. *Pharmacology, Biochemistry and Behavior, 36,* 311–315.

Foltin, R. W., & Fischman, M. W. (1989). Ethanol and cocaine interactions in humans: Cardiovascular consequences. *Pharmacology, Biochemistry and Behavior, 31,* 877–883.

Foltin, R. W., Fischman, M. W., Pedroso, J. J., & Pearlson, G. D. (1987). Marijuana and cocaine interactions in humans: Cardiovascular consequences. *Pharmacology, Biochemistry and Behavior, 28,* 459–464.

Foltin, R. W., Fischman, M. W., Pippen, P. A., & Kelly, T. H. (1993). Behavior effects of cocaine alone and in combination with ethanol or marijuana in humans. *Drug and Alcohol Dependence, 32* 93–106.

Gorelick, D. A. (1992). Alcohol and Cocaine: Clinical and pharmacological interactions. *Recent Developments in Alcoholism, 10,* 37–56.

Grant, B. F., & Harford, T. C. (1990). Concurrent and simultaneous use of alcohol with cocaine: Results of national survey. *Drug and Alcohol Dependence, 25,* 97–104.

Hadjimiltiades, S., Covalesky, V., Manno, B. V., Haas, W. S., & Mintz, G. S. (1988). Coronary arteriographic findings in cocaine abuse-induced myocardial infarction. *Catheter Cardiovascular Diagnoses, 17,* 33–36.

Hearn, W. L., Rose, S., Wagner, J., Ciarleglio, A., & Mash, D. C. (1991). Cocaethylene is more potent than cocaine in mediating lethality. *Pharmacology, Biochemistry and Behavior, 39,* 531–533.

Hedaya, M. A., & Pan, W. (1996). Cocaine and alcohol interactions in naive and alcohol-pretreated rats. *Drug Metabolism and Disposition, 24,* 807–812.

Henning, R. J., & Wilson, L. D. (1996). Cocaethylene is as cardiotoxic as cocaine but is less toxic than cocaine plus ethanol. *Life Sciences, 57,* 615–627.

Henning, R. J., Wilson, L. D., Glauser, J., Lavins, E., Sebrosky, G., & Sutheimer, C. A. (1994). Cocaine plus ethanol is more cardiotoxic than cocaine or ethanol alone. *Critical Care Medicine, 22,* 1896–1906.

Higgins, S. T., Bickel, W. K., Hughes, J. R., Lynn, M., Capeless, M. A., & Fenwick, J. W. (1990). Effects of intranasal cocaine on human learning, performance and physiology. *Psychopharmacology, 102,* 451–458.

Higgins, S. T., Budney, A. J., Bickel, W. K., Foerg, F. E., & Badger, G. J. (1994). Alcohol dependence and simultaneous cocaine and alcohol use in cocaine-dependent patients. *Journal of Addictive Diseases, 13* 177–189.

Higgins, S. T., Budney, A. J., Bickel, W. K., Foerg, J. R., & Badger, G. (1993). Achieving cocaine abstinence with a behavioral approach. *American Journal of Psychiatry, 150,* 763–769.

Higgins, S. T., Budney, A. J., Bickel, W. K., Hughes, J. R., & Foerg, F. (1993). Disulfiram therapy in patients abusing cocaine and alcohol. *American Journal of Psychiatry, 150,* 675–676.

Higgins, S. T., Budney, A. J., Hughes, J. R., Bickel, W. K., Lynn, M. & Mortensen, A. (1994). Influence of cocaine use on cigarette smoking. *Journal of American Medical Association, 272,* 1724.

Higgins, S. T., Delaney, D. D., Budney, A. J., Bickel, W. K., Hughes, J. R., Foerg, F., & Fenwick, J. W. (1991). A behavioral approach to achieving initial cocaine abstinence. *American Journal of Psychiatry, 148,* 1218–1224.

Higgins, S. T., Roll, J. J., & Bickel, W. K. (1996). Alcohol pretreatment increases preference for cocaine over monetary reinforcement. *Psychopharmacology, 123,* 1–8.

Higgins, S. T., Rush, C. R., Bickel, W. K., Capeless, M. A., Hughes, J. R., & Lynn, M. (1992). Effects of alcohol and cocaine, alone and in combination on human learning and performance. *Journal of Experimental Analysis of Behavior, 48,* 87–105.

Higgins, S.T., Rush, C.R., Hughes, J. R., Bickel, W. K., Lynn, M., & Capless, M. A. (1993). Acute behavioral and cardiac effects of cocaine and alcohol combinations in humans. *Psychopharmacology, 111,* 285–294.

Jatlow, P. (1993). Cocaethylene: Pharmacologic activity and clinical significance. *Therapeutic Drug Monitoring, 15,* 533–536.

Jatlow, P., Elsworth, J. D., Bradberry, C. W., Winger, G., Taylor, J. R., Russell, R., & Roth, R. H. (1991). Cocaethylene: A neuropharmacologically active metabolite associated with concurrent cocaine–ethanol ingestion. *Life Sciences, 48,* 1787–1794.

Kandel D., & Yamaguchi K. (1993). From beer to crack: Developmental patterns of drug involvement. *American Journal of Public Health, 83,* 851–855.

Karch, S. B., & Billinghan, M. E. (1988). The pathology and etiology of cocaine-induced heart disease. *Archives of Pathology and Laboratory Medicine, 112,* 225–230.

Katz, J. L., Terry, P., & Witkin, J. M. (1992). Comparative behavioral pharmacology and toxicology of cocaine and its ethanol-derived metabolite, cocaine ethyl-ester (cocaethylene). *Life Sciences, 50,* 1351–1361.

Kidorf, M., & Stitzer, M. L. (1993). Descriptive analysis of cocaine use of methadone patients. *Drug and Alcohol Dependence, 32,* 267–275.

Kosten, T. R., Gawin, F. H., Rounsaville, B. J., & Kleber, H. D. (1986). Cocaine abuse among opioid addicts: Demographic and diagnostic factors in treatment. *American Journal of Drug and Alcohol Abuse, 12,* 1–16.

Kreek, M. J. (1987). Multiple drug abuse patterns and medical consequences. In H. Y. Meltzer (Ed.), *Psychopharmacology: The third generation of progress* (pp. 1597–1604). New York: Raven Press.

Landry, M. J. (1992). An overview of cocaethylene, an alcohol-derived, psychoactive, cocaine metabolite. *Journal of Psychoactive Drugs, 24,* 273–276.

Lange, R. A., Cigarroa, R. G., & Yancy, C. W., Jr. (1989). Cocaine-induced coronary-artery vasoconstriction. *New England Journal of Medicine, 321,* 1557–1562.

Lukas, S. E., Lundahl, S. E., Sholar, M., & Wines, J. (1996). The acute effects of intranasal cocaine differ in tobacco smokers and non-smokers. *Abstracts: College on Problems of Drug Dependence, 58,* 83.

Lukas, S. E., Sholar, M., Kouri, E., Fukuzako, H., & Mendelson, J. H. (1994). Marijuana smoking increases plasma cocaine levels and subjective reports of euphoria in male volunteers. *Pharmacology, Biochemistry and Behavior, 48,* 715–721.

Mannelli, P., Janiri, L., Tempesta, E., & Jones, R. T. (1993). Prediction in drug abuse: Cocaine interactions with alcohol and buprenorphine. *British Journal of Psychiatry, 163,* 39–45.

McCance, E. F., Price, L. H., Kosten, T. R., & Jatlow, P. I. (1995). Cocaethylene: Pharmacology, physiology and behavioral effects in humans. *Journal of Pharmacology and Experimental Therapeutics, 274,* 215–223.

McCance-Katz, E. F., Price, L. H., McDougle, C. J., Kosten, T. R., Black, J. E., & Jatlow, P. I. (1993). Concurrent cocaine-ethanol ingestion in humans: Pharmacology, physiology, behavior, and the role of cocaethylene. *Psychopharmacology, 111,* 39–46.

Meandzija, B., O'Connor, P. G., Fitzgerald, B., Rounsaville, B. J., & Kosten, T. R. (1994). HIV infection and cocaine use in methadone maintained and untreated intravenous drug users. *Drug and Alcohol Dependence, 36,* 109–113.

Miller, N. S., & Gold, M. S. (1988). Cocaine and alcoholism: Distinct or part of a spectrum? *Psychiatric Annals, 18,* 538–539.

Miller, N. S., Gold, M. S., & Belkin, B. M. (1990). The diagnosis of alcohol and cannabis dependence in cocaine dependence. *Advances in Alcohol and Substance Abuse, 8,* 33–42.

Miller, N. S., Gold, M. S., & Klahr, A. L. (1990). The diagnosis of alcohol and cannabis dependence (addiction) in cocaine dependence (addiction). *The International Journal of the Addictions, 25,* 735–744.

Miller, N. S., Gold, M. S., & Millman, R. B. (1989). The prevalence of alcohol dependence in cocaine dependence in an inpatient population. *Annals of Clinical Psychiatry, 1,* 93–97.

Miller, N. S., Millman, R. B., & Keskinen, S. (1989). The diagnosis of alcohol, cocaine, and other drug dependence in an inpatient treatment population. *Journal of Substance Abuse, 6,* 37–40.

Miller, N. S., Summers, G. L., & Gold, M. S. (1993). Cocaine dependence: Alcohol and other drug dependence and withdrawal characteristics. *Journal of Addictive Diseases, 12,* 25–35.

Minor, R. L., Scott, B. D., Brown, D. D., & Winniford, M. D. (1991). Cocaine-induced myocardial infarction in patients with normal coronary arteries. *Annals of Internal Medicine, 115,* 797–806.
Moliterno, D. J., Willard, J. E., Lange, R. A., Negus, B. H., Boehrer, J. D., Glamann, D. B., Landau,
C., Rossen, J. D., Winniford, M. D., & Hillis, L. D. (1994). Coronary-artery vasoconstriction
induced by cocaine, cigarette smoking or both. *New England Journal of Medicine, 330,* 454–459.
Nanji, A. A., & Filipenko, J. D. (1984). Asystole and ventricular fibrillation associated with cocaine intoxication. *Chest, 85,* 132–133.
Nemeth-Coslet, R., Henningfield, J. E., Katz, J. L., & Goldberg, S. R. (1986). Effect of cocaine on rate
of cigarette smoking. *Pharmacology, Biochemistry and Behavior, 25,* 300.
Nemoto, T. (1994). Patterns of cocaine use in HIV infection among injection drug users in a methadone
clinic. *Journal of Substance Abuse, 6,* 169–178.
Oliveto, A. H., Rosen, M. I., Woods, S. W., & Kosten, T. R. (1995). Discriminative stimulus, self-reported and cardiovascular effects of orally administered cocaine in humans. *Journal of Pharmacology and Experimental Therapeutics, 272,* 231–241.
Perez-Reyes, M. (1994). The order of drug administration: Its effects on the interaction between cocaine and ethanol. *Life Sciences, 55,* 451–550.
Perez-Reyes, M. (1993). Subjective and cardiovascular effects of cocaethylene in humans. *Psychopharmacology, 113,* 144–147.
Perez-Reyes, M., & Jeffcoat, A.R. (1992). Ethanol/cocaine interaction: Cocaine and cocaethylene plasma concentrations and their relationship to subjective and cardiovascular effects. *Life Sciences, 51.*
553–563
Perez-Reyes, M., Jeffcoat, A. R., Myers, M., Sihler, K., & Cook, C. E. (1994). Comparison in humans
of the potency and pharmacokinetics of intravenously injected cocaethylene and cocaine. *Psychopharmacology, 116,* 428–432.
Perkins, K. A., DiMarco, A., Grobe, J. E., Scierka, A., & Stiller, R. L. (1994). Nicotine discrimination
in male and female smokers. *Psychopharmacology, 116,* 407–413.
Perwitz, M. J., Willard, J.E., Landau, C., Lange, R. A., Glamann, D. B., Kessler, D. J., Foerster,
E. H.,Todd, E., & Hillis, L. D. (1995). Influence of cocaine, ethanol, or their combination on
epicardial coronary arterial dimensions in humans. *Archives of Internal Medicine, 144,* 1186–
1191.
Preston, K. L., & Bigelow, G. E. (1991). Subjective and discriminative effects of drugs. *Behavioural
Pharmacology, 2,* 293–313.
Preston, K. L., & Sullivan, J. T., Strain, E. C., & Bigelow, G. E. (1996). Enhancement of cocaine's-
abuse liability in methadone maintenance patients. *Psychopharmacology, 123,* 15–25.
Rod, J. L., & Zucker, R. P. (1987). Acute myocardial infarction shortly after cocaine inhalation. *American Journal of Cardiology, 59,* 161.
Roll, J. M., Higgins, S. T., Budney, A. J., Bickel, W. K., & Badger, G. J. (1996). A comparison of cocaine-dependent cigarette smokers and non-smokers on demographic, drug use and other characteristics. *Drug and Alcohol Dependence, 40,* 195–201.
Roll, J. M., Higgins, S. T., & Kennedy, M. (1996). *Cocaine use can increase cigarette smoking.* Paper
presented at the annual meeting of the College on Problems of Drug Dependence, San Juan, Puerto Rico.
Rose, J. S. (1994). Cocaethylene: A current understanding of the active metabilite of cocaine and
ethanol. *American Journal of Emergency Medicine, 12,* 489–490.
Rush, C. R., Critchfield, R. S., Troisi II, J. R., & Griffiths, R. R. (1995).Discriminative stimulus effects
of diazepam and buspirone in normal volunteers. *Journal of the Experimental Analysis of Behavior, 63,* 277–294.
Rush, C. R., & Griffiths, R. R. (1996). Acute subject-rated and behavioral effects of alprazolam and
buspirone, alone and in combination with ethanol, in normal volunteers. *Experimental and Clinical Psychopharmacology,* in press.
Rush, C. R., Higgins, S. T., Bickel, W. K., Wiegner, M. S., & Hughes, J. R. (1994). Acute behavioral
and cardiac effects of alcohol and caffeine, alone and in combination, in humans. *Behavioral Pharmacology, 4,* 562–572.

SAMHSA (1995). *National Household Survey on drug Abuse: Main Findings 1993.* Public Health Service: U.S. Department of Health and Human Services, Rockville, MD. DHHS Publication No. (SMA) 95-3020. Washington, DC: U.S. Government Printing Office.

Schechter, M.D. (1994). Discriminative effects of cocaethylene in rats trained to discriminate cocaine or ethanol. *Life Sciences, 55,* 1033–1043.

Schnoll, S. H., Daghestani, A. N., Karrigan, J., Kitchen, S. B., & Hansen, T. (1985). Characteristics of cocaine users in threatment in L. S. Harris (Ed.), *Problems of drug dependence, 1985.* NIDA Research Monograph 67 (pp. 397). Washington DC: U.S. Government Printing Office.

Schuster, C. R., Fischman, M. W., & Johanson, C. E. (1981). Internal stimulus control and the subjective effects of drugs. In C. E. Johanson & T. Thompson (Eds.), *Behavioral pharmacology of human drug dependence,* Rockville, MD Research Monograph 37. National Institue on Drug Abuse. Public Health Service: Alcohol, Drug Abuse, and Mental Health Administration, Rockville, MD. U.S. Department of Health and Human Services, Washington, DC: U.S. Government Printing Office. (pp. 116–129).

Schuster, C. R., & Johanson, C. E. (1988). Relationship between the discriminative stimulus properties and subjective effects of drugs. In F. C. Colpaert., & R. L. Balster (Eds.), Berlin: Springer-Verlag, Transduction mechanisms of drug stimuli (pp. 161–175).

Siegal, H. A., Carlson, R. G., Wang, J., Falck, R. S., Stephens, R. C., & Nelson, E. D. (1994). Injection drug users in the midwest: An epidemiologic comparison of drug use patterns in four Ohio cities. *Journal of Psychoactive Drugs, 26,* 265–275.

Siegal, R. K. (1980). Cocaine substitutes. *New England Journal of Medicine, 302,* 817–819.

Smart, R. G., Ogborne, A. C., & Newton-Taylor, B. (1990). Drug abuse and alcohol problems among cocaine abusers in an assessment/referral service. *British Journal of Addiction, 85,* 1595–1598.

Smith, H. W. B., III, Liberman, H. A., Brody, S. L., Battey, L. L., Donohue, B. C., & Morris, D. C. (1987). Acute myocardial infarction temporally related to cocaine use: Clinical, angiographic, and pathophysiologic observations. *Annals of Internal Medicine, 107,* 13–18.

Stillman, R., Jones, R. T., Moore, D., Walker, J., & Welm, S. (1993). Improved performance 4 hours after cocaine. *Psychopharmacology, 110,* 415–420.

Strain, E. C., Stitzer, M. L., Liebson, I. A., & Bigelow, G. E. (1993). Methadone dose and treatment outcome. *Drug and Alcohol Dependence, 33,* 105–117.

Walsh, S. L., Sullivan, J. T., Preston, K. L., Garner, J. E., & Bigelow, G. E. (1996). Effects of naltrexone on responses to intravenous cocaine, hydromorphone, and their combination in humans. *Journal of Pharmacology and Experimental Therapeutics, 279,* 524–538.

Weiss, R. D., Mirin, S. M., & Griffin, M. L. (1988). Psychopathology in cocaine abusers: Changing trends. *The Journal of Nervous and Mental Disease, 176,* 719–725.

Welti, C. V., & Wright, R. K. (1979). Death caused by recreationa cocaine use. *JAMA, 214,* 2519–2522.

Woolverton, W. L., & Schuster, C. R. (1983). Behavioral and pharmacological aspects of opioid of dependence: Mixed agonist-antagonists. *Pharmacological Reviews, 35,* 33–52.

Zimmerman, F. H., Gustafson, G. M., & Kemp, H. G., Jr. (1987). Recurrent myocardial infarction associated with cocaine abuse in a young man with normal coronary arteries: Evidence for coronary artery spasm culminating in thrombosis. *Journal of the American College of Cariology, 9,* 964–968.

11

COCAINE EFFECTS
ON BRAIN FUNCTION

SCOTT E. LUKAS AND PERRY F. RENSHAW

McLean Hospital
Harvard Medical School
Belmont, Massachusetts

INTRODUCTION

SUMMARY OF TECHNIQUES AND AIMS

Recently, important advances in the understanding of the basic pharmacological mechanism of cocaine's effect on the central nervous system (CNS) have occurred due to the use of various brain imaging techniques that can assess different components of brain activity/function in a living organism. Briefly, computed tomography (CT) (Pascual-Leone, Dhuma & Anderson, 1991a,b), magnetic resonance imaging (MRI) (Volkow, Valentine, & Kulkarni, 1988; Amass, Nardin, Mendelson, Teoh, & Woods, 1991), positron emission tomography(PET) (Volkow et al., 1990; London & Morgan, 1993), and single-photon emission computerized tomography (SPECT) (Holman et al., 1991; Pearlson et al., 1993) have all been used to characterize the acute and/or chronic effects of cocaine. Functional MRI (fMRI) is still in its infancy, and its potential for assisting in the understanding of cocaine's effects on brain function have yet to be fully realized. Preliminary results of its utility in studying cocaine abuse will be provided in this chapter.

Cocaine stimulates the CNS and elevates the mood in a dose-related manner. After a generalized "alerting" effect, subjects report a profound sense of increased well-being that often includes increases in self-confidence, emotional state, and sexual feelings (Fischman, 1988; Gawin, 1991; Van Dyke, Ungerer, Jatlow, Barash, & Byck, 1982; Withers, Pulvirenti, Koob, & Gillin, 1995). This intense good feeling state has been called "euphoria" or a "rush" of pleasure that lasts several seconds and is followed by several minutes of persistent but lower level euphoria. The euphorigenic effects of cocaine appear and disappear rapidly after acute administration, regardless of the route of administration. Although above techniques offer excellent spacial resolution of the brain, a technique with short temporal resolution is needed to detect CNS changes associated with the cocaine-induced reward.

The chapter focuses on the use of brain electrical activity and various forms of MR technology to study the acute and chronic effects of cocaine. These techniques offer great promise as they can be fine-tuned to track the rapidly oscillating neural networks that elicit changes in mood state and behavior. Further, a method for coregistering these two neuroimaging techniques to provide an additional dimension to understanding the source and mechanism of action of cocaine will be described.

EFFECTS OF COCAINE ON BRAIN ELECTRICAL ACTIVITY

GENERAL METHODOLOGY

Electroencephalography (EEG) is a technique for measuring the electrical activity of neurons located in both the cerebral cortex and subcortical nuclei. The analog EEG signal is typically digitized and then stored on disk for subsequent analysis. Computerized analysis of the signals is frequently performed using a Fast Fourier Transformation, which quantifies the amount of energy as a function of frequency (cf. Lukas, 1991a). Four major bands of spontaneous EEG activity have proven to be most useful: delta (1–3 Hz), theta (4–7 Hz), alpha (8–13 Hz), and beta (13–25 Hz). Both the alpha and beta bands are further subdivided to improve precision of measurements: slow (8–10 Hz) and fast (11–13 Hz) alpha and slow (13.5–19.5 Hz) and fast (20–26 Hz) beta bands have been used to differentially measure the effects of psychoactive drugs (Cohen et al., 1993, Lukas et al., 1989). Alpha activity is the most prominent rhythm seen during wakefulness and is generally localized over the posterior and occipital regions of the head.

Event-related potentials (ERPs) are specific alterations in brain electrical activity that occur in response to specific auditory, visual, or tactile stimuli. They are frequently generated by repeatedly presenting a stimulus while averaging the resultant brain electrical activity to filter extraneous activity that is unrelated to the processing of the stimuli. ERPs are often used to measure the functional status of the CNS because the speed of neuronal signal propagation is known. Evoked potentials (EP) differ somewhat in that they occur much faster after stimulus presentation (typically <50 msec) and are not affected by cognitive function.

Each type of ERP (e.g., auditory, visual) has a characteristic waveform that varies according to the number and latency of positive and negative waves that appear after the stimulus. The resultant positive and negative peaks are named by their electrical polarity and their latency after stimulus presentation in milliseconds. Cognitive ERPs have been used in recent years to characterize the effects of drugs on brain function and are characterized by its key components as follows:

N100 and N200—largest negative waves with latency of 90–130 ms and 180–220 ms, respectively; P200—largest positive wave with a latency of 180–250 ms; P300—the largest positive wave with a latency of 250–500 ms after delivery of a specific stimulus. Maximal amplitudes are observed at parietal and central midline electrode sites and almost any element of surprise within an experimental setting elicits a P300 (Sutton, Braren, Zubin, & John, 1965).

The P300 component of the ERP is the most extensively studied in drug abuse, because it is generated by information processes related to memory and cognition. There are several procedures used to elicit the P300 response, although the most common involves a simple two-stimuli discrimination task, or the *oddball paradigm* (Duncan-Johnson & Donchin, 1977) The procedure involves presenting two different stimuli to which the subject is asked to count only one. Brain wave activity in response to the "target" stimulus is averaged independent of the responses to the frequent stimulus.

Topographic brain electrical activity mapping is a technique that was first used in 1971 (Duffy, 1982) to amalgamate EEG or ERPs from numerous scalp sites into a single display of electrical activity at a single point in time. The voltage is measured at each electrode site while 3- or 4-point interpolation techniques are used to calculate the power values of the area between electrodes. The final image is a color- or gray-scaled map of the electrical activity of the entire surface of the head and colors/shades represent different voltage values (Buchsbaum et al, 1982; Dubinsky & Barlow, 1980; Duffy, Burchfiel, & Lombrose, 1979).

EFFECTS IN VOLUNTEERS

Hans Berger was the first to report that a subcutaneous dose of 30 mg of cocaine increased EEG alpha (Berger, 1931) and beta activity (Berger, 1937). More recently, three laboratories (Herning, Jones, Hooker, Mendelson, & Blackwell 1985a; Lukas, 1991b; Mannelli, Janiri, Tempesta, & Jones, 1993) have studied the EEG effects of a low dose of cocaine in occasional users. These authors also reported an increase in alpha and beta activity. Upon closer examination, alpha activity rapidly disappears along with the cocaine-induced euphoria, leaving a desynchronized state with predominantly beta activity (Lukas, 1991a,b).

EFFECTS IN COCAINE-EXPERIENCED SUBJECTS

Few studies have evaluated the EEG activity of subjects with a history of cocaine abuse or dependence. Alper, Chabot, Kim, Prichep, and John (1990) reported that recovering crack cocaine-dependent patients had significantly more alpha power. Other authors (Pascual-Leone et al., 1991b) found significant increases in delta, theta, and beta power and a significant decrease of alpha power in chronic, habitual abusers, but many subjects were receiving neuroleptic treatment. Bauer and his colleagues (Bauer, 1994; Bauer & Kranzler, 1994) failed to demonstrate any abnormalities in EEG activity among cocaine-dependent patients.

EFFECTS ON THE P300 ERP

The P300 ERP has been used to study the acute and chronic effects of cocaine. In general, P300 amplitude is reduced by acute cocaine (Herning, Jones, Hooker, & Tulunay, 1985b; Herning, Hooker, & Jones, 1987; Lukas, 1991b), suggesting that it may disrupt stimulus evaluation. Changes in auditory P300 amplitude and latency can reflect the progress of individuals as they are detoxified from cocaine (Lukas, Woods, Mendelson, 1987). The increased P300 latency returned to control levels by the fourth week of detoxification, but the amplitude remained elevated. Branchey, Buydens-Branchey, & Horvath, (1993) evaluated 10 patients dependent on cocaine and/or opioids in recovery after detoxification, showing that P300 amplitude was significantly reduced compared to a group of age matched controls, whereas P300 latency was not affected. Two studies (Amass, Lukas, Weiss, & Mendelson, 1990; Katbamma et al., 1993) have evaluated patients with a history of alcohol and cocaine abuse during recovery. They found elevated latencies of the middle latencies ERPs (Katbamma, Metz, Adelman, & Thodi, 1993), and an increased P300 latency and an attenuated P300 amplitude (Amass et al., 1990). Although some of these results may seem contradictory, they consistently reflect alterations in cognitive information processing after acute and chronic cocaine use.

The cocaine-induced alterations in brain electrical activity reflect a generalized reduction of neural activity (Alper et al., 1990; Amass et al., 1990; Lukas et al., 1987; Pascual-Leone et al., 1991b). This is consistent with studies reporting decreases in cortical glucose utilization (London & Morgan, 1993) and blood flow (Pearlson et al., 1993), which reflect slowed brain metabolism. This slowing may be associated with the brain cortical atrophy (Pascual-Leone et al., 1991a; Strickland et al., 1993) and may underlie the neuropsychological alterations reported in this population.

SOURCE LOCALIZATION OF BRAIN WAVE ACTIVITY

Attempts to locate the pacemaker for the observed rhythmic activity of the human EEG have centered on the thalamus (Dempsey, Morison, & Morison, 1941). Specifically, the intralaminar nuclei project bilaterally over the cortex and influence levels of consciousness from sleeping states to awake and alert. These neuroanatomical pathways account for the excellent correlation between EEG activity and behavioral states of alertness (Lindsley, 1952; Wikler, 1957). As there are good correlations between such patterns and altered levels of consciousness (and drugs of abuse can modify consciousness), the search for the source of a particular brain wave pattern can have important implications for the similarities and differences among various drugs of abuse. Furthermore, the degree to which drug-induced altered levels of consciousness resemble those that are attained naturally can help understand the biological basis of drug abuse. Because the EEG is sensitive to changes in degrees of consciousness, both natural and those induced by environmental or pharmacological intervention, it is an excellent model for this line of research.

There are two methods for exploring the source of a brain wave pattern: the *forward* solution and the *inverse* solution. The former is achieved by actually calculating the field distribution over the surface of the scalp that is generated by a known source and magnitude, whereas the inverse solution involves calculating the source on the basis of the measured field distribution. The inverse solution is not unique because there are many possible answers to any particular topographic map (Wood, 1982).

COCAINE-INDUCED EUPHORIA—CORRELATES WITH BRAIN FUNCTION

EEG EFFECTS OF ACUTE COCAINE

When measuring the pharmacological effects of a drug it is desirable to reduce or eliminate as many confounding variables as possible. This is particularly important in studies that are designed to detect subtle, but important, changes in brain function that are associated with specific mood states. A successful documentation of such a relationship was made possible by studying individuals in an experimental chamber (Figure 11.1) and asking them to report changes in mood state or behavior using a nonverbal joystick device. Thus, spontaneous changes in behavior were captured on a continual basis, ensuring that a transient change in behavior or mood state is not missed. The instructional set of this experiment is as follows: The subjects are told to move the position of the joystick either forward, to the side, or release it to report first detection, intense, or certainty and offset of cocaine effects, respectively. Two buttons are also available to report intense good feelings or euphoria and/or intense bad feelings or dysphoria. As the buttons were independent, subjects could report good and bad effects simultaneously (Lukas, Mendelson, Benedikt, & Jones, 1986). A typical nonverbal report of cocaine-induced intoxication as generated via the joystick device is depicted in Figure 11.2. The subject quickly detected the 0.9 mg/kg in dose of cocaine, which was followed by multiple short episodes of euphoria. Frequently, this latter phase is accompanied by a relative reduction in alpha activity and an increase in EEG beta activity. With the exception of the *crash,* this behavioral pattern after acute cocaine administration mimics that observed after acute administration of ethanol, morphine, and marijuana.

The corresponding EEG topographic maps during various phases of the experiment are plotted above the behavioral data to provide a temporal framework for directly comparing the electrophysiological and behavioral data. The baseline levels of EEG alpha activity increase during self-reported episodes of euphoria while it is markedly reduced during dysphoria. Figure 11.3 depicts the increase in EEG alpha activity during euphoria from a group of 6 subjects who were challenged with a 0.9 mg/kg dose of cocaine.

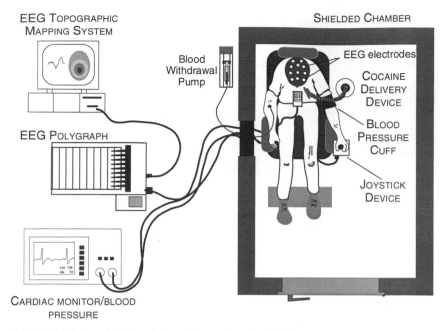

FIGURE 11.1   Artist's rendering of the top view of a clinical neuropsychopharmacology laboratory. The subject is depicted with electroencephalogram (EEG) and electrocardiogram (EKG) electrodes and a blood pressure cuff for automatic assessment of vital signs. The walls of the larger room
are sealed in copper screen to provide an electrically isolated environment. The joystick device is located next to the subject's left hand and the output is directed to the EEG computer.

DRUG-INDUCED CHANGES IN EEG ALPHA ACTIVITY

Alterations in brain electrical activity as a measure of drug-induced intoxication are useful because of the covariance between alterations in brain electrical activity and behavior in both normal and abnormal states (Begleiter, 1977; Glaser,
1963; Koukkou & Lehmann, 1975). The mood state euphoria is not unique to psychoactive drugs, but has eluded precise definition. This is because the term *euphoria* is frequently used without an objective measure of a drug's rewarding effects. Thus, a major reason for pursuing this line of research using topographic
mapping techniques is that the power, predominant frequency, distribution, and
time course of brain electrical activity can be simultaneously measured over the
entire scalp to provide a complete assessment of rapid neurophysiological events
likely to be associated with rapidly changing behavioral states. Furthermore, as-
similation of data from drugs belonging to various pharmacological classes strongly suggests that alterations in brain electrical activity correlate with specific, drug-
induced behavioral states and that paroxysmal increases in EEG alpha activity may
be linked to drug-induced euphoria-a response that is shared among many different drugs. In fact, such a relationship exists because studies have shown that drug-

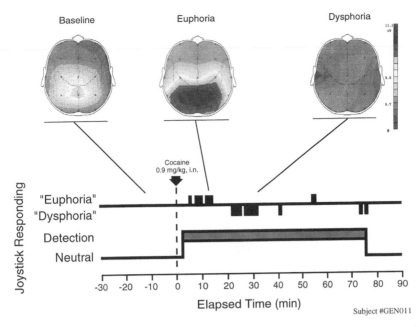

FIGURE 11.2 Joystick responding of a typical male subject after an acute dose of cocaine (0.9 mg/kg). The subject had continuous access to the joystick device. Topographic maps of EEG alpha activity (10.0–10.5 Hz) are plotted along the same time axis to permit direct comparisons of brain function during baseline and cocaine-induced euphoria and dysphoria. The scale is in μV.

induced euphoria is associated with abrupt increases in EEG alpha activity after ethanol (Alper et al., 1990; Ehlers, Wall, & Schuckit, 1989; Lukas, 1991a; Lukas & Mendelson, 1988; Lukas et al., 1986; 1987; 1989; 1990; 1991; Cohen, Porjesz, & Begleiter, 1993), and marijuana (Lukas, Mendelson, & Benedikt, 1995). In addition, chronic marijuana smokers display more EEG alpha activity than controls (Struve, Straumanis, Patrick, & Price, 1989). These data suggest that rapid changes in EEG alpha may reflect CNS processes that are associated with the positive reinforcing effects of various drugs of abuse.

Such similarities among drug classes would be of theoretical importance because they imply that a common neurophysiological process contributes to or modulates the reinforcing effects of drugs from several classes. However, there are several important *practical* applications as well. First, discrete alterations in brain electrical activity have been shown to discriminate between individuals on the basis of familial history of alcoholism in men (Church & Williams, 1982; Ehlers & Schuckit, 1991; Gabrielli et al., 1982) and women (Lukas, Mendelson, Woods, Mello & Teoh, 1989a), and may prove useful as neurophysiological markers of *vulnerability* to drug abuse. Additional confidence that this relationship exists is found in the studies demonstrating that patterns of brain electrical activity also are genetically related (Propping, Kruger, & Janah, 1980; Vogel, Schalt, Kruger, Prop-

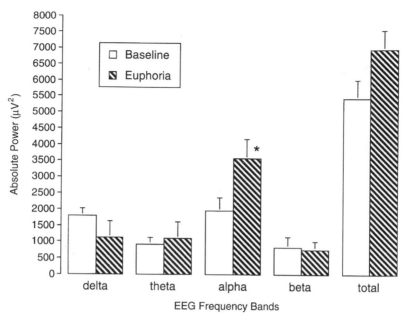

FIGURE 11.3 Group changes in EEG activity before and during cocaine-induced euphoria. The euphoric episodes were identified by the subjects using a joystick device. Data are from 3–4 euphoric episodes from six male subjects who received 0.9 mg/kg cocaine.

ping, & Lehnert, 1979). Second, applying these techniques during prospective evaluations of putative pharmacological treatments for drug abuse will provide basic information on the mechanism by which such medications are effective. Third, a common process among different drugs of abuse opens up new areas of research to explore alternative methods of managing or treating drug abuse and drug dependence. Fourth, detoxification from a drug of abuse may be managed more effectively if specific physiological and behavioral responses can be predicted.

CHANGES IN P300 TOPOGRAPHY DURING COCAINE SELF-ADMINISTRATION

The neurophysiological concomitants of drug-seeking behavior remain a mystery, but knowledge of the neuronal processes that precede drug taking may provide new insights into how to curb such behavior in the first place as well as help prevent relapse. We conducted a study to assess the electrophysiological correlates of cocaine-seeking behavior. At 30-min intervals, female subjects were given four opportunities to self-administer an intranasal dose of cocaine (two placebos 0.45 and 0.9 mg/kg) on a random basis. Subjects were told that they would receive the dose that they selected immediately upon completing an auditory P300 ERP task.

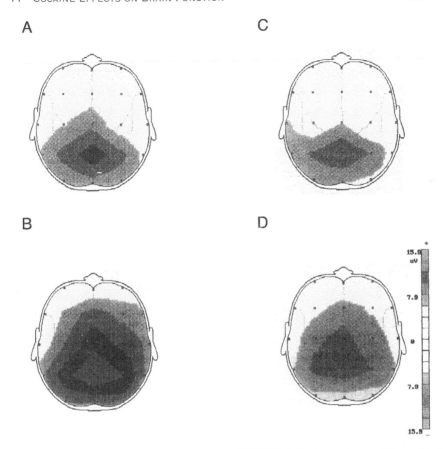

FIGURE 11.4 Topographic maps of auditory P300 ERPs during (A) resting conditions and just prior to the delivery of (B) placebo, (C) low (0.45 mg/kg), or (D) high (0.9 mg/kg) dose of cocaine. Data are the grand averages of four healthy adult women who used cocaine on an occasional basis.

This strategy permitted us to measure the electrophysiological events that immediately *preceded* the delivery of a known dose of cocaine. Figure 11.4 shows the group topographic distribution of the P300 ERP while subjects expected delivery of cocaine or placebo. The reduction in P300 amplitude prior to cocaine suggests that cocaine-seeking behavior places demands on the subject's attentional and cognitive processes that are not present when the subject knows that a placebo dose will be given. Because cocaine craving was markedly elevated at this time, these electrophysiological changes may be a measure of cocaine-seeking behavior. Such robust changes in P300 topography during the moments just preceding delivery of a known dose of cocaine provides a unique *snapshot* of a brain function during an important behavior.

SUMMARY

As the technology improved over the years, researchers have integrated EEG measures into studies that seek out the relationship between brain function and behavior. It is now apparent that such measures can also yield insights to the processes that contribute to the vulnerability of individuals to drug abuse. For example, P300 amplitudes are smaller in the children of alcoholics than in sons of control fathers (Begleiter, Porjesz, Bihari, & Kissin, 1984; Cohen, Wang, Porjesz, & Begleiter, 1995; Hill, Steinhauer, Park, & Zubin, 1990; Polich, Pollock & Bloom, 1994; Steinhauer & Hill, 1993). This finding suggest that the reduced P300 amplitude may be a heritable trait that antecedes the development of alcoholism and thus it may function as a critical neurophysiological marker of a genetic predisposition for alcoholism. A similar relationship for cocaine has not yet been explored.

The significance of drug-induced increases in EEG alpha activity is that high activity is normally associated with a pleasurable, free-floating and extremely relaxed state (Brown, 1970; Lindsley, 1952; Matejcek, 1982; Wallace, 1970) similar to that induced during transcendental meditation (Wallace, 1970). The covariance between increased EEG alpha activity and subjective reports of euphoria after use of various drugs of abuse (such as cocaine, marijuana, and ethanol) suggests that this neurophysiologic response may be associated with drug-induced reinforcement. If increased EEG alpha activity is associated with drug-induced reinforcement in general, and is not selective for a single drug class, then this interpretation is consistent with the notion that drug-seeking behavior is a form of stimulus self-administration that produces a change in behavior state. Whether the direction of the effect is stimulating or sedating is unimportant.

Because drugs from different pharmacological classes are frequently used together, it is likely that there are pharmacological reasons for these combinations. By measuring neurophysiological activity antecedent to drug-taking behavior we may be able to identify basic processes that are shared among drugs of abuse. Alternatively, we may discover that one drug counteracts negative or undesirable effects of another. Such information may explain why certain combinations are preferred over others. Measuring these processes using an multidisciplinary approach increases our chances of discovering the basic mechanisms that subserve drug reinforcement.

MAGNETIC RESONANCE IMAGING AND MAGNETIC RESONANCE SPECTROSCOPY

MAGNETIC RESONANCE IMAGING

MRI exploits the intrinsic magnetic properties of the hydrogen atoms within brain water. In a static magnetic field, the protons within the hydrogen nuclei will

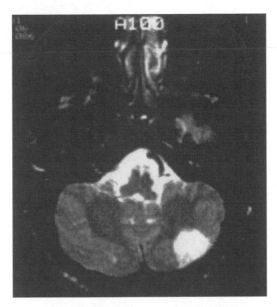

FIGURE 11.5   T2-weighted magnetic resonance imaging (MRI) of the brain of a woman with a clinical history of polysubstance abuse. This image demonstrates a silent cerebellar infarction, which appears as a hyperintense white spot in the lower right side of the image.

align with or against the field. Since aligning with the field is a lower energy state than aligning against it, slightly more nuclei will be in the lower energy state than in the higher energy state. Consequently, radio frequency (RF) irradiation at a specific resonance frequency (e.g., 64 MHz at 1.5 Tesla [T]) may be used to convert some of the lower energy nuclei to the higher energy state. When the RF pulse is stopped, the nuclei that have aligned against the field will return to the lower energy state and in so doing, will give off RF energy at the resonance frequency. The emitted RF energy may be detected using a suitable coil, or antenna, and amplified by an MR scanner. Images, which are essentially maps of the location from which these RF signals arise, are constructed with the use of magnetic field gradients to achieve spatial localization (Kucharczyk, Moseley, & Barkovich, 1994).

In clinical practice, brain MR images may be referred to as being T1-weighted or T2-weighted, where T1 and T2 are relaxation times that describe the rate at which the hydrogen nuclei return to equilibrium following RF irradiation at the resonance frequency. In general, T1-weighted images demonstrate the features of structural neuroanatomy in great detail, with clear delineation of gray matter, white matter, and cerebrospinal fluid (CSF) containing structures. Images that are T2-weighted are often very useful for highlighting areas of pathology, for example tumors, infarctions, and demyelination, which demonstrate characteristic changes in image signal intensity. Magnetic resonance contrast agents may also be used to further define suspicious areas (Bradley, Yuh, & Bydder, 1993). These agents, which typically contain a paramagnetic ion such as gadolinium, will penetrate a disrupted blood–brain barrier (BBB) but not an intact one. Thus, in situations in which the BBB is inflamed (e.g., acute multiple sclerosis, lupus) or infiltrated (e.g., tumors), contrast will extravasate, and postcontrast MR images are said to enhance.

Attribution of any particular brain anomaly to the use or abuse of cocaine is confounded by the fact that other etiologies are always possible and by the fact that cocaine is typically used in combination with other substances. Nonetheless, brain MRI studies of cocaine-abusing populations have identified a number of cerebrovascular complications, including cortical and subcortical infarctions and hemorrhage, which appear to be associated with the use of cocaine (Brown, Prager, Lee, & Ramsey, 1992). Figure 11.5 depicts this effect in a cocaine-abusing woman. These findings are also supported by the results of a recent, prospective autopsy study in the state of Connecticut (Nolte, Brass, & Fletterick, 1996). Over a 1-year period, 10 out of 17 nontraumatic, intracranial hemorrhages were associated with a positive toxicology examination for the presence of cocaine. In another large study, perinatal cocaine exposure has been associated with an increased incidence of cortical infarction and midline CNS malformations (Heier et al., 1991).

Overall, the presence of clinically apparent cerebrovascular compromise is relatively low. However, structural MRI studies may not be sufficient to fully characterize the "clinically silent brain dysfunction" which occurs in many substance abusers (Volkow et al., 1992). In this regard, the use of MRS and fMRI which are described below, may provide greater insight into the effects of acute and chronic cocaine use.

MAGNETIC RESONANCE SPECTROSCOPY

MRS employs standard MRI devices in order to determine brain levels of both exogenous and endogenous compounds. Although the technology is relatively new, the present and future utility of MRS for evaluating individuals with psychiatric illness (Dager & Steen, 1992) and substance abuse disorders (Kaufman, Levin, Christensen, & Renshaw, 1996a) has been reviewed. Psychotropic medications that have been detected in humans using MRS include lithium (Renshaw & Wicklund, 1988) and some fluorinated polycyclic drugs such as fluoxetine and trifluperazine (Komoroski, Newton, Karson, Cardwell, & Sprigg, 1990). For the evaluation of endogenous metabolites, two different MRS-visible nuclei have been studied most extensively: phosphorus (^{31}P) and hydrogen (^{1}H). Phosphorus MR spectra provide information on the concentration of high-energy phosphate compounds (e.g., phosphocreatine, nucleoside triphosphate) as well as phospholipid metabolites (phosphomonoesters and phosphodiesters). Hydrogen (also called proton) MR spectra detect signals from an established neuronal marker, N-acetyl-aspartate (Tsai & Coyle, 1995), creatine and phosphocreatine, cytosolic choline-containing compounds, myo-inositol, and lactate.

COCAINE EFFECTS ON HIGH-ENERGY PHOSPHATES

In animals, the acute administration of cocaine has been associated with decreased levels of intracellular free magnesium, which may be related to the vasoconstrictive effects of cocaine (Altura, 1993). The ^{31}P MRS assessment of free magnesium levels is made by evaluating the relative frequency difference between the inorganic phosphate and the nucleoside triphosphate resonances. In humans, ^{31}P MRS studies have focused on changes in brain chemistry that are related to cocaine use in the context of polysubstance abuse. MacKay, Meyerhoff, Dillon, Weiner, & Fein, (1993) have reported decreased levels of both phosphomonoesters (PME), which are lipid precursors, and phosphodiesters (PDE), which are lipid catabolites, in white matter structures of cocaine-dependent, polysubstance abusers. In contrast, Christensen et al. (1996) have reported different patterns of metabolic change in a cohort of heavy polysubstance abusers in early remission. Specifically, these investigators noted an increase in (PME) and a decrease in the level of nucleoside triphosphate (NTP) through an axial slice of brain.

Because the vast majority of brain NTP is adenosine triphosphate (ATP), decreases in the brain NTP resonance strongly suggest that bioenergetic impairment may be associated with active polysubstance use. No change was noted in brain levels of phosphocreatine (PCr), which is unusual in that the brain generally maintains NTP levels at the expense of PCr because of its higher phosphate group transfer potential. However, studies of partial ischemia and reperfusion in animals have consistently demonstrated decreases in brain NTP without decrement in PCr levels (Aurelli et al., 1994; Corbett, Lapptook, & Olivares, 1991).

Proton MRS also has been used to study the effects of both acute and chronic stimulant use. Acute administration of amphetamine to the rat is associated with increases in both brain lactate and cerebral blood flow (CBF) (Detre, Williams, & Koretzky, 1990). Two groups have recently reported results of ^{1}H MRS studies of acute cocaine administration. Christensen et al. (1996) evaluated the effects of two doses of cocaine (0.4 mg/kg and 0.2 mg/kg iv) and placebo on basal ganglia metabolites in a cohort of 30 subjects with a history of occasional cocaine use. They noted dose-dependent, statistically significant increases in the intracellular N-acetyl-aspartate, cytosolic choline-containing compound, and myo-inositol resonance intensities. These findings were interpreted to be most consistent with intracellular swelling, leading to increased metabolite transverse relaxation (T2) times (Cady et al., 1994). This swelling could be due either to the vasoconstrictive effects of cocaine and/or to the direct effects of dopamine on Na/K ATPase (Bertorello, Hopfield, Aperia, & Greengard, 1990). In contrast, an increase in the line width of the water resonance was found without any change in intensity. This result was interpreted to reflect an increase in the vascular concentration of deoxyhemoglobin, leading to a greater dephasing of the freely mobile water protons (Ogawa, Lee, Kay, & Tank, 1990).

Li et al.(1996) evaluated changes in ^{1}H MR spectra of the basal ganglia and the frontal lobe before and 30–60 min after the intravenous injection of 70 mg cocaine over a 90-min period to 14 subjects with a history of cocaine dependence. They noted an increase in the intensity of the N-acetyl-aspartate resonance area to the creatine area ratio in the frontal lobe without a corresponding change in the basal ganglia. This result was attributed to an increase in the level of N-acetyl-aspartate, although the possibility of differential changes in metabolite relaxation times was not considered.

At baseline, Li et al (1996) also noted that subjects with a history of cocaine abuse had decreased N-acetyl-aspartate-to-creatine ratios in both the basal ganglia and frontal lobes compared to healthy control subjects. This finding is of considerable interest because N-acetyl-aspartate appears to exist principally in neurons and decreased brain levels of N-acetyl-aspartate have been demonstrated in subjects with a range of neurodegenerative disorders (Tsai & Coyle, 1995). However, Chang, Ernst, & Strickland (1996) have recently reported ^{1}H MRS results obtained from midfrontal gray and white matter voxels of 38 abstinent cocaine users and 27 matched comparison subjects. Elevated absolute concentrations of cytosolic-choline-containing compounds, creatine and phosphocreatine, and myo-inositol were observed in the white matter voxels for the male subjects only. No differences were noted in either the gray matter or the white matter for the female subjects and no differences were noted in the gray matter for the male subjects.

In summary, MRS provides a noninvasive window on brain chemistry. The limited number of studies performed to date suggests that both acute and chronic cocaine use may be associated with changes in brain chemistry. Abnormalities of compounds involved in lipid metabolism and bioenergy have been documented using ^{31}P MRS. Proton MRS studies have also suggested that there may be changes in lipid metabolism that arise from chronic cocaine use and that there may also be a decrease in brain levels of N-acetyl-aspartate, an established neuronal marker, in some brain regions. Although it is disappointing that the results of studies reported to date have not been more consistent, these investigations have generally involved a small number of subjects. Moreover, these studies also have been conducted during a period of rapid technical advances in MRS methods.

FUNCTIONAL MAGNETIC RESONANCE IMAGING

Functional neuroimaging studies have historically been limited both by the need to use radionuclides and by poor temporal and spatial resolution. Recent advances in the area of MRI may surmount these difficulties. In particular, the development of high-speed, echo planar imaging (EPI) devices has greatly enhanced the temporal resolution of MRI (Stehling, Turner & Mansfield, 1991). With EPI, single-image planes may be acquired in 50–100 ms and multiple image planes may be acquired each second. The development of EPI has greatly hastened the development of a family of techniques that are generally referred to as fMRI. These methods are generally designed so that changes in CBF or volume lead to changes in image signal intensity.

fMRI studies maybe divided into two separate classes: *noncontrast* techniques, which make use of endogenous physiological factors to detect changes in cerebral activation (Kwong et al., 1992; Ogawa et al., 1990), and *contrast* techniques, which require the intravenous injection of a paramagnetic agent (Belliveau et al., 1990; 1991). Noncontrast techniques employ either T1-weighted pulse sequences to detect changes in blood flow or, more commonly, T2-weighted pulse sequences to detect changes in the local concentration of paramagnetic deoxyhemoglobin. The latter method has been referred to as blood-oxygen-level-dependent (BOLD) imaging. BOLD experiments take advantage of the fact that regional brain activation is associated with changes in both blood flow and blood volume, with the magnitude of the former exceeding that of the latter, leading to a washout of paramagnetic deoxyhemoglobin, decreased phase dispersion of surrounding water protons, and increased local signal intensity (Ogawa et al., 1993).

A major drawback to BOLD studies is low sensitivity; at 1.5 T, the magnitude of the observed signal changes is relatively small. For instance, photic stimulation, which induces a 70% increase in occipital cortical blood flow, produces only a 2–4% increase in MR signal intensity (Ogawa et al., 1993; Hathout et al., 1994). Additionally, recent reports have indicated that the magnitude of BOLD signal intensity changes varies as a function of subject age, gender, hematocrit, and medication status (Levin et al., 1995c, 1996a; Ross et al., 1998).

The contrast technique, which is referred to as dynamic susceptibility contrast (DSC) MRI, utilizes the bolus injection of a paramagnetic contrast agent in order to produce changes in tissue magnetic susceptibility and MR image intensity (Belliveau et al., 1990). During the first pass of the contrast agent, MR signal intensity may change by as much as 20–40% at 1.5 T and this change in signal intensity may be related to the local cerebral blood volume (CBV) using indicator dilution methods. DSC MRI data may be used to map cerebral blood volume at rest (Harris et al., 1996) or, by using multiple injections of contrast, to measure changes associated with specific behavioral or pharmacological challenges (Belliveau et al., 1991; Levin et al., 1995a).

The promise that fMRI holds for studies of individuals with mental illness and substance abuse disorders has been reviewed (Levin, Ross, & Renshaw, 1995b; Kaufman et al., 1996a). To this point, few fMRI studies have addressed the issue of the extent to which drug effects may be determined. Despite the relative insensitivity of the BOLD technique, signal changes in response to administration of the vasodilator acetazolamide (Vorstrup, Henriksen, & Pruson, 1984) have been detected in rats (Graham et al., 1994). Levin et al. (1995b, 1996b) have pointed out that DSC MRI may offer a more robust means to evaluate the acute effects of drugs on cerebral hemodynamics and have devised a multiple bolus method to minimize artifacts that might result from prior administration of contrast. Kaufman et al. (1996b) have recently used this technique to evaluate the vasoconstrictive effects of an acute intravenous injection of cocaine. They reported that 0.4 mg/kg cocaine is associated with an 18% decrease in global CBV as well as a significantly shorter mean transit time for the contrast to pass through the CNS.

There have also been relatively few reports of fMRI investigations of individuals with substance abuse disorders, despite the fact that radionuclide imaging studies have consistently demonstrated changes in cerebral perfusion and metabolism in substance abusers (Mathew & Wilson, 1991). However, looking forward, there are likely to be several important areas for fMRI research. One example would include the use of BOLD fMRI to document changes in regional cerebral hemodynamics in response to drug-related cues (Childress et al., 1993). Another area of research might include the use of fMRI to document the efficacy of interventions designed to ameliorate the vasoconstrictive properties of cocaine (Nolte et al., 1996). Given the improvements in spatial and temporal resolution afforded by fMRI, as well as the fact that radioactive tracers are not required, it is clear that fMRI will ultimately play a very important role in clinical substance abuse research.

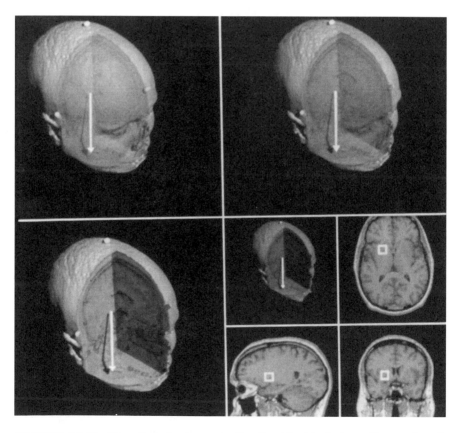

FIGURE 11.6   Three-dimensional reconstruction of a subject's brain along with a coregistered negative alpha wave. The top two and bottom left panels are sequential computerized surgery of the outer layers to reveal the source of the electrical signal. The lower right panel is a composite of standard two-dimensional images. The vitamin E capsules can be easily seen.

COREGISTRATION OF IMAGING TECHNOLOGIES

It is now clear that MRI technology can be merged with EEG/ERP data to provide direct neuroanatomical verification of the source of specific brain-wave patterns. Such a feat requires that a number of technical problems be solved. The first was to obtain an accurate measure of the electrode location. Upon the completion of many of the EEG studies described above, the scalp electrodes were removed and the individual electrode sites were marked by gluing a Vitamin E capsule to the sites (Torello, Phillips, Hunter & Csuri, 1987). Subjects were then escorted to the Brain Imaging Center at McLean Hospital and serial MRIs were obtained using a G.E. 1.5 Tesla Signa Magnetic Resonance Whole body Imager.

Estimates of the EEG sources were calculated using an *inverse* solution using a commercially available software package (Dipole, Bio-logic Co., Mundelein, IL). The topographic data from all electrode sites spanning a 20-ms window that included the P3 peak were analyzed and were applied to a 3-shell model to calculate a single-dipole source. The inverse solution involves setting an initial *guess* of the source near the origin (i.e., x,y,z) and performing a series of iterations to determine the momentary solution of a sample point. The process involves calculating the field distribution of voltages that would be predicted from the dipole solution. The resultant data set provided an estimate of the location, direction, and magnitude of the P3 source. The dipole data were converted to ASCII format and presented in two equivalent formats in millimeter units. A right-handed Cartesian coordinate system was used to define sources in dipole space. This information was merged with a three-dimensional reconstructed MR image (Figure 11.6). The first three panels peel away the scalp, skull, and brain to reveal the source of the potential that was recorded on the surface.

SUMMARY AND CONCLUSIONS

Our understanding of cocaine's effects on brain function have been propelled by the development of a number of important technological advances. These advances have not proceeded in a vacuum, but rather have continued in a manner such that discoveries in one area are applied to another. Thus, while EEG and ERP measures have been in use for nearly a century, many of the basic principles for measuring brain electrical activity apply to other imaging modalities.

The ultimate goal of these efforts is to gain a better understanding of cocaine's reinforcing effects so that new and improved methods for preventing and treating cocaine use can be developed. Activation of mesolimbic and/or mesocortical dopaminergic neurons with a concomitant increase in brain dopamine levels is not unique to cocaine and other CNS stimulants. In fact, many drugs of abuse that belong to different pharmacologic classes share this ability to elevate mesolimbic dopamine neurotransmission. These include amphetamine, methamphetamine, methylphenidate, fentanyl, nicotine, methadone, morphine, phencyclidine, and even ethanol. This common action of diverse drugs suggests that a single path of drug-induced reinforcement may exist and thus holds promise for developing treatments for polydrug abuse, a trend that has been consistently increasing.

The data reviewed and presented in this chapter emphasize the value of a multidisciplinary approach to studying cocaine's reinforcing effects. By combining a nonverbal method of reporting mood state changes with measures of spontaneous brain electrical activity, a neurophysiological correlate of cocaine-induced euphoria was obtained—this same correlate occurs with other drugs of abuse as well. With the addition of MRI, the source of this activity was confirmed to be in the thalamus. Thus, coregistration of data between imaging modes has a tremendous impact on the precision of the data collected.

Finally, MR imaging and spectroscopy are both maturing very rapidly, and their use in drug abuse research in the very near future will help solve some of the mysteries associated with cocaine's acute and chronic effects. Of all the new techniques, fMRI has the potential to make the greatest impact because its temporal resolution can easily match that of the rapidly changing behaviors that occur just prior to and after cocaine administration.

REFERENCES

Alper, K. R., Chabot, R. J., Kim, A. H., Prichep, L. S., & John E. .R (1990). Quantitative EEG correlates of crack cocaine dependence. *Psychiatry Research: Neuroimaging, 35,* 95–105.

Altura, B. (1993). Cocaine induces rapid loss of intracellular free Mg in cerebral vascular smooth muscle. *European Journal of Pharmacology and Molecular Pharmacology, 246,* 299–301.

Amass, L., Lukas, S. E., Weiss, R. D., & Mendelson, J. H. (1990). Evaluation of cognitive skills in ethanol- and cocaine-dependent patients during detoxification using P300 evoked response potentials (ERPs). *NIDA Research Monograph, 95,* 353–354.

Amass, L., Nardin, R., Mendelson, J. H., Teoh, S. K., & Woods, B. T. (1991). Quantitative magnetic resonance imaging in heroin- and cocaine-dependent men: A preliminary study. *Psychiatry Research: Neuroimaging, 45,* 15–23.

Aurelli, T., Miccheli, A., DiCocco, M. E., Ghirardi, O., Giulani, A., Ramucci, M. T., & Conti, F. (1994). Effect of acetyl-carnitine on recovery of brain phosphorus metabolites and lactic acid level during reperfusion after cerebral ischemia in the rat—Study by 31P and 1H NMR spectroscopy. *Brain Research, 643,* 92–99.

Bauer, L. O. (1994). Photic driving of EEG alpha activity in recovering cocaine-dependent and alcohol-dependent patients. *American Journal on Addictions, 3,* 49–57.

Bauer, L. O., & Kranzler, H. R. (1994). Electroencephalographic activity and mood in cocaine-dependent outpatients: Effects of cocaine cue exposure. *Biological Psychiatry, 36,* 189–197.

Begleiter, H. (Ed.). (1977). *Evoked brain potentials and behavior* (Vol. 2 of the Downstate Series of Research in Psychiatry and Psychology). New York: Plenum Press.

Begleiter, H., Porjesz, B., Bihari, B., & Kissin, B. (1984). Event-related brain potentials in boys at risk for alcoholism. *Science, 225,* 1493–1496.

Belliveau, J. W., Rosen, B. R., Kanto, H. L., Rzedian, R. R., Kennedy, K. N., McKinstry, R. C., Vevea, J. M., Cohen, M. S., Pykett, I. L., & Brady, T. J. (1990). Functional cerebral imaging by susceptibility contrast imaging. *Magnetic Resonance in Medicine, 14,* 538–546.

Belliveau, J. W., Kennedy, D. N., McKinstry, R. C., Buchbinder, B. R., Wiesskoff, R. M., Cohen,

M. S., Vevea, J. M. Brady, T. J., & Rosen, B. R. (1991). Functional mapping of the human visual cortex by magnetic resonance imaging. *Science, 254,* 716–719.

Berger, H. (1931). Ober das Elektrenkephalogramm des Menschen. Dritte Mitteilung. *Archives of Psychiatry, 94,* 16–60.

Berger, H. (1937). Ober das Elektrenkephalogramm des Menschen. XIII. Mitteilung. *Archives of Psychiatry, 94,* 577–584.

Bertorello, A. M., Hopfield, J. F., Aperia, A., & Greengard, P. (1990). Inhibition by dopamine of (Na+,K+) ATPase activity in neostriatal neurons through D1 and D2 dopamine receptor synergism. *Nature, 347,* 386–388.

Bradley, W. G., Yuh, W. T. C., & Bydder, G. M. (1993). Use of MR imaging contrast agents in the brain. *Journal of Magnetic Resonance Imaging, 3,* 199–218.

Branchey, M. H., Buydens-Branchey, L., & Horvath, T. B. (1993). Event-related potentials in substance-abusing individuals after long-term abstinence. *American Journal on Additions, 2,* 141–148.

Brown, B. B. (1970). Recognition of aspects of consciousness through association with EEG alpha activity represented by a light signal. *Psychophysiology, 6,* 442–452.

Brown, E., Prager, J., Lee, H.-Y, & Ramsey, R. G. (1992). CNS complications of cocaine abuse: Prevalence, pathophysiology, and neuroradiology. *AJA American Journal of Roentgenology, 159,* 137–147.

Buchsbaum, M. S., Rigal, F., Coppola, R., Cappelletti, J., King, C., & Johnson, J. A. (1982). A new system for gray-level surface distribution maps of electrical activity. *Electroencephalography and Clinical Neurophysiology, 53,* 237–242.

Cady, E. B., Lorek, A., Penrice, J., Wylexinska, M., Cooper, C. E., Brown, G. C., Owen-Reece, H., Kirkbride, V., Wyatt, J. S., Osmund, E., & Reynolds, R. (1994). Brain metabolite transverse relaxation times in magnetic resonance spectroscopy increase as adenosine triphosphate depletes during secondary energy failure following acute hypoxia-ischaemia in the newborn piglet. *Neuroscience Letter, 182,* 201–204.

Chang, L., Ernst, T., & Strickland, T. L. (1996). Neurochemical abnormalities and gender effects in abstinent asymptomatic cocaine users. *Proceedings of the International Society of Magnetic Resonance in Medicine,* p 992, New York, April.

Childress, A. R., Hole, A. V., Ehrman, R. N., Robbins, S. J., McLellan, A. T., & O'Brien, C. P. (1993). Cue reactivity and cue reactivity interventions in drug dependence. *NIDA Research Monograph, 137,* 73–95.

Christensen, J. D., Kaufman, M. J., Levin, J. M., Mendelson, J. H., Holman, B. L., Cohen, B. M., & Renshaw, P. F. (1996). Abnormal cerebral metabolism in polydrug abusers during early withdrawal: A 31P MR spectroscopy study. *Magnetic Resonance in Medicine, 35,* 658–663.

Church, M. W., & Williams, H. L. (1982). Dose- and time-dependent effects of ethanol on brain stem auditory evoked responses in young adult males. *Electroencephalography and Clinical Neurophysiology, 54,* 161–174.

Cohen, H. L., Porjesz, B., & Begleiter, H. (1993). Ethanol-induced alterations in electroencephalographic activity in adult males. *Neuropsychopharmacology, 8,* 365–370.

Cohen, H. L., Wang, W., Porjesz, B., & Begleiter, H. (1995). Auditory P300 in young alcoholics: Regional response characteristics. *Alcoholism: Clinical and Experimental Research, 19,* 469–475.

Corbett, R. J. T., Lapptook, A. R., & Olivares, E (1991). Simultaneous measurement of cerebral blood flow and energy metabolites in piglets using deuterium and phosphorus magnetic resonance. *Journal of Cerebral Blood Flow and Metabolism, 11,* 55–65.

Dager, S. R., & Steen, G. R. (1992). Applications of magnetic resonance spectroscopy to the investigation of neuropsychiatric disorders. *Neuropsychopharmacology, 6,* 249–266.

Dempsey, E. W., Morison, R. S., & Morison, B. R. (1941). Some afferent diencephalic pathways related to cortical potentials in the cat. *American Journal of Physiology, 131,* 718–731.

Detre, J. A., Williams, D. S., & Koretsky, A. P. (1990). Nuclear magnetic resonance determination of flow, lactate, and phosphate metabolites during amphetamine stimulation in rat brain. *NMR in Biomedicine, 3,* 272–278.

Dubinsky, J., & Barlow, J. S. (1980). A simple dot-density topogram for EEG. *Electroencephalography and Clinical Neurophysiology, 48,* 473–477.

Duffy, F. H. (1982). Topographic display of evoked potentials: Clinical applications of brain electrical activity mapping (BEAM). In I. Bodis-Wollner (Ed.), *Annals of the New York Academy of Sciences Evoked potentials* (Vol. 388) (pp. 183–196) New York: Ann. NY Acad Sci.

Duffy, F. H., Burchfiel, J. L., & Lombrose, C. T. (1979). Brain electrical activity mapping (BEAM): A method for extending the clinical utility of EEG and evoked potential data. *Annals of Neurology, 5,* 309–321.

Duncan-Johnson, C. & Donchin, E. (1977). On quantifying surprise: The variation of the event-related potentials with subjective probability. *Psychophysiology, 14,* 456–467.

Ehlers, C. L., & Schuckit, M. A. (1991). Evaluation of EEG alpha activity in sons of alcoholics. *Neuropsychopharmacology, 4,* 199–205.

Ehlers, C. L., Wall, T. L., & Schuckit, M. A. (1989). EEG spectral characteristics following ethanol administration in young men. *Electroencephalography and Clinical Neurophysiology, 73,* 179–187.

Fischman, M.W. (1988). Behavioral pharmacology of cocaine. *Journal of Clinical Psychiatry, 49(Suppl),* 7–10.

Gabrielli, W. F., Mednick, S. A., Volavka, J., Pollock, V. E., Schulsinger, F., & Itil, T. M. (1982). Electroencephalograms in children of alcoholic fathers. *Psychophysiology, 19,* 404–407.

Gawin, F. H. (1991). Cocaine addiction: Psychology and neurophysiology. *Science, 251,* 1580–1586.

Glaser, G. H. (Ed.) (1963). *EEG and behavior.* New York: Basic Books, Inc.

Graham, G. D., Zhong. J., Petroff, O. A., Constable, R. T., Prichard, J. W., & Gore, J. C. (1994). BOLD MRI monitoring of changes in cerebral perfusion induced by acetazolamide and hypercarbia in the rat. *Magnetic Resonance Medicine, 31,* 557–560.

Harris, G. J., Lewis, R. F., Satlin, A., English, C. D., Scott, T. M., Yurgelun-Todd, D. A., & Renshaw, P. F. (1996). Dynamic susceptibility contrast MRI of regional cerebral blood volume in Alzheimer's disease. *American Journal of Psychiatry, 153,* 721–724.

Hathout, G. M., Kirlew, K. A. T., So, G. J. K., Hamilton, D. R., Zhang, J. X., Sinha, U., Sayre, J., Gozal, D., Harper, R. M., et al. (1994). MR imaging signal response to sustained stimulation in human visual cortex. *Journal of Magnetic Resonance Imaging, 4,* 537–543.

Heier, L. A., Carpanzanom C. R., Mast., J, Brill, P. W., Winchester, P., & Deck, M.D. (1991). Maternal cocaine abuse: The spectrum of radiologic abnormalities in the neonatal CNS. *American Journal of Neuroradiology, 12,* 951–956.

Herning, R. I., Jones, R. T., Hooker, W. D., Mendelson, J. H., & Blackwell, L. (1985a).Cocaine increases EEG beta: a replication and extension of Hans Berger's historic experiments. *Electroencephalography and Clinical Neurophysiology, 60,* 470–477.

Herning, R. I., Jones, R. T., Hooker, W. D., & Tulunay F. C. (1985b). Information processing components of the auditory event related potential are reduced by cocaine. *Psychopharmacologia, 87,* 178–185.

Herning, R. I., Hooker, W. D., & Jones, R. T. (1987). Cocaine effects on electroencephalographic cognitive event-related potentials and performance. *Electroencephalograhy and Clinical Neurophysiology, 66,* 34–42.

Hill, S. Y., Steinhauer, S. R., Park, J., & Zubin, J. (1990). Event-related potential characteristics in children of alcoholics from high density families. *Alcoholism: Clinical and Experimental Research, 14,* 6–16.

Holman, B. L., Carvalho, P. A., Mendelson, J., Teoh, S. K., Nardin, R., Hallgring, E., Hebben, N., & Johnson, K. A. (1991). Brain perfusion is abnormal in cocaine-dependent polydrug users: A study using Technetium-99m-HMPAO and ASPECT. *Journal of Nuclear Medicine, 32,* 1206–1210.

Katbamma, B.,Metz, A., Adelman, C. L., & Thodi. C. (1993). Auditory-evoked responses in chronic alcohol and drug abusers. *Biological Psychiatry, 33,* 750–752.

Kaufman, M. J., Levin, J. M., Christensen, J. D., & Renshaw, P. F. (1996a). Magnetic resonance studies of substance abuse. *Seminars in Clinical Neuropsychiatry, 1,* 61–75.

Kaufman, M. J., Levin, J. M., Christensen, J. D., Lukas, S. E.,Mendelson, J. H., Maas, L. C., Rose, S. L., Cohen, B. M., & Renshaw, P. F. (1996b). Dynamic susceptibility contrast MR measurement of cerebral blood volume reduction following intravenous cocaine administration to human subjects. *Proceedings of the International Society of Magnetic Resonance in Medicine,* p 448, New York, April.

Komoroski, R. A., Newton, J. E. O., Karson, C., Cardwell, D., & Sprigg, J. (1990). Detection of psychoactive drugs in humans using 19F NMR spectroscopy. *Biological Psychiatry, 29,* 711–714.

Koukkou, M., & Lehmann, D. (1975). Human EEG spectra before and during cannabis hallucinations. *Biological Psychiatry, 11,* 663–667.

Kucharcyzk, J., Mosely, M., & Barkovich, A. J. (Eds.) (1994). *Magnetic Resonance Neuroimaging.* Boca Raton: CRC Press.

Kwong, K. K., Belliveau, J. W., Chesler, D. A., Goldberg, I. E., Weisskoff, R. M., Poncelet, B. P., Kennedy, D. N., Happel, B. E., Cohen, M. S., Turner, A., et al. (1992). Dynamic magnetic resonance imaging of human brain activity during primary sensory stimulation. *Proceedings of the National Academy of Sciences U.S.A., 89,* 5675–5679.

Levin, J. M., Kaufman, M. J., Ross, M. H., Mendelson, J. H., Maas, L. C., Cohen, B. M., & Renshaw, P. F. (1995a). Sequential dynamic susceptibility contrast MR experiments in human brain: Residual contrast agent effect, steady state, and hemodynamic perturbation. *Magnetic Resonance Medicine, 34* 655–663.

Levin, J. M., Ross, M. H., & Renshaw, P. F. (1995b). Clinical applications of functional MRI in neuropsychiatry, *Journal of Neuropsychiatry and Clinical Neuroscience, 7,* 511–522.

Levin, J. M., Ross, M. H., Mendelson, J. H., Kaufman, M. J., Yurgelun-Todd, D. A., Cohen, B. M., & Renshaw, P. F. (1995c, August). Reduction in BOLD response to photic stimulation after ethanol administration. *Proceedings of the International Society of Magnetic Resonance in Medicine,* (p. 162). Nice, France.

Levin, J. M., Ross, M. H., Mendelson, J. H., Mello, N. K., Cohen, B. M., & Renshaw, P. F. (1996a, April). Gender differences in BOLD response to photic stimulation. *Proceedings of the International Society of Magnetic Resonance in Medicine,* (p. 278), New York.

Levin, J. M., Wald, L. L., Ross, M. H., Kaufman, M. J., Cohen, B. M., & Renshaw, P. F. (1996b, April). Investigation of T1 effects as basis for residual contrast agent effects seen in sequential dynamic susceptibility contrast experiments. *Proceedings of the International Society of Magnetic Resonance in Medicine* (p. 441). New York.

Li, S. J., Prost, R. W., Harsch, H., Pankiewica, J., Bloom, A. S., & Stein, E. A. (1996, April). Reversible neurochemical alterations in cocaine abusers assessed by 1H magnetic resonance spectroscopy. *Proceedings of the International Society of Magnetic Resonance in Medicine,* (p. 993) New York.

Lindsley, D. B. (1952). Psychological phenomena and the electroencephalogram. *Electroencephalography and Clinical Neurophysiology, 4,* 443–456.

London, E. D., & Morgan, M. J. (1993). Positron emission tomography studies on the acute effects of psychoactive drugs on brain metabolism and mood. In E. D. London (Ed.), *Imaging drug action in the brain* (pp 265–280). Boca Raton: CRC Press.

Lukas, S. E. (1991a). Brain electrical activity as a tool for studying drugs of abuse. In N. K. Mello (Ed.), *Advances in substance abuse: Behavioral and biological research* (Vol 4, pp. 1–88). London: Jessica Kingsley Ltd.

Lukas, S. E. (1991b). Topographic brain mapping during cocaine-induced intoxication and self-administration. In G. Rascagni, N. Brunello, & T. Fukuda (Eds.), *Biological psychiatry* (Vol. 2, pp. 25–29). Amsterdam: Elsevier Science Publishing Co., Inc.

Lukas, S. E., Mendelson, J. H., Benedikt, R. A., & Jones, B. (1986). EEG alpha activity increases during transient episodes of ethanol-induced euphoria. *Pharmacology, Biochemistry and Behavior, 25,* 889–895.

Lukas, S. E.,, & Mendelson, J. H. (1988). Electroencephalographic activity and plasma ACTH during ethanol-induced euphoria. *Biological Psychiatry, 23,* 141–148.

Lukas, S.E., Mendelson, J. H., Woods, B. T., Mello, N. K., & Teoh, S. K. (1989). Topographic distribution of EEG alpha activity during ethanol-induced intoxication in women. *Journal of Studies on Alcohol, 50,* 176–185.

Lukas, S. E., Mendelson, J. H., Kouri, E. M., Bolduc, M. & Amass, L. (1990). Ethanol-induced alterations in EEG alpha activity and apparent source of the auditory P300 evoked response potential. *Alcohol, 7,* 471–477.

Lukas, S. E., Mendelson, J. H., Amass, L., Benedikt, A. R., & Henry, N. J. (1991). Electrophysiological correlates of ethanol reinforcement. In R. E. Mere, G. A. F. Knob, & M. G. Luis (Eds.), *Neuropharmacology of ethanol: New approaches* (pp. 202–231). Cambridge, MA: Birkhauser.

Lukas, S. E., Mendelson, J. H., & Benedikt, R. (1995). Electroencephalograhic correlates of marihuana-induced euphoria. *Drug and Alcohol Dependence, 37,* 131–140.

Lukas, S. E., Woods, B. T., & Mendelson, J. H. (1987). Brain electrical activity mapping (BEAM) during ethanol-induced intoxication in human females. *Federation Proceedings, 46,* 538.

MacKay, S., Meyerhoff, D., Dillon, W., Weiner, M. W., & Fein, G. (1993). Alteration of brain phospholipid metabolites in cocaine-dependent polysubstance abusers. *Biological Psychiatry, 34,* 261–264.

Mannelli, P., Janiri, L., Tempesta, E., & Jones, R. T. (1993). Prediction in drug abuse: Cocaine interactions with alcohol and buprenorphine. *British Journal of Psychiatry, 163* (suppl 21), 39–45.

Matejcek, M. (1982). Vigilance and EEG: Psychological, physiological and pharmacological aspects. In W. M. Hermann (Ed.), *EEG in drug research* (pp. 405–508). Stuttgart: Gustav Fischer.

Mathew, R. J., & Wilson, W. H. (1991). Substance abuse and cerebral blood flow. *American Journal of Psychiatry, 148,* 292–305.

Nolte, K. B., Brass, L. M., & Fletterick, C. F. (1996). Intracranial hemorrhage associated with cocaine abuse: A prospective autopsy study. *Neurology, 46,* 1291–1296.

Ogawa, S., Lee, T. M., Kay, A. R., & Tank, D. W. (1990). Brain magnetic resonance imaging with contrast dependent on blood oxygenation. *Proceedings of the National Academy of Sciences U.S.A., 87,* 9868–9872.

Ogawa, S., Menon, R. S., Tank, D. W., Kim, S. G., Merkle, H., Ellerman, J. M., & Ugurbil, K. (1993). Functional brain mapping by blood oxygenation level dependent contrast magnetic resonance imaging. *Biophysical Journal, 6,* 803–812.

Pascual-Leone, A., Dhuna, A. K., & Anderson, D. C. (1991a). Cerebral atrophy in habitual cocaine abusers: A planimetric CT study. *Neurology, 41,* 34–38.

Pascual-Leone, A., Dhuna, A. K., & Anderson, D. C. (1991b). Longterm neurological complications of chronic, habitual cocaine abuse. *Neurotoxicology, 12,* 393–400.

Pearlson, G. D., Jeffrey, P. J., Harris, G. J., Ross, C. A., Fischman, M. W., & Camargo, E. E. (1993). Correlation of acute cocaine-induced changes in local cerebral blood flow with subjective effects. *American Journal of Psychiatry, 150,* 495–497.

Polich, J., Pollock, V. E., & Bloom, F. E. (1994). Meta-analysis of P300 amplitude from males at risk for alcoholism. *Psychological Bulletin, 115,* 55–73.

Propping, P., Kruger, J., & Janah, A. (1980). Effect of alcohol on genetically determined variants of the normal electroencephalogram. *Psychiatry Research, 2,* 85–98.

Renshaw, P. F., & Wicklund, S. (1988). In vivo measurement of lithium in humans by nuclear magnetic resonance spectroscopy. *Biological Psychiatry, 23,* 265–475.

Ross, M. H., Yurgelun-Todd, D. A., Renshaw, P. F., Mass, L. C., Mendelson, J. H., Mello, N. K., Cohen, B. M., & Levin, J. M. (1998). Age-related reduction in functional MRI response to photic stimulation. *Neurology, 48,* 173–176.

Stehling, M. K., Turner, R., & Mansfield, P. (1991). Echo-planar imaging: magnetic resonance imaging in a fraction of a second. *Science, 254,* 43–49.

Steinhauer, S. R., & Hill, S. Y. (1993). Auditory event-related potentials in children at high risk for alcoholism. *Journal of Studies on Alcohol, 54,* 408–421.

Strickland, T. L., Mena, I., Villanueva-Meyer, J., Miller, B. L., Cummings, J., Mehringer, C. M., Satz, P., & Meyers, H. (1993). Cerebral perfusion and neuropsychological consequences of chronic cocaine use. *Journal of Neuropsychopharmacology and Clinical Neuroscience, 5,* 419–427.

Struve, F. A., Straumanis, J. J., Patrick, G., & Price, L. (1989) Topographic mapping of quantitative EEG variables in chronic heavy marijuana users: Empirical findings with psychiatric patients. *Clinical Electroencephalography, 20,* 6–23.

Sutton, S., Braren, M., Zubin, J., & John, E. (1965). Evoked potential correlates of stimulus uncertainty. *Science, 150,* 1187–1188.

Torello, M. W., Phillips, T., Hunter, W. W., & Csuri, C. A. (1987). Combinational imaging: Magnetic resonance imaging and EEG displayed simultaneously. *Journal of Clinical Neurophysiology, 4,* 274–275.

Tsai, G., & Coyle, J. T. (1995). N-acetylaspartate in neuropsychiatric disorders. *Progress in Neurobiology, 46,* 531–540.

Van Dyke, C., Ungerer, J., Jatlow, P., Barash, P., & Byck, R. (1982). Intranasal cocaine: Dose relationships of psychological effects and plasma levels. *International Journal of Psychiatry in Medicine, 12,* 1–13.

Vogel, W., Schalt, E., Kruger, J., Propping, P., & Lehnert, K. F. (1979). The electroencephalogram (EEG) as a research tool in human behavior genetics: Psychological examinations in healthy males with various inherited EEG variants. *Human Genetics, 47,* 1–45.

Volkow, N. D., Valentine, A., & Kulkarni, M. (1988). Radiological and neurological changes in the drug abuse patient: A study with MRI. *Journal of Neuroradiology, 15,* 288–293.

Volkow, N. D., Fowler, J. S., Wolf, A. P., Schyler, D., Shiue, C. Y., Alpert, A., Dewey, S. L., Logan, J., Christman, D., & Bendriem, B. (1990). Effects of chronic cocaine abuse on postsynaptic dopamine receptors. *American Journal of Psychiatry, 147,* 719–724.

Volkow, N., Hitzemann, R., Wang, G., Fowler, J. S., Wolf, A. P., Dewey, S. L., & Handlesman, L. (1992). Long-term frontal brain metabolic changes in cocaine abusers. *Synapse, 11,* 184–190.

Vorstrup, S., Henriksen, L., & Pauson, O.B. (1984). Effect of acetazolamide on cerebral blood flow and cerebral metabolic rate for oxygen. *Journal of Clinical Investigation, 74,* 1634–1639.

Wallace, R. K. (1970). Physiological effects of transcendental meditation. *Science, 167,* 1751–1754.

Wikler, A. (1957). *The relation of psychiatry to pharmacology.* Baltimore: Williams and Wilkins.

Withers, N. W., Pulvirenti, L., Koob, G. F., & Gillin J. C. (1995). Cocaine abuse and dependence. *Journal of Clinical Psychopharmacology, 15,* 63–78.

Wood, C. C. (1982). Application of dipole localization methods to source identification of human evoked potentials. In I. Bodis-Wollner (Ed.), *Annals of the New York Academy of Sciences Evoked Potentials* (Vol. 388, pp. 139–155) New York: Ann. NY Acad Sci.

12

THE CONTRIBUTION OF GENETIC FACTORS IN COCAINE AND OTHER DRUG ABUSE

GREGORY I. ELMER

Maryland Psychiatric Research Center
University of Maryland
School of Medicine
Baltimore, Maryland

LUCINDA L. MINER

Office of Science Policy and Communications
National Institute on Drug Abuse
Rockville, Maryland

ROY W. PICKENS

Clinical Neurogenetics Section
Intermural Research Program
National Institute on Drug Abuse
Baltimore, Maryland

INTRODUCTION

Cocaine is a potent reinforcer with significant abuse potential. However, not everyone who tries cocaine continues using cocaine, and not everyone who uses cocaine develops debilitating addiction (Pickens, Elmer, LaBuda, & Uhl, 1996). Research in behavior genetics is designed to better understand individual differences in behavior. The underlying factors responsible for individual differences in response to cocaine can be broadly categorized into genetic- and environmental-based factors. Genetic factors are heritable differences in genotype (i.e., genes that are passed from parent to offspring). Environmental factors are simply all non-genetic factors, although they usually refer to past experience and current environmental conditions.

A goal of behavior genetic research is to identify the relative proportion of variability due to genetic and environmental factors. There are several reasons for partitioning this variance. A primary reason is to help target research emphasis. For example, the demonstration of a "heritable" component in the response to cocaine would justify molecular biological efforts aimed at discovering differences in gene function and, by inference, the relationship between genetically transcribed elements and behavior. An equally significant reason for partitioning the variance is to demonstrate the importance of environmental factors in the etiology of drug abuse and to segregate the source of environmental influence into various components. Last, partitioning sources of variance is a first step in characterizing the interplay between genetic and environmental factors. No organism can become addicted to cocaine without first having access, and all historical and current environmental conditions must necessarily exert their effect on a "genotype."

Vulnerability to drug abuse is a complex trait determined by both genetic and environmental influences. The purpose of this chapter will be primarily to examine strategies for studying genetic influences in drug abuse, drawing both from animal and human research. However, because genotype and environmental influences are inextricably linked, environmental factors that contribute to drug abuse are also briefly reviewed. Special attention is paid to the need for additional research on gene and environment interactions in drug abuse, as the effect of the genotype depends on the environment (past history and current circumstance), and the effect of the environment depends on the genotype.

GENETIC INFLUENCE IN VULNERABILITY
TO DRUG ABUSE

Identification of genes influencing drug abuse vulnerability involves both human and animal studies. Animal studies allow genotype to be experimentally manipulated and the effects of specific genes to be studied under controlled environmental conditions. Animal studies are involved in efforts to describe specific gene influences on individual components of addiction, to determine mode of inheritance of the traits, and to map candidate loci. Recent advances in murine genetics provide powerful tools for investigating the behavioral effects of experimental manipulations at the level of the genome. Human studies, on the other hand, take advantage of "experiments in nature" (e.g., twins, adoptees) to study genetic influences in both natural and laboratory environments. Human studies are involved in efforts to determine the presence and extent of genetic influence in human disease, and to identify factors that contribute to genetic heterogeneity in disease expression. In addition, statistical methods are available for determining if specific gene markers are associated with diseases. Animal and human studies function in a complementary manner to enhance our understanding of genetic influences in drug abuse (Pickens & Svikis, 1991), and together provide useful data for gene identification and cloning.

**STRATEGIES FOR IDENTIFYING A GENETIC INFLUENCE
AND THE SPECIFIC GENES INVOLVED
IN VULNERABILITY TO DRUG ABUSE**

Animal Strategies

Strategies for identifying a genetic influence or specific genes that underlie complex traits require systematic characterization of the degree to which a gene or set of genes influence a particular behavior. Numerous methods have been used to identify genetic contributions to drug abuse in animal models. Experimental approaches that manipulate the sample population's genotype through choice of inbred strain, systematic breeding protocols, or genetic engineering are important elements in vulnerability research. Currently, inbred strains and selection programs are commonly used to describe the degree of influence genotype has on a trait and the nature of covariant biochemical and behavioral traits, classical cross paradigms are used to determine the mode of inheritance, quantitative trait loci characterization in recombinant inbred strains are used to map candidate loci, and transgenic and knockout technologies are used to manipulate specific genomic components to test molecular hypotheses.

Determining the Degree of Genetic Influence

Inbred Strains   The use of inbred strains in experimental studies can provide one of the basic means for identifying a genetic influence in vulnerability to drug abuse. Inbred strains are produced by brother–sister mating for 20 or more generations, resulting in greater than 99% identical genotypes (Lyon, 1989). By definition, subjects within an inbred strain are essentially identical twins. For experimental purposes, the genotype of the subject can be manipulated as an independent variable to ascertain the degree of influence genotype has on the behavior. Thus, when inbred strains are reared and studied in identical environments, differences across inbred strains in response to a drug (i.e., locomotor stimulation, drug self-administration) are due to differences in the genotype of the individual. The use of inbred strains allows for partitioning individual differences in behavior into genetic and environmental components (see Falconer, 1989; McClearn, 1991). Phenotypic variance (V_p) is the measure that describes variance in behavior that is composed of genetic (V_g) and environmental (V_e) components ($V_p = V_g + V_e$). An estimate of broad sense heritability (or the coefficient of genetic determination) can be obtained from the ratio V_g/V_p. This measure describes the extent to which individual differences in behavior are determined by genotype. Although this approach does not describe which genetic factors are involved in response to a drug, it can clearly demonstrate the importance of genetic factors in determining the behavioral effects of cocaine.

Cocaine produces a number of well-characterized effects in animals, including locomotor stimulation, stereotypy, seizures, tachycardia, and, following chronic administration, sensitization to the locomotor stimulant effects. The genotype of the animal has been shown to significantly affect the quantitative and sometimes qualitative effects of cocaine in all of these measures (for a review see Seale, 1991). The extent to which individual differences in behavior are determined by genotype (coefficient of genetic determination) in many of these studies was not directly calculated; however, locomotor experiments in our laboratory suggest that up to 38% of the observed individual variability in locomotor behavior could be accounted for by the genotype of the subject (Elmer, Gorelick, Goldberg, & Rothman, 1996). Because most of the preclinical studies directly related to measures of cocaine reward and addiction have been done in inbred strains, the remaining portion of this section will describe results of inbred strain studies using assays designed to measure reward.

Numerous assays are used to assess vulnerability to drug addiction in animals; each assay determines different aspects of drug intake and reward. Two-bottle choice procedures, conditioned place preference (CPP), intracranial self-stimulation (ICSS), and operant self-administration are four of the most commonly used assays (Bozarth, 1987). Two-bottle choice procedures measure the relative preference for the drug (vs. vehicle) and amount of drug the subject will consume. CPP measures the time spent in the drug-associated location following repeated pairing of experimenter-administered drug or vehicle and is designed to measure conditioned reinforcement properties of abused drugs. Studies using two-bottle choice procedures (Alexander, Duda, Garth, Vogel & Berrettini, 1993; George & Goldberg, 1988; Jones, Reed, Radcliffe & Erwin, 1993) and CPP procedures (Seale & Carney, 1991; Guitart et al., 1993; Kosten, Miserendino, Chi & Nestler, 1994) have found genotype to qualitatively and quantitatively influence the phenotype. ICSS measures behavior maintained by electrical stimulation of specific brain regions. Administration of abused drugs will decrease the amount or frequency of electrical stimulation needed to maintain self-stimulation behavior. To date, no study has determined if there are genetic differences in cocaine-induced changes in rate or threshold for ICSS behavior.

The preclinical operant self-administration paradigm closely approximates human drug-taking behavior both in terms of compounds that will serve as reinforcers in humans and in terms of behavioral profiles elicited when response contingencies are matched (Goldberg & Henningfield, 1988). The operant self-administration paradigm operationally defines the behavior in a context designed to investigate primary reinforcement processes and thus provides a valuable model in vulnerability research. The results of studies using inbred strains reveal a significant effect of genotype on behavior reinforced by cocaine injections. Using an intravenous self-administration model, cocaine was found to serve as a positive reinforcer in DBA/2J and C57BL/6J mice; cocaine maintained greater amounts of behavior than vehicle and showed orderly dose-related changes in behavior in both the DBA and C57 mice (Grahame & Cunningham, 1995). C57BL/6J mice acquired self-administration behavior (as defined by a predetermined criteria) more rapidly than DBA/2J mice and self-administered greater amounts of cocaine once self-administration behavior was established. Genetic differences in the direct rate-disrupting effects of cocaine on operant responding do not appear to be responsible for the observed differences in self-administration behavior (Heyser, McDonald, Beauchamp, Koob, & Gold, 1997). In another study of operant intravenous cocaine self-administration in mice, cocaine served as a positive reinforcer in C57BL/6J × SJL mice but not in BALB/cByJ mice under several experimental conditions (Deroche et al., 1997). The inbred rat strains Lewis and F344 have been used in numerous studies to demonstrate a significant genetic influence in vulnerability to drug abuse; these two genotypes differ in cocaine preference (George & Goldberg, 1988, 1989) and cocaine-induced CPP (Guitart, Beitner, Marby, Kosten, & Nestler, 1992; Kosten et al., 1994). Under a progressive ratio schedule of cocaine-reinforced behavior, F344 rats demonstrate significantly greater amounts of drug-seeking behavior than ACI or Brown Norway rats (Ward, Li, Luedtke, & Emmett-Oglesby, 1996). Interestingly, selective dopamine antagonist pretreatment suggests that different mechanism may mediate cocaine-reinforced behavior across the three genotypes tested.

The results obtained across measures of vulnerability or drug reward (i.e., preference, CPP, and operant self-administration) highlight the importance of a clearly defined phenotype and the potentially unique measurements obtained in each paradigm. For example, most studies using DBA/2J mice and F344 rats have found both genotypes to avoid cocaine solutions and to show avoidance or a neutral response to environments previously paired with cocaine (Alexander et al., 1993; Jones, Reed, Radcliffe, & Erwin, 1993; Seale & Carney, 1991). However, DBA/2J mice will self-administer cocaine in a manner consistent with cocaine serving as a positive reinforcer, and F344 rats emit a significant amount of behavior in order to obtain cocaine under progressive ratio schedules (Ward et al., 1996). Similar discrepancies are found between predictions made from CPP studies and the operant self-administration results in the BALB/cByJ mice; BALB/cByJ mice exhibit strong positive cocaine-induced CPP (Seale & Carney, 1991) yet display no positive reinforcement following cocaine injections in self-administration procedures (Deroche et al., 1997). Thus, contrary to the qualitative indications of the preference and CPP models, cocaine does serve as a positive reinforcer in the DBA/2J mice and F344 genotypes and not in the BALB/cByJ mice. The contradictions should not be taken to imply the sole use of a single paradigm to measure vulnerability. Although the correlation between two-bottle choice, CPP, and operant self-administration in both mice and rats appears to be weak, two points must be kept in mind. First, in most cases only pair-wise comparisons can be made between measures (with zero degrees of freedom); second, each dependent variable may mirror important but distinct aspects of the addiction and thereby reflect a subset of variables that contribute to vulnerability. When taken as a whole, the combination of several phenotypes may have more predictive value than each individual phenotype (see McClearn, 1993).

Selective Breeding   Selective breeding is another useful tool that can provide valuable genetic information. Through a careful breeding program (Falconer, 1989) of mating animals that are similar for a trait of interest, investigators can derive new lines of animals that differ dramatically on the selected trait. In a properly controlled selection procedure, only these gene(s) that influence the behavior (high and low line) will be segregated, all other genes will be randomly distributed across the two lines. During this breeding process information can be obtained on the magnitude of the genetic influence; for example, if a trait has no genetic basis (narrow sense heritability (h^2) = 0), selective breeding will have no effect, at the other extreme, if the trait is due entirely to genetic factors (h^2 = 1.0), selection will proceed very rapidly. The response to selection seen in offspring is used to calculate narrow sense heritability. In addition, an estimate of the number of genes influencing the selected trait can also be calculated (see Falconer, 1989, for further detail). Of greatest interest in many cases is information on other phenotypes that are correlated with the selection phenotype. Selected lines differ primarily in genes influencing the selected phenotype; therefore other behavioral differences observed between the lines suggest that the selected genes have other effects. Conversely, when other nonselected phenotypes also differ between the lines, these phenotypes may have common underlying mechanisms.

Selective breeding has been most widely used to select for ethanol-related phenotypes. Selectively bred lines of mice and rats exist for several ethanol responses including loss of righting reflex, open-field activity, withdrawal and ethanol preference. Other groups have selected for sensitivity to nicotine, levorphanol, diazepam, and pentobarbital. There are currently two phenotypes for which initial sensitivity to cocaine has been selectively bred, cocaine-induced conditioned place preference and cocaine-induced locomotor activity. Selective breeding in heterogeneous N/Nih rats for conditioned place preference following 10 mg/kg cocaine resulted in divergent populations through three generations; however, no heritability estimates were given (Schechter, 1992). The discriminative stimulus properties of cocaine in a two-lever task did not differ in third-generation rats. Selection studies for cocaine-induced locomotor activity in heterogeneous HS/Ibg mice have bred mice for high- and low-activity levels after a 10 mg/kg dose of cocaine (Smolen & Marks, 1991; Marley, Arros, Henricks, Marley, & Miner, 1998). As is the case for many of these drugs, the high- and low-responding cocaine-sensitive lines were still diverging after many generations, indicating that this trait is likely being influenced by a number of genes. Interestingly, the cocaine-insensitive line has no stimulant effect following cocaine administration up to 40 mg/kg but is still responsive to amphetamine (Marley et al., in press). These results are in agreement with a proposed genetic dissociation between the locomotor stimulant properties of amphetamine and cocaine (George, Porrino, Ritz, & Goldberg, 1991).

Determining the Mode of Inheritance

Classical Cross   Another breeding design that has been utilized to examine the mode of inheritance is the classical cross design. This breeding program involves mating individuals from two progenitor inbred strains to produce an F_1 generation. Individual animals from the F_1 generation are then either intercrossed with each other to produce an F_2 generation or mated with animals from either of the progenitor strains to produce the backcross generations. The mode of inheritance, whether a trait is inherited in a primarily additive fashion or whether dominance is occurring, can be determined by examining the mean responses of each generation for the particular trait of interest. For example, if a trait is being affected by genes acting solely in an additive manner, the mean response of the F_1 generation should be an average of the two progenitor strains responses on that same trait. Any deviation from that average is a reflection of genes acting in a dominant or partial dominant manner. In addition, the backcross and F_2 generations can give estimates of interactions among genes at several loci (Mather & Jinx, 1982). Classical cross-breeding designs have been used to examine inheritance patterns for a number of responses to drugs of abuse, including morphine, nicotine, and ethanol as well as several sedative-hypnotic compounds. Recently, cocaine-induced locomotor activation and conditioned place preference were characterized in two mouse strains (C57BL/6J, 129/SvJ) and their outcrossed F1 generation (Miner, 1997). Cocaine-induced conditioned place preference was induced in the C57BL/6J mice and F1 generation but not the 129/SvJ mice. These results, in combination with studies on spontaneous locomotor activity, suggest that these phenotypes are not inherited in a simple additive manner and demonstrate the potential importance of dominance and epistatic interactions when mating two inbred genotypes. These issues become especially important considering the frequency of polygenic backgrounds commonly used in recombinant DNA technology.

Identifying Specific Loci Relevant to Vulnerability

Quantitative Trait Loci   Recent progress in the field of molecular genetics has allowed us to move beyond the traditional genetic approaches that provide genetic information that is primarily descriptive in nature, such as heritability and mode of inheritance, to actually attempt to identify specific genes influencing these complex behavioral traits. The continuing expansion of high-density maps of chromosomal markers, such as restriction fragment polymorphisms (RFLPs) and simple sequence-length polymorphisms (SSLPs), as well as improved statistical methodology has enhanced the ability of geneticists to ultimately identify genes contributing to the expression of complex, polygenic behavioral traits. In recent years a number of chromosomal loci or quantitative trait loci (QTL) have been identified that are associated with a variety of drug-related responses. QTL for ethanol, methamphetamine, and morphine phenotypes have been recently identified (see

Crabbe, Belknap, & Buck, 1994). Cocaine-stimulated locomotor activity has been associated with several QTL, including identification by two independent groups of regions on chromosomes 5, 9, and 16 (Miner & Marley, 1995b; Tolliver, Belknap, Woods & Carney, 1994). A small number of overlapping amphetamine QTLs suggest the possibility of some similar mechanisms accounting for genetically based variation in response to these two drugs (Alexander, Wright, & Freed, 1996; Grisel, Belknap, O'Toole, Helms, Wenger, & Crabbe, 1997). The nature of these analyses, however, can lead to a high probability of false-positive identifications, so many of these QTLs are considered conditional and await verification by additional testing. Interestingly, none of the QTLs identified for cocaine-induced activity and seizures overlap, and thus far none are located at the dopamine transporter (Lossie, Vandenbergh, Uhl, & Camper, 1994). It remains to be seen if RFLPs or SSLPs will identify the dopamine transporter as a significant determinant in reward-related behaviors. Thus far variations in whole brain binding or affinity do not covary with differences in cocaine self-administration behavior in a limited number of rat strains (George, Porrino, Ritz, & Goldberg, 1991; Ward et al., 1996).

Congenic   The identification of QTL gives investigators a promising chromosomal neighborhood in which to search for genes influencing the associated phenotype. One strategy that can be used to narrow the search for genes is to breed congenic strains. Through successive generations of backcrossing and selection, it is possible to produce congenic strains that are genetically identical except in a small region surrounding the gene of interest. This differential region can be small enough to permit chromosome walking to the target gene. In fact, it is possible to transfer a region of 5 centimorgans in ten generations of backcrossing (Silver, 1995). Currently, congenic strains are being developed to allow positional cloning of QTLs influencing several ethanol-related traits, including preference, conditioned place preference, and withdrawal from ethanol (Crabbe et al., 1994).

Transgenic/Knockout   Transgenic techniques can be used to examine the role of candidate genes in drug responsiveness. The production of overexpression transgenics as well as knockout mice, in which the candidate gene of interest has been deleted using homologous recombination in embryonic stem cells, have been utilized to create several new mouse models in which to explore the neurobiology of drug response. Several new genetically engineered strains show great promise for increasing the understanding of cocaine's behavioral effect. Presently, several dopamine-related knockout mice have been produced, including the dopamine (DAT) and vesicular monoamine transporter (VMAT2) knockouts and dopamine receptor 1, 2, 3, and 4 knockouts (*DAT,* Giros, Jaber, Jones, Wightman, & Caron, 1996; *VMAT2,* Wang et al., 1997; *D1,* Xu et al., 1994; *D2,* Baik et al., 1995; Kelly et al., 1997; *D3,* Accili et al., 1996; *D4,* Rubenstein et al., 1997). The behavioral consequences of gene elimination has been quantitative and in some cases qualitative in nature. Cocaine-induced stimulation of locomotor activity is eliminated in DAT and D1 knock-out mice (Giros et al., 1996), not affected in D3 knockout mice (Xu et al., 1997), and increased in VMAT2 heterozygous knockout (Takahashi et al., 1997; Wang et al., 1997) and D4 homozygous knockout mice (Ruben-stein et al., 1997). Cocaine-induced conditioned place preference is unaffected in the D1 knockout mice (Miner, Drago, Chamberlain, Donavan, & Uhl, 1995) and VMAT heterozygous knockout mice (Takahashi et al., 1997). Cocaine-related phe-notypes in the D2 knockout have not been reported. The results of these studies suggest that altered expression of some dopamine neurotransmission-related pro-teins may influence individual response to cocaine. Another study of interest that directly assessed the reinforcing properties of cocaine points to the importance of neurotransmitter systems outside the dopamine system in modulating components of the addiction process. Elimination of the serotonin 5HT1b-receptor significant-ly increases the rate of acquisition of cocaine self-administration yet does not af-fect the maintenance of cocaine self-administration once the behavior is acquired (Rocha, Ator, Emmett-Oglesby, & Hen, 1997). Further studies strategically as-sessing the reinforcing effects of cocaine in dopamine-related and nondopamine systems will shed light on the types of neurotransmitter interactions underlying the efficacy of cocaine as a reinforcer.

Although the power of transgenic technology in producing new animal models to assess the roles of selected candidate genes in drug responsiveness is undisput-ed, there are some cautions that must be taken in the interpretation of the results. One is the likelihood of developmental events that may have occurred to com-pensate for the loss of the deleted proteins. Another confounding factor is the ge-netic background of the transgenic animal (see Miner, 1997) and quality of the breeding regimen of these animals. Another factor to consider is related to the use of genetically engineered animals to assess mechanisms underlying vulnerability. To the extent that complete ablation of the targeted protein would be an extreme endpoint in vulnerability studies, information concerning the gene dosage-depen-dent nature of behavioral consequences provides additional value in determining predisposing factors. For example, complete eliminations of DAT results in com-plete insensitivity to the locomotor stimulant effects of cocaine, yet decreases up to 50% in DAT (heterozygous mice) do not affect the locomotor stimulant effects of cocaine (Giros et al., 1996). Therefore, although the integral role of DAT in the behavioral effects of cocaine may be strongly supported by ablation experiments, the degree of variability in the normal population may not be expected to exceed a 50% reduction, and therefore have no impact on issues of vulnerability. Includ-ing heterozygote mice and additional mice with a range of targeted protein ex-pression levels will broaden the utility of genetically engineered animals models from a predominantly mechanistic role to one of determining underlying genetic predispositions to specific drug effects as well.

Human Strategies

Clinical methods capitalize on naturally occurring events and also on laborato-ry studies to investigate genetic influences in a trait or disorder. Four main types of nonlaboratory studies include family, adoption, twin, and genotype-identifica-tion (association, linkage) studies. In addition, laboratory studies are employed to identify biological markers of genetic risk.

Family Studies

Family studies provide an upper-limit estimate of heritability: if a disorder does not run in families it is unlikely to have a genetic influence. Family studies compare rates of a disorder in first-degree relatives of affected individuals (probands) to rates of the disorder in unaffected individuals (controls). Increased prevalence of the disorder in relatives of probands suggests a possible genetic influence. Although there have been a number of family studies of alcoholism, relatively few family studies of other drug abuse have been reported, with most focusing on familial transmission of opioid dependence. In general, relatives of opioid-dependent probands have higher rates of drug dependence and other psychopathology than relatives of nondependent controls (Maddux & Desmond, 1989; Mirin, Weiss, Griffin, & Michael, 1991; Mirin, Weiss, Sollogub & Michael, 1984; Rounsaville et al., 1991). Parents and siblings of cocaine abusers show excessive rates of drug abuse, alcoholism, and antisocial personality (Kosten, Anton, & Rounsaville, 1992; Luthar, Anton, Merikangas, & Rounsaville, 1992), suggesting not only a possible genetic involvement in drug abuse but also a possible genetic interrelationship between drug abuse and alcoholism and certain psychopathology (Pickens, Svikis, McGue, & LaBuda, 1995).

Adoption Studies

Family studies show only that genetic influences may be involved. Familial transmission may be due to genetic and/or environmental influences. To specifically show that genetic influences are involved, either adoption or twin studies must be employed. In adoption studies, prevalence of a disorder is determined in two groups of adoptees: offspring of biological parents having the disorder and offspring of biological parents not having the disorder. Since both groups of adoptees are separated from their biological parents early in life and reared by nonaffected adoptive parents, the method largely separates the genetic contributions of the biological parents from the environmental contributions of the adoptive parents. Higher rates of the disorder in adopted-away offspring of biological parents with the disorder than in adopted-away offspring of biological parents without the disorder suggest the presence of genetic factors in the etiology of the disorder. No adoption studies of cocaine dependence have been reported, although drug abuse in adoptees has been found to be correlated with alcohol abuse in biological parents (Cadoret, O'Gorman, Troughton, & Heywood, 1986).

Twin Studies

Twin studies capitalize on the fact that monozygotic (MZ) and dizygotic (DZ) twins differ in terms of number of shared genes. MZ twins come from a single fertilized ovum, and therefore both members of a pair share the same genes. However, DZ twins come from two separately fertilized ova, with both members on the average sharing only about half of their genes. To the extent that both types of twins share equally similar rearing environments, higher concordance for the disorder in MZ than DZ twins suggests the presence of genetic factors in the etiology of the disorder. With twin studies, an indication of genetic influence can be obtained by comparing concordance rates in MZ and DZ twins (assuming equal environmental similarity of MZ and DZ twins). For observed traits (e.g., diagnosis, quantity of drug consumption), heritability as the ratio of genetic variance (V_g) to total phenotypic variance (V_p) can be estimated by comparing variations in MZ and DZ twins. An increasingly used approach to estimate the relative contribution of genetic and environmental influences is structural equation modeling (path analysis). With modeling techniques, variance contributing to a disorder can be decomposed into additive genetic (h^2), common environmental (c^2), and unique environmental (e^2) influences. Significance of estimated latent genetic and environmental influences can be evaluated by comparing X^2 fit of nested models including all factors, to a model in which specific latent components have been omitted.

As with adoption studies, few twin studies of drug abuse have been reported. In a twin sample of alcoholic probands, heritability of other Diagnostic and Statistical Manual of Mental Disorders, 3rd edition (*DSM-III*) drug abuse/dependence was $h^2 = .31$ for males and $h^2 = .22$ for females (Pickens et al., 1991). More recently, in a male twin sample where both pair members served in the U.S. military during the Vietnam War era, heritability for any illicit *DSM-IIIR* drug use disorder was $h^2 = .34$ (Tsuang et al., 1996). In a twin sample of psychiatric clinic admissions, MZ twins were found to have higher correlations (.31) for extent of illicit drug use (none, tried, greater than 5 times, abuse, dependence) than DZ twins (.19), in a direction suggestive of a genetic effect (Gynther, Carey, Gottesman, & Vogler, 1995). However, in neither case was heritability for cocaine abuse specifically reported.

Genotype-Identification Studies

Genotype-identification studies include both association and linkage studies. In association studies, an effort is made to determine if a genetic marker is associated with a disorder in a population; that is, whether the marker occurs more often in unrelated people with the disorder than in unaffected people. In linkage studies, an effort is made to determine if a gene marker is present in family members with the disorder but not in family members without the disorder. Two linkage studies of alcoholism have been reported (Hill, Aston, & Rabin, 1988; Tanna, Wilson, Winokur, & Elston, 1988), but the results must be interpreted with caution given that neither lod score reached the generally accepted minimal statistical criteria for genetic linkage (i.e., a lod score equal to or exceeding 3.0) and that neither result has been replicated. No linkage studies of substance abuse other than alcoholism have been reported.

Blum et al. (1990) achieved considerable public and scientific attention with the report that the D_2 dopamine receptor (DRD$_2$) gene was associated with alcoholism. This generated a number of studies to determine the association between DRD$_2$ markers and other types of substance abuse and psychiatric disorders. Data from several association studies reported that A1 and B1 markers of DRD$_2$ appear more often in polysubstance abusers than in controls (Comings, Muhleman, Ahn, Gysin & Flanagan, 1994; Gelernter, Goldman & Risch, 1993; Noble et al., 1993; O'Hara, Smith, Cutting & Uhl, 1993; Smith et al., 1992). In addition, higher frequencies of A1 and B1 DRD$_2$ gene markers were found in the most severe substance abusers (Uhl, Blum, & Smith, 1993). More recently, Noble and colleagues (1993) reported an allelic association between DRD$_2$ and cocaine dependence. Prevalence of the A1 allele was found in 51% of cocaine-dependent subjects, as compared to only 16% in nonsubstance-abusing controls (Noble et al., 1993). However, methodological issues have been raised about these association studies, and interpretation of the results requires caution. Disproportionate sampling of abusers or controls from population subgroups with atypical allelic frequencies could yield spurious results (Lander & Schork, 1994). In addition, subsequent studies of alcoholism transmission within families revealed no DRD$_2$ linkage (Bolos et al., 1990; Parsian et al., 1991).

Laboratory Studies

Laboratory studies are available for identifying the specific risk factors that may be inherited in substance abuse. In the at-risk study design, for example, individuals at increased risk are compared to individuals at low risk prior to their entry into the risk period to identify measures that distinguish the two groups. Since offspring of alcoholics are at higher risk for alcoholism than offspring of nonalcoholics, differences between the two groups prior to the initiation of regular alcohol use may identify specific risk factors that mediate alcoholic risk. A number of studies have shown that offspring of alcoholics have higher rates of other substance abuse and show altered response to alcohol as compared to offspring of nonalcoholics (Schuckit et al., 1991). Interestingly, from a genetic perspective, they also show differences in response to barbiturates and benzodiazepines (McCaul, Turkkan, Svikis, & Bigelow, 1990, 1991). No reports of differences in response to cocaine have appeared to date.

At-risk studies have also been instrumental in identifying biological markers for genetic risk in substance abuse. When offspring of alcoholics are compared to offspring of nonalcoholics, several important differences are seen, including reduced amplitude in the P$_{300}$ component of event-related potentials elicited by visual stimuli (Begleiter, Porjesz, Bihari, & Kissin, 1984) and increased body sway (static ataxia) in the absence of alcohol challenge (Hill, Armstrong, Steinhauer, Baughman, & Zubin, 1987) and a number of additional biological and subjective differences in response to alcohol challenge.

ENVIRONMENTAL INFLUENCE
IN VULNERABILITY TO DRUG ABUSE

Although vulnerability to drug abuse is genetically influenced, most estimates from both animal and human studies suggest that only about one-third of the variance in cocaine response is due to genetic influence. As with genetic influences, both animal and human research contributes to identification of environmental factors in drug abuse. Clinical research strategies can examine heritability within broadly defined environmental contexts (e.g., before and after policy changes, in different geographical regions). Animal research can more precisely define and control environmental stimuli and study environmental and genetic influences within that context, but cannot always duplicate conditions that exist at the human level. As in the study of genetic influences, human and animal studies provide a helpful complement to understanding the influences of genetic and environmental influences on behavior.

AVAILABILITY, STRUCTURE, AND ROUTE OF ADMINISTRATION

A number of environmental factors are known to influence drug abuse. One of the more obvious of these is drug availability: if a drug is not available, use (and consequently dependence) is not possible. Often overlooked, however, are the environmental factors of the drug itself and the method of drug administration. A drug is identified by its chemical structure, which is a major determinant of abuse liability. Drugs with certain chemical structures are more likely to be abused than drugs with other chemical structures. Although almost any drug can be self-administered under appropriate circumstances, most drugs that are abused have rather specific chemical structures. Even modest structural variations in the cocaine molecule results in a significant variation in drug self-administration behavior in animals (Ritz, Lamb, Goldberg, & Kuhar, 1987). Similarly, route of administration determines the speed with which a drug reaches the brain, which is believed to be related to abuse liability. In general, those routes that quickly get a drug to the brain are believed to have the higher abuse potential. As an example, acquisition of intravenous cocaine self-administration behavior in animals occurs more rapidly and maintains greater amounts of drug-seeking behavior than oral deliveries of cocaine (Henningfield & Keenan, 1993; Meisch & Lemaire, 1993). In humans, cocaine has been found to have a greater abuse liability, greater propensity for dependence, and more severe consequences when smoked (inhalation) or injected intravenously than when administered by the intranasal route (Cone, 1995; Hatsukami & Fischman, 1996).

ENVIRONMENTAL STIMULI ASSOCIATED WITH DRUG ADMINISTRATION

Environmental stimuli associated with drug administration can have a pronounced effect on the behavioral and neurochemical effects of the drug. The mere presentation of stimuli previously associated with the administration of cocaine (conditioned stimuli) can produce hyperlocomotion, increased heart rate, and increased neuronal activities following the presentation of cocaine paired cues (Brown, Robertson, & Fibiger, 1992; Ehrman, Robbins, Childress, & O'Brien, 1992; Panlilio & Schindler, 1997; Pert, Post, & Weiss, 1990). Importantly, environmental stimuli can have a considerable effect on drug-seeking and drug-taking behavior (Henningfield, Nemeth-Coslett, Katz, & Goldberg, 1987; Schindler, Katz, & Goldberg, 1988). Previously neutral stimuli paired with drug injections significantly enhance the acquisition and asymptotic level of drug-taking behavior. Clinically noteworthy effects are the impact of conditioned stimuli on the persistence of drug-seeking behavior in the absence of drug availability and on the reacquisition of drug-taking behavior following its absence. Recent work also suggests that the combination of conditioned stimuli that independently augment self-administration behavior have greater than additive effects on drug-seeking behavior and drug intake; compound stimulus presentations increased drug intake during maintenance conditions twofold while increasing drug-seeking behavior during extinction trials threefold (Panlilio, Weiss, & Schindler, 1996). In humans, stimuli previously associated with cocaine use can elicit cocaine craving in laboratory environments and produce increases in glucose metabolism in cortical and limbic regions involved in memory (Grant et al., 1996). These results clearly support the importance of current stimulus conditions and associative learning processes in the expression of drug-taking behavior.

ALTERNATIVE REINFORCERS

An important current environmental circumstance found in all natural settings is the availability of nondrug, alternative reinforcers (Higgins, 1997). Experimental settings designed to assess human and animal models of drug self-administration typically make only one reinforcer (drug) available during experimental sessions. Recent animal and human investigations using behavioral economic principles (Bickel, DeGrandpre, & Higgins, 1995; Higgins, 1996) emphasize the importance of "unit cost" to obtain cocaine and the effectiveness of alternative reinforcers in suppressing drug-seeking behavior. In animal studies, when alternative reinforcers such as saccharin or food are made available during experimental sessions, the rate of acquisition of cocaine self-administration and the level of drug intake during steady-state conditions is decreased (Carroll, 1993; Carroll & Lac, 1993; Comer, Lac, Wyvell, & Carroll, 1996). In all cases, the magnitude of the reduction is a function of the level of work required to obtain drug and the relative availability of an alternative reinforcer (although see Nader et al., 1993). The alternative reinforcer is most efficacious in reducing drug-seeking behavior when the response cost for obtaining drug is high. A similar result is found in humans allowed to choose between 10 mg of intranasal cocaine or money (0–$2/choice). Making the alternative reinforcer (money) available decreased cocaine selections (Higgins, Bickel, & Hughes, 1994).

STRESS

Most attention to environmental influences in drug abuse have focused on past history and current environmental circumstance. One environmental factor believed to influence drug self-administration is stress. Stressful events in animal models can take the form of nonphysical events (social isolation and predator exposure) or direct physical contact (footshock-, restraint-, and aggressor-induced stress). The behavioral response to stress can vary substantially as a function of the type of stressor and context. The acute neurochemical response to stress typically involves the hypothalamic-pituitary-adrenal axis; mediobasal hypothalamic release of corticotrophin-releasing factor (CRF) increases the release of adreno-cortocotropin (ACTH), which stimulates adrenal glucocorticoid and medullary catecholamine release. However, there are quantitative and qualitative differences in the magnitude and neurochemical response to stress that vary in an intensity-, stressor-, and genotype-dependent manner (i.e., Pieper, Forester, & Elmer 1997). Importantly, individual differences in stressful events during development could have long-term consequences. Early stressful events have been shown to produce long-term changes in neurochemistry that last well into adulthood (i.e., glucocorticoid and 5HT2 receptor density and distribution) (Meaney et al., 1996; Smythe, Rowe, & Meaney, 1994).

Stressful events can significantly alter drug-seeking and drug-taking behavior. Stress facilitates the acquisition, maintenance, and reacquisition of drug-taking behavior in animals (see Piazza & Le Moal, 1996). In drug-naive animals, direct stressors such as footshock and resident aggressive models (Goeders & Guerin, 1994; Haney et al., 1995) and indirect stressors such as social isolation and the observation of stress in cohorts (Ramsy & Van Ree, 1993) increase the rate of acquisition of cocaine self-administration behavior. Although no study has used stress in a cocaine reinstatement paradigm, recent findings using heroin have shown that a single stressful experience can reinstate drug self-administration behavior in animals after an extended extinction phase (Shaham & Stewart, 1995). At the human level, stress covers many things, ranging from internal states (e.g., anxiety, depression) to external events (e.g., failing marriage, difficult job, having problems with children, environmental privations). A number of these have been associated with both drug use and dependence. Clinicians and their clients have long maintained that stress aggravates drug problems. Some support for this view is provided by research with drug-dependent humans (e.g., Gottheil et al., 1987). The relationship between stress and alcohol use is well known. In one study, men were 27 times more likely to develop alcohol abuse/dependence if employed in a job having high psychological demands and low control relative to men in low-strain employment (Crum Muntaner, Eaton, & Anthony, 1995). Because such studies usually rely on correlational designs or retrospective self-report data, however, precise conclusions about the effects of stress on drug use remain elusive.

HOW DO GENES AND THE ENVIRONMENT INTERACT?

It could be argued that either genetic or environmental factors alone are responsible for drug addiction. For example, elimination of the dopamine transporter through homologous recombination may completely eliminate the behavioral effects of cocaine necessary for addiction (Giros et al., 1996). Thus, one alteration at a single gene would dictate vulnerability. Alternatively, it could be argued that addiction results from general behavioral principles (i.e., classical and operant conditioning). As an example, current and past stimulus conditions can be arranged in such a manner as to cause electric shock to serve as a reinforcer in animals; it would follow from this example that it is environmental factors (i.e., schedule of presentation) that are the determinants of vulnerability (Dews, 1973). Convincing arguments can be made in each case. Although it is conceivable that cocaine addiction occurs by environmental or genetic factors, the probability of the causes being related to environmental or genetic factors is likely quite low. The consistent observation in behavior genetic studies is the demonstrated importance of genotype and environment in the etiology of traits/disorders.

Several animal studies have explored gene and environment interactions in the context-specific nature of tolerance and sensitization (Cabib, 1993; Elmer, Mathura, & Goldberg, 1993; Elmer et al., 1996); however, few studies have specifically examined gene and environment interactions thought to be involved in measures of vulnerability to drug abuse. In a study specifically designed to partition genotype and environmental factors in the relationship between locomotor reaction to a novel environment and acquisition of intravenous morphine self-administration behavior, Ambrosio and colleagues (Ambrosio, Goldberg, & Elmer, 1995) found that environmental factors influencing both traits was expressed in a genotype-dependent manner. The pure environmental correlation between these two variables could be determined within each of the inbred strains because genotype across individuals within the inbred strain was identical (Falconer, 1989; Wright, 1968). The degree to which common environmental factors influenced both traits (environmental correlation) in the Lewis, F344, and NBR rats was nonsignificant; $r = $ .21, .33, and .11, respectively. However, there was a significant environmental correlation between locomotor response and rate of acquisition in the ACI rats ($r = $ .71). Thus, the study population (genotype) significantly influenced the relationship under investigation. ACI rats may be particularly sensitive to environmental factors affecting both the reaction to a novel environment and acquisition of self-administration.

Some additional examples of genotype by environment (G $\times$ E) interactions can be found for intracranial self-stimulation (ICSS) and ethanol self-administration behavior using stress and work requirement, respectively. The effects of stress alter behavior maintained by electrical stimulation of the nucleus accumbens in a genotype-dependent manner. Stress (electrical shock) increases (BALB/cByJ), decreases (DBA/2J), or has no effect (C57BL/6J) on ICSS behavior (Zacharko, Lalonde, Kasian, & Anisman, 1987). Thus, the response to an environmental stressor is dependent on the genotype. Increasing the amount of work required to obtain ethanol deliveries selectively decreases the amount of reinforcers obtained in a genotype-dependent manner (Ritz, Garcia, Protz, Rael, & George, 1994). AA-, NP- and HAD-selected rat lines readily find ethanol to be a reinforcer when ratio requirements are low. However, when the work requirement is increased significantly, only the P rats will continue to work for ethanol. Thus, the degree to which an animal is willing to work for drug delivery is dependent, in part, on the genotype.

There have been even fewer human studies examining gene and environment interaction. Although genotype and environment cannot be manipulated as directly as in animal studies, human studies of gene and environment interaction can nevertheless be conducted. Strategies for studying gene and environment interaction in humans involve estimating heritability for a trait under two (or more) sets of environmental conditions. For example, Heath et al., (1985) examined the heritability of educational attainment in two samples of Norwegian twins—those born before and after the introduction of more liberal social and educational policies following World War II. In twins born before 1940, 41% of the variance in educational attainment was due to additive genetic influences, with no evidence of sex differences in familial transmission. In twins born after 1940, significant sex differences in familial transmission were found. For females, heritability was similar to that before 1940. For males, however, variance due to additive genetic influence increased to 67–74%, suggesting greater dependence of educational attainment on innate ability.

Alternatively, heritability may be examined in groups of people distinguished by current environmental circumstance (e.g., city vs. rural populations). As examples of how genetic influences may be studied under different (although not necessarily entirely environmental) conditions, McGue, Pickens and Svikis (1992) found greater heritability in males for *DSM-III* Alcohol Abuse/Dependence in probands with an early ($h^2 = .73$) rather than late ($h^2 = .30$) onset. Similarly, higher heritability has been found for males ($h^2 = .60$) than females ($h^2 = .42$) for *DSM-III* diagnosis of alcohol dependence (Pickens et al., 1991). Also, when evidence of genetic influences in alcohol dependence were examined in a set of twins with and without comorbidity for drug or mental disorders, evidence of genetic influence in alcoholism was found only when comorbidity for a drug or mental disorder was present in the proband. No difference in MZ and DZ concordance was seen in probands without a comorbid drug or mental disorder (Pickens et al., 1995).

More attention needs to be paid to the role of gene and environment interaction in drug abuse (for examples in psychiatric illness see Kendler & Eaves, 1986; Kendler et al., 1995). This is particularly true of cocaine abuse, where the drug may be taken in different unit doses and by different administration routes to yield marked differences in reinforcing effects. With cocaine, genetic effects may be most evident under environmental conditions where the drug's potential reinforcing effects were minimum, and least evident under environmental conditions where the drug's potential reinforcing effects were maximum. Similarly, environmental effects (e.g., reinforcement sensitivity) may be greatest under conditions where genetic influences are the weakest, and the weakest under conditions where genetic influences are the strongest.

Understanding the interaction between genes and environment is important to understanding drug abuse, because genetic influences may not manifest under all environmental conditions. Finding environmental conditions that inhibit expression of genetically based vulnerabilities may be a target for prevention efforts and may improve our ability to treat drug abuse.

REFERENCES

Accili, D., Fishburn, C., Drago, J., Steiner, H., Lachowicz, J., Park, B.-H., EB, G., Lee, E., Cool, M., Sibley, D., & Westphal, H. (1996). A targeted mutation of the D3 dopamine receptor gene is associated with hyperactivity in mice. *Proceedings National Academy of Sciences, 93,* 1945–1949.

Alexander, R. C., Duda, J., Garth, D., Vogel, W., Berrettini, W. H. (1993). Morphine and cocaine preference in inbred mice. *Psychiatric Genetics, 3,* 33–37.

Alexander, R. C., Wright, R., & Freed, W. (1996). Quantitative trait loci contributing to phencyclidine-induced and amphetamine-induced locomotor behavior in inbred mice [published erratum appears in *Neuropsychopharmacology* 1996 Dec;15(6):609]. *Neuropsychopharmacology, 15,* 484–490.

Ambrosio, E. A., Goldberg, S. R., & Elmer, G. I. (1995). Behavior genetic investigation of the relationship between spontaneous locomotor activity and the acquisition of morphine self-administration behavior. *Behaviour Pharmacology, 6,* 229–237.

Baik, J. H., Picetti, R., Saiardi, A., Thiriet, G., Dierich, A., Depaulis, A., Le Meur, M., & Borrelli, E. J. A. (1995). Parkinsonian-like locomotor impairment in mice lacking dopamine D2 receptors. *Nature, 377,* 424–428.

Begleiter, H., Porjesz, B., Bihari, B., & Kissin, B. (1984). Event-related potentials in boys at risk for alcoholism. *Science, 225,* 1493–1496.

Bickel, W. K., DeGrandpre, R. J., & Higgins, S. T. (1995). The behavioral economics of concurrent drug reinforcers: a review and reanalysis of drug self-administration research. *Psychopharmacology, 118,* 250–259.

Blum, K., Noble, E. P., Sheridan, P. J., Montgomery, A., Ritchie, T., Jagadeeswaran, P., Nogami, H., Briggs, A. H., & Cohn, J. B. (1990). Allelic association of human dopamine D2 receptor gene in alcoholism. *Journal American Medical Association, 263,* 2055–2060.

Bolos, A. M., Dean, M., Lucas-Derse, S., Ramsburg, M., Brown, G. L., & Goldman, D. (1990). Population and pedigree studies reveal a lack of association between the dopamine D2 receptor gene and alcoholism. *Journal American Medical Association, 264,* 3156–3160.

Bozarth, M. A. (Ed.). (1987). *Methods of assessing the reinforcing properties of abused drugs.* New York: Springer-Verlag.

Brown, E. E., Robertson, G. S., & Fibiger, H. C. (1992). Evidence for conditional neuronal activation following exposure to a cocaine-paired environment: Role of forebrain limbic structures. *Journal of Neuroscience, 12,* 4112–21.

Cabib, S. (1993). Strain-dependent behavioural sensitization to amphetamine: role of environmental influences. *Behavioral Pharmacology, 4,* 367–374.

Cadoret, R. J., O'Gorman, T., Troughton, E., & Heywood, E. (1986). An adoption study of genetic and environmental factors in drug abuse. *Archives of General Psychiatry, 43,* 1131–1136.

Carroll, M. E. (1993). The economic context of drug and non-drug reinforcers affects acquisition and maintenance of drug-reinforced behavior and withdrawal effects. *Drug Alcohol Dependence, 33,* 201–210.

Carroll, M. E., & Lac, S. T. (1993). Autoshaping i.v. cocaine self-administration in rats: Effects of non-drug alternative reinforcers on acquisition. *Psychopharmacology, 110,* 5–12.

Comer, S. D., Lac, S. T., Wyvell, C. L., & Carroll, M. E. (1996). Combined effects of buprenorphine and a nondrug alternative reinforcer on i.v. cocaine self-administration in rats maintained under FR schedules. *Psychopharmacology, 125,* 355–360.

Comings, D. E., Muhleman, D., Ahn, C., Gysin, R., & Flanagan, S. D. (1994). The dopamine D2 receptor gene: a genetic risk factor in substance abuse. *Drug and Alcohol Dependence, 34,* 175–180.

Cone, E. J. (1995). Pharmacokinetics and pharmacodynamics of cocaine. *Journal of Anal Toxicology, 19,* 459–478.

Crabbe, J., Belknap, J., & Buck, K. (1994). Genetic animal models of alcohol and drug abuse. *Science, 264,* 1715–1723.

Crum, R. M., Muntaner, C., Eaton, W. W., & Anthony, J. C. (1995). Occupational stress and the risk of alcohol abuse and dependence. *Alcoholism Clinical Experimental Research, 19,* 647–55.

Deroche, V., Caine, S. B., Heyser, C. J., Polis, I., Koob, G. F., & Gold, L. H. (1997). Differences in the liability to self-administer intravenous cocaine between C57BL/6 X SJL and BALB/cByJ mice. *Pharmacology, Biochemistry and Behavior, 57,* 429–440.

Dews, P. B. (1973). The behavioral context of addiction. In L. Goldberg & F. Hoffmeister (Eds.), *Psychic dependence, Bayer-Symposium IV* (pp. 36–46). Berlin: Springer-Verlag.

Ehrman, R. N., Robbins, S. J., Rose-Childress, A., & O'Brien, C. P. (1992). Conditioned responses to cocaine-related stimuli in cocaine abuse patients. *Psychopharmacology* 107:523–529.

Elmer, G. I., Gorelick, D. A., Goldberg, S. R., & Rothman, R. B. (1996). Acute sensitivity vs. context-specific sensitization to cocaine as a function of genotype. *Pharmacology, Biochemistry and Behavior, 53,* 623–628.

Elmer, G. I., Mathura, C. B., & Goldberg, S. R. (1993). Genetic factors in conditioned tolerance to the analgesic effects of etonitazene. *Pharmacology, Biochemistry and Behavior, 45,* 251–254.

Falconer, D. S. (Ed.). (1989). *Introduction to quantitative genetics.* New York: Longman Scientific and Technical and John Wiley and Sons.

Gelernter, J., Goldman, D., & Risch, N. (1993). The A1 allele at the D2 dopamine receptor gene and alcoholism. A reappraisal. *Journal American Medical Association, 269,* 1673–1677.

George, F., & Goldberg, S. (1989). Genetic approaches to the analysis of addiction processes. *Trends in Pharmacological Science, 10,* 78–83.

George, F. R., & Goldberg, S. R. (1988). Genetic differences in response to cocaine. *NIDA Research Monograph,* 239–249.

George, F., Porrino, L., Ritz, M., & Goldberg, S. (1991). Inbred rat strain comparisons indicate different sites of action for cocaine and amphetamine locomotor stimulant effects. *Psychopharmacology (Berl), 104,* 457–462.

Giros, B., Jaber, M., Jones, S. R., Wightman, R. M., & Caron, M. G. (1996). Hyperlocomotion and indifference to cocaine and amphetamine in mice lacking the dopamine transporter. *Nature, 379,* 606–612.

Goeders, N. E., & Guerin, G. F. (1994). Non-contingent electric footshock facilitates the acquisition of intravenous cocaine self-administration in rats. *Psychopharmacology, 114,* 63–70.

Goldberg, S. R., & Henningfield, J. E. (1988). Reinforcing effects of nicotine in humans and experimental animals responding under intermittent schedules of i.v. drug injection. *Pharmacology, Biochemistry and Behavior, 30,* 227–234.

Gottheil, E. (1992). Psychosocial factors and treatment. Overview. *Recent Developments in Alcoholism, 10,* 111–113.

Grahame, N. J., & Cunningham, C. L. (1995). Genetic differences in intravenous cocaine self-administration between C57BL/6J and DBA/2J mice. *Psychopharmacology, 122,* 281–291.

Grant, S., London, E. D., Newlin, D. B., Villemagne, V. L., Liu, X., Contoreggi, C., Phillips, R. L., Kimes, A. S., & Margolin, A. (1996). Activation of memory circuits during due-elicited cocaine craving. *Proceedings National Academy of Sciences, 93,* 12040–12045.

Grisel, J. E., Belknap, J. K., O'Toole, L. A., Helms, M. L., Wenger, C. D., & Crabbe, J. C. (1997). Quantitative trait loci affecting methamphetamine responses in BXD recombinant inbred mouse strains. *Journal of Neuroscience, 17,* 745–754.

Guitart, X., Beitner, J. D., Marby, D. W., Kosten, T. A., & Nestler, E. J. (1992). Fischer and Lewis rat strains differ in basal levels of neurofilament proteins and their regulation by chronic morphine in the mesolimbic dopamine system. *Synapse, 12,* 242–253.

Guitart, X., Kogan, J. H., Berhow, M., Terwilliger, R. Z., Aghajanian, G. K., & Nestler, E. J. (1993). Lewis and Fischer rat strains display differences in biochemical electrophysiological and behavioral parameters: studies in the nucleus accumbens and locus coeruleus of drug naive and morphine-treated animals. *Brain Research, 611,* 7–17.

Gynther, L. M., Carey, G., Gottesman, I. I., & Vogler, G. P. (1995). A twin study of non-alcohol substance abuse. *Psychiatry Research, 56,* 213–220.

Hatsukami, D. K., & Fischman, M. W. (1996). Crack cocaine and cocaine hydrochloride: are the differences myth or reality? *Journal American Medical Association, 276,* 1480–1588.

Heath, A. C., Berg, K., Eaves, L. J., Solaas, M. H., Corey, L. A., Sundet, J., Magnus, P., & Nance, W. E. (1985). Education policy and the heritability of educational attainment. *Nature, 314,* 734–736.

Henningfield, J. E., & Keenan, R. M. (1993). Nicotine delivery kinetics and abuse liability. *Journal of Consulting Clinical Psychology, 61,* 743–750.

Henningfield, J. E., Nemeth-Coslett, R., Katz, J. L., & Goldberg, S. R. (1987). Intravenous cocaine self-administration by human volunteers: Second-order schedules of reinforcement. *NIDA Research Monograph, 76,* 266–273.

Heyser, C. J., McDonald, J. S., Beauchamp, V., Koob, G. F., & Gold, L. H. (1997). The effects of cocaine on operant responding for food and locomotor activity in several strains of mice. *Psychopharmacology, 132,* 202–208.

Higgins, S. T. (1996). Some potential contributions of reinforcement and consumer-demand theory to reducing cocaine use. *Addictions Behavior, 21,* 803–816.

Higgins, S. T. (1997). The influence of alternative reinforcers on cocaine use and abuse: a brief review. *Pharmacology, Biochemistry and Behavior, 57,* 419–427.

Higgins, S. T., Bickel, W. K., & Hughes, J. R. (1994). Influence of an alternative reinforcer on human cocaine self-administration. *Life Science, 55,* 179–187.

Hill, S. Y., Armstrong, J., Steinhauer, S. R., Baughman, T., & Zubin, J. (1987). Static ataxia as a psychobiological marker for alcoholism. *Alcoholism: Clinical and Experimental Research, 11,* 345–348.

Hill, S. Y., Aston, C., & Rabin, B. (1988). Suggestive evidence of genetic linkage between alcoholism and the MNS blood group. *Alcoholism: Clinical and Experimental Research, 12,* 811–814.

Jones, B. C., Reed, C. L., Radcliffe, R. A., & Erwin, V. G. (1993). Pharmacogenetics of cocaine: I. Locomotor activity and self-selection. *Pharmacogenetics, 3,* 182–188.

Kelly, M. A., Rubinstein, M., Asa, S. L., Zhang, G., Saez, C., Bunzow, J. R., Allen, R. G., Hnasko, R., Ben-Jonathan, N., Grandy, D. K., & Low, M. J. (1997). Pituitary lactotroph hyperplasia and chronic hyperprolactinemia in dopamine D2 receptor-deficient mice. *Neuron, 19,* 103–113.

Kendler, K. S., & Eaves, L. J. (1986). Models for the joint effect of genotype and environment on liability to psychiatric illness. *American Journal of Psychiatry, 143,* 279–289.

Kendler, K. S., Kessler, R. C., Walters, E. E., MacLean, C., Neale, M. C., Heath, A. C., & Eaves, L. J. (1995). Stressful life events, genetic liability, and onset of an episode of major depression in women. *American Journal of Psychiatry, 152,* 833–842.

Kosten, T. A., Anton, S. F., & Rounsaville, B. J. (1992). Ascertaining psychiatric diagnoses with the family history method in a substance abuse population. *Journal of Psychiatric Research, 26,* 135–147.

Kosten, T. A., Miserendino, M. J., Chi, S., & Nestler, E. J. (1994). Fischer and Lewis rat strains show differential cocaine effects in conditioned place preference and behavioral sensitization but not in locomotor activity or conditioned taste aversion. *Journal of Pharmacology Experimental Therapy, 269,* 137–144.

Lander, E. S., & Schork, N. J. (1994). Genetic dissection of complex traits. *Science, 265,* 2037–2048.

Lossie, A. C., Vandenbergh, D. J., Uhl, G. R., & Camper, S. A. (1994). Localization of the dopamine transporter gene, Dat1, on mouse chromosome 13. *Mammalian Genome, 5,* 117–118.

Luthar, S. S., Anton, S. F., Merikangas, K. R., & Rounsaville, B. J. (1992). Vulnerability to drug abuse among opioid addict's siblings: Individual, familial, and peer influences. *Comprehensive Psychiatry, 33,* 190–196.

Lyon, M. F. (1989). Rules for nomenclature of inbred strains. In M. F. Lyon & A. G. Searle (Eds.), *Genetic variants and strains of the laboratory mouse* (pp. 632–635). New York: Oxford University Press.

Maddux, J. F., & Desmond, D. P. (1989). Family and environment in the choice of opioid dependence or alcoholism. *American Journal of Drug & Alcohol Abuse, 15,* 117–134.

Marley, R. J., Arros, D. M., Henricks, K. K., Marley, M. E., & Miner, L. L. (in press). Sensitivity to cocaine and amphetamine among mice selectively bred for differential cocaine sensitivity. *Psychopharmacology.*

Mather, K., & Jinks, J. K. (Eds.). (1982). *Biometrical genetics.* London: Chapman and Hall.

McCaul, M. E., Turkkan, J. S., Svikis, D. S., & Bigelow, G. E. (1990). Alcohol and secobarbital effects as a function of familial alcoholism: Acute psychophysiological effects. *Alcohol Clinical Experimental Research, 14,* 704–712.

McCaul, M. E., Turkkan, J. S., Svikis, D. S., & Bigelow, G. E. (1991). Alcohol and secobarbital effects as a function of familial alcoholism: Extended intoxication and increased withdrawal effects. *Alcohol Clinical Experimental Research, 15,* 94–101.

McClearn, G. E. (1991). The tools of pharmacogenetics. In J. C. Crabbe & R. A. Harris (Eds.), *The genetic basis of alcohol and drug actions* (pp. 1–24). New York: Plenum.

McClearn, G. E. (1993). Genetics, systems, and alcohol. *Behavior Genetics, 23,* 223–230.

McGue, M., Pickens, R. W., & Svikis, D. S. (1992). Sex and age effects on the inheritance of alcohol problems: A twin study. *Journal of Abnormal Psychology, 101,* 3–17.

Meaney, M. J., Diorio, J., Francis, D., Widdowson, J., LaPlante, P., Caldji, C., Sharma, S., Seckl, J. R., & Plotsky, P. M. (1996). Early environmental regulation of forebrain glucocorticoid receptor gene expression: Implications for adrenocortical responses to stress. *Developmental Neuroscience, 18,* 49–72.

Meisch, R. A., & Lemaire, G. A. (1993). Drug self-administration. In F. van Haaren (Ed.), *Methods in behavioral pharmacology* (pp. 257–300). New York: Elsevier Science Publishers.

Miner, L. L. (1997). Cocaine reward and locomotor activity in C57BL/6J and 129/SvJ inbred mice and their F1 cross. *Pharmacology Biochemistry Behavior, 58,* 25–30.

Miner, L. L., Drago, J., Chamberlain, P. M., Donovan, D., & Uhl, G. R. (1995). Retained cocaine conditioned place preference in D1 receptor deficient mice. *Neuroreport, 6,* 2314–2316.

Miner, L. L., & Marley, R. J. (1995a). Chromosomal mapping of loci influencing sensitivity to cocaine-induced seizures in BXD recombinant inbred strains of mice. *Psychopharmacology, 117,* 62–66.

Miner, L. L., & Marley, R. J. (1995b). Chromosomal mapping of the psychomotor stimulant effects of cocaine in BXD recombinant inbred mice. *Psychopharmacology, 122,* 209–214.

Mirin, S. M., Weiss, R. D., Griffin, M. L., & Michael, J. L. (1991). Psychopathology in drug abusers and their families. *Comprehensive Psychiatry, 32,* 36–51.

Mirin, S. M., Weiss, R. D., Sollogub, A., & Michael, J. (1984). Psychopathology in the families of drug abusers. In S. M. Mirin (Ed.), *Substance abuse and psychopathology* (pp. 80–106). Washington, DC: American Psychiatric Association.

Nader, M. A., Hedeker, D., & Woolverton, W. L. (1993). Behavioral economics and drug choice: Effects of unit price on cocaine self-administration by monkeys. *Drug Alcohol Dependence, 33,* 193–199.

Noble, E. P., Blum, K., Khalsa, M. E., Ritchie, T., Montgomery, A., Wood, R. C., Fitch, R. J., Ozkaragoz, T., Sheridan, P. J., Anglin, M. D., & et al. (1993). Allelic association of the D2 dopamine receptor gene with cocaine dependence. *Drug and Alcohol Dependence, 33,* 271–285.

O'Hara, B. F., Smith, S. S., Cutting, G. R., & Uhl, G. R. (1993). Racial differences in dopamine D2 receptor taq1 alleles and their association with substance abuse. *Human Heredity, 43,* 209–218.

Panlilio, L. V., & Schindler, C. W. (1997). Conditioned locomotor-activating and reinforcing effects of discrete stimuli paired with intraperitoneal cocaine. *Behavioural Pharmacology, 8,* 691–698.

Panlilio, L. V., Weiss, S. J., & Schindler, C. W. (1996). Cocaine self-administration increased by compounding discriminative stimuli. *Psychopharmacology, 125,* 202–208.

Parsian, A., Todd, R. D., Devor, E. J., O'Malley, K. L., Suarez, B. K., Reich, T., & Cloninger, C. R. (1991). Alcoholism and alleles of the human D2 dopamine receptor locus. *Archives of General Psychiatry, 48,* 655–663.

Pert, A., Post, R., & Weiss, S. (1990). Conditioning as a critical determinant of sensitization induced by psychomotor stimulants. *NIDA Research Monographs, 97,* 208–241.

Piazza, P. V., & Le Moal, M. L. (1996). Pathophysiological basis of vulnerability to drug abuse: Role of an interaction between stress, glucocorticoids, and dopaminergic neurons. *Annual Review Pharmacology Toxicology, 36,* 359–378.

Pickens, R. W., Elmer, G. I., LaBuda, M., & Uhl, G. (1996). Genetic vulnerability to substance abuse. In C. R. Schuster & M. J. Kuhar (Eds.), *Pharmacological aspects of drug dependence: Toward an integrated neurobehavioral approach* (pp. 1–52). Berlin: Springer-Verlag.

Pickens, R. W., & Svikis, D. S. (1991). Genetic influences in human substance abuse. *Journal of Addictive Disease, 10,* 205–213.

Pickens, R. W., Svikis, D. S., McGue, M., & LaBuda, M. C. (1995). Common genetic mechanisms in alcohol, drug, and mental disorder comorbidity. *Drug Alcohol and Dependence, 39,* 129–138.

Pickens, R. W., Svikis, D. S., McGue, M., Lykken, D. T., Heston, L. L., & Clayton, P. J. (1991). Heterogeneity in the inheritance of alcoholism. A study of male and female twins. *Archives of General Psychiatry, 48,* 19–28.

Pieper, J. O., Forester, D. F., & Elmer, G. I. (1998). *Predator and footshock stress-induced analgesia.* Unpublished manuscript.

Ritz, M. C., Lamb, R. J., Goldberg, S. R., & Kuhar, M. J. (1987). Cocaine receptors on dopamine transporters are related to the self-administration of cocaine. *Science, 237,* 1219–1223.

Ritz, M. R., Garcia, J. M., Protz, D., Rael, A.-M., & George, F. R. (1994). Ethanol-reinforced behavior in P, NP, HAD and LAD rats: Differential genetic regulation of reinforcement and motivation. *Behaviour Pharmacology, 5,* 521–531.

Rocha, B. A., Ator, R., Emmett-Oglesby, M. W., & Hen, R. (1997). Intravenous cocaine self-administration in mice lacking 5-HT1B receptors. *Pharmacology Biochemistry Behavior, 57,* 407–412.

Rounsaville, B. J., Kosten, T. R., Weissman, M. M., Prusoff, B., Pauls, D. L., Anton, S. F., & Merikangas, K. (1991). Psychiatric disorders in relatives of probands with opiate addiction. *Archives of General Psychiatry, 48,* 33–42.

Rubinstein, M., Phillips, T. J., Bunzow, J. R., Falzone, T. L., Dziewczapolski, G., Zhang, G., Fang, Y., Larson, J. L., McDougall, J. A., Chester, J. A., Saez, C., Pugsley, T. A., Gershanik, O., Low, M. J., & Grandy, D. K. (1997). Mice lacking dopamine D4 receptors are supersensitive to ethanol, cocaine, and methamphetamine. *Cell, 90,* 991–1001.

Schechter, M. D. (1992). Rats bred for differences in preference to cocaine: Other behavioral measurements. *Pharmacology, Biochemistry Behavior, 43,* 1015–1021.

Schindler, C. W., Katz, J. L., & Goldberg, S. R. (1988). The use of second-order schedules to study the influence of environmental stimuli on drug-seeking behavior. *NIDA Research Monographs, 84,* 180–195.

Schuckit, M. A., Hauger, R. L., Monteiro, M. G., Irwin, M., Duthie, L. A., & Mahler, H. I. M. (1991). Response of three hormones to diazepam challenge in sons of alcoholics and controls. *Alcohol Clinical Experimental Research, 15,* 537–542.

Shaham, Y., & Stewart, J. (1995). Stress reinstates heroin-seeking in drug-free animals: an effect mimicking heroin, not withdrawal. *Psychopharmacology, 119,* 334–341.

Seale, T. W. (1991). Genetic differences in response to cocaine and stimulant drugs. In J. C. Crabbe & R. A. Harris (Eds.), *The genetic basis of alcohol and drug actions* (pp. 279–321). New York: Plenum Press.

Seale, T. W., & Carney, J. M. (1991). Genetic determinants of susceptibility to the rewarding and other behavioral actions of cocaine. *Journal of Addiction Diseases, 10,* 141–161.

Silver, L. M. (Ed.). (1995). *Mouse genetics: Concepts and applications.* New York: Oxford University Press.

Smith, S. S., O'Hara, B. F., Persico, A. M., Gorelick, D. A., Newlin, D. B., Vlahov, D., Solomon, L., Pickens, R., & Uhl, G. R. (1992). Genetic vulnerability to drug abuse: The D2 dopamine receptor Taq I B1 restriction fragment length polymorphism appears more frequently in polysubstance abusers. *Archives of General Psychiatry, 49,* 723–727.

Smolen, A., & Marks, M. J. (1991). Genetic selections for nicotine and cocaine sensitivity in mice. *Journal of Addictive Disease, 10,* 7–28.

Smythe, J. W., Rowe, W. B., & Meaney, M. J. (1994). Neonatal handling alters serotonin (5-HT) turnover and 5-HT2 receptor binding in selected brain regions: Relationship to the handling effect on glucocorticoid receptor expression. *Brain Research Development Brain Research, 80,* 183–189.

Takahashi, N., Miner, L. L., Sora, I., Ujike, H., Revay, R., Kostic, V., Przedborski, S., & Uhl, G. (1997). VMAT2 knockout mice: Heterozygotes display reduced amphetamine-conditioned reward, enhanced amphetamine locomotion and enhanced MPTP toxicity. *Proceedings of National Academy of Sciences, 94,* 9938–9943.

Tanna, V. L., Wilson, A. F., Winokur, G., & Elston, R. C. (1988). Possible linkage between alcoholism and esterase-D. *Journal of Studies on Alcohol, 49,* 472–476.

Tolliver, B. K., Belknap, J. K., Woods, W. E., & Carney, J. M. (1994). Genetic analysis of sensitization and tolerance to cocaine. *Journal of Pharmacology Experimental Therapeutics, 270,* 1230–1238.

Tsuang, M. T., Lyons, M. J., Eisen, S. A., Goldberg, J., True, W., Lin, N., Meyer, J. M., Toomey, R., Faraone, S. V., & Eaves, L. (1996). Genetic influences on *DSM-III-R* drug abuse and dependence: A study of 3,372 twin pairs. *Am J Med Genet* 67:473–7.

Uhl, G. R., Blum, K., & Smith, S. S. (1993). Substance abuse vulnerability and D2 receptor genes. *Trends in Neuroscience, 16,* 83–88.

Wang, Y. M., Gainetdinov, R. R., Fumagalli, F., Xu, F., Jones, S. R., Bock, C. B., Miller, G. W., Wightman, R. M., & Caron, M. G. (1997). Knockout of the vesicular monoamine transporter 2 gene results in neonatal death and supersensitivity to cocaine and amphetamine. *Neuron, 19,* 1285–1296.

Ward, A. S., Li, D. H., Luedtke, R. R., & Emmett-Oglesby, M. W. (1996). Variations in cocaine self-administration by inbred rat strains under a progressive-ratio schedule. *Psychopharmacology, 127,* 204–212.

Wright, S. (1968). *Genetic and biometric foundations.* Chicago: University of Chicago.

Xu, M., Hu, X. T., Cooper, D. C., Moratalla, R., Graybiel, A. M., White, F. J., & Tonegawa, S. (1994). Elimination of cocaine-induced hyperactivity and dopamine-mediated neurophysiological effects in dopamine D1 receptor mutant mice. *Cell, 79,* 945–955.

Zacharko, R. M., Lalonde, G., Kasian, M., & Anisman, H. (1987). Strain-specific effects of inescapable shock on intracranial self-stimulation from the nucleus accumbens. *Brain Research, 426,* 164–168.

13

VULNERABILITY
TO COCAINE ABUSE

HOWARD D. CHILCOAT

Departments of Psychiatry and Biostatistics
Henry Ford Health Sciences Center
Detroit, Michigan

CHRIS-ELLYN JOHANSON

Departments of Psychiatry and Behavioral Neurosciences
Wayne State University
Detroit, Michigan

INTRODUCTION

Although the present book covers many aspects of cocaine research and provides a plethora of information on the behavioral and pharmacological determinants and consequences of excessive cocaine use, many readers who approach this text will be seeking an answer to "why" a particular person begins using cocaine. That is, what determines whether a person is willing to try cocaine even once and then on a more regular basis? Is there something different about a cocaine user that we can identify? Do systems in the user's body, particularly in the brain, process cocaine differently? Are there life experiences that lead an individual into the world of cocaine addiction? Is a person who has other behavioral or psychiatric problems more likely to use cocaine?

Unfortunately, the answer to the "why" question is neither understood nor is the answer likely to be simple. There are not only multiple pathways leading to serious involvement with cocaine but the nature of the determinant, or the sphere of influence, can range from the biological to the cultural. Furthermore, it is unlikely that an individual would start to use cocaine because of a single cause; instead, use is a function of interactions among several factors from the universe of determinants. Adding to this complexity, the type of factor (for example, biological, psychological, or social) that might promote use at one stage of development may be without potential impact at other stages. Finally, drug use might be part of a

---

Cocaine Abuse: Behavior, Pharmacology,
and Clinical Applications

313

constellation of behavior problems or a symptom, manifestation, or consequence of another, preexisting, disorder in the individual.

GOALS OF THE CHAPTER

So how do we answer the question "why?" for cocaine use and dependence? In this chapter we will not attempt to give a complete answer to the question because it does not exist, although we will illustrate some findings. Instead, we have set out to accomplish three major goals. Our first goal is to discuss the use of epidemiologic methods as a tool for answering these questions, with a particular focus on findings from the National Household Survey on Drug Abuse (NHSDA). The second is to describe a conceptual framework synthesized from several models that have been used to explain the initiation and continued use of cocaine. These models incorporate developmental, infectious, and psychopathological perspectives and represent major current theories of etiology. In addition, we will describe a new conceptual model that features reinforcement processes and their potential impact on drug use, although the preliminary status of this model needs to be kept in mind. After setting the stage by describing a synthesis of etiologic models, our third goal is to present specific examples of research on the determinants of cocaine use. These examples illustrate two important domains: the family and the neighborhood. In describing these findings, we will discuss the potential influence of other types of determinants and interactions among spheres of influence.

UNIVERSE OF DETERMINANTS

Within the framework synthesized from these models, the myriad of factors that might influence drug use initiation and maintenance can be conceptually organized into several categories that constitute the universe of determinants. Broadly speaking, these categories can be divided into those that operate on the level of the individual (e.g., genetic endowment, physiological systems, psychological traits, psychiatric syndromes) versus those that are environmental in origin (e.g., intrauterine experience, interpersonal factors, societal conditions). These categories can be further differentiated. For instance, interpersonal factors may derive from the family, school, peers, or fellow workers. However, even the broad categories may not be mutually exclusive. For instance, perturbations in the intrauterine environment (e.g., from drugs) may affect gene expression of physiological systems that in turn place an individual at risk.

In most etiologic studies, elements from the universe of determinants that are considered in the analyses are restricted, a fact that is often unappreciated by the nonexpert. For instance, investigators who view substance abuse as environmentally determined and largely a function of family disruption are unlikely to find that differences in brain chemistry have an influence on the initiation of drug use. Likewise, geneticists may fail to ask important questions about psychosocial context.

EPIDEMIOLOGIC STUDIES

The first goal of this chapter is to acquaint the reader with strategies used to determine the prevalence and incidence of drug use. A number of sources has been used as indicators of cocaine use and related problems, ranging from anecdotal and media reports to large-scale population-based surveys. Although anecdotal and clinical case reports of cocaine use can serve as useful indicators of cocaine problems, they have high potential for bias because these indicators focus on existing "cases" (e.g., teenage crack use; deaths due to cocaine use) while ignoring the sample base from which these "cases" arise. As a result, rare events can appear more common than they actually are. In addition, data from sources that are not representative of the general population can distort associations between suspected risk factors and cocaine outcomes. Epidemiological studies, which measure "cases," as well as the population base from which these "cases" emerge, minimize the potential for bias. Additionally, these studies can be used to identify risk factors, thereby providing clues about the etiology of cocaine use. In this section, we describe several major epidemiologic sources of data on the use of cocaine and related problems in the United States.

CROSS-SECTIONAL STUDIES

Most epidemiologic studies of the use of cocaine (as well as other drugs) in the United States rely on data collected in surveys of the general population. Usually, survey data are collected cross-sectionally, meaning that all information, including both data on risk factors and outcomes (i.e., drug use), is collected at the same time. Information generally is collected using standardized questionnaires administered individually in face-to-face interviews or in group settings, such as classrooms. The most widely used data from cross-sectional surveys are prevalence estimates of cocaine outcomes, which can be produced for the entire sample, as well as for subgroups (e.g., females, adolescents). As defined in epidemiology, prevalence is the proportion of the population with "disease" (in this case, a cocaine outcome) in a specified period of time (Lillienfeld & Stolley, 1994). Lifetime prevalence of cocaine use refers to the occurrence of cocaine use at any point in the lifetime, whereas past-year prevalence refers to any occurrence in the year prior to the survey interview (but first use could have occurred much earlier). In order for prevalence to be estimated, the cocaine outcome must be operationalized as a dichotomous variable, such as cocaine use versus no use or cocaine dependence versus nondependence. Various analytic strategies can then be used to estimate the size and direction of associations between these specified cocaine outcomes and suspected risk factors. To the extent that surveys ask meaningful questions and use state-of-the-art sampling and analytic techniques that maximize validity and reliability, we can make informative inferences about the distribution of cocaine use in the population. Surveys that do not sample and analyze data appropriately or are driven by political motives can be misleading, wasteful, and dangerous. Furthermore, if surveys are driven by a particular perspective (e.g., psychological), other domains from the universe of determinants are likely to be ignored. This is particularly likely in the case of biological determinants because appropriate assessments (e.g., analysis of genetic markers using blood) are difficult to accomplish within traditional survey methods. These assessments often are too expensive given the large number of individuals sampled in population-based studies and may place excessive burden on respondents. On the other hand, alternative sampling methods, such as those used in nested case-control studies, can be used to incorporate biologic measures in a cost efficient manner (Clayton & Hills, 1993).

PROSPECTIVE STUDIES

Even the best cross-sectional surveys can only suggest etiologic factors that influence cocaine use and abuse. To shed light on etiologic factors, more sophisticated strategies incorporating measurements of individual or contextual characteristics prior to the onset of drug use or abuse are needed. However, these studies can be extremely expensive to conduct and, by definition, they cannot provide immediate results. In these prospective studies (also termed cohort studies), individuals who have not yet experienced the drug use outcome, but who vary along dimensions considered potential determinants of drug use (as indicated perhaps by findings from cross-sectional studies), are followed over time (e.g., Kellam, Simon, & Ensminger, 1983). Typically, in prospective studies of drug use, a cohort is selected as a sample for initial participation in a survey, and then reinterviewed at one or more subsequent time intervals to compare the risk of drug use outcomes by preexisting risk factors (for examples, see Chen & Kandel, 1995; Chilcoat, Dishon, & Anthony, 1995). Comparisons are then made in terms of the risk of becoming a cocaine user (or experiencing another specified cocaine-related outcome such as dependence) among those with a given risk factor relative to those without the factor. More specifically, incidence is used as the direct measure of risk and is defined as the number of new cases of "disease" in the population during a specified period of time, divided by the number of people at risk of experiencing the outcome (Lillienfeld & Stolley, 1994). In the present context, relative risk is then estimated by the ratio of the incidence of a specified cocaine outcome in the "exposed" group (i.e., those with a specified risk factor) to the incidence in the "unexposed" group (i.e., those without a specified risk factor). In order to estimate the incidence of cocaine use during a defined follow-up interval, individuals who have initiated cocaine use prior to the start of the interval are not considered at risk and are excluded from the numerator and denominator in the estimation of the incidence of cocaine use. To illustrate, we will estimate the relative risk of cocaine use as a function of early aggressive behavior among males, using data from a 26-year follow-up of participants in the Woodlawn study (Kellam & Ensminger, 1980) as presented by Mayer and Warsi (1997). Aggressive behavior was assessed when the participants were 6 years old, *prior* to the onset of cocaine use. Among the 90 males in the high aggressive behavior group at age 6, 30 reported cocaine use at the 26-

year follow-up (incidence = 33%). There were 254 male participants in the low aggressive behavior group, of whom 52 reported cocaine use at follow-up (incidence = 20%). Therefore, the relative risk of cocaine use in the high versus low aggressive behavior groups was 0.33/0.20 = 1.63. This can be interpreted as meaning that a male with high levels of aggression at age 6 is 1.63 times more likely to become a cocaine user compared to a male with low levels of aggression.

There are a number of advantages to a prospective approach that make it a more powerful analytic strategy than cross-sectional studies. The most obvious advantage is that the temporal sequence of the outcome and risk factor is fixed so that the risk factor is known to precede the outcome—a necessary, although not sufficient, condition for establishing causal relationships (Rothman, 1986). An additional advantage is that it reduces correlated error, such as response tendencies, which could result in a spurious association between the risk factor and outcome (Chilcoat & Anthony, 1996). For example, a bias could exist in which respondents who report a high level of a specific risk factor (e.g., antisocial behavior) are more likely to *report* cocaine use than those without this risk factor, by virtue of the characteristics of antisocial behavior (e.g., lying, exaggerating). As a result, the estimate of the cocaine–antisocial behavior association would be biased in favor of a positive association. Because respondents who report cocaine use at baseline are eliminated from the prospective analysis, including those with a tendency to overreport use, the potential for bias is reduced.

TRENDS IN COCAINE USE: EPIDEMIOLOGIC FINDINGS FROM NATIONAL STUDIES

Despite the advantages of prospective studies, much can be learned from cross-sectional surveys, as we previously noted, and in addition, few prospective studies focusing on cocaine use have been conducted. As an illustration of a cross-sectional survey that can be used to shed light on the etiology of cocaine use, we will briefly summarize basic findings from NHSDA, the major epidemiological survey of illicit drug use among children *and* adults in the United States (SAMHSA, 1995). In addition, we will present results from a school-based survey of drug use in the United States, the Monitoring the Future (MTF) study (Johnston, O'Malley, & Bachman, 1995). The MTF has been conducted since 1975 using high school seniors as respondents; since 1991, the MTF has added younger respondents (8th and 10th grades). Typically, both of these surveys are used to estimate prevalence of drug use; however, they can be used to search for determinants of cocaine use that go beyond sex, age, region, and ethnicity, the major risk factors reported in official government publications, although this is rarely done.

The NHSDA has been collecting information on the use of cocaine and other drugs for about 20 years. The NHSDA uses a multistage probability sample of households to estimate drug use in the civilian, noninstitutionalized population of the United States, age 12 and older. African-Americans, Hispanics, and young people are oversampled to increase the precision of estimates for these groups.

Interviews are conducted in the home by trained interviewers. In order to maximize the validity of responses and to minimize underreporting, respondents use self-administered answer sheets to answer questions about issues that might be considered sensitive, such as illicit drug use. Since its inception in 1979, the NHSDA has increased the sample size and frequency of the survey and currently over 25,000 interviews are completed in the NHSDA surveys, now carried out annually.

Figure 13.1 shows the past-year and past-month prevalence rates for cocaine use since 1979. As can be seen these rates increased steadily reaching a peak for past-month use in 1985 and then steadily declined until 1992, remaining at this level through 1995. In 1985 there were almost 6 million people who had used cocaine (including crack) at least once in the past 30 days. By 1994, this number had decreased to 1.3 million. On the other hand, among respondents reporting use in the past year, the numbers who had used it at least once a week or more remained the same (between 650,000 to 800,000) over this same time period. Thus, the more frequent, problematic use of cocaine remains at peak levels. In general, the MTF has shown the same general trends in cocaine use as the NHSDA. For instance, the MTF showed that cocaine use in high school seniors reached its peak in 1985 and declined until 1993. In 1985, 13.1% of high school seniors reported that they had taken cocaine during the past year, whereas in 1992, this number had declined to 3.1%.

Among adolescents, there has been a slight but statistically significant increase in the prevalence of cocaine use in both the NHSDA and MTF. For instance, in the MTF, past-year prevalence of cocaine use among 8th graders has risen from 0.7% in 1991 to 1.6% in 1995. This reversal in the trends for cocaine use, which has also

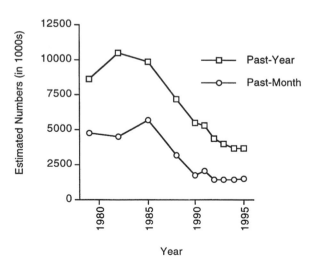

FIGURE 13.1   Past-month and past-year prevalence of cocaine (including crack) use from the National Household Survey on Drug Abuse from 1979 to 1995.

been found for marijuana and other drugs of abuse, has aroused concern in the general public and public health authorities. We should note that the reliability of the estimates for 8th graders is limited by the relatively small number of users in the sample. Nonetheless, the trends are reason for alarm, especially because early initiation of drug use signals increased risk of drug problems (Anthony & Petronis, 1995; Robins & Przybeck, 1985).

DEMOGRAPHIC TRENDS IN COCAINE USE

In addition to changes in overall prevalence, there has been a change in current demographic patterns of cocaine use, compared to those in the late 1970s and early 1980s. Although cocaine was then the "drug of choice" among the "elite," its use has become increasingly prevalent in other portions of the population. Data from the 1991 NHSDA showed that the past-year and past-month prevalence rates for cocaine use were significantly higher in those who had not completed high school compared to those with a high school diploma. The difference was particularly striking for crack cocaine use, for which the past-month prevalence was four times greater among those who did not finish high school compared to college graduates. This is in contrast to the situation in 1982 when high school and college graduates were two to three times more likely to have used cocaine in the past month than those who had not finished high school. Further, in 1993, cocaine use in the past month among the unemployed was three times higher than in the employed. The difference was even greater for crack cocaine. Recent statistics from the National Institute of Justice show that the rates of cocaine-positive urine among both male and female arrestees in major cities remain near peak levels of 40 to 80% (National Institute of Justice, 1993). Thus, it would appear that the decreasing trend in prevalence rates of cocaine use observed in the general population is absent or significantly less in the educationally, economically, and socially disadvantaged.

RACIAL AND ETHNIC DIFFERENCES IN COCAINE USE

There has been an increasing effort to probe the meaning of differences in the prevalence of drug use for groups varying by demographic characteristics. One characteristic that has received attention in this regard is race/ethnicity. For most drugs, regardless of gender or age, African Americans report lower rates of use. However, in both the 1988 and 1990 NHSDA, lifetime prevalence rates for crack cocaine were over twice as high among African-Americans compared to White-Americans. However, analyses that controlled for neighborhood of residence, thereby holding constant shared characteristics such as drug availability and social conditions, found that the odds of crack cocaine use did not differ by race/ethnicity (Chilcoat & Schütz, 1995; Lillie-Blanton, Anthony, & Schuster, 1993). Thus, it appears that neighborhood characteristics that promote the use of crack cocaine are equally effective, regardless of racial or ethnic status. African-

Americans, however, are much more likely than White-Americans to live in neighborhoods with these characteristics, thus leading to the higher overall prevalence of crack use among African-Americans. It must be remembered, however, that because of the relatively smaller size of the African-American population than the White-American population in the United States, the majority of crack users are white. Differences in reported use of crack have also been noted in Hispanic populations. In 1988, the lifetime prevalence of crack use for Hispanic-Americans was 2.1% compared to 1.0% for White-Americans. However, there was no difference in the odds of crack use when neighborhood factors were controlled (Lillie-Blanton et al., 1993). In addition, in the 1990 NHSDA, the lifetime prevalence for Hispanic-Americans was not significantly different from that for White-Americans. In fact, when Chilcoat and Schütz (1995) adjusted for neighborhood, Hispanic-Americans were found to have significantly lower odds of being a crack user compared to Whites.

ADDITIONAL POPULATION-BASED STUDIES
OF COCAINE ABUSE AND DEPENDENCE

Besides the NHSDA and MTF, there are other sources of information about cocaine use and dependence. In the interest of space we will not describe the findings of these alternative sources but a brief description will be provided. Although not designed specifically to measure prevalence of drug *use,* the National Comorbidity Study (NCS) used a nationally representative sample of 15–54-year-olds to assess the comorbidity among drug use disorders and mental health disorders in the United States (Anthony et al., 1994; Kessler et al., 1994). The primary advantages of the NCS relative to the NHSDA, in terms of drug outcomes, is that the NCS used a structured psychiatric interview to assess drug *abuse and dependence* in addition to use. Similarly, the Epidemiologic Catchment Area (ECA) Study also measured the prevalence (and incidence) of psychiatric disorders, including drug use disorders; however, it sampled from five distinct but presumably representative areas of the country (New Haven, CT; Baltimore, MD; St. Louis, MO; Los Angeles, CA; Durham, NC) (Anthony & Helzer, 1991) rather than from a national sampling frame. It also used a different structured psychiatric interview that was based on *DSM-III* (American Psychiatric Association, 1980), as opposed to *DSM-IIIR* disorders assessed in the NCS.

OTHER INDICATORS OF COCAINE USE
IN THE UNITED STATES

There are a number of other data sources that serve as indicators of aspects of cocaine use or dependence in the United States. Two widely used data sources are the Drug Use Forecasting Program (DUF; National Institute of Justice, 1993), which provides estimates of drug use based on urine samples collected from arrestees, and the Drug Abuse Warning Network (DAWN), which collects drug use data from emergency rooms and coroner's reports (SAMHSA, 1994). Although data from these sources can provide some indication of trends of cocaine use, they cannot estimate prevalence directly. Instead, these two data sources serve as indicators of the *consequences* of drug use (e.g., being arrested, experiencing a life-threatening effect requiring medical assistance), and because of their limited sampling frame, their generalizability to the population is extremely limited. For example, given that drug abusers are often involved in drug-related crimes, the fact that DUF estimates of cocaine use are extremely high should not be surprising. Nevertheless, it has been suggested that the DUF program provides more accurate estimates of crack use among minority youth than the NHSDA (Kleber, 1994). However, we feel that although the NHSDA does not sample the small proportion of minority youth that are institutionalized or homeless, the estimates obtained by the NHSDA are more valid because the sample is nationally representative, unlike the DUF sample.

CONCEPTUAL FRAMEWORK

To guide our understanding of etiologic factors leading to cocaine dependence, we have attempted to synthesize several distinct theoretical models into a conceptual framework. Although some of these models have been described by others, our goal in integrating these models is to provide a framework that will help researchers identify factors that are potential targets for effective intervention strategies. The first model conceptualizes drug use as a series of transitional stages, in which an individual can progress from being exposed to drug-using opportunities to developing drug dependence. The second model draws from the theory of infectious disease epidemiology. The integration of an infectious disease perspective into the framework is motivated by Robins (1984), who stated that drug dependence is the area in mental health epidemiology that is most analogous to infectious disease because prevalence varies across time and space and transmission occurs person-to-person. Finally, we draw from the perspective of behavioral pharmacology to explore a new model of reinforcement processes that promote initiation and escalation of cocaine use.

STAGE MODEL

From the stage perspective, it is clear that the path to cocaine dependence is not a simple one. As Kandel points out (Kandel & Yamaguchi, 1993), initial use of cocaine almost always occurs subsequent to use of alcohol, cigarettes, and marijuana. On the other hand, most people who try these other substances do not initiate cocaine use. Furthermore, only a fraction of those who have tried cocaine, as well as other drugs, progress to drug dependence (Anthony, Warner, & Kessler, 1994). Therefore, it is critical that we identify those risk factors that promote the progression from earlier stages of drug use to more problematic drug involvement.

Equally important is the identification of protective factors that block this progression.

Although the pathway from drug use to dependence most likely follows a continuum (Glantz & Pickens, 1992), it is useful conceptually to divide this transitional phenomenon into discrete stages (Graham, Collins, Chung, & Hansen, 1991). This enables us to probe the extent to which specific factors signal risk of making a *transition* between these stages. As shown in Figure 13.2, we have hypothesized four stages of drug involvement: opportunity to use, drug sampling, patterned drug use, and drug problems. Each stage is a necessary, although not sufficient, condition for progression to the subsequent stage. As Newcomb (1995) points out, the conceptualization of drug use occurring in stages is probabilistic, rather than deterministic, in nature—status in one stage infers nothing about status in subsequent stages, it merely indicates that all previous stages have been traversed.

The first stage in the model is exposure to the opportunity to use a drug, a critical component in the transition to drug use that often is overlooked. In this stage, cocaine is made available to an individual, who either does or does not initiate use. In general, opportunities to use are provided directly by other individuals, typically peers. It also is possible that an individual might seek an opportunity on his or her own, such as a child who has access to the parents' liquor supply.

If use occurs at a given opportunity, the individual progresses to the next stage, which we have described using the term "drug sampling," to capture the notion that an individual is trying the drug for the first time. Although drug sampling by itself might not be problematic, it nonetheless represents a critical behavioral transition from nonuser to user. Progression to the next stage is characterized by an es-

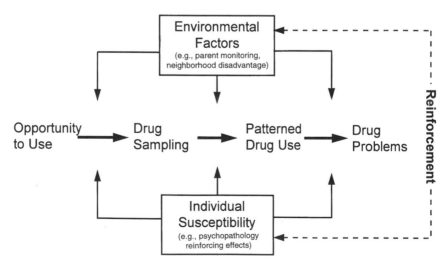

FIGURE 13.2   The hypothesized impact of individual and environmental factors on progression through stages of cocaine use.

calation of use from sampling to patterned use. In this stage, quantity and frequency increase to a level at which problems related to use can develop. More time is spent using and acquiring the drug, and an increasing proportion of the behavioral repertoire consists of drug-related behaviors.

The transition to problems of drug dependence, such as those defined by *DSM* or International Classification of Disease (*ICD*) classification systems (American Psychiatric Association, 1994; World Health Organization, 1993), marks the final stage. These problems include a great deal of time spent obtaining and using the drug; loss of control of use; continued use despite health, social, or occupational problems related to use; and physiologic symptoms of tolerance and withdrawal. From a public health standpoint, this final stage is most important, and prevention of these problems is the ultimate goal.

The stage model provides many options for prevention. Theoretically, blocking the transition into any of the stages leading up to cocaine dependence could thwart the development of problematic cocaine use. However, risk or protective factors that are important at one stage of drug involvement will not necessarily be important at other stages. By dividing the progression of drug involvement into defined stages, it is possible to segregate the potential etiologic factors at any given stage.

In this regard, the stage model can be elaborated further using a developmental perspective. More specifically, risk factors for transition to a specific stage of drug use may be different depending on the point in the developmental lifecourse at which the transition occurs. For instance, antisocial behaviors, an individual risk factor, are linked more strongly with drug sampling that starts in late childhood or early adolescence versus that initiated later in life (Shedler & Block, 1990). In another example, Chilcoat and Schütz (1995) found that there was not difference in the odds of crack cocaine use by race/ethnicity at younger ages (less than 18), but that a difference did exist for older individuals (over 35). That is, race/ethnicity was not a risk factor at younger ages but did become one later in adulthood. The developmental perspective also helps us understand differences in the trajectory of drug involvement as a function of the age at which drug initiation occurs. For example, drinking alcohol is considered normative when it occurs in early adulthood: legal restrictions to drinking are reduced, and the vast majority of the population uses alcohol at least occasionally at this age. In contrast, self-initiated use of alcohol in childhood is normative and signals greater risk of problematic use later on (i.e., a greater risk of a trajectory to later stages). A number of investigators (Anthony & Petronis, 1995; Robins & Przybeck, 1985) have found that the earlier drug use is initiated, the more likely the development of drug problems, even when duration of use is taken into account. As a result, Robins and Przybeck (1985) suggested that a useful prevention strategy would be to delay the onset of drug use until after age 18. In their discussion of the risk-focused approach to drug prevention, Hawkins, Catalano, and Miller (1992) argued that, given the small proportion of adolescent problem drug users relative to the number who experiment with drugs (i.e., users), prevention efforts should target factors related to abuse rather than use. That is, prevention efforts should focus on risk factors that operate at later stages. We feel, however, that when a developmental perspective is used, the importance of preventing earlier stages of use becomes more evident.

INFECTIOUS DISEASE ANALOGY

We have extended Robins's infectious disease analogy, borrowing from Frost's theory of infectious disease epidemiology (Frost, 1941) as a guide in the search for factors that influence the likelihood that an individual will make the transition from one stage of cocaine use to the next. Frost stated that changes in disease prevalence are due to changes in (a) the conditions that determine whether exposure to an infectious agent occurs or (b) conditions that determine whether disease develops once exposure has occurred (e.g., susceptibility within individuals, reinforcing strength of the drug). Adapting Frost's theory to the stage model, cocaine becomes the "infectious agent" and cocaine outcomes (e.g., stage of cocaine use) are substituted for disease. The utility of Frost's explanation of changes in disease prevalence is in its delineation of the separate but interacting roles of the environment, individual, and the infectious agent. Frost stated that environmental factors are important determinants of whether an individual is exposed to an infectious agent, a necessary, but not sufficient condition for an infectious disease to occur. Similarly, cocaine dependence, as well as each of the previous stages of cocaine involvement, cannot occur without exposure to cocaine-using opportunities (Anthony & Helzer, 1995). The environmental factors that bring the host (individual) into contact with the agent (cocaine) generally operate by increasing the availability of the drug. In addition to opportunities to initiate use of cocaine, the transition to each of the subsequent stages of drug involvement is controlled, in part, by environmental factors that influence the availability of cocaine. Over the course of the last century, cocaine availability has varied across time and place due to a number of environmental factors. For example, at a societal level, changes in regulatory laws have influenced the availability of cocaine. In addition, differences in availability can exist among different regions of the country or at the level of the neighborhood and school. At the level of the individual, affiliating with drug-using peers can also increase availability of cocaine.

In the second part of his explanation of changes in disease prevalence, Frost points out that individual susceptibility is an important determinant of whether disease develops after exposure to the infectious agent. As represented in Figure 13.2, we hypothesize that variations in susceptibility at the level of the individual signal differential risk of making a transition from one stage of cocaine use to the next. For example, the observation that a minority of those who initiate cocaine use develop dependence (Anthony et al., 1994) could be explained in part by differences in individual susceptibility, such as genetic factors, as discussed in chapter 12, Elmer et al., this volume. In addition, we have extended this model to allow for interaction between environmental factors and individual susceptibility, as indicated by the arrow connecting the two in Figure 13.2.

INDIVIDUAL SUSCEPTIBILITY—PSYCHIATRIC COMORBIDITY

Studies of community samples have shown that the diagnosis of alcoholism or drug abuse/dependence is associated with higher prevalence rates of a wide variety of psychiatric disorders (Kilbey, Breslau, & Andreski, 1992). In a study that evaluated the psychiatric status of individuals seeking treatment for cocaine abuse or dependence (Rounsaville et al., 1991), both high current (55.7%) and lifetime (73.5%) prevalence rates for psychiatric disorders other than substance abuse were reported. The principal types of coexisting psychiatric disorders were: major depression, minor bipolar conditions, anxiety disorders, antisocial personality, and a history of attention deficit hyperactivity disorder (ADHD). Prospective studies have shown that adolescents with both ADHD and conduct disorder who show residual symptoms of ADHD and also have developed antisocial personality disorder have higher rates of substance abuse problems (Mannuzza, Klein, Bessler, Malloy, & LaPadula, 1993). However, for those who reached adulthood and no longer showed symptoms of ADHD or antisocial personality, the odds of being a drug abuser were no different than controls (Mannuzza et al., 1993).

One of the complications in determining the role of psychiatric disorders in the development of substance abuse problems is that drug use itself might cause a psychiatric syndrome. Although there is continuing debate about the etiologic significance of psychiatric disorders in the development of substance abuse (e.g., Biederman et al., 1997), there is general agreement that substance abuse and other psychiatric problems coexist and that substance-abusing treatment clients with comorbid psychiatric disorders have poorer treatment outcome. Appropriate pharmacological or psychotherapeutic treatment of the comorbid psychiatric disorder has been shown to improve the outcome of substance abuse treatment (Woody, McLellan, Luborsky, & O'Brien, 1985).

INDIVIDUAL SUSCEPTIBILITY—GENETIC DIFFERENCES

Although there is evidence of genetic differences among individuals who are drug users (Blum et al., 1990; Smith et al., 1992; Uhl, Perisco, & Smith, 1992), the specific genetic differences remain controversial and how differences in genetic structure translate into behavioral risk is not known. For instance, it has been demonstrated that the prevalence of an allelic variant of a gene that controls the expression of dopamine receptors is higher in certain groups of drug users (Smith et al., 1992). However, how individuals who possess this genetic variant differ at other levels of analysis has not been investigated. One possibility is that the drug itself produces a different spectrum of effects in these individuals. Because dopamine pathways are known to be important determinants of the reinforcing effects of cocaine (Fischman & Johanson, 1996; Johanson & Schuster, 1995; Koob & Bloom, 1988), these genetic differences might translate into differences in reinforcing effects. A more detailed discussion of the role of genetic factors in cocaine dependence is presented in chapter 12, Elmer et al., this volume.

REINFORCEMENT PROCESSES

With this idea in mind, we will now elaborate on another theory that may be useful in guiding our understanding of how risk and protective factors at the level of the individual interact with those in the environment to influence the progression through stages of cocaine use (Figure 13.2). This perspective, namely reinforcement, derives from the experimental work of behavioral pharmacologists and largely has gone untested as an etiologic model of vulnerability. Over the last three decades there has emerged a large body of evidence that drugs of abuse such as cocaine are readily taken by nonhumans under a wide range of experimental conditions (Johanson, 1978). One of the first studies that demonstrated animals would self-administer drugs of abuse used cocaine (Deneau, Yanagita, & Seevers, 1969). Rhesus monkeys were surgically prepared with an intravenous catheter through which drug could be infused. When the monkey made a response on a manipulandum, the infusion equipment was programmed to deliver an injection of cocaine. Under these simple conditions, with no training or coercion, all rhesus monkeys made the required response repetitively and took cocaine in a pattern that resembled human pattern of binges alternating with periods of little or no intake (Deneau et al., 1969). In behavioral terms, cocaine functioned as a reinforcer (Johanson, 1978). The history of subsequent self-administration studies with cocaine in both animals and humans can be found in chapter 8, by Fischman & Foltin. The important point in the present context is that the powerful reinforcing effects of cocaine are indisputable; there are many investigators who would even suggest that cocaine is THE most reinforcing drug.

Behavioral research on cocaine as a reinforcer has been expanded to demonstrate the biological basis of this property. It is now well accepted that the biological mechanisms underlying the ability of cocaine to function as a reinforcer are intimately connected with the biological substrates for normal motivational systems, many of which involve dopamine (Fischman & Johanson, 1996; Johanson & Schuster, 1995; Koob & Bloom, 1988). It is our contention that the salience of these reinforcing effects has not been considered in etiologic models. At the most radical level, we would suggest that the accumulation of evidence of the normalcy of cocaine reinforcement changes the question that epidemiologists should ask from "What are the risk factors for cocaine abuse?" to "Why aren't we all abusing cocaine?" A more reasonable conclusion is not that we are all inherent cocaine abusers but that the probability of drug-seeking behavior is far greater than most epidemiologists ever consider. Said another way, we are all at some risk and this risk is not trivial. Furthermore, the extent of the risk may be genetically determined, as suggested previously.

COUNTERVAILING INFLUENCES—ENVIRONMENTAL FACTORS

If we all have some biological predisposition to use cocaine, why does the vast majority of our citizenry resist? Most of us do not become involved with cocaine because there are countervailing influences that for almost everyone have prevented the expression of an underlying biological process. The implication of this view is that instead of only focusing on risk factors that might increase the appeal of cocaine, or increase the probability of drug taking, we should also focus on factors that decrease the impact of our biological risk. Although to some extent this is a matter of semantics (e.g., a risk factor may be simply the absence of a protective factor or vice versa), the recognition that individuals are biologically vulnerable may help sharpen etiologic research and include assessment of domains that could be characterized as countervailing influences.

Animal research using cocaine self-administration paradigms has provided some indications of the types of environmental factors that can decrease drug-seeking behavior and thus be considered countervailing influences. These include punishment, response cost, and the availability of alternative sources of reinforcement. For instance, in Bergman and Johanson's (1981) study of rhesus monkeys, the administration of electric shock, contingent upon responding maintained by cocaine, decreased cocaine self-administration. Furthermore, the decrease was proportional to the magnitude of the punishment. However, that study also showed that animals adapted to this punishment and, over time, levels of cocaine self-administration returned to nonpunished levels. This habituation, which occurs with other types of behavior decreased by punishment (Azrin, 1959), clearly limits the utility of this type of countervailing influence. Punishment has also been shown to have other liabilities as an effective means of controlling behavior. For instance, the delivery of punishment often elicits counteraggression (Cherek, Spiga, Bennett, & Grabowski, 1991). Even when punishment can be shown to be effective when delivered immediately, if its delivery is delayed, effectiveness is reduced in proportion to its delay (Azrin & Holz, 1966). Finally, the predictability of punishment is important with intermittent or uncertain delivery having reduced effectiveness (Azrin & Holz, 1966). Anyone who examines our present-day judicial system of prosecution and imprisonment with these criteria in mind (punishment must be certain and immediate) can easily understand why its effectiveness might not be optimal.

On the other hand, there are more proximal sources of punishment that may be used effectively because they can be delivered consistently and immediately. For instance, parents can exercise considerable control over behavior with the judicious delivery of appropriate punishment (e.g., restricting privileges, verbal admonishments). This may very well be one of the mechanisms by which parent monitoring, a factor reviewed in a subsequent section of this chapter, mediates its effect on decreasing initiation of drug use. Moral or religious training and, at the secular level, health education, often seek to exercise control over drug-taking behavior using threats of punishment. These approaches may be quite effective at certain stages of development or with individuals without other behavioral problems. However, if one accepts the strong biological basis of cocaine reinforcement, it may not seem surprising that these approaches sometimes have minimal impact. In particular, their effectiveness may be compromised in situations where someone has already begun taking cocaine and in individuals whose behavioral pathology (e.g., antisocial personality) is such that traditional moral and educational training may not be effective.

Another factor that can modulate the reinforcing effects of cocaine is availability, as influenced by the effort required to obtain the drug. In animal experimental studies, this has been evaluated using a paradigm that requires animals to emit more and more responses to obtain the same drug dose. This paradigm is called the progressive ratio schedule (Hodos, 1961). Initially, a drug might be available if the animal emitted only two responses, then four, etc., until a point is reached, termed the breaking point, when the animal ceases responding. Over two decades ago, Yanagita (1973) demonstrated that the breaking point at which rhesus monkeys ceased responding differed considerably across drugs. Interestingly, the breaking point for cocaine was generally higher than for other drugs. Nevertheless, even with cocaine, if the difficulty of obtaining the drug is increased, drug consumption will decrease. The implications for this finding for prevention of drug use are obvious. On the other hand, the *ability* to increase the difficulty of obtaining drugs in a democratic society may be limited.

Another type of countervailing influence is the availability of alternative reinforcers. Animal studies have provided several examples of the ability of alternative reinforcers to decrease cocaine self-administration. For instance, Carroll, Lac, and Nygaard (1989) demonstrated that rats did not initiate the self-administration of cocaine when they already had the opportunity to engage in a behavioral task reinforced by a highly palatable food. Even in animals that had already initiated cocaine self-administration, levels of drug taking decreased when they were allowed to select the food instead of cocaine. Woolverton and his colleagues (Nader & Woolverton, 1991; Nader, Hedeker, & Woolverton, 1993) also showed that cocaine self-administration by rhesus monkeys decreased as an increasing number of food pellets was made available. In other laboratory studies, Fischman and her colleagues (Fischman & Foltin, 1992) have demonstrated that when cocaine users are allowed to choose between taking cocaine versus engaging in a behavior that results in obtaining money, cocaine self-administration decreases as a function of the amount of money offered for the alternative behavior. One way of interpreting these results is that the availability of activities that are sources of alternative reinforcement can compete with drug taking. A recent epidemiological study found that youths who prayed, read the Bible, and went to church functions at least two times each week and also went to a revival or crusade at least a few times each month were about one-fifth as likely to have started taking drugs (Johanson, Duffy, & Anthony, 1996). In addition, a number of studies have shown that cocaine use, as well as that of other drugs, is less likely to occur in adults who take on traditional social roles, such as getting married and having children (Kandel & Raveis, 1989). These findings could easily be interpreted as demonstrating that having alternatives can act as a countervailing influence. Compared to punishment and response cost, the use of alternatives may be a more constructive approach to decreasing initiation and continuance of drug use and actually appears to be the foundation for many prevention and treatment approaches. For instance, one of the most successful treatments for cocaine abuse has been the use of contingency management procedures, where clients essentially have the choice of continuing drug use or receiving vouchers exchangeable for goods and services (Higgins et al., 1991). This treatment approach is described in Higgins & Wong, this volume.

COUNTERVAILING INFLUENCES—INDIVIDUAL SUSCEPTIBILITY

As characterized above, the origin of potential countervailing influences is the environment. However, countervailing influences may also be biological in origin. For instance, the rate of alcoholism is reduced in certain ethnic populations that metabolize alcohol differently, producing a metabolic product that makes people nauseous (Thomasson et al., 1991). There is also evidence from self-administration studies in humans that psychomotor stimulants produce aversive effects in some individuals, which in turn appear to decrease their drug-taking behavior. For instance, de Wit, Uhlenhuth, & Johanson (1986) demonstrated that individuals differed in terms of the extent to which they preferred amphetamine over placebo in an experimental laboratory study. In this choice situation, some individuals chose amphetamine (although they were not aware of what type of drug they were taking) on every opportunity, whereas another group of individuals avoided amphetamine. This variability in preference (i.e., reinforcing effects) was related to subjective effects. Although amphetamine choosers reported mood changes, such as increases in arousal and elation, nonchoosers reported significant increases in negative moods, such as anxious and depressive affect. Similar individual differences in mood in response to amphetamine were reported as early as the 1930s and have continued to be noted in subsequent studies (Angrist, Corwin, Bartlik, & Cooper, 1987; Davidoff & Reifenstein, 1937; von Felsinger, Lasagna, & Beecher, 1955). Whether these aversive subjective effects play a causal role in the failure of these individuals to self-administer amphetamine cannot be established from correlational studies (Johanson & de Wit, 1989). Nevertheless, a parsimonious explanation of the observed individual differences is that the aversive effects produced by amphetamine functioned as a countervailing influence.

COUNTERVAILING INFLUENCES— ENVIRONMENT–INDIVIDUAL INTERACTIONS

In summary, cocaine is a powerful reinforcer capable of controlling the initiation and maintenance of behavior leading to its administration. In animal self-administration studies, it is rare for animals to fail to acquire the behavior. All that is needed is simple availability. The implication of these findings is that most humans would also self-administer cocaine if it were accessible. However, we are postulating that there are countervailing influences that mitigate against this biological reality, and it is these countervailing influences, which may be biological or environmental in origin, that protect the vast majority from using cocaine. Further-more, as with all physiological processes, one would expect variability, with dif-ferences perhaps related to gene expression. Therefore, one of the biological con-straints we can consider is that the magnitude of the reinforcing effects of cocaine are normally distributed. Those for whom cocaine is more reinforcing, speaking relatively, would require a greater degree of protection from environmental sources, whereas for those with less biological vulnerability (i.e., cocaine's rein-forcing effects are relatively smaller), the efforts required to keep the individual drug-free would be considerably less. Some recent studies in which animals were allowed to self-administer amphetamine lend credence to the idea of the variabil-ity of reinforcing effects. For instance, Piazza, Deminiere, LeMoal, and Simon (1989) demonstrated that rats with certain characteristics, in this case greater lo-comotor activity in a novel environment, were more likely to begin to self-ad-minister amphetamine, and these differences were related to measures of brain function (Piazza et al., 1991a,b). However, it was still relatively easy to arrange conditions that resulted in the acquisition of self-administration in all rats. In this case, a few days of noncontingent drug administration converted the nonrespon-ders to responders (Piazza et al. 1991a,b).

ENVIRONMENTAL RISK FACTORS
FOR COCAINE USE

Hawkins et al. (1992) identified two major categories of environmental factors that might have a causal impact on drug use among adolescents and young adults: contextual and interpersonal. Contextual factors include risk factors that exist in the broad social context, such as laws and norms affecting drug-using behavior, extreme economic deprivation, and neighborhood deterioration. Much of the re-search on interpersonal factors has focused on adolescent drug use and, conse-quently, has encompassed three domains most relevant to this age group: family, peers, and school (Hawkins et al., 1992). The occupational domain can also be in-cluded (or substituted for school) when considering cocaine use by adults. Each of these domains contains a variety of risk and protective factors. For instance, the broadest domain cited by Hawkins et al. (1992), the family, encompassed a range of factors, including family drug-using behavior and attitudes, family management practices, family conflict, and low bonding among family members. Although do-mains often are considered to be distinct, there can be no question they influence each other. For instance, Patterson (1982) has demonstrated that ineffective fami-ly behavior management practices, such as poor discipline and parent–child inter-action, increase the likelihood that a child will associate with deviant and drug-us-ing peers, the strongest single risk factor for an individual's use of drugs.

In the remainder of the chapter, we will focus on two examples of environ-mental risk factors that have been shown to signal cocaine use: parent monitoring and neighborhood characteristics. In terms of the reinforcement model, both of these factors are suspected as playing an important role in the availability of cocaine, as well as other drugs. Also, as pointed out in our discussion of the reinforcement model, parent monitoring is a necessary condition for delivery of appropriate punishment. Neighborhood characteristics can be important determinants of the availability of alternative reinforcers, such as after-school activities for children and employment opportunities for adults. Although individual biological risk factors may be informative etiologically, at this point in the evolution of prevention and treatment strategies, their success will depend on the identification of environmental risk and protective factors. That is, environmental factors are particularly important, even if future research identifies specific genetic pathways to cocaine dependence, because at this point in time, they are easier to change than genetic factors (Kahn, 1996). Thus, malleability is a critical characteristic for any risk or protective factor that is to be the target of an intervention strategy. For this reason, parenting behaviors, including monitoring and supervision, have been identified as potential targets for intervention programs, which have tended to focus on children and their peers. Although neighborhood characteristics may be less malleable, they nonetheless can provide important clues for successful intervention approaches.

PARENT MONITORING

Our research on the impact of parent monitoring on drug sampling was motivated by research conducted at the Oregon Social Learning Center (e.g., Patterson et al., 1992), which identified family behavior management strategies as a potentially malleable target for interventions designed to reduce the risk of drug use and related problems. High levels of parent monitoring imply frequent surveillance and control over a child's environment and tracking his or her interactions within environments that extend beyond home or school. In addition, parent monitoring has been posited as the cornerstone for other important parenting behaviors (Dishion & McMahon, 1998). For instance, parents who fail to monitor their children's activities and are unaware of problem behavior cannot discipline their children effectively (i.e., deliver punishment with certitude). Consequently, it was hypothesized that parent monitoring could have an important impact on children's drug-using behavior through direct and indirect paths. Parent monitoring could have a direct influence on youthful drug taking by limiting opportunities for initiation and escalation of drug use. It also could influence drug use indirectly by limiting access to drug-using peers, the most powerful risk factor for drug use among children. Although a number of studies had found cross-sectional associations between parent monitoring and drug use, the lack of prospective studies left the causal role of parent monitoring unexplored. In addition, because previous studies on parent monitoring focused on adolescents rather than on children, many participants had already initiated drug use, so it was not possible to disentangle the temporal relationship between parent monitoring and drug sampling.

In our first prospective study of parent monitoring (Chilcoat et al., 1995), we compared the one year *incidence* of drug sampling by level of parent monitoring in an epidemiologically defined sample of 8–10-year-old urban-dwelling elementary school children in Baltimore, Maryland. These children originally were recruited for participation in a prevention trial to test interventions directed toward mental health and problem behavior. All children entering first grade in 19 public schools in Baltimore City in 1985 and 1986 were eligible for participation in the intervention, conducted as a collaboration between Baltimore City Public Schools and the Prevention Research Center, directed by Dr. Sheppard G. Kellam. The intervention is described in greater detail elsewhere (Kellam, 1991; Kellam et al., 1991).

Beginning in the spring of 1989, when the children were in third and fourth grades, annual assessments of the children's drug use and related behaviors were conducted. Each assessment consisted of a standardized interview conducted separately with each child, in private, by a trained interviewer in the child's school. A total of 1,112 children completed the assessments in 1989 and 1990 with complete data on parent monitoring and drug use, and these children form the sample for this prospective analysis.

To sharpen the focus on incidence of drug sampling and to control for the temporal sequencing of parent monitoring in relation to the initiation of drug use, our analysis was restricted to those children who did not report drug sampling at any time prior to the baseline interview. As a result, 165 students were excluded from analysis because their interview responses indicated drug use prior to the 1989 assessment, leaving 947 children who were at risk for initiating drug sampling.

Parent monitoring was measured by ten items adapted from Capaldi and Patterson (1988), which measured the presence of supervisory rules and surveillance of the child's whereabouts and behaviors outside the school. The parent monitoring items included parenting behaviors such as whether there were clear rules about when the child should come home after school or on weekends, whether adult supervision was present within one hour of the child coming home after school, and whether the child knew how to contact parents if they were not at home. Drug sampling was defined as taking alcohol without parental permission or using tobacco, marijuana, cocaine, or inhalants, at least once in the 1-year interval since the baseline interview. At this age, drug sampling was almost completely limited to alcohol and tobacco.

As hypothesized, lower levels of parent monitoring signaled increased risk of drug sampling. The 1-year incidence of drug sampling among children in the lowest quartile of parent monitoring was four times higher than for those in the highest quartile (7.7% vs. 1.9%, respectively). Parent monitoring was significantly associated with drug sampling even when we accounted for level of peer drug use and antisocial behaviors, two of the strongest predictors of drug use (Relative Risk = 3.62, 95% CI = 1.1–11.9, adjusted for age, sex, minority status, peer drug use, and overt antisocial behavior) (Figure 13.3). Furthermore, this relationship was maintained regardless of family composition and neighborhood of residence.

In a subsequent study (Chilcoat & Anthony, 1996), we extended the follow-up

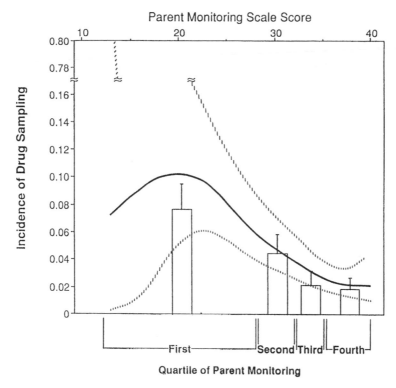

FIGURE 13.3   One-year incidence of drug sampling in relation to baseline parent monitoring for 947 children aged 8–10 years. Bars represent incidence of drug sampling for each quartile of parent monitoring (± SE). Quartile divisions correspond to parent monitoring scale scores. The fitted curve (solid line) with 95% confidence intervals (dotted lines) was estimated using generalized additive models.

interval 2 more years, through the assessment in spring 1992, so that we could examine the relationship between drug sampling and parent monitoring up to age 13 years. The sample base for this study consisted of 926 children who were interviewed each spring from 1989 to 1992. Results from this study indicated that as children enter adolescence, a period in which the incidence of alcohol and tobacco use increases, the apparent protective effect of parent monitoring diminishes. Survival analysis indicated that after age 11 the cumulative incidence of drug sampling did not vary by level of parent monitoring (as measured at the baseline assessment in 1989), although, as described above, parent monitoring signaled increased risk of drug sampling at ages 8 to 10. However, when we restricted our analysis to the initiation of illicit drugs (marijuana, inhalants, and cocaine), we found a striking difference in the incidence of use of these drugs by level of parent monitoring through this follow-up period (from 1990 to 1992). The 2-year incidence of initiating marijuana, inhalants, or cocaine in the lowest and highest

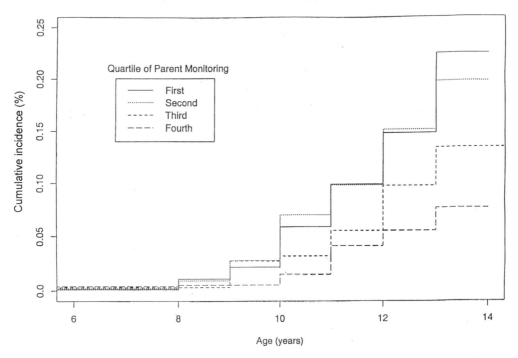

FIGURE 13.4   Cumulative incidence of marijuana, inhalant, or cocaine use at each age through the end of follow-up in spring 1992, stratified by quartile of parent monitoring. Cumulative incidence estimates were obtained by subtracting Kaplan-Meier survival estimates from one (log-rank test = 16.3, df = 3, $p < .001$).

quartiles of parent monitoring (measured in 1989) was 11 and 4%, respectively. In contrast to the cumulative incidence curves for initiation of any drug use, which became parallel after age 10 years, the corresponding curves for initiation of marijuana, cocaine, or inhalant use by quartile of parent monitoring continued to diverge through age 13 years, the oldest age at the end of follow-up (Figure 13.4). In addition, we found that a decreasing level of parent monitoring over time also signaled increased risk of starting to use these drugs. These findings suggest that parent monitoring is an environmental factor that plays a causal role in the initiation of drug sampling at relatively young ages, although the etiologic role of this factor can only be proven in experimental field trials.

In terms of our theoretical framework, parent monitoring reduces the likelihood of the transition to drug sampling as an environmental factor that limits youths' contact with opportunities to use drugs or prevents use once exposure opportunities occur. It also can be viewed as a countervailing influence, one perhaps involving punishment of behavior that is seen as drug-related. Because we focused on drug sampling as the outcome in these studies, which combines the first two stages in our model (exposure opportunities as well as drug sampling), we cannot distinguish on which of these stages parent monitoring has the strongest impact. Nonetheless, it is reasonable to conclude that it affects both of these stages. Because children with higher levels of parent monitoring are less likely to associate with drug-using peers, a primary source of drug availability, it appears that parents who effectively monitor their children limit drug-using opportunities indirectly by restricting contact with drug-using peers. In addition, high levels of parent monitoring signaled lower risk of drug use even among children at higher risk of drug use due to their own antisocial behaviors and friends' drug use. This finding suggests that parent monitoring blocks the transition to drug use even for children who are likely to have been exposed to opportunities to use drugs.

NEIGHBORHOOD

In this section, we report on several studies from our research group that have investigated neighborhood as a factor influencing cocaine use. The neighborhood provides a context that can alter an individual's risk of starting and escalating cocaine use. A basic premise in each of these studies is that the overall risk of cocaine use varies by neighborhood and therefore individual residents' risk of cocaine use varies as a function of the neighborhood in which they live. Although residents differ in their individual risk of cocaine use, there is a background risk contributed by the neighborhood. Therefore, an individual with a specific profile of individual risk factors (e.g., greater individual susceptibility to the reinforcing effects of the drug) would be at greater risk of using cocaine if he or she resided in one neighborhood versus another. Cocaine availability is hypothesized to be a major component of the risk contributed by the neighborhood, as well as residents' shared attitude toward use and socioeconomic factors at the level of the neighborhood, such as employment opportunities (Lillie-Blanton et al., 1993). In terms of our conceptual framework, the neighborhood is an important environmental factor that influences contact between the host and agent. Furthermore, it can have an impact at all stages of drug use. Finally, it can be seen as the source of alternative reinforcers or their lack.

Two studies that we discuss below examine whether children's perception of their neighborhood environment signals greater risk of transitions into the first two stages of use. The first study (Crum, Lillie-Blanton, & Anthony, 1996) focuses on exposure to opportunities to use cocaine, and the second study (Schütz, Chilcoat, & Anthony, 1993) focuses on the transition to drug sampling. We also will provide additional details on two studies mentioned earlier in this chapter (Chilcoat & Schütz, 1995; Lillie-Blanton et al., 1993), which sought to determine whether neighborhood of residence might explain the racial/ethnic differences in the prevalence of crack cocaine use.

In the first study, Crum et al. (1996) hypothesized that children living in disadvantaged neighborhoods would have greater exposure to opportunities to use drugs, especially for those that are less ubiquitous, such as cocaine. To investigate this hypothesis, they analyzed data from 1,416 urban-dwelling 11–14-year-old children who were interviewed in 1992 as part of the Prevention Research Center study, described above, comparing the prevalence of exposure opportunities for using various drugs by children's perceived level of neighborhood disadvantage. Neighborhood disadvantage was measured using an 18-item scale, which was a modification of an instrument developed by Elliot et al. (1989). Children's scale scores, determined by summing their responses, were divided into tertiles, in which the highest tertile included children living in the most disadvantaged neighborhoods, based on their reports. Results indicated that children in the highest tertile of neighborhood disadvantage were most likely to report past exposure opportunities for using each drug. The strongest association was found for cocaine, in which the odds of exposure opportunities for cocaine use among those in the highest tertile of neighborhood disadvantage was 5.6 times that of those in the lowest tertile (95% CI = 2.0–16.2). Children in the middle tertile had intermediate odds of exposure opportunities for all drugs, although these estimates generally were not statistically different from those in the lowest tertile.

In another study, Schütz et al. (1993) used the same scale of perceived neighborhood disadvantage to probe whether the cumulative incidence of drug sampling (i.e., any use of tobacco, alcohol without parents' permission, marijuana, cocaine, or inhalants) was highest among those children who rated their neighborhood as more disadvantaged. Following 925 children from the PRC study who were interviewed each year from 1989 to 1992, they employed survival analytic strategies to compare the cumulative incidence of drug sampling by tertile of neighborhood disadvantage. As was the case for exposure opportunities, neighborhood disadvantage signaled greater risk for drug sampling in the 3-year follow-up interval.

Instead of using direct measures of neighborhood characteristics, Lillie-Blanton et al. (1993) applied an alternative strategy to evaluate the influence of neighborhood on drug use. This analytic approach was designed to hold constant unmeasured characteristics of the neighborhood that influence use of crack cocaine and that are assumed to be shared by all its residents. It was conceivable that higher prevalence of crack use among African-Americans was determined to some extent by neighborhood factors because of the social conditions influencing the spread of the crack epidemic (Dunlap & Johnson, 1992; Hamid, 1992). Therefore, it was hypothesized that neighborhood-specific factors might account for the observed differences by race/ethnicity. Lillie-Blanton et al. (1993) used data from the 1988 NHSDA to test this hypothesis.

In order to hold constant neighborhood factors influencing the use of crack-cocaine, Lillie-Blanton et al. (1993) poststratified the NHSDA sample into area segments, which generally overlap census tracts and can be used as an indicator of neighborhood. Respondents were divided into risk sets that included at least one respondent who reported ever using crack cocaine and all other respondents in the same area segment. Risk sets were informative only if they included at least one crack user. Conditional logistic regression models were used to estimate the odds of crack use in African-Americans relative to Whites, conditioning on neighborhood. Use of conditional logistic regression models enabled statistical control of neighborhood factors related to crack use without measuring these factors directly. As hypothesized, when neighborhood was held constant by means of this analytic strategy, differences in crack-cocaine use by race/ethnicity disappeared. The odds of crack use for African-Americans relative to Whites was 0.85 (95% CI = 0.37–1.93) and 0.88 for Hispanics relative to Whites (95% CI = 0.47–1.67).

Chilcoat and Schütz (1995) sought to replicate these findings using data from the subsequent NHSDA, carried out to 1990. Using the same analytic strategy, they found similar results. The relative odds of crack use for African-Americans compared to Whites, which was 2.8 when neighborhood was not held constant, dropped to 1.37 (95% CI = 0.82–2.29), using the poststratification approach described above. Interestingly, as mentioned previously, although Hispanics had higher odds of lifetime crack use than Whites in the unadjusted data (RO [Relative Odds] = 1.46), they had lower odds after controlling for neighborhood of residence (RO = 0.52, 95% CI = 0.28–0.95). In addition, an interaction was detected between age and race/ethnicity. For African–Americans relative to Whites, there was no difference at younger ages; however, there was evidence of a difference at older ages, particularly in the 30–34-year-old age group. Using our conceptual framework, this difference might be explained, in part, by the lack of alternate reinforcers, such as employment opportunities among older (25–40 years old) African-Americans.

In summary, these studies provide additional evidence that factors at the level of the neighborhood might play an important etiologic role in transitions to various stages of drug use, especially exposure to drug-using opportunities and initiation of drug use. Additional research is needed to further our understanding of the specific mechanisms through which the neighborhood influences drug use outcomes. Based on the findings of Crum et al. (1996) in which neighborhood disadvantage was associated most strongly with cocaine exposure but not with more ubiquitous drugs, such as alcohol and tobacco, we speculate that the neighborhood's main influence is through street-level and residential patterns of availability. This is a testable hypothesis that can be investigated in future research.

CONCLUSION

In this chapter, we have set forth a conceptual framework combining the authors' distinctive perspectives from epidemiology and behavioral pharmacology, with the aim of guiding the search for factors that influence vulnerability to cocaine use and dependence. In particular, it is our hope that this integration of models will encourage researchers, clinicians, and policy makers to examine potential targets for intervention that can block the transition to each of the specified stages of drug use. The search for these factors should pay particular attention to the specific stage of drug use that is to be prevented, with the realization that the factors that have an influence on one stage of cocaine use might not have an impact at other stages. In addition, the target population's position in the developmental life course must also be taken into consideration. It is our hope that future research will be stimulated by the examples that we have presented. Clearly, important strides have been made in the understanding of cocaine vulnerability, but there can be no doubt that research integrating a range of scientific perspectives will produce a significantly greater yield.

ACKNOWLEDGMENTS

The authors would like to acknowledge Jim Anthony and Naomi Breslau for their intellectual guidance in the preparation of this chapter. CEJ would like to thank Charles Schuster for his encouragement and support.

REFERENCES

American Psychiatric Association. (1994). *Diagnostic and statistical manual of mental disorders,* (4th ed.). Washington, DC: American Psychiatric Association.

Angrist, B., Corwin, J., Bartlik, B., & Cooper, T. (1987). Early pharmacokinetics and clinical effects of oral d-amphetamine in normal subjects. *Biological Psychiatry, 22,* 1357–1368.

Anthony, J., & Helzer, J. (1991). Syndromes of drug abuse and dependence. In L. Robins & D. Regier (Eds.), *Psychiatric disorders in America.* (pp. 116–154). New York: Free Press.

Anthony, J. C., & Helzer, J. E. (1995). Epidemiology of drug dependence. In M. T. Tsuang, M. Tohen, & G. E. P. Zahner (Eds.), *Textbook in psychiatric epidemiology.* New York: John Wiley and Sons.

Anthony, J. C., & Petronis, K. R. (1995). Early-onset drug use and risk of later drug problems. *Drug and Alcohol Dependence, 40,* 9–15.

Anthony, J. C., Warner, L. A., & Kessler, R. C. (1994). Comparative epidemiology of dependence on tobacco, alcohol, controlled substances, and inhalants: Basic findings from the National Comorbidity Survey. *Experimental Clinical Psychopharmacology, 2,* 244–268.

Azrin, N. (1959). Punishment and recovery during fixed-ratio performance. *Journal of Experimental Analysis and Behavior, 3,* 301–305.

Azrin, N. H., & Holz, W. C. (1966). Punishment. In W. Honig (Ed.), *Operant behavior: Areas of research and application.* New York: Appleton-Century-Crofts.

Bergman, J., & Johanson, C. E. (1981). The effects of electric shock on responding maintained by cocaine in rhesus monkeys. *Pharmacology, Biochemistry & Behavior, 14,* 423–426.

Biederman, J., Wilens, T., Mick, E., Faraone, S. V., Weber, W., Curtis, S., Thornell, A., Pfister, K., Jetton, J. G., & Soriano, J. (1997). Is ADHD a risk factor for psychoactive substance use disorders: Findings from a four-year prospective follow-up study. *Journal of the American Academy of Children and Adolescent Psychiatry, 36,* 21–29.

Blum, K., Noble, E. P., Sheridan, P. J., Montgomery, A., Ritchie, T., Jagadeeswaran, P., Nogami, H., Briggs, A. H., & Cohn, J. B. (1990). Allelic association of human dopamine D_2 receptor gene in alcoholism. *Journal of the American Medical Association, 263,* 2055–2060.

Capaldi, D., & Patterson, G. (1988). *Psychometric properties of fourteen latent constructs from the Oregon Youth Study.* New York: Springer-Verlag.

Carroll, M. E., Lac, S. T., & Nygaard, S. T. (1989). A concurrently available nondrug reinforcer prevents the acquisition or decreases the maintenance of cocaine-reinforced behavior. *Psychopharmacology, 97,* 23–29.

Chen, K., & Kandel, D. (1995). The natural history of drug use from adolescence to the mid-thirties in a general population sample. *American Journal of Public Health, 85,* 41–47.

Cherek, D., Spiga, R., Bennett, R., & Grabowski, J. (1991). Human aggressive and escape responding: Effects of provocation frequency. *Psychological Records, 41,* 3–17.

Chilcoat, H., & Anthony, J. (1996). Impact of parent monitoring on initiation of drug use through late childhood. *Journal of the American Academy of Child and Adolescent Psychiatry, 35,* 91–100.

Chilcoat, H., Dishion, T., & Anthony, J. (1995). Parent monitoring and the incidence of drug sampling in urban elementary school children. *American Journal of Epidemiology, 141,* 25–31.

Chilcoat, H., & Schütz, C. (1995). Racial/ethnic and age differences in crack use within neighborhoods. *Addiction Research, 3,* 103–111.

Clayton, D., & Hills, M. (1993). *Statistical models in epidemiology.* Oxford: Oxford University Press.

Crum, R., Lillie-Blanton, M., & Anthony, J. (1996). Neighborhood environment and opportunity to use cocaine in late childhood and early adolescence. *Drug and Alcohol Dependence, 43,* 155–161.

Davidoff, E., & Reifenstein, E. G. (1937). The stimulating action of benzedrine sulfate. *Journal of the American Medical Association, 108,* 1770–1776.

de Wit, H., Uhlenhuth, E. H., & Johanson, C. E. (1986). Individual differences in the reinforcing and subjective effects of amphetamine and diazepam. *Drug and Alcohol Dependence, 16,* 341–360.

Deneau, G., Yanagita, T., & Seevers, M. H. (1969). Self-administration of psychoactive substances by the monkey. *Psychopharmacologia, 16,* 30–48.

Dishion, T., & McMahon, R. (1998). Parent monitoring and the prevention of problem behavior: A conceptual and empirical reformulation. *Clinical Child and Family Psychology Review 1,* 61–73.

Dunlap, E., & Johnson, B. (1992). The setting for the crack era: Macro forces, micro consequences (1960–1992). *Journal of Psychoactive Drugs, 24,* 307–321.

Elliott, D., Huizinga, D., & Menard, S. (1989). *Multiple problem youth: Delinquency, substance use, and mental health problems.* New York: Springer-Verlag.

Fischman, M. W., Foltin, R. W. (1992). Self-administration of cocaine by humans: A laboratory perspective. In *Cocaine: Scientific and social dimensions* (pp. 165–180). Chichester, UK: Wiley and Sons.

Fischman, M. W., & Johanson, C. E. (1996). Cocaine. In C. R. Schuster & M. I. Kuhar (Eds.), *Pharmacological aspects of drug dependence: Toward an integrated neurobehavioral approach. Handbook of Experimental Pharmacology.* (pp. 159–195). Berlin: Springer-Verlag.

Frost, W. (1941). *The papers of Wade Hampton Frost.* London: Oxford University Press.

Glantz, M., & Pickens, R. (Eds.). (1992). *Vulnerability to drug abuse.* Washington, DC: American Psychological Association.

Graham, J., Collins, L., Se, W., Chung, N., & Hansen, W. (1991). Modeling transitions in latent stage-sequential processes: A substance use prevention example. *Journal of Consulting Clinical Psychology, 59,* 48–57.

Hamid, A. (1992). The developmental cycle of a drug epidemic: The cocaine smoking epidemic of 1981–1991. *Journal of Psychoactive Drugs, 24,* 337–348.

Hawkins, J. D., Catalano, R. F., & Miller, J. Y. (1992). Risk and protective factors for alcohol and other drug problems in adolescence and early adulthood: Implications for substance abuse prevention. *Psychological Bulletin, 112,* 64–105.

Higgins, S. T., Delaney, D. D., Budney, A. J., Bickel, W. K., Hughes, J. R., Foerg, F., & Fenwick, J. W. (1991). A behavioral approach to achieving initial cocaine abstinence. *American Journal of Psychiatry, 148,* 1218–1224.

Hodos, W. (1961). Progressive ratio as a measure of reward strength. *Science, 134,* 943–944.

Johanson, C., Duffy, F., & Anthony, J. (1996). Associations between drug use and behavioral repertoire in urban youths. *Addiction, 91,* 523–534.

Johanson, C. E. (1978). Drugs as reinforcers. In D. E. Blackman, & D. J. Sanger (Eds.), *Contemporary research in behavioral pharmacology* (pp. 325–390). New York: Plenum Press.

Johanson, C. E., & de Wit, H. (1989). The use of choice procedures for assessing the reinforcing properties of drugs in humans. In M. W. Fischman & N. Mello (Eds.), *Assessing the abuse liability of drugs in humans.* (pp. 171–209). Monograph Series #92. Washington, DC: National Institute on Drug Abuse.

Johanson, C. E., & Schuster, C. R. (1995). Cocaine. In F. E. Bloom & D. J. Kupfer (Eds.), *Psy-*

chopharmacology: The fourth generation of progress (pp. 1685–1697). New York: Raven Press, Ltd.

Johnston, L., O'Malley, P., & Bachman, J. (1995). *National survey results on drug use from the Monitoring the Future Study, 1975–1994.* Washington, DC: National Institute on Drug Abuse.

Kahn, P. (1996). Coming to grips with genes and risk. *Science, 274,* 496–498.

Kandel, D. B., Raveis, V. H. (1989). Cessation of illicit drug use in young adulthood. *Archives of General Psychiatry, 46,* 109–116.

Kandel, D. B., & Yamaguchi, K. (1993). From beer to crack: Developmental patterns of involvement in drugs. *American Journal of Public Health, 83,* 851–855.

Kellam, S., & Ensminger, M. (1980). Studying children epidemiologically. In F. Earls (Ed.), *Theory and method in child psychiatric epidemiology.* Watson, NY: International Monograph Series in Psychosocial Epidemiology.

Kellam, S. G. (1991). A developmental epidemiological research program for the prevention of mental distress and disorder, heavy drug use, and violent behavior. In W. Parry-Jones & N. Queloz (Eds.), *Mental health and deviance in inner cities* (pp. 101–108). Geneva, Switzerland: World Health Organization.

Kellam, S. G., Simon, M. B., & Ensminger, M. E. (1983). Antecedents in first grade of teenage substance abuse and psychological well-being: A ten-year community-wide prospective study. In D. Ricks & B. S. Dohrenwend (Eds.), *Origins of psychopathology* (pp. 17–42). Cambridge, UK: Cambridge University Press.

Kellam, S. G., Wertheimer-Larsson, L., Dolan, L., Brown, C. H., & Mayer, L. (1991). Developmental epidemiologically based preventive trials: Baseline modeling of early target behaviors and depressive symptoms. *American Journal of Community Psychology, 19,* 563–583.

Kessler, R. C., McGonagle, K. A., Zhao, S., Nelson, C., Hughes, M., Eshleman, S., Wittchen, H.-U., & Kendler, K. (1994). Lifetime and 12-month prevalence of DSM-III-R psychiatric disorders in the United States: Results from the National Comorbidity Survey. *Archives of General Psychiatry, 51,* 8–19.

Kilbey, M. M., Breslau, N., & Andreski, P. (1992). Cocaine use and dependence in young adults: Associated psychiatric disorders and personality traits. *Drug and Alcohol Dependence, 29,* 283–290.

Kleber, H. (1994). The war on drugs (letter). *New England Journal of Medicine, 331,* 129.

Koob, G. F., & Bloom, F. E. (1988). Cellular and molecular mechanisms of drug dependence. *Science, 242,* 715–723.

Lillie-Blanton, M., Anthony, J. C., & Schuster, C. R. (1993). Probing the meaning of racial/ethnic group comparisons in crack-cocaine smoking. *Journal of the American Medical Association, 269,* 993–997.

Lillienfeld, D., & Stolley, P. (1994). *Foundations of epidemiology (3rd ed.).* New York: Oxford University Press.

Mannuzza, S., Klein, R. G., Bessler, A. Malloy, P., & LaPadula, M. (1993). Adult outcome of hyperactive boys. *Archives of General Psychiatry, 50,* 565–576.

Mayer, L. S., & Warsi, G. (1997). *Attributable risks and prevented fractions in a discrete mediational model.* Unpublished manuscript.

Nader, M. A., & Woolverton, W. L. (1991). Effects of increasing the magnitude of an alternative reinforcer on drug choice in a discrete-trials choice procedure. *Psychopharmacology, 105,* 169–174.

Nader, M. A., Hedeker, D., & Woolverton, W. L. (1993). Behavioral economics and drug choice: Effects of unit price on cocaine self-administration. *Drug and Alcohol Dependence, 33,* 193–199.

National Institute of Justice. (1993). Drug use forecasting: 1992 annual report: Drugs and crime in America's cities. Washington, DC: Department of Justice.

Newcomb, M. (1995). Drug use etiology among ethnic minority adolescents. In G. Botvin, S. Schinke, & M. Orlandi (Eds.), *Drug abuse prevention with multiethnic youth* (pp. 105–129). Thousand Oaks, CA: Sage Publications.

Patterson, G. (1982). *Coercive family process.* Eugene, OR: Castalia Publishing Co.

Patterson, G., Reid, J. R., Dishion, T. J. (1992). *Antisocial boys.* Eugene, OR: Castalia Publishing Co.

Piazza, P. V., Deminiere, J.-M., LeMoal, M., & Simon, H. (1989). Factors that predict individual vulnerability to amphetamine self-administration. *Science, 245,* 1511–1513.

Piazza, P. V., Deminiere, J.-M., Maccari, S., LeMoal, M., Mormede, P., & Simon, H. (1991a). Individual vulnerability to drug self-administration: Action of corticosterone on dopaminergic neuronal systems as a possible pathophysiological mechanism. In P. Wilner & S. Scheel-Kruger (Eds.), *The mesolimbic dopamine system: From motivation to action* (pp. 473–495).

Piazza, P. V., Maccari, S., Deminiere, J.-M., LeMoal, M., Mormede, P., & Simon, H. (1991b). Corticosterone levels determine individual vulnerability to amphetamine self-administration. *Proceedings of the National Academy of Science USA, 88,* 2088–2092.

Robins, L. (1984). The natural history of adolescent drug use. *American Journal of Public Health, 74,* 656–657.

Robins, L. N., & Przybeck, T. R. (1985). Age of onset of drug use as a factor in drug and other disorders. In *Implications for Prevention: National Institute on Drug Abuse Research Monograph* (pp. 178–192). Washington, DC: U.S. Government Printing Office.

Rothman, K. (1986). *Modern epidemiology.* Boston, MA: Little, Brown and Co.

Rounsaville, B. J., Anton, S. F., Carroll, K., Budde, D., Prusoff, B. A., & Gawin, F. (1991). Psychiatric diagnoses of treatment-seeking cocaine abusers. *Archives of General Psychiatry, 48,* 43–51.

Schütz, C., Chilcoat, H., & Anthony, J. (1993). *Disadvantaged neighborhoods and early initiation of drug use.* Presented at the World Psychiatric Association, Section of Epidemiology and Community Psychiatry, Groningen, Netherlands.

Shedler, J., & Block, J. (1990). Adolescent drug use and psychological health: A longitudinal inquiry. *American Psychology, 45,* 612–630.

Smith, S. S., O'Hara, B. F., Persico, A. M., Gorelick, D. A., Newlin, D. B., Vlahoy, D., Solomon, L., Pickens, R., & Uhl, G. R. (1992). Genetic vulnerability to drug abuse: The dopamine D2 receptor TaqI B1 RFLP appears more frequently in polysubstance abusers. *Archives of General Psychiatry, 49,* 723–727.

Substance Abuse and Mental Health Services Administration (SAMHSA). (1994). *Data from the Drug Abuse Warning Network* (DAWN) *Annual Emergency Room Data 1992.* Washington, DC: US Government Printing DHHS Publication No. (SMA) 94-2080.

Substance Abuse and Mental Health Services Administration (SAMHSA). (1995). *National Household Survey on Drug Abuse: Main Findings 1993.* Washington, DC: US Government Printing Office DHHS Publication No. (SMA) 95-3020.

Thomasson, H., Edenberg, H., Crabb, D., Mai, X., Jerome, R., Li, T., Want, S., Win, Y., Lu, R., & Yin, S. (1991). Alcohol and aldehyde dehydrogenase genotypes and alcoholism in Chinese men. *American Journal of Human Genetics, 48,* 677–681.

Uhl, G. R., Perisco, A. M., & Smith, S. S. (1992). Current excitement with D2 dopamine receptor alleles in substance abuse. *Archives of General Psychiatry, 49,* 157–160.

von Felsinger, J. M., Lasagna, L., & Beecher, H. K. (1955). Drug-induced mood changes in man. I. Personality and reactions to drugs. *Journal of the American Medical Association, 157,* 1113–1119.

Woody, G. E., McLellan, A. T., Luborsky, L., & O'Brien, C. P. (1985). Sociopathy and psychotherapy outcome. *Archives of General Psychiatry, 42,* 1081–1086.

World Health Organization. (1993). *The ICD-10 Classification of Mental and Behavioral Disorders: Diagnostic Criteria for Research.* Geneva, Switzerland: World Health Organization.

Yanagita, T. (1973). An experimental framework for evaluation of dependence liability in various types of drugs in monkeys. *Bulletin on Narcotics, 25,* 57–64.

14

TREATING COCAINE ABUSE: WHAT DOES RESEARCH TELL US?

STEPHEN T. HIGGINS

Departments of Psychiatry and Psychology
University of Vermont
Burlington, Vermont

CONRAD J. WONG

Department of Psychology
University of Vermont
Burlington, Vermont

INTRODUCTION

Despite significant decreases during the past decade in the overall number of cocaine users in the United States, the number of heavy users and the amount of cocaine that they consume has remained stable or increased (Everingham & Rydell, 1994; Substance Abuse and Mental Health Services Administration (SAMHSA), 1997). It is these heavy users who contribute most to the serious adverse individual and societal effects associated with cocaine abuse, including crime and incarceration, drug-exposed neonates, AIDS and other infectious disease, poverty, trauma, and violence (Konkol & Olsen, 1996; Montoya & Atkinson, 1996; National Institute of Justice, 1997; SAMHSA, 1997; Tardiff et al., 1994).

As heavy cocaine use and associated problems persist, treatment demand for cocaine abuse is growing. According to the most recent report by the National Association of State Alcohol and Drug Abuse Directors, for example, treatment admissions for primary cocaine abuse increased approximately 1.7-fold between 1989-1995 (Figure 14.1, National Association of State Alcohol and Drug Abuse Directors, 1997). No significant downturn in that trend is expected soon. In light of such well-documented need and demand for cocaine abuse treatment, the pur-

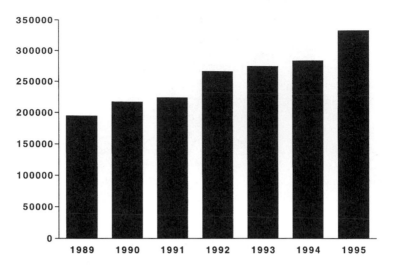

FIGURE 14.1   Number of admissions for primary cocaine abuse to state-funded drug abuse treatment facilities in the United States from 1989–1995. (From National Association of State Alcohol and Drug Abuse Directors, 1997.)

pose of this chapter is to review what has been learned scientifically about how to effectively treat this disorder. This chapter focuses on individuals who are seeking or enrolled in treatment for cocaine abuse (i.e., primary cocaine abusers). Interested readers should see chapter 15 by Silverman et al., this volume for a discussion of treatments for cocaine abuse among individuals seeking or enrolled in treatment for opioid dependence.

TREATING COCAINE ABUSE

IN-HOSPITAL VERSUS OUT-OF-HOSPITAL PATIENT CARE

A primary question that must be addressed in treating cocaine abuse is whether hospitalization is necessary for a positive outcome. The goal is to use the least restrictive setting likely to facilitate a positive outcome (e.g., American Psychiatric Association, 1995).

There are two published reports explicitly examining this issue. In an uncontrolled study, cocaine abusers seeking treatment at a private psychiatric hospital ($N = 149$) were compared to cocaine abusers seeking treatment at a publicly funded outpatient clinic ($N = 149$) (Budde, Rounsaville, & Bryant, 1992). Based on intake interviews, those seeking inpatient care used more cocaine and alcohol, had greater drug-related social impairment and psychopathology, and were more socioeconomically advantaged than those seeking outpatient care. A subsample of

94 individuals from the two settings combined (32% of original sample) were assessed 1 year after the intake interview. Inpatients showed greater improvements in the severity of cocaine abuse and psychopathology at follow-up than outpatients, even after controlling for differences in socioeconomic status. Although no causal inferences can be made based on this uncontrolled study, the results suggested that inpatient settings may attract a more impaired population and, despite that apparent disadvantage, produce greater clinical improvements than outpatient settings.

In a randomized trial, 111 male veterans who met criteria for cocaine dependence and were free of acute medical problems requiring hospitalization were randomly assigned to 1 month of inpatient care or day-hospital treatment (Alterman et al., 1994). More of those assigned to inpatient than day hospital completed the recommended 1-month treatment (89% vs. 54%), but a larger proportion of day hospital than inpatient treatment completers participated in a recommended regimen of aftercare (83% vs. 35%). There were no differences between the two treatments at a 7-month follow-up on measures of cocaine use or the need for additional treatment. Both treatment groups decreased cocaine and other drug use compared to pretreatment levels, and only a quarter to a third of patients in the two groups required additional treatment during the follow-up period. The most striking differences observed between the two treatments were that average provider cost per subject for inpatient treatment was $6,146 versus $2,260 for those assigned to day hospital, and wage loss by patients in inpatient versus day-hospital treatment was $18/day versus $8/day.

Based on the available evidence, inpatient treatment is difficult to justify as a first-choice intervention for cocaine abuse. Inpatient care is much more expensive than less restrictive settings and there is no evidence from controlled trials demonstrating that it produces superior outcomes. Moreover, to our knowledge, there has yet to be a controlled clinical trial reported demonstrating the efficacy of inpatient treatment for cocaine abuse. By contrast, several such trials have been reported for outpatient settings and, at least, one for a day-hospital setting (see pp. 349–354). There is no doubt that some individuals may require inpatient treatment due to the recalcitrance of their cocaine use when treated in less restrictive settings, because of complications related to a psychiatric or other medical condition, or for some other reason. Unfortunately, criteria to a priori identify individuals needing inpatient treatment are not available (McKay, McLellan, & Alterman, 1992). At this time, outpatient or day-hospital settings appear to be the appropriate first choice for treating cocaine abuse.

EARLY ATTRITION

A serious problem in treating cocaine abuse is that as many as half of those who contact clinics seeking treatment fail to show for their initial appointment (Festinger, Lamb, Kountz, Kirby, & Marlowe, 1995; Festinger, Lamb, Kirby, & Marlowe, 1996). In a retrospective study conducted in an urban outpatient clinic, the only significant predictor of attendance at the intake appointment was the number of days between initial phone contact and the scheduled appointment (Festinger et al., 1995). Those who were provided an appointment within 24 h of the initial contact were 26% more likely (83% vs. 57%) to attend that initial appointment than those scheduled at a later time. Those findings were supported in a subsequent prospective study in which 78 cocaine abusers seeking outpatient treatment were randomly assigned to either an accelerated or standard intake condition (Festinger et al., 1996). In the accelerated condition, interviews were scheduled on the same day as the initial contact or on the morning of the next business day, while in the standard condition they were scheduled 1–3 days after the initial contact. Fifty-nine percent (23/39) of those assigned to the accelerated protocol attended their scheduled interview versus 33% (13/39) assigned to the standard protocol. No significant differences in treatment retention rates were discerned between patients who entered via the accelerated or standard intake procedures, suggesting that this intervention was doing more than simply entering "less motivated" individuals who would then go on to have higher dropout rates.

Another trial conducted with a mixed sample of drug abusers (35% primary cocaine abusers) produced comparable results in terms of the efficacy of the accelerated intake in reducing attrition (Stark et al., 1990). However, during-treatment dropout rates appeared to be higher in the accelerated than standard conditions in that study, suggesting that the benefits of the accelerated intake might be offset by higher rates of later attrition.

Overall, accelerated intakes appear to be a low-cost and effective method for reducing the high attrition rates commonly observed between the initial clinic contact and intake interview. Additional research is needed to determine whether accelerated intakes reliably increase during-treatment attrition rates and, if so, whether they do so to an extent that negates any clinical benefits that might accrue from the decreases in early attrition that they produce. Other methods for reducing early attrition (e.g., incentives to attend intake sessions) should be investigated as well.

TREATMENT DURATION, INTENSITY, AND FORMAT

What is an optimal duration, frequency, and format (group vs. individual) of therapy for cocaine abuse? Unfortunately, there has been little experimental investigation of these treatment parameters. Reports from nonexperimental studies with illicit-drug abusers indicate that patients who are retained in treatment for 3 or more months have significantly better outcomes than those who terminate earlier (Hubbard et al., 1984; Simpson, 1984). Similar relationships were noted in several more recent studies with cocaine abusers, with subjects who received more treatment having better 6- and 12-month outcomes (Carroll, Power, Bryant, & Rounsaville, 1993; Wells, Peterson, Gainey, Hawkins, & Catalano, 1994), but there are exceptions (Kang et al., 1991). Treatment durations of 3 to 6 months are typical in clinical trials with cocaine abusers, but whether such durations improve outcomes compared to briefer interventions is unknown (Carroll, Rounsaville, Gordon, et al., 1994; Higgins, Budney, Bickel, et al., 1994; Wells et al., 1994).

Also common in clinical trials are regimens of at least once weekly therapy sessions plus additional clinic contact for urinalysis testing and other monitoring of progress during the initial 3 or more months of treatment (Carroll, Rounsaville, Gordon, 1994; Higgins, Budney, Bickel, Foerg, Donham, et al., 1994). How those frequencies of treatment delivery and other clinic contact influence outcome is unknown. In a comparison of cocaine-dependent individuals assigned (not randomized) to 2 weeks of orientation and then 4 weeks of 6 vs. 12 h per week of day hospital, pre- to posttreatment outcomes were positive and comparable across the two intensities (Alterman et al., 1996).

Regarding the issue of group versus individual therapy, we are aware of only one controlled trial on this topic (Oswald, Schmitz, Jacks, Day, & Grabowski, 1996). The study was a randomized comparison of group versus individually delivered Relapse-Prevention therapy during aftercare with cocaine-dependent adults. Pre- to posttreatment outcomes were positive and did not differ between the group and individual therapy formats.

Caution needs to be exercised in drawing conclusions based on the Alterman et al. (1996) and Oswald et al. (1996) studies. Pre- to posttreatment improvements are not grounds to infer that treatment produced the observed changes. Differential changes between treatment groups (i.e., treatment effects) are needed to support such causal inferences. In the absence of treatment effects, one cannot be sure whether the treatments under investigation were active. If it so happened that they were not, then parametric manipulations are going to produce negative results. We have no way of knowing whether that was the case in these two studies, but such a possibility should be considered.

We know of no other studies explicitly addressing the effects of treatment intensity, duration, or format with cocaine abusers. Prospective, experimental studies on these topics are sorely needed. Empirically based recommendations for clinical practice at this time must come from the results described above in combination with information from those controlled clinical trials that have demonstrated treatment effects (see pp. 349–354). Based on that information, a treatment duration of 3 or more months, with a minimum frequency of once-per-week therapy, including individual therapy, coupled with at least weekly or more frequent urine toxicology screening and other monitoring of clinical status is recommended.

TREATMENT CONTENT

The next question is one of treatment content: What treatments have been shown to be efficacious in reducing cocaine abuse in controlled clinical trials?

Behavioral Treatments

We describe next the behavioral, or psychosocial, interventions demonstrated thus far to be efficacious in controlled clinical trials with cocaine abusers, and hence the ones that, in our opinion, are to be recommended at this time. These interventions generally share a common feature of utilizing well-established psychological principles, including those from operant and respondent conditioning and social-learning theory. Treatments that include incentives delivered contingent on documented cocaine abstinence, either in the form of vouchers exchangeable for retail items or work or housing opportunities with homeless abusers, have the greatest empirical support at this time.

Community Reinforcement Approach Plus Contingency Management

Four controlled trials support the efficacy of an outpatient intervention based on operant conditioning, which combines contingency management and the Community Reinforcement Approach (CRA) (Higgins et al., 1991; Higgins et al., 1993b; Higgins, Budney, Bickel, Foerg, Donham, et al., 1994; Higgins & Silverman, in press). Additional trials support the efficacy of particular components of this multielement treatment (e.g., see chapter 15 by Silverman et al., this volume).

The primary contingency-management procedure in this treatment is one in which patients earn vouchers exchangeable for retail items contingent on urinalysis testing documenting recent cocaine abstinence. Urinalysis monitoring is conducted thrice weekly for 12 weeks and then twice weekly during weeks 13–24 of the 24-week intervention. The voucher system is in effect for weeks 1–12 of treatment, and during weeks 13–24 subjects receive a $1.00 state lottery ticket per negative specimen. The average value of incentives earned across the 24 weeks has been approximately $3.50 per treatment day.

CRA is delivered by professional therapists during twice weekly therapy sessions of 1.5-h duration during weeks 1–12 and once weekly during weeks 13–24. All counseling is delivered in individual-therapy sessions. The goal of CRA is to systematically alter the drug user's environment so that reinforcement density from nondrug sources is relatively high during sobriety and low during drug use. The typical components of CRA are disulfiram therapy in conjunction with procedures to support medication compliance for those patients who also abuse alcohol; reciprocity relationship counseling for those who have spouses; a job-finders intervention for unemployed clients or those wishing to change jobs; social-skills training; assistance in altering social and recreational practices; and drug refusal and other skills training.

Two trials examined the efficacy of this treatment by comparing it to standard outpatient drug abuse counseling (Higgins et al., 1991; Higgins et al., 1993b). The first trial was 12 weeks in duration and patients were assigned sequentially to the two treatment groups. The second trial was 24 weeks in duration and patient assignment to the two treatment groups was random. In both trials, the behavioral treatment retained patients significantly longer and documented significantly longer periods of continuous cocaine abstinence than standard counseling. For example, in the randomized trial, 58% of patients assigned to the behavioral treatment completed 24 weeks of treatment versus 11% of those assigned to standard counseling. Furthermore, 68% and 42% of patients in the behavioral group were documented to have achieved 8 and 16 weeks of continuous cocaine abstinence versus 11 and 5% of those in the counseling group.

In a third trial, patients were randomly assigned to receive CRA with or without vouchers (Higgins, Budney, Bickel, Foerg, Donham, et al., 1994). Vouchers significantly improved treatment retention and cocaine abstinence. Seventy-five percent of patients in the group with vouchers completed 24 weeks of treatment versus 40% in the group without vouchers. Average duration of continuous cocaine abstinence that would be documented via urinalysis testing were 11.7 ± 2.0 weeks in the former versus 6.0 ± 1.5 weeks in the latter (Figure 14.2). At the end of the 24-week treatment period, significant decreases from pretreatment scores were observed in both treatment groups on the ASI family/social and alcohol scales, with no differences between the groups. Both groups also decreased on the ASI drug scale, but the magnitude of changes was significantly greater in the voucher than the no-voucher group. Only the voucher group showed a significant improvement on the ASI psychiatric scale.

Follow-up results at 6, 9, and 12 months after treatment entry were reported from the randomized trial comparing the CRA plus vouchers treatment to drug abuse counseling and from the trial comparing CRA with and without vouchers

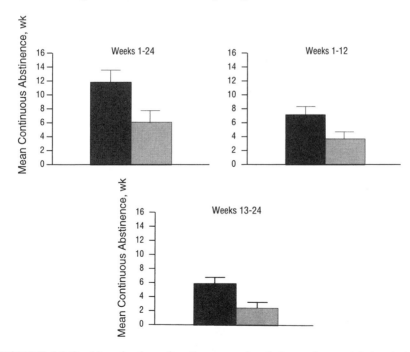

FIGURE 14.2 Mean durations of continuous cocaine abstinence documented via urinalysis testing are shown for each treatment group during the entire 24-week treatment, and separately for periods when vouchers were available (weeks 1–12) and unavailable (weeks 13–24). Voucher and no-voucher groups are represented by solid and shaded bars, respectively; bars represent 1 SEM. (From Higgins et al., 1994a. Copyright © 1994, American Medical Association.)

(Higgins et al., 1995). In the trial comparing CRA with vouchers to drug abuse counseling, significantly greater cocaine abstinence was documented via urinalysis at 9- and 12-month follow-ups in the former; both groups showed comparable and significant improvements on the ASI. In the trial comparing CRA with and without vouchers, there were no significant differences in urinalysis results. However, the magnitude of improvement on the ASI composite drug scale was significantly larger in the voucher group throughout follow-up, and only the voucher group showed significant improvement on the ASI psychiatric scale.

A fourth trial supporting the efficacy of the voucher program was recently completed (Higgins, Wang, Budney, English, & Kennedy, 1997). Seventy cocaine-dependent adults were randomly assigned to receive CRA plus contingent or noncontingent vouchers. In the contingent group, vouchers were only delivered if urinalysis results documented recent cocaine abstinence, whereas in the noncontingent group vouchers were delivered independent of urinalysis results. In preliminary analyses, the contingent group averaged approximately 8.5 weeks of continuous cocaine abstinence during the 24-week trial versus approximately 6.0 weeks in the control group, which is not a statistically significant difference. However, greater than three fold more patients in the contingent group (36% vs. 12%) achieved 12 or more weeks of continuous cocaine abstinence, which is a significant difference.

Studies examining the efficacy of the disulfiram component of this treatment are described below (see p. 355). Lastly, another component that was investigated was the use of a contingency contract between patients and significant others wherein the significant other provided social reinforcement contingent on the patient providing cocaine-negative urinalysis results. Having a significant other participate in treatment in this manner was a significant predictor of positive treatment outcomes in a retrospective study of this intervention (Higgins, Budney, Bickel, & Badger, 1994). That study was followed up by a randomized trial (Higgins, unpublished data). Fifty-eight cocaine-dependent patients were randomized to two treatment groups. One group was permitted to include a significant other in treatment and to engage in the behavioral contracting while the other group could not. No significant treatment differences were discernible on retention or during-treatment cocaine abstinence. Follow-up results have not yet been analyzed.

Day Treatment plus Contingent Housing and Work Therapy

A treatment combining day treatment (same as day hospital but in a nonmedical setting) with access to work therapy and housing contingent on drug abstinence has been demonstrated to be efficacious with homeless substance abusers (72% were primary crack cocaine abusers) (Milby et al., 1996). Subjects were 176 individuals who met diagnostic criteria for one or more substance abuse disorders and McKinny Act criteria for homelessness. They were randomized to receive enhanced or usual care. Enhanced care involved 2 months of clinic attendance for 5.5 h each weekday, transportation to and from the clinic, clinic-provided lunch, psychoeducational groups, and individualized counseling. During the last 4 months of the 6-month treatment, intensity of day treatment was reduced to meeting two afternoons per week, and subjects were eligible to participate in a work-therapy program refurbishing condemned houses and also to reside in the refurbished housing for a modest rental fee. Participation in the work program and housing were contingent on drug abstinence documented through weekly, random urinalysis testing. Drug-positive results precluded subjects from working and required them to vacate their apartment within 2 weeks. Work could be resumed and housing reoccupied by submitting two consecutive drug-free urine specimens (2 weeks of abstinence). Usual care consisted of a twice weekly, 12-step-oriented group and individual counseling, medical evaluation and treatment or referral for identified problems, and referrals to community agencies for housing and vocational services. Usual care was provided without a specified end-point, although the frequency of services decreased as subjects progressed. AIDS education and a monthly support group were available to subjects in both treatment conditions.

Enhanced care increased cocaine abstinence significantly at the 2-month but not the 6- or 12-month assessments. Enhanced care also produced greater reductions in alcohol use at each assessment and significantly fewer days homeless at the 6- and 12-month assessments. No significant differences between the groups were observed in measures of employment.

Preliminary results from a second trial supporting the efficacy of day treatment plus contingent work therapy and housing in the treatment of homeless cocaine abusers were presented at a recent national meeting (Milby et al., 1997).

Relapse Prevention

Relapse prevention (RP) is based in social learning theory and teaches patients to recognize high-risk situations for drug use, to implement alternative coping strategies when confronted with high-risk events, and to apply strategies to prevent a full-blown relapse should an episode of drug use occur (Marlatt & Gordon, 1985). As is described here, the evidence supporting the efficacy of RP is encouraging but mixed.

The first trial reported on this topic was conducted with 42 adults who met criteria for cocaine abuse or dependence (Carroll, Rounsaville, & Gawin, 1991). Patients were randomly assigned to RP or Interpersonal Psychotherapy (IP), which teaches strategies for improving social and interpersonal problems (Carroll et al., 1991). Both treatments were delivered by professional therapists during 12 weeks of weekly therapy. All patients also received weekly monitoring of cocaine use and other aspects of functioning and random urinalysis monitoring. Retention generally was better with RP than IP throughout treatment, although a statistically significant difference was observed only at week 4 of the 12-week trial, when 86% of RP patients remained in treatment versus 57% of IP patients. Nonsignificant trends were evidence in the same direction for continuous cocaine abstinence, with 57% of those who received RP versus 33% of those who received IP achieving ≥ 3 weeks of continuous cocaine abstinence during the 12-week trial.

In a second trial, RP and case management were compared in a 2 × 2 design in which patients also received either desipramine or placebo (Carroll, Rounsaville, Gordon, et al., 1994). One hundred thirty-nine patients were randomized to one of four treatment groups. Clinic management was designed to provide a nonspecific therapeutic relationship and an opportunity to monitor patients' clinical status. Both treatments were delivered in weekly therapy sessions during 12 weeks of treatment. All patients also received weekly urinalysis testing and other clinical monitoring. All treatment groups improved from pre- to posttreatment on measures of cocaine use and the Addiction Severity Index (ASI) drug, alcohol, family/social, and psychiatric composite scales, but there were no significant main effects for psychosocial (RP vs. case management) or drug treatment (desipramine vs. placebo). At 1-year follow-up, those patients who received RP reported significantly higher levels of cocaine abstinence than patients who received clinic management (Figure 14.3) (Carroll, Rounsaville, Nich, et al., 1994). Differences in cocaine use were not discernible in urinalysis testing. RP focuses on teaching skills to prevent relapse, and it seems logical that those skills may have contributed to the difference in cocaine use observed during follow-up.

Wells et al. (1994) reported negative results in their trial with RP. One hundred ten cocaine abusers were alternatively assigned to RP or 12-step-based counseling. RP and counseling were delivered in group formats by professional, male–female cotherapy teams. One member of each team was trained in the respective treatment approach and the other was trained more eclectically. Groups met for 2-h sessions twice weekly for 2 weeks, then once weekly for the next 10 weeks, and finally at 4-week intervals for the remainder of the 24-week intervention period. Random urinalysis monitoring was conducted monthly. No significant differences

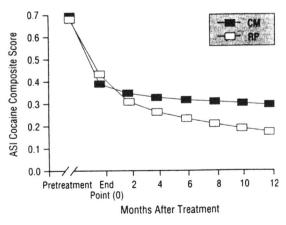

FIGURE 14.3   Addiction Severity Index (ASI) cocaine composite scores are shown for the clinic management (closed symbols) and relapse prevention (open symbols) groups at pretreatment, end-of-treatment, and every 2 months during 1-year follow-up. (From Carroll et al., 1994b. Copyright © 1994, American Medical Association.)

between the two groups were discerned in retention or cocaine use during the 24-week outpatient trial or at a 6-month follow-up evaluation.

Other Interventions

Several other treatments for cocaine abuse appear promising based on preliminary findings reported at scientific meetings, mentioned in book chapters, and elsewhere. These include active-cue-exposure therapy (Childress et al., 1993), coping-skills training (Rohsenow, 1993), neurobehavioral treatment (Rawson et al., 1995), and contingency management with special populations (Elk, 1997; Higgins & Silverman, in press; Shaner et al., 1995). Several of these interventions are currently being evaluated in randomized trials.

Two additional interventions were evaluated in published, randomized trials (Hall et al., 1994; Hughes et al., 1995). In the study by Hughes et al., 53 women entering residential treatment for cocaine abuse were randomly assigned to a condition in which one or two of their children were permitted to reside with them or to a usual-care condition in which children were placed with the best available caretaker. Average length of stay in treatment was approximately threefold longer in the experimental than control conditions (300.4 vs. 101.9 mean days of retention). No other measures of outcome were reported.

Hall et al.'s (1994) study focused on the evaluation of desipramine therapy and procedures for improving treatment participation. Subjects were 94 male veterans who met diagnostic criteria for cocaine dependence and reported freebase or crack smoking as their primary mode of cocaine use. These individuals were randomized to desipramine or placebo and to what was termed enhanced continuity or standard treatment conditions in a 2×2 research design. All subjects began treatment as inpatients, typically for 2 weeks. Following inpatient treatment, patients could continue therapy in the outpatient center of the same medical complex. Therapy consisted of weekly individual therapy that was reduced during the course of treatment to once monthly, and 3-h group therapy sessions that were scheduled weekly throughout the 12-week intervention. Different therapists conducted individual and group sessions. In the enhanced continuity condition, participation in the outpatient regimen began during the inpatient stay and patients kept the same individual and group therapists throughout the inpatient and outpatient phases. In the standard condition, outpatient treatment began after the inpatient stay and subjects were assigned new individual and group therapists upon entering the outpatient phase.

There were no significant effects of pharmacotherapy. Compared to standard care, enhanced care increased cocaine abstinence at the 3-week assessment (63% vs. 42% abstinence), but not the 8- or 12-week assessments, and increased the mean number of individual therapy sessions attended (4.8 $\pm$ 3.0 vs. 3.6 $\pm$ 3.1). No other significant treatment effects were reported.

Pharmacological Treatments

There is not yet an effective pharmacotherapy for cocaine abuse. Research on this topic has been reviewed extensively elsewhere and is only briefly summarized here (e.g., Gorelick, 1994; Kleber, 1995; Mendelson & Mello, 1996). (See chapter 15 by Silverman et al., this volume, for a discussion of pharmacotherapies for cocaine abuse in patients with comorbid cocaine and opiate abuse.)

Pharmacotherapies for Primary Cocaine Abuse

Pharmacotherapy research for cocaine abuse was spurred initially by an open-label trial followed by a double-blind, randomized trial supporting the efficacy of desipramine, a tricyclic antidepressant, in producing short-term reductions in cocaine use and craving in outpatients (Gawin & Kleber, 1984; Gawin, Kleber et al., 1989). In the randomized trial, 59% of cocaine-dependent patients treated for 6 weeks with desipramine achieved 3 or more weeks of continuous cocaine abstinence versus 25% and 17% of those treated with lithium or placebo (Gawin, Kleber, et al., 1989). Unfortunately, those promising results have not been replicated in subsequent controlled trials with desipramine (e.g., Carroll, Rounsaville, Gordon, Nich, et al., 1994; Weddington et al., 1991) or imipramine, another tricyclic antidepressant (Nunes et al., 1995). Evidence that subgroups with less severe cocaine dependence may benefit from treatment with desipramine and imipramine was presented in at least two reports and merits further study (Carroll, Rounsaville, Gordon, Nich et al., 1994; Nunes et al., 1995).

Other antidepressants that have been investigated in primary cocaine abusers include fluoxetine (Grabowski et al., 1995), maprotiline (Brotman et al., 1988), and gepirone (Jenkins et al., 1992). Studies are still in progress with some of these compounds, but none have demonstrated reliable efficacy in reducing cocaine craving or use in controlled trials.

Because of cocaine's dopaminergic activity, a number of dopaminergic drugs have been researched as possible treatment agents, including amantadine, bromocriptine, bupropion, flupenthixol, carbidopa-L-dopa, mazindol, methylphenidate, and tyrosine (Chadwick, Gregory, & Wendling, 1990; Gawin, Allen, & Humblestone, 1989; Grabowski et al., 1996; Kampman et al., 1996; Moscovitz et al., 1993; Rosen, Flemenbaum, & Slater, 1986; Stine, Krystal, Kosten, & Charney, 1995). Open-trial data have sometimes looked promising, but no reliable positive effects have been observed with any of these compounds in randomized trials. The same is true for the anticonvulsant carbamazepine (Kranzler, Bauer, Hersh, & Klinghoffer, 1995). Use of disulfiram therapy in patients with comorbid cocaine and alcohol abuse looks promising and is discussed in a later section (see p. 355).

Treating Comorbid Psychiatric Problems Other Than Substance Abuse

The inability of these pharmacotherapies to decrease cocaine use should not obscure their potential importance for treating other psychiatric disorders common among cocaine abusers. Approximately three-quarters of cocaine abusers meet lifetime diagnostic criteria for a psychiatric disorder other than substance abuse, including increased rates of affective disorders, anxiety disorders, antisocial personality, and attention-deficit disorder (Rounsaville et al., 1991). These disorders merit appropriate medical treatment in cocaine abusers just as they do in other populations. At this time, such interventions should be considered as treatments for these other psychiatric disorders, and not primary or secondary treatments for cocaine abuse. For example, Carroll and colleagues (Carroll, Nich, & Rounsaville, 1995) conducted exploratory analyses examining treatment response in depressed and nondepressed cocaine-dependent patients using results from their randomized trial comparing desipramine versus placebo with and without RP. Desipramine was significantly more effective than placebo in reducing depressive symptomatology in depressed patients (i.e., was an efficacious antidepressant), but was not more effective in reducing cocaine use.

Multiple Drug Use and Abuse

Use and abuse of alcohol, caffeine, marijuana, nicotine, and opioids is common among cocaine abusers (see chapter 10 by Rush et al., this volume). Treatment of comorbid opioid and cocaine abuse is discussed in chapter 15 by Silverman et al., this volume. Treatment of comorbid alcohol and cocaine abuse has been evaluated in controlled trials and disulfiram therapy with monitoring to assure compliance with the medication regimen appears promising for reducing use of both substances. To our knowledge, treatments of other forms of multiple drug abuse among cocaine abusers have not been evaluated in controlled clinical trials.

Alcohol Use

Prevalence of alcohol dependence among cocaine-dependent individuals is 60% or higher, and as many as 97% of current cocaine users also report current alcohol use (Carroll, Rounsaville, & Bryant, 1993; Grant & Harford, 1990; Higgins, Budney, Bickel, Foerg, & Badger, 1994). Disulfiram therapy with monitoring to assure medication compliance was used as a standard component in the contingency-management-plus-CRA studies described above. A chart review was conducted on 16 cocaine-dependent individuals who received that treatment (Higgins et al., 1993a). Disulfiram therapy was associated with significant decreases in drinking and, unexpectedly, cocaine use. The percentage of cocaine-positive specimens during disulfiram therapy was 11% ± 3 versus 25% ± 6 off the medication. Of course, being a chart review, no causal inferences can be made regarding the contribution of disulfiram to those effects.

Carroll, Rounsaville, and Bryant (1993) reported results consistent with these findings in a pilot, randomized trail. In that study, disulfiram therapy was compared to naltrexone therapy in a population of 18 outpatients who abused cocaine and alcohol. Disulfiram therapy resulted in threefold or greater reductions in drinking and cocaine use than naltrexone therapy. Finally, a larger randomized trial on the efficacy of disulfiram therapy was completed recently by Carroll and colleagues and again cocaine use was significantly reduced by disulfiram therapy (K. M. Carroll, personal communication).

Marijuana Use

Marijuana use is the most prevalent form of other illicit-drug use among cocaine abusers, with 25–90% of clinical samples of cocaine abusers reporting concurrent use and approximately 30% meeting criteria for marijuana dependence

(Budney, Higgins, & Wong, 1996). The only experimental report we are aware of on treating marijuana and cocaine abuse was a contingency-management study conducted with two subjects who abused cocaine and marijuana, but who sought treatment for only the former (Budney, Higgins, Delaney, Kent, & Bickel, 1991). The voucher-based intervention described above was implemented initially to establish cocaine abstinence only and subsequently to establish cocaine and marijuana abstinence. Both subjects successfully abstained from cocaine while continuing to use marijuana when contingencies of reinforcement required abstinence from only the former. When the contingencies were modified to require abstinence from both cocaine and marijuana, the two subjects successfully abstained from both substances. At a follow-up assessment completed 1 year after treatment termination, both subjects continued to abstain from cocaine but had resumed marijuana use, suggesting that at least in these two individuals there was no functional relationship between the use of cocaine and marijuana.

A retrospective analysis of pretreatment and during-treatment marijuana use on cocaine abstinence was conducted with 95 cocaine-dependent outpatients who received contingency management plus CRA treatment (Budney et al., 1996). Neither marijuana use or dependence adversely influenced treatment outcome. Although consistent with the experimental results from Budney et al. (1991), the negative results from this retrospective analysis are inconsistent with results from a similar study in which marijuana use was predictive of relapse to cocaine use following outpatient and inpatient treatment (Rawson, Obert, McMann, & Mann, 1986).

Caffeine and Nicotine Use

Regular use of caffeinated beverages is common in cocaine-dependent patients, although somewhat lower than in an age- and gender-matched community sample (68% vs. 83%) (Budney, Higgins, Hughes, & Bickel, 1993). To our knowledge, how caffeine use affects treatment outcome for cocaine abuse has not been reported.

The prevalence of regular cigarette smoking is much higher in cocaine-dependent patients than in an age- and gender-matched community sample (75% vs. 22%) (Budney et al., 1939). To our knowledge, there have been no experimental studies examining relationships between smoking and cocaine use in treatment settings. The influence of regular cigarette smoking on treatment outcome for cocaine abuse was examined in a retrospective study of patients who received contingency management plus CRA treatment (Roll, Higgins, Budney, Bickel, & Badger, 1996). Smokers were a more impaired group in terms of initiating cocaine use at an earlier age, using cocaine more frequently, and preferring intravenous or smoked over intranasal cocaine administration. Cigarette smoking was not a significant predictor of treatment outcome.

SUMMARY

Treatment demand for cocaine abuse in the United States remains high despite significant reductions in the overall number of cocaine users. Studies of treatment outcome among cocaine abusers document large pre- to posttreatment reductions in cocaine use, but often leave unanswered the contribution of treatment to those changes. A review of controlled clinical trials conducted with cocaine abusers supports a position that the disorder generally can be managed in outpatient or day-hospital settings. High rates of attrition in outpatient settings is a problem, but progress is being made in devising cost-effective strategies to engage and retain cocaine abusers in treatment. The optimal duration, frequency, and format of treatment delivery remains unclear. Regarding treatment content, the efficacy of several psychosocial interventions have been supported in randomized clinical trials, including the use of voucher-based reinforcement of abstinence in combination with the CRA, day treatment plus contingent work therapy, and housing with homeless individuals, and Relapse Prevention therapy. Additional interventions including special residential accommodations for drug-abusing mothers and strategies to increase continuity of care between inpatient and outpatient settings appear promising. There is not yet a reliably effective pharmacotherapy for cocaine abuse, although studies examining the efficacy of monitored disulfiram therapy in the sizable subsample of patients who abuse cocaine and alcohol look promising for reducing use of both substances. Overall, the challenge of treating cocaine abuse remains daunting, but careful scientific study of the problem has resulted in encouraging advances.

ACKNOWLEDGMENTS

Preparation of this chapter was supported by Research grants DA06113 and DA08076, and National Training Award DA07242 from the National Institute on Drug Abuse.

REFERENCES

Alterman, A. I., O'Brien, C. P., McLellan, T., August, D. S., Snider, E. C., Droba, M., Cornish, J. W., Hall, C. P., Raphaelson, A. H., & Schrade, F. X. (1994). Effectiveness and costs of inpatient versus day hospital cocaine rehabilitation. *The Journal of Nervous and Mental Disease, 152,* 157–163.

Alterman, A. I., Snider, E. C., Cacciola, J. S., May, D. J., Parikh, G., Maany, I., & Rosenbaum, P. R. (1996). A quasi-experimental comparison of the effectiveness of 6- versus 12-hour per week outpatient treatments for cocaine dependence. *The Journal of Nervous and Mental Disease, 184,* 54–56.

American Psychiatric Association. (1995). Practice guidelines for the treatment of patients with substance use disorders: alcohol, cocaine, opioids. *American Journal of Psychiatry, 152,* 5–59.

Brotman, A., Witkie, S. M., Gelenberg, A. J., Falk, W. E., Wojcik, J., & Leahy, L. (1988). An open trial of maprotiline for the treatment of cocaine abuse: a pilot study. *Journal of Clinical Psychopharmacology, 8,* 125–127.

Budde, D., Rounsaville, B., & Bryant, K. (1992). Inpatient and outpatient cocaine abusers: clinical comparisons at intake and one-year follow-up. *Journal of Substance Abuse Treatment, 9,* 337–342.

Budney, A. J., Higgins, S. T., Delaney, D. D., Kent, L., & Bickel, W. K. (1991). Contingent reinforcement of abstinence with individuals abusing cocaine and marijuana. *Journal of Applied Behavior Analysis, 24,* 657–665.

Budney, A. J., Higgins, S. T., Hughes, J. R., & Bickel, W. K. (1993). Nicotine and caffeine use in cocaine-dependent individuals. *Journal of Substance Abuse, 5,* 117–130.

Budney, A. J., Higgins, S. T., & Wong, C. J. (1996). Marijuana use and treatment outcome in cocaine-dependent patients. *Journal of Clinical and Experimental Psychopharmocology, 4,* 1–8.

Carroll, K. M., Nich, C., & Rounsaville, B. J. (1995). Differential symptom reduction in depressed cocaine abusers treated with psychopathology and pharmacotherapy. *Journal of Nervous and Mental Disease, 183,* 251–259.

Carroll, K. M., Power, M-E. D., Bryant, K., & Rounsaville, B. J. (1993). One-year follow-up status of treatment seeking cocaine abusers: psychopathology and dependence severity as predictors of outcome. *The Journal of Nervous and Mention Disease, 181,* 71–79.

Carroll, K. M., Rounsaville, B. J., & Bryant, K. J. (1993). Alcoholism in treatment-seeking cocaine abusers: clinical and prognostic significance. *Journal of Studies on Alcohol, 54,* 199–208.

Carroll, K. M., Rounsaville, B. J., Gawin, F. H. (1991). A comparative trial of psychotherapies for ambulatory cocaine abusers: relapse prevention and interpersonal psychotherapy. *American Journal of Drug and Alcohol Abuse, 17,* 229–247.

Carroll, K. M., Rounsaville, B. J., Gordon, L. T., Nich, C., Jatlow, P. Bisighini, R. M., & Gawin, F. H. (1994). Psychotherapy and pharmacotherapy for ambulatory cocaine abusers. *Archives of General Psychiatry, 51,* 177–187.

Carroll, K. M., Rounsaville, B. J., Nich, C., Gordon, L. T., Wirtz, P. W., & Gawin, F. (1994). One-year follow-up of psychotherapy and pharmacotherapy for cocaine dependence. *Archives of General Psychiatry, 51,* 989–997.

Carroll, K., Ziedonis, D., O'Malley, S., McCance-Katz, E., Gordon, L., & Rounsaville, B. (1993). Pharmacologic interventions for alcohol- and cocaine-abusing individuals: a pilot study of disulfiram vs. naltrexone. *The American Journal on Addictions, 2,* 77–79.

Chadwick, M. J., Gregory, D. L., & Wendling, G. (1990). A double-blind aminoacids, L-tryptophan and L-tyrosine, and placebo study with cocaine dependent subjects in an inpatient chemical dependency treatment center. *American Journal of Drug and Alcohol Abuse, 16,* 275–286.

Childress, A. R., Hole, A. V., Ehrman, R. N., Robbins, S. J., McLellan, A. T., & O'Brien, C. P. (1993). Cue reactivity and cue reactivity interventions in drug dependence. In L. S. Onken, J. D. Blaine & J. J. Boren (Eds.), *NIDA Research Monograph No. 137. Behavioral Treatments for Drug Abuse and Dependence.* (NIH Publication No. 93-3684, pp. 73–95). National Institute on Drug Abuse, Rockville, MD: U.S. Government Printing Office.

Elk, R. (1997). Contingency management interventions in the treatment of cocaine-dependent pregnant women. In L. S. Harris (Ed.), *NIDA Research Monograph: Problems of Drug Dependence 1996: Proceedings of the 58th Annual Scientific Meeting of the College on Problems of Drug Dependence.* Rockville, MD: National Institute on Drug Abuse, p. 59.

Everingham, S. S., & Rydell, C. P. (1994). *Modeling the demand for cocaine.* ISBN: 0-8330-1553-2, Santa Monica, CA: RAND.

Festinger, D. S., Lamb, R. J., Kirby, K. C., & Marlowe, D. B. (1996). The accelerated intake: A method for increasing initial attendance to outpatient cocaine treatment. *Journal of Applied Behavior Analysis, 29,* 387–389.

Festinger, D. S., Lamb, R. J., Kountz, M., Kirby, K. C., & Marlowe, D. (1995). Pre-treatment dropout as a function of treatment delay and client variables. *Addictive Behaviors, 20,* 111–115.

Gawin, F. H., Allen, D., & Humblestone, B. (1989). Outpatient treatment of 'crack' cocaine smoking with flupenthixol decanoate: A preliminary report. *Archives of General Psychiatry, 46,* 322–325.

Gawin, F. H., & Kleber, H. D. (1984). Cocaine abuse treatment. Open pilot trial with desipramine and lithium carbonate. *Archives of General Psychiatry, 41,* 903–909.

Gawin, F. H., Kleber, H. D., Byck, R., Rounsaville, B. J., Kosten, T. R., Jatlow, P. I., & Morgan, C. (1989). Desipramine facilitation of initial cocaine abstinence. *Archives of General Psychiatry, 46,* 117–121.

Gorelick, D. A. (1994). Pharmacologic therapies for cocaine addiction. In N. S. Miller & M. Gold (Eds.), *Pharmacological therapies for alcohol and drug addictions.* New York, NY: Marcel Dekker, Inc., pp. 143–157.

Grabowski, J., Roache, J., Schmitz, J. M., Rhoades, H., Elk, R., & Thompson, W. (1996). Methylphenidate (MP): An adjunct for cocaine dependence. In L. S. Harris (Ed.), *Problems of drug* dependence, 1995: Proceedings of the 57th annual scientific meeting, the College on Problems of Drug Dependence, Inc., NIDA Research Monograph Series 162, NIH No. 96-4116, Rockville, MD: National Institute on Drug Abuse, pp. 150.

Grabowski, J., Rhoades, H., Elk, R., Schmitz, J., Davis, C., Creston, D., & Kirby, K. (1995). Fluoxetine is ineffective for treatment of cocaine dependence and concurrent opiate dependence: two placebo controlled double-blind trials. *Journal of Clinical Psychopharmacology, 15,* 163–174.

Grant, B. F., & Harford, T. C. (1990). Concurrent and simultaneous use of alcohol with cocaine: results of national survey. *Drug and Alcohol Dependence, 25,* 97–104.

Hall, S. M., Tunis, S., Triffleman, E., Banys, P., Clark, H. W., Tusel, D., Stewart, P., & Presti, D. (1994). Continuity of care and desipramine in primary cocaine abusers. *Journal of Nervous and Mental Disease, 182,* 570–575.

Higgins, S. T., Budney, A. J., & Badger, G. J. (unpublished data). [Effects of contingent reinforcement from significant others on cocaine use]. Unpublished raw data.

Higgins, S. T., Budney, A. J., Bickel, W. K., & Badger, G. J. (1994). Participation of significant others in outpatient behavioral treatment predicts greater cocaine abstinence. *American Journal of Drug and Alcohol Abuse, 20,* 47–56.

Higgins, S. T., Budney, A. J., Bickel, W. K., Foerg, F. E., & Badger, G. J. (1994). Alcohol dependence and simultaneous cocaine and alcohol use in cocaine-dependent patients. *Journal of Addictive Diseases, 13,* 177–189.

Higgins, S. T., Budney, A. J., Bickel, W. K., Foerg, F. E., Donham, R., & Badger, G. J. (1994). Incentives improve treatment retention and cocaine abstinence in ambulatory cocaine-dependent patients. *Archives of General Psychiatry, 51,* 568–576.

Higgins, S. T., Budney, A. J., Bickel, W. K., Foerg, F. E., Ogden, D., & Badger, G. J. (1995). Outpatient behavioral treatment for cocaine dependence: One-year outcome. *Experimental and Clinical Psychopharmacology, 3,* 205–212.

Higgins, S. T., Budney, A. J., Bickel, W. K., Hughes, J. R., & Foerg, F. (1993a). Disulfiram therapy in patients abusing cocaine and alcohol. *American Journal of Psychiatry, 150,* 675–676.

Higgins, S. T., Budney, A. J., Bickel, W. K., Hughes, J. R., Foerg, F., & Badger, G. (1993b). Achieving cocaine abstinence with a behavioral approach. *American Journal of Psychiatry, 150,* 763–769.

Higgins, S. T., Delaney, D. D., Budney, A. J., Bickel, W. K., Hughes, J. R., Foerg, F., & Fenwick, J. W. (1991). A behavioral approach to achieving initial cocaine abstinence. *American Journal of Psychiatry, 148,* 1218–1224.

Higgins, S. T., & Silverman, K. (Eds.) (in press). *Motivating behavior change among illicit-drug abusers: contemporary research on contingency-management interventions.* Washington, DC: APA Books, American Psychological Association.

Higgins, S. T., Wong, C. J., Budney, A. J., English, K. T., & Kennedy, M. H. (1997). Efficacy of incentives during outpatient behavioral treatment for cocaine dependence. In L. S. Harris (Ed.), *NIDA Research Monograph: Problems of Drug Dependence 1996: Proceedings of the 58th Annual Scientific Meeting of the College on Problems of Drug Dependence.* Rockville, MD: National Institute on Drug Abuse, p. 75.

Hubbard, R. L., Rachal, J. V., Craddock, S. G., & Cavanaugh, E. R. (1984). Treatment outcome prospective study (TOPS): client characteristics and behaviors before, during, and after treatment. In F. M. Tims & J. P. Ludford (Eds.), *Drug abuse treatment evaluation: strategies, progress, and prospects. NIDA Research Monograph #51.* Washington, DC: US Government Printing Office (ADM) 84-1329, pp. 42–68.

Hughes, P. H., Coletti, S. D., Neri, R. L., Umann, C. F., Stahl, S., Sicilian, D. M., & Anthony, J. C. (1995). Retaining cocaine-abusing women in a therapeutic community: the effect of a child live-in program. *American Journal of Public Health, 85,* 1149–1152.

Jenkins, S. W., Warfield, N. A., Blaine, J. D., Cornish, J., Ling, W., Rosen, M. I., Urschel, H., Wesson, D., & Ziedonis, D. (1992). A pilot trial of gepirone vs. placebo in the treatment of cocaine dependency. *Psychopharmacology Bulletin, 28,* 21–26.

Kampman, K., Volpicelli, J. R., Alterman, A., Cornish, J., Weinrieb, R., Epperson, L., Sparkman, T., & O'Brien, C. P. (1996). Amantadine in the early treatment of cocaine dependence: a double-blind, placebo-controlled trial. *Drug and Alcohol Dependence, 41,* 25–33.

Kang, S.-Y., Kleinman, P. H., Woody, G. R., Millman, R. B., Todd, T. C., Kemp, J., & Lipton, D. S. (1991). Outcomes for cocaine abusers after once-a-week psychosocial therapy. *American Journal of Psychiatry, 148,* 630–635.

Kleber, H. D. (1995). Pharmacotherapy, current and potential, for the treatment of cocaine dependence. *Clinical Neuropharmacology, 18* (supplement 1), S96–S109.

Konkol, R. J., & Olsen, G. D. (Eds.) (1996). *Prenatal cocaine exposure.* New York: CRC Press.

Kranzler, H. R., Bauer, L. O., Hersh, D., & Klinghoffer, V. (1995). Carbamazepine treatment of cocaine dependence: a placebo-controlled trial. *Drug and Alcohol Dependence, 38,* 203–211.

Marlatt, G. A., & Gordon, J. R. (1985). *Relapse prevention.* New York: Guilford.

McKay, J. R., McLellan, A. T., & Alterman, A. I. (1992). An evaluation of the Cleveland criteria for inpatient treatment of substance abuse. *American Journal of Psychiatry, 149,* 1212–1218.

Mendelson, J. H., & Mello, N. K. (1996). Management of cocaine abuse and dependence. *The New England Journal of Medicine, 334,* 965–972.

Milby, J. B., Schumacher, J. E., McNamara, C., Wallace, D., McGill, T., Strange, D., & Michael, M. (1997). Abstinent contingent housing enhances day treatment for homeless cocaine abusers. In L. S. Harris (Ed.), *NIDA Research Monograph: Problems of Drug Dependence 1996: Proceedings of the 58th Annual Scientific Meeting of the College on Problems of Drug Dependence,* Rockville, MD: National Institute on Drug Abuse, p.77.

Milby, J. B., Schumacher, J. E., Raczynski, J. M., Caldwell, E., Engle, M., Michael, M., & Carr, J. (1996). Sufficient conditions for effective treatment of substance abusing homeless persons. *Drug and Alcohol Dependence, 43,* 23–38.

Montoya, I. D., & Atkinson, J. S. (1996). Determinants of HIV seroprevalence rates among sites participating in a community-based study of drug use. *Journal of Acquired Immune Deficiency Syndromes and Human Retrovirology, 13,* 169–176.

Moscovitz, H., Brookoff, D., & Nelson, L. (1993). A randomized trial of bromocriptine for cocaine users presenting to the emergency department. *Journal of General Internal Medicine, 8,* 1–4.

National Association of State Alcohol and Drug Abuse Directors. (1997). *State resources and services related to alcohol and other drug problems for fiscal year 1995: An analysis of state alcohol and drug abuse profile data.* Washington, DC: National Association of State Alcohol and Drug Abuse Directors, Inc.

National Institute of Justice. (1997). *1996 Drug Use Forecasting annual report on adult and juvenile arrestees.* Rockville, MD: National Institute of Justice Clearinghouse.

Nunes, E. V., McGrath, P. J., Quitkin, F. M., Ocepek-Welikson, K., Stewart, J. W., Koenig, T., Wager, S., & Klein, D. F. (1995). Imipramine treatment of cocaine abuse: possible boundaries of efficacy. *Drug and Alcohol Dependence, 39,* 185–195.

Oswald, L. M., Schmitz, J. M., Jacks, D., Day, S., & Grabowski, J. (1996). Relapse prevention treatment for cocaine dependence: group versus individual format. In L. S. Harris (Ed.), *Problems of drug dependence, 1995: Proceedings of the 57th annual scientific meeting, the College on Problems of Drug Dependence, Inc., NIDA Research Monograph Series 162* (p. 98). (NIH No. 96-4116). Rockville, MD: National Institute on Drug Abuse.

Rawson, R. A., Obert, J. L., McCann, M. J., & Mann, A. J. (1986). Cocaine treatment outcome: cocaine use following inpatient, outpatient, and no treatment. In L. S. Harris (Ed.), *Problems of Drug Dependence, NIDA Research Monograph 67* (pp. 271–277). Washington, DC: US Government Printing Office.

Rawson, R. A., Shoptaw, S. J., Obert, J. L., McCann, M. J., Hasson, A. L., Marinelli-Casey, P. J., Brethen, P. R., & Ling, W. (1995). An intensive outpatient approach for cocaine abuse treatment: the Matrix Model. *Journal of Substance Abuse Treatment, 12,* 117–127.

Rosen, H., Flemenbaum, A., & Slater, V. L. (1986). Clinical trial of carbidopa-L-dopa combination for cocaine abuse. *American Journal of Psychiatry, 143,* 1493.

Rohsenow, D. (1993, September). *Social skills training for cocaine dependent individuals.* Paper presented at the NIDA Technical Review Meeting, Outcomes for treatment of cocaine dependence, Bethesda, MD.

Roll, J. M., Higgins, S. T., Budney, A. J., Bickel, W. K., & Badger, G. J. (1996). A comparison of cocaine dependent cigarette smokers and non-smokers on demographic, drug use, and other characteristics. *Drug and Alcohol Dependence, 40,* 195–201.

Rounsaville, B. J., Anton, S. F., Carroll, K. Budde, D., Prusoff, B. A., & Gawin, F. (1991). Psychiatric diagnoses of treatment-seeking cocaine abusers. *Archives of General Psychiatry, 48,* 43–51.

Shaner, A., Eckman, T. A., Roberts, L. J., Wilkins, J. N., Tucker, D. E., Tsuang, J. W., & Mintz, J. (1995). Disability income, cocaine use, and repeated hospitalization among schizophrenic cocaine abusers. *New England Journal of Medicine, 12,* 777–783.

Simpson, D. D. (1984). National treatment system evaluation based on the drug abuse reporting program (DARP) followup research. In F. M. Tims & J. P. Ludford (Eds.), *Drug abuse treatment evaluation: strategies, progress, and prospects. NIDA Research Monograph #51.* (pp. 29–41). Washington, DC: US Government Printing Office (ADM) 84–1329.

Stark, M. J., Campbell, B. K., & Brinkerhoff, C. V. (1990). "Hello, May we help you?" A study of attrition prevention at the time of the first phone contact with substance-abusing clients. *American Journal of Drug and Alcohol Abuse, 16,* 67–76.

Stine, S. M., Krystal, J. H., Kosten, T. R., & Charney, D. S. (1995). Mazindol treatment for cocaine dependence. *Drug and Alcohol Dependence, 39,* 245–252.

Substance Abuse and Mental Health Services Administration. (1997). *National household survey on drug abuse: main findings 1996.* Rockville, MD: Substance Abuse and Mental Health Services Administration, Office of Applied Studies.

Tardiff, K., Marzuk, P. M., Leon, A. C., Hirsch, C. S., Stajic, M., Portera, L., & Hartwell, N. (1994). Homicide in New York City: cocaine use and firearms. *Journal of the American Medical Association, 272,* 43–46.

Weddington, W. W., Brown, B. S., Haertzen, C. A., Hess, J. M., Mahaffey, J. R., Kolar, A. F., & Jaffe, J. H. (1991). Comparison of amantadine and desipramine combined with psychotherapy for treatment of cocaine dependence. *American Journal of Drug and Alcohol Abuse, 17,* 137–152.

Wells, E. A., Peterson, P. L., Gainey, R. R., Hawkins, J. D., & Catalano, R. F. (1994). Outpatient treatment for cocaine abuse: a controlled comparison of relapse prevention and twelve-step approaches. *American Journal of Drug and Alcohol Abuse, 20,* 1–17.

15

TREATMENT OF COCAINE
ABUSE IN METHADONE
MAINTENANCE PATIENTS

KENNETH SILVERMAN, GEORGE E. BIGELOW,
AND MAXINE L. STITZER

Department of Psychiatry and Behavioral Sciences
Johns Hopkins University School of Medicine
Baltimore, Maryland

INTRODUCTION

Heavy use of cocaine has increased dramatically in the United States over the past 30 years (Everingham & Rydell, 1994). Consistent with this pattern, cocaine use has increased to alarming rates among a select group of chronic drug abusers enrolled in treatment, methadone-maintenance patients (Condelli, Fairbank, Dennis, & Rachal, 1991; Dunteman, Condelli, & Fairbank, 1992; Rawson, McCann, Hasson, & Ling, 1994). The high rates of cocaine use among methadone patients is particularly troubling because of the range of associated adverse conditions. Cocaine use in methadone patients has been associated with increased rates of HIV infection (Chaisson et al., 1989), unemployment (Zanis, Metzger, & McLellan, 1994), criminal activity (Hunt, Spunt, Lipton, Goldsmith, & Strug, 1986), and complications during pregnancy (Chasnoff, Burns, Schnoll, & Burns, 1985).

This chapter reviews interventions used to treat cocaine use in methadone patients. The chapter has four main sections. The first section reviews research on the effects of methadone itself on cocaine use. The high rates of cocaine use in methadone patients has prompted concern that methadone itself may increase cocaine use, either directly or indirectly. To look thoroughly for evidence of potential undesirable effects of methadone on cocaine use, this section reviews a number of descriptive studies relevant to this issue, in addition to controlled studies. The next three sections review controlled trials of the three major types of interventions that have been employed in drug abuse treatment: pharmacological, psychosocial, or behavioral, and other less conventional types of treatment.

Studies were included in this chapter only if data on cocaine use were provided separate from data on other drug use, if the rates of cocaine use were high enough to see potential decreases by an effective intervention (i.e., $\geq$ 15% of patients in any study group showed evidence of cocaine use at any point in the study), and if the study was published in a peer-reviewed journal. Sections of the chapter reviewing controlled trials include only studies that employed random assignment of subjects to the study conditions or an accepted within-subject design (e.g., reversal design; Hersen & Barlow, 1976). The primary outcome measures used to determine whether conditions were effective were those based on urinalysis results (e.g., percent cocaine-positive).

METHADONE

As noted above, the high rates of cocaine use in methadone patients has prompted concern that methadone itself may increase cocaine use. The concern has been heightened by anecdotal reports that suggest that methadone may diminish cocaine's adverse effects (Barglow & Kotun, 1992; Hunt et al., 1984; Kosten, Rounsaville, & Kleber, 1987), and by controlled laboratory research that suggests that methadone may enhance cocaine's reinforcing effects (Bilsky, Montegut, Delong, & Reid, 1992; Preston, Sullivan, Strain, & Bigelow, 1996). There has also been concern that cocaine may substitute for heroin, when heroin use is decreased by methadone treatment (Hunt, Lipton, Goldsmith, & Strug, 1984; Kosten, Rounsaville, & Kleber, 1987). This section reviews descriptive and experimentally controlled studies that examine the relationship between methadone treatment and cocaine use.

COCAINE USE AFTER ENTRY
IN METHADONE TREATMENT

A number of descriptive studies have examined the effects of entry into methadone maintenance on cocaine use. One early study (Kosten, Gawin, Rounsaville, & Kleber, 1986) compared reports of recent cocaine use in a group of patients being admitted to treatment ($n = 204$) with reports of recent use in patients who had been in methadone maintenance for at least 3 months ($r = 120$). Seventy-four percent of the newly admitted patients reported recent cocaine use, whereas only 20% of the longer-term methadone patients reported recent cocaine use. In both samples, patients reporting the highest rates of heroin use also reported the highest rates of cocaine use.

Several studies have attempted to assess the impact of methadone treatment on cocaine use by comparing patients' reports of the frequency and amount of cocaine prior to entry into methadone treatment with their reports of cocaine use during treatment. Chaisson et al. (1989) studied 633 intravenous drug abusers enrolled in methadone treatment. Although the relationship between methadone treatment and heroin use was clear (between 92 and 95% of patients reported stopping or decreasing their heroin use), the relationship between methadone treatment and cocaine use was less clear: Between 57 and 68% of the cocaine-using methadone patients reported decreasing their use of cocaine during methadone treatment relative to pretreatment, but 24% reported initiating or increasing their cocaine use. Magura, Siddiqi, Freeman, and Lipton (1991a) and Magura, Siddiqi, Freeman, and Lipton (1991b) found similar patterns of results, although some patients reported different patterns of changes in cocaine use following admission to treatment, there were overall decreases in cocaine use relative to intake.

The large-scale Treatment Outcome Prospective Study (TOPS) included interviews with individuals ($N = 526$) admitted to 17 public methadone programs (Dunteman, Condelli, & Fairbank, 1992; Fairbank, Dunteman, & Condelli, 1993). In that study, overall cocaine use decreased during methadone treatment: 36% of patients reported using cocaine during the year prior to treatment entry, whereas 22% reported using at a 1-year follow-up. In addition, patients who remained in methadone treatment for most or all of the year prior to the 1-year follow-up interview were no more or less likely to use cocaine than those who had dropped out of treatment. Cocaine use at the follow-up interview was significantly associated with cocaine use prior to intake and current use of heroin.

These studies show that entry into methadone treatment is associated with overall decreases in cocaine use more often than increases. At the same time, the data raise the possibility that methadone treatment results in the initiation of or increases in cocaine use in some patients. Of course, the descriptive nature of these studies does not allow conclusions as to whether or not methadone produced the observed changes. For example, the study by Chaissen et al. (1989) has been frequently cited as providing evidence that methadone may be responsible for some patients initiating or increasing their cocaine use (e.g., Condelli et al., 1991). However, the authors of that study noted that cocaine use was increasing in general in the geographic area in which the methadone clinics were located, so it is possible that the increases observed in the study reflected that general increase in cocaine use (e.g., due to increases in the availability and use of cocaine in the geographic area) and was unrelated to the methadone treatment.

Yancovitz et al. (1991) conducted an elegant controlled evaluation of the effects of methadone treatment on heroin and cocaine use that addresses these limitations. They randomly assigned 301 individuals on waiting lists for 23 methadone clinics to receive an interim methadone treatment or to a "frequent contact" control condition; frequent contact control patients were switched to methadone treatment after 1 or more months. The interim methadone patients received daily methadone (up to 80 mg), biweekly interviews and urine tests, and free condoms. Although the two groups did not differ in their heroin or cocaine use (based on self-reports or urinalysis) at intake to the study, at the 1-month follow-up assessment heroin use among the interim methadone patients was significantly lower than heroin use among the control patients (29% vs. 60% opiate positive, respectively); there was no difference between the two groups in their cocaine use (68% vs. 70% cocaine positive, respectively) at follow-up. Within the interim methadone group, heroin use decreased significantly from intake to the 1-month follow-up (63% to 29% opiate positive, respectively). That group also showed a small but insignificant decrease in cocaine use across the two time points (77% to 68% cocaine positive, respectively). Control patients showed no difference from intake to follow-up in either heroin (62% to 60% positive, respectively) or cocaine (71% to 70% positive, respectively) use. Cocaine use at the 1-month follow-up assessment predicted heroin use at that follow-up independent of treatment group. This study provides perhaps the clearest evidence to date that methadone treatment does not increase cocaine use in methadone patients.

EFFECTS OF METHADONE DOSE ON COCAINE USE

Correlational Analyses of Patients at Different Methadone Doses

The effects of methadone on cocaine use also can be examined in studies that assess the effects of varying methadone dose. One descriptive study (Hartel et al., 1995) of 652 patients receiving methadone doses between 20 and 100 mg per day showed that although high-dose methadone (> 70 mg) was associated with decreased use of heroin, there was no significant relationship between methadone dose and cocaine use. At all methadone doses, cocaine use was greatest in patients who continued to use heroin.

Uncontrolled Assessments of Progressive Dose Increases

Several uncontrolled descriptions of treatments for cocaine-abusing methadone patients have involved monitoring of cocaine use while increasing methadone dose. In two reports (Stine, Burns, & Kosten, 1991; Stine, Freeman, Burns, Charney, & Kosten, 1992), increasing methadone dose up to 120 mg per day contingent on cocaine-positive urines was not associated with increases in cocaine use.

Strain, Stitzer, Liebson, and Bigelow (1994b) monitored opiate and cocaine use in a trial comparing buprenorphine and methadone in 164 opioid-dependent patients. Both medications were administered using a flexible dose procedure in which doses were increased (up to 16 mg and 90 mg, respectively) based on patient request and opiate-positive urine tests. Comparison of urines before and after patients received dose increases showed that the methadone dose increases were associated with significant decreases in the percent of opiate-positive urines (79.6% vs. 66.1% positive), but no significant change in the percent of cocaine-positive urines (58.1% vs. 54.2% positive). There were no significant differences between the two medications on opiate or cocaine urinalysis results. Further analyses of the 86 patients who completed the study (43 in each group) showed similar results (Strain, Stitzer, Liebson, & Bigelow, 1996).

Another study (Strain, Stitzer, Liebson, & Bigelow, 1994a) compared buprenorphine and methadone in 51 cocaine-abusing, opioid-dependent individuals. Both medications were administered using a flexible dosing procedure in which doses were increased (up to 16 mg and 90 mg, respectively) based on continued opiate or cocaine-positive urinalysis results. Although this study did not show differences between buprenorphine and methadone on cocaine use, the study did show significant reductions in rates of both opiate- and cocaine-positive urines over time for patients who completed the main 16-week treatment phase of the study ($n =$ 28).

Controlled Comparisons of Methadone Doses

A few controlled studies have assessed the effects of varying methadone dose on cocaine use. One study randomly assigned 247 consecutive admissions to a methadone program to receive 0 mg, 20 mg, and 50 mg methadone during a 20-week treatment period (Strain, Stitzer, Liebson, & Bigelow, 1993a). An intent-to-treat analysis showed significant and dose-related increases in retention, decreases in opiate use (74%, 68%, and 56% of urines positive for opiates, respectively), and decreases in cocaine use (67%, 62%, and 53% of urines positive for cocaine, respectively). Subsequent analyses were conducted (Strain et al., 1993b) using data from patients who completed the entire 20-week treatment condition (17, 34, and 44 patients from the 0-, 20-, and 50-mg conditions, respectively). This analysis also showed that 50-mg methadone significantly decreased opiate use (36% opiate positive) compared to both 20 mg (60% positive) and 0 mg (73% positive). Although the overall analysis of data from this study did not show significant reductions in cocaine use as a function of methadone dose, post hoc analysis showed that the 50-mg dose significantly reduced cocaine use during selected weeks (weeks 9–12) relative to the other two doses.

In another study, designed primarily to assess the efficacy of buprenorphine as a treatment for opioid dependence, Johnson, Jaffe, and Fudala (1992) randomly assigned 162 opioid-dependent patients to receive 8 mg buprenorphine, 20 mg methadone, or 60 mg methadone throughout a 17-week period. Although the study showed that both 60 mg methadone and 8 mg buprenorphine significantly increased retention and decreased the percent of opiate-positive urines, there were no differences across groups in the percent of urines positive for cocaine.

Another study (Oliveto, Kosten, Schottenfeld, Ziedonis, & Falcioni, 1994), also designed to evaluate buprenorphine, randomly assigned 100 opioid-dependent cocaine users to receive buprenorphine (2 mg or 6 mg per day) or methadone (35 or 65 mg per day). The methadone doses selected for comparison in this study produced lower levels of opiate use as measured by urinalysis than the doses of buprenorphine; however, there were no differences across groups in cocaine urinalysis results. The percentage of cocaine- and opiate-positive urines were significantly correlated in all groups except the 2 mg buprenorphine group.

One study (Grabowski, Rhoades, Elk, Schmitz, & Creson, 1993), described briefly in a letter, reported some potentially conflicting results in a 2 × 2 randomized controlled study comparing two frequencies of clinic visits (achieved by varying the number of take-home doses provided to patients; 2 vs. 5 visits per week) and two methadone doses (50 and 80 mg per day). The high dose of methadone was associated with significant decreases in the percentage of urines positive for opiates, but significant increases in the percentage of urines positive for cocaine. Of all the studies reviewed, this study provides the only evidence that methadone increases overall cocaine use. However, close inspection of the data in this study (provided in a full description of the study in an unpublished manuscript) reveals a possible confound in that cocaine use at intake was highest in one of the two 80-mg methadone groups (approximately 60% cocaine-positive urinalysis results for patients in the 80 mg, 5 visits per week group compared to below 45% cocaine-positives for the two low-dose methadone groups). That 80-mg group increased from about 60% cocaine-positive at intake to a maximum of about 65% cocaine positive during treatment; patients in the other three groups either showed no consistent change (50 mg, 2 visits per week and 80 mg, 2 visits per week) or decreased their cocaine use (50 mg, 5 visits per week), relative to intake. The fact that this study conflicts with all studies described above suggests that the results are probably due to the pretreatment group differences.

CONCLUSIONS

The overwhelming majority of these studies show that methadone treatment is associated with either no overall change in cocaine use or with overall decreases in cocaine use. Although the descriptive studies described above do not provide a firm basis for drawing conclusions, the consistency of results across these studies and the failure to show that methadone is associated with overall increases in cocaine use provide important support to the findings of the randomized controlled studies. One of the most consistent observations across these studies is that opiate and cocaine use tend to covary. That is, cocaine use is most common in patients with the highest rates of heroin use, not in patients who stop their heroin use during methadone treatment. This later observation strongly suggests that patients do not use cocaine as a substitute for heroin once heroin use is diminished or eliminated by methadone treatment. These conclusions refer to the overall pattern of cocaine use in groups of methadone patients. Whether some individuals exposed to methadone treatment (or to increasing methadone doses) increase their cocaine use while others decrease their use, producing no overall change or overall decreases in the group as a whole, is not known. But the overall pattern of results in these studies provides little or no evidence that methadone exacerbates problems of cocaine abuse in methadone patients, and provides a small amount of evidence that methadone can have some overall beneficial effects.

PHARMACOLOGICAL TREATMENTS

A number of investigations have been conducted to evaluate the effectiveness of potential pharmacological treatments for cocaine use. (See Higgins & Wong, chapter 14, this volume, and Mendelson & Mello, 1996, for discussions of research in other subgroups of cocaine abusers). This section reviewed controlled evaluations of pharmacotherapies for cocaine abuse in methadone patients.

A PHARMACOTHERAPEUTIC ALTERNATIVE
TO METHADONE: BUPRENORPHINE

Buprenorphine, a partial μ-opioid agonist that is currently under development for the treatment of opioid dependence, has been considered as a possible medication for the treatment of cocaine abuse in opioid-dependent patients (Kosten, Rosen, Schottenfeld, & Ziedonis, 1992; Mello & Mendelson, 1995; Mendelson & Mello, 1996). Although most proposed pharmacotherapies for cocaine abuse have been given to patients as adjunctive therapies to methadone treatment, buprenorphine has been used as an alternative to methadone because it effectively treats opioid dependence. Preclinical studies have provided strong evidence that buprenorphine can reduce cocaine self-administration in laboratory animals (Mello & Negus, 1996), making this a very attractive compound for evaluation in treatment studies.

Gastfriend, Mendelson, Mello, Teoh, and Reif (1993) randomly assigned 22 cocaine- and opiate-dependent individuals to receive either 4 mg or 8 mg buprenorphine in a 12-week trial. Opiate use, as measured by urine toxicology, decreased significantly from intake to treatment for both buprenorphine groups; however, only the 4-mg group showed a significant decrease in cocaine use. There were no significant differences between the 4-mg and 8-mg groups on any measures, making conclusions about the effects of buprenorphine on cocaine use difficult.

Schottenfeld, Pakes, Ziedonis, and Kosten (1993) exposed 15 opioid- and cocaine-dependent patients to a series of ascending and then descending doses of buprenorphine (minimum of 2 mg and maximum of 16 mg). Opiate use (based on urine toxicology and self-reports) decreased as buprenorphine dose increased during the ascending phase of the study, and increased again as buprenorphine dose decreased in the descending dose phase. Increasing buprenorphine dose was associated with decreases in cocaine use; however, cocaine use remained low when the buprenorphine dose was decreased during the descending dose phase of the study. Thus, although this study provided some indication that buprenorphine can decrease cocaine use, the study did not provide a clear experimental demonstration of the effect.

Johnson et al. (1995) conducted a double-blind, placebo-controlled, randomized trial comparing 0 mg, 2 mg, and 8 mg buprenorphine in 150 opioid-dependent patients in a brief, 7-day treatment period. Although buprenorphine significantly reduced opiate use as assessed by urinalysis, it did not affect cocaine urinalysis results. Finally, several studies have compared buprenorphine to methadone (see section on methadone), but all failed to show significant differences in the effects of the two medications on cocaine use (Strain et al., 1994a, 1994b; Strain et al., 1996; Johnson et al., 1992; Oliveto et al., 1994).

Taken together, these studies suggest that buprenorphine treatment may be associated with decreases in cocaine use; however, such decreases have yet to be experimentally linked to buprenorphine. There is no evidence that buprenorphine produces greater reductions in cocaine use than methadone.

ADJUNCTIVE PHARMACOTHERAPIES FOR COCAINE ABUSE IN METHADONE PATIENTS

There are a number of published reports on the effects of nonopioid medications on cocaine use in methadone patients (Mendelson & Mello, 1996; Gorelick, 1994; Johanson & Schuster, 1995); however, only a limited number of reports describe controlled studies. The medications that have been evaluated in methadone patients fall into one or both of two categories: antidepressant medications or drugs that affect dopaminergic function (Mendelson & Mello, 1996). Antidepressants have been considered because depression is thought to precede and precipitate cocaine use, and to result from cessation of cocaine use (Mendelson & Mello, 1996). Also, many antidepressant agents share pharmacological properties with cocaine (i.e., inhibition of monamine reuptake). If cocaine use is maintained by the alleviation or avoidance of depression, then medications that reduce depression may also reduce cocaine use. Medications that affect dopaminergic function have been considered because cocaine's reinforcing effects are thought to be mediated through the dopaminergic system. Cocaine binds to the dopamine transporter and blocks reuptake of dopamine. This effect of cocaine has been linked with cocaine's reinforcing effects (Ritz, Lamb, Goldberg, & Kuhar, 1987; Johanson & Schuster, 1995). A medication that binds to the same site on the dopamine transporter could potentially block this effect of cocaine and thereby block its reinforcing effects (Gorelick, 1994). In addition, chronic cocaine use is thought to result in diminished dopaminergic function, which may be associated with cocaine withdrawal. Dopamine agonists have been considered as a treatment medication for cocaine abuse because they might restore dopaminergic function, alleviate cocaine withdrawal, and thereby reduce cocaine use (Gorelick, 1994).

Fluoxetine

Grabowski et al. (1995) compared the antidepressant fluoxetine (20 mg per day) to placebo in a double-blind, randomized controlled, 2-month study in 21 methadone patients. Although fluoxetine did not produce an overall decrease in the proportion of urines that were cocaine positive relative to the control group, the proportion of cocaine-positive urines was significantly lower for fluoxetine patients during weeks 3 and 4 of the 8-week study.

Desipramine and Amantadine

Arndt, Dorozynsky, Woody, McLellan, and O'Brien, (1992) assessed the effects of the tricyclic antidepressant desipramine in 79 methadone patients in a 12-week double-blind, placebo-controlled, randomized trial. Desipramine significantly decreased retention relative to placebo; among the subgroup of patients who completed treatment ($n = 59$), desipramine appeared to produce significantly better psychiatric status, but had no effect on cocaine use (Arndt, McLellan, Dorozynsky, Woody, & O'Brien, 1994).

Two double-blind, placebo-controlled, 12-week studies in methadone patients compared the effects of desipramine, a tricyclic antidepressant, and amantadine, an indirect dopamine agonist that is effective in treating Parkinson's disease. One of these studies (Kolar et al., 1992; $N = 22$) found that desipramine increased retention relative to placebo, had no overall effects on cocaine urinalysis results, but appeared to increase the proportion of cocaine-free urines during the final 2 weeks of treatment in those patients who remained in treatment. Amantadine had no effects on retention or cocaine urinalysis. The other study (Kosten, Morgan, Falcione, & Shottenfeld, 1992; $N = 94$) found no differences in retention across groups, transient effects of the medications on self-reported cocaine use, and no effects of either medication on cocaine urinalysis results. Further analyses were conducted in which patients were categorized as depressed ($n = 20$) or nondepressed ($n = 74$) to determine if the medications had differential effects in patients meeting the Diagnostic and Statistical Manual of Mental Disorders (3rd ed.) (*DSM-III-R*) criteria for major depression or dysthymia (Ziedonis & Kosten, 1991). Analyses of urine results failed to show a significant interaction of medication and depression diagnosis on any of the time periods assessed (i.e., first 2 weeks, weeks 5 and 6, last 2 weeks). Secondary analyses of data from depressed patients only comparing the change in the percentage of cocaine-free urines from the first to the last 2 weeks of the study showed a significant reduction with active medication. Other similar analyses did not provide any clear evidence that the medications were effective either in patients meeting the criteria for antisocial personality disorder or in patients who did not fulfill those criteria (Leal, Ziedonis, & Kosten, 1994).

In a double-blind, placebo-controlled, random assignment study, Handelsman et al. (1995) assessed the effects of two doses of amantadine (200 and 400 mg per day) on cocaine use. Fifty-nine patients participated in this trial, which lasted 9 weeks and revealed no effects of amantadine on any measures of cocaine use.

Mazindol

The effectiveness of mazindol, another dopamine reuptake inhibitor, was evaluated in a 2-week protocol using a placebo-controlled, crossover design (Kosten, Steinberg, & Diakogiannis, 1993). In that study, 19 methadone-maintained, cocaine-dependent patients were treated with 1 week of mazindol and 1 week of placebo in counterbalanced order. The study showed no effects of mazindol on cocaine use.

Buproprion

Finally, Margolin et al. (1995) conducted a 12-week, multisite, placebo-controlled, randomized, double-blind trial comparing buproprion, an antidepressant and dopamine reuptake blocker, to placebo in 149 cocaine-dependent methadone-maintenance patients. Buproprion failed to significantly effect any measure of cocaine use. However, exploratory analyses of data from the 36 patients who were categorized as depressed (HAM-D scores above 12) showed that buproprion significantly decreased the percent of urine tests positive for cocaine (89% positive at baseline to 60% positive at week 12) relative to placebo (99% positive at baseline to 93% positive at week 12).

CONCLUSIONS

Overall, none of the medications evaluated in these controlled clinical trials has proven effective in reducing cocaine use in methadone-maintenance patients in general. One study showed that fluoxetine may have a small, transient effect, and two of the studies suggest that some medications (desipramine and buproprion) may be effective in depressed, cocaine-abusing methadone patients.

PSYCHOSOCIAL AND BEHAVIORAL TREATMENTS

A variety of psychosocial and behavioral treatments have been evaluated in controlled trials with methadone patients. Some of these trials were designed specifically to evaluate the effect of an intervention on cocaine use; however, many address illicit drug use in general.

NODE-LINK MAPPING

Node-link mapping is a counseling method that involves the use of flowcharts to diagram relationships between thoughts, actions, feelings and drug use or related problems. Maps are drawn by the counselor, typically in collaboration with a client, starting with a core problem or issue and then expanded (Dansereau, Joe, & Simpson, 1995). Patients enrolled in three public methadone clinics in Texas between May 1990 and April 1992 were randomly assigned to receive standard counseling or to receive node-link-mapping-enhanced counseling (Czuchry, Dansereau, Dees, & Simpson, 1995; Dansereau et al., 1995; Joe, Dansereau, & Simpson, 1994). Counselors in each of the clinics were randomly assigned to learn and administer the node-link mapping intervention. Data for clients enrolled in treatment for at least 6 months ($N = 311$) showed that node-link mapping significantly decreased the proportion of cocaine-positive urines (59% positive at intake and 37% positive at 6 months) relative to the standard counseling control (49% positive at intake and 47% positive at 6 months). It should be noted that some of the difference between treatment conditions may have resulted from the fact that patients in the node-link mapping condition had higher rates of cocaine-positive tests at intake; no data were provided to show that the two groups differed significantly in their levels of cocaine-positive results at the 6-month time point. Two other analyses involving different subgroups of patients (Czuchry et al., 1995; Dansereau et al., 1995) suggest that node-link mapping can decrease drug use, although those analyses do not determine the specific effects of the intervention on cocaine use. These studies suggest that node-link mapping deserves further evaluation.

NEUROBEHAVIORAL TREATMENT

Magura et al. (1994) evaluated the effectiveness of a "neurobehavioral treatment" for cocaine-abusing methadone patients developed by Rawson and colleagues (1990). This treatment employs relapse-prevention techniques, focuses on developing a therapeutic alliance, and guides patients through "observed neuropsychogical stages of recovery from stimulant abuse, classified by the model as "withdrawal," "honeymoon," "the wall," "adjustment," and "resolution" (Magura et al., 1994; p. 145). In this study, 62 methadone patients were randomly assigned to receive either the neurobehavioral treatment or standard counseling (control). Retention did not differ between groups. Neurobehavioral patients showed a significant reduction in the percentage of urines that were cocaine positive from baseline (the 4 weeks prior to study admission) to follow-up (final 4 weeks of the 6-month period or 4 weeks before discharge, whichever was later) (81% to 66% positive, respectively), whereas control patients showed no change (69% to 71% positive). Also, neurobehavioral patients showed a significant reduction in the percentage of patients that provided at least one cocaine-positive urine test during baseline versus follow-up (95% vs. 74% of patients, respectively), whereas control patients showed no change (79% vs. 79% of patients). Although the neurobehavioral group showed decreases in cocaine use not shown by the control patients, they had somewhat higher baseline use. Conclusions from this study are somewhat clouded due to the fact that the neurobehavioral and control groups did not differ substantially at the end of treatment (6-month time point), either in the percentage of urines that were cocaine positive (66% vs. 71%) or in the percentage of patients that provided at least one cocaine-positive urine test (74% vs.79%). Further, multivariate analysis showed that treatment condition did not predict urinalysis results at the 6-month time point. Thus, the study failed to show efficacy for the use of the neurobehavioral approach in cocaine-abusing methadone patients.

SUPPORTIVE-EXPRESSIVE PSYCHOTHERAPY

Supportive-expressive psychotherapy has produced some positive results in the treatment of selected subgroups of methadone patients (Woody et al., 1983; Woody et al., 1984). The supportive techniques are designed to help patients feel free to talk about their personal experiences. The expressive techniques are designed to help patients explore and work on problems in their relationships. When these techniques are used for substance abuse patients, the therapist focuses on drug dependence, the role that drugs play in troubling feelings and behaviors, as well as how to resolve problems without drugs (Woody, McLellan, Luborsky, & O'Brien, 1995). The effects of supportive-expressive psychotherapy specifically on cocaine use in methadone patients was demonstrated in an excellent study by Woody et al. (1995). Eighty-four patients were selected from 300–350 newly admitted patients in three community-based methadone programs. It is important to note that over half of the original 300–350 patients (202 patients) were not included in the study either because they said that they were not interested in receiving the additional counseling or psychotherapy that would be provided in the study or because they failed to attend a minimum number of counseling and/or psychotherapy sessions during the first 6 weeks of the study. Patients were randomly assigned to receive weekly supportive-expressive psychotherapy (delivered mostly by doctoral-level therapists) in addition to the weekly drug counseling (delivered by high school and college graduates) for 6 months, or to receive drug counseling only. To keep the amount of contact with a professional constant across the two groups, patients in the drug counseling group were assigned a second drug counselor who provided an additional drug counseling session each week. Supportive-expressive therapy had no clear effects on opiate urinalysis results relative to drug counseling alone (an average of 45% versus 43% opiate positive across weeks, respectively); however, the supportive-expressive therapy did appear to produce a significant decrease in the percentage of cocaine-positive urines (an average of 22% versus 36% cocaine positive across weeks, respectively). Figure 15.1 shows the percent of co-

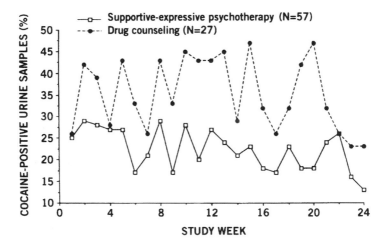

FIGURE 15.1   Percentage of cocaine-positive urine samples, by study week, in opiate-dependent patients receiving methadone and drug counseling plus either supportive-expressive psychotherapy ($n = 57$) or additional drug counseling ($n = 27$). (From Woody et al., *American Journal of Psychiatry, 152,* 1302–1308, 1995. Copyright © 1995, the American Psychiatric Association. Reprinted with permission.)

caine-positive samples provided per week by patients in the two groups. Thus, this type of professionally delivered therapy may be beneficial for reducing drug use in patients who are particularly interested in receiving the therapy.

CONTINGENCY-MANAGEMENT PROCEDURES

Contingency-management procedures have been used with considerable effectiveness to reduce abuse of a variety of licit and illicit substances (Stitzer & Higgins, 1995). These procedures typically involve providing desirable consequences (e.g., money or privileges) to patients contingent on patients providing objective evidence of drug abstinence.

Take-Home Methadone Doses

Stitzer, Iguchi, and Felch (1992) evaluated the use of take-home methadone doses in 53 methadone-maintenance patients. After a 12-week baseline period of standard treatment, patients were randomly assigned to receive take-home methadone doses either contingent on drug-free urines or on a noncontingent basis for 6 months. Patients in the contingent group received one, two, and three take-homes per week after providing 2, 4, and 6 or more consecutive weeks of drug-free urines, respectively. Contingent take-home methadone doses significantly increased the percentage of patients who met a criterion for clinical improvement (i.e., 10% increase in percentage of drug-free urines from baseline condition and 4 weeks of consecutive drug-free urines), relative to the noncontingent condition (32% vs. 8% of patients, respectively). However, the effect of the take-home intervention on cocaine use was not sufficiently robust to produce significant decreases in overall rates of positive urines.

Contingent Access to Methadone Treatment

Kidorf and Stitzer (1993) assessed the effects of providing continued methadone treatment contingent on cocaine abstinence. In that study, 47 individuals who were eligible for methadone maintenance and who provided a cocaine-positive urine at intake were enrolled in a 90-day premaintenance probationary period and were randomly assigned to an experimental or control group. Patients in the experimental group were transferred to a 2-year methadone-maintenance program contingent on providing 2 consecutive weeks of cocaine-negative urines; patients failing to meet this criterion were given 6-week methadone detoxifications at the end of the 90-day probationary period. Control patients were given access to continued methadone treatment on a noncontingent basis using a yoked procedure. Significantly more patients in the experimental than control group achieved 2 consecutive weeks of cocaine-free urines (Figure 15.2). Experimental patients also provided a higher percentage of cocaine-free urines (29%) than controls (13%), although that difference between groups was not significant.

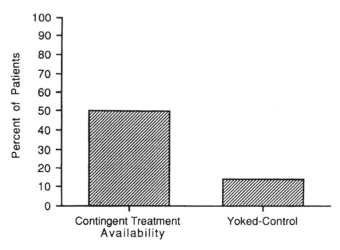

FIGURE 15.2   The percentage of patients in each treatment condition ($N = 22$) who met the cocaine-abstinence criteria (2 consecutive weeks of cocaine-free urines) during the premaintenance probationary period. (From Kidorf & Stitzer, *Experimental and Clinical Psychopharmacology, 1,* 200–206, 1993. Copyright © 1993 by the American Psychological Association. Reprinted with permission.)

Voucher-Based Reinforcement

Silverman et al. (1996) assessed the effectiveness of voucher-based reinforcement of cocaine abstinence in methadone patients. The intervention was originally developed and shown effective for primary cocaine-dependent patients (Higgins et al., 1994; Higgins & Wong, chapter 14, this volume). Thirty-seven patients who continued to use cocaine during the first 5 weeks of methadone treatment were randomly assigned to receive vouchers contingent on providing cocaine-free urines or to receive vouchers on a noncontingent basis during a 12-week intervention period. All vouchers had monetary values and were exchangeable for goods and services purchased by the staff at the patient's request. For patients in the contingent group, vouchers initially had a low monetary value ($2.50), but the value of the vouchers increased steadily as a function of the number of consecutive cocaine-free urines provided. Patients in this group could earn a maximum of $1,155 in vouchers for providing cocaine-free urines throughout the 12-week intervention period. During the 12-week intervention period, patients receiving vouchers for cocaine-free urines achieved significantly longer durations of sustained cocaine abstinence (Figure 15.3) and significantly more weeks of cocaine abstinence (Figure 15.4) than patients in the noncontingent group. Overall, the study showed that voucher-based reinforcement of cocaine abstinence can produce substantial periods of sustained cocaine abstinence in cocaine-abusing methadone patients.

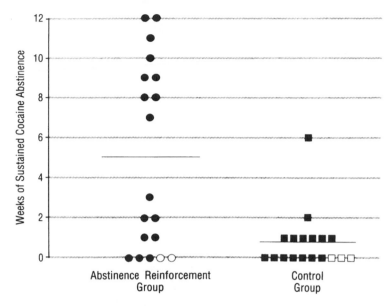

FIGURE 15.3   Longest duration of sustained cocaine abstinence achieved during the 12-week voucher condition. Each point represents data for an individual patient and the lines represent group means. The 19 abstinence reinforcement patients are displayed in the left column (circles) and the 18 control patients in the right (squares). Open symbols represent patients who dropped out of the study early. (From Silverman et al., *Archives of General Psychiatry, 53,* 409–415, 1996.)

MULTICOMPONENT TREATMENTS

McLellan, Arndt, Metzger, Woody, and O'Brien (1993) assessed the effects of increasing the amount and type of treatment services available to 92 male, intravenous opiate-using methadone patients. Patients were randomly assigned to one of three 6-month treatment conditions: Minimum, Standard, or Enhanced Methadone Services. The Minimum Services condition was "designed to provide the lowest level of supervised care possible under current Food and Drug Administration standards." Patients in this group received daily methadone of up to 90 mg per day, two take-home methadone doses per week, monthly brief (15 min) contacts with a counselor, and weekly random urine testing. Patients in the Standard Services condition received daily methadone as in the Minimum Services condition, regular counseling sessions, weekly random urine testing, and a contingency management procedure in which they could earn up to two take-home methadone doses per week for providing drug-free urines and evidence of employment. The Enhanced Services condition included all "Standard Services," but in addition counselors referred patients for additional help from other professionals (i.e., full-time psychiatrist, half-time employment counselor, and a half-time

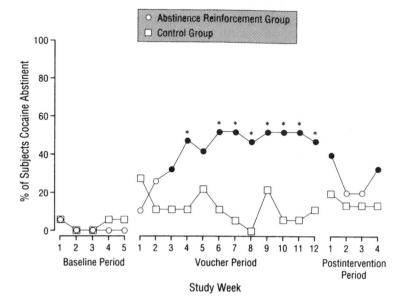

FIGURE 15.4   Percentage of patients abstinent during 25 successive study weeks. Circles represent data from the abstinence reinforcement group and squares represent the control group. A patient was considered cocaine abstinent for a given week if all of the three urine samples for that week were negative for cocaine. Filled points and asterisks indicate the weeks on which the abstinence reinforcement group value differed significantly from the control group value according to planned comparisons based on a repeated measures analysis of variance ($p \leq 0.05$ and $p \leq 0.01$, respectively). Data for the 4-week postintervention period are based on the urinalysis results from subjects who completed the postintervention period (i.e., 15 control and 15 abstinence reinforcement subjects). (From Silverman et al., *Archives of General Psychiatry, 53,* 409–415, 1996.)

family therapist) in the clinic. Figure 15.5 shows that Minimum Services patients had significantly higher rates of opiate- and cocaine-positive urines than patients in the other two groups. Compared to Standard Services, Enhanced Services were associated with significant reductions in opiate but not cocaine urine-positive test results. Thus, this study showed adding regular counseling and providing take-home methadone doses contingent on drug-free urines and evidence of employment (i.e., Standard Services) was sufficient to decrease cocaine use in this population. However, providing additional services (psychiatric services, employment counseling, and family therapy) did not produce additional reductions in cocaine use.

In a small randomized clinical trial (Carroll, Chang, Behr, Clinton, & Kosten, 1995), 14 pregnant methadone patients were randomly assigned to receive standard or enhanced methadone-maintenance treatment. Standard treatment consisted of daily methadone, weekly group counseling, and urine testing (three times per week). Patients in the enhanced treatment group received weekly prenatal care,

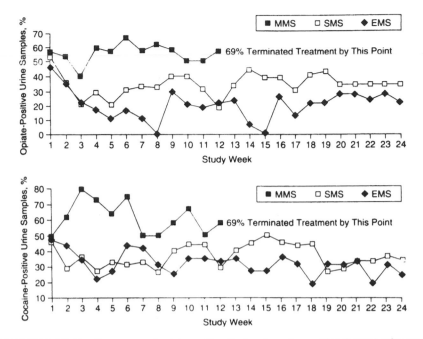

FIGURE 15.5   Percentages of opiate-positive (top) and cocaine-positive (bottom) urine samples, per treatment group (minimum services, MMS; standard methadone services, SMS; and enhanced methadone services, EMS), by study week. Sixty-nine percent of patients in the MS condition were protectively transferred to the Standard care condition within the first 3 months, so only data for the first 3 months are presented for the MS condition. (From McLellan et al., *Journal of the American Medical Association, 269,* 1953–1959. Copyright 1993, American Medical Association. Reprinted with permission.)

weekly relapse-prevention groups, and $15 for every three consecutive drug-free urine samples that they provided. Treatment retention was similar for both groups (22.3 and 25.1 weeks for patients in the standard and enhanced groups, respectively) and there were no differences in the percentage of cocaine-positive urines provided by patients in the two groups (39.8% and 39.4% cocaine-positive, respectively).

CONCLUSIONS

Studies of psychosocial and behavioral interventions provide the clearest evidence that cocaine abuse in methadone patients is a treatable problem. Four interventions were effective in reducing cocaine in methadone patients: supportive-expressive psychotherapy, contingent access to methadone treatment, voucher-based reinforcement of cocaine abstinence, and multidimensional treatment that involved counseling and contingent take-home methadone doses.

OTHER TREATMENTS

A variety of treatments have been used in clinical practice such as acupuncture, biofeedback, and hypnosis that do not fit neatly in the categories listed above; however, only acupuncture has been evaluated in a controlled clinical trial in methadone patients. Although it is not known why acupuncture may affect drug abuse, some have speculated that acupuncture may result in release of endogenous opioids, which may modulate "neural circuits in the midbrain also affected by drugs of abuse" (Margolin, Avants, Chang, & Kosten, 1993, p. 195). Two studies (Avants, Margolin, Chang, Kosten, & Birch, 1995; Wells et al., 1995) have randomly assigned methadone patients to receive either acupuncture at points commonly used in treating drug abuse or to receive sham acupuncture (i.e., at locations assumed to be inactive). Both studies showed that acupuncture had no effects on treatment retention, or on cocaine or opiate use based on urinalysis results or self-report.

SUMMARY AND CONCLUSIONS

A wide range of interventions for cocaine use in methadone patients have been evaluated in controlled studies. These controlled studies are summarized in Table 15.1. Three important points should be made about this body of research. First, contrary to some common concerns and speculations, the controlled studies show that methadone itself does not produce overall increases in cocaine use in methadone patients. In general, methadone appears to have no overall effect on cocaine use, although there is limited evidence that methadone may produce small overall decreases in cocaine use. At the same time, the studies show clearly that methadone alone does not adequately control cocaine use, even at doses in the high range of those approved for general use by the Food and Drug Administration.

Second, the limited effectiveness of the diverse group of interventions evaluated in these studies highlights the fact that cocaine use in methadone patients is extremely difficult to treat effectively. Of the different interventions that were evaluated in controlled studies, only four interventions (supportive-expressive psychotherapy, contingent methadone treatment, voucher-based reinforcement of cocaine abstinence, multicomponent treatment) were clearly shown to reduce cocaine use in methadone patients. Two additional treatments (desipramine and buproprion) show potential effectiveness in depressed methadone patients, and two others (methadone and fluoxetine) show some evidence of at least transient effectiveness. The limited effectiveness is particularly striking considering the wide variety of treatments that have been evaluated. Furthermore, some of the effective treatments, particularly supportive-expressive psychotherapy, were effective in only a select group of patients; and no treatment was effective with a large majority of patients. The magnitude of effects produced by these four interventions can be seen in Figures 1–5, which show the cocaine urinalysis results ob-

TABLE 15.1 Experimentally Controlled Evaluations of Treatments for Cocaine Abuse in Methadone Patients

Intervention	N	Groups	Design	Experimental conditions	Duration	Effect on cocaine urinalysis[a]	Citation
Methadone							
Methadone	301	2	Random assignment; parallel group	Waiting list vs. ≈80 mg methadone	1 month	None	Yancovitz et al., 1991
Methadone	247	3	Random assignment; parallel group	Placebo vs. 20 mg methadone vs. 50 mg methadone	20 weeks	↓	Strain et al., 1993a,b
Methadone	162	3	Random assignment; parallel group	20 mg methadone vs. 60 mg methadone vs. 8 mg buprenorphine	17 weeks	None	Johnson et al., 1992
Methadone	100	4	Random assignment; parallel group	35 and 65 mg methadone vs. 2 and 6 mg buprenorphine	24 weeks	None	Oliveto et al., 1994
Methadone	107	4	Random assignment; parallel group	50 mg methadone vs. 80 mg	26 weeks	Uncertain	Grabowski et al., 1993
Buprenorphine							
Buprenorphine	162	3	Random assignment; parallel group	20 mg methadone vs. 60 mg methadone vs. 8 mg buprenorphine	17 weeks	None	Johnson et al., 1992
Buprenorphine	164	2	Random assignment; parallel group	Flexible dosing methadone vs. flexible dosing buprenorphine	26 weeks	None	Strain et al., 1994a; Strain et al., 1996
Buprenorphine	51	2	Random assignment; parallel group	Flexible dosing methadone vs. flexible dosing buprenorphine	16 weeks	None	Strain et al., 1994b
Buprenorphine	100	4	Random assignment; parallel group	2 and 6 mg buprenorphine vs. 35 and 65 mg methadone	24 weeks	None	Oliveto et al., 1994
Buprenorphine	22	2	Random assignment; parallel group	4 mg buprenorphine vs. 8 mg buprenorphine	12 weeks	None	Gastfriend et al., 1993
Buprenorphine	15	1	Ascending–descending doses	2–16 mg buprenorphine	21 weeks	Uncertain	Schottenfeld et al., 1993
Buprenorphine	150	3	Random assignment; parallel group	Placebo vs. 2 mg buprenorphine and 8 mg buprenorphine	1 week	None	Johnson et al., 1995

(continues)

TABLE 15.1 (*Continued*)

Intervention	N	Groups	Design	Experimental conditions	Duration	Effect on cocaine urinalysis[a]	Citation
Adjunctive Pharmacotherapies							
Fluoxetine	21	2	Random assignment; parallel group	Placebo vs. 20 mg fluoxetine	8 weeks	Decrease in weeks 3 and 4	Grabowski et al., 1995
Desipramine	79	2	Random assignment; parallel group	Placebo vs. 250–500 mg desipramine	12 weeks	None	Arndt et al., 1992
Desipramine	22	3	Random assignment; parallel group	Placebo vs. 200 mg desipramine vs. mg amantadine	12 weeks	None	Kolar et al., 1992
Desipramine	94	3	Random assignment; parallel group	Placebo vs. 150 mg desipramine vs. 300 mg amantadine	12 weeks	Decrease in depressed patients only	Kosten, Morgan, et al., 1992; Ziedonis & Kosten, 1991; Leal et al., 1994
Amantadine	22	3	Random assignment; parallel group	Placebo vs. 200 mg desipramine vs. mg amantadine	12 weeks	None	Kolar et al., 1992
Amantadine	94	3	Random assignment; parallel group	Placebo vs. 150 mg desipramine vs. 300 mg amantadine	12 weeks	None	Kosten, Rosen, et al., 1992; Ziedonis & Kosten, 1991; Leal et al., 1994
Amantadine	59	3	Random assignment; parallel group	Placebo vs. 200 mg amantadine vs. 400 mg amantadine	9 weeks	None	Handlesman et al., 1995
Mazindol	19	2	Random assignment; crossover	Placebo vs. 2 mg mazindol	1 week	None	Kosten et al., 1993
Buproprion	149	2	Random assignment; parallel group	Placebo vs. 300 mg buproprion	12 weeks	Decrease in depressed patients only	Margolin et al., 1995
Psychosocial and behavioral treatments							
Node-link mapping	311	2	Random assignment; parallel group	Standard counseling vs. node-link mapping	6 months	Uncertain	Joe et al., 1994
Neurobehavioral	62	2	Random assignment; parallel group	Standard counseling vs. neurobehavioral	6 months	Uncertain	Magura et al., 1994

Treatment	N		Design	Comparison	Duration		Reference
Supportive-expressive	84	2	Random assignment; parallel group	Standard counseling vs. supportive-expressive psychotherapy	6 months	→	Woody et al., 1995
Contingency management							
Contingent take-home doses	53	2	Random assignment; parallel group	Contingent vs. noncontingent take-home doses	6 months	None	Stitzer et al., 1992
Contingent access to treatment	47	2	Random assignment; parallel group and partial crossover	Contingent vs. noncontingent treatment	90 days	→	Kidorf & Stitzer, 1993
Voucher-based reinforcement	37	2	Random assignment; parallel group	Contingent vs. noncontingent vouchers	12 weeks	→	Silverman et al., 1996
Multicomponent treatments							
Standard services (regular counseling and contingent take-home doses)	92	3	Random assignment; parallel group	Minimal vs. standard vs. enhanced	6 months	→	McLellan et al., 1993
Enhanced services (standard services plus psychiatric, employment, family)	92	3	Random assignment; parallel group	Minimal vs. standard vs. enhanced	6 months	→	McLellan et al., 1993
Enhanced treatment (relapse prevention plus contingent money)	14	2	Random assignment; parallel group	Standard vs. enhanced	6 months	None	Carroll et al., 1995
Other treatment							
Acupuncture	60	2	Random assignment; parallel group	Acupuncture vs. sham acupuncture	6 months	None	Wells et al., 1995
Acupuncture	40	2	Random assignment; parallel group	Acupuncture vs. sham acupuncture	6 weeks	None	Avants et al., 1995

[a] ↓ Significant decrease ($p \le .05$) relative to control condition.

383

tained in the studies. It may be interesting to note that these five figures were selected for inclusion in this chapter because they are the *only* published figures that show significant effects of treatment interventions on cocaine use from all of the studies reviewed.

Finally, although these studies show that cocaine abuse in methadone patients is difficult to treat effectively, the studies also show that it is treatable. The four effective treatments were demonstrated effective in randomized, controlled clinical trials using an objective measure of cocaine use (i.e., urinalysis results). Thus, these are clear and credible demonstrations. But these demonstrations should represent only a beginning to a research-based process of developing effective treatments for cocaine abuse in methadone patients. The effectiveness of the interventions need to be replicated across sites and research groups. In addition, the interventions need to be improved to affect the behavior of a larger proportion of patients, to produce greater reductions in cocaine use, and to produce long-term effects.

The treatments evaluated in experimentally controlled clinical trials described in this chapter represent only a portion of the cocaine abuse interventions in use today and a fraction of the treatments under development. Efforts to identify an effective pharmacotherapy for cocaine abuse in methadone patients are ongoing and could be critical to developing optimally effective treatment packages. Other psychosocial and behavioral treatments (e.g., therapeutic communities) may be effective as well, but have yet to be evaluated in experimentally controlled clinical trials. Although many of these unevaluated treatments, both pharmacological and psychosocial/behavioral, may appear promising, logical, or appealing, their effectiveness cannot be assumed based on uncontrolled observations. This review of carefully controlled experimental studies has revealed only a handful of effective interventions that withstood the scrutiny of carefully controlled clinical trials. The list of "effective" treatments would have been many times longer if "effectiveness" was based on all uncontrolled published studies such as studies comparing pretreatment to posttreatment levels of cocaine use, or studies comparing an intervention to historical controls or to nonrandomized patients who self-select an alternative treatment. Further development of treatments for cocaine abuse is clearly needed, but this development must proceed using carefully controlled, experimental evaluations that provide rigorous screens of treatment effectiveness.

ACKNOWLEDGMENTS

Supported by grants R01 DA09426 and P50 DA09258 from the National Institute on Drug Abuse.

REFERENCES

Arndt, I. O., Dorozynsky, L., Woody, G. E., McLellan, A. T., & O'Brien, C. P. (1992). Desipramine treatment of cocaine dependence in methadone-maintained patients. *Archives of General Psychiatry, 49,* 888–93.

Arndt, I. O., McLellan, A. T., Dorozynsky, L., Woody, G. E., & O'Brien, C. P. (1994). Desipramine treatment for cocaine dependence: Role of antisocial personality disorder. *Journal of Nervous and Mental Disease, 182,* 151–156.

Avants, S. K., Margolin, A., Chang, P., Kosten, T. R., & Birch, S. (1995). Acupuncture for the treatment of cocaine addiction: Investigation of a needle puncture control. *Journal of Substance Abuse Treatment, 12,* 195–205.

Barglow, P., & Kotun, J. M. (1992). Methadone and cocaine. *Hospital & Community Psychiatry, 43,* 1245–1246.

Bilsky, E. J., Montegut, M. J., Delong, C. L., & Reid, L. D. (1992). Opioidergic modulation of cocaine conditioned place preferences. *Life Sciences, 50,* 85–90.

Carroll, K. M., Chang, G., Behr, H., Clinton, B., & Kosten, T. R. (1995). Improving treatment outcome in pregnant, methadone-maintained women. Results from a Randomized Clinical Trials. *The American Journal on Addictions, 4,* 56–59.

Chaisson, R. E., Bacchetti, P., Osmond, D., Brodie, B., Sande, M. A., & Moss, A. R. (1989). Cocaine use and HIV infection in intravenous drug users in San Francisco. *Journal of the American Medical Association, 261,* 561–5.

Chasnoff, I. J., Burns, W. J., Schnoll, S. H., & Burns, K. A. (1985). Cocaine use in pregnancy. *New England Journal of Medicine, 313,* 666–669.

Condelli, W. S., Fairbank, J. A., Dennis, M. L., & Rachal, J. V. (1991). Cocaine use by clients in methadone programs: Significance, scope, and behavioral interventions. *Journal of Substance Abuse Treatment, 8,* 203–212.

Czuchry, M., Dansereau, D. F., Dees, S. M., & Simpson, D. D. (1995). The use of node-link mapping in drug abuse counseling: The role of attentional factors. *Journal of Psychoactive Drugs, 27,* 161–166.

Dansereau, D. F., Joe, G. W., & Simpson, D. D. (1995). Attentional difficulties and the effectiveness of a visual representation strategy for counseling drug-addicted clients. *International Journal of the Addictions, 30,* 371–386.

Dunteman, G. H., Condelli, W. S., & Fairbank, J. A. (1992). Predicting cocaine use among methadone patients: Analysis of findings from a national study. *Hospital & Community Psychiatry, 43,* 608–611.

Everingham, S. S., & Rydell, C. P. (1994). *Modeling the demand for cocaine.* Santa Monica, CA: RAND.

Fairbank, J. A., Dunteman, G. H., & Condelli, W. S. (1993). Do methadone patients substitute other drugs for heroin? Predicting substance use at 1-year follow-up. *American Journal of Drug Alcohol Abuse, 19,* 465–74.

Gastfriend, D. R., Mendelson, J. H., Mello, N. K., Teoh, S. K., & Reif, S. (1993). Buprenorphine pharmacotherapy for concurrent heroin and cocaine dependence. *American Journal on Addictions, 2,* 269–278.

Gorelick, D. A. (1994). Pharmacologic therapies for cocaine addiction. In N. S. Miller and M. Gold (Eds.), *Pharmacological Therapies for Alcohol and Drug Addictions* (pp. 143–157). New York: Dekker.

Grabowski, J., Rhoades, H., Elk, R., Schmitz, J., & Creson, D. (1993). Methadone dosage, cocaine and opiate abuse [letter]. *American Journal of Psychiatry, 150,* 675.

Grabowski, J., Rhoades, H., Elk, R., Schmitz, J., Davis, C., Creson, D., & Kirby, K. (1995). Fluoxetine is ineffective for treatment of cocaine dependence or concurrent opiate and cocaine dependence: Two placebo-controlled, double-blind trials. *Journal of Clinical Psychopharmacology, 15,* 163–174.

Handelsman, L., Limpitlaw, L., Williams, D., Schmeidler, J., Paris, P., & Stimmel, B. (1995). Amantadine does not reduce cocaine use or craving in cocaine-dependent methadone maintenance patients. *Drug and Alcohol Dependence, 39,* 173–180.

Hartel, D. M., Schoenbaum, E. E., Selwyn, P. A., Kline, J., Devenny, K., Klein, R. S., & Friedland, G. H. (1995). Heroin use during methadone maintenance treatment: The importance of methadone dose and cocaine use. *American Journal of Public Health, 85,* 83–88.

Hersen, M., Barlow, D. H. (1976). Single case experimental designs: Strategies for studying behavior change. New York: Pergamon Press.

Higgins, S. T., Budney, A. J., Bickel, W. K., Foerg, F. E., Donham, R., & Badger, M. S. (1994). Incentives improve outcome in outpatient behavioral treatment of cocaine dependence. *Archives of General Psychiatry, 51,* 568–576.

Hunt, D. E., Lipton, D. S., Goldsmith, D., & Strug, D. (1984). Street pharmacology: Uses of cocaine and heroin in the treatment of addiction. *Drug and Alcohol Dependence, 13,* 375–387.

Hunt, D. E., Spunt, B., Lipton, D., Goldsmith, D. S., & Strug, D. (1986). The costly bonus: Cocaine related crime among methadone treatment clients. Annual Meeting of the American Society of Criminology (1983, Denver, Colorado). *Advances in Alcohol & Substance Abuse, 6,* 107–122.

Hunt, D. E., Strug, D. L., Goldsmith, G. S., Lipton, D. S., Spunt, B., Truitt, L., & Robertson, K. A. (1984). An instant shot of "aah": Cocaine use among methadone clients. *Journal of Psychoactive Drugs, 16,* 217–227.

Joe, G. W., Dansereau, D. F., & Simpson, D. D. (1994). Node-link mapping for counseling cocaine users in methadone treatment. *Journal of Substance Abuse, 6,* 393–406.

Johanson and Schuster. (1995). Cocaine. In F. E. Bloom and D. J. Kupfer (Eds.), *Psychopharmacology: The Fourth Generation of Progress* (pp. 1685–1698). New York: Raven Press, Ltd.

Johnson, R. E., Eissenberg, T., Stitzer, M. L., Strain, E. C., Liebson, I. A., & Bigelow, G. E. (1995). A placebo controlled clinical trial of buprenorphine as a treatment for opioid dependence. *Drug and Alcohol Dependence, 40,* 17–25.

Johnson, R. E., Jaffe, J. H., & Fudala, P. J. (1992). A controlled trial of buprenorphine treatment for opioid dependence. *Journal of the American Medical Association, 267,* 2750–2755.

Kidorf, M., & Stitzer, M. L. (1993). Contingent access to methadone maintenance treatment: Effects on cocaine use of mixed opiate-cocaine abusers. *Experimental and Clinical Psychopharmacology, 1,* 200–206.

Kolar, A. F., Brown, B. S., Weddington, W. W., Haertzen, C. C., Michaelson, B. S., & Jaffe, J. H. (1992). Treatment of cocaine dependence in methadone maintenance clients: A pilot study comparing the efficacy of desipramine and amantadine. *International Journal of the Addictions, 27,* 849–868.

Kosten, T. R., Gawin, F. H., Rounsaville, B. J., & Kleber, H. D. (1986). Cocaine abuse among opioid addicts: demographic and diagnostic factors in treatment. *American Journal of Drug Alcohol Abuse, 12,* 1–16.

Kosten, T. R., Morgan, C. M., Falcione, J., & Schottenfeld, R. S. (1992). Pharmacotherapy for cocaine-abusing methadone-maintained patients using amantadine or desipramine. *Archives of General Psychiatry, 49,* 894–898.

Kosten, T. R., Rosen, M. I., Schottenfeld, R., & Ziedonis, D. (1992). Buprenorphine for cocaine and opiate dependence. *Psychopharmacology Bulletin, 28,* 15–19.

Kosten, T. R., Rounsaville, B. J., & Kleber, H. D. (1987). A 2.5-year follow-up of cocaine use among treated opioid addicts: Have our treatments helped? *Archives of General Psychiatry, 44,* 281–284.

Kosten, T. R., Steinberg, M., & Diakogiannis, I. A. (1993). Crossover trial of mazindol for cocaine dependence. *American Journal on Addictions, 2,* 161–164.

Leal, J., Ziedonis, D., & Kosten, T. (1994). Antisocial personality disorder as a prognostic factor for pharmacotherapy of cocaine dependence. *Drug and Alcohol Dependence, 35,* 31–35.

Magura, S., Rosenblum, A., Lovejoy, M., Handelsman, L., Foote, J., & Stimmel, B. (1994). Neurobehavioral treatment for cocaine-using methadone patients: a preliminary report. *Journal of Addictive Diseases, 13,* 143–60.

Magura, S., Siddiqi, Q., Freeman, R. C., & Lipton, D. S. (1991a). Changes in cocaine use after entry to methadone treatment. *Journal of Addictive Diseases, 10,* 31–45.

Magura, S., Siddiqi, Q., Freeman, R. C., & Lipton, D. S. (1991b). Cocaine use and help-seeking among methadone patients. *Journal of Drug Issues, 21,* 617–633.

Margolin, A., Avants, S. K., Chang, P., & Kosten, T. R. (1993). Acupuncture for the treatment of cocaine dependence in methadone-maintained patients. *American Journal on Addictions, 2,* 194–201.

Margolin, A., Kosten, T. R., Avants, S. K., Wilkins, J., Ling, W., Beckson, M., Arndt, I. O., Cornish, J.,

Ascher, J. A., Li, S-H., & Bridge, P. (1995). A multicenter trial of buproprion for cocaine dependence in methadone-maintained patients. *Drug and Alcohol Dependence, 40,* 125–131.

McLellan, A. T., Arndt, I. O., Metzger, D. S., Woody, G. E., & O'Brien, C. P. (1993). The effects of psychosocial services in substance abuse treatment. *Journal of the American Medical Association, 269,* 1953–1996.

Mello, N. K., & Mendelson, J. H. (1995). Buprenorphine treatment of cocaine and heroin abuse. In A. Cowan and J. W. Lewis (Eds.), Buprenorphine: Combating Drug Abuse with a Unique Opioid (pp. 241–287). New York: Wiley-Liss.

Mello, N. K., & Negus, S. S. (1996). Preclinical evaluation of pharmacotherapies for treatment of cocaine and opioid abuse using drug self-administration procedures. *Neuropsychopharmacology, 14,* 375–424.

Mendelson, J. H., & Mello, N. K. (1996). Management of cocaine abuse and dependence. *New England Journal of Medicine, 334,* 965–972.

Oliveto, A. H., Kosten, T. R., Schottenfeld, R., Ziedonis, D., & Falcioni, J. (1994). Cocaine use in buprenorphine- vs. methadone-maintained patients. *American Journal on Addictions, 3,* 43–48.

Preston, K. L., Sullivan, J. T., Strain, E. C., & Bigelow, G. E. (1996). Enhancement of cocaine's abuse liability in methadone maintenance patients. *Psychopharmacology, 123,* 15–25.

Rawson, R. A., McCann, M. J., Hasson, A. J., & Ling, W. (1994). Cocaine abuse among methadone maintenance patients: Are there effective treatment strategies? *Journal of Psychoactive Drugs, 26,* 129–136.

Rawson, R. A., Obert, J. L., McCann, M. J., Smith, D. P., Ling, W. (1990). Neurobehavioral treatment for cocaine dependency. *Journal of Psychoactive Drugs, 22,* 159–171.

Ritz, M. C., Lamb, R. J., Goldberg, S. R., Kuhar, M. J. (1987). Cocaine receptors on dopamine transporters are related to self-administration of cocaine. *Science, 237,* 1219–1223.

Schottenfeld, R. S., Pakes, J., Ziedonis, D., & Kosten, T. R. (1993). Buprenorphine: Dose-related effects on cocaine and opioid use in cocaine-abusing opioid dependent humans. *Biological Psychiatry, 34,* 66–74.

Silverman, K., Higgins, S. T., Brooner, R. K., Montoya, I. D., Cone, E. J., Schuster, C. R., & Preston, K. L. (1996). Sustained cocaine abstinence in methadone maintenance patients through voucher-based reinforcement therapy. *Archives of General Psychiatry, 53,* 409–415.

Stine, S. M., Burns, B., & Kosten, T. (1991). Methadone dose for cocaine abuse. *American Journal of Psychiatry, 148,* 1268.

Stine, S. M., Freeman, M., Burns, B., Charney, D. S., & Kosten, T. (1992). Effect of methadone dose on cocaine abuse in a methadone program. *American Journal on Addictions, 1,* 294–303.

Stitzer, M. L., & Higgins, S. T. (1995). Behavioral Treatment of Drug and Alcohol Abuse. In F. E. Bloom and D. J. Kupfer (Eds.), *Psychopharmacology: The Fourth Generation of Progress* (pp. 1807–1819). New York: Raven Press, Ltd.

Stitzer, M. L., Iguchi, M. Y., & Felch, L. J. (1992). Contingent take-home incentive: Effects on drug use of methadone maintenance patients. *Journal of Consulting and Clinical Psychology, 60,* 927–934.

Strain, E. C., Stitzer, M. L., Liebson, I. A., & Bigelow, G. E. (1993a). Dose-response effects of methadone in the treatment of opioid dependence. *Annals Internal Medicine, 119,* 23–27.

Strain, E. C., Stitzer, M. L., Liebson, I. A., & Bigelow, G. E. (1993b). Methadone dose and treatment outcome. *Drug and Alcohol Dependence, 33,* 105–117.

Strain, E. C., Stitzer, M. L., Liebson, I. A., & Bigelow, G. E. (1994a). Buprenorphine versus methadone in the treatment of opioid-dependent cocaine users. *Psychopharmacology, 116,* 401–406.

Strain, E. C., Stitzer, M. L., Liebson, I. A., & Bigelow, G. E. (1994b). Comparison of buprenorphine and methadone in the treatment of opioid dependence. *American Journal of Psychiatry, 151,* 1025–1030.

Strain, E. C., Stitzer, M. L., Liebson, I. A., & Bigelow, G. E. (1996). Buprenorphine versus methadone in the treatment of opioid dependence: Self-reports, urinalysis, and Addiction Severity Index. *Journal of Clinical Psychopharmacology, 16,* 58–67.

Strug, D. L., Hunt, D. E., Goldsmith, D. S., Lipton, D. S., & Spunt, B. (1985). Patterns of cocaine use among methadone clients. *International Journal of the Addictions, 20,* 1163–75.

Wells, E. A., Jackson, R., Diaz, O. R., Stanton, V., Saxon, A. J., & Krupski, A. (1995). Acupuncture as an adjunct to methadone treatment services. *American Journal on Addictions, 4,* 198–214.

Woody, G. E., McLellan, A. T., Luborsky, L., & O'Brien, C. P. (1995). Psychotherapy in community methadone programs: A validation study. *American Journal of Psychiatry, 152,* 1302–1308.

Woody, G. E., Luborsky, L., McLellan, A. T., O'Brien, C. P., Beck, A. T., Blaine, J., Herman, I., & Hole, A. (1983). Psychotherapy for opiate addicts. Does it help? *Archives of General Psychiatry, 40,* 639–645.

Woody, G. E., McLellan, A. T., Luborsky, L., O'Brien, C. P., Blaine, J., Fox, S., Herman, I., & Beck, A. T. (1984). Severity of psychiatric symptoms as a predictor of benefits from psychotherapy: The Veterans Administration-Penn Study. *American Journal of Psychiatry, 141,* 1172–1177.

Yancovitz, S. R., Des, J. D., Peyser, N. P., Drew, E., Friedmann, P., Trigg, H. L., & Robinson, J. W. (1991). A randomized trial of an interim methadone maintenance clinic. *American Journal of Public Health, 81,* 1185–91.

Zanis, D. A., Metzger, D. S., & McLellan, A. T. (1994). Factors associated with employment among methadone patients. *Journal of Substance Abuse Treatment, 11,* 443–7.

Ziedonis, D. M., & Kosten, T. R. (1991). Depression as a prognostic factor for pharmacological treatment of cocaine dependence. *Psychopharmacology Bulletin, 27,* 337–43.

16

RELAPSE TO COCAINE USE

SHARON M. HALL, DAVID A. WASSERMAN,
BARBARA E. HAVASSY, AND PEG MAUDE-GRIFFIN

Department of Psychiatry
University of California, San Francisco
San Francisco, California

It is difficult to write an introduction to a chapter on relapse to any drug of abuse without lapsing into overworn phrases and repetitious reminders of the importance and unknown nature of the relapse process. This is especially the case with cocaine abuse, where information about relapse determinants and the relapse process is sparse indeed. The data are slowly accumulating, however, and interesting questions, if not definitive answers, are presenting themselves.

DEFINITIONS

"Relapse" denotes at least one episode of drug use following a period of no use. Some authors differentiate a lapse from a relapse. Usually, a lapse is defined as a brief episode of drug use quickly followed by a resumption of abstinence. A relapse lasts longer than a lapse and may continue indefinitely. No consensus exists on how to operationalize a relapse, however. With respect to cocaine relapse, McKay, Rutherford, Alterman, Cacciola, and Kaplan (1995) have been among the few to attempt an operational definition. They defined relapse as "one day or more of cocaine use, surrounded by abstinence periods of at least two weeks in duration, during a period in which the subject was trying to not use cocaine" (p. 37). The usefulness of this definition is not yet clear. This pattern may not best describe relapse for individuals who have infrequent, but severe, cocaine binges. Other authors have contended that at least 1 month (Rawson, Obert, McCann, Smith, & Ling, 1990) or even 3 months (Washton & Stone-Washton, 1990) of abstinence must be achieved before true relapse can occur.

It may be that the term "relapse" is simply too imprecise. A tripartite strategy might be the most useful. "Complete relapse" could be defined as return to baseline levels of use. A "lapse" would be any use of cocaine. Any amount of use in between these two would be "partial relapse."

Definitions of relapse are also complicated by emerging definitions of positive cocaine treatment outcomes. Scientists are now using multiple outcome measures besides absolute abstinence. These "softer" outcome measures reflect several factors. First, they are a response to the generally poor track record of cocaine treatments in producing long periods of abstinence. Second, they are an outgrowth of changing treatment populations with more intractable problems and lower motivation to quit using cocaine. Last, they reflect a more sophisticated view of what is realistic and clinically useful in treatment outcome. Examples of "softer" measures are days of cocaine use, days to first use, days since last use, number of incidents of use, amount of drugs used, money spent on drugs, urinary concentrations of benzoylecgonine (the primary cocaine metabolite), number or proportion of drug-positive (or drug-negative) urine screens, degree of drug craving, and quality of drug high. Researchers also are looking at broader outcomes beyond drug use, such as treatment retention and compliance, criminal activity, family problems, and employment difficulties. The current emphasis on demonstrating *reductions* in cocaine use and cocaine-associated problems, rather than *elimination* of use, suggests that we may be moving toward a harm-reduction approach to cocaine treatment.

Development of definitions of cocaine relapse is hampered by the lack of descriptive data on relapse episodes. For example, data on the length of a typical relapse episode are lacking. We do not know how often a lapse is halted, then followed by a long period of nonuse, as opposed to the lapse developing directly into a relapse.

These definitional concerns are further complicated by the existence of at least three widely used routes of cocaine administration that may result in different patterns of use, and therefore in different patterns of relapse. These include cocaine inhalation, or crack smoking; intranasal use of powdered cocaine; and injection cocaine use, often combined with heroin ("speedball"). It is generally assumed that smokers and intranasal users tend to use cocaine in a binge–abstinence pattern, but that injection users do not. Again, we lack data about the naturalistic consumption patterns of cocaine abuse, so it is difficult to develop definitions of relapse unique to route of administration of cocaine.

THEORETICAL MODELS OF RELAPSE

There are several models of drug use and relapse, including the conditioning models, (for example, Baker, Morse, & Sherman, 1987; Wikler, 1972), many of which have a neurobiological underpinning (Wise, 1988). There are also social learning models (Marlatt & Gordon, 1980, 1985), which emphasize cognitive and environmental events.

The conditioning models emphasize the importance of the environmental context of drug administration and withdrawal and propose that these contextual stimuli can become conditioned stimuli through Pavlovian conditioning. When the person is presented with these conditioned stimuli without drug administration, conditioned responses occur that are experienced as urges and cravings for the drug of abuse.

Those models with neurobiological underpinnings posit underlying neurological mechanisms that drive craving, which in turn drives drug use. The modifications in neurotransmitters are assumed to be the direct result of cocaine ingestion and conditioning. Most recent neurobiological models have focused on dopamine modulation as driving relapse. Events leading to cocaine ingestion can result in conditioned changes in dopaminergic activity, even when cocaine is not self-administered.

The social learning model acknowledges the existence of conditioned cues and responses, but asserts that these factors account for a small percentage of relapses. More important, according to this model, are the high-risk situations that exist independent of physical withdrawal or drug-related stimuli, and a person's cognitive appraisal of these risky situations. Cravings are the individual's positive outcome expectations for the initial effects of the drug, for example, change in mood or relief from withdrawal or pain (Marlatt & Gordon, 1985).

These conditioning, neurobiological, and social learning models make different assumptions and predictions about the nature of antecedent stimuli and responses to these cues, but they share a common assumption—that internal or external stimuli elicit cravings that significantly increase the probability of relapse. These models cannot account for the retrospective reports of relapsed addicts that their relapses were rarely caused by craving (for example, Wallace, 1990).

Only one theoretical model can account for relapses in the absence of craving (Tiffany, 1990). In this model, drug use behavior is conceptualized as an automatized series of behaviors that are triggered by a fixed set of stimulus configurations. Cravings, which are governed by nonautomatic processes, arise when the usually effortless implementation of these automatized behaviors is impeded, either by some external contingency (for example, drug unavailability) or by the individual's desire to remain abstinent. Relapses that occur in the absence of self-reported urges are understood as instances where the automatic drug use behaviors are engaged and completed without activation of the nonautomatic processes that generate urge responding. This can occur when the addict is distracted or overwhelmed by negative affect (that is, nonautomatic processing is devoted to some other task) or when the stimulus configurations are particularly supportive of drug use (i.e., all of the cues are present and drug is readily available).

There are few direct tests of these varied models. One can argue that the many tests of pharmacological agents that modify dopaminergic activity provide indirect tests of the usefulness of the pharmacologic model. Nevertheless, treatment studies are poor tests of theoretical constructs, due to the many complex factors that influence outcome.

PREDICTION OF RELAPSE TO COCAINE

Numerous biological, psychological, social, and situational factors may influence relapse to cocaine. Research on most of these factors is still sparse. We discuss those with the strongest empirical support.

DEMOGRAPHIC CHARACTERISTICS

Although demographic information (e.g., gender, age, marital status, socioeconomic status [SES], race/ethnicity) is almost always provided on cocaine research samples, authors rarely report whether and how these characteristics are related to immediate treatment outcomes or to long-term abstinence. In the absence of these reports, it is impossible to know if these relationships were not investigated or if the analyses were done and no significant findings emerged. When demographic variables have been examined, the most interesting—and problematic—results have concerned SES and race/ethnicity. Data showing a relationship between lower SES or non-white race/ethnicity and relapse (e.g., Hall, Havassy, & Wasserman, 1991) are often difficult to interpret. SES and race/ethnicity overlap with route of cocaine administration and with each other. Persons who are more advantaged and white, compared to those less advantaged and non-white, are more likely to be intranasal users rather than smokers or injection users, and intranasal users have markedly better treatment outcomes (Hall et al., 1991). Thus, evidence that purports to show a protective effect for higher SES or being white may be better interpreted as demonstrating that intranasal users are easier to treat successfully. SES and race also may be proxies for numerous social environmental variables (e.g., drug availability, access to resources) that make it harder to maintain abstinence from cocaine (Lillie-Blanton, Anthony, & Schuster, 1993). Silverman et al. (1996), in their voucher-based contingency study with cocaine-abusing methadone-maintenance patients, found no treatment effects for race. This may have been because all subjects used more severe administration routes; however, no information on route was presented.

PSYCHOPATHOLOGY

Epidemiological studies have shown a strikingly high prevalence of psychiatric disorders among cocaine patients compared to the general population (e.g., Halikas, Crosby, Pearson, Nugent, & Carlson, 1994; Havassy & Wasserman, 1996; Kleinman et al., 1990; Rounsaville et al., 1991; Wasserman, Havassy, & Boles, 1997; Ziedonis, Rayford, Bryant, & Rounsaville, 1994). Surprisingly, the role of psychopathology in cocaine relapse has seldom been addressed systematically, despite a widespread belief that drug abusers with co-occurring psychiatric disorders are more problematic to treat. Havassy and Wasserman (1996), reporting on a sample of 450 cocaine patients in private inpatient and outpatient drug abuse treatment, found that no Diagnostic and Statistical Manual of Mental Disorders (3rd ed.) (*DSM-III-R*) psychiatric disorders predicted relapse to cocaine use at 3, 6, or 12 months after treatment entry. Several disorders, however (major depressive episode, generalized anxiety disorder, and agoraphobia), predicted continuous cocaine *abstinence* at at least one of these timepoints. Data in this study were from the Diagnostic Interview Schedule (DIS-III-R), administered 14–21 days after treatment entry.

Other recently published studies also have found a "protective" effect for selected psychiatric disorders, especially depression. Carroll, Nich, and Rounsaville (1995), in their 2 × 2 study of the antidepressant desipramine crossed with psychosocial treatments, hypothesized that "depression would be a positive prognostic factor . . . through association with greater subjective distress, heightened perceptions of negative consequences of cocaine use, and motivation for treatment" (p. 252). This hypothesis was borne out. Moreover, depressed subjects had better treatment retention. Reductions in cocaine use and depressive symptoms were closely associated throughout treatment. Few published data suggest that co-occurring psychiatric disorders attenuate the effectiveness of cocaine treatment, although Arndt, McLellan, Dorozynsky, Woody, and O'Brien (1994), in another desipramine treatment trial, showed that antisocial personality disorder was a negative prognostic factor.

Positive associations between co-occurring psychiatric disorders and cocaine abstinence are somewhat counterintuitive. Patients with no additional psychiatric problems beyond their cocaine use might be expected to fare better, not worse, after quitting cocaine. As Carroll et al. (1995) suggested, however, patients with some types of psychiatric symptoms (e.g., depression) may be more motivated to avoid cocaine than patients who are in less distress. Perhaps an *improvement* in psychiatric symptoms, rather than their initial presence, is beneficial. To investigate this, future studies should include repeated psychiatric assessments over time. Several research groups already have noted decreases in depressive and other symptoms after the start of treatment. In the inpatient–outpatient study led by Havassy, for example, distress scores on the Symptom Checklist-90-R (Derogatis, 1983) decreased markedly between treatment entry and 4 weeks after treatment entry (unpublished data).

The effect of psychopathology as a positive prognostic factor may be limited to the mood and anxiety disorders. The role of more severe psychopathology (e.g., schizophrenia) in cocaine relapse may be different. Also, psychiatric disorders that are present at the start of treatment may have very different effects from disorders that originate after a period of abstinence. As noted above, disorders diagnosed at the start of treatment may remit or decrease in intensity once abstinence has been established and have little impact on future cocaine use. Disorders that begin or recur following abstinence may have a potentially large negative impact. Research that addresses the effects of onset of new disorders during cocaine abstinence has yet to be conducted.

MOODS AND STRESS

Much of the relapse literature suggests that both negative and positive affect are associated with relapse; however, negative affect is more consistently associated with relapse than is positive affect. Positive affect and negative affect may not be two anchors on a single continuum. Diener and Emmons (1984) have proposed that positive and negative moods are separate dimensions.

Many studies about drug and alcohol relapse support this perspective. Shiffman (1982) and Marlatt and Gordon (1980) found that negative affect and stress were associated with a large percentage of relapse episodes; however, sizable percentages of relapse episodes were associated with positive affect or were precipitated by positive stimuli, for example, eating, drinking, and relaxation. McKay et al. (1995), in one of the few studies of cocaine relapse processes, found that treated cocaine-dependent subjects associated both positive and negative affective states with the period during relapse. Negative affective states most frequently described the period prior to relapse and the period of termination of cocaine use.

Our work concerning relapse to tobacco, alcohol, opiates (Hall, Havassy, & Wasserman, 1990), and cocaine (Hall et al., 1991) also suggests the importance of negative and positive affective states and indicates that these are different constructs rather than opposite ends of a continuum. The first study (Hall et al., 1990) showed that lower levels of positive and higher levels of negative moods were correlated with first drug use, but only when moods and drug use were assessed concurrently. Prospective (lagged) analyses in which drug use was predicted from earlier mood scores failed to show significant relationships.

The second study (Hall et al., 1991) replicated the methodology used in the first study with 104 treated cocaine users. This study assessed the effects of stress variables (negative moods, hassles, symptoms, and life events) and of positive mood on relapse to cocaine. In concurrent analyses, each of the measures of mood and stress had a main effect on abstinence: higher scores on positive moods were correlated with a lower risk of relapse, whereas higher scores on all of the stress measures were correlated with a higher risk. In prospective analyses using lagged correlations, only positive mood had an effect on abstinence; higher positive mood scores yielded lower risk of relapse. Results of these studies suggest that subjective well-being may be crucial for maintaining abstinence among treated cocaine users.

Baker, Morse, and Sherman (1986) have proposed a psychobiological model that provides additional support for the mutual exclusivity of positive and negative affect. In their proposed "two-affect model of urges and drug motivation" described in their work on a psychobiological analysis of urges, they postulate two mutually inhibitory, distinct, incompatible urge networks, positive and negative. This work includes elaborate descriptions of positive and negative urge networks and neurobiological support for these networks. This model concerns itself with motivation to use drugs, and although withdrawal states are incorporated and can be explained within this context, relapse is not discussed.

CRAVING

Few psychological constructs have captured the attention of the field of cocaine abuse as has the construct of craving. Much of the interest appears to stem from implied acceptance of a biological model of dependence, which assumes that craving that arises from neurotransmitter imbalance is causal in drug use. Nevertheless, evidence for the usefulness of the construct is mixed at best.

Retrospective surveys of relapsed alcoholics, cigarette smokers, and drug addicts challenge the assumption that urges and cravings always precede and initiate relapse (Bradley, Phillips, Green, & Gossop, 1989; Litman, Stapleton, & Oppenheim, 1983; Ludwig, 1972; Marlatt, 1978; Marlatt & Gordon, 1980; O'Connell & Martin, 1987; Shiffman, 1986). Across the different samples, a minority of respondents—from 1 to 23%—attributed their relapses to cravings. More frequently, respondents cited dysphoric moods, social pressure, interpersonal conflict, drug availability, and positive emotional states as causative factors in their relapse to drug use. Wallace (1989) found a similarly low percentage of crack cocaine smokers, less than 6%, who listed craving as the proximate cause of their relapse. All of these studies are limited by their retrospective designs, the unreliability of long-term memory, unverified self-reports, self-presentation biases, and differences in methodology. Despite these limitations, it seems reasonable to suggest that relapse is multidetermined, and that urges and cravings are only one factor in facilitating relapse. Some authors have gone even further, suggesting that urges and cravings are not necessary for the initiation of drug use after a period of abstinence (Tiffany, 1990).

Although one explanation for the weak results for craving is that craving is simply not that important in relapse or remission, the empirical relationship between craving and subsequent drug use may be attenuated by a number of methodological factors, including poor measurement of the craving construct. Most studies that have measured self-reported craving, either as a predictor or dependent variable, have relied exclusively on a single Likert scale or other rating thermometer technique. While intuitively appealing, the use of a single item is often psychometrically unreliable, may not adequately sample the different semantic categories that addicts use to describe their urges and cravings (Kozlowski & Wilkinson, 1987), and sheds little light on theories of drug craving. Recognition of these problems has led to the development of more sophisticated self-report instruments (Halikas, Kuh, Crosby, Carlson, & Crea, 1991; Tiffany, Singleton, Haertzen, & Henningfield, 1993), but these have not yet been incorporated into cue reactivity laboratory studies or treatment outcome studies to determine their utility.

Several studies have attempted to create a laboratory analog of conditioned cocaine craving. In these studies, subjects are exposed to cocaine-related or neutral stimuli, and their physiological responses and self-reported urges are monitored. Recently, this work has been extended to cocaine abusers (Berger et al., 1996; Ehrman, Robbins, & Childress, 1992; Kranztler & Bauer, 1992; Robbins, Ehrman, Childress, & O'Brien, 1992; Satel, Krystal, Delgado, Kosten, & Chaney, 1995).

These studies have been criticized for a number of methodological reasons (Laberg, 1986; McCaul, Turken, & Stitzer, 1989; Newlin, Hotchkiss, Cox, Rauscher, & Li, 1989; Tiffany, 1990). Most important for the current discussion is the observation that the magnitude and duration of changes in self-reported craving that have been demonstrated thus far are so modest that they are of questionable clinical significance (Drummond, Cooper, & Glautier, 1990). Furthermore, it is unclear whether these laboratory-generated phenomena have any clinically important relation to active relapse. Most often the studies emphasize physiological responses such as skin conductance that may or may not be directly linked to drug use (cf. Cooney, Baker, Pomerleau, & Josephy, 1984). Even in those studies that include a measure of drug consumption in the laboratory (Hodgson, Rankin, & Stockwell, 1979; Rankin, Hodgson, & Stockwell, 1979; Rickard-Figueroa & Zeichner, 1985; Stockwell, Hodgson, & Taylor, 1982), it is unclear whether these effects bear any relation to actual relapse outside of the laboratory. The cue reactivity paradigm offers a methodology for evaluating theories of drug use and relapse, for example, determining whether a "conditioned" response is counterdirectional or isodirectional to the direct drug effect. Nonetheless, further investigation is needed into the relations between laboratory responses and real-world relapse.

SOCIAL SUPPORT

The underlying hypothesis in the study of social relationships in the context of drug abuse is that social support may provide a protective factor with regard to maintaining abstinence from drug use. The foundation for this hypothesis is derived from several decades of research on morbidity and mortality associated with social isolation (e.g., Durkheim, 1951, cited by House, Landis, & Umberson, 1988). Social relationships are protective of health, and, in patients with chronic disease, those with greater levels of support have better health outcomes (see Cassel, 1976; Cobb, 1976; House et al., 1988).

With regard to drug use behaviors, social learning models assert that addiction is a set of learned responses reinforced by the presence of role models, conditioned cues, and cognitive factors that promote continued drug use. Within this model, social support for healthy behaviors and a nondrug-using lifestyle could promote abstinence. Supportive others may motivate, influence, or assist individuals treated for addiction to attain and maintain abstinence, and the absence of a strong, prosocial, nondrug-involved social network may be a major contributor to post-treatment relapse.

At least three frequently used social support constructs appear in the drug and alcohol literature: social integration, functional support, and abstinence-specific support. (For further description, see Cohen & Syme, 1985).

Social integration (frequently labeled "structural support"), a quantitative construct concerned with amount of social involvement, is measured by numbers of relatives, friends, and important others with whom one maintains contact; numbers of social groups to which one belongs; number of activities attended; and size and composition of social networks. The second construct, *functional support,* is qualitative and addresses the perceived adequacy of and satisfaction with support, both emotional support and tangible support. *Abstinence-specific support* is related to efforts to maintain abstinence or pressures to use drugs, and may be either of the structural or functional type.

Studies of social support, particularly those of smokers and alcoholics, have indicated that greater support is associated with higher abstinence rates at the end of treatment and at posttreatment follow-up (Coppotelli & Orleans, 1985; Finney, Moos, & Mewborn, 1980; Havassy, Hall, & Wasserman, 1991; Mermelstein, Lichtenstein, Baer, & Kamarck, 1986). The measure of support most consistently and significantly associated with drug use outcomes is social integration. A higher degree of social integration, versus isolation, is positively associated with better outcomes. This is consistent with the relationships found in the chronic medical illness-social support literature.

In our study of 104 cocaine users who were followed for 6 months after completing abstinence-oriented treatment (Havassy, Wasserman, & Hall, 1995), the effect of social integration was conditional on race. For Caucasian subjects, the adjusted odds of sustaining abstinence increased 2.48 times with each additional point increase on a social integration measure, the Social Participation Index. There was no effect of social integration on abstinence for African-American subjects. African-American and Caucasian subjects did not differ in their endorsement pattern on the SPI, and both groups were highly variable in how they attained their scores. Controlling for the effects of demographic and other background variables, the main effect for emotional support was significant. Higher levels of emotional support predicted sustained abstinence, and lower levels predicted a lapse to cocaine use. Instrumental support and interpersonal conflict did not have significant effects.

Analyses indicated that having no current users in networks versus having one or more was not related to cocaine abstinence. In contrast, a "friendship" variable, having no friends versus having one or more friends who were current users versus having no cocaine-using friends, did predict relapse, conditional on race. For Caucasian subjects, those with friends but no cocaine-using friends were protected against relapse (69.6% stayed abstinent for 12 weeks), and those who reported no friends at all were at an increased risk for relapse (25.0% stayed abstinent).

Few studies in the addictions that consist of experimental interventions have included aspects of social relationships and support. So far as we could find, only one study, completed by members of our group and comparing the clinical and cost-effectiveness of private sector inpatient and outpatient treatment programs for a sample of 450 cocaine-dependent adults (Havassy, Wasserman, Tschann, Weisz, & Schmidt, in press; Havassy, Wasserman, Weisz, & R. Maude-Griffin, 1996), has addressed the posttreatment period and therefore has direct implications for relapse. Preliminary analyses (Weisz, Havassy, & Wasserman, 1994) indicated no main effects on outcomes for social support variables examined individually. Nevertheless, there were pronounced changes in social support variables from treatment entry through 6 months. Levels of emotional, tangible, and abstinence-specific support increased over time between treatment entry and the first postentry assessment at 6 weeks, then began to drop. Across assessments, subjects who were abstinent at 6 months reported higher levels of social support than subjects who had used cocaine. Significant interactions indicated that increases in support were better maintained by subjects who were abstinent than by those who were not. Regardless of abstinence status, subjects reported a significant decrease in proportion of social network members who used cocaine between the first two assessments (treatment entry and 6 weeks). This decrease was maintained at 6 months. African-Americans reported less social network cocaine use than Caucasians, across assessments and independent of abstinence status. Women reported higher levels of emotional support than men. Significant interactions for emotional, tangible, and abstinence-specific support indicated pronounced differences between abstinent versus nonabstinent men: nonabstinent men reported lower levels of support, especially at early assessments. Nonabstinent men had the lowest levels of support across assessments. There were few differences between nonabstinent versus abstinent women. Results of analyses suggest that high levels of social support are correlated with maintaining abstinence. Because predictive analyses are still preliminary, whether any elements of social relationships contribute to the models predicting abstinence is not yet known.

Data from both these studies point to a potentially positive role for social relationships in the maintenance of abstinence following treatment. Although there were some differences according to race and gender, aspects of social environments may either facilitate abstinence or contribute to relapse. As in other studies, the data indicate that contributions of structural support or social participation to abstinence are more consistent than the contributions of functional support.

GOALS FOR FUTURE ABSTINENCE

In our work (Hall et al., 1991), patients who had a commitment to absolute cocaine abstinence at the end of treatment, that is, who did not entertain the possibility of using ever again, even once, were significantly more likely (adjusted relative risk = 2.4) to remain continuously abstinent after treatment than patients who endorsed weaker abstinence goals (e.g., wanted to remain abstinent but realized they might slip, or wished to reconsider in the future whether they would use again). The positive effect of a commitment to absolute abstinence appears robust across drug treatment populations. In our earlier study of alcoholics, cigarette smokers, and heroin addicts (Hall et al., 1990), we also found a significant association between abstinence goal and future abstinence. In both studies, subjects completed abstinence-oriented treatment programs. Thus, the most rigorous goal choice was congruent with treatment program goals. We do not know whether the effect would hold in patients completing other types of programs (e.g., those using a harm reduction model) or in self-quitters.

EXPECTANCIES

Other cognitive variables that may play a role in cocaine relapse are positive and negative cocaine expectancies. Research on expectancies in cocaine patients lags far behind parallel research on alcoholics and cigarette smokers. The importance of expectancies in bringing about cocaine relapse is unknown. Nevertheless, it is conceivable that persons with high levels of positive expectations about cocaine's effects, or low levels of negative expectations, would be prone to relapse. Clinically, this is generally believed to be the case. Washton (1989), for example, has written about the dangers of "euphoric recall," a phenomenon in which abstinent cocaine users remember their positive experiences with cocaine and forget or minimize the negative. Jaffe and Kilbey (1994) have developed a self-report measure, the Cocaine Expectancy Questionnaire, to assess beliefs about the effects of cocaine. Their solution for the scale includes grandiosity/euphoria, enhancement of abilities, increased energy/arousal, sexual enhancement, and paranoia. Studies to evaluate the effects of different categories of expectancies on treatment outcome would be useful. As Jaffe and Kilbey point out, expectancies are potentially modifiable. If it can be shown that certain expectancies are associated with future relapse, interventions that target these expectancies may be effective.

THE COCAINE RELAPSE PROCESS

For a given individual, the cocaine relapse process may involve one or several of the above variables. The relapse process has been studied retrospectively by McKay et al. (1995), and Kirby, Lamb, Iguchi, Husband, and Platt (1995). McKay et al., using a structured interview, studied the onset, course, and termination of the cocaine relapse process in 95 patients. The most common experiences reported on the day of relapse were wanting drugs, having a lot of free time, being alone, having money, feeling extremely bored and lonely, and not participating in self-help programs. Factors important in regaining abstinence after relapse were painful internal states, help seeking, and other coping responses. McKay et al. also identified three relapse pathways: Unpleasant Affect, Positive Affect, and Sensation Seeking. The Sensation Seeking pathway was associated with more cocaine use days during the relapse.

Kirby et al. (1995) interviewed 265 cocaine-experienced methadone patients about antecedents of cocaine use and their strategies for avoiding cocaine use. Although not a relapse study per se, the data may shed light on which factors are most important in relapse. Antecedents were categorized as either environmental stimuli, activities, or emotions. The most frequently identified antecedents were having the drug present, being offered the drug, and having money available. Having nothing to do was the most frequently endorsed activity, and boredom was the most frequently endorsed emotion. Reporting fewer types of situations that occasioned cocaine use was associated with longer periods of lifetime abstinence. Kirby et al. classified abstinence strategies as either reactive, proactive, or unplanned. Overall, the three most often identified strategies were avoiding people and places, thinking about what one could lose if one used, and leaving the high-risk situation. The strategies most associated with abstinence were thinking about what one would lose, leaving the situation, moving to a new area, and using a different drug. Most of these methadone subjects were regular cocaine users, and their responses might not generalize to persons who had been abstinent from cocaine for longer periods or to primary cocaine abusers.

TREATMENTS TO PREVENT COCAINE RELAPSE

DRUG TREATMENT INTERVENTIONS AND RELAPSE

Studies of treatment interventions have contributed little to our knowledge of the factors that predict relapse, or how to prevent it. This lack can be traced to several factors. First, most clinical trials in the field are drug studies. For example, we found over 30 studies evaluating the effects of pharmacotherapy on cocaine use. Six of these were on desipramine (Arndt, Dorozynsky, Woody, McLellan, & O'Brien, 1992; Carroll, Rounsaville, Gordon, Nich, Jatlow, et al., 1994; Gawin & Kleber, 1984; Gawin et al., 1989; Kosten, Morgan, Falcione, & Schottenfeld, 1992; Levin & Lehman, 1991), four on amandatine (Alterman et al., 1992; Handelsman et al., 1995; Kampman et al., 1996; Weddington et al., 1991), four on mazindol (Berger, Gawin, & Kosten, 1989; Kosten, Steinberg, & Diakogiannis, 1991; Margolin, Avants, & Kosten, 1995; Stine, Krystal, Kosten, & Charney, 1995), and four on fluoxetine (Batki, Washburn, Delucchi, & Jones, 1996; Grabowski et al., 1995; Grabowski, Kirby, Elk, Cowan, & Rhoades, 1992; Pollack & Rosenbaum, 1991). The remaining studies used imipramine (Galloway, Newmeyer, Knapp, Stalcup, & Smith, 1994; Nunes et al., 1995; Rosencrans, 1991), bromocriptine (Dackis & Gold, 1985), methylphenidate (Khantzian, Gawin, Kleber, & Riordan, 1984), carbidopa-L-dopa (Rosen, Flemenbaum, & Slater, 1986), carbamazapine (Cornish et al., 1995; Halikas, Crosby, Pearson, & Graves, 1997; Kranzler, Bauer, Hersh, & Klinghoffer, 1995; Montoya, Levin, Fudala, & Gorelick, 1995), flupenthixal (Gawin, Allen, & Humblestone, 1989), and lithium (Gawin & Kleber, 1984). Unfortunately, none of these drugs has, as yet, shown sufficient efficacy during treatment to suggest they might be useful in preventing relapse. Therefore, these many pharmacological studies have contributed little to our understanding of relapse. (See Higgins & Wong, chapter 14, this volume, for a fuller discussion of pharmacological treatment studies.)

BEHAVIORAL RELAPSE PREVENTION STRATEGIES

Relapse prevention (RP) is a relatively recent technology for promoting abstinence from drugs of abuse as well as cessation of nondrug problematic behaviors (DeJong, 1994). RP strategies, which are grounded in social learning theory, were first presented in a systematic fashion by Marlatt and Gordon (1985). Based on widespread clinical acceptance and positive showing in a number of treatment studies across drugs of abuse, RP components are now incorporated into almost all psychosocial treatment conditions and combined psychosocial/pharmacologic conditions utilized in cocaine treatment trials.

RP strategies aim to prevent initial lapses in newly abstinent users as well as prevent lapses from become relapses. Rawson, Obert, McCann, and Marinelli-Casey (1993) described seven groups of RP interventions: psychoeducation, identification of high-risk situations for relapse and warning signs for relapse, development of coping skills, development of new lifestyle behaviors, increased self-efficacy, dealing with relapse, and drug/alcohol monitoring. In the 1980s, the RP approach was rapidly integrated into numerous cocaine treatment approaches and protocols (e.g., McAuliffe & Albert, 1992; Rawson, Obert, McCann, Smith, & Ling, 1990; Rawson et al., 1995; Wallace, 1990; Washton, 1989). Several research groups (e.g., Carroll and associates at Yale; Wells and associates at the University of Washington) have created RP-based treatments for cocaine users and tested these treatments in clinical trials. Carroll et al. (1991) compared RP to interpersonal therapy. Although both treatment conditions resulted in decreased cocaine use, RP appeared especially effective with severe users. Carroll and her associates have continued to explore the effectiveness of the RP approach, sometimes crossed with pharmacologic therapies, with largely encouraging results (Carroll, Rounsaville, Gordon, et al., 1994; Carroll, Rounsaville, Nich, et al., 1994, 1995). Wells, Petersoni, Gainey, Hawkins, and Catalano (1994) tested a cognitive–behavioral RP treatment against a 12-step recovery support group. In that trial, little evidence was found for differential effects of the two treatments. In a recent review, Carroll (1996) concluded that relapse prevention treatment has shown considerable promise when compared to no-treatment controls; however, its superiority to discussion control groups or other treatments is still unknown. As noted by Marlatt (1996), one reason for this is that many RP interventions fail to distinguish between abstinence initiation and relapse management. Most drug abuse treatments, both psychological and pharmacological, strive to help patients achieve abstinence. However, the hallmark characteristic of RP, and the feature that distinguishes it from other behavioral therapies, is the emphasis on intervening after a lapse has occurred in order to minimize the duration and severity of the relapse. That successfully treated patients learn to do that for themselves may account for the delayed emergence of positive RP effects found with cocaine abusers (Carroll, Rounsaville, Nich, et al., 1994b), alcoholics (Chaney, O'Leary, & Marlatt, 1978), and problem drinkers (Marlatt, Baer, & Latimer, 1995). As clinical researchers continue to elucidate the critical change mechanisms and how they affect outcome over time, conduct comparative evaluations of RP with other theoretically distinct interventions, combine RP with pharmacological treatments, and investigate interactions between patient characteristics and RP, the relationship between RP and posttreatment relapse will become clearer. (See Higgins and Wong, chapter 14, this volume, and Silverman et al., chapter 15, this volume, for more comprehensive discussions of behavioral treatment studies.)

SUMMARY

Relapse to cocaine use presents an interesting and complex set of problems to the scientist. Relapse itself is difficult to define due to differing routes of administration and insufficient data about the natural history of cocaine use. Theoretical models of relapse abound, but there are few direct tests of them. Nevertheless, some variables consistently predict continued abstinence, at least among cocaine abusers who are attempting to achieve abstinence in formal treatment programs. These include the presence of some forms of psychopathology, especially depression; perceived well-being; adequate social support; and rigorous goals with respect to abstinence. Cocaine craving does not appear to be a major factor, although this may reflect the many methodological difficulties that surround its measurement. As is so frequently the case in the treatment of drug abuse disorders, despite the fact that much is still to be learned about cocaine relapse, well-controlled clinical trials suggest that cognitive–behavioral relapse prevention strategies may be of use in increasing long-term abstinence rates.

REFERENCES

Alterman, A. I., Droba, M., Antelo, R. E., Cornish, J. W., Sweeney, K. K., Parikh, G. A., & O'Brien, C. P. (1992). Amantadine may facilitate detoxification of cocaine addicts. *Drug and Alcohol Dependence, 31,* 19–29.

Arndt, I. O., Dorozynsky, I., Woody, G. E., McLellan, T. A., & O'Brien, C. P. (1992). Desipramine treatment of cocaine dependence in methadone-maintained patients. *Archives of General Psychiatry, 49,* (November), 888–893.

Arndt, I. O., McLellan, A. T., Dorozynsky, L., Woody, G. E., & O'Brien, C. P. (1994). Desipramine treatment for cocaine dependence: Role of antisocial personality disorder. *Journal of Nervous and Mental Disease, 182,* 151–156.

Baker, T. B., Morse, E., & Sherman, J. E. (1987). The motivation to use drugs: A psychobiological analysis of urges. In P. C. Rivers (Ed.), *The Nebraska symposium on motivation: Alcohol and addictive behavior* (pp. 257–324). Lincoln: University of Nebraska Press.

Batki, S. L., Washburn, A. M., Delucchi, K., & Jones, R. T. (1996). A controlled trial of fluoxetine in crack cocaine dependence. *Drug and Alcohol Dependence, 41,* 137–142.

Berger, P., Gawin, F., & Kosten, T. (1989). Treatment of cocaine abuse with mazindol. *The Lancet, February 4,* 283.

Berger, S. P., Hall, S., Mickalian, J. D., Reid, M. S., Crawford, C. A., Delucchi, K. L., Carr, K., & Hall, S. M. (1996). Haloperidol antagonism of cue-elicited cocaine craving. *Lancet, 347,* 504–508.

Bradley, B. P., Phillips, G., Green, L., & Gossop, M. (1989). Circumstances surrounding the initial lapse to opiate use following detoxification. *British Journal of Psychiatry, 154,* 354–359.

Carroll, K. M. (1996). Relapse prevention as a psychological treatment: A review of controlled clinical trials. *Experimental and Clinical Psychopharmacology, 4,* 46–54.

Carroll, K. M., Rounsaville, B. J., Gordon, L. T., Nich, C., Jatlow, P., Bisighini, R. M., & Gawin, F. H. (1994). Psychotherapy and pharmacotherapy for ambulatory cocaine abusers. *Archives of General Psychiatry, 51,* 177–187.

Carroll, K. M., Rounsaville, B. J., Nich, C., Gordon, L. T., Wirtz, P. W., & Gawin, F. (1994). One-year follow-up of psychotherapy and pharmacotherapy for cocaine dependence: Delayed emergence of psychotherapy effects. *Archives of General Psychiatry, 51,* 989–997.

Carroll, K. M., Nich, C., & Rounsaville, B. J. (1995). Differential symptom reduction in depressed cocaine abusers treated with psychotherapy and pharmacotherapy. *Journal of Nervous and Mental Disease, 183,* 251–259.

Carroll, K. M., Rounsaville, B. J., & Gawin, F. H. (1991). A comparative trial of psychotherapies for ambulatory cocaine abusers: Relapse prevention and interpersonal psychotherapy. *American Journal of Drug and Alcohol Abuse, 17* (3), 229–247.

Cassell, J. (1976). The contribution of the social environment to host resistance. *American Journal of Epidemiology, 104,* 107–123.

Chaney, E. F., O'Leary, M. R., & Marlatt, G. A. (1978). Skill training with alcoholics. *Journal of Consulting and Clinical Psychology, 46* (5), 1092–1104.

Cobb, S. (1976). Social support as a moderator of life stress. *Psychosomatic Medicine, 38,* 300–314.

Cohen, S., & Syme, S. L. (1985). Issues in the study and application of social support. In S. Cohen & S. L. Syme (Eds., *Social support and health* (pp. 3–22). New York: Academic Press.

Cooney, N. L., Baker, L. H., Pomerleau, O. F., & Josephy, B. (1984). Salivation to drinking cues in alcohol abusers: Toward the validation of physiological measure of craving. *Addictive Behaviors, 9,* 91–94.

Coppotelli, H. C., & Orleans, C. T. (1985). Partner support and other determinants of smoking cessation maintenance among women. *Journal of Consulting and Clinical Psychology, 53,* 455–460.

Cornish, J. W., Maany, I., Fudala, P. J., Neal, S., Poole, S. A., Volpicelli, P., & O'Brien, C. P. (1995). Carbamazepine treatment for cocaine dependence. *Drug and Alcohol Dependence, 38,* 221–227.

Dackis, C. A., & Gold, M. S. (1985). Bromocriptine as treatment of cocaine abuse. *Lancet, 1,* (8348), 1151–1152.

DeJong, W. (1994). Relapse prevention: An emerging technology for promoting long-term drug abstinence. *The International Journal of the Addictions, 29,* 681–705.

Derogatis, L. R. (1983). *The SCL-90-R.* Towson, MD: Clinical Psychometric Research.

Diener, E., & Emmons, R. A. (1984). The independence of positive and negative affect. *Journal of Personality and Social Psychology, 47,* 1105–1117.

Drummond, D. C., Cooper, T., & Glautier, S. P. (1990). Conditional learning in alcohol dependence: Implications for cue exposure treatment. *British Journal of Addiction, 85,* 725–743.

Durkheim, E. (1951). *Suicide.* New York: Free Press. (Original work published 1897).

Finney, J. W., Moos, R. H., & Mewborn, C. R. (1980). Posttreatment experiences and treatment outcome of alcoholic patients six months and two years after hospitalization. *Journal of Consulting and Clinical Psychology, 48,* 17–29.

Ehrman, R. N., Robbins, S. J., & Childress, A. R. (1992). Conditioned responses to cocaine-related stimuli in cocaine abuse patients. *Psychopharmacology, 107,* (4), 523–529.

Galloway, G. P., Newmeyer, J., Knapp, T., Stalcup, S. A., & Smith, D. (1994). Imipramine for the treatment of cocaine and methamphetamine dependence. *Journal of Addictive Diseases, 13* (4), 201–216.

Gawin, F. H., Allen, D., & Humblestone, B. (1989). Outpatient treatment of 'crack' cocaine smoking with flupenthixol decanoate. A preliminary report. *Archives of General Psychiatry, 46,* 322–325.

Gawin, F. H., & Kleber, H. D. (1984). Cocaine abuse treatment II: An open pilot trial with lithium and desipramine. *Archive of General Psychiatry, 41,* 903–909.

Gawin, F. H., Kleber, H. D., Byck, R., Rounsaville, B. J., Kosten, T. R., Jatlow, P. I., & Morgan, C. (1989). Desipramine facilitation of initial cocaine abstinence. *Archives of General Psychiatry, 46,* 117–121.

Grabowski, J., Kirby, K., Elk, R., Cowan, C.,& Rhoades, H. (1992). Fluoxetine and behavioral factors in the treatment of cocaine dependence. In L. S. Harris (Ed.), *Problems of drug dependence 1991: Proceedings of the 53rd Annual Scientific Meeting. The College on the Problems of Drug Dependence.* NIDA Research Monograph Series, *119,* 362. DHMS Publ. No. (ADM) 92–1888. Washington, DC: U.S. Government Printing Office.

Grabowski, J., Rhoades, H., Elk, R., Schmitz, J., Davis, C., Creson, D., & Kirby, K. (1995). Fluoxetine is ineffective for treatment of cocaine dependence or concurrent opiate and cocaine dependence: Two placebo controlled double-blind trials. *Journal of Clinical Psychopharmacology, 15,* 163–174.

Halikas, J. A., Crosby, R. D., Pearson, V. L., & Graves, N. M. (1997). A randomized double-blind study of carbamazepine in the treatment of cocaine abuse. *Clinical Pharmacology and Therapeutics, 62,* 89–105.

Halikas, J. A., Crosby, R. D., Pearson, V. L., Nugent, S. M., & Carlson, G. A. (1994). Psychiatric co-morbidity in treatment-seeking cocaine abusers. *American Journal on Addictions, 3,* 24–34.

Halikas, J. A., Kuhn, K. L., Crosby, R. D., & Carlson, G. A. (1991). The measurement of craving in cocaine patients using the Minnesota Cocaine Craving Scale. *Comprehensive Psychiatry, 32,* (1), 22–27.

Hall, S. M., Havassy, B. E., & Wasserman, D. A. (1990). Commitment to abstinence and acute stress in relapse to alcohol, opiates, and nicotine. *Journal of Consulting and Clinical Psychology, 58,* 175–181.

Hall, S. M., Havassy, B. E., & Wasserman, D. A. (1991). Effects of commitment to abstinence, positive moods, stress, and coping on relapse to cocaine use. *Journal of Consulting and Clinical Psychology, 59,* 526–532.

Hall, S. M., Tunis, S. L., Triffleman, E., Banys, P., Clark, H. W., Tusel, D., Stewart, P., & Presti, D. (1994). Continuity of care and desipramine in primary cocaine abusers. *The Journal of Nervous and Mental Disease, 182,* (10), 570–575.

Handelsman, L., Limpitlaw, L., Williams, D., Schmeidler, J., Paris, P., & Stimel, B. (1995). Amantadine does not reduce cocaine use or craving in cocaine-dependent methadone maintenance patients. *Drug and Alcohol Dependence, 39* (3), 173–180.

Havassy, B. E., Wasserman, D. A., Tschann, J. M., Weisz, C., & Schmidt, C. J. (in press). Outcomes of inpatient and outpatient treatments for cocaine dependence. In F. Turns, J. Blaine, L. Onkin, & B. Tain (Eds.), *Treatment of cocaine dependence: Outcome research.* Washington, DC: NIDA Research Monograph.

Havassy, B. E., Hall, S. M., & Wasserman, D. A. (1991). Social support and relapse: Commonalities among alcoholics, opiate users, and cigarette smokers. *Addictive Behaviors, 16,* 235–246.

Havassy, B. E., & Wasserman, D. A. (1996). *Cocaine dependence, comorbidity, and outcomes in private chemical dependency treatment programs.* Unpublished manuscript.

Havassy, B. E., Wasserman, D. A., & Hall, S. M. (1995). Social relationships and abstinence from cocaine in an American treatment sample. *Addiction, 90,* 699–710.

Havassy, B. E., Wasserman, D. A., Weisz, C., & Maude-Griffin, R. (1996). *Effectiveness of inpatient and outpatient private treatment for cocaine dependence.* Unpublished manuscript.

Hodgson, R., Rankin, H., & Stockwell, T. (1979). Alcohol dependence and the priming effect. *Behavior Research and Therapy, 17,* 379–387.

House, J. S., Landis, K. R., & Umberson, D. (1988). Social relationships and health. *Science, 241,* 540–545.

Jaffe, A. J., & Kilbey, M. M. (1994). The Cocaine Expectancy questionnaire (CEQ). Construction and predictive utility. *Psychological Assessment, 6,* 18–26.

Kampman, K., Volpicelli, J. R., Alterman, A., Cornish, J., Weinrieb, R., Epperson, L., Sparkman, T., & O'Brien, C. P. (1996). Amantadine in the early treatment of cocaine dependence: A double-blind, placebo-controlled trial. *Drug and Alcohol Dependence, 41,* 25–33.

Khantzian, E. J., Gawin, F., Kleber, H. D., & Riordan, C. E. (1984). Methylphenidate (Ritalin) treatment of cocaine dependence—a preliminary report. *Journal of Substance Abuse Treatment, 1* (2), 107–112.

Kirby, K. C., Lamb, R. J., Iguchi, M. Y., Husband, S. D., & Platt, J. J. (1995). Situations occasioning cocaine use and cocaine abstinence strategies. *Addiction, 90,* 1241–1252.

Kleinman, P. H., Miller, A. B., Millman, R. B., Woody, G. E., Todd, T., Kemp, J., & Lipton, D. S. (1990). Psychopathology among cocaine abusers entering treatment. *Journal of Nervous and Mental Disease, 178,* 442–447.

Kosten, T. R., Morgan, C. M., Falcione, J., & Schottenfeld, R. S. (1992). Pharmacotherapy for cocaine-abusing methadone-maintained patients using amantadine or desipramine. *Archives of General Psychiatry, 49,* (11), 894–898.

Kosten, T. R., Steinberg, M., & Diakogiannis, I. A. (1993). Crossover trial of mazindol for cocaine dependence. *American Journal of Addictions, 2* (2), 161–164.

Kozlowski, L. T., & Wilkinson, D. A. (1987). Use and misuse of the concept of craving by alcohol, tobacco, and drug researchers. *British Journal of Addiction, 82,* 31–36.

Kranzler, H. R., & Bauer, L. O. (1992). Bromocriptine and cocaine cue reactivity in cocaine-dependent patients. *British Journal of Addiction, 81,* (11), 1537–1548.

Kranzler, H. R., Bauer, L. O., Hersh, D., & Klinghoffer, V. (1995). Carbamazepine treatment of cocaine dependence. A placebo-controlled trial. *Drug and Alcohol Dependence, 38,* 203–211.

Laberg, J. C. (1986). Alcohol and expectancy: Subjective, psychophysiological and behavioral responses to alcohol stimuli in severely, moderately, and nondependent drinkers. *British Journal of Addiction, 81,* 797–808.

Levin, F. R., & Lehman, A. F. (1991). Meta-analyses of desipramine as an adjunct in the treatment of cocaine addiction. *Journal of Clinical Psychopharmacology, 11* (6), 374–378.

Lillie-Blanton, M., Anthony, J. C., & Schuster, C. R. (1993). Probing the meaning of racial/ethnic group comparisons in crack cocaine smoking. *Journal of the American Medical Association, 269,* 993–997.

Litman, G. K., Stapleton, J., & Oppenheim, A. N. (1983). Situations related to alcoholism relapse. *British Journal of Addiction, 78,* 381–389.

Ludwig, A. M. (1972). On and off the wagon: Reasons for drinking and abstaining by alcoholics. *Quarterly Journal of Studies on Alcohol, 33,* 91–96.

Margolin, A., Avants, S. K., & Kosten, T. R. (1995). Mazindol for relapse prevention to cocaine abuse in methadone-maintained patients. *American Journal of Drug and Alcohol Abuse, 21,* 469–481.

Marlatt, G. A. (1996). Models of relapse and relapse prevention: A commentary. *Experimental and Clinical Psychopharmacology, 4* (1), 55–60.

Marlatt, G. A. (1978). Craving for alcohol, loss of control, and relapse: Cognitive behavioral analysis. In P. E. Nathan, G. A. Marlatt, & T. Loberg (Eds.), *Alcoholism: New directions in behavioral research and treatment* (pp. 271–314). New York: Plenum Press.

Marlatt, G. A., Baer, J. S., & Latimer, M. E. (1995). Preventing alcohol abuse in college students: A harm-reduction approach. In G. M. Boyd, J. Howard, & R. A. Zucker (Eds.), *Alcohol problems among adolescents: Current directions in prevention research* (pp. 147–172). Northvale, NJ: Erlbaum.

Marlatt, G. A., & Gordon, J. R. (1980). Determinants of relapse: Implications for the maintenance of behavior change. In P. O. Davidson & S. M. Davidson (Eds.), *Behavioral medicine: Changing health lifestyles* (pp. 410–472). New York: Brunner/Mazel.

Marlatt, G. A., & Gordon, J. R. (Eds.). (1985). *Relapse prevention: Maintenance strategies in the treatment of addictive behaviors.* New York: Guilford Press.

McAuliffe, W. E., & Albert, J. (1992). *Clean start: An outpatient program for initiating cocaine recovery.* New York: Guilford Press.

McCaul, M. E., Turken, J. S., & Stitzer, M. L. (1989). Psychophysiological effects of alcohol related stimuli. I. The role of stimulus intensity. *Alcoholism: Clinical and Experimental Research, 13,* 386–391.

McKay, J. R., Rutherford, M. J., Alterman, A. I., Cacciola, J. S., & Kaplan, M. R. (1995). An examination of the cocaine relapse process. *Drug and Alcohol Dependence, 38,* 35–43.

Mermelstein, R., Cohen, S., Lichtenstein, E., Baer, J. S., & Kamarck, T. (1986). Social support and smoking cessation and maintenance. *Journal of Consulting and Clinical Psychology, 54,* 447–453.

Montoya, I. D., Levin, F. R., Fudala, P. J., & Gorelick, D. A., (1995). Double-blind comparison of carbamazepine and placebo for treatment of cocaine dependence. *Drug and Alcohol Dependence, 38,* 213–219.

Newlin, D. B., Hotchkess, B., Cox, W. M., Rauscher, F., & Li, T. K. (1989). Autonomic and subjective responses to alcohol stimuli with appropriate control stimuli. *Addictive Behaviors, 14,* 625–630.

Nunes, E. V., McGrath, P. J., Quitkin, F. M., Ocepek-Welikson, K., Stewart, J. W., Koenig, T., Wager, S., & Klein, D. F. (1995). Imipramine treatment of cocaine abuse: Possible boundaries of efficacy. *Drug and Alcohol Dependence, 39* (3), 185–195.

O'Connell, K. A., & Martin, E. J. (1987). Highly tempting situations associated with abstinence, temporary lapse, and relapse among participants in smoking cessation programs. *Journal of Consult-*

ing and Clinical Psychology, 55, 367–371.

Pollack, M. H., & Rosenbaum, J. F. (1991). Fluoxetine treatment of cocaine abuse in heroin addicts. *Journal of Clinical Psychiatry, 52,* 31–33.

Rankin, H., Hodgson, R., & Stockwell, T. (1979). The concept of craving and its measurement. *Behaviour Research and Therapy, 17,* 389–396.

Rawson, R. A., Obert, J. L., McCann, M. J., & Marinelli-Casey, P. (1993). Relapse prevention strategies in outpatient substance abuse treatment. *Psychology of Addictive Behaviors, 7,* 85–95.

Rawson, R. A., Obert, J. L., McCann, M. J., Smith, D. P., & Ling, W. (1990). Neurobehavioral treatment for cocaine dependency. *Journal of Psychoactive Drugs, 22,* 159–171.

Rawson, R. A., Shoptaw, S. J., Obert, J. L., McCann, M. J., Hasson, A. L., Marinelli-Casey, P. J., Brethen, P. R., & Ling, W. (1995). An intensive outpatient approach for cocaine abuse treatment: The Matrix Model. *Journal of Substance Abuse Treatment, 12,* 117–127.

Rickard-Figueroa, K., & Zeichner, A. (1985). Assessment of smoking urge and its concomitants under an environmental smoking cue manipulation. *Addictive Behaviors, 10,* 249–256.

Robbins, S. J., Ehrman, R. N., Childress, A. R., & O'Brien, C. P. (1992). Using cue reactivity to screen medications for cocaine abuse: A test of amantadine hydrochloride. *Addictive Behaviors, 17* (5), 491–499.

Rosen, H., Flemenbaum, A., & Slater, V. L. (1986). Clinical trial of carbidopa-L-dopa combination for cocaine abuse. *American Journal of Psychiatry, 143,* 1493.

Rounsaville, B. J., Anton, S. F., Carroll, K., Budde, D., Prusoff, B. A., & Gawin, F. (1991). Psychiatric diagnoses of treatment-seeking cocaine abusers. *Archives of General Psychiatry, 39,* 161–166.

Satel, S. L., Krystal, J. H., Delgado, P. L., Kosten, T. R., & Chaney, E. F. (1995). Tryptophan depletion and attenuation of cue-induced craving for cocaine. *American Journal of Psychiatry, 152* (5), 778–783.

Shiffman, S. (1982). Relapse following smoking cessation: A situational analysis. *Journal of Consulting and Clinical Psychology, 50,* 71–86.

Shiffman, S. (1986). A cluster-analytic classification of smoking relapse episodes. *Addictive Behaviors, 11,* 295–307.

Silverman, K., Higgins, S. T., Brooner, R. K., Montoya, I. D., Cone, E. J., Schuster, C. R., & Preston, K. L. (1996). Sustained cocaine abstinence in methadone maintenance patients through voucher-based reinforcement therapy. *Archives of General Psychiatry, 53,* 409–415.

Stine, S. M., Krystal, J. H., Kasten, T. R., & Charney, D. S. (1995). Mazindol treatment for cocaine dependence. *Drug and Alcohol Dependence, 39,* 245–252.

Stockwell, T. R., Hodgson, R., & Taylor, C. (1982). Alcohol dependence, beliefs and the priming effect. *Behaviour Research and Therapy, 20,* 513–522.

Tiffany, S. T. (1990). A cognitive model of drug urges and drug-use behavior: Roles of automatic and nonautomatic processes. *Psychological Review, 97* (2), 147–168.

Tiffany, S. T., Singleton, E., Haertzen, C. A., & Henningfield, J. E. (1993). The development of a cocaine craving questionnaire. *Drug and Alcohol Dependence, 34,* 19–28.

Wallace, B. C. (1989). Psychological and environmental determinants of relapse in crack cocaine smokers. *Journal of Substance Abuse Treatment, 6,* 95–106.

Wallace, B. C. (1990). Treating crack cocaine dependence: The critical role of relapse prevention. *Journal of Psychoactive Drugs, 22,* 149–158.

Washton, A. M. (1989). *Cocaine addiction: Treatment, recovery, and relapse prevention.* New York: W. W. Norton.

Washton, A. M., & Stone-Washton, N. (1990). Abstinence and relapse in outpatient cocaine addicts. *Journal of Psychoactive Drugs, 22,* 135–147.

Wasserman, D. A., Havassy, B. E., & Boles, S. (1997). Traumatic events and post-traumatic stress disorder in cocaine users entering private treatment. *Drug and Alcohol Dependence, 46,* 1–8.

Weddington, W. W., Brown, B. S., Haertzen, C. A., Hess, J. M., Mahaffrey, J. R., Kolar, A. F., & Jaffe, J. H. (1991). Comparison of amantadine and desipramine combined with psychotherapy for treatment of cocaine dependence. *American Journal of Drug and Alcohol Abuse, 17,* 137–152.

Weisz, C., Havassy, B. E., & Wasserman, D. A. (1994). Changes over time in social support and net-work drug use among treated cocaine users. In L. Harris (Ed.), *Problems of drug dependence, 1993: Proceedings of the 55th Annual Scientific Meeting* (p. 157). The College on Problems of Drug Dependence. NIDA Research Monograph Series, *141*, Vol. 2. Washington, DC: U.S. Government Printing Office.

Wells, E. A., Petersoni, P. L., Gainey, R. R., Hawkins, J. D., & Catalano, R. F. (1994). Outpatient treatment for cocaine abuse: A controlled comparison of relapse prevention and twelve-step approaches. *American Journal of Drug and Alcohol Abuse, 10,* 1–17.

Wikler, A. (1972). Sources of reinforcement for drug using behavior—a theoretical formulation. *Pharmacology and the Future of Man. Proceedings of the 5th International Congress of Pharmacology, 1,* 18–30.

Wise, R. A. (1988). The neurobiology of craving: Implications for the understanding and treatment of addiction. *Journal of Abnormal Psychology, 97* (2), 118–132.

Ziedonis, D. M., Rayford, B. S., Bryant, K. J., & Rounsaville, B. J. (1994). Psychiatric comorbidity in White and African-American cocaine addicts seeking substance abuse treatment. *Hospital and Community Psychiatry, 45,* 43–49.

17

COCAINE LEGALIZATION: DESIGNING THE EXPERIMENTS

THOMAS J. CROWLEY AND
J. T. BREWSTER

Addiction Research and Treatment Services
Department of Psychiatry
University of Colorado School of Medicine
Denver, Colorado

INTRODUCTION

Americans spent about $31 billion on black market cocaine in 1993 (Office of National Drug Control Policy, 1995). Some suggest that "legalizing" cocaine would drive black market dealers out of business (Nadelman, 1989, 1996; Schmoke, 1990, 1996; Smith, 1988).

We define "cocaine legalization" as reducing controls to make inexpensive cocaine available legally to users. Discussions of legalization draw on retrospective data, rather than prospective research, to support cost-benefit predictions. Thus, drug-abuse researchers who do prospective studies have written little about legalization. An English-language Medline search for 1993–1996, using the keywords "cocaine" and "legalization," found only one publication, an historical analysis (Pauly, 1994). However, before drugs are approved for new uses scientists conduct prospective randomized clinical trials. Only treatments that are safe and efficacious then earn approval. How might trials be designed to test cocaine legalization?

We review different levels of drug legalization already operating in the United States. We explore which ones offer models for legalizing cocaine, considering scientific data that suggest the possible consequences from adopting each model. Then, having selected a possibly feasible model, we examine the "nuts-and-bolts" of designing prospective studies of its safety and efficacy.

Cocaine Abuse: Behavior, Pharmacology,
and Clinical Applications

BRIEF HISTORY OF CONTROLS
ON COCAINE AVAILABILITY

In the late 1800s "the aura of enthusiasm that surrounded cocaine's entry into U.S. commerce, as well as the actual euphoriant effect of the drug, rapidly spread cocaine's use throughout the United States" (Musto, 1992). Although epidemiologic data from that time are not available, cocaine was included in numerous patent medicines and in Coca-Cola. Then, with increased public awareness of adverse effects, reinforced by the Harrison Narcotic Act of 1914, cocaine's black market use decreased. However, in the late 1960s a renaissance of cocaine use began, with rapid acceleration in the 1970s and 1980s. Still, for many people cocaine remained prohibitively expensive, costing over $100 per gram.

In inner cities use increased after the mid-1980s with the advent of crack cocaine, which was sold in small, inexpensive quantities. Despite efforts to limit importation from South America, cocaine production nearly tripled from 1988 to 1991, from 360 to 1,000 metric tons (Weiss, Mirin, & Bartel, 1994). Cocaine now is one of the most commonly encountered drugs of abuse.

From the mid-1880s until passage of the Pure Food and Drug Act in 1906, cocaine was readily available and completely unregulated in the United States. However, amid growing concerns about cocaine's adverse effects, the Harrison Act made cocaine a prescription-only drug, restricting importation and subjecting nonprescription users to criminal penalties. The Controlled Substances Act of 1970 revised and unified Federal drug-control laws (DEA, 1990). It established five lists (or Schedules) of controlled substances. Schedule I drugs "have no established medical use in the United States and have a high abuse potential." Those in Schedules II-V have medical indications. Schedule II drugs also "have a high abuse potential with severe psychic or physical dependence liability"; cocaine is in Schedule II. Drugs in Schedules III, IV, and V are thought to have successively lower abuse potentials.

COCAINE LEGALIZATION: HYPOTHESES
VERSUS VALUE STATEMENTS

Arguments for or against legalization may be empirically testable hypotheses or untestable assertions about values. Although we recognize the importance (and in some cases, the primacy) of untestable value judgments, they fall outside the scope of this chapter. By separating testable hypotheses from value judgments, we can consider what research may be needed to clarify whether cocaine legalization would improve people's lives.

Examples of potentially testable hypotheses are (a) current legal controls on cocaine suppress cocaine-related mortality and morbidity; (b) making cocaine legally available will reduce crime, gang involvement, and incarcerations; (c) if cocaine controls are reduced, overall use initially will rise, but then will fall below current levels; (d) reducing controls on cocaine will reduce harm to nonusers.

The following are examples of value judgments not testable in scientific experiments. Despite their importance, they lie outside our present scope: (a) individual drug use is a right; people have the right to make choices without fear of criminal sanctions; (b) drug abuse is an illness, not a crime, and it is wrong to punish illnesses; (c) drug prohibition erodes civil liberties; as police powers grow to capture drug criminals, citizens' freedoms are eroded; (d) if cocaine legalization resulted in many more deaths among addicts but also reduced crime, that net change would be acceptable.

FACTORS INFLUENCING PREVALENCE
OF USE

A major concern is that legalization of cocaine might increase the prevalence of its use. Over the years that prevalence has swung widely in America. For example, for many years researchers have asked 12th grade students about their cocaine use (Johnston, O'Malley, & Bachman, 1995). Figure 17.1 shows remarkable rises and falls in those data; between 1985 and 1992 reports of "last-month" cocaine use fell more than five-fold.

Figure 17.2, drawn from the same study, shows the prevalence of use in the last month for cocaine and cigarettes. Obviously, there were many fewer cocaine users than cigarette users. Also, trends in the two curves are not parallel. Although cigarette smoking declined overall between 1975 and 1980, cocaine use rose. Then,

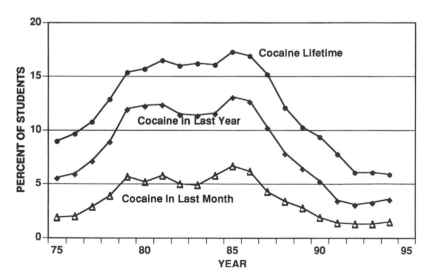

FIGURE 17.1 Prevalence of cocaine use among twelfth-grade students, 1975–1994 (data from Johnston et al., 1995).

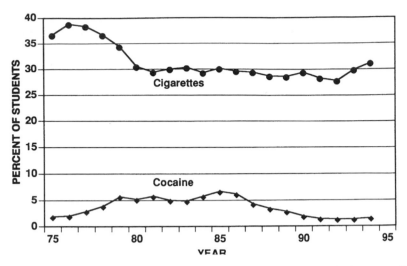

FIGURE 17.2   Prevalence of cigarette smoking and cocaine use in the last 30 days among high school seniors, 1975–1994 (data from Johnston et al., 1995).

despite a net decline in cocaine use from 1980 through 1994, cigarette use changed little. If the two curves rose and fell together, the year-by-year Pearson correlation of cigarette and cocaine use would be high, but the nonsignificant correlation of −.16 indicates that the curves do not move in tandem.

Cocaine legalization studies should avoid increasing the prevalence of cocaine use. What causes the prevalence of use to rise or fall across time, or to be so much different among different drugs? And why are trends in drug use not parallel for different substances? Two factors probably influence these variations.

AVAILABILITY

The first factor is availability of the drug. "Availability" is measured by the ease of obtaining the substance (e.g., its cost, number of persons or places offering it, the times when those places are open, etc.). For example, *khat* is a Middle Eastern shrub that contains a stimulant drug (Halbach, 1980). Although khat is widely used in the Middle East, it essentially is unavailable in the United States. Being unavailable here, it is not used here. Availability influences the prevalence of khat use.

Cigarette-rolling machines, introduced in the late 1800s, made cigarettes conveniently available. The prevalence of cigarette smoking then steadily rose to about 40% of adult Americans by 1964 (review of Davis & Novotny, 1989). Machines made cigarettes more available and that increased their use.

Lower cost also makes a drug more available to users. Alcohol consumption clearly increases when alcohol prices fall (de Lint & Schmidt, 1971).

Similarly, cocaine generally was unavailable and little used in the United States a generation ago. However, drug smugglers made cocaine much more available in the 1970s and 1980s, and the prevalence of use increased dramatically with availability. Then as with cigarettes, marketing cocaine as "crack" in small, easily smoked, individually affordable doses enhanced sales. This evidence all suggests that increasing cocaine's availability will increase cocaine use.

ACCEPTANCE

The second factor influencing cocaine use is acceptance of that use within the society. "Acceptance" of cocaine is reflected in the number of places or circumstances where use is permitted or encouraged and in the society's net balance of rewards or punishments for use. Caffeine, generally accepted in America, is widely used at meals, on the highway, at work, and so forth. At the other extreme, heroin use is widely condemned, and in repeated National Household Surveys (SAMSHA, 1996) only about 1% of Americans reported ever trying heroin. Comparables figures for cocaine were 8.7 to 11.5%, placing it between the extremes of caffeine and heroin.

Drugs perceived as too risky to use are less accepted; acceptance of use is, in part, the converse of risk perception. Annual surveys among high school seniors clearly show that classes perceiving cocaine as very risky (i.e., less acceptable) have a lower prevalence of cocaine use (Johnston et al., 1995, p. 195).

Social acceptance of a drug influences its prevalence of use in several ways. First, if the drug is widely used by others, new initiates easily learn how to get it into the body. For example, most American children know that people burn tobacco but pour boiling water over coffee. An American given khat leaves might experiment with those procedures but might not suck on the leaves, the successful Middle Eastern method.

Second, users reinforce one anothers' drug use, and there are more users to do so if the drug is widely accepted. For example, when cocaine use is planned at a party, invitations may go only to users. A person who starts using may get to more parties. Users also may cheer and celebrate a new initiate's use as a shared, rebellious, antiestablishment act. However, this can occur only if the drug is accepted and used at least somewhere in the society. A khat-possessing American would not win social approval from other khat users, since there are almost none in America.

Third, the use of a less accepted drug meets more negative, punitive consequences. Acceptance of tobacco has declined in the United States, and now users must sit in special sections of restaurants and abstain at work, in airplanes, or in others' homes. For illegal drugs the sanctions are stronger, including arrest and jailing. Such legal sanctions do appear to suppress use. Compared to the West, Moslem countries with alcohol prohibitions have much less alcoholism, as reflected in less liver cirrhosis (Crowley, 1988). Similarly, although it often is said that alcohol prohibition failed, cirrhosis rates declined precipitously during prohibition in Canada, as well as in the United States (Popham, 1956). Prohibition also reportedly reduced psychiatric hospital admissions for alcoholic psychoses, as well as arrests for public drunkenness and disorderly conduct (Moore, 1989). It appears that Prohibition's punishment of alcohol use did reduce drinking and its adverse consequences. Thus, more acceptance of cocaine (including fewer legal sanctions against its use) probably will increase cocaine use.

Accordingly, to avoid increasing the prevalence of cocaine use, studies of cocaine legalization should minimize increases in availability and acceptance of cocaine. Of course, this is difficult, since legalization means reducing restrictions and increasing availability.

COCAINE TOXICITY

Cocaine is toxic to physiology and behavior (Johanson & Fischman, 1989; Benowitz, 1993). Toxicity is one reason for controls on the drug.

BEHAVIORAL TOXICITY

Depending on doses and individual idiosyncracies, laboratory subjects receiving cocaine may develop moderate, transient psychiatric symptoms (Sherer, Kumor, Cone, & Jaffe, 1988; Foltin et al., 1990). Laboratory subjects are carefully screened for mental disorders, but in the general population about half of drug-dependent persons have such disorders (Regier et al., 1990), some of which are exacerbated by cocaine. Moreover, unlike the laboratory, on-the-street doses are not medically controlled, and high-dose use may continue for hours, days, or weeks. Cocaine users then sometimes develop disinhibition, impaired judgment, grandiosity, impulsiveness, hypersexuality, hypervigilance, compulsively repeated actions, psychomotor activation, severe transient panic, and paranoid psychosis (Gawin & Ellinwood, 1988; Manschreck, Allen, & Neville, 1987). Delirium, delusional disorders, pathologic mood and anxiety syndromes, and hallucinosis may occur during cocaine intoxication, and pathologic mood and anxiety may accompany cocaine withdrawal (Crowley, 1994a). Fortunately, most cocaine symptoms gradually decline with abstinence (Weddington et al., 1990).

We know of no scientific reports of cocaine administration to cocaine-dependent human outpatients. However, we examined cocaine's effects on behavior in a monkey group in a naturalistic outdoor pen with access to an attached building (Crowley, Mikulich, Williams, Zerbe, & Ingersoll, 1992; Crowley, Williams, Mikulich, & Ingersoll, 1993). Single doses of cocaine produced bizarre disruptions of normal social behavior lasting several hours. Those observations (Crowley et al., 1992) suggest problems that might arise during cocaine dosing of human outpatients:

Another serious outcome followed a 1.5 mg/kg dose in Monkey 3, who briefly ran, and then sat quietly for 30 min, very alert and intently watching the others. He then bolted across the yard, vocalizing as though pursued, although we saw no precipitating threat by others. Apparently in response, Monkey 12 then chased 3, which fled indoors. After 2–3 min No. 3 returned to the yard, sitting stiff and alert with No. 12 about 7 m away, oriented toward No. 3. At 47 min postdose No. 3 began an even wilder, more rapid, screaming flight without apparent provocation. He ran across the corral, crashing into and digging beneath the fence (a behavior we had not seen before). Again No. 12 chased, and No. 3 retreated to the building where we isolated him, ending observations. A few hours later he rejoined the others without incident. Without cocaine monkeys never made such intense, apparently fear-driven, unprovoked flights. (pp. 208–210)

A clinic might need to offer doses comparable to this to compete successfully against black market dealers. However, it is difficult to imagine operating an outpatient clinic producing such behavior.

PHYSIOLOGICAL TOXICITY

Transient medical problems necessitating withdrawal from studies occasionally develop in carefully screened laboratory subjects receiving controlled doses of cocaine under medical supervision (e.g., Foltin, Fischman, Pedroso, & Pearlson, 1988; Hatsukami et al., 1994). Without such careful controls cocaine may produce severe toxicity (Benowitz, 1993): hypertension, cardiac arrhythmia, myocardial and renal infarction, limb ischemia, myocarditis, shock, headaches, seizures, transient focal neurologic deficits, strokes, toxic encephalopathy, pneumomediastinum, pneumothorax, pulmonary edema, respiratory arrest, hyperthermia, rhabdomyolosis, spontaneous abortion, abruptio placentae, placenta praevia, premature rupture of membranes, and sudden death. Other reported problems include severe asthma (Albertson, Walby, & Derlet, 1995) and obstetrical complications, including reduced fetal weight (Zuckerman et al., 1989). Again, it is difficult to conceptualize operating a clinic when the treatment may produce such severe pathology.

TOXICITY AND ETHICS

Of course, toxicity does not rule out the medical use of a drug. Anticancer drugs, for example, are highly toxic but improve overall survival rates. A drug treatment need not be without adverse effects if it improves overall outcome in the target population. Therefore, we should ask if the target population for cocaine legalization is current users, possible future users, or society as a whole. Is the proposed outcome to improve the health and welfare of current users, to keep new users from starting, or to cut crime in deteriorated neighborhoods? Would there be ethical concerns in offering very cheap cocaine to addicts if it harms them but cuts crime in their neighborhoods? We address these questions in a later section.

WHAT TO STUDY: MODELS OF LEGALIZATION

"Legalization" discussions sometimes seem to presume that drugs either are, or are not, regulated. In fact, nations place graded levels of legal control on different drugs. The level depends in part on a substance's "abuse potential"—its innate capacity to drive repeated drug taking by animals or humans. Historically, alcohol and nicotine were less regulated than their now-known abuse potentials would have allowed. Tightening their regulation from those earlier, less restrictive levels has not been easy.

Drug regulations may aim at controlling availability, at controlling purity, at providing safe and effective doses, or at assuring honest advertising. Only the first is the focus of this chapter. The different levels of availability-controlling regulations applied to different drugs (Table 17.1) offer alternative models of how cocaine might be regulated (see Moore, 1990). We now consider those models.

OVER-THE-COUNTER DRUGS, TOBACCO, AND ALCOHOL

Over-the-Counter Drugs

Over-the-counter (OTC) drugs, such as nonnarcotic pain relievers and cold remedies, have minor abuse potential. Table 17.1 shows that almost no regulations control their availability. Indeed, their sales produce tax revenues, so states may have some interest in continuing or expanding those sales. Moreover, manufacturers of these drugs can use part of their profits as "campaign donations" to legislators, thereby defeating bills that might limit availability of the substances. OTC drugs do not cause addiction, so selling such a drug to persons addicted to it is "not applicable" (N/A) in Table 17.1.

Nicotine gum and patches now are classified as OTC drugs, although nicotine has major abuse potential. Table 17.1 shows that it is not illegal to sell nicotine gum and patches to nicotine-dependent tobacco smokers. Sale to minors is illegal, but in practice minors probably will be able to obtain this OTC drug easily.

With cocaine legalized at OTC levels, it would be sold in grocery and convenience stores, at newsstands, and from vending machines. Suppliers would compete for sales through enticing packaging, marketing, pricing, and through print, electronic, and billboard advertising. Adolescents and previous nonusers readily could purchase cocaine in unlimited quantities. Cocaine suppliers could use campaign contributions to support legislation allowing sales and profits to increase, thereby blocking legislation to reinstate controls if relaxed restrictions eventually were deemed unwise.

Tobacco

Few regulations limit tobacco's availability (Table 17.1). Stores may need local or state licenses to sell it, and it cannot legally be sold to minors. In some jurisdictions possession by minors is prohibited. Although not advertised on televi-

TABLE 17.1 Models for Controlling Drug Availability[a]

	Over-the-counter	Nicotine replacement	Tobacco	Alcohol	Unscheduled prescription drugs	Schedule II-V drugs	Opioid maintenance drugs	Schedule I drugs
License to sell required			Y	Y	Y	Y	Y	Stricter
Special training to prescribe, dispense, or sell					Y	Y	Y	Stricter
Sales from machines prohibited				Y	Y	Y	Y	Y
Prescription required					Y	Y	Y	Stricter
Sale to minors prohibited		Y	Y	Y			Y	Y
Possession by minors prohibited			Y	Y				Y
Advertising to public restricted			Y				Y	Stricter
Profits difficult to divert to legislators					N/A	N/A	N/A	Y
Dose determined by prescribers								Stricter
Illegal to possess without prescription					Y	Y	Y	Stricter
Illegal to sell or prescribe to addicts	N/A				N/A	Y	Y	Stricter
Special government supervision and licensing					Y	Y	Y	Stricter
Illegal to make or use						Y	Y	Y

[a]Abbreviations: Y, yes; N/A, not applicable; Stricter, regulation is more strict than this.

sion, tobacco is heavily advertised in print and on billboards. It can be sold to tobacco-dependent persons, including those with severe tobacco-induced illness. Tobacco interests are among the largest contributors to state and national legislators, assuring that bills limiting tobacco's availability are vigorously opposed. Since tobacco sales produce much tax revenue, governments may have some interest in maintaining sales.

If cocaine's controls were like tobacco's, grocery stores, gas stations, convenience stores, bars, and other facilities in some jurisdictions would need local licenses to sell cocaine. Sale to minors would be illegal, but that would be difficult to enforce because of vending-machine sales. Cocaine would be advertised heavily in print sources, but not on television. Adults could possess unlimited quantities; some local jurisdictions would prohibit possession by adolescents. Governments might develop some interest in maintaining or expanding tax revenues from cocaine sales. Marketing, competition for sales, and legislative influence otherwise would be like those described above for OTC drugs.

Alcohol

Alcohol's regulations are similar to tobacco's (Table 17.1). Sellers must have state licenses. However, alcohol sales from vending machines are prohibited, limiting access by minors, to whom sales are illegal. Many jurisdictions prohibit possession of alcohol by minors. Sales to alcoholic adults are not restricted; indeed, they buy great quantities of alcohol. Alcohol is advertised strongly in all media, including television. Governments may have some interest in maintaining sales for tax revenues. As with tobacco, alcohol manufacturers heavily influence legislatures through campaign donations.

If cocaine's regulations paralleled alcohol's, only adults could buy cocaine, and only in special places like bars and liquor stores. There, new adult users (but not adolescents) would have ready access to cocaine. The drug extensively would be advertised and marketed by competing suppliers. In other respects the restrictions would be like tobacco's.

Cocaine Prevalence, Morbidity, and Mortality under Over-the-Counter, Tobacco, or Alcohol Models

These models almost certainly would increase the prevalence of cocaine use. Based on the statement that "The nation is now awash in illicit drugs. Anyone who wants them can get them," Smith (1988, p. 6) asserted that drug use was unlikely to rise if cocaine were "available without prescription to all adults," (Smith, 1988, p. 5) an OTC model. However, legal tobacco, sold with more restrictions than the OTC model provides, is *much more widely used* than illegal cocaine. Figure 17.2 shows this difference for high school seniors. For all Americans over age 11 the difference is even greater; only 0.7% of respondents in the 1995 National Household Survey said that they had used cocaine in the last month, while 28.8% had used tobacco (SAMHSA, 1996).

As prevalence increased, cocaine's toxicity probably would lead to increased morbidity and mortality. We estimated (Crowley, 1994b) that the United States had about 8,000 cocaine deaths and about 105,000 alcohol deaths, a 13-fold difference, in a recent year. Nadelman (1989) notes that with cocaine being illegal, "there is overwhelming evidence that most users of cocaine do not get into trouble with the drug." He further asserts, "there is good reason to doubt that many Americans would inject cocaine . . . into their veins even if given the chance to do so legally" (p. 954). Of course, smoking and "snorting" cocaine avoid the needle barrier. However, if cocaine became as available and as acceptable as alcohol, given its toxicity and abuse potential, we find no data suggesting that cocaine would produce fewer fatalities than alcohol does. That possibility of a 13-fold increase in cocaine deaths (and related personal and social morbidity) probably would be seen as unacceptable. Therefore, legalization in the OTC, tobacco, or alcohol models seems improbable.

"UNSCHEDULED" AND "SCHEDULED" PRESCRIPTION DRUGS

Controls on Prescription Drugs

Prescription drugs have serious risks and side effects and are more controlled than OTC drugs (Table 17.1). Abuse potentials are thought to be minor for unscheduled prescription drugs and modest to severe for scheduled ones. *Unscheduled drugs* include, for example, antibiotics, anticancer drugs, or diuretics. Prescriptions control the amount of unscheduled drugs that the patient may purchase, and thus the doses used. Pharmacies dispensing these drugs, and the pharmacists themselves, must be licensed. It is illegal to obtain or possess unscheduled drugs without a prescription. Because prescribers (rather than patients) usually choose which drug to use, these drugs are mostly advertised to doctors, rather than to the public. Because that is a practical business decision rather than a regulation, it is marked N/A in Table 17.1. Similarly, since people do not become addicted to unscheduled drugs, Table 17.1 considers as N/A the question of sales to addicts. Governments may be interested in maintaining a strong prescription-drug industry, in part because of taxes the industry pays. Pharmaceutical companies and workers can influence legislative decisions about these drugs through campaign donations.

Scheduled drugs are those in five government lists ("Schedules I–V"). Schedule I drugs are said to have no role in medical practice and a high abuse potential. The drugs in Schedules II–V have accepted roles in medicine but also have abuse potential, producing "psychological or physical dependence." Drugs thought to have the greatest risk of abuse appear in Schedule II, with risks ranging downward to those in Schedule V. Schedule II drugs include cocaine, as well as, for example, morphine, amphetamine, and secobarbital.

Scheduled drugs have all of the regulatory controls placed on other prescription drugs, but also are subject to additional, special government supervision and licensing. Legal manufacturing, shipping, storing, prescribing and selling of scheduled drugs are intensely monitored by the Drug Enforcement Agency. Although these drugs can be prescribed for other legitimate medical uses, they cannot be prescribed for treating addiction per se. Thus, physicians cannot prescribe cocaine to "help" addicts through times when the drug is unavailable on the street. Local and federal police pursue illicit sellers of scheduled drugs. The success of that effort, of course, underlies the debate about cocaine legalization. Cocaine's dependence-producing characteristics, emphasized throughout this volume, will not be amplified here. However, cocaine's Schedule II classification is proper under current rules, since it has both high abuse potential and medical value as a local anesthetic.

Cocaine Prevalence, Morbidity, and Mortality under a Prescription Drug Model

If cocaine were reclassified from Schedule II into Schedules III, IV, or V it still would not be prescribed for addiction. No scheduled drug presently can be prescribed for maintenance of addicts outside of specially licensed maintenance clinics (we discuss that model in a later section). Thus, merely reducing cocaine's schedule status among prescription drugs probably will not increase its legal availability to addicts, and probably would not affect cocaine's prevalence of use, morbidity, or mortality.

MODIFIED RULES FOR SCHEDULED DRUGS

If American regulations were changed, general physicians could prescribe scheduled drugs to maintain addicts, presumably displacing street dealers. Some authorities fear that with that option naive or venal physicians might grossly overprescribe addictive substances. Physicians, reportedly with little problem, do prescribe methadone this way in Amsterdam (van Brussel, 1995). On the other hand, several heavily prescribing physicians in London in the 1960s probably contributed to a spreading heroin problem there. One of them, Lady Isabella Frankau, single-handedly prescribed 6 kg of heroin, some 600,000 analgesic doses, in 1962 (Judson, 1973). Her patients received up to 2400 mg (240 doses) per day, much of which they probably sold. Some American physicians have abused prescribing privileges, but the evidence is mixed on how great this problem of diverting cocaine into the black market might become if all doctors could prescribe cocaine to addicts.

Aside from that possible problem, a much larger question is whether the history of opioid prescribing really informs us about cocaine, a much different drug. We address that question next.

OPIOID MAINTENANCE DRUGS

Controls on Opioid Maintenance Drugs

Methadone and acetylmethadol, addicting relatives of heroin and morphine, are prescribed as opioid-maintenance drugs to heroin addicts (Table 17.1). The drugs provide legal substitutes for heroin, while involving patients in treatment programs. Controls on opioid-maintenance drugs are like those for Schedule II drugs, but physicians prescribing opioid-maintenance drugs must have special federal approval and must work in rigorously regulated clinics. The doctors are prohibited in most cases from prescribing to minors, can prescribe only to persons with proved addictions, and only can give the drugs orally, not by injection. Patients initially come to the clinic for each day's dose; later they may take some doses at home. These controls succeed reasonably well in blocking diversion of opioid maintenance drugs to the black market. Under regulations similar to these a few British physicians apparently prescribe cocaine to some addicts, but outcome reports are extremely sketchy (Brewer, 1995). Brenner (1989) proposed this model for cocaine legalization in America.

If Americans regulated cocaine as they do opioid-maintenance drugs, only adults with known addictions could receive cocaine in special clinics, preventing access of new users to the drug. Most doses would be administered at the clinic, but stable patients might take some doses home. Physicians would control dose sizes, although patients might supplement prescribed doses from illegal sources. Cocaine would be advertised to prescribing doctors, but less so to the public. If regulations paralleled those for opioid maintenance, all dosing would be oral. Cocaine is orally active (Wilkinson, Van Dyke, Jatlow, Barash, & Byck, 1980), but addicts certainly have not favored this route.

Pharmaceutical-industry profits from cocaine-maintenance clinics probably would be modest, since cocaine is an old drug, no longer covered by patents. Moreover, the market would be small (only about 100,000 Americans are in methadone-maintenance programs), and many patients would be medically indigent. Thus, drug companies probably would have little motivation to influence legislatures on cocaine issues.

Cocaine legalization aims to eliminate illicit dealers by underselling them. Accordingly, maintenance-clinic cocaine would have to cost patients less than street cocaine. Therefore, governments certainly would not get taxes from such clinics and might need to subsidize them. Thus, governments would not be disposed to expand clinics for tax revenues.

Cocaine Prevalence, Morbidity, and Mortality under an Opioid Maintenance Model

In this model cocaine would cost less in a treatment clinic than on the street, but only for treatment-seeking, cocaine-dependent persons. Thus, this model (unlike an OTC model) probably would have little impact on cocaine's overall availability. Therefore, general population rates of cocaine use, and rates of associated morbidity and mortality, probably would not increase.

SCHEDULE I DRUGS

These compounds are considered to have high abuse potential and no role in medical treatment. Examples are mescaline, marijuana, and LSD. Schedule I drugs may not be manufactured, distributed, prescribed, or possessed, except for rigidly regulated research purposes. These regulations are more strict than those outlined elsewhere in Table 17.1, resulting in the numerous statements of "Stricter" in Table 17.1. Dealers in these drugs, as outlaws, probably find it difficult to channel campaign contributions to legislators. Accordingly, these dealers probably are less well represented in state and national legislatures than tobacco or alcohol suppliers.

Legalization of cocaine implies a lessening of controls. Obviously then, since tightening controls by moving cocaine to Schedule I is not relevant in this discussion, we consider it no further here.

A GOVERNMENT-AS-DEALER MODEL

We review one more model, not represented in current drug-control procedures, for the sake of completeness. Nonclinical cocaine-use stations could provide unlimited quantities of low-cost cocaine for on-site use by certified cocaine-dependent persons, who could snort, inject, or smoke the drug at will for as long as they wished. Without doctors or counselors, such operations would not conflict with medical ethics. The stations would undersell street dealers, cutting into street markets and probably driving at least some dealers out of business. Strict controls could keep the drug on the premises, so the stations would not increase cocaine's availability in the community. Clients could be required to stay after their last dose, until they were sufficiently detoxified to return home safely. Like skid-row shelters, the stations could provide bedding and some food, although people usually eat and sleep very little while using cocaine.

We know of no studies of unlimited cocaine use by human beings. However, clinical experience suggests that cocaine in unlimited quantities is highly compelling. Cocaine-dependent wealthy people, who can buy as much as they wish, sometimes exhaust their fortunes before seeking treatment. Two rhesus monkeys, free to inject cocaine around the clock, both died within 5 days (Johanson, Balster, & Bonese, 1976). Cocaine-use stations might partially succeed in driving black market dealers from the street by underselling them. However, cocaine's compelling abuse potential and serious toxicity, in a situation where price would not serve to moderate use, probably would lead to unacceptably high morbidity and mortality. If these stations tried to control dosing by raising prices (or by other means), they would lose their "market advantage" over street dealers, and patients might return to street suppliers.

RESEARCH NEEDS

Our review suggests that an OTC–tobacco–alcohol model for cocaine legalization probably will increase sharply the prevalence of cocaine use and cocaine deaths; that model therefore is unlikely to be adopted. We suggest that nontreatment cocaine-use stations also probably would produce unacceptably high morbidity and mortality. The review further indicates that rescheduling cocaine within the group of prescription drugs probably would change minimally the availability to addicts, so rescheduling cocaine seems irrelevant to this discussion. Having general physicians prescribe cocaine to addicts presents some unresolved questions about drug diversion, but more importantly, shares with the opioid-maintenance model numerous uncertainties about cocaine safety, efficacy, and ethics. We now further consider that opioid-maintenance model.

The opioid-maintenance model seems the best choice to study. It would make cocaine more available to addicts in a treatment program, probably with minimal increases in the general-population prevalence of cocaine use or cocaine mortality. Schmoke (1990) calls for the establishment of cocaine-maintenance clinics. However, despite possible advantages for this model, unresolved questions about safety, efficacy, and ethics remain. These questions would have to be answered in controlled, prospective research before cocaine-maintenance clinics could be opened generally.

DOSE, FREQUENCY, AND ROUTE OF ADMINISTRATION

First, will some combination of cocaine dose, frequency, and route of administration attract cocaine-dependent persons away from street dealers and into treatment clinics? How large could the dose be while remaining safe? Research subjects have taken 10 to about 150 mg of cocaine by nose ("snorting") and 4–48 mg iv. Peruvian research subjects smoked cigarettes containing 75 mg of cocaine; bioavailability, the proportion entering the body, was estimated at 70%. American subjects smoked doses of 10–50 mg. These studies (Fischman et al., 1976; Fischman, Schuster, Javaid, Hatano, & Davis, 1985; Foltin, Fischman, Pippen, & Kelly, 1993; Hatsukami et al., 1990; Hatsukami et al., 1994; Higgins, Bickel, & Hughes, 1994; Javaid, Fischman, Schuster, Dekirmenjian, & Davis, 1978; Jeffcoat, Perez-Reyes, Hill, Sadler, & Cook, 1989; Lukas, Sholar, Kouri, Fukuzako, & Mendelson, 1994; Paly, Jatlow, Van Dyke, Jeri, & Byck, 1982; Perez-Reyes, Di Guiseppi, Ondrusek, Jeffcoat, & Cook, 1982; Pirwitz et al., 1995; Resnick, Kestenbaum, & Schwartz, 1977) suggest that an experimental cocaine maintenance clinic might provide with reasonable safety single doses of 50–100 mg by nose, 50 mg by injection, or 75 mg for smoking.

However, repeated dosing may have effects different from single doses. Cocaine remains in the body briefly (mean half life of about an hour; Javaid, Musa, Fischman, Schuster, & Davis, 1983; Jeffcoat et al., 1989), so addicts might request frequent doses around the clock. For example, Crowley (1987) reported a user of pharmaceutical cocaine who developed severe symptoms from taking as much as 45 g per week, with some 60 injections per day. Fischman et al. (1985) gave successive doses of 48 mg iv and 96 mg iv an hour later. In 1-h daily sessions for 2 weeks, subjects have taken up to 224 mg in some sessions (Fischman & Schuster, 1982). Peruvian research subjects smoked up to 10 cigarettes, each containing 75 mg of cocaine, in 90 min (Paly et al., 1982). Another study permitted smoking of four 50-mg doses in daily 1-h sessions for 4 days (Foltin et al., 1990). Still another allowed smoking of 35 mg every 15 min across 2.5 hs, a total of 350 mg (Hatsukami et al., 1994). Thus, an experimental cocaine-maintenance clinic might provide 200 mg (or more) per hour. We do not know how long this could go on. However, intranasal doses of 96 mg every 35 min usually produced unacceptable blood pressure elevations after five doses (Foltin et al., 1988). In the interest of safety, clinics probably would need some cap on hourly and daily doses.

Would patients supplement capped clinic doses with street cocaine, and would this defeat the goal of driving dealers from the streets? We know that opioid-maintenance treatment produces opioid satiety, reducing both the desire for, and use of, heroin-like drugs (Jones & Prada, 1975). However, cocaine may not produce cocaine satiety. In at least two studies a dose of cocaine almost immediately *increased* craving for cocaine (Jaffe, Cascella, Kumor, & Sherer, 1989; Perez-Reyes et al., 1982). Another showed that higher doses of cocaine increased craving *more than* lower doses (Hatsukami et al., 1994). Thus, clinic cocaine might increase, rather than decrease, black market cocaine sales, *stimulating* the use of street cocaine. This hypothesis needs careful study before establishment of cocaine-maintenance clinics.

Moreover, in laboratory studies physicians with emergency equipment stand by during and after dosing. Patients, at least initially, would need continued medical monitoring in their experimental cocaine clinics for several hours after dosing. Furthermore, laboratory subjects are screened to exclude those with medical or psychiatric disorders that might be worsened by cocaine. Studies would need to determine which disorders should contraindicate admission to cocaine-maintenance clinics. Exclusion of too many candidates, and the inconvenience of remaining at the clinic under medical supervision, might prevent clinics from luring many addicts away from street dealers.

To summarize, these questions about cocaine dose, frequency, and route of administration need answers before cocaine-dispensing clinics could be opened: What dose of cocaine would be large enough to attract patients away from street dealers and into clinics, but still small enough to be safe? By what route (intranasal, smoking, intramuscular, intravenous) and how often could patients take these doses, again balancing attractiveness versus safety? If the frequency or size of doses were capped in the interest of safety, would cocaine-dependent persons supplement clinic doses with black market cocaine? Would clinic-administered cocaine stimulate, rather than suppress, craving and black market purchases? Would safety considerations exclude many addicts with preexisting disorders from maintenance clinics? Would the inconvenience of medical monitoring prevent clinics from attracting users away from street dealers?

TREATMENT OUTCOME

Will cocaine-dispensing clinics improve patients' outcomes? Clinic-administered cocaine would have some clear advantages over street supplies. The risk of transmitting HIV and hepatitis via contaminated needles would approach zero in clinics, and the cocaine would be of known purity and potency. Physicians would supervise dose size and frequency and provide emergency medical care. However, at least two questions about the welfare of patients in such a clinic remain.

First, with cocaine costing little or nothing, will patients escalate doses to dangerous levels? Legalization aims to drive black market dealers from the street by underselling them. To keep patients from using street suppliers, clinics might have to provide as much cocaine as patients request. At least some cocaine-dependent persons with access to large amounts of cocaine take potentially fatal quantities. If clinics cap doses, patients might defeat the clinics' purpose by returning to street suppliers to supplement their clinic doses. Supplementation, of course, would increase cumulative doses, producing potentially grave toxicity. If clinics did not cap doses, patients might be safer with street suppliers, where price and availability provide caps. In short, research would have to show whether addicts in communities with, or without, maintenance clinics used less cocaine and had better outcomes.

Second, would cocaine-dispensing clinics increase or decrease the number of patients eventually pursuing abstinence through drug-free treatment? Clinic counselors presumably would encourage abstinence and drug-free therapy for patients receiving cocaine, and this might increase the number eventually abstaining. However, addicts often enter treatment saying, "The hassle on the street was too much for me." With hassle-free cocaine available in clinics, perhaps fewer patients would enter drug-free treatment and achieve good outcomes. Again, only research can answer this question.

ETHICS: BENEFITS FOR INDIVIDUALS OR SOCIETY?

Much empirical research (rather than armchair debate) would be needed to show whether cocaine-maintenance treatment would benefit or harm patients. If such clinics harmed patients, could they ethically continue operating to reduce community crime rates? Some might argue that they should. However, medical ethics dating to the Nuremburg trials firmly require that medical treatment must aim at benefiting the patient receiving it. "The right decision is the one that is *good* for this patient—not patients in general, nor what is good for physicians, for science, or even for society as a whole" (Pellegrino, 1983, p. 97). Ethically, cocaine maintenance treatment can be implemented only if research demonstrates that it benefits its recipients.

An alternative, of course, would be to eliminate any suggestion of treatment, building instead simple cocaine-use stations, as described above. It might be argued, "They do it to themselves on the street; why not let them do it in a cocaine-use station?" However, cocaine is very compelling; on-the-street dose size is limited by price. A use-station that provided unlimited quantities at low cost (to keep users from returning to street dealers) would probably generate very high-dose, toxic use with unacceptable mortality and morbidity.

CONCLUSIONS

• Controls on cocaine that paralleled OTC-alcohol-tobacco controls almost certainly would sharply increase prevalence of use in the general population, producing much more cocaine-related morbidity and mortality. It appears improbable to us that this model would be adopted.

• Simply changing cocaine's listing to a lower schedule would have little impact, since controls on the five schedules are quite similar.

• It is unclear whether changing Schedule II regulations so that all physicians could prescribe cocaine for addiction maintenance would (or would not) increase diversion of cocaine from medical channels. This option also shares the safety and ethical uncertainties of maintenance clinics, summarized next.

• Cocaine-maintenance clinics, patterned after opioid-maintenance clinics, probably would not contribute to widespread cocaine use by the general population. However, extensive research would be required to show that clinically safe cocaine doses would draw users away from street dealers and into clinics, and that such doses would benefit those receiving them. Two steps are required to get support for such medical research. First, researchers first must convince other clinical scientists at their own institutions that the risk to those who volunteer as human research subjects would be outweighed by the potential value of the findings. The researchers then must convince a national panel of experts that the studies, in competition with other proposed studies, are important enough to deserve funding. Our interpretation of current evidence is that (with clinics competing against high street doses) cocaine dosing probably would not be clinically safe; that dosing in clinics probably would stimulate (rather than suppress) street sales; and that combined street and clinic doses probably would be worse for patients than street doses alone. Thus, we doubt that such studies currently could be funded.

However, today's scientific data always are incomplete. New evidence might change our view. For example, if British doctors fully described their cocaine-dosing experience (Brewer, 1995), that experience might recommend further, cautious studies. If such studies eventually showed that cocaine-maintenance clinics benefited patients, we then would support establishing such clinics. Conversely, we emphasize that it would severely breach civilized medical ethics to operate such clinics if on balance they harmed their patients, regardless of any perceived benefits (such as crime reduction) for others. We further emphasize that questions of safety and efficacy require empirical clinical research and cannot be settled through deductive reasoning in television debates and magazine editorials (Buckley, 1996).

• Cocaine use-stations, offering no treatment but virtually limitless quantities of cocaine to cocaine-dependent persons, probably would draw many users away from street dealers. However, current evidence predicts much suffering and death in such places. Some may argue that dealers already place users at high risk, harming the rest of society as a by-product, and that if government merely assumed the dealers' role, society would benefit. Against that argument we close, not with an hypothesis, but with a value judgment: It would be immoral to offer potentially fatal cocaine-use stations to cocaine-dependent persons who are ill equipped to resist the stations' attractions. The body politic should not adopt the morals of cocaine dealers, arguably our least moral citizens, to solve cocaine addiction.

REFERENCES

Albertson, T. E., Walby, W. F., & Derlet, R. W. (1995). Stimulant-induced pulmonary toxicity. *Chest, 108,* 1140–1149.

Benowitz, N. L. (1993). Clinical pharmacology and toxicology of cocaine. *Pharmacology and Toxicology, 72,* 3–12.

Brenner, T. A. (1989). The legalization of drugs: Why prolong the inevitable? *Capital University Law Review, 18,* 237–255.

Brewer, C. (1995). Recent developments in maintenance prescribing and monitoring in the United Kingdom. *Bulletin of the New York Academy of Medicine, 72*(2), 359–370.

Buckley, W. F. (1996, February 12). The war on drugs is lost. *National Review,* pp. 35–38.

Crowley, T. J. (1987). Clinical issues in cocaine abuse. In S. Fisher, A. Rasking, & E. H. Uhlenhuth (Eds.), *Cocaine: Clinical and biobehavioral aspects* (pp. 193–211). New York: Oxford University Press.

Crowley, T. J. (1988). Learning and unlearning drug abuse in the real world: Clinical treatment and public policy. In B. Ray (Ed.), *Learning factors in substance abuse* (NIDA Research Monograph No. 84, pp. 100–121). Washington, DC: U.S. Government Printing Office.

Crowley, T. J., Mikulich, S. K., Williams, E. A., Zerbe, G. O., & Ingersoll, N. C. (1992). Cocaine, social behavior, and alcohol-solution drinking in monkeys. *Drug and Alcohol Dependence, 29,* 205–223.

Crowley, T. J., Williams, E. A., Mikulich, S. K., & Ingersoll, N. (1993). Buprenorphine and cocaine effects on social behavior of monkeys. *Drug and Alcohol Dependence, 31,* 235–245.

Crowley, T. J. (1994a). The organization of intoxication and withdrawal disorders. In T. A. Widiger, A. J. Frances, H. A. Pincus, M. B. First, R. Ross, & W. Davis (Eds.), *DSM-IV Sourcebook* (pp. 93–107). Washington, DC: American Psychiatric Association.

Crowley, T. J. (1994b). Any man's death: Presidential address. In L. S. Harris (Ed.), *Problems of drug dependence, 1983* (NIDA Research Monograph No. 140, pp. 5–10). Washington, DC: U.S. Government Printing Office.

Davis, R. M., & Novotny, T. E. (1989). The epidemiology of cigarette smoking and its impact on chronic obstructive pulmonary disease. *American Review of Respiratory Disease, 140*(3), Part 2, S82–S84.

de Lint, J., & Schmidt, W. (1971). Consumption averages and alcoholism prevalence: A brief review of epidemiological investigations. *British Journal of Addictions, 66,* 97–107.

Drug Enforcement Administration. (1990). *Physician's manual: An information outline of the controlled substances act of 1970.* Washington, DC: U.S. Government Printing Office.

Fischman, M. W., Schuster, C. R., Resnekov, L., Shick, J. F. E., Krasnegor, N. A., Fennell, W., & Freedman, D. X. (1976). Cardiovascular and subjective effects of intravenous cocaine administration in humans. *Archives of General Psychiatry, 33,* 983–989.

Fischman, M. W., & Schuster, C. R. (1982). Cocaine self-administration in humans. *Federation Proceedings, 41,* 241–246.

Fischman, M. W., Schuster, C. R., Javaid, J., Hatano, Y., & Davis, J. (1985). Acute tolerance development to the cardiovascular and subjective effects of cocaine. *The Journal of Pharmacology and Experimental Therapeutics, 235,* 677–682.

Foltin, R. W., Fischman, M. W., Pedroso, J. J., & Pearlson, G. D. (1988). Repeated intranasal cocaine administration: Lack of tolerance to pressor effects. *Drug and Alcohol Dependence, 22,* 169–177.

Foltin, R. W., Fischman, M. W., Nestadt, G., Stromberger, H., Cornell, E. E., & Pearlson, G. D. (1990).

Demonstration of naturalistic methods for cocaine smoking by human volunteers. *Drug and Alcohol Dependence, 26,* 145–154.

Foltin, R. W., Fischman, M. W., Pippen, P. A., & Kelly, T. H. (1993). Behavioral effects of cocaine alone and in combination with ethanol or marijuana in humans. *Drug and Alcohol Dependence, 32,* 93–106.

Gawin, F. H., & Ellinwood, E. H. (1988). Cocaine and other stimulants: Actions, abuse, and treatment. *The New England Journal of Medicine, 318*(18), 1173–1182.

Halbach, H. (1980). Khat: The problem today. In L. S. Harris (Ed.), *Problems of drug dependence, 1979* (NIDA Research Monograph No. 27, pp. 318–319). Washington, DC: U.S. Government Printing Office.

Hatsukami, D., Keenan, R., Carroll, M., Colon, E., Geiske, D., Wilson, B., & Huber, M. (1990). A method for delivery of precise doses of smoked cocaine-base to humans. *Pharmacology, Biochemistry and Behavior, 36,* 1–7.

Hatsukami, D. K., Pentel, P. R., Glass, J., Nelson, R., Brauer, L. H., Crosby, R., & Hanson, K. (1994). Methodological issues in the administration of multiple doses of smoked cocaine-base in humans. *Pharmacology, Biochemistry and Behavior, 47,* 531–540.

Higgins, S. T., Bickel, W. K., & Hughes, J. R. (1994). Influence of an alternative reinforcer on human cocaine self-administration. *Life Sciences, 55*(3), 179–187.

Jaffe, J. H., Cascella, N. G., Kumor, K. M., & Sherer, M. A. (1989). Cocaine-induced cocaine craving. *Psychopharmacology, 97,* 59–64.

Javaid, J. I., Fischman, M., Schuster, C. R., Dekirmenjian, H., & Davis, J. M. (1978). Cocaine plasma concentration: Relation to physiological and subjective effects in humans. *Science, 202,* 227–228.

Javaid, J. I., Musa, M. N., Fischman, M., Schuster, C. R., & Davis, J. M. (1983). Kinetics of cocaine in humans after intravenous and intranasal administration. *Biopharmaceutics and Drug Disposition, 4,* 9–18.

Jeffcoat, A. R., Perez-Reyes, M., Hill, J. M., Sadler, B. M., & Cook, C. E. (1989). Cocaine disposition in humans after intravenous injection, nasal insufflation (snorting), or smoking. *Drug Metabolism and Disposition, 17*(2), 153–159.

Johanson, C. E., Balster, R. L., & Bonese, K. (1976). Self-administration of psychomotor stimulant drugs: The effects of unlimited access. *Pharmacology, Biochemistry and Behavior, 4,* 45–51.

Johanson, C. E., & Fischman, M. W. (1989). The pharmacology of cocaine related to its abuse. *Pharmacological Reviews, 141*(1), 3–52.

Johnston, L. D., O'Malley, P. M., & Bachman, J. G. (1995). *National survey results on drug abuse from the Monitoring the Future study. 1975–1994: Volume 1, Secondary school students* (NIH Publication No. 95-4026). Washington, DC: U.S. Government Printing Office.

Jones, B. E., & Prada, J. A. (1975). Drug-seeking behavior during methadone maintenance. *Psychopharmacologia, 41,* 7–10.

Judson, H. F. (1973, September 24). The British and heroin - 1. *New Yorker, 49,* 76–86.

Lukas, S. E., Sholar, M., Kouri, E., Fukuzako, H., & Mendelson, J. H. (1994). Marijuana smoking increases plasma cocaine levels and subjective reports of euphoria in male volunteers. *Pharmacology, Biochemistry and Behavior, 48*(3), 715–721.

Manschreck, T. C., Allen, D. F., & Neville, M. (1987). Freebase psychosis: Cases from a Bahamian epidemic of cocaine abuse. *Comprehensive Psychiatry, 28*(6), 555–564.

Moore, M. H. (1989, October 16). Actually, prohibition was a success. *New York Times.*

Moore, M. H. (1990). Drugs: Getting a fix on the problem and the solution. *Yale Law and Policy Review, 8,* 701–728.

Musto, D. F. (1992). Cocaine's history, especially the American experience. In *Cocaine: Scientific and Social Dimensions* (pp. 7–19). Ciba Foundation Symposium No. 166. New York: John Wiley and Sons.

Nadelmann, E. A. (1996, February 12). The war on drugs is lost. *National Review,* pp. 38–40.

Nadelmann, E. A. (1989). Drug prohibition in the United States: Costs, consequences, and alternatives. *Science, 245,* 939–947.

Office of National Drug Control Policy. (1995). *What America's users spend on illegal drugs, 1988–1993.*

Paly, D., Jatlow, P., Van Dyke, C., Jeri, F. R., & Byck, R. (1982). Plasma cocaine concentrations during cocaine paste smoking. *Life Sciences, 30,* 731–738.

Pauly, P. J. (1994). Is liquor intoxicating? Scientists, prohibition, and the normalization of drinking. *American Journal of Public Health, 84,* 305–313.

Pellegrino, E. D. (1983). To be a physician. In N. Adams & M. D. Buckner (Eds.), *Medical ethics: A clinical textbook and reference for the health care professions* (pp. 94–97). Cambridge, MA: MIT Press.

Perez-Reyes, M., Di Guiseppi, S., Ondrusek, G., Jeffcoat, A. R., & Cook, C. E. (1982). Free-base cocaine smoking. *Clinical Pharmacology and Therapeutics, 32*(4), 459–465.

Pirwitz, M. J., Willard, J. E., Landau, C., Lange, R. A., Glamann, B., Kessler, D. J., Foerster, E. H., Todd, E., & Hillis, L. D. (1995). Influence of cocaine, ethanol, or their combination on epicardial coronary arterial dimensions in humans. *Archives of Internal Medicine, 155,* 1186–1191.

Popham, R. E. (1956). The Jellinek alcoholism estimation formula and its application to Canadian data. *Quarterly Journal Studies on Alcohol, 17,* 559–593.

Regier, D. A., Farmer, M. E., Rae, D. S., Locke, B. Z., Keith, S. J., Judd, L. L., & Goodwin, F. K. (1990). Comorbidity of mental disorders with alcohol and other drug abuse: Results from the Epidemiologic Catchment Area (ECA) Study. *Journal of the American Medical Association, 264*(19), 2511–2518.

Resnick, R. B., Kestenbaum, R. S., & Schwartz, L. K. (1977). Acute systemic effects of cocaine in man: A controlled study by intranasal and intravenous routes. *Science, 195,* 696–698.

Schmoke, K. L. (1990). Drug laws ignore addicts while helping criminals. *Addiction Review, 2,* 1–4.

Schmoke, K. L. (1996, February 12). The war on drugs is lost. *National Review,* pp. 38–40.

Sherer, M. A., Kumor, K. M., Cone, E. J., & Jaffe, J. H. (1988). Suspiciousness induced by four-hour intravenous infusions of cocaine: Preliminary findings. *Archives of General Psychiatry, 45,* 673–677.

Smith, M. A. (1988). The drug problem: Is there an answer? *Federal Probation: A Journal of Correctional Philosophy and Practice, 52* (1), 3–6.

Substance Abuse and Mental Health Services Administration (SAMHSA). (1996). *National household survey on drug abuse: Population estimates 1995* (DHHS Publication No. SMA 96-3095). Washington, DC: U.S. Department of Health and Human Services.

van Brussel, G. (1995). Methadone treatment by general practitioners in Amsterdam. *Bulletin of the New York Academy of Medicine, 72*(2), 348–358.

Weddington, W. W., Brown, B. S., Haertzen, C. A., Cone, E. J., Dax, E. M., Herning, R. I., & Michaelson, B. S. (1990). Changes in mood, craving, and sleep during short-term abstinence reported by male cocaine addicts: A controlled, residential study. *Archives of General Psychiatry, 47,* 861–868.

Weiss, R. D., Mirin, S. M., & Bartel, R. L. (1994). *Cocaine* (2nd ed., p. 9). Washington, DC: American Psychiatric Press.

Wilkinson, P., Van Dyke, C., Jatlow, P., Barash, P., & Byck, R. (1980). Intranasal and oral cocaine kinetics. *Clinical Pharmacology and Therapeutics, 27,* 386–394.

Zuckerman, B., Frank, D. A., Hingson, R., Amaro, H., Levenson, S. M., Kayne, H., Parker, S., Vinci, R., Aboagye, K., Fried, L. E., Cabral, H., Timperi, R., & Bauchner, H. (1989). Effects of maternal marijuana and cocaine use on fetal growth. *The New England Journal of Medicine, 320,* 762–768.

INDEX

Abruptio placentae, cocaine-related
  human studies, 163
  in nonhuman subjects, 167
Abstinence, *see* Cocaine abstinence
Abstinence-specific support, construct of social
  support, 397
Acceptance, societal, affecting cocaine use,
  413–414
Access
  alternative nondrug reinforcers, 93
  cocaine, experimental session length and peri-
    od of access, 88
  methadone, cocaine abstinence contingent on,
    375
  unlimited, and dysregulated cocaine intake,
    63–64
Accumbens shell, dopaminergic antagonist infusions, 37–39
Acetylmethadol, opioid-maintenance, controls
  on, 420–421
Acquisition
  amphetamine self-administration, 27
  cocaine-reinforced behavior
    drug history role, 90–91
    effects of feeding conditions, 91–92
Acupuncture, methadone patients using cocaine,
  380
Acute interaction procedure, human cocaine
  challenge studies using, 218–224
Adenylate cyclase, inhibition by DAMGO, 10

Adipsia, in nigrostriatal lesioned rat, 22
Adolescents
  drug sampling and parent monitoring, 333–334
  prevalence of cocaine use, 318–319
Adoption studies, role of genetics in drug abuse,
  298
(+)-AJ 76, dopamine autoreceptor antagonist,
  149–150
Affect, positive and negative, mutual exclusivity, 394
Age, interaction with ethnicity in use of crack,
  337
Aggressive behavior, male, and relative risk of
  cocaine use, 316–317
Agonist substitution, approach to pharmacotherapy, 210
Alcohol
  availability, regulations, 418
  dependence, among cocaine-dependent indi-
    viduals, 356
  effects on cocaine self-administration,
    241–242
Alcohol–cocaine combination
  cardiovascular effects, 246–248
  cocaethylene role in mediating effects, 248
  performance effects, 244–246
  subject-rated effects, 242–243
Alfentanil
  reinforcing effect, 153
  responding maintained by, 148

Amantadine, effect on cocaine use in methadone patients, 370–371
AMPA, cross-sensitization to, 115, 118
Amphetamine
  anorectic effects in accumbens-lesioned rat, 22–23
  cross-sensitization to cocaine, 7
  discriminative-stimulus effects, 60
  intra-accumbens
    reproducing cocaine stimulus effects, 27–29
    subsequent responding, 39
  selectively bred phenotypes responsive to, 294
  self-administration, acquisition, 27
Amygdala
  basolateral
    excitotoxic lesions, 35
    lesioned, effect on cocaine-maintained responding, 42
  central nucleus, dopaminergic antagonist infusions, 37–39
  extended, excitotoxic lesions, 36
  lesions, blocking of cocaine sensitization, 117
  6-OHDA-lesioned, cocaine-maintained responding following, 35–36
  role in development of conditioned fear response, 121–122
Antibodies, to cocaine, 150–152
Aphagia, in nigrostriatal lesioned rat, 22
Apomorphine
  cocaine substitution
    in drug discrimination studies, 60
    effect on cocaine self-administration, 23–25
  paired with cocaine, contralateral rotation following, 117
Association studies, in genotype-identification studies in humans, 299–300
Attrition, early, in cocaine treatment, 346–347
Autoshaping procedure, in acquisition study, 92
Availability
  cocaine
    environmental factors, 324
    history of controls on, 410
  cocaine or alternative reinforcers, as countervailing influences, 328–329
  drugs
    affecting prevalence of use, 412–413
    effect on drug abuse, 301
    neighborhood environment effect, 335, 337
Avoidance, passive or active, prenatal cocaine exposure effect, 169

Bayley Scales of Infant Development, 165
Bed nucleus of stria terminalis, dopaminergic antagonist infusions, 37–39
Behavioral economics, evaluation of reinforcing efficacy, 84–87
Behavioral effects, cocaine
  medial prefrontal cortical destruction effect, 31–32
  self-administered, amygdala role, 35–39
  single dopamine transporter binding site regulating, 3
  tolerance and sensitization to, 122–127
  ventral subiculum role, 39–40, 43
Behavioral interventions
  cocaine abusers, 348–354
  cocaine-abusing methadone patients, 372–379
Behavioral toxicity, cocaine, 414–415
Benzoylecgonine, distribution in fetus, 159–160
Binge-and-crash phenomenon, 63–64
Binging, acute tolerance role, 110–111
Blood, anticocaine antibodies retained in, 151–152
Blood-oxygen-level-dependent imaging, low sensitivity, 279–280
Brain
  dopaminergic depletions, 22–23
  electrical activity, cocaine effects, 266–269
  functioning, correlates with cocaine-induced euphoria, 269–274
  MRI, 274–276
  weight, prenatal cocaine exposure effect, 169–170
Brain stem auditory response, prenatal cocaine exposure effect, 170
Break point
  decrease, suggesting tolerance, 111
  measure of progressive ratio schedules, 83
  SCH 23390 effect, 148–149
Bromocriptine
  effect on cocaine self-administration, 145, 147
  evaluation in acute interaction studies, 220
Buprenorphine
  as alternative to methadone, 369–370
  compared with methadone, in opioid-dependent patients, 366–367
  discriminative stimulus effects, 138
  effects
    reinstatement of responding, 90
    self-administration of μ-opioids, 143, 153

evaluation in
  acute interaction studies, 221–222
  chronic interaction studies, 228–230
  plus nondrug reinforcers, effect on cocaine re-
    inforcement, 93–95
  testing as potential cocaine pharmacotherapy,
    199–202
  treatment for opioid abuse, 136
Buproprion, effect on cocaine use in methadone
  patients, 371–372

Caffeine, regular usage among cocaine-dependent patients, 357
Carbamazepine, evaluation in chronic interaction studies, 226–228
Cardiovascular effects
  cocaine–alcohol combination, 246–248
  cocaine–marijuana combination, 253–254
  cocaine–nicotine combination, 256
  cocaine–opioid combination, 250–252
Cardiovascular monitoring, during cocaine administration, 185
Cardiovascular problems, in neonates exposed
  to cocaine, 161
Case studies, cocaine use during pregnancy,
  160–162
Catecholamines, depletion by 6-OHDA, 22
Caudate putamen
  cocaine effects *in vivo*, 6–8
  dopamine uptake, cocaine effect, 2–4
  opioid receptor density, 10
cDNA, dopamine transporter, 11–12
Central nervous system
  mechanisms of tolerance, 126
  stimulants, effects on cerebral dopamine lev-
    els, 281–282
Chemical structure, drug, effect on drug abuse
  liability, 301
Children
  in disadvantaged neighborhoods, drug expo-
    sure, 335–336
  8- to 10-year-olds, parent monitoring study, 332
Chlordiazepoxide, effect on suppression of cocaine self-administration, 72–73
Chloride ions, and sodium ions, cotransported
  with dopamine, 2
Choice
  cocaine dose and route of administration in
    research protocols, 190–193
  between drug and nondrug reinforcers,
    68–69, 84–86, 93, 242

Cholinergic nucleus basalis magnocellularis, excitotoxic lesions, 40
Chronic interaction procedure, human cocaine
  challenge studies using, 224–232
Cigarettes
  availability and acceptance, and prevalence of
    use, 412–413
  smoking, *see* Nicotine
Cis-flupenthixol, testing as potential cocaine
  pharmacotherapy, 198
Classical conditioning, responses to drug-associated stimuli, 57
Clinic management, compared with relapse prevention protocol, 352
Clinics, experimental cocaine-maintenance,
  423–426
Cocaethylene, role in mediating effects of cocaine–alcohol combination, 248
Cocaine
  acute interaction design studies, 218–224
  antibodies, 150–152
  availability
    environmental factors, 324
    history of controls on, 410
  chronic interaction design studies, 224–232
  craving
    as challenge to laboratory research, 195
    desipramine effect, 196, 225
    pergolide effect, 198
  dependence, etiological theoretical models,
    321–325
  effects
    brain electrical activity, 266–269
    high-energy phosphates, 277–278
    euphoria induced by, correlates with brain
      function, 269–274
  interactions with
    dopamine agonists, 139–140
    dopamine antagonists, 140–141
    medications, methodology, 234
  legalization
    hypotheses *vs.* value statements, 410–
      411
    models, 416–422
  maintenance treatment, ethics, 425
  pharmacodynamic profile in humans,
    212–217
  prevalence
    under opioid maintenance model, 421
    under over-the-counter models, 418–419
    under prescription drug model, 420
  relapse, *see* Relapse

Cocaine *(continued)*
  route of administration
    as choice of research participant, 190–193
    research questions with respect to legaliza-
      tion, 423–424
  toxicity, 414–415
Cocaine abstinence
  future, goals for, 398
  initiation, distinction from relapse manage-
    ment, 401
  methadone access contingent on, 375
  in relation to relapse, 389–390
  voucher program effect, 349–350, 376
Cocaine abuse
  in-hospital *vs.* out-of-hospital care, 344–345
  liability
    determinants, 51–74
    subjective index, 213
  in methadone patients, adjunctive pharma-
    cotherapies, 370–372
  and multiple drug abuse, patterns, 240–241
  patients with history of, EEG activity, 267
  tolerance and sensitization, 122–127
    interactive roles, 108
  treatment
    content, 347–356
    duration and intensity, 346–347
    early attrition, 345–346
    group *vs.* individual therapy, 347
    in methadone maintenance patients,
      363–384
    use of models of opioid abuse treatment,
      136–137
  vulnerability, 313–338
Cocaine–alcohol combination
  cardiovascular effects, 246–248
  cocaethylene role in mediating effects, 248
  performance effects, 244–246
  subject-rated effects, 242–243
Cocaine binding site, dopamine transporter, 1,
  3–4
Cocaine dose
  as choice of research participant, 190–193
  and regulation of drug intake, 87
  reinforcing strength closely related to, 67–68
  research questions with respect to legaliza-
    tion, 423–424
  and test medication, ascending sequences, 234
Cocaine–marijuana combination
  cardiovascular effects, 253–254
  performance effects, 253
  subject-rated effects, 252–253

Cocaine–nicotine combination
  cardiovascular effects, 256
  self-administration studies, 255–256
  subject-rated effects, 256
Cocaine–opioid combination
  cardiovascular effects, 250–252
  increase of adverse effects, 249
  performance effects, 250
  subject-rated effects, 250
Cocaine self-administration
  alcohol effects, 241–242
  alternatives, 67–70
  and changes in sensitivity to reinforcing ef-
    fects, 113–114
  and development of sensitization, 125–126
  direct effects occurring independently of,
    53–56
  dopamine agonist effects, 145–147
  dopamine antagonist effects, 147–150
  human research participants, 187–193
  mesoaccumbens dopamine depletion effects,
    23–27
  nicotine pretreatment effect, 255–256
  P300 topography changes during, 272–273
  role in informing cocaine pharmacotherapy,
    194–202
  schedules, 62–66
Cocaine use
  buprenorphine effects, 369–370
  after entry in methadone treatment, 364–366
  environmental risk factors, 330–337
  prevalence, affecting factors, 411–414
  racial and ethnic differences, 319–320
  trends
    demographic, 319
    epidemiological findings from national
      studies, 317–319
  in United States, data sources, 320–321
Community reinforcement approach, treating
  cocaine abuse, 348–350
Comorbidity
  drug and mental disorders, 305
  National Comorbidity Study, 320
  psychiatric
    and individual susceptibility, 325
    treatments, 354–355
Comparisons, controlled, methadone dose effects on cocaine use, 367–368
Compensation, volunteers in cocaine research, 186
Concurrent schedules
  preference role, 83
  two-lever, role of time-out periods, 69–70

Conditioned place preference, in studies of vulnerability to drug abuse, 292–293
Conditioned stimuli
effect on persistence of drug-seeking behavior, 302
eliciting effects similar to those produced by drug, 118–120
Conditioning
importance to sensitization, 116–118
neuroanatomy, 120–122
Conditioning models, cocaine relapse, 391
Confidentiality, volunteers in cocaine research, 186
Confounding factor
causative role of cocaine independent of, 166–167
in controlled comparisons of methadone doses, 368
polydrug use as, 171
in transgenic technology, 297
Congenic strains, and cloning quantitative trait loci, 296
Contingency management
in community reinforcement approach, 349–351
methadone access contingent on cocaine abstinence, 375
take-home methadone doses, 375
voucher-based reinforcement, 376
Corticosterone, elevated during cocaine reinforcement, 95–96
Cortico-striato-pallido-thalamic circuitry, implications for, 41–43
Counseling, for cocaine use in methadone patients, 374–375
Countervailing influences, to using cocaine
environmental factors, 326–329
environmental/individual interactions, 329–330
individual susceptibility, 329
Crack smoking
animal experiment under fixed-ratio, 94–95
demographic trends, 319
ethnic differences
neighborhood environment effect, 336–337
and racial differences, 319–320
route of administration in research protocols, 189, 191–193
as substitute reinforcer, 86
Craving
cocaine
as challenge to laboratory research, 195

desipramine effect, 196, 225
pergolide effect, 198
relapse in absence of, 391
relationship to relapse to cocaine, 395–396
role in continued drug use and relapse, 216–217
Cross-sectional studies, in epidemiological study of cocaine use, 315–316
Cross-sensitization
AMPA, 115, 118
amphetamine to cocaine, 7
between stimulants and opiates, 123–124
Cross-tolerance, between cocaine and other psychomotor stimulants, 110–113

DAMGO, inhibition of adenylate cyclase activity, 10
D_1 dopamine agonists, as candidate medications, 61
D_2 dopamine agonists, reinstatement by, 60–61
Delivery
cocaine effects in nonhuman subjects, 167–168
preterm labor, cocaine-associated, 163
Demand, in behavioral economics, 84–86
Demographics
in predicting relapse to cocaine, 392
trends in cocaine use, 319
Depression, in relation to cocaine use, treatment retention, 393
Design considerations, pharmacological interaction studies, 217–218
Desipramine
effect on cocaine use in methadone patients, 370–371
evaluation in chronic interaction studies, 225–226
intervention for cocaine abuse, 353
testing in cocaine choice/self-administration paradigm, 196
therapeutic efficacy, 354
Determinants, universe of, influencing drug use initiation, 314
Developmental perspective, stage model elaborated by, 323–324
Direct effects
biasing assessment of reinforcing efficacy, 82
cocaine, on operant behavior, 74
occurring independently of self-administration, 53–56
role in reinstatement phenomenon, 59

Direct effects *(continued)*
  and satiation, effects on reinforcement,
    96–100
Discriminative-stimulus effects, cocaine
  dose–response function, 124
  in relation to abuse potential, 56–62
  tolerance, 109–111
Disulfiram
  evaluation in acute interaction studies, 223
  mechanism of action, 211
  therapy with cocaine abusers, 354–355
Dopamine
  brain levels, effects of central nervous system
    stimulants, 281–282
  cocaine-related increase in conditioned ani-
    mals, 118–120
  depletion in mesoaccumbens, effect on co-
    caine self-administration, 23–27
  extracellular, increase in cocaine-sensitized
    animals, 114
Dopamine receptors
  D_1 and D_2
    acute and chronic cocaine effects, 8–9
    antagonists, 140–141
  D_2 and D_3, relative binding affinities, 137
  D_3, agonists selective for, 139–140
Dopamine transporter
  cDNA, 11–12
  cocaine effects, acute and chronic, 2–4
Dose
  changes in, drug intake across, 97–99
  cocaine, *see* Cocaine dose
  magnitude, within-session changes in,
    99–100
  methadone
    effect on cocaine use, 366–368
    take-home, 375
  opioids, antagonist effect dependent on,
    143–145
  test medication, acute pretreatment, 217–218
Dose–response function
  cocaine and ethanol, 247
  for discriminative stimulus effects, 124
  under progressive ratio schedule of reinforce-
    ment, 112
Drug abuse
  multiple, among cocaine abusers, 240–241,
    257, 356–357
  vulnerability
    environmental influence, 300–303
    genetic influence
      animal strategies, 291–297
      human strategies, 297–300

Drug Abuse Warning Network, 240, 249, 252,
    255, 320–321
Drug discrimination
  procedure, 137–138
  role in cocaine combinations with other
    drugs, 258
Drug history, affecting rate of acquisition of co-
    caine-reinforced behavior, 90–91
Drug interactions
  cocaine with other abused drugs in humans,
    240–258
  opioids and potential treatment medications,
    138
  and therapeutic efficacy, 73
Drugs
  availability
    affecting prevalence of use, 412–413
    effect on drug abuse, 301
  classes, common neurophysiological process,
    271–272
  concurrent exposure, effect on cocaine-rein-
    forced responding, 91
  dopaminergic, possible treatment agents, 355
  intake across changes in dose, 97–99
  magnitude of dose, within-session changes,
    99–100
  over the counter, 416
  prescription, controls on, 419–420
  sampling by children, parent monitoring
    study, 332–334
  schedule I, regulations, 421–422
Drug-seeking behavior
  environmental stimulus role, 66, 301–302
  in relation to P300 changes, 273
  sensitization role, 108
Drug use
  continuance following laboratory research,
    184
  and development of tolerance, 123
  initiation and maintenance, universe of deter-
    minants, 314
Drug Use Forecast, 320–321
DS121, dopamine autoreceptor antagonist, 141
Duration, treatment for cocaine abuse, 346–347
Dynamic susceptibility contrast MRI, mapping
    cerebral blood volume, 279
Dynorphin, striatonigral, chronic cocaine ef-
    fect, 9
Echo planar imaging, enhancement of MRI res-
    olution, 278
EEG, *see* Electroencephalogram
Elasticity, cross-price, in behavioral economics,
    84–86

Electrical activity, brain
  cocaine effects, 266–269
  measured over entire scalp, 270
Electric shock, rates of responding maintained
  by, 54–56
Electroencephalogram
  acute cocaine effects, 269
  alpha activity
    drug-induced changes, 270–272, 274
    in volunteers after cocaine administration,
      267
  and ERP, coregistration with MRI technology,
    281
Electrophysiological responses, striatal neurons,
  reinforcer effects, 119–120
β-Endorphin, chronic cocaine effect, 9
Environment
  effect on vulnerability to drug abuse,
    300–303
  interaction with
    genes, role in drug addiction, 303–306
    individual, as countervailing influence,
      329–330
    related factors, as countervailing influences,
      326–329
  role in conditioning, 119
Environmental stimuli
  associated with drug administration, 301–302
  modulating cocaine reinforcement, 88–90
  role in drug-seeking behavior, 66
Epidemiological studies
  cocaine exposure during pregnancy, 162–166
  prevalence and incidence of drug use,
    315–321
ERP, see Event-related potentials
Ethical issues
  administering cocaine to humans, 182–186
  cocaine-maintenance treatment, 425
  and cocaine toxicity, 415
Ethnic differences, see also Racial differences
  cocaine use, 319–320
  crack use, neighborhood environment effect,
    336–337
  social integration effect on abstinence,
    397–398
Etiologic factors, leading to cocaine dependence, conceptual framework, 321–325
Etiology, cocaine abuse, 181–182
Euphoria
  cocaine-induced, correlates with brain func-
    tion, 269–274
  disappearance after acute administration, 265
  measures of, 216–217

Event-related potentials
  characteristic waveform, 266–267
  and EEG, coregistration with MRI technolo-
    gy, 281
  P300, see P300 ERP
Excitotoxic lesions
  basolateral amygdala, 35
  cholinergic nucleus basalis magnocellularis,
    40
  pedunculopontine tegmental nucleus, 40
  structures receiving accumbens afferents, 36
  ventral subiculum of hippocampal formation,
    39–40
Experimental events, affecting cocaine reinforcement, 87–90
Extinction-like behavior, in severe accumbens
  dopamine depletion, 25, 27

Family studies, role of genetics in drug abuse,
  298
Fear response, conditioned, amygdala role,
  121–122
Feeding conditions, effect on cocaine reinforcement, 91–93
Fetus
  benzoylecognine distribution, 159–160
  cocaine-exposed, brain hemorrhage, 161
Fixed-interval schedule, behavior acceleration
  in, 64–65
Fixed-ratio schedule
  cocaine reinforcement, 63–64
  reinforcing and punishing events under, 71
  in relation to rate dependency, 53–54
  responding rate changes under, 113
  role of time-outs, 83
Fluoxetine
  evaluation in chronic interaction studies,
    226
  in methadone patients, effect on urines posi-
    tive for cocaine, 370
  testing as potential cocaine pharmacotherapy,
    199
Food
  behavior maintained by, satiation and direct
    effects, 97
  reinforcement, increase in magnitude, 68
  responding maintained by
    chlordiazepoxide effect, 72–73
    cocaine-related pause, 54
  restriction, and corticosterone levels, 96
Functional support, construct of social support,
  397

GBR 12909
  cocaine-selective effect, 65
  discriminative stimulus effects, 139–140,
    152
  effect on cocaine self-administration, 146
GBR 12935
  binding sites on dopamine transporter, 3–4
  local infusion, effect on monoamine levels, 6
Genes
  immediate early, expression after chronic co-
    caine treatment, 115–116
  interaction with environment, role in drug ad-
    diction, 303–306
Genetic differences, and individual susceptibility, 325
Genetics, vulnerability to drug abuse
  animal strategies, 291–297
  human strategies, 297–300
Genotype-identification studies, association and
  linkage components, 299–300
Gestation
  cocaine-associated decrease, 162–163
  cocaine effects in nonhuman subjects,
    167–168
Glutamate, role in learned component of sensitization, 118
Glycosylation sites, dopamine transporter, 13
GNC–KLH, immunization, 151
Government-as-dealer model, nonclinical cocaine-use stations, 422, 426–427

Habituation, impaired by prenatal cocaine exposure, 165
Haloperidol
  antagonism of discriminative stimulus effects,
    140–141
  D_2-like antagonist effects, 147
  evaluation in acute interaction studies, 221
Hemorrhage
  brain, in cocaine-exposed fetus, 161
  intracranial, cocaine-associated, 276
Heroin
  methadone treatment effects, controlled eval-
    uation, 365–366
  naltrexone treatment, 136
  response rates maintained by, 36
  self-administered, tolerance development, 88
Hippocampus, lesions, effect on cocaine behavioral effects, 39–40
Housing, and work therapy, contingent on drug
  abstinence, 350–351

Human strategies
  gene–environment interactions, 305–306
  genetic influence in vulnerability to drug
    abuse, 297–300
[^{3}H]WIN 35,428, identification of binding sites
  on dopamine transporter, 12
Hydromorphone, in naltrexone–cocaine interaction study, 231–232
6-Hydroxydopamine lesions
  amygdala, cocaine-maintained responding af-
    ter, 35–36
  depletion of brain catecholamines, 22
  effect on cocaine self-administration, 23–
    27
  mesoaccumbens pathway, 41–42
  subsequent dopamine turnover increase, 32
Hyperactivity, rats prenatally exposed to cocaine, 169
Hypertonia, in cocaine-exposed infants, 165

Immunization
  with catalytic monoclonal antibody to co-
    caine, 152
  GNC–KLH, 151
Inbred strains, in determining genetic influence
  in vulnerability to drug abuse, 291–294
Individual susceptibility
  as countervailing influence to using cocaine,
    329
  and genetic differences, 325
  and psychiatric comorbidity, 325
Infectious disease analogy, cocaine dependence,
  324
Inheritance, mode, use of classical cross design,
  295
Intensity
  cocaine abuse treatment 346–347
  of demand, in behavioral economics, 84–86
Interoceptive effects, cocaine, and abuse potential, 56–62
Intracranial self-stimulation
  genotype by environment interactions for,
    304
  in studies of vulnerability to drug abuse,
    292
Intraprefrontal infusions
  cocaine, responding maintained by, 32–33
  SCH 23390, decrease of cocaine-maintained
    responding, 33–35
IQ scores, effect of prenatal exposure to cocaine, 166

Knockout mice
dopamine-related, 296–297
dopamine transporter, 13

Laboratory challenge method
pharmacodynamic profile of cocaine in humans, 212–217
pharmacological interaction studies: design, 217–218
studies using
acute interaction design, 218–224
chronic interaction design, 224–232
Laboratory models, cocaine pharmacotherapy testing, 194–195, 202–203
Laboratory studies
controlled, cocaine plus other drugs of abuse, 239–258
human, approaches to pharmacotherapy development, 211–212, 233–234
identification of inherited risk factors of substance abuse, 300
Language delays, as long-term effect of prenatal exposure to cocaine, 166
Lapse, prevention from becoming relapse, 401
Learned behavior, cocaine stimulant effects, 53
Learning theory, tolerance and sensitization in context of, 123–124
Legalization
cocaine, hypotheses vs. value statements, 410–411
models
government-as-dealer, 422
opioid maintenance drugs, 420–421
over-the-counter drugs, tobacco, and alcohol, 416–419
schedule I drugs, 421–422
unscheduled and scheduled prescription drugs, 419–420
Linkage studies, in genotype-identification studies in humans, 299
Localization, source of brain wave activity, 268–269

Magnetic resonance imaging
brain, weighting and contrast agents, 274–276
coregistration with EEG/ERP, 281
functional
impact on drug research, 282
noncontrast and contrast, 278–280

Magnetic resonance spectroscopy
analysis of exogenous and endogenous compounds, 276
^{31}P MRS, cocaine effects, 277–278
Marijuana
cocaine abusers using, treatment protocols, 356–357
sampling by children, parent monitoring study, 333–334
Marijuana–cocaine combination, 241
cardiovascular effects, 253–254
performance effects, 253
subject-rated effects, 252–253
Mazindol
effects
cocaine self-administration, 145
cocaine use in methadone patients, 371
evaluation in acute interaction studies, 220–221
Memory, representational and habit, 120
Men
aggressive behavior, and relative risk of cocaine use, 316–317
social support effect on abstinence, 398
and women, differential responses to cocaine, 193
Mesoaccumbens
dopamine depletion, effect on cocaine self-administration, 23–27, 41–42
role in behavior maintained by cocaine, 43
Methadone
buprenorphine as alternative, 369–370
cocaine abusers maintained by, buprenorphine effect, 200–202
in cocaine–buprenorphine challenge studies, 230
discriminative stimulus effects, 138
dose
effect on cocaine use, 366–368
take-home, 375
effectiveness as treatment drug, 135–136, 152–153
evaluation in chronic interaction studies, 228–229
opioid-maintenance, controls on, 420–421
treatment regimen, cocaine use after entry in, 364–366
Methohexital, behavior maintained by, 72–73
Methylphenidate, raclopride displaced by, 126–127
Microdialysis, measurement of cocaine levels in brain, 6

Monitoring the Future studies, 317–318
Monoamine oxidase-B, irreversible inhibition by selegiline, 224
Mood
  correlation with risk of relapse to cocaine, 394
  positive-mood effects of cocaine–alcohol combinations, 243
Morbidity, *see also* Comorbidity
  cocaine, under various models of legalization, 418–421
Morphine
  in cocaine–buprenorphine challenge studies, 229–230
  combined with cocaine, controlled laboratory studies, 250–252
Morphine-6-hemisuccinyl-bovine serum albumin, effect on cocaine self-administration, 151
Mortality, cocaine, under various models of legalization, 418–421
Motor behaviors, role of brain dopaminergic depletions, 22
MRI, *see* Magnetic resonance imaging
Multiple drug abuse, *see also* Polydrug use
  among cocaine abusers, 240–241, 257, 356–357
Multiple schedule
  electric shock-maintained responding, 54–56
  time-out period in, 64

Naloxone
  effect on cocaine toxicity, 11
  evaluation in acute interaction studies, 222
Naltrexone
  effect on reinforcing effects of opioids, 143–145
  evaluation in chronic interaction studies, 230–232
  interaction with opioid agonists, 138
  pharmacotherapeutic value, 210–211
  treatment for heroin abuse, 136
National Comorbidity Study, 320
National studies, epidemiological findings on trends in cocaine use, 317–319
Neighborhood, as environmental factor influencing cocaine use, 335–337
Neonatal behavioral assessment scale, 164–165
Neonate, prenatal exposure to cocaine
  cardiovascular problems, 161
  nonhuman experimental studies, 168–170
  retarded physical measurements, 163–164

Neuroanatomical control studies, importance for, 30–31
Neuroanatomy, of conditioning, and conditioned drug effects, 120–122
Neurobehavioral development
  human neonate, prenatal cocaine effect, 164–165
  nonhuman neonate, prenatal cocaine effect, 168–169, 171
Neurobehavioral treatment, for cocaine-abusing methadone patients, 373
Neurobiology, sensitization, 114–116
Neurochemical effects, cocaine, *in vivo* measurements, 5–8
Neurotensin, increased binding after iv cocaine, 11
Neurotoxic effects, chronic cocaine treatments, 4
Neurotransmitter systems, prenatal cocaine exposure effect, 170
Nicotine, regular usage among cocaine-dependent patients, 356
Nicotine–cocaine combination
  cardiovascular effects, 256
  self-administration studies, 255–256
  subject-rated effects, 256
Nifedipine, evaluation in acute interaction studies, 223
Nigrostriatal dopaminergic pathway, role in amphetamine effects, 22–23
Node-link mapping, for cocaine-abusing methadone patients, 372–373
Nomifensine
  binding sites on dopamine transporter, 4
  induced increase in dopamine levels in brain, 6–7
  intra-accumbens self-administration, 28–29
Nonhuman experimental studies, prenatal cocaine exposure, 166–170
Nonspecific effects, in relation to tolerance, 112–114
Norepinephrine transporter, cocaine acute and chronic effects, 5
Noxious stimuli, suppressant effects, relationship to cocaine reinforcing effects, 71–72
Nucleoside triphosphate, brain levels, decrease, 277
Nucleus accumbens
  amphetamine infusions, 27–29
  cocaine effects *in vivo*, 6–8
  dopamine antagonist infusions, 29–31
  dopaminergic transmission, 32–33

dopamine uptake, cocaine effect, 2–4
microinjected AMPA, cross-sensitization in sensitized animals, 115
opioid receptor density, 10

6-OHDA, *see* 6-Hydroxydopamine
7-OH-DPAT
  effect on cocaine self-administration, 146–147
  selective for D$_3$ site, 139–140
Opioid abuse, approaches to reduction, 135–137
Opioid–cocaine combinations
  cardiovascular effects, 250–252
  performance effects, 250
  subject-rated effects, 250
Opioid receptors, μ- and κ-, acute and chronic cocaine effects, 9–11
Opioids
  behavior and relapse maintained by, 57
  interactions with potential treatment medications, 138
  maintenance drugs, controls, 420–421
  self-administration
    methadone effect, 142–143
    naltrexone effect, 143–145
Outcome measures, multiple, besides absolute abstinence, 390

Palliation, pharmacotherapeutic category, 211
Parent monitoring, effect on youthful drug taking, 331–335
Patient care, cocaine abuse, in-hospital *vs.* out-of-hospital, 344–345
Patient outcomes, in hypothetical cocaine-dispensing clinics, 424–425
PD 128483, effect on cocaine self-administration, 145–146
PD 128907, selective for D$_3$ site, 139–140
Pedunculopontine tegmental nucleus, excitotoxic lesions, 40
Performance effects
  cocaine–alcohol combination, 244–246
  cocaine–marijuana combination, 253
  cocaine–opioid combinations, 250
Pergolide, testing as potential cocaine pharmacotherapy, 198
P300 ERP
  acute and chronic effects of cocaine, 268
  elicitation, 267

topography, changes during cocaine self-administration, 272–273
Pharmacodynamic profile, cocaine in humans, 212–217
Pharmacotherapy
  anticocaine, pharmacology, 233–234
  cocaine self-administration role, 194–202
  development, approaches to, 211–212
  mechanisms, 210–211
  potential, studies using laboratory challenge method, 212–232
  for primary cocaine abuse, 354
Physical measurements
  human neonate, effect of prenatal exposure to cocaine, 163–164
  nonhuman neonate, effect of prenatal exposure to cocaine, 168
Physicians, prescribing scheduled drugs, 420
Physiological response, cocaine, 214–215
Physiological toxicity, cocaine, 415
Placenta, cocaine transfer across, 159
Plasma levels, cocaine, alcohol effect, 243
Polydrug use, *see also* Multiple drug abuse
  among cocaine users, 193
  as confounding factor, 171
Positive-mood effects, cocaine–alcohol combinations, 243
Prediction
  continued abstinence, 402
  relapse to cocaine, demographics role, 392
Preference, measure of concurrent schedules, 83
Prefrontal cortex
  medial, effect of destruction on cocaine behavioral effects, 31–32, 42
  role in cocaine sensitization, 115
Pregnancy, cocaine use during
  case studies, 160–162
  epidemiological studies, 162–166
Prenatal care, effect on cocaine-exposed fetus, 162, 164
Pretreatment
  nicotine, effect on cocaine self-administration, 255–256
  test medication, dose, 217–218
Prevalence
  cocaine
    under opioid maintenance model, 421, 423
    under over-the-counter models, 418–419, 426
    under prescription drug model, 420

Prevalence *(continued)*
  cocaine use
    affecting factors, 411–414
    in national studies, 317–319
Prevention
  options, provided by stage model, 321–323
  relapse
    in behavioral interventions, 351–353
    behavioral strategies, 400–401
Price, in behavioral economics, 84–86
Priming
  injection
    other drugs: effect on cocaine reinstatement, 89–90
    reinstatement of self-administration, 58–61
  mediated by interoceptive cocaine effects, 56
Prodynorphin, striatal, chronic cocaine effect, 9
Prognostic factor, positive, psychopathology effect as, 393
Progressive ratio schedule
  break point role, 83
  tolerance to cocaine reinforcing effects under, 111–112
Prospective studies, in epidemiological study of cocaine use, 316–317
Protein kinase C, role in cocaine effects, 11
Proton MRS, study of effects of stimulant use, 277–278
Psychomotor stimulants
  and cocaine, cross-tolerance, 110–111
  increase of locomotor activity, 1
  reinforcing and direct effects, 52–56
Psychopathology, relapse to cocaine, 392–393
Psychosis, retriggered by low dose of drug, 126
Psychosocial interventions, cocaine-abusing methadone patients, 372–379
Psychotherapy, supportive-expressive, for cocaine use in methadone patients, 373–375
Punishment, as countervailing influence to using cocaine, 327

Quadazocine, effect on reinforcing effects of opioids, 143–145
Quantitative trait loci, relevant to vulnerability to drug abuse, 295–296

Racial differences, *see also* Ethnic differences
  cocaine use, 319–320
Raclopride, displaced by methylphenidate, 126–127
Radiofrequency irradiation, in MRI, 275

Rating scales, cocaine euphorigenic and stimulant properties, 216
Regional differences, dopamine transporters, 12–13
Reinforcement
  cocaine
    effects of treatment plus nondrug reinforcers, 93–95
    experimental events affecting, 87–90
    satiation effects and direct effects, 96–100
    stress effects, 95–96
  community, approach to treating cocaine abuse, 349–351
  processes, countervailing influences to using cocaine, 326–330
  schedules, 83–84
  voucher-based, 376
Reinforcers
  alternative nondrug
    access to, 93
    availability, 328–329
    combined with pharmacological treatment, 93–95
    effect on vulnerability to drug abuse, 302
    environments rich in, 100
  as substitutes and as complements, 86
Reinforcing effects, cocaine
  alteration by accumbens dopamine depletion, 25
  contextual determinants, 62–74
  importance of rate-dependent effects, 53–56
  opioid antagonist effects, 10–11
  sensitization to, 125–126
  tolerance, 111–114
Reinforcing efficacy
  behavior maintenance, 82
  confounding by direct effects, 83
  evaluation by behavioral economics, 84–87
Reinforcing strength, closely related to dose, 67–68
Reinstatement
  cocaine self-administration, 57–58
  extinguished responding, 89–90, 92–93
  with priming injections of other drugs, 59–60
  serving as model of relapse, 58–62
Relapse
  definitions, 389–390
  demographic characteristics, 392
  drug treatment interventions and, 400
  prevention
    in behavioral interventions, 351–352
    behavioral strategies, 400–401
  process, 399–400

psychopathology, 392–393
reinstatement as model, 58–62
relationship to craving, 395–396
risk, mood and stress effects, 394
role of positive and negative cocaine expectancies, 399
to self-administration behavior, 56–58
social support role, 396–398
theoretical models, 390–391
Research
cocaine self-administration in humans
choice of dose and route, 190–193
general methodology, 187–188
routes of administration, 188–190
human laboratory: response to cocaine challenge, 209–235
volunteer recruitment for, 183–185
Research needs, for legalizing cocaine, 422–425
Resolution, MRI, enhancements, 278, 280
Responding
cocaine-maintained
6-OHDA-lesioned amygdala effect, 35–36
suppression, 70–74
cocaine-reinforced, concurrent drug exposure effect, 91
extinguished, reinstatement, 89–90
food-maintained, cocaine-related pause, 54
operant
intraprefrontal cocaine infusion effect, 32–33
role of genetic differences, 293
Responding, rate of
decrease in 6-OHDA-lesioned animals, 26–27
electric shock-maintained, 54–56
Reuptake, monoamines, inhibition, 1
Risk factors
environmental, for cocaine use, 330–337
known to precede outcomes, in prospective studies, 316–317
for transition between stages of use/abuse, 321–324
Rotational effects, cocaine, sensitization to, 116–117
Route of administration
cocaine
as choice of research participant, 190–193
research questions with respect to legalization, 423–424
cocaine dynamic effects dependent on, 214–215

effects
cocaine reinforcing behavior, 87–88
drug abuse, 301
self-administered cocaine in research protocols, 188–190

Safety issues, administering cocaine to humans, 185
Satiation, and direct effects, modulation of reinforcement, 96–100
SCH 23390
antagonism of discriminative stimulus effects, 140–141
effect on cocaine self-administration, 148–149
SCH 23390 infusions
intra-accumbens, effect on cocaine self-administration, 30–31
intra-amygdala, 37–39
intraprefrontal, decrease of cocaine-maintained responding, 33–35
Scheduled drugs
regulatory controls, 419–420
schedule I, regulations, 421–422
Second-order schedule, reinforcement, 65–66
Selective breeding, in determining genetic influence in vulnerability to drug abuse, 294
Selegiline, evaluation in acute interaction studies, 224
Self-administration
amphetamine, acquisition, 27
cocaine, see Cocaine self-administration
heroin, tolerance development, 88
intravenous opioids
agonist effects, 142–143
antagonist effects, 143–145
nomifensine, intra-accumbens, 28–29
Sensitization
conditioning role, 116–118
to effects of cocaine, 7–8
neurobiology, 114–116
and tolerance, in cocaine abuse, 122–127
Serotonin transporter, cocaine acute and chronic effects, 5
SKF 38393, effect on cocaine reinforcing effects, 149
Smoking
cigarette, see Nicotine
crack, see Crack smoking
Social integration, construct of social support, 396–397

Social learning model
  cocaine relapse, 391
  promotion of abstinence, 396
Social support, protective factor for maintaining abstinence, 396–398
Sodium ions, and chlorine ions, cotransported with dopamine, 2
Speedball combination, in naltrexone–cocaine interaction study, 231–232
Spiperone, effect on cocaine reinforcing effects, 149
Stage model, cocaine dependence, 321–324
Stimulus effects, cocaine
  dopaminergic antagonist effects, 29–31
  reproduced by dopaminergic agonists, 27–29
Stress
  correlation with risk of relapse to cocaine, 394
  effects
    cocaine reinforcement, 95–96
    vulnerability to drug abuse, 302–303
Striatum
  dopamine transporter binding sites, increase, 4
  ventral, neuronal electrophysiological response to reinforcers, 119–120
Structure–activity relationships, dopamine transporter binding sites, 5
Subjective effects, cocaine
  buprenorphine effect, 200
  in evaluation of pharmacotherapy, 215–216
  tolerance, 109–111
Subject-rated effects
  cocaine–alcohol combination, 242–243
  cocaine–marijuana combination, 252–253
  cocaine–nicotine combination, 256
  cocaine–opioid combinations, 250
Sulpiride, effect on cocaine-maintained responding, 33
Supportive-expressive psychotherapy, cocaine-using methadone patients, 373–375
Suppression, cocaine-maintained responding, 70–74

Terguride, effect on cocaine self-administration, 146
Testing, potential pharmacotherapies, 195–202
Therapy
  group vs. individual, for cocaine abuse, 347, 353
  work, and housing, contingent on drug abstinence, 351–352

Time course, peak dopamine levels, 7–8
Time dependence
  local effects of intracerebral dopaminergic antagonists, 30–31
  SCH 23390 diffusion away from infusion site, 37
Time-out period
  under multiple schedules, 64
  role in
    fixed-ratio schedule, 83
    two-lever concurrent schedule, 69–70
Tobacco, availability, regulations, 416–417
Token economy, in cocaine self-administration research, 190–191
Tolerance, see also Cross-tolerance
  cocaine locomotor-activating effects with continuous infusion, 8
  to reinforcing effects of cocaine, 111–114
  role in drug abuse, 108
  to self-administered heroin, 88
  and sensitization, in cocaine abuse, 122–127
  to subjective and discriminative stimulus effects of cocaine, 109–111
Topography, P300, changes during cocaine self-administration, 272–273
Toxicity, cocaine
  behavioral, 414–415
  and ethics, 415
  physiological, 415
Transgenic techniques, study of candidate gene role in drug responsiveness, 296–297
Transition
  to drug sampling by children, parent monitoring effect, 334–335
  between stages of use/abuse, risk factors, 321–324
Trazodone, evaluation in acute interaction studies, 222
Treatment
  behavioral repertoire reconstitution role, 70
  cocaine abuse
    content, 347–356
    duration and intensity, 346–347
    early attrition, 345–346
    group vs. individual therapy, 347
    in-hospital vs. out-of-hospital care, 344–345
    use of models of opioid abuse treatment, 136–137
  cocaine abusers seeking: inclusion in research, 185

methadone, cocaine use after entry in, 364–366

multicomponent, for cocaine-using methadone patients, 377–379

outcomes, in hypothetical cocaine-dispensing clinics, 424–425

pharmacological
adjunctive, in methadone patients, 370–372

buprenorphine, 369–370

combined with alternative nondrug reinforcers, 93–95

phases, 61

potential medications, interactions with cocaine, 139–141

prevention of cocaine relapse, 400–401

treatment with primary cocaine abusers, 353–355

Tryptophan depletion, evaluation in acute interaction studies, 223–224

Twin studies
gene–environment interactions, 305

role of genetics in drug abuse, 298–299

Tyrosine hydroxylase, distribution in brain, prenatal cocaine exposure effect, 170

United States, cocaine use, data sources, 320–321

Unit price, as responses per milligram dose, 86–87

Unlimited access, and dysregulated cocaine intake, 63–64

Unscheduled drugs, regulatory controls, 419

Value statements, in regard to cocaine legalization, 410–411

Variability, individual, in sensitization to cocaine, 117–118

Variance partitioning, and goals of behavior genetic research, 290

Ventral pallidum, excitotoxic lesions, 36

Ventral subiculum of hippocampal formation
excitotoxic lesions, 39–40

role in cocaine behavioral effects, 43

Ventral tegmental area
cocaine-induced monoamine increase, 6

6-OHDA-lesioned, effect on cocaine self-administration, 25–27

Volunteers
cocaine challenge studies, profile of subjective responses, 215–216

EEG alpha activity after cocaine administration, 267

receiving vs. not receiving concurrent methadone, 228–229

recruitment for cocaine research, 183–185

Voucher program
effect on treatment retention and cocaine abstinence, 349–350

reinforcement of cocaine abstinence based on, 376

Vulnerability
to acquire cocaine-reinforced behavior, 95–96

cocaine abuse, 313–338

drug abuse
environmental influence, 300–303

genetic influence
animal strategies, 291–297

human strategies, 297–300

Within-subject crossover design
decreased variability in, 218

in study of
desipramine–cocaine interaction, 225–226

naltrexone–cocaine interaction, 230–231

Women
and men, differential responses to cocaine, 193

pregnant
cocaine use, associated social and lifestyle factors, 160

methadone-maintenance treatment, 378–379

reduced sensitivity to some of cocaine's effects, 198

social support effect on abstinence, 398

Work therapy, and housing, contingent on drug abstinence, 350–351